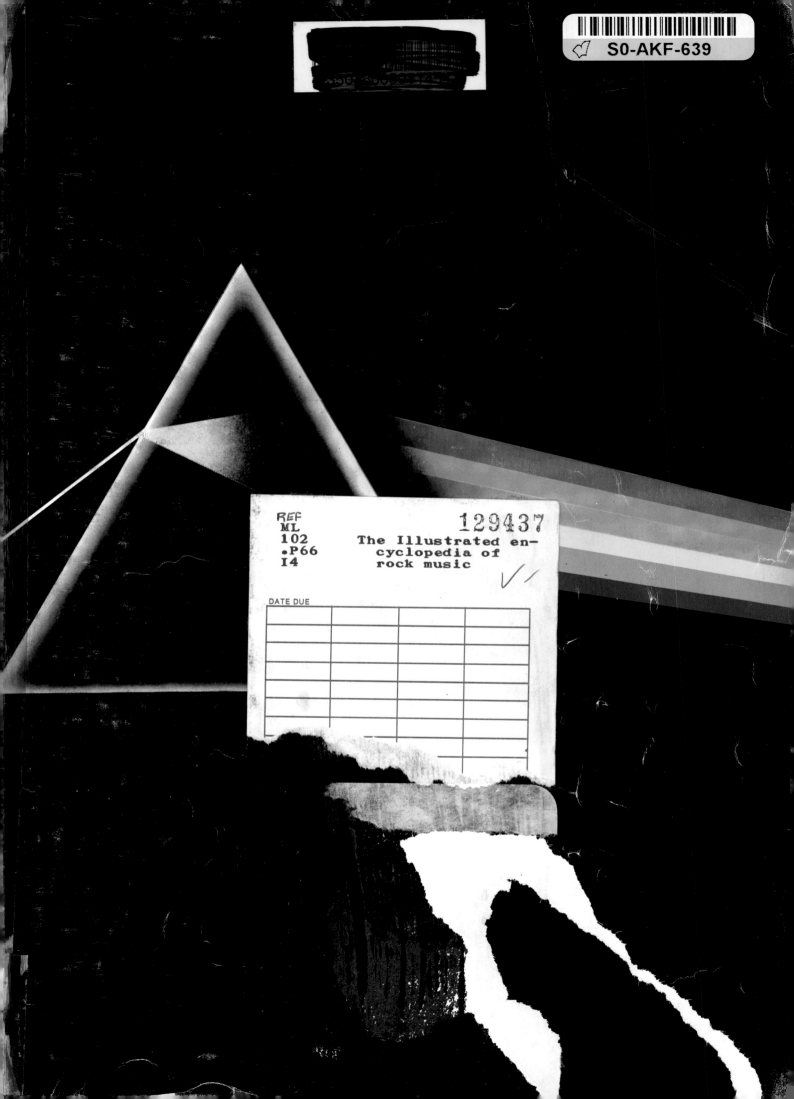

THE ILLUSTRATED
ENCYCLOPEDIA OF
ROCK

THE ILLUSTRATED ENCYCLOPEDIA OF
ROCK

a Salamander book

Published by

H·A·R·M·O·N·Y B·O·O·K·S
NEW YORK

A Salamander Book

First published, 1977, by Harmony Books, a
division of Crown Publishers, Inc. All Rights
Reserved under International Copyright Union by
Harmony Books. No part of this book may be
reproduced or utilized in any form or by any
means, electronic or mechanical, including
photocopying, recording, or by any information
storage and retrieval system without permission
in writing from the Publisher

Harmony Books, a division of Crown Publishers, Inc.
One Park Avenue, New York, New York 10016

Published simultaneously in Canada by
General Publishing Company Limited

Library of Congress Catalog Card Number: 76 40219

First published in the United Kingdom in 1976 by
The Hamlyn Publishing Group Limited

© Salamander Books Ltd 1976
52 James Street, London W1, United Kingdom

© Text Nick Logan, Bob Woffinden
& IPC Magazines Ltd 1976
King's Reach Tower, Stamford Street, London SE1,
England

Parts of this book have already appeared in the
music paper New Musical Express and also in a
Star Book paperback published by Wyndham
Publications, Ltd, London, England

Filmset by SX Composing Limited,
Leigh-on-Sea, Essex, England

Colour reproduction by Metric Reproductions Ltd,
Chelmsford, Essex, and
Alan Pooley Printing Ltd,
Tunbridge Wells, Kent, England

Printed and bound by Henri Proost,
Turnhout, Belgium

All correspondence concerning the content of this
volume should be addressed to Salamander Books
Limited

Credits

Authors: Nick Logan and Bob Woffinden
Additional research: John Tobler
Picture research: Angela Errigo

Acknowledgments

The authors would like to give special thanks to
Max Bell, Miles, Charles Shaar Murray, Ian
MacDonald, Roy Carr, David Redshaw, Tony
Tyler, Steve Clarke, Neil Spencer, Al Clark, Fred
Dellar, Tony Stewart, Julie Webb, Nick Kent, Fiona
Foulger, Kathy Kelly.

The publishers would like to thank the following
who gave their permission to use record sleeves
as illustrations in this book; A&M, Anchor, Arista,
Atlantic, Blue Thumb, Bronze, Capitol, Capricorn,
CBS, Charisma, Chrysalis, Roger Dean, Decca,
DJM, E.G. Management, Elektra/Asylum, EMI,
Fantasy, Harvest, Island, Jethro Tull, MCA,
Mountain Managements, NEMS, Nonesuch,
Phonogram, Polydor, Private Stock, Procol Harum,
Pye, RAK, RCA, Rolling Stones Records, R.S.O.,
Swan Song, Tamla Motown, Transatlantic, United
Artists, Virgin, WEA and Yes.

We should also like to thank Virgin Records,
Marble Arch, London for supplying record sleeves
for photography and Bruce Scott for photographing
all the record sleeves.

Picture Credits

The following companies and organisations provided
publicity photographs for use in the book, and we are
very grateful for these; ABC/Dunhill Records,
Asylum Records, Atlantic, Avco, Blackhill Enterprises,
Brunswick Records, CBS, Chess Records, Chrysalis,
Columbia Records, Cotillion Records, Decca,
Directional Enterprises, Elektra, Epic, Armet Frances,
Arthur Howes Agency, Island, King Crimson Management
Ltd, Konk, Liberty, William Morris Agency, NEMS,
New Musical Express, Popsie, Private Stock Records,
Pye Records, RSO, Reprise, Stars Inc, Robert Stigwood
Organisation, Warner Bros, WEA.

Only the non-publicity photographs are listed by page
number. If there is more than one photograph on that
page the column number is given in brackets after the
page number.

Cover (front and back): Robert Ellis. Endpapers:
EMI/Harvest. Page 5: Design and photography – Graham
Hughes. 11: London Features International Limited*. 14:
Paragon Publicity. 17: LFIL. 22 (2/3): LFIL. 25: Associated
Press. 28: South London Photo Agency. 30 (3/4): Alan
Johnson. 34 (4): Joseph Stevens. 37 (3/4): Joseph Stevens.
39: LFIL. 43: Robert Ellis. 48 (1/2): Derek Taylor. 55 (4): Joll
Furmanousky. 62 (4): London Photo Agency. 67 (3/4):
Napier Russell. 68 (2): LFIL; (4): Joseph Stevens. 75 (2):
Robert Ellis. 77 (1/4): LFIL. 83 (inset): David Block Limited.
88 (4): Gered Mankowitz. 90 (3/4): Robert Ellis. 95: LFIL.
99: Joseph Stevens. 101 (2/4): Arthur Pine Associates.
102: Joseph Stevens. 104: Syndication International. 106 (1/2):
Joseph Stevens. 112 (1/2): Pennie Smith; (2/4): Barry
Plummer. 113 (1/2): LFIL. 117 (1/3): LFIL; (4/both): Joseph
Stevens. 120: (1/2): Graham F. Page. 121: LFIL. 126: LFIL.
130 (2/4): LFIL. 133: Brian Cooke. 135 (1/4): LFIL. 136: LFIL.
138 (3/4): LFIL. 139 (2/4): LFIL. 141 (3): London Photo
Agency. 145: LFIL. 152 (1): SKR Photos International; (2/4):
LFIL. 155 (1): Robert Ellis. 159 (2/4): LFIL. 160 (1/4): LFIL.
168 (3/4): Pennie Smith. 169 (1/4): LFIL. 173: Chuck Pulin
© 1975. 179 (1/3): LFIL. 181: LFIL. 184 (2/4): Pennie Smith.
185 (3/4): LFIL. 192: Mick Rock. 198 (1/4): Hiro. 205 (2/3):
London Photo Agency. 207 (2): Chalkie Davis. 209 (2):
Dagmar. 210 (1/4): LFIL. 211: LFIL. 214: Monitor. 218 (3/4):
LFIL. 222: LFIL. 224: LFIL. 230: LFIL. 231 (3/4): LFIL. 237:
Mick Gold. 242 (3/4): LFIL. 243 (1/4): LFIL. 244: Ian Dickson.
246: LFIL. 248 (2/3): Pennie Smith. 251: LFIL. 252: LFIL.

*London Features International Limited is abbreviated
hereafter to LFIL. LFIL photos are by Mike Putland, Jill
Furmanousky, Fredric Golchan, Preston/Kent, Stuart
Richman and David Hill.

*Right: Roger Daltrey, as rampant centaur, on the sleeve
of his second solo album, Ride A Rock Horse. The design
and photography was the work of Graham Hughes, and it
won him the Design and Art Director's silver award in
1976 for the most outstanding record sleeve photography.*

129437

Introduction

Compiling a rock encyclopedia is, of course, an undertaking of extreme foolishness. Since rock music is fundamentally ephemeral, there are innumerable problems to overcome. The most immediate of these is that, even though the field is relatively undocumented, there is sufficient information readily available to fill a dozen volumes, and enough apocryphal material on top of that to furnish several tomes.

The rock business is hardly known for its inherent stability. Most bands have notoriously turbulent histories, for example. Also, in a world where you're only as good as last night's gig, performers can change their image and musical direction at a moment's notice, while others will rise from the dole queue to become the proverbial overnight success – which, if such a transition doesn't actually happen overnight, can certainly be accomplished in less time than it takes to publish an illustrated book.

And that's only the start. Since some of the momentum in rock 'n' roll has traditionally been provided by so-called One Hit Wonders, the next problem is who to include and why. First you need to negotiate the tricky dilemma of who is a rock performer and who isn't. Impossible to resolve this, since rock has always been a most eclectic music form, borrowing in varying degrees from folk, blues, soul, R&B and country traditions. We've relied on our instinct and a modicum of common sense to sort this out: we've included all those acts who purvey what might be described as mainstream rock music (both those who are eternally in the public eye, and those who are almost legendary – in the pure sense of the word – performers). Also we have recognized as many peripheral performers as

we could fit in, hopefully including all those, like Ray Charles and Hank Williams, who have exercised a measure of personal influence.

There are even more mundane problems to work out. Who gets filed where and why? An as-yet unheralded British band rejoice in the appellation A Band Called O, and could presumably be listed under 'A', 'B' or 'O' according to taste (we've plumped for 'O'). Fixed rules would prove hazardous, so again we've been pragmatic. T. Rex are listed under Marc Bolan, for example, and The Mothers Of Invention under Frank Zappa, without whom . . . .

The actual alphabetical order follows the traditional manner; individual artists are listed under surnames, bands under their full title; if an artist has given his name to a group, then it's listed as a band – eg the Edgar Broughton Band is under 'E', the Sensational Alex Harvey Band under 'S'.

This was the order of play originally worked out when the Book of Rock was first conceived (by Nick Logan). It was then a series of ten weekly pull-out supplements in *New Musical Express* back in 1973, and was afterwards reproduced in paperback form as *The NME Book Of Rock.*

That was the starting-point for this book, but as it has since been totally revised, completely overhauled, and fully illustrated there is now little similarity between that publication and this.

EVEN THOUGH this book is being rushed out in record time (and the printers haven't even had the benefit of altitude training) there have inevitably been some events that have overtaken us. Phil May, whom we refer to as the last surviving original member of the Pretty Things, has

Left: The Animals circa 1964, l to r, Chas Chandler, Alan Price, Hilton Valentine, Eric Burdon, John Steel.

Recordings:

The Animals (MGM/Columbia)
Animals On Tour (MGM/—)
Animal Tracks (MGM/Columbia)
Animalisms (MGM/Decca)
In Concert From Newcastle (Springboard/DJM)

Compilations:

Most Of The Animals (—/ Columbia)
Best Of The Animals (MGM/—)
Animalization (MGM/—)

Area Code 615

Mac Gayden lead guitar, vocals
Charlie McCoy harmonica, vocals
Bobby Thompson banjo, guitar
Wayne Moss guitar, bass
Buddy Spicher fiddle, viola, cello
David Briggs keyboards
Norbert Putnam bass, cello
Kenny Buttrey drums
Weldon Myrick pedal steel

Although by late '60s the Nashville sound had peaked, musicians there were still regarded with reverential awe. It was there that Dylan went to record **Nashville Skyline**, with aid of local sessionmen Buttrey and McCoy (both of whom had also worked on **Blonde On Blonde**).

These two were joined by other local musicians who decided to capitalise on their collective reputation – Area Code 615 was never a gigging band, but just an 'ad hoc' assembly of musicians who played together all the time anyway. The group was never a serious long-term consideration. **Area Code 615**, however, sparked off enough of an enthusiastic response in 1969 to encourage follow-up, **Trip In The Country,** the following year. Both displayed much instrumental versatility, as would have been expected, and a real gutsy, kick-out-the-jams approach; **Stone Fox Chase,** from **Trip In The Country,** has been used as theme for BBC-TV rock programme "The Old Grey Whistle Test" since 1971.

After **Trip In The Country,** the personnel resumed routine session work. Many of ex-members played gigs outside U.S. for first time in May '75 when they backed Billy Swan (♦) at Paris Olympia. Wayne Moss now plays with another Nashville-based group, Barefoot Jerry (♦), and David Briggs has played with Elvis Presley in Las Vegas and Joan Baez on her 1975 U.S. tour.

Both albums repackaged 1974 as double set.

Recordings:
Area Code 615 (Polydor)
Trip In The Country (Polydor)

Argent

Rod Argent keyboards, vocals
John Verity guitar, vocals
Jim Rodford bass
Robert Henrit drums

Formed 1969 by Rod Argent (b. St. Albans, England, June 14, 1945) after demise of his previous band, the more pop-oriented Zombies (♦). Original line-up, after several unsuccessful try outs, comprised Argent, his cousin Jim Rodford, Bob Henrit and singer/composer/guitarist Russ Ballard. Their music, revolving around the piano and organ playing of Rod Argent, took much of initial inspiration from Zombies – as evidenced on group's 1970 debut album.

Having made their U.K. debut spring '69 Argent visited U.S.A. for their first tour 1970, but it wasn't until the 1971 **Ring Of Hands** set that the group established an independent identity on record. This second album aroused much interest and sales on both sides of the Atlantic, and put Argent on the brink of a breakthrough into the "flash-rock" hierarchy populated so lucratively by likes of ELP, Yes and Genesis.

However, the third album, the 1972-released **All Together Now,** showed them veering away from the impressive restraint and dynamic control of the second – possibly the result of too much touring – and by the fourth release, **In Deep** (1973), Argent were displaying a tendency towards self-indulgence interpreted as presaging crisis point among some rock critics.

Between these two albums, group did manage to notch up success in singles chart in Britain and America with the cuts **Hold Your Head Up** (1972) and **God Gave Rock And Roll To You** (1973).

However, the February 1974 **Nexus** collection did little to lift doubts about the band's direction and, towards the end of that same month, Russ Ballard, whose compositional ability had been one of band's strengths from beginning, announced his departure in favour of solo career (♦ Russ Ballard).

Guitarist John Grimaldi was brought in as replacement and, a few months later, singer/guitarist John Verity, whose own John Verity Band had previously played a U.K. tour as support to Argent, was similarly recruited, bringing the group up to a quintet.

The late 1974 **Encore** release was a live double album featuring in-concert workouts of some of the group's best-known material, including the two aforementioned singles.

Circus appeared early 1975 before a label switch to RCA-distributed Good Earth, for whom they recorded **Counterpoint** after some nine months off road. However, Grimaldi quit early in 1976 and the group subsequently folded. Rod Argent is now working on a solo album.

Recordings:
Argent (Epic/CBS)
Ring Of Hands (Epic/CBS)
All Together Now (Epic/CBS)
In Deep (Epic/CBS)
Nexus (Epic/CBS)
Encore (Epic/CBS)
Circus (Epic/CBS)
Counterpoint (RCA – Good Earth)

Compilation:
**The Best Of Argent –
An Anthology** (Epic)

Joan Armatrading

Born St. Kitts, West Indies, this singer/songwriter is now U.K.-based. Recorded first album for British Cube label 1974 before signing with A&M for second 1975. Has been working recently with fellow A&M act, The Movies.

Recordings:
Whatever's For Us (A&M/Cube)
Back To The Night (A&M)

Peter Asher

After stint with Gordon Waller as successful British pop duo Peter & Gordon (biggest hits included Lennon/McCartney composition **World Without Love** and Buddy Holly's **True Love Ways**), Asher developed into one of most important producer/managers in music business.

Asher was very friendly with Paul McCartney, who had been dating his sister, actress Jane Asher, for the better part of four years. When the Beatles set up Apple organisation, Asher was made head of A&R.

One of his first signings was James Taylor (♦), whose debut album was undoubtedly promising; but Asher became disillusioned with the Beatles' dilettante approach to their business, and he and Taylor moved on to Los

Angeles and superstardom.

Asher produced Taylor's first three albums for Warner Bros, the first two of which went platinum. He then managed The Section (◆), a group of session musicians who worked with Taylor and Carole King, and the enormously successful Linda Ronstadt (◆). Still produces her albums, but has bowed out of Taylor's last two.

Asleep At The Wheel

Chris O'Connell vocals
Ray Benson guitar, vocals
Lucky Oceans (Reuben Gosfield) pedal steel
Leroy Preston rhythm guitar
Floyd Domino piano
Tony Garnier bass
Scott Hennige drums
Ed Vizard alto, tenor saxophones
Denny Levin fiddle

Nucleus of band was originally Benson, Preston and Oceans, who moved from East Coast to Paw Paw, West Virginia, to play both country music of such as Hank Williams and George Jones and original compositions of Preston, who then played drums. They were joined by Chris O'Connell, a secretary from Virginia, as lead vocalist. Like Commander Cody before them, they moved to San Francisco Bay Area, in an attempt to increase their following; at that time Domino joined as pianist, bringing strong swing influence to band, who cut their debut album, **Comin' Right At Ya**, in March 1973, with Gene Dobkin on bass.

The addition of bassist Garnier increased swing orientation, and band settled in Austin, Texas. Second album, **Asleep At The Wheel** (with Richard Casanova on fiddle) issued Feb '74, and band achieved moderate U.S. success with single from it, their version of Louis Jordan's **Choo Choo Ch'Boogie**. They increased personnel to accommodate more big-band material in their act, bringing in Hennige (Preston switching to rhythm guitar), Vizard and, to complete country-swing sound, Levin on fiddle. **Texas Gold** released Spring '76.

Recordings:
Comin' Right At Ya (United Artists)
Asleep At The Wheel (Epic)
Texas Gold (Capitol)

Pete Atkin/ Clive James

Atkin grew up in Cambridge, England, playing piano in local dance bands, before going up to St. John's College Cambridge and becoming involved with the Footlights revue, where he met loquacious Australian Clive James. Alerted by their common love for Rodgers & Hart to the possibility of pursuing a career together, they began working in partnership – James putting lyrics to Atkin's songs.

After pressing two albums themselves, and distributing them locally, Atkin went to London in 1969, where he was given a publishing and then a recording con-

tract, and made two albums for Philips – the folksy **Beware Of The Beautiful Stranger** and the more instrumentally-ambitious **Driving Through Mythical America**. (Both of which were reissued on RCA in 1973.)

Meanwhile Atkin, after going to the U.S. with the Footlights revue, also landed two late-night revue shows for television, with Julie Covington.

When Atkin & James signed to RCA in 1972, the wheels began to turn more smoothly, as the songwriting partnership received critical acclaim and James turned out material prolifically, some of it observant and witty, some just too clever by half. From touring folk clubs, Atkin graduated to performing concerts with a backing band in 1974, but it wasn't until 1975 that James joined him for a nationwide trek.

As each successive album receives good reviews, but makes little commercial impact, so the residual impression is that the humour is just too cerebral and contrived to be actually funny. **Live Libel,** released in 1975, an elaborate satire on several pop personalities, was rather too diffuse to be effective.

James is now well-known for his own appearances on television, and also his vituperative comments on the appearance of others, as television critic of the "Observer".

Recordings:
Beware Of The Beautiful Stranger (—/Fontana)
Driving Through Mythical America (—/Philips)
A King At Nightfall (—/RCA)
The Road Of Silk (—/RCA)
Secret Drinker (—/RCA)
Live Libel (—/RCA)

Chet Atkins

Born Luttrell, Tennessee, June 20, 1924, Atkins is the doyen of Nashville cats. In 1946 he was signed up by Steve Sholes of RCA Victor, and achieved fame through his guitar instrumentals. He started working with the Carter family, moved to Nashville, and began to appear at Grand Old Opry. In 1949, Sholes started using Atkins as studio guitarist for RCA Nashville sessions, and by 1957 he was head of RCA Nashville operations, where he was involved with recording such artists as Jim Reeves and Elvis Presley (◆).

Although Atkins was indubitably a country artist, he helped to shape course of rock 'n' roll by broadening appeal of Presley's records, incorporating such devices as loud electric guitars, drums and backing vocal groups, all of which only alienated the established C&W audience.

As a Nashville producer, Atkins was also involved with recording career of that other phenomenon of early rock music – the Everly Brothers (◆).

He led a local band which included Floyd Cramer on keyboards, and which formed nucleus of Nashville studio band. Atkins himself was largely responsible for popularising and defining Nashville sound, which was typified by over-blown arrangements and ample use of pedal steel and strings – especially with artists such as Charley Pride and George Jones – and which has become in-

creasingly self-parodying in recent years.

Despite it all, Atkins remains the most respected figure in Nashville music circles.

Atlanta Rhythm Section

Barry Bailey guitar
Ronnie Hammond vocals
Paul Goddard ~~guitar~~ bass
Robert Nix drums
J. R. Cobb second guitar
Dean Daughtry keyboards

Like Booker T. & M.G.s (◆), Atlanta Rhythm Section are a band who came together through collective experience working as studio session band – in this case, at Studio One, Doraville, Georgia. Prime mover was Buddy Buie, who owned studios and became band's manager. All had had professional experience playing in South; Bailey, Goddard, Nix and Daughtry had all formerly toured with Roy Orbison (◆) as members of The Candymen. Additionally, Bailey had played with Allen Toussaint, Felix Pappalardi and Mylon Le Fevre; and Daughtry with Al Kooper and Mylon Le Fevre. Nix has recorded with Lynyrd Skynyrd and Ike and Tina Turner.

Original vocalist was Rodney Justo, who left after debut album, **Atlanta Rhythm Section**, and was replaced by Hammond, a multi-instrumentalist as well as singer. Since then the line-up has been stable, as the band have concentrated (by going out on the road in 1975) on improving their brand of Southern rock, which is very much in style of Allman Brothers' **Idlewild South**.

Recordings:
Atlanta Rhythm Section (Atlantic)
Back Up Against The Wall (Atlantic)
Third Annual Pipe Dream (Polydor)
Dog Days (Polydor)
Red Tape (Polydor)

Atomic Rooster

Vincent Crane keyboards
Johnny Mandala guitar
Rick Parnell drums

British group, formed late 1969 by Vincent Crane and Carl Palmer, both from Arthur Brown's Crazy World outfit. (Crane had written Brown's 1968 **Fire** hit.) Palmer quit later same year to join Emerson Lake And Palmer (◆), and Rooster suffered several subsequent personnel changes.

Had two hit singles in U.K. charts 1971 with **Tomorrow Night** and **Devil's Answer**, and were joined by R&B veteran Chris Farlowe (◆) as vocalist following year. Farlowe subsequently quit after recording of fifth album, the 1973 **Nice 'n' Greasy.**

Recordings:
Atomic Rooster (—/B&C)
Death Walks Behind You (Elektra/B&C)
In Hearing Of (Elektra/B&C)
Made In England (Elektra/Dawn)
Nice 'n' Greasy (Elektra/Dawn)
Compilations:
Assortment (—/B&C)

Audience
◆ Howard Werth

Brian Auger

Born 1939, this keyboards-playing Londoner began musical career early '60s, leading jazz trio on piano. Abandoned jazz idiom 1964, augmenting trio with John McLaughlin on guitar for short spell, before establishing first Brian Auger Trinity with Rick Brown (bs) and Micky Waller (drms – later of Jeff Beck Group), Auger himself switching from piano to organ.

Long John Baldry (◆) joined as vocalist, having rid himself of own band. Baldry brought Rod Stewart (◆) – previously second string vocalist to Baldry in The Hoochie Coochie Men – with him.

Guitarist Vic Briggs was added to line-up and Auger's manager, Giorgio Gomelsky, suggested putting his secretary Julie Driscoll alongside Baldry and Stewart to provide three-strong vocal front line.

Above: Julie Driscoll and, l to r, Clive Thacker, Brian Auger, Dave Ambrose.

Thus, by mid-64, Steampacket was born. The band was self-contained road show: Auger's Trinity (line-up of which went through several changes) played their jazz-oriented R&B instrumentals, as well as backing Julie Driscoll's soul repertoire, Stewart's mixture of Motown and blues, and Baldry, whom Auger considered the "best white blues singer of his period". The entire Steampacket would finish each gig on stage together.

Full of tempestuous personalities, band survived stormy history until summer 1966 when first Stewart left (to join Shotgun Express) and later Baldry quit after row with Auger. Due to different contractual obligations only **Early Days**, on 2001 label, survives from this period.

Auger held re-organised Trinity – (Dave Ambrose (bs), Clive Thacker (drms), Gary Boyle (gtr) – together with Julie Driscoll as lead vocalist, and in 1968 they had international hit with Dylan's **This Wheel's On Fire.** Follow up single flopped and Ms Driscoll quit during subsequent U.S. tour.

More problems followed, not least of which was 15-month spell without a record release, and the strain of sustaining public interest by gigs alone eventually caused complete break-up – once again in U.S. – in July 1970.

Auger subsequently formed new outfit, Oblivion Express, which at one time included present Average White Band drummer Steve Ferrone, and has concentrated activities in U.S. with some success.

Recordings:
Brian Auger Trinity:
Open (Marmalade)
Streetnoise (Marmalade)
Befour (RCA)
Oblivion Express:
Oblivion Express (RCA)
Better Land (RCA)
Second Wind (RCA)
Closer To It (RCA)
Straight Ahead (RCA)
Reinforcements (RCA)
Live Express Vol. 2 (RCA)

Average White Band

Alan Gorrie bass, vocals
Hamish Stuart guitar, vocals
Onnie McIntyre rhythm guitar, vocals
Steve Ferrone drums
Roger Ball keyboards, saxes
Malcolm Duncan tenor sax

Formed Scotland early 1972, first break was as support band to Eric Clapton on come-back gig at London Rainbow, Jan 1973. Regarded by many as closest a British band has come to authentic soul music. First album, released in U.K. 1973, was critically well-received but it wasn't until switch to Atlantic for 1974-recorded **Average White Band**, produced by Arif Mardin, that public took notice. From second set came million-selling U.S. and U.K. smash single **Pick Up The Pieces,** and in February 1975 AWB were topping both U.S. charts.

Tragically, on point of breakthrough, band's original drummer Robbie McIntosh died of heroin poisoning at party in Los Angeles September 1974. Replacement was Ferrone, an Englishman previously with Brian Auger's Oblivion Express and Bloodstone.

Currently working primarily in U.S., partly due to English tax laws. Third album (1975) has also struck gold status.

Recordings:
Show Your Hand (MCA)
Average White Band (Atlantic)
Cut The Cake (Atlantic)
Soul Searching (Atlantic)

Hoyt Axton

Born in Oklahoma, Axton opted early on for singing career, and in 1958 was performing own songs in folk clubs in San Francisco Bay Area. By this time his mother, Mae Axton, who had taken up composition herself, had written million-seller **Heartbreak Hotel**

for Elvis Presley (➧).

Axton performed his songs and bummed around, and came to recognition only gradually as his compositions began to be recorded by major artists – **Greenback Dollar** by Kingston Trio in 1962, **The Pusher** by Steppenwolf (➧) in 1967, and **Joy To The World** by Three Dog Night (➧) in 1970. During this time, Axton himself recorded up to a dozen albums, mostly for small companies.

It wasn't until he signed with A&M in early '70s that his own recording career became viable. **Less Than The Song** again provided much material for other artists such as Joan Baez, but it was his sequel, **Life Machine,** that gave him substantial hit on the U.S. country charts with **When The Morning Comes.** With his next album, **Southbound,** he reverted to form; it profited him little more than respect, but did well for other people, especially Ringo Starr, who took **No No Song** to a U.S. No. 1.

Recordings:
Less Than The Song (A&M)
Life Machine (A&M)
Southbound (A&M)
Fearless (A&M)

The Confessions Of Dr Dream. Courtesy Island Records. The first of Ayers' three albums for Island, Confessions (1974) came closest to commercial success. In 1975 he briefly retired, and re-signed to Harvest 1976.

Kevin Ayers

Born 1944 at Herne Bay, Kent, England, Ayers spent pre-teen years in Malaysia. Leaving school at 16, moved to Canterbury where he helped form Soft Machine (➧) as bassist in 1966. On quitting Softs 1968, engaged in variety of activities including touring U.S. with Jimi Hendrix and writing songs in Ibiza before recording first solo album **Joy Of A Toy** in 1970 with support from various Softs and composer David Bedford (➧).

Bedford joined Ayers soon after in latter's The Whole World, a group also featuring Lol Coxhill (saxes) and Mike Oldfield (gtr, bs). This band made two albums, **Shooting At The Moon** (released U.K. 1971) and **Whatevershebringswesing** (1972), before disbanding. Ayers subsequently switched permanently to guitar and continued in company of Whole World bassist Archie Legget to create U.K. stage show Banana Follies, the material from which comprised his fourth album **Bananamour** (1973).

For **The Confessions Of Dr Dream**, released U.K. 1974 and his most commercially successful venture to date, Ayers signed to Island label – in June of that year joining Island stablemates Eno, Nico and John Cale for celebrated London Rainbow gig recorded live on the album, **June 1 1974.**

From this peak, 1975-released **Sweet Deceiver** saw Ayers'

artistic stock slump alarmingly. A prime example of the unevenness of his work, many critics regard it as the nadir of Ayers' output. However, although he's yet failed to attract the attention his earlier work suggested he would merit, Ayers has to be recognised as a sophisticated (if erratic) rock composing/performing talent. His recent managerial shift to John Reid stable (Elton John, Queen) ought to presage renaissance of artistic and commercial potential.

Compilation set **Odd Ditties** (1976) is not "best of" as such, but comprises six never-before-released tracks plus eight previously on obscure and/or deleted singles.

Recordings:
Joy Of A Toy (—/Harvest)
Shooting At The Moon (—/Harvest)
Whatevershebringswesing (—/Harvest)
Bananamour (—/Harvest)
The Confessions Of Dr Dream (Island)
June 1 1974 (Island)
Sweet Deceiver (Island)
Compilations:
Odd Ditties (Harvest)

Babe Ruth

Ellie Hope vocals
Ray Knott bass
Steve Gurl keyboards
Ed Spevock drums
Bernie Marsden guitar

Formed in Hatfield, Hertfordshire, England, 1971 and originally called Shacklock after founder-member Alan Shacklock (gtr). Dave Hewitt (bs) also member of original four-strong line up, gig as lead vocalist going after auditions to Janita "Jenny" Haan, born in Edgware, England, but raised in U.S. from age 12 to 17.

On release of **First Base**, 1972, band changed name to Babe Ruth, after American baseball legend. Londoner Spevock joined group for **Amar Cabalero**. Meanwhile first album began to pick up U.S. chart action and went gold in Canada.

Babe Ruth, their third album, introduced another new recruit, Steve Gurl from Wild Turkey, and reached No. 75 in U.S. lists. Resulting U.S. tour demands, however, caused founder Shacklock to quit band shortly after. Bernie Marsden, also ex-Wild Turkey, brought in as replacement.

However, in Spring 1976, band rocked again by sudden departure of Jenny Haan and Dave Hewitt. Replacements Ellie Hope and Ray Knott made debuts on **Kid's Stuff** (Capitol).

Recordings:
First Base (Harvest)
Amar Cabalero (Harvest)
Babe Ruth (Harvest)
Stealin' Home (Capitol)
Kid's Stuff (Capitol)

Burt Bacharach

Born Kansas City May 12, 1928, is one of the most prolific and successful composers of popular music (usually in collaboration with lyricist Hal David).

After army service in the early '50s he found work as conductor and arranger with various record companies, and also worked for three years with Marlene Dietrich's night club act. Towards end of '50s began to establish himself as songwriter of distinction with **Story Of My Life** (a hit for Marty Robbins in U.S. and Michael Holliday, U.K.) and **Magic Moments**, a No. 1 for Perry Como in U.K.

In early '60s began association with Dionne Warwick, for whom he and Hal David wrote many songs now considered standards – **Walk On By, Anyone Who Had A Heart, This Girl's In Love With You** and **I Say A Little Prayer**. Also became involved with movie industry (initially through his marriage to actress Angie Dickinson), and scored "What's New Pussycat?" (the title-song of which established Tom Jones as a U.S. star), as well as "Butch Cassidy And The Sundance Kid", for which he received two Oscars – one for the score, one for theme song **Raindrops Keep Falling On My Head**.

Bacharach also had U.K. hit of his own, **Trains And Boats And Planes**, and wrote hit Broadway musical, "Promises, Promises". Makes occasional live appearances; also albums with his orchestra for A&M label. His remarkable success is probably due to fact that he brought a new concept to popular composition by visualising arrangement and melody together, and making the two virtually inseparable.

Not Fragile. Courtesy Mercury/Phonogram.

Bachman-Turner Overdrive

Randy Bachman vocals, guitar
Fred Turner vocals, bass
Blair Thornton guitar
Robbie Bachman drums

Leader Randy Bachman was founder-member of Canadian hit singles band Guess Who (◆) which he left in 1970 after illness and inter-group friction. Returning to native Canada, Bachman cut solo album **Axe** for RCA before forming outfit Brave Belt with brother Robbie, singer/bassist Fred Turner and erstwhile Guess Who founder Chad Allan. Originally with Reprise, for whom they recorded two albums, became BTO when Allan quit and third Bachman brother, Tim, joined line-up as additional guitarist. Band switched labels to Mercury for release of first album, the riff-happy **Bachman-Turner Overdrive**.

Tim Bachman quit after second (gold) album to study engineering and production, replaced by guitarist Thornton. Third album, **Not Fragile**, achieved platinum sales and provided U.S. and U.K. million-selling single **You Ain't Seen Nuthin' Yet** (1974). 1975 album **Four Wheel Drive** also achieved gold status.

Recordings:
Bachman-Turner Overdrive (Mercury)
Bachman-Turner Overdrive II (Mercury)
Not Fragile (Mercury)
Four Wheel Drive (Mercury)
Head On (Mercury)

Back Door

Colin Hodgkinson bass, vocals
Ron Aspery saxes, keyboards, flute, clarinet
Adrian Tilbrook drums

Unknown jazz-rock trio from Blakey, Yorkshire, N. England, when they cut and released first album, **Back Door**, in 1972 on small local label. Then featured Tony Hicks on drums. All three considerable musicians, though initial interest in Back Door largely due to bass playing of Colin Hodgkinson, whose revolutionary technique – including full chording – drew wide critical acclaim.

After "discovery" by U.K. rock press, signed by Warner Bros, which re-issued first album on

that label in 1973. Second album, **8th Street Blues** (1974) recorded in New York with producer Felix Pappalardi. **Activate** (1976) was produced by Carl Palmer.

Recordings:
Back Door (Warner Bros)
8th Street Blues (Warner Bros)
Another Fine Mess (Warner Bros)
Activate (Warner)

Bad Company

Paul Rodgers vocals
Mick Ralphs guitar
Boz Burrell bass
Simon Kirke drums

British band formed late 1973, played debut gig Newcastle March 9, 1974. Rodgers and Kirke formerly of Free (◆); Ralphs a founder member of Mott The Hoople (◆); Burrell, least known of four, previously with King Crimson (◆) where he learned bass under tuition of Robert Fripp.

Straight Shooter. Courtesy Island Recs.

Boasting the considerable vocal talents of Paul Rodgers (Rod Stewart has been on record on numerous occasions describing Rodgers as best singer in British rock) and managerial abilities of Led Zeppelin bossman Peter Grant, band met with considerable success on first U.S. tour in 1974.

Subsequently topped both U.S. charts with first album and debut single **Can't Get Enough** (1974). Ralphs had originally written the song for Mott The Hoople. However, Mott singer Ian Hunter lacked range to handle this and other Ralphs' compositions – and this was one reason for Ralphs leaving the band.

In 1974, Bad Company became the most successful new British band in the States – achieving almost instant recognition as a top flight heavyweight attraction. (In fact they had gone to the U.S. planning to be there for six weeks. Instead, starting as a support band, they went down a storm, were rapidly promoted to headlining status and didn't return to English homes until some three months later.)

Second and third albums released 1975 and 1976, all three appearing in U.S. on Led Zeppelin's Swan Song label.

Recordings:
Bad Company (Swan Song/Island)
Straight Shooter (Swan Song/Island)
Run With The Pack (Swan Song/Island)

Right: Joan Baez, Queen of Folk Protest to Dylan's King. Between 1963-65 they were lovers, their break-up being graphically documented in "Don't Look Back".

Badfinger

Pete Ham vocals, guitar, piano
Tom Evans vocals, bass
Mike Gibbins drums
Joey Molland vocals, guitar

In the summer of 1968, The Iveys submitted tapes to the Beatles' Apple Corps Ltd., and as a result were taken on by Apple. They were almost The Beatles writ small; Molland and Evans were from Liverpool (and Ham and Gibbins from Swansea), and the band had something of their vocal style. Possibly McCartney saw in them something of his own youth; certainly Molland was a McCartney look-alike.

After an early single **Maybe Tomorrow** was a hit everywhere except Britain, they worked in late '69 on soundtrack of "The Magic Christian" (starring Ringo and Peter Sellers) with McCartney, who wrote **Come And Get It** for the movie and them. The Iveys changed their name, and **Come And Get It** became the first hit for Badfinger.

While touring the U.S., they scored again with **No Matter What** and then worked on their album **No Dice**, which attracted universally favourable reviews and which contained the song **Without You** – a 1972 U.K. No. 1 for Nilsson (◆). Although McCartney had composed **Come And Get It**, the band were gaining most acceptance as songwriters rather than performers.

With a second U.S. tour behind them, band were invited by George Harrison to return to take part in Concert for Bangla Desh, and also helped out on various Beatle recording sessions (including those for Harrison's **All Things Must Pass**, Lennon's **Imagine**, and Ringo's single, **It Don't Come Easy**.) Their own album, **Straight Up**, produced by Todd Rundgren (◆) and released at beginning of '72, provided them with a U.S. No. 1 single – **Day After Day** – and they toured the U.S. twice that year.

For reasons which are not at all clear, but which might have something to do with increasing dispersal of The Beatles and also their own management difficulties, Badfinger surrendered this bridgehead before they had fully capitalised on it. The album **Ass** was released only after they had left Apple and signed for Warner Bros. Despite the presence there of former Apple associate Derek Taylor, the new contract yielded little for either party. Both **Badfinger** and **Wish You Were Here** were virtually stillborn.

Days after quitting the band, Pete Ham committed suicide on May 1, 1975, and Badfinger capitulated.

Recordings:
Magic Christian Music (Apple)
No Dice (Apple)
Straight Up (Apple)
Badfinger (Warner Bros)
Ass (Apple)
Wish You Were Here (Warner Bros)

Joan Baez

Originally traditional folk-singer with voice so pure it could shatter glass and dark beauty to match. Became darling of intellectual left in the U.S. and in the '60s emerged as most important, and most controversial, female performer.

Born New York, Jan 9, 1941, her father a Mexican physicist, her mother a teacher of English and Scottish drama, both her grandfathers were ministers. Her youth was spent moving between American campuses – a very middle-class upbringing.

Early experience singing in local choirs. Learned to play guitar and sing in Boston, Mass., before appearing regularly at Club 47, Cambridge, Mass. Enormous success at 1959 Newport Folk Festival brought her widespread national acclaim.

In 1960 she recorded **Joan Baez,** an album of traditional folk material, including many Scottish ballads. Album had quite unprecedented success and entered music charts in both U.S. and U.K.

With regular concert appearances, began making impact as – in Lilian Roxon's phrase – a "bargain-basement Pete Seeger"; but her popularity rapidly outstripped narrow confines of folk establishment.

Joan Baez, Vol. II and **In Concert, Vols. I & II** followed at yearly intervals, and helped enhance her reputation by adhering to proven formula of traditional songs, beautifully delivered, with a minimum of accompaniment – though nothing was ever to recapture the concentrated magic of **Joan Baez.**

Joan Baez In Concert included a song that came to be identified with her – **We Shall Overcome** – which was taken up as all-purpose protest song throughout Western hemisphere. It was an early indication of her burgeoning political awareness, and she sang it at a stream of much-publicised civil rights marches in the U.S., culminating in the 1963 Freedom March on Washington.

During this period, she was also associated with emergence of the young Bob Dylan. She enabled him to reach a wide public by introducing him regularly at her concerts (although later, on a European tour, he was not to return the favour).

Dylan wrote sleeve-notes for **Joan Baez In Concert, Vol. II** and from 1963 to 1965 they were lovers and regularly in each other's company – truly the King and Queen of Folk Protest. Towards the end of 1965 their relationship terminated, Joan walking out on Dylan in a scene recorded in the documentary film "Don't Look Back". He later reputedly wrote **Visions Of Johanna** about her, and 10 years later, Joan reflected on their relationship in **Diamonds And Rust.**

From **Joan Baez 5** onwards, she began to include on her albums more and more material by contemporary songwriters, and especially Dylan himself. **Any Day Now** was an entire double-album of Dylan songs.

Of those who populated protest platforms of the early '60s, Baez was the one whose commitment increased most demonstrably, and politics became the major concern of her life. In 1964 she was one of outside agitators denounced by the police for her activities in Berkeley demonstrations. She was a very active pacifist.

In 1965, in Carmel Valley, she founded Institute for Study Of Non-Violence, refused to pay taxes which would contribute towards American war effort in Vietnam, and became national symbol of protest. The idolization she had first experienced turned to hatred and contempt.

In 1968 published her autobiography, "Daybreak", and also a book of poems; also married student protest leader David Harris – at 22, five years her junior. He went to prison for draft evasion in 1969 and during this time **David's Album** and **One Day At A Time** were released.

The 1970 film, "Carry It On" (U.K. title: "Joan"), told of the marriage and her political activities. Significantly, there were few songs. In 1971 she publicly announced the break-up of her marriage; she has one child, Gabriel.

Blessed Are . . ., Carry It On and **Come From The Shadows** contained much original material, composed either by herself or sister Mimi Farina (➡); her commitment on record then peaked with **Where**

Are You Now, My Son?, side two of which was a documentary recording made in Hanoi during a U.S. bombing attack. **Gracias A La Vida** was entirely in Spanish (her inability to speak Spanish had been one of Joan's childhood regrets).

She then made a "volte-face" – claimed it was a long time since she'd made music for music's sake, and also announced that in any case she was short of money. **Diamonds And Rust** was arguably her first-ever commercial album; it was thoroughly enjoyable, containing some of her own strongest compositions, as well as material by Stevie Wonder and Jackson Browne. It was her biggest seller for a decade or more, and also the first time she'd used an electric band to such stimulating effect.

Diamonds And Rust seemed to recharge her career, although not at the expense of her principles to which she remained as fervently committed as ever. In 1975 she went out on the road with a band – David Briggs (kybds), Dan Ferguson (gtr), Larry Carlton (gtr), James Jamerson (bs) and Jim Gordon (drms). **From Every Stage** was a double-album of live recordings from this tour. Thus revivified, she played a prominent part later in the year in Bob Dylan's Rolling Thunder tour and once again there seemed to be a special chemistry between them. At the beginning of 1976 her career seemed in healthier shape than it had for years.

Recordings:
Joan Baez (Vanguard)
Joan Baez, Vol. II (Vanguard)
Joan Baez In Concert (Vanguard)
Joan Baez In Concert, Vol. II (Vanguard)
Joan Baez 5 (Vanguard)
Farewell Angelina (Vanguard)
Noel (Vanguard)
Joan (Vanguard)
Baptism – A Journey Through Our Time (Vanguard)
Any Day Now (Vanguard)
David's Album (Vanguard)
One Day At A Time (Vanguard)
Blessed Are . . . (Vanguard)
Carry It On (Vanguard)
Come From The Shadows (A&M)
Where Are You Now, My Son? (A&M)
Gracias A La Vida (A&M)
Diamonds And Rust (A&M)
From Every Stage (A&M)

Compilations:
The First Ten Years (Vanguard)
also contributions to:
Woodstock (Atlantic)
Celebration At Big Sur (Ode)

*Gracias A La Vida.
Courtesy A&M Records.*

Peter 'Ginger' Baker

Born Lewisham, London, 1939. First played trumpet as teenager, but switched to drums and played in a number of jazz bands, including those led by British trad jazzers Acker Bilk and Terry Lightfoot, before replacing Charlie Watts in Alexis Korner's Blues Incorporated in 1962.

Left Blues Inc (◗ British R&B) in February following year with Graham Bond and Jack Bruce to form Graham Bond Trio – later Graham Bond (◗) Organization – and remained with Bond for more than three years.

Formed Cream (◗) with Eric Clapton and Jack Bruce in summer 1966. After end of Cream in late 1968, teamed up again with Clapton following year for short-lived Blind Faith (◗). In January 1970 formed ill-fated, top heavy Air Force aggregation around nucleus of Steve Winwood, Graham Bond, Denny Laine, Chris Wood, Rick Grech and Remi Kabaka. Before they split in disarray, recorded the two albums listed below, both first released in 1970, the second being a live set.

Disillusioned by Air Force experience, Baker pursued growing interest in African music which led him, in 1971, to buy a plot of land to build own studio in Akeja, Nigeria. Performed sporadically during this period with Fela Ransome-Kuti and briefly led a mainly Nigerian band, Salt, until he quit performing temporarily early in 1973 to concentrate on studio which he opened in January that year. (Paul McCartney's **Band On The Run** recorded there later in the year.)

Recordings:
Air Force 1 (Atco/Polydor)
Air Force 2 (Atco/Polydor)
Fela Ransome-Kuti And Ginger Baker Live (Signpost/EMI)
Stratavarious (Atco/Polydor)
Compilations:
Ginger Baker At His Best (RSO)

Baker Gurvitz Army

Peter "Ginger" Baker drums
Adrian Gurvitz guitar
Paul Gurvitz bass
Snips vocals
Peter Lemer keyboards

Emerged out of Three Man Army: formed late 1974 by Baker (◗) and Gurvitz brothers, formerly of British outfit Gun, who had 1967 U.K. No. 1 single with **Race With The Devil**. Snips recruited later from remnants of Sharks (◗), and jazz-based Peter Lemer from Seventh Wave. Albums first released in U.K. 1974 and 1975. Adrian Gurvitz has also recorded with Graeme Edge of Moody Blues (◗). Peter Lemer left in 1976.

Recordings:
Baker Gurvitz Army (Janus/ Vertigo)
Elysian Encounter (Atco/ Mountain)
Hearts On Fire (Atco/Mountain)

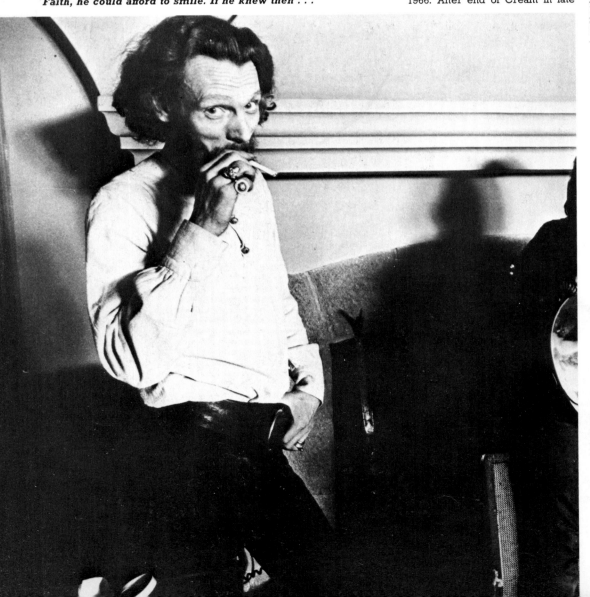

Below: Peter "Ginger" Baker looking like the cat who ate the cream (ouch). Having just joined the money-spinning Blind Faith, he could afford to smile. If he knew then . . .

*Elysian Encounter.
Courtesy Mountain.*

Long John Baldry

Born London 1940, "Long" prefix derives from height (6ft 7in). Of interest due to role played in U.K. blues and R&B booms (♦ Blues – British and British R&B) and in careers of Elton John (♦) and Rod Stewart (♦). Possessed of powerful rasping voice ideal for genre, Baldry appeared with Alexis Korner's Blues Inc (♦ Alexis Korner) and subsequently as second vocalist to Cyril Davies (♦) in latter's All Stars, one of earliest R&B bands, which he took over and renamed The Hoochie Coochie Men after Davies' death in 1964. Recordings from this period compiled on **Long John's Blues**.

Rod Stewart then became Baldry's second vocalist, the pair of them subsequently joining Brian Auger and Julie Driscoll in touring R&B revue Steampacket.

Baldry teamed with Bluesology, Elton John then being his keyboards player, but then committed unpardonable "sin" of denying his roots to make stab for stardom in MOR field. He seemed to have pulled it off when, in 1967, his **Let The Heartaches Begin** ballad went to No. 1 in U.K. charts, but when he failed to sustain success Baldry slipped away into limbo, despite 1971 return to rock LP **It Ain't Easy** co-produced (one side each) by Rod Stewart and Elton John. Albums listed below omit pop period.

Recordings:
Long John's Blues (United Artists)
It Ain't Easy (Warner Bros)
Everyone Stops For Tea (Warner Bros)

Hank Ballard

Born Nov 18, 1936, Detroit, U.S. In 1953 joined The Royals, who changed their name to Hank Ballard and the Midnighters and went on to enjoy some success for King records of Cincinnati.

Originally, Ballard was famous for recording a series of suggestive R&B records (among them **Work With Me Annie** and **Annie Had A Baby**) which, in the directness of lyrics and rawness of rhythm, could claim to be true precursors of rock 'n' roll. Although the records sold well in Negro communities, they were banned from airwaves and hence never achieved widespread success; but this was an early demonstration of the fact that rock 'n' roll could expect to be bowdlerised before it could reach mass commercial acceptance.

After this initial flurry, they did little more of interest until major 1958 hit, **Teardrops On My Letter** – the B-side of which was **The Twist**, which two years later, in a more commercial form, became a multi-million seller for Chubby Checker – possibly the most successful single of all time (it topped the U.S. charts in 1960 and 1961). Again, Ballard missed out, as even though his version also sold a million, it never registered on any charts. Ballard had other hits – **Finger Poppin' Time, Let's Go, Let's Go, Let's Go** – but by the mid-'60s had hit hard times; the band broke up, and he played as solo performer, usually in smaller clubs on soul circuit. However, because of the rawness of his early sound he remained a

Right: Music From Big Pink. Courtesy Capitol Records/EMI.

major influence, to both black and white musicians. Among others, The Allman Brothers (♦) have acknowledged a debt to him.

In 1974 his own career was resuscitated somewhat when he was signed to the small but perky All Platinum label.

Russ Ballard

For seven years lead guitarist/vocalist for British outfit Argent (♦) which he quit Feb 1974 to pursue solo career. Previously with Adam Faith's Roulettes and Unit 4 + 2 at time of their **Concrete And Clay** U.K. hit (1965). Ballard was responsible for much of Argent material, including the song **Liar** which Three Dog Night re-worked for U.S. million-seller. First solo album released 1975, second in following year.

Recordings:
Russ Ballard (Epic)
Winning (Epic)

Banco

Pier Luigi Calderoni drums
Gianni Nocenzi keyboards, clarinet
Renato D'Angelo bass
Rodolfo Maltese guitars, trumpet
Vittorio Nocenzi keyboards
Franceso Di Giacomo vocals

Formed Rome, Italy, 1971 through amalgamation of two top Italian rock bands Fiori Di Campo and Experience. First album, **Banco del Mutuo Succorso**, made No. 1 in Italian LP lists 1972, as did second, **Darwin** (1973), and third, **Io Sono Nato Libero** (later same year).

Prime exponents of what has been dubbed "Spaghetti Rock", Banco were signed following year to Emerson Lake and Palmer's newly-formed Manticore label for whom they recorded first U.K. and U.S. release, **Banco**, in London 1975.

Recordings:
Banco (Manticore)

The Band

Jaime Robbie Robertson guitar
Richard Manuel piano, vocals
Levon Helm drums, vocals
Garth Hudson organ, saxophone
Rick Danko bass, vocals

Together professionally since early '60s, The Band backed rock 'n' roller Ronnie Hawkins (as the Hawks) in Canada, and then began a professional relationship with Bob Dylan on his 1966 U.K. tour (during which the famous Albert Hall concert, which was subsequently bootlegged, took place). In 1967, after Dylan's motorcycle accident, they recorded the legendary Basement Tapes with him at Big Pink – their communal home in Woodstock – while he was recuperating.

In the following year their debut

Stage Fright. Courtesy Capitol Records/EMI.

album, **Music From Big Pink**, caused minor sensation in music circles, and the brilliant sequel, **The Band**, proved to be every bit as good as Eric Clapton and George Harrison's advance opinions had suggested; it achieved classic status immediately.

The Band established unique style based on Robbie Robertson's songwriting (he took his inspiration from the rich vein of U.S. rural traditions and folk-lore) and the economical and effortless playing of group as a whole.

Stage Fright may have lacked the intense dramatic qualities of **The Band**, but was outstanding nevertheless. Then things began to go wrong – **Cahoots** is interesting (and includes a bonus item – a track created in partnership with Van Morrison), but it lacked the firm sense of direction of earlier work, and it was to be over four

years before another album of original Robertson material was produced.

After their appearance on Dec 31, 1971, at the New York Academy Of Music (recorded as live **Rock Of Ages**, which featured mostly material from previous albums) they did nothing until they performed at Watkins Glen festival in July '73.

Ostensibly The Band spent their time in studio, but emerged with little to show for their efforts. Robertson's ambitious project, a complex, thematic work was shelved, and eventually they released **Moondog Matinee**, a precisely arranged labour of love, a memorial to their rock 'n' roll roots in the early '50s.

In 1974 they resumed live work with Dylan in the U.S., with a tour that was later immortalised on the **Before The Flood** album. (They were co-credited on this, as they were on **The Basement Tapes** when that was finally issued in 1975.) Also they provided all the back-up work on Dylan's **Planet Waves**.

In late '75, The Band's own long-awaited album of new material materialised. **Northern Lights – Southern Cross** was almost inevitably disappointing, but it showed they had not lost their instrumental tightness, or Robertson his ear for melody. Only the lyrics were below par – the astronomical implications of title were never explored.

The members of the group are shy and retiring, and have never aspired to the exclusive circles of the professional rock elite, preferring to lead quiet family lives. They have hardly ever guested on other albums – they made an exception for Ringo Starr's **Ringo** album, but played on one track only. **Stage Fright** is a song about themselves. But they have produced some of the most picturesque and enchanting of all rock music.

Robertson's latest solo project is the production of a Neil Diamond album, **Beautiful Noise**.

Below: Time Honoured Ghosts.

Recordings:
Music From Big Pink (Capitol)
The Band (Capitol)
Stage Fright (Capitol)
Cahoots (Capitol)
Rock Of Ages (Capitol)
Moondog Matinee (Capitol)
Northern Lights – Southern Cross (Capitol)

Above: The first publicity pic of The Band, getting ethnic at Big Pink. L to r, Manuel, Hudson, Helm, Robertson, Danko.

TIME HONOURED GHOSTS

Barclay James Harvest

Stewart "Wooly" Wolstenholme keyboards, vocals
Melvin Pritchard drums
Les Holroyd bass, vocals
John Lees guitar, vocals

British group, formed early 1967 around Oldham, Lancashire area – Wolstenholme and Lees at art school together – signing to Harvest label following year (EMI reputedly named their new label after them). Released first album in U.K. 1969. Line-up has remained intact since inception, as has music, which fits loosely into "flash-rock" categorization, leaning heavily on Wolstenholme's use of mellotron and keyboards. Although not always favoured with critical approval, BJH have on a number of occasions (for instance, when they switched labels in U.K. to Polydor) appeared to be on brink of major commercial breakthrough.

In U.K., however, are established as consistently in-demand gigging band with relatively small but ardent following. Second, third and fourth albums, as listed below, first released in U.K. 1970, '71 and '72. Albums five and six both released 1974, their most recent set in 1975 recorded in San Francisco with producer Eliot Mazer. In U.K. compilation set **Early Morning Onwards** re-leased on Starline label 1972.

Recordings:
Barclay James Harvest (Capitol/Harvest)
Once Again (Capitol/Harvest)
Short Stories (Capitol/Harvest)
Baby James Harvest (Capitol/Harvest)
Everyone Is Everybody Else (Polydor)
Barclay James Harvest "Live" (Polydor)
Time Honoured Ghosts (Polydor)

Barefoot Jerry

Wayne Moss rhythm guitar
Jim Colvard lead guitar
Russ Hicks steel guitar
Si Edwards drums
Terry Dearmore bass, vocals
Warren Hartman keyboards

Group emerged from the ashes of Area Code 615 (➧) with Moss, the band's producer and now the only surviving original member, as the main protagonist. As with Area Code 615, the band is composed of experienced session musicians based in Nashville, who divide their time between work for the band and other diverse assignments. Hence they tour as a unit only occasionally, and have

more interesting rock specimen
than might first appear. First gig
in music business was as staff
songwriter with Liberty Records
in U.K. Later promoted to A&R
manager, he produced first album
for Groundhogs (➡) and instigated
fleeting psychedelic phenomenon,
Haphash And The Coloured Coat.
As independent writer/producer
recorded series of orchestral
albums for British Silverline Records (arrangements of Beatles,
Stones material); did synthesiser
album for Pye label; arranged
strings on first celebrated Family
album, **Music In A Doll's House,**
and wrote TV advertising jingles
for likes of Guinness beer, Rice
Krispies and Smarties sweets.
Since setting up Wombles "hit
factory" (five U.K. hits and three
albums over two years), Batt has
enjoyed two hits in U.K. charts
under own name and in 1975
produced album for Steeleye
Span (➡), their most commercially
successful.

The Bay City Rollers

Leslie McKeown vocals
Stuart Wood guitar
Ian Mitchell bass
Eric Faulkner guitar
Derek Longmuir drums

Originally known as The Saxons,
the Bay City Rollers, from Edinburgh, became in 1975 the biggest
phenomenon to hit U.K. pop music
scene since The Beatles.

Band line-up shuffled quite regularly in early '70s, but manager
Tam Paton kept driving Rollers
onward, overlooking fact that
members of the band as it finally
evolved possessed no more than
ordinary talents. It was Paton's
astute management, and a suc-

never played outside the U.S. as
Barefoot Jerry.

They are all country musicians
moving into the rock field, and
their strength lies in Colvard's
guitar-playing, though Moss himself is a highly respected and versatile musician. He had his own
studios in Nashville by 1962, and
is a veteran of hundreds of sessions, including those for Bob
Dylan's **Blonde On Blonde.
Grocery,** issued in 1976, is a
double-album of previously unissued material that post-dates the
Area Code 615 sessions.

Recordings:
Watchin' TV (Monument/—)
**You Can't Get Off With Your
Shoes On** (Monument)
Grocery (Monument/—)

Syd Barrett

Born Roger Keith Barrett in Cambridge, England, Jan 1946, as
founder member of Pink Floyd (➡)
his quizzical, surrealistic lyrics
and visionary obsessions with
interplanetary mysticism formed
hard core of British psychedelia,
circa 1967. Formed and named
Pink Floyd 1965 while student at
Camberwell Art School, London.

Responsible for original concept
of band, writing both their early
U.K. hit singles, **Arnold Layne** and
See Emily Play (both 1967), and
group's first album, **Piper At The
Gates Of Dawn** (same year).

Dropping acid and becoming
increasingly withdrawn and ec-

centric, personality problems
gradually turned Barrett from
asset to liability and in April 1968,
he was replaced by David Gilmour.

Set about recording solo album
The Madcap Laughs in early
1970, completing half of it in just
two days with assistance from
Gilmour and Roger Waters, and
in November same year complet-
ed a second solo set, **Barrett,** with
Gilmour, Rick Wright and drummer Jerry Shirley. Although there
was/has been much talk of a third
solo album, Barrett hasn't been
heard on record since.

Over past five years various
stories and legends have grown
around him (a U.K. Syd Barrett
Appreciation Society continues to
publish a monthly newsletter
"Terrapin") one being that he's
spent most of recent times holed
up in a Cambridge cellar. Early
Floyd manager Peter Jenner
made futile attempt to record him
in 1974, and most recent story was
that when Floyd mixed **Shine On
You Crazy Diamond** (dedicated
to memory of Barrett) for 1975
Wish You Were Here album, Syd
turned up in studio uninvited and
unexpected and announced that
he was "ready to do his bit".

Dave Gilmour has said of him:
"... one of the three or four
greats, along with Bob Dylan."

Albums below subsequently re-
issued as Harvest double-set.

Recordings:
The Madcap Laughs (Harvest)
Barrett (Harvest)

Mike Batt

Principally known in U.K. as
creator and songwriter for hit-
making spin-off group from children's TV series "The Wombles",
Southampton-born Batt is a much

Below: Barrett. Harvest.

cession of carefully chosen singles – mostly written by Bill Martin and Phil Coulter (bespoke song-writers for many years; they had composed Britain's first outright winner of the Eurovision Song Contest, Sandie Shaw's **Puppet On A String**) – that enabled Rollers to hit such impregnable peaks. Accusations that they didn't play on their records just became irrelevant.

They are more than a pop group, they are an entire cult, an opportunity for their pubescent audience to imitate their Tartan gear. Although they are Scotland's own, their success is unconfined.

First hit U.K. charts in late '71 with **Keep On Dancing**, and through a string of teen-appeal ditties like **Summerlove Sensation** and **Shang-A-Lang**, just got bigger and bigger, until they peaked in Spring '75 with an old Four Seasons' song, **Bye Bye Baby**, and a nationwide tour which was given daily coverage by a rapacious national press. At last, the new phenomenon – Rollermania. Their albums might seem leadenly uninspired, but they have all gone gold anyway.

This achieved, the Rollers set out with calm deliberation to conquer the U.S. A No. 1 single – **Saturday Night** – augured well; as U.S. success was consolidated in 1976. Alan Longmuir left, and Mitchell was drafted in.

Recordings:
Rolling (—/Bell)
Once Upon A Star (—/Bell)
Wouldn't You Like It (—/Bell)
Rock 'n' Roll Love Letter (Arista/—)

Left: The Beach Boys, when it looked like good vibrations all the way. From bottom left, clockwise: Al Jardine, Dennis, Brian, Carl Wilson, Mike Love.

Beach Boys

Brian Wilson vocals
Carl Wilson vocals, guitar
Dennis Wilson vocals, drums
Mike Love vocals
Al Jardine vocals, guitar

Formed Los Angeles 1961 by Wilson brothers Carl (born Dec 21, 1946), Dennis (Dec 4, 1944) and compositional genius Brian (June 20, 1942) – all from middle-class district of Hawthorne, California. While at school, the brothers harmonised in friends' and relatives' homes along with cousin Mike Love (Mar 15, 1941) and Al Jardine (Sept 3, 1942).

Played high school hops as Carl And The Passions and later Kenny And The Cadets (Brian was Kenny) until the Brian Wilson composition **Surfin'** in 1961. It was Dennis who was the surfer in the group, and who one day suggested it to brother Brian – who had studied music theory at school – that he write a song on that subject. **Surfin'**, recorded in demo studio, came out on small Candix label – group choosing name Beach Boys to fit the song – and became local and then national hit. (Other Candix material contained on U.S. only **Greatest Hits 1961-63** compilation.)

In one swoop, from very few influences, Brian Wilson had created a whole new genre – surf music. As Nik Cohn said in his book, "Awopbopaloobop": "He (Wilson) worked a loose-limbed group sound and added his own falsetto. Then he stuck in some lazy twang guitar and rounded it all out with jumped up Four Freshmen harmonies. No sweat, he'd created a bonafide surf music out of nothing. More, he had invented California".

The group made their debut on New Years Eve 1961, following with their first tour in early 1962 – Wilsons' neighbour David L. Marks taking Al Jardine's place for six months while latter attended dental college.

From Candix to mighty Capitol label and two more hits, **Surfin' Safari** (1962) and **Surfin' U.S.A.** (1963), on which Brian Wilson hooked surf lyrics to Chuck Berry's **Sweet Little Sixteen** riff. **Surfer Girl** and **Little Deuce Coupe**, the latter marking Brian's new interest in hot rods and dragster racing, followed, and in same year the elder Wilson composed the million-selling Jan & Dean hit **Surf City**. **Surfin' U.S.A.**

album (1963) earned first gold record, a success repeated by **Surfer Girl**.

Fun Fun Fun, Little Honda and **I Get Around** made singles lists in 1964, but it wasn't until the unusually-complex last-named – backed with "forgotten masterpiece" **Don't Worry Baby** – that the Beach Boys began to obtain serious critical attention.

Towards end of same year, however, Brian Wilson began to suffer pressures of stress and over-work. With nervous breakdown early 1965, Brian announced decision to stop touring with band and instead mastermind their recording career from behind the scenes. Bruce Johnston was drafted in as replacement, after brief stay by Glen Campbell (➧).

By now, singles like **Help Me Rhonda** and **California Girls** were beginning to evolve new subtleties in composition and production, a direction re-enforced by Brian's first post-touring album **Beach Boys – Today** (1965). Albums **Summer Days And Summer Nights** and **Beach Boys Party** followed in same year, after which Brian set himself to work on major project **Pet Sounds** with lyricist Tony Asher.

Slowly, however, the Beach Boys and their creative mastermind had begun to drift apart. While group toured world, Brian started hanging out with one Van Dyke Parks (➧), later to write Beach Boys lyrics, started dropping acid and went through a period of attempting to disown his musical past.

The masterwork **Pet Sounds** was, in fact, put together under heavy contractual pressures from Capitol and not at all approved by rest of group when they returned to U.S. On release in 1966, it was received well by critics and by Beach Boys aficionados in U.K. but bombed in the U.S.

However, though not as influential as contemporary Beatles album **Revolver, Pet Sounds** did set totally new standards in arrangement and production that diverted pop on to unforeseen track.

Beatles status at time is of more than passing interest here, because Brian Wilson was by all accounts possessed of quite acute feelings of competitiveness towards the British group. Thus, the commercial failure of **Pet Sounds** dented his pride badly – a blow only slightly eased by gold record sales for revolutionary **Good Vibrations**, one of finest pop singles of all time, later same year.

There then followed the most enigmatic period in the Brian Wilson/ Beach Boys career – the **Smile** album project with new lyricist Van Dyke Parks. With the group on his back to produce more commercial

Above: Pet Sounds. Courtesy Capitol Records/EMI.

Above: Surf's Up. Courtesy Warner Bros Records.

material (they also harboured a deep resentment towards Parks), Wilson saw **Smile** as his tour de force – his masterpiece which would give the Beatles their come-uppance and show the watching world that Brian Wilson, the artistic genius, was where the direction of pop was really at.

Yet the new album was plagued by bad vibes and slow to materialise, and when, in spring 1967, the Beatles released **Sgt Pepper** to unprecedented universal acclaim, Brian Wilson withdrew into a state of sustained paranoia. One theory is that Wilson realised **Smile** could only come out second best in comparison to **Sgt Pepper** and thus decided to withdraw from "battle".

Whatever the truth, Wilson took only three or four of the songs prepared for **Smile** – omitting the epic **Surf's Up** – wrote a bunch of new material and released same under the title **Smiley Smile** (1967), which even in its revamped state is one of rock's most maligned and misunderstood albums. (Some 15 tracks were originally composed for **Smile,** nine of which have subsequently turned up on various BBs albums.)

A sequence of critically-unfavoured albums followed – first of which, **Wild Honey** (1968) – was recorded by group in Brian's living room and marked return to simpler music. By this time, burgeoning San Francisco rock scene was beginning to break out nationally and Beach Boys in comparison drew bad press for their all-American persona and

whole "plastic L.A. trip".

Brian Wilson, suffering from a hearing defect, was a disillusioned man; and Dennis Wilson, after breakdown of his marriage, was having own problems – it was in this period he became involved with Charles Manson, a story well-documented in press at time.

Other members of band – Mike Love in particular – became involved in transcendental meditation, an influence evident on the 1968 **Friends** album which was released in wake of near-disastrous U.S. tour.

By 1970 – despite 1969 **Do It Again** hit from **Friends** – Beach Boys were at their lowest ebb. They had left Capitol for Warner-Reprise (changeover in U.K. not until 1972) and first album for new label, **Sunflower,** represented group at a new low. (It was also last BBs album personally directed by Brian until **15 Big Ones** in 1976.)

In 1970, however, came chance for a renaissance. Group went down well with critics and audience at a Monterey Festival, hitched on to ecology bandwagon in series of benefit gigs, and jammed with Grateful Dead at Fillmore West summer 1971 – an event witnessed by Bob Dylan who was heard to mutter "they're great" within earshot of at least one reporter.

For next album, **Surf's Up,** the Brian Wilson/V. D. Parks epic for **Smile** was rescued from vaults and released mid-1971 to critical acclaim and healthy sales, resuscitating interest in group and returning them to rightful place among world's leading rock bands.

Below: Endless Summer. Courtesy Capitol Records/EMI.

Below: Holland. Courtesy Warner Bros Records.

South Africans Ricky Fataar and Blondie Chaplin (now departed) came in to fill out stage sound. Yet, despite acclaimed concert appearances, Beach Boys as recording group failed to take advantage of second-wind reputation. **Carl And The Passions**, a double set uniting **Pet Sounds** with new material, was one of poorest ever albums, and the early 1973 **Holland** album – recorded in Amsterdam – was, so the story goes, at one point in danger of being rejected by Warner-Reprise until label bosses brought in Van Dyke Parks and forced Brian Wilson to complete embryonic part-written composition **Sail On Sailor.**

That track aside, Brian Wilson's output since late '60s has been virtually non-existent – descending further still into his role as confused genius. In Nick Kent's lengthy Brian Wilson article in "New Musical Express" 1975, one-time Beatles and Beach Boys PR Derek Taylor is quoted thus: "Brian though – one day he's coherent . . . bright, and then the next he can be so damn illogical . . . strange . . . scarey."

Ironically, however, American public – somewhat behind U.K. – has spent last couple of years rediscovering Beach Boys history. Frustrating group's own efforts to de-emphasize their past, a well-compiled classics anthology, **Endless Summer**, topped U.S. charts mid-1974, and that and the similarly-retrospective **Spirit Of America** have since gone platinum. 1974 Reprise **In Concert** album, a live double set, has also achieved U.S. gold status.

For three years no new studio product was forthcoming. When a new album did appear (ballyhooed as Brian Wilson's return) it was anti-climatic in the extreme. **15 Big Ones** – a reference to the number of tracks, and the age of the band – did indeed feature Brian singing, writing and "directing", but it was a perplexingly forlorn collection that appeared to indicate a total dearth of direction and ideas.

Much as they might be lost in the '70s, however, the importance of Brian Wilson and the Beach Boys can never be undermined.

Recordings:	
Surfin' Safari (Capitol)	**Friends** (Capitol)
Surfin U.S.A. (Capitol)	**20/20** (Capitol)
Surfer Girl (Capitol)	**Sunflower** (Reprise/Stateside)
Little Deuce Coupe (Capitol)	**Surf's Up** (Reprise/Stateside)
Shut Down Vol. II (Capitol)	**Carl And The Passions/**
All Summer Long (Capitol)	**So Tough** (Reprise)
Christmas Album (Capitol)	**Holland** (Reprise)
Beach Boys – Today (Capitol)	**In Concert** (Reprise)
Beach Boys In Concert (Capitol)	**15 Big Ones** (Reprise)
Summer Days And Summer	Compilations:
Nights (Capitol)	**The Beach Boys Greatest Hits**
Beach Boys Party (Capitol)	**1961-63** (Orbi/—)
Pet Sounds (Capitol)	**Endless Summer** (Capitol)
Smiley Smile (Capitol)	**Spirit Of America** (Capitol)
Wild Honey (Capitol)	**Good Vibrations** (Warner Bros)
	20 Golden Greats (—/Capitol)

The Beatles

John Lennon guitar, vocals	**George Harrison** guitar, vocals
Paul McCartney bass, vocals	**Ringo Starr** drums, vocals

All four born in Liverpool – Lennon Oct 9, 1940; McCartney June 18, 1942; Harrison Feb 25, 1943; Starr July 7, 1940. Originally Lennon had formed a school group called The Quarrymen, and had met McCartney, who in turn had introduced Lennon to school-friend of his, Harrison. When they left school in 1959, all were keen to continue playing together. Lennon went on to Liverpool College Of Art where he met Stuart Sutcliffe, whom he persuaded to take up bass.

They thus had three guitarists and a bass-player, though Sutcliffe was hardly competent. After playing locally, they obtained an audition with one of U.K.'s leading impresarios, Larry Parnes, who was sufficiently impressed to send them on a short tour of Scotland backing Johnny Gentle. It was at this time that they started calling themselves the Silver Beatles, although even then it seemed they preferred the simple abbreviation, The Beatles.

Still they needed a regular drummer, and found one in Pete Best, son of the owner of Liverpool's Casbah Club. The need had been made more pressing by the fact that on returning from Scotland the band were offered a residency in Hamburg – which turned out to be the first of five such stints. It was there they were to learn the endurance and stage extroversion which enabled them to make such a dramatic impact back home. Nevertheless, the first visit was cut short when the German authorities discovered that George was under-age to be playing in public performance in bars and clubs.

Back in Liverpool they were rawer and cruder, their stamina and inventiveness considerably strengthened. They began to make solid reputations for themselves in the North-West. When they played a return engagement in Hamburg (during which they made their first recordings, under the direction of Bert Kaempfert, as backing musicians for Tony Sheridan), Stu Sutcliffe opted to stay on and continue his art education, and McCartney took up bass. In April 1962, Sutcliffe tragically died of a brain haemorrhage.

When they returned to Liverpool, the group were taken in hand by local record shop owner Brian Epstein (➔). After he'd arranged an unproductive audition for them at Decca Records, the band returned to Hamburg, where they were telegrammed by Epstein. George Martin at EMI records liked their demo tapes, and a recording session had been fixed.

With this decisive step in front of them, Lennon, McCartney and Harrison decided to oust Best, and offered the job to Ringo Starr, who'd met the others in Hamburg while playing with Rory Storme and the Hurricanes.

The last piece thus in position, The Beatles came back to take up a contract with EMI Records in September 1962, and take their first tentative steps to becoming the most phenomenal recording artists ever known.

Under the guidance of producer George Martin – henceforward to play an important part until almost the very end – the first single, **Love Me Do**, was a minor hit towards the end of the year; but it was not until 1963 and **Please Please Me**, which topped the U.K. charts, that the ball started rolling for what the national press was to dub "Beatle-mania".

Two more hits – **From Me To You, She Loves You** – followed, as well as their debut album, **Please Please Me**, but it was not until their fifth single, **I Want To Hold Your Hand**, was promoted by Capitol records in the U.S. that the group achieved recognition there in 1964. By the time of their first U.S. tour in April 1964 their records were, incredibly, filling the top five places of the "Cashbox" singles chart.

With The Beatles both capitalised on their first overseas success and consolidated their, by now, unprecedented reputation at home.

By mid-64 the band were touring almost continuously in the U.K., Europe, the U.S. and Australia, and after their sixth hit, **Can't Buy Me Love**, withdrew momentarily to make their first feature film, "A Hard Day's Night", directed by Dick Lester from a script by Alun Owen.

A departure from the pop-film tradition, "A Hard Day's Night" did not attempt to portray The Beatles as singing actors in the stereotyped dramatic situations of an Elvis Presley or Cliff Richard feature, but used documentary techniques linked by surreal episodes to illustrate the life-style the band were actually living.

The film was an unequivocal commercial and critical success, and opened even more avenues for the band as fully-fledged entertainers, not merely musicians. This could be discerned in two ways. Firstly, The Beatles were granted an open sesame to literary and intellectual company everywhere. In 1964, after the publication of John Lennon's first book "In His Own Write", he was invited to be guest of honour at Foyle's literary lunch. And secondly, The Beatles had now become the first rock band to bridge the generation gap; theirs was no longer merely an adolescent audience – they really did appeal to everyone from eight to 80.

A Hard Day's Night. Courtesy Parlophone Records/EMI.   *Please Please Me. Courtesy Parlophone Records/EMI.*

The soundtrack album **A Hard Day's Night** was equally well-received, and the title-track provided the band with their seventh consecutive hit single in Britain.

In the latter half of 1964 **Beatles For Sale** was released, retreating in format from **A Hard Day's Night** which had been entirely composed of original material, to that of **Please Please Me** and **With The Beatles** which featured eight Beatles' originals, plus six compositions by other artists. **I Feel Fine** saw out the year as the No. 1 single in both the U.K. and U.S. It was The Beatles' eighth U.K. hit, their sixth consecutive No. 1.

From here on though, the band virtually ignored all outside sources, and 1965 showed the group beginning to consciously reject the instant commercial material of the previous two years, beginning with the highly personal **Ticket To Ride** which, despite managerial misgivings, was no less successful than earlier hits.

"Help!", their second movie, again directed by Lester, somewhat jumped the gun on The Beatles' new-found self-consciousness, and its surreal humour emerged as self-indulgent, although the accompanying album, **Help!**, was the biggest yet. Once again the title-track, issued as a single, was a worldwide hit – but this time the group did not return to touring, retiring instead to the recording studio to work on **Rubber Soul.**

In many ways **Rubber Soul** started a new kind of break-through. The songs were powerful, the music sophisticated and well-produced (though Beatles' songs had never been anything but), the lyrics by turn acerbic and wittily ironic, often relating to personal experience. The aim was nearly always true.

Their work was henceforth infused with a new positivism. With **Paperback Writer** they took further the process initiated on **Rubber Soul,** and focussed more sharply on lyrics and the technical side of electric sound-production. The major fruits of this phase, though, were

Right: They went up the stairs. They came down the stairs. The flash-bulbs duly popped. This particular shot dates from Sept 1964, and could have been taken almost anywhere in the world. For the record, they are leaving New York.

provided by **Revolver,** which many regard as their most consistently successful album. The painstaking care granted to each track was quite unique, as was both the scope and the unimpaired brilliance of their inventiveness. It all showed that touring for them had become something more than an irritating duty; it had become a positive obstacle to their progress, and in the latter half of 1966 they abandoned it altogether.

Growing in confidence, they issued at the beginning of 1967 what is normally considered the best pop single of all time – **Penny Lane/Strawberry Fields Forever.** They followed even this in the most devastating manner possible. **Sergeant Pepper's Lonely Hearts Club Band,** released June 1, 1967, is traditionally regarded as the apex not only of their career, but of rock music per se. Conceived as an unbroken series of songs, it featured an impressive array of styles, some dazzling and innovatory production techniques and climaxed astonishingly in the literally mind-blowing **A Day In The Life.** The intricate design of the sleeve set entirely new standards of record art-work (and the idea of printing the lyrics on the sleeve similarly started a whole new thing).

It has not aged well, but its contemporary effect was incalculable. August critics who had previously put their reputations on the line for the band now found their faith triumphantly vindicated. The world at large received it rapturously.

Epstein had had reservations about the whole enterprise, and by now The Beatles' need of a manager was minimal – but it was nevertheless a traumatic blow when he died later that year. At this time the band members were up to their necks in Eastern mysticism and assorted drugs; from now on they became more prone to wild errors of judgment; of which opening an Apple boutique in Baker Street, London, was merely the first. (Though the subsequent chaotic Apple organisation showed none of The Beatles had a head for business.)

If hubris now ran rampant in The Beatles' camp, nemesis was just over the horizon in the shape of their third film, "Magical Mystery Tour". It was an hour-long television presentation, premiered in the U.K. on Dec 26, 1967; a self-indulgent affair of jumbled lunacy, ill-conceived witticisms and trick photography which they had made entirely themselves; it showed the Achilles heel at last.

They were chastened by the experience, and consequently spent months on the enormous, sprawling **The Beatles,** which finally appeared at the very end of 1968, some months after the biggest latterday hit **Hey Jude/Revolution,** the first single to appear on their own Apple label. The latter song revealed Lennon's awakening political consciousness, even though he was then still rejecting facile solutions.

Though full of good tracks **The Beatles** (usually referred to as The White Album) was the work of a disintegrating unit, and the appearance of the ominous single, **Ballad Of John And Yoko,** reflected the inner turmoil of a band which was visibly coming to the end of its tether in front of the cameras for the film "Let It Be" at Twickenham studios.

Before that though they had initiated another fascinating project – the cartoon film, "Yellow Submarine", directed by George Dunning. Though The Beatles' involvement was minimal, they did provide the odd joke and wrote some new material.

Let It Be – originally to be called Get Back – was recorded and left in the can; once again The Beatles were undermined by soaring ambition. They delayed the release of the album because they wanted it to be a multi-media entertainment, accompanied by the film and a book. **Abbey Road** was put together and released in its place – the last tracks, chronologically, that The Beatles cut together. Ironically, it showed them still as buoyant as ever.

Let It Be was eventually released in 1970, in a version doctored by Phil Spector and in company with an almost worthless book of photographs, at a very inflated price, and the career of The Beatles, who by then were no longer interested in working with one another, closed on a sour note.

For subsequent careers, ➧ Harrison, Lennon, McCartney and Starr.

The importance of The Beatles' recorded work in the shaping of contemporary rock is incalculable and is approached in significance only by the career of Bob Dylan (➧). By far the best songwriting team in the field, Lennon-McCartney, supported increasingly by Harrison after **Revolver,** provided the basic material for a series of albums monumental in scope, imagination and technical expertise.

Most of the basic production precepts of today came into being as innovations on particular Beatles tracks and it is extremely unlikely that rock, as it is presently commercially structured, will ever again offer the claustrophobic, hot-house urgency of the conditions in which The Beatles made their most revolutionary music.

In 1974 a successful Liverpool play by local writer Willy Russell, "John, Paul, George, Ringo . . . And Bert" was produced on the London stage and in the U.S. by Robert Stigwood, who also staged a version of "Sergeant Pepper's Lonely Hearts Club Band" in New York. There is rumoured to be a documentary film in preparation, and a Hollywood biopic must be on the cards. This could all be forestalled, of course, if The Beatles themselves reunited for a concert; after over five years of public squabbling, litigation and finally reconciliation, they might all just be ready to take up one of the priceless purses that are currently being proferred by various promoters.

Of the many books about their career, "The Beatles" by Hunter Davies is the authorised biography, "Love Me Do – The Beatles' Progress" by Michael Braun is a lively and intelligent memoir of the early days of fame, and "The Beatles: An Illustrated Record" by Tony Tyler and Roy Carr is a thorough and illuminating account of their recording career. "Lennon Remembers" by Jann Wenner is the full text of an extremely lengthy, highly tendentious and consistently fascinating interview with Lennon from "Rolling Stone".

Let It Be. Courtesy Apple/EMI.

Revolver. Courtesy Parlophone Records/EMI.

U.K. Album Releases:	
Please Please Me (Parlophone)	**Sergeant Pepper's Lonely Hearts Club Band** (Parlophone)
With The Beatles (Parlophone)	
A Hard Day's Night (Soundtrack) (Parlophone)	**The Beatles** (Apple)
Beatles For Sale (Parlophone)	**Yellow Submarine** (Soundtrack) (Apple)
Help! (Soundtrack) (Parlophone)	**Abbey Road** (Apple)
Rubber Soul (Parlophone)	**Let It Be** (Apple)
Revolver (Parlophone)	**The Beatles 1962-66** (Apple)
A Collection Of Beatles Oldies . . . But Goldies (Parlophone)	**The Beatles 1967-70** (Apple)
	Rock 'n' Roll Music (Parlophone)

U.S. Album Releases:	
Meet The Beatles (Capitol)	**Sergeant Pepper's Lonely Hearts Club Band** (Capitol)
The Beatles' Second Album (Capitol)	
A Hard Day's Night (Capitol)	**Magical Mystery Tour** (Capitol)
Something New (Capitol)	
Beatles '65 (Capitol)	**The Beatles** (Apple)
The Early Beatles (Capitol)	**Yellow Submarine** (Apple)
Beatles VI (Capitol)	**Abbey Road** (Apple)
Help! (Capitol)	**Hey Jude** (Apple)
Rubber Soul (Capitol)	**Let It Be** (Apple)
Yesterday . . . And Today (Capitol)	**The Beatles 1962-66** (Apple)
Revolver (Capitol)	**The Beatles 1967-70** (Apple)
	Rock 'n' Roll Music (Capitol)

Above: Backstage after their first headlining tour, Beatles, Pacemakers, Roy Orbison. Left: Abbey Road. Apple/EMI.

Beaver and Krause

Born in Detroit, Bernie Krause gained erratic experience as a folk singer, moving around the cities in the East, before Lee Hays offered him the chair Pete Seeger was vacating in The Weavers. That was in 1963, and when the group finally disbanded at the end of the year, Krause moved on to San Francisco, doing some production work for Motown in Detroit on the way. In 1967 Elektra hired him as a producer, and it was there he met Paul Beaver.

Beaver had been born in the mid-west in 1925 and was a veteran of '40s and '50s jazz clubs, before becoming a highly-qualified Moog musician. In 1953 he had worked on "The Magnetic Monster", which was the first film to use electronic effects as an integral part of its score. He was a pioneer in the field of electronic instrumentation, and by the time he met Krause had already experimented with ring modulation, filter and oscillation devices. In the later '60s he contributed Moog music to the scores of "Catch-22", "The Graduate", "Candy", "Performance" and "Rosemary's Baby".

Together Krause and Beaver began work on the electronic aspects of recording, and Krause conceived something called The Martin/Parasound String-Controlled Synthesiser – which was a synthesiser installed in a guitar body so that it could be played on stage.

Their music was referred to simply as electronic, but they preferred to think of it as a new form of audio-expressionism. In 1968 they signed for Warner Bros and recorded **In A Wild Sanctuary**, but their "tour de force" is generally reckoned to be **Gandharva**, recorded live in Grace Cathedral, San Francisco, Feb 10-11, 1971, with the participation of rock musician Mike Bloomfield and noted jazz musician Gerry Mulligan. Their third and final recording **All Good Men** included the first complete recording of **A Real Slow Drag**, written by ragtime composer Scott Joplin for his opera "Treemonisha", which was never publicly performed until 1975.

Though Beaver and Krause were innovators in their field, their preeminence was undermined as electronic instruments rapidly became commonplace. Early in 1975, Paul Beaver died of a stroke in Los Angeles.

Recordings:
In A Wild Sanctuary (Warner Bros)
Gandharva (Warner Bros)
All Good Men (Warner Bros)

Be-Bop Deluxe

Bill Nelson guitar, vocals
Charlie Tumahai bass
Andrew Clarke keyboards
Simon Fox drums

Above: The Jeff Beck Group, early version. From left: Aynsley Dunbar, who occupied the drum seat for a fortnight, Beck, Rod Stewart, Ron Wood. Revered by U.S. audiences, they could have been where Zeppelin are today. Beck, by his almost self-destructive nature, blew it – and his group just fell apart.

Highly touted new British band based around not inconsiderable guitar-playing ability of Wakefield-born Nelson. A one-time local government officer, Nelson worked with two Yorkshire bands – Global Village and later the gospel-based Gentle Revolution – recording three albums, **A To Austr, Astral Navigations** and **Northern Dream,** at Holyground "home studio" in his native Wakefield in what was described as "an exercise in alternative record production". Though last named has since become collectors' piece, all three had limited pressings, selling only in local record shops.

However, one of 250 pressings of **Northern Dream** found its way to DJ John Peel, who gave Nelson first air-play and helped attract interest of major EMI label.

First incarnation of Be-Bop Deluxe featured Nelson, Robert Bryan (bs), Nicholas Chatterton-Dew (drms), Ian Parkin (rhy gtr) and Richard Brown (kybds), though latter quit shortly before recording of band's first album **Axe Victim,** released U.K. on EMI's Harvest label in 1974.

Band's first major tour same year was as support to Cockney Rebel, during which Nelson became dissatisfied with colleagues, disbanding group in August that year. From similarly disarrayed Cockney Rebel, Milton Reame-James (kybds) and Paul Jeffreys (bs) joined Be-Bop with former Hackensack drummer Simon Fox completing new line up. However, presence of ex-Rebels was shortlived, and third incarnation of Be-Bop Deluxe started with enlistment of New Zealander Tumahai.

As three piece, band cut second album **Futurama** at Rockfield Studios in Wales with Queen producer Roy Thomas Baker, Andrew Clarke (kybds) joining after album's release in U.K. mid-1975. Nelson himself produced ambitious **Sunburst Finish,** released in U.K. early 1976 coincidental with major U.K. tour obviously designed to push Be-Bop Deluxe into heavyweight heirarchy.

Recordings:
Axe Victim (Harvest)
Futurama (Harvest)
Sunburst Finish (Harvest)

Jeff Beck

Born Surrey, England, June 1944, studied at Wimbledon Art College. Established himself as one of U.K.'s all-time great hero axemen during two-year stint with Yardbirds (♦) from whom he split in 1966.

In 1967 had U.K. hit solo single with out-of-character **Hi Ho Silver Lining** (re-issued and hit second time round in U.K. 1972) and following year with even more bizarre **Love Is Blue,** before forming The Jeff Beck Group with Rod Stewart (vcls), Ron Wood (bs), Micky Waller (drms) and later Nicky Hopkins (pno).

Enhanced already considerable reputation with series of rowdy, outrageous gigs – mostly in U.S. – and two patchily excellent albums, **Truth** (1968) and **Beck-Ola** (1969). Their music basically bluesy hard rock, Wood and Stewart contributed one or two originals but it was band's exciting reworkings of blues and contemporary material that pulled the crowds. Also, the teaming of Beck and Stewart (privately the two were frequently at each others' throats) was like nothing heard in rock before, and like nothing that was to be heard again until Jimmy Page squared off to Robert Plant in Led Zeppelin.

A continually hassle-prone outfit, The Beck Group eventually burned itself out in 1969 and Wood and Stewart went to join Faces (♦). Beck made attempts to

form band with Tim Bogert and Carmine Appice, late of Vanilla Fudge (♦), but project fell through when the guitarist sustained injuries in car smash. He was out of action for 18 months.

Bogert/Appice formed Cactus (♦), and Beck resurfaced late 1971 with another Jeff Beck Group, featuring Cozy Powell (drms), Max Middleton (pno), Clive Chaman (bs), and Robert Tench (vcls). This band made two albums, **Rough And Ready** (1971) and **Jeff Beck Group** (1972), but Beck declared it unsatisfactory.

Break up of Cactus subsequently allowed him to form group he had long wanted – Beck Bogert & Appice (♦), but this too was relatively short-lived.

Rough And Ready.
Courtesy Epic/CBS.

One of greatest guitar players to emerge in rock – only Clapton and Hendrix can truly be said to have surpassed him for imagination, excitement, technique and sheer fuel – Beck's tragedy is that he's also thoroughly inconsistent and law purely unto himself.

1975 double album, **Blow By Blow,** however, returned him some measure of commercial success.

First two albums later coupled for double-album re-issue by Epic 1975.

Recordings:
Truth (Epic/Columbia-EMI)
Beck-Ola (Epic/Columbia-EMI)
Rough And Ready (Epic)
Jeff Beck Group (Epic)

Blow By Blow (Epic)
Wired (Epic)

Beck, Bogert & Appice

Jeff Beck guitar, vocals
Tim Bogert bass, vocals
Carmine Appice drums, vocals

Formed 1972 when Americans Appice and Bogert left Cactus (♦) and English axe hero Beck (♦) disbanded last Jeff Beck Group. A thunderously exciting power trio, instrumentally impeccable but suffering from dearth of worthwhile material. Cut one and only album 1973 and broke up following year (though there is an in-concert album **Live In Japan** available on import in U.S. only).

Recordings:
Beck Bogert & Appice (Epic)

David Bedford

British-born composer/arranger, studied at Royal Academy of Music. As arranger worked on first Kevin Ayers (♦) solo album, before joining Ayers' The Whole World band on keyboards for two albums. Subsequently formed duo with fellow Whole Worlder Lol Coxhill (♦). His first solo album, **Nurses Song With Elephants,** released U.K. 1972 (not in U.S.), featured Ayers and Mike Oldfield (♦).

Went on to pursue variety of activities including music teaching and arranging for likes of Ayers, Oldfield, Roy Harper and Edgar Broughton Band.

Next appeared on U.K. Virgin label for **Star's End** project, a Bedford composition commissioned by Royal Philharmonic and performed at London Festival Hall in November 1974. Record features Mike Oldfield on guitar, as does **The Orchestral Tubular Bells** (1975), Bedford's orchestral arrangement of Oldfield's million-seller, and **The Rime Of The Ancient Mariner** (again 1975),

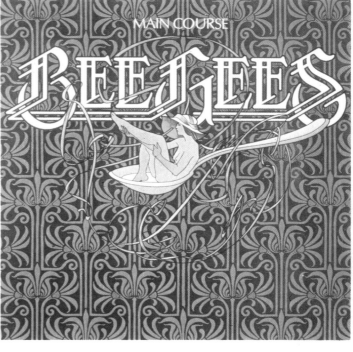

Above: Whatever his short-comings in other departments, Beck remains one of the greatest guitarists to emerge in rock.

his evocation of Samuel Cole-ridge's epic poem with narration by actor Robert Powell.

Recordings:
Nurses Song With Elephants (—/Dandelion)
Star's End (Virgin)
The Orchestral Tubular Bells (Virgin)
The Rime Of The Ancient Mariner (Virgin)

Captain Beefheart

Beefheart was born Don Van Vliet in Glendale, California in 1941. At high school in Lancaster, early artistic leanings led to offer of art scholarship, which he declined, before meeting and becoming firm friends with Frank Zappa.

After joining a band called The Blackouts, Van Vliet took the name Captain Beefheart and formed the Magic Band in 1964. The band successfully purveyed a blues-rock sound, signed to A&M Records, and issued a single **Diddy Wah Diddy** (a Bo Diddley original); the first album, **Safe As Milk,** was turned down by A&M as being too bleak lyrically, so Beefheart took it to Kama Sutra. The album was composed entirely of original tunes, based on coun-try-blues styles and making fine use of slide guitars and synco-pation. It won guarded approval from the critics, mainly for its avant-garde techniques. It also spurred interest in the Magic Band, which led to a successful tour of Europe.

At this time the Magic Band con-sisted of Van Vliet, plus Ry Cooder (gtr), Jimmy Semens (gtr), Herb Bermann (bs) and John French (drms). Cooder and Bermann presently departed to be replaced by Alex St. Claire

and Jerry Handley respectively, and the new line-up cut **Mirror Man,** an album not released until years later and not considered part of the Beefheart canon.

For **Strictly Personal** in 1968, Semens was replaced by Jeff Cotton; the album was mixed by Bob Krasnow without Beefheart's supervision, and the futuristic blend of blues, rock and free-form jazz remains obscured by phasing.

It was not until his old friend Zappa signed Beefheart to his own Straight label in 1968, and allowed him to make an album free of all constraints that the original qualities of the music were enabled to pass unhampered by post-production work. Recalling

Above: Your Captain speaking.

Semens, Van Vliet built the Magic Band again from scratch, giving the members outlandish names. The new line-up was: Bill Harkleroad (Zoot Horn Rollo), gtr; Mark Boston (Rockette Morton), bs; Antennae Jimmy Semens, gtr; The Mascara Snake, clrnt. The music this line-up put together was quite remarkable, all of it outstanding in the rock field. **Trout Mask Replica** is still one of the most advanced overall concepts in rock music.

In 1971 Beefheart took the band on a nationwide tour, recalling French (Drumbo) as drummer. After this, Zappa and Beefheart quarrelled, and the latter switched labels again, this time to Reprise,

Above: Main Course. Courtesy RSO. Released 1975, this re-established the Bee Gees in the U.S., and yielded the million-selling Jive Talkin'.

and again reshuffled the Magic Band pack, bringing in Artie Tripp (Ed Marimba) on marimba and Elliott Ingber (Winged Eel Fingerling) on guitar, both of whom were ex-Mothers Of In-vention. For the manic-depressive **The Spotlight Kid,** Beefheart unexpectedly returned to his blues roots.

This line-up didn't work out, and when Ingber left, Morton moved up to guitar, and Roy Estrada (Orejon) took over bass for **Clear Spot,** a more straight-forward and considerably hap-pier record.

Alex St. Claire Snouffer rejoined, and the band used on **Uncondi-tionally Guaranteed** – his most melodic and accessible set since **Safe As Milk** – was Rollo, Morton, St. Claire, Tripp and Mark Mar-cellino on keyboards. Although **Unconditionally Guaranteed,** Beefheart's debut release on Virgin Records, effectively re-launched him as a commercial proposition, his quick-fire sequel **Bluejeans And Moonbeams** was disappointing and de-escalated the momentum.

In 1975, amid much rancour, he parted company with the nucleus of the Magic Band (who went on to work under the name Mallard (◆)) and then toured with Frank Zappa, the two having by now patched up their differences. They made an album together, **Bongo Fury,** which was the subject of a legal dispute in the U.K. Beef-heart meanwhile set to re-assembling a Magic Band, and brought back Drumbo, Winged Eel Fingerling and Indian Ink.

A complete original, Beefheart exerts next to no influence on the rest of the rock scene, while con-tinuing to plough his own con-sistently startling furrow. In recent years his music has become more conventional, but his early albums remain important for their raw inventiveness.

Recordings:
Safe As Milk (known alternatively as **Dropout Boogie**) (Kama Sutra)
Mirror Man (Kama Sutra)
Strictly Personal (Blue Thumb/Liberty)
Trout Mask Replica (Straight)
Lick My Decals Off Baby (Straight)
The Spotlight Kid (Reprise)
Clear Spot (Reprise)
Unconditionally Guaranteed (Virgin)
Blue Jeans And Moonbeams (Virgin)
With Frank Zappa:
Bongo Fury (Discreet/—)

Above: The brothers Gibb.

Bee Gees

Barry Gibb vocals
Robin Gibb vocals
Maurice Gibb vocals, keyboards

Nucleus of the Bee Gees has always been the brothers Gibb, Barry (b. Sept 1946) and twins Robin and Maurice (b. Dec 1949), whose parents emigrated from Manchester, England, to Austra-lia in 1958. They had already shown leanings towards enter-tainment business back in Man-chester, appearing in talent con-test when Barry was nine and the twins seven. After only a few months in Australia, the Gibbs had made their first appearance in similar talent show, this time on local radio, and while in early teens they quickly graduated to secure their own weekly TV series.

In 1963, Australia's Festival Records released their first single, **Three Kisses Of Love,** which went Top 20. More followed and by 1965–66, through better-known hits, **Spicks And Specks, I Was A Lover And A Leader Of Men, Wine And Women,** the Bee Gees (name taken from Barry Gibb's initials) were Australia's No. 1 group.

Signed to management by Robert Stigwood (➤), the group returned for an assault on the U.K. teen market with a fourth member in tow – drummer and former Australian child actor ("Smiley", "The Scamp") Colin Petersen. Shortly after arrival, they added a fifth member, highly-rated Australian guitarist Vince Melouney, and with this line-up cut first post-Australia album, **Bee Gees First.**

Within a matter of months they had smashed into U.K. charts. The 1967 hit **New York Mining Disaster 1941** gave them their first bite, and the Bee Gees rose rapidly to status of teenybop idols when million-selling follow-up **Massachussetts** hit No. 1 in U.K. later same year, both singles being written by brothers Gibb.

Above: Robin Gibb.

Melodic strength of Gibbs' song-writing (also the way Stigwood astutely handled their career) invited early comparisons with Beatles and ensured impressive run of hits over next two years in U.K. and U.S.: e.g. **World, Words,** and the U.S. gold **I Gotta Get A Message To You.** Vince Melouney didn't stay around long however, splitting to form own ill-fated group.

Melouney's departure, though of his own choosing, was an early omen of sorts, because internal disagreements always threatened stability of the group. In 1969, Robin Gibb decided he could do without his brothers and struck out for a solo career. After commercially bright start with 1970-released **Robin's Reign** album, and hit single **Saved By The Bell,** he subsequently found it wasn't that easy. For a while the Bee Gees existed in a limbo: Maurice attempted acting career, married Scottish pop singer Lulu (who later divorced him), appeared frequently on his wife's TV specials; while Barry seemed more intent on keeping himself and his girl-friend in national press than his avowed intent – songwriting.

In late 1971, their differences settled, the brothers re-united. Maurice and Barry having dis-

carded the services of Colin Petersen, none too harmoniously, the year before.

However, despite two 1971 U.S. million-selling singles, **Lonely Days** and **How Can You Mend A Broken Heart?** the brothers Gibb never quite managed to regain the early impetus that at one time looked set to carry them to virtually Beatle-type status.

Since re-union, they have been more successful outside native country, though they made impressive U.K. comeback (rising high in U.S. lists too) with 1975 hit **Jive Talkin',** produced by Arif Mardin. In U.S., **Nights On Broadway** followed it into charts, as did the albums **Mr. Natural** and **Main Course,** which also yielded the U.S. hit, **Fanny.**

However, in one area alone the Bee Gees are assured of status (and lucrative royalties) for years to come – songwriting. Their extensive catalogue of material has attracted attention of some of the major international music biz stars; talents as diverse as Frank Sinatra, Elvis Presley, Janis Joplin, Nina Simone, Dean Martin and hundreds more.

Recordings:
Bee Gees First (Atco/Polydor)
Horizontal (Atco/Polydor)
Rare, Precious And Beautiful (Atco/Polydor)
Idea (Atco/Polydor)
Rare, Precious And Beautiful Vol. II (Atco/Polydor)
Odessa (Atco/Polydor)
Cucumber Castle (Atco/Polydor)
Sound Of Love (Atco/Polydor)
Trafalgar (Atco/Polydor)
To Whom It May Concern (Atco/Polydor)
Life In A Tin Can (RSO)
Mr Natural (RSO)
Main Course (RSO)
Compilations:
Best Of Bee Gees (Atco/Polydor)
Best Of Bee Gees Vol. II (Atco/Polydor)
Robin Gibb:
Robin's Reign (Atco/Polydor)

Maggie Bell

Born Jan 12, 1945, in poor area of Glasgow, Scotland. Quit school at 15 to work as window dresser by day and singer by night, a path that led eventually to now defunct Stone The Crows (➤).

On Crows break up 1973 Maggie pursued solo career, recording 1974-released **Queen Of The Night** album in New York with famed Atlantic producer Jerry Wexler and such eminent soul sessionmen as Cornell Dupree and Chuck Rainey. Despite sympathetic press, critical acclaim and numerous U.K. music paper readers poll awards, however, Maggie solo has so far failed to shift tickets and albums any better than did Stone The Crows. Title of

second solo album derives from Maggie's aunt Doris Droy, who worked Scottish music halls under name Suicide Sal.

Recordings:
Queen Of The Night (Atlantic/Polydor)
Suicide Sal (Swan Song/Polydor)

Chuck Berry

One of the enduring legends of rock 'n' roll, and its single most influential figure.

Born Charles Edward Berry in St. Louis, Missouri, Oct 18, 1931, he learned guitar while in teens, though the halcyon calm of his adolescent years was shattered by a three-year spell in reform school for attempted robbery. Returned home in 1947 and worked for time for General Motors,

before taking up career in hairdressing. Took increasing interest in music, partly to supplement his income and support a wife and two children. In 1955 he moved to Chicago, and his career took off after he'd persuaded Muddy Waters (➤) to let him sit in on a session. Waters was highly impressed with his guitar technique and fluent style, so he recommended Berry to Leonard Chess, head of Chess Records, who signed up many local black acts.

Berry was offered a contract, and recorded his first tracks, **Maybellene** and **Wee Wee Hours.** Though Berry himself preferred the latter, the former was released as the A-side after it had been co-credited to Alan Freed (➤), who possibly suggested modifications to enhance its commercial potential. With the radio exposure Freed was able to

Right: the acceptable face of the Chuck Berry legend – a '70s version of the famous duck-walk. From Maybellene in 1955 through Sweet Little Sixteen, Roll Over Beethoven, Johnny B. Goode, Memphis Tennessee and dozens more, Berry was rock's single most influential figure. And all this from a man who used to cut hair.

supply, the song was an immediate U.S. Top 10 hit.

For the next four years, Berry then went on to produce a stream of utterly incomparable, archetypal rock 'n' roll songs, among which were **Roll Over Beethoven, Johnny B. Goode, Sweet Little Sixteen** and **Brown-Eyed Handsome Man.** Some of his most dexterous compositions, such as **Memphis Tennessee,** were not even issued as singles during this period.

His sources were those of rock 'n' roll itself – a blend of R&B and C&W (he had listened to country music on radio at home in St. Louis), although he had also acquired an appreciation of blues (obviously, since he was working in Chicago). In contrast to other early rockers, he concentrated on clarity of diction, so that his witty and often acerbic lyrics could be plainly heard – indeed, he was responsible for introducing a disciplined lyricism to early rock music.

He also notched up appearances in four films at this time – "Rock Rock Rock", "Mr. Rock And Roll", "Go Johnny Go", and "Jazz On A Summer's Day" – the latter a film of the 1959 Newport Jazz Festival, where he sang **Sweet Little Sixteen** and demonstrated his famous duck-walk, which he had developed in 1956 and which virtually completed the Berry charisma. He was one of the few black performers getting across to a largely white teenage audience and his popularity was enormous.

But Berry was something of a "bête noire" in the eyes of the U.S. music establishment, possibly because more than anyone else he made manifest the spirit of youthful rebellion that was inherent in rock music, possibly just because he was rich and successful and black.

In 1959, like another prominent entertainer before him – Charles Chaplin – he was indicted for offences under the Mann Act. Unlike Chaplin, he was found guilty after a trial lasting almost two years and sentenced to two years' imprisonment. Though Berry has never ceased to assert his innocence, the episode shattered his marriage and threatened to shatter his career.

When he was released, the climate of rock had changed, though arguably to Berry's advantage. When The Beatles and the Rolling Stones had given back to rock the strength and vitality it had been lacking at the turn of the decade, they had done so partly by digging into Berry's repertoire. **Roll Over Beethoven** was one of the few early Beatle million-sellers they didn't write themselves, and the Stones, who to date have recorded more than 12 of his numbers, made Berry's **Come On** their debut single. The Beach Boys merely re-wrote **Sweet Little Sixteen** as **Surfin' USA** to score one of their earliest hits.

The success of **Memphis Tennessee,** issued in 1964, acted as a harbinger of his release from prison, and then the result of his first studio sessions in almost five years was another string of hits – **Nadine, No Particular Place To Go, You Never Can Tell.**

Though his chart success soon waned, his popularity in live performance was undiminished, and he has worked unstintingly in this area for the last decade, often using a pick-up band in U.K. This is one of the aspects that has continued to make him a controversial personality; another is his alleged bad temper, and a third is the fact that in his recording career he has shown no compunction about repeating the same song many times over with only minor adjustments. It's possible that his experience of U.S. justice soured him; certainly he seems to have emerged from prison a harder, more shrewd businessman.

In 1966 he signed a lucrative contract with Mercury Records, but by 1969 had returned to Chess, and made **Back Home** and **San Francisco Dues,** arguably his finest-ever "albums". He also benefitted from the renewed interest in rock 'n' roll, and worked in some of Richard Nader's revival shows, as well as being given a prominent part in the film, "Let The Good Times Roll".

A U.K. appearance at the Lanchester Arts Festival in 1972 not only gave him one-half of a double album, **London Sessions,** but also, strangely, his biggest-ever chart success. The gently ribald **My Ding-A-Ling** was his first-ever No. 1 on both sides of the Atlantic. Strangely, because the song had been in and out of his stage show since he first turned professional.

In 1974 he began to feature his daughter, Ingrid Gibson, in his stage shows – she contributes vocals to **Chuck Berry '75.**

Berry is now a rich man, and can afford to live in style and comfort. Despite the occasionally shoddy form that his hardened professionalism takes, there is no doubt that his contribution to the history of rock music has been unique; even in recent years, his old songs have continued to prove ready-made hit material – as Elvis Presley showed with **Promised Land,** and ELO with **Roll Over Beethoven. Golden Decade, Vols. I** and **II** form the hard-core of his seminal work; the other releases listed are those since he rejoined the Chess label.

Recordings:
Golden Decade (Chess)
Golden Decade, Vol. II (Chess)
Golden Decade, Vol. III (Chess)
Back Home (Chess)
San Francisco Dues (Chess)
London Sessions (Chess)
Bio (Chess)
St. Louis To 'Frisco To Memphis (Mercury/Philips)
Chuck Berry '75 (Chess)

Golden Decade Vol Three. Courtesy Chess/Phonogram.

Big Brother & The Holding Company
➔ Janis Joplin

Big Star

Brainchild of Memphis-born boy genius Alex Chilton who with U.S. group The Box Tops (Chilton vcls, gtr) had million-selling hits with **The Letter** (1967) and **Cry Like A Baby** (1968). First named was later recorded by Joe Cocker. Cutting four albums for Bell, last in 1969, Box Tops were among most successful exponents of so-called "blue-eyed soul" along with Righteous Bros and Roy Head.

Aged 17 at time of **The Letter,** Chilton headed for New York Greenwich Village folk circuit when Box Tops split, returning to Memphis 1971 to form Big Star which on first album featured Chris Bell (gtr, vcls), Andy Hummell (bs), Jody Stephenson (drms). Bell had left by second album, which like its predecessor was critically lauded but commercially a non-happener (there was third album, never released, copies of which are collectors'

Left: Charles Edward "Chuck" Berry grants a rare (early) smile at no charge – though he may invoice us for it later! Like most of the veteran rock stars, Berry probably got short-changed many times over in his early years, which may be one reason for his notoriously jaundiced attitude towards the business side of rock.

items in U.S.). Nevertheless, Big Star accrued certain cult following both in U.K. and U.S.

Chilton last heard of working solo in Memphis.

Recordings:
Big Star 1 (Ardent/Stax)
Radio City (Ardent/—)

Elvin Bishop

Born in Tulsa, Oklahoma, Bishop met Paul Butterfield at University of Chicago in 1960 and developed a very fruitful professional partnership with him. They formed the nucleus of the Butterfield Blues Band (➧) in the first half of the '60s, Bishop playing lead guitar until Mike Bloomfield arrived when he switched to second guitar.

In 1968 Bishop left to form his own band, though his records (none of which were particularly successful) were released under his own name. Certainly, his music evinced no radical departure from that of the Butterfield Blues Band.

At the end of 1973, he was introduced to Allman Bros manager Phil Walden by Richard Betts, and he signed for the former's Capricorn Records. His first album for the label, **Let It Flow,** featured guest appearances by Betts, Toy Caldwell of the Marshall Tucker Band, and Charlie Daniels. The album showed that Bishop had left behind the electric 12-bar blues. He enjoyed commercial success in 1976 with **Struttin' My**

Stuff, and the single taken from it.

Recordings:
Elvin Bishop (Fillmore)
Feel It (Fillmore)
Rock My Soul (Epic)
Crabshaw Rising – The Best Of Elvin Bishop (Epic)
Let It Flow (Capricorn)
Juke Joint Jump (Capricorn)
Struttin' My Stuff (Capricorn)

Black Oak Arkansas

Jim Dandy vocals
Stan 'Goober' Knight guitar, vocals
Ricky Reynolds guitar, vocals
Pat Daugherty bass, vocals
Jimmy Henderson guitar
Tommy Aldridge drums

From the small community of Black Oak in Arkansas, first came together around 1964-65, choosing name from roots (they were previously Knowbody Else) when they arrived in Los Angeles 1969. Former school rebels led by the ebullient, extrovert Dandy (real name Jim Mangrum, b. Mar 30, 1948, Black Oak), established early reputation on strength of dynamic presentation though sometimes suspect musical ability.

A prolific recording outfit, released first album 1970 but didn't really start to break in U.S. until **Raunch And Roll Live** (1973) and **High On The Hog** (1974).

First visited U.K. spring 1974 as

support on tour with Black Sabbath, making immediate impact. Consistent box-office, large-grossing concert attraction in U.S. **Black Oak, Raunch And Roll Live** and **Keep The Faith** albums have since gone gold.

After **Street Party** set (1974), original guitarist Harvey Jett replaced by Jimmy Henderson from Jackson, Mississippi. Further re-organisation in early '76 brought in Ruby Starr (vcls) and four-girl vocal unit Hot Buttered Soul to augment for concerts.

Group live in own community in Oakland, Arkansas, where they have purchased parcels of land and made considerable financial donations to local causes.

Recordings:
Black Oak Arkansas (Atlantic/—)
Keep The Faith (Atlantic/—)
If An Angel (Atlantic/—)
Raunch And Roll Live (Atlantic)
High On The Hog (Atlantic)
Street Party (Atlantic)
Ain't Life Grand (Atlantic)
X-Rated (MCA)
Live Mutha (Atlantic)
Balls Of Fire (MCA)

Black Sabbath

Ozzie Osbourne vocals
Tony Iommi guitar
Geezer Butler bass
Bill Ward drums

In late 1969, a group from Bir-

mingham, U.K., who had established a strong local reputation changed name from Earth to Black Sabbath and arrived on national U.K. rock scene on a wave of mystical beliefs and associations with occult, backed up by huge barrage of sound. First album hit U.K. charts with very little publicity – and, though band met certain amount of critical scorn, theirs was very much an "underground" breakthrough by-passing usual media channels.

International success followed remarkably swiftly – in fact on strength of second album, **Paranoid,** the title track of which gave band huge 1970 hit. Subsequent albums achieved gold status and, although Sabbath remained unfashionable among rock critics on both sides of Atlantic, group established itself as one of U.K.'s first and most successful heavy metal exports.

After 1973 fifth album, **Sabbath Bloody Sabbath,** however, band ran up against acute managerial hassles which forced cessation of recording and performing until **Sabotage** on new U.K. label towards end of 1975. Same time made concert come-back with first U.S. and later U.K. tour.

Line-up unchanged since inception, though Gerald Woodruffe augmented on keyboards for recent gigs.

Recordings:
Black Sabbath (Warner Bros/Vertigo)
Paranoid (Warner Bros/Vertigo)
Master Of Reality (Warner Bros/Vertigo)
Black Sabbath Volume 4 (Warner Bros/Vertigo)
Sabbath Bloody Sabbath (Warner Bros/World-Wide Artists)
Sabotage (Warner Bros/NEMS)
Compilations:
We Sold Our Soul For Rock 'n' Roll (Warner Bros/NEMS)

We Sold Our Soul For Rock 'n' Roll. Courtesy NEMS Records.

Ritchie Blackmore

Born Western - Super - Mare, England, on April 14, 1945, Blackmore was guitarist and a founder-member of British heavy rock outfit Deep Purple (➧) up to his departure from the band after much speculation in June 1975.

Taking former Elf members Ronnie Dio (vcls), Craig Gruber (bs), Gary Driscoll (drms) and Micky Lee Soule (kybds), Blackmore formed his own outfit, Ritchie Blackmore's Rainbow for a debut album (1975) and extensive U.S. tour. Thus far, relatively successful in concert and record areas.

Recordings:
Ritchie Blackmore's Rainbow (Polydor)
Rainbow Rising (Oyster)

Ronee Blakley

Born in Idaho and raised in the U.S. North-West, Ronee Blakley began studying piano at the age of eight; she later entered Stanford University and graduated in music. She also has a degree from the Juillard School of Music in New York, and has composed a film score and given a Moog synthesiser recital at Carnegie Hall.

Apart from being so musically versatile, she was also writing her own material, and in 1971 began playing clubs in the Los Angeles area. She made one album, **Ronee Blakley**, for Elektra in 1972.

Having heard that album and seen her perform, Richard Baskin recommended her for the part of the country star Barbara Jean in Robert Altman's critically-acclaimed movie, "Nashville". Her performance, for which she gained an Academy Award nomination, was particularly commendable.

With this stimulus, she was able to pick up her recording career again, with an album for Warner Bros in 1975, **Welcome**, entirely self-composed, and recorded in Muscle Shoals, with many of the resident sessioneers participating and Jerry Wexler producing. At the end of the year, she was one of the stars of Bob Dylan's Rolling Thunder tour.

Despite the fact that she was apparently riding a tidal wave of success, Warner Bros were dissatisfied with **Welcome** and dropped her from the label early in 1976; nevertheless, she is one of the more promising performers to emerge in the second half of the '70s.

Recordings:
Ronee Blakley (Elektra)
Welcome (Warner Bros)

Bobby 'Blue' Bland

Born Robert Calvin Bland in Rosemark, Tennessee, Jan 27, 1930. Formed own high school blues band in early '40s, but by end of decade had moved into R&B, as part of group known as Beale Streeters, which also included Johnny Ace, Rosco Gordon and B. B. King (♦).

In mid-'50s, signed to Duke Records and had first major hit with **Farther Up The Road**, and by 1960 was clearly established as one of leading vocalists in his field. Bland consolidated reputation in '60s with singles like **I Pity The Fool, Stormy Monday** and **Ain't That Loving You**. He was by now a distinctive vocal stylist, and one of most highly paid concert performers; his band included his musical director Joe Scott and the highly-touted guitar-

ist Wayne Bennett.

Like many of his contemporaries, Bland's career was in eclipse in later '60s, though he hung on in there with irregular hits. In 1972 Duke Records was taken over by ABC/Dunhill, and, after a lifetime of selling records largely to the black market, Bland was finally pointed in the direction of the white rock audience with **His California Album**, produced by Steve Barri.

The experiment was successful, mainly because Bland was able to demonstrate his total mastery of almost any kind of material. **His California Album** contained **It's Not The Spotlight**, later recorded by Rod Stewart (ever the Bland devotee), and gave Bland a couple of single hits, as did the follow-up, the equally fine **Dreamer**. Bland's career is buoyant again, despite an off-target **Bobby Bland And B. B. King – Live Together For The First Time**, which was weighed down by too much mutual respect.

Dreamer. Courtesy ABC Records.

Recordings:
Best Of Bobby Blue Bland (Duke)
Best Of . . . Volume II (Duke)
Spotlighting The Man (Duke)
Touch Of The Blues (Duke)
His California Album (ABC)
Dreamer (ABC)
Live Together For The First Time (with B. B. King) (ABC)
Get On Down With Bobby Bland (ABC)

Blind Faith

Steve Winwood keyboards, guitar, vocals
Eric Clapton guitar, vocals
Ginger Baker drums
Rick Grech bass, violin, vocals

An early example of rock's incipient fragmentation, Blind Faith was prototype "supergroup" – a phenomenon brought into being by a period in which public interest centred upon individual players instead of groups.

The fact that the musicians, pressured by this interest into taking unpremeditated steps to justify their sudden eminence, were not as confident in their own capacity as were their devotees, is reflected in the rather pointed name the four members of the first such band chose for themselves.

For the formation of Blind Faith 1969, Clapton and Baker were available from the disbanded Cream (♦) and Winwood from the then temporarily defunct Traffic (♦). Grech was tempted mid-tour from Family (♦). They cut one album, albeit a million-seller, too fast, made debut in open-air

festival before 100,000 audience at London's Hyde Park June 1969, played one traumatic U.S. tour and broke up within months of formation.

Blind Faith. Courtesy Polydor Records.

In retrospect their one album ironically shows the bare bones of a very promising group, containing as it does a number of good Winwood compositions and the Clapton classic **Presence Of The Lord.**

Recording:
Blind Faith (Atco/Polydor)

Blodwyn Pig

Mick Abrahams guitar, vocals
Jack Lancaster flute, sax
Andy Pyle bass
Ron Berg drums

Original guitarist for Jethro Tull (♦), Abrahams formed Pig on leaving Tull 1968. Albums enjoyed moderate sales to support consistent gigging reputation. When Abrahams left to form Wombat and later Mick Abrahams Band (latter recorded two albums, **A Musical Evening With Mick Abrahams,** and **At Last**), Peter Banks joined for short spell until Blodwyn (as they were then known) split altogether in 1970.

There was attempted short-lived re-formation of Blodwyn Pig early 1974 with originals Abrahams, Lancaster and Pyle, plus original Jethro drummer Clive Bunker, but project slumped into oblivion after a handful of gigs. In 1975 Abrahams turned out tuition album for U.K.-based SRT label – **Have Fun Learning Guitar.**

Recordings:
Ahead Rings Out (A&M/Island)
Getting To This (A&M/Island)

Blood Sweat And Tears

David Clayton-Thomas vocals
Bobby Colomby drums
Tony Klatka saxes, trombone
Larry Willis keyboards
George Wadenius guitar
Dave Bargeron trombone
Ron McClure bass
Bill Tillman saxes

Formed New York 1967 by Al Kooper (♦), Steve Katz and Bobby Colomby, BS&T was designed as means to coerce rock into conventional musical literacy by technical example – a move many older critics felt long overdue and maintained could best be contrived by a fusion with the politer forms of jazz.

On **Child Is Father To The Man,** their 1968 first album, the mixture was still raw enough (partly the influence of Kooper) to be acceptable. But **Blood Sweat And Tears,** their million-selling second release, recorded after Kooper had departed to go super-sessioning, gave the high-cultural game away and rock audiences have never really forgiven the group their initial patronizing hollowness, a situation not helped by the stampede of AM stations and audiences to take group to their hearts. (From that second LP, **You Made Me So Very Happy, Spinning Wheel, And When I Die** were all million-selling singles in quick succession.)

BS&Ts later albums, though not as pretentious as the second, have been about equal blends of cold technique and ersatz emotion, this disintegratory trend reaching a nadir with the more posturingly meaningless performances of vocalist David Clayton-Thomas.

Since third album, personnel changes have occurred with perplexing frequency – in fact, only Bobby Colomby now remains of original line-up. London-born Clayton-Thomas quit in 1972 to pursue solo career (see below), his place being taken by succession of vocalists – Bobby Doyle, Jerry Fisher, Jerry LeCroix etc – until he re-united with BS&T in late '74 for **New City.**

By 1976 BS&T had travelled far from original vision of Kooper, Katz and Co., and have lost out with rock audiences in process. Though still a commercial viability with older, cabaret-oriented audiences, they remain a significantly pointless cul-de-sac off the very road of rock they set out to re-surface.

Recordings:
Child Is Father To The Man (Columbia/CBS)
Blood Sweat And Tears (Columbia/CBS)
Three (Columbia/CBS)
BS&T 4 (Columbia/CBS)
New Blood (Columbia/CBS)
No Sweat (Columbia/CBS)
Mirror Image (Columbia/CBS)
New City (Columbia/CBS)
Compilations:
Greatest Hits (Columbia/CBS)
More Than Ever (Columbia/CBS)
David Clayton-Thomas solo:
David Clayton-Thomas (Columbia/CBS)
Tequila Sunrise (Columbia/CBS)
Harmony Junction (RCA)

Mike Bloomfield

A monumentally bizarre figure, whose vast potential has remained irritatingly unfulfilled. Chicago-born Bloomfield's astounding guitar work with the original Paul Butterfield Blues Band (♦) circa 1965-66 gained him a considerable reputation which his work on Bob Dylan's **Highway 61 Revisited** only served to enhance. At that time he was thought of as one of the great white blues guitarists.

Leaving Butterfield in 1967, Bloomfield formed the brilliant but erratic and short-lived Electric Flag (♦), which also included Buddy Miles and Nick Gravenites.

His next venture was **Super Session**, an album of jams with Steve Stills (➧) and Al Kooper (➧), cut in 1968. This collaboration was an enormous success – as was its successor, a live double-album **The Live Adventures Of Mike Bloomfield And Al Kooper.**

After that his activities temporarily became vaguer and vaguer. **It's Not Killing Me**, a rather disappointing solo album followed and, apart from occasional jams with various old friends, Bloomfield became more and more reclusive. He and Gravenites collaborated on the soundtrack of "Steelyard Blues", which was effective as a soundtrack if not as an album release, and also worked with Dr. John (➧) and John Paul Hammond on the disastrously tedious **Triumvirate.** After that he restricted himself to such non-constructive activities as TV commercials, but has since stepped out from the shadows again as a founder-member of KGB (➧).

Recordings:
Super Session (Columbia/CBS)
The Live Adventures Of Mike Bloomfield And Al Kooper (Columbia/CBS)
It's Not Killing Me (Columbia/CBS)
Steelyard Blues (Original Soundtrack) (Warner Bros/—)

David Blue

Born 1942, migrated to Green-wich Village as an actor in 1960 under real name David Cohen. He was part of the circle that included Bob Dylan, Tom Paxton, Eric Andersen, et al. Partly as result of these connections, he he was selected to do three tracks on **Singer Songwriter Project,** with Patrick Sky, Richard Farina and Bruce Murdoch, and subsequently made **David Blue,** again for Elektra.

In 1966 Blue got together with a band called American Patrol, although none of their recordings together were ever released. As a result he joined Reprise Records, and reverted temporarily to his real name with **Me, S. David Cohen.** With still no great commercial success to his credit, he changed his name back to Blue and signed recording deal with David Geffen's Asylum records, Geffen being a personal friend. Since then his albums have appeared at regular intervals, liberally spiced with superstar names like Bob Dylan and Joni Mitchell.

While no single album has ever worked as well as it might, **David Blue, Me S. David Cohen, Nice Baby And The Angel** and **Com'n Back For More,** the last named released in '75, provide an accurate indication of Blue's progress through 12 years of recording.

Recordings:
Singer Songwriter Project (Elektra)
David Blue (Elektra)
These 23 Days In September (Reprise/—)

Me, S. David Cohen (Reprise/—)
Stories (Asylum)
Nice Baby And The Angel (Asylum)
Com'n Back For More (Asylum)

Blue Oyster Cult

Eric Bloom vocals, guitar
Allen Lanier keyboards, synthesiser
Albert Bouchard drums, vocals
Joe Bouchard bass, vocals
Donald (Buck Dharma) Roeser guitar, vocals

Widely considered foremost extant U.S. exponent of heavy metal rock. Made two unreleased albums for Elektra label as Stalk Forrest Group and Soft White Underbelly before signing with U.S. Columbia late 1971 as Blue Oyster Cult. Released eponymous first album same year, following with **Tyranny And Mutation** in 1973 (though latter's release was delayed in U.K.).

Received critical acclaim on both sides of Atlantic, particularly for 1974 third album, **Secret Treaties,** which contained Patti Smith-composed **Career Of Evil,** and the live double set, **On Your Feet Or On Your Knees,** the following year.

A dynamically aggressive live band, after several false starts completed debut U.K. tour, 1975.

Above: Eric Bloom, BOC.

Agents Of Fortune (1976) features Patti Smith "guest" vocals, as well as two writing credits.

Recordings:
Blue Oyster Cult (Columbia/CBS)
Tyranny And Mutation (Columbia/CBS)
Secret Treaties (Columbia/CBS)
On Your Feet Or On Your Knees (Columbia/CBS)
Agents Of Fortune (Columbia/CBS)

Blue Ridge Rangers
➧ John Fogerty

Blues – American

Blues was essentially the folk-music of the Negroes who had been transported from Africa to work as slaves on the cotton plantations in the southern states of America – although blues as it developed was not primarily African in origin and owed at least as much to European folk ballad traditions. The music served both to ameliorate the negro's lot (however briefly) and to remind him of its nature. As a standard musical form, blues can probably be said to have evolved by the end of the 19th century.

Slightly different forms were developed in different areas, and each region had its champion – Charley Patton in the Mississippi Delta, Blind Lemon Jefferson in Dallas. There was also Heddie Leadbetter (Leadbelly), who was acquainted with Jefferson in Dallas at the beginning of the century. Leadbelly was born in Mooringsport, Louisiana, Jan 20, 1889, of black and Cherokee Indian stock; he helped develop a blues form that was based on the work songs and hollers of those, like himself, doing hard labour in state penitentiaries. Many of his songs were adapted by the British skiffle groups of '50s, but his most famous composition was **Goodnight Irene**, which sold two million copies in 1950, just a year after his death.

Meanwhile, Bessie Smith, from Chattanooga, Tennessee, became one of the first people to take

Left: On Your Feet Or On Your Knees. Courtesy CBS Records. A critically well-received double live set, BOC have since said they hated it.

blues into the concert hall and also one of first to make extensive recordings (for Columbia). She often sang with jazz musicians, although she was herself considered a classic blues singer; her career nose-dived after the stock market crash of 1929, and she died after an automobile accident in that year.

Things began to change, in fact, with the depression. Thousands of unemployed negroes migrated north in search of work; they settled in the great industrial centres, particularly Chicago and Detroit. It was Chicago that came to dominate the Northern blues scene, in the same way that Memphis became the natural centre for those who had stayed in the south. A dichotomy began to develop between delta blues and urban blues because, with the trek north, styles began to change. Packed noisy clubs called for louder, more brash music than the traditional acoustic blues style of the south, and many of the more distinguished singers added keyboards, percussion and bass to form their own groups. The softer style of '30s performers like Big Bill Broonzy was gradually outmoded.

Chicago's own really unique sound evolved with the arrival of Muddy Waters and others in the post-war years; in 1934 the young Waters had heard Robert Johnson in Clarksdale, Mississippi, and the impression was a lasting one. Johnson was one of the most inventive blues singers and, though he was murdered in 1938 at the age of 24, was the single most important influence on the Chicago blues of the '50s and '60s.

The rise of the Chess record company (originally known as Aristocrat) also assisted in spreading the gospel of blues music. Len and Phil Chess, Jewish immigrants from Poland, arrived in the U.S. in 1928 and developed a chain of night-clubs and bars in the black sections of Chicago. The Chess label itself was formed in 1950, with talent scouts like Ike Turner and Sam Phillips in Memphis, and soon afterwards black musicians were flocking to Chicago; Sonny Boy Williamson II and Howlin' Wolf arrived, as well as Muddy Waters.

Howlin' Wolf was born June 10, 1910 near Tupelo in Mississippi delta, and was very influenced by Charley Patton. He was originally recorded in Memphis by Sam Phillips for the Sun label, before he signed to Chess, and then moved to Chicago 1952. His real nane was Chester Burnett; he was a huge man with a brooding and utterly distinctive style of singing, who even had a minor hit with his classic **Smokestack Lightnin'.**

After several visits to Britain, he worked, like other blues singers, with respectful rock musicians, and in 1969 recorded the controversial and cleverly titled **This Is Howlin' Wolf's New Album. He Doesn't Like It. He Didn't Like Electric Guitar At First Either,** and in 1971 he made **London Sessions** for Rolling Stones Records, with the assistance of Eric Clapton, Stevie Winwood, Charlie

Right: Muddy Waters, one of the most influential of bluesmen. Bottom right: Willie Dixon, who played in Muddy's band. Top: John Lee Hooker.

Watts and Bill Wyman. He died in 1976, by which time heavy rock bands like Led Zeppelin had recycled much of his material.

Muddy Waters was born McKinley Morganfield in Rolling Fork, Mississippi, April 4, 1915. After moving to Chess, he made a series of magnificent blues recordings in the '50s, introducing the world to songs such as **Hoochie Coochie Man** and **I Just Wanna Make Love To You.** Then when he began to be brought over to Britain, his innovative use of amplification at first riled the purists, but it did persuade people like Alexis Korner and Cyril Davies to plug in, and hence directly influenced the Stones. Waters, too, aimed directly at the rock market in the later '60s with **Electric Mud** and **After The Rain.**

Before Waters' personal success his band had proved the fount of much talent – namely his half-brother Otis Spann, who died in 1970, and harmonica player Little Walter, who died in 1968. Perhaps more important, though, was his bass-player, Willie Dixon, who wrote numerous blues standards including **You Shook Me** and **Little Red Rooster.** He acted as a link-man between the artists and the Chess label, arranging the business side as well as playing on most of the sessions. Further, he recorded with people like Chuck Berry and Bo Diddley, and was probably the most important individual link between the blues and rock 'n' roll.

John Lee Hooker was born in Clarksdale, Mississippi in 1917, and was based in Detroit in the post-war years. A stylist whose guitar playing is characterized by constantly shifting rhythms, he was a major influence on the British R&B boom of early '60s, with songs like **Boom Boom** and **Dimples.** (The former was successfully covered by The Animals; the latter became an unlikely hit single for him). He too, inevitably, went on to recording sessions with rock artists, making **Hooker 'n' Heat** with Canned Heat (♦).

The Story Of The Blues, Vol One. Courtesy CBS Records.

Sonny Terry and Brownie McGhee, a harmonica and guitar partnership, made a strong impression on blues revivalism, being themselves articulate commentators on the genre. They recorded prolifically in the '50s, before they too directed themselves towards the white market,

issuing an album with rock musicians on A&M in 1973.

In Kansas City, a more raucous and extrovert blues style was developed by artists like Joe Turner, who became known as blues shouters. This too played an important formative part in rock 'n' roll as Bill Haley (to give just one example) tended to base his style and presentation on that of the shouters.

Hence, the effect of the blues on rock 'n' roll is quite incalculable. The Beatles, Rolling Stones and Animals were all heavily influenced by these bluesmen and their styles of music. Bob Dylan's debut album was composed almost entirely of old blues standards.

In the U.S. it wasn't until success of Paul Butterfield (♦), who'd learned his blues direct from Chicago's dive-bars where people like Muddy Waters, Howlin' Wolf, Little Walter and Otis Rush were still delivering their music, that these performers came to be appreciated for themselves. In the wake of the '60s blues boom, many achieved fame, though few made fortunes, despite their gladiatorial entry into the rock arena. The truth is they were living legends all, and by the time the world became aware of that, most were too old to play or even to benefit in any material form.

British audiences, on the other hand, discovered the blues via the works of groups such as John Mayall's Bluesbreakers and

Fleetwood Mac (➧ British Blues). On the whole, also, it was more often the British performers who opted to work directly with the legendary American bluesmen.

The Story Of The Blues, Vols. I & II (Columbia/CBS), compiled by Paul Oliver to accompany his book of the same title, is one of the most thoroughly-researched compilations of blues music, illustrating its many forms.

Blues – British

The British Blues Boom, which flowered from 1965–68, began as extension of earlier R&B phase (➧ British R&B) and finally petered out, leaving nucleus of formidable instrumentalists with abiding knowledge of blues form and the technique to carry these ideas forward in creating new types of virtuoso rock 'n' roll.

Dates given above indicate "peaking" of interest in British Blues; but several respected "founding fathers" – John Mayall, Alexis Korner, John Baldry and Graham Bond – had run blues-oriented outfits for years.

Genre ranged from bottleneck/tambourine "delta" blues to all-electric "city" blues based on Chicago and Detroit downtown guitar styles. Early Rolling Stones material shows marked influence of former style, but real boom came when British guitarists like Eric Clapton, Peter Green, (➧ Fleetwood Mac), Stan Webb (➧ Chicken Shack) and Alvin Lee (➧ Ten Years After) emerged as masters of "city" style already used by legendary U.S. guitar giants such as B. B. King, Buddy Guy, Otis Rush, Albert King and Freddy King.

Seminal British outfit during Blues Boom was John Mayall's Bluesbreakers. With Clapton, then Green and later Mick Taylor (➧ Rolling Stones) as guitar frontmen, Mayall's reputation as boss-man of U.K. blues scene held throughout late '60s.

Other bands (Fleetwood Mac, early Jethro Tull, TYA, Savoy Brown, Chicken Shack) and the occasional blues soloist (Duster Bennett) spread the word – and impressario/producer Mike Vernon founded a new label, Blue Horizon, expressly to expose this wealth of talent.

Boom's real legacy lies in later development of new, instrumental standards in British rock 'n' roll and a style based on instrumental virtuosity and epic soloing later to form platform for '70s U.K. invasion of U.S. rock market.

Although loath to copy their own national sources, American guitarists assiduously learned the style second hand; rock guitar received its biggest boost in technique for ten years and these influences remain.

Blues Project

Al Kooper keyboards
Steve Katz guitar
Danny Kalb guitar
Andy Kulberg bass, flute
Roy Blumenfeld drums

Seminal New York City group, first recorded with above line-up. Artie Traum and Tommy Flanders also involved with band in em-

bryonic stage. Possibly N.Y.'s first real white blues band, achieved semi-legendary status working East Coast 1965-66, Al Kooper (➧) having played sessions for Dylan, Steve Katz boasting similar reputation via associations with New York folk scene (Dave Van Ronk, Even Dozen Jug Band etc).

Project landed residency at Cafe Au Go Go in Greenwich Village – see first album – and word of mouth reputation spread fast. By summer '66, band had played three huge open-air concerts in Central Park. Albums of time now collectors' pieces in States.

Original group disintegrated, however, when Kooper and Katz went off to form Blood Sweat & Tears (➧). A revival of Blues Project was attempted in 1971 by Kalb and Blumenfeld with aforementioned Tommy Flanders, plus Don Kretmar from Seatrain and keyboards player David Cohen. This band made **Lazarus** album, which was produced by Shel Talmy, same year. In 1972, guitarist Bill Lussenden augmented line-up for **Blues Project** album on Capitol. Blues Project split second time round shortly after.

Re-united by Al Kooper early 1973 for one-off Central Park gig, out of which came MCA album listed below. In early 1976, Steve Katz launched new band American Flyer on United Artists.

Recordings:
Live At The Cafe Au Go Go (Verve)
Blues Project/Projections (Verve)
Blues Project At Town Hall (Verve)
Lazarus (Capitol)
Blues Project (Capitol)
Reunion In Central Park (MCA)

Colin Blunstone

Born June 24, 1945 and began career at school in St. Albans, U.K. with group The Zombies (➧). After demise of band, and disenchanted with music business, took office job in London suburbs only once venturing out of self-imposed exile to record a remake of Zombies' song **She's Not There** under pseudonym Neil MacArthur, a minor U.K. hit 1968.

Returned to music full-time with the 1971 solo album **One Year**, from which came 1972 hit with the Denny Laine song **Say You Don't Mind**. After second album same year, went on road in U.K. with band which included Pete Wingfield (➧) on keyboards. Slumped into period of inactivity after 1974 **Journey** and is now with Elton John's Rocket Records.

Recordings:
One Year (Epic)
Ennismore (Epic)
Journey (Epic)

Marc Bolan (& T. Rex)

Born Mark Feld in Hackney, East

Right: My People Were Fair And Had Sky In Their Hair . . .

London, 1948, Bolan was youthful mod and budding male model before he broke into music scene at same time as other struggling young songwriters, David Bowie and Cat Stevens.

Changed name to Marc Bolan when Decca released **The Wizard** single in 1966 before becoming member of John's Children, who have claims to being first-ever glam rock band. This outfit had two minor British hits on Track label, **Desdemona** and **Go Go Girl**, the latter actually a backing track for Bolan's later **Mustang Ford** with vocals added after he had left group. Around this time, also cut recordings for Track album, **Beginning Of Doves**, although this was not released until 1974.

Tanx. Courtesy EMI.

Bolan subsequently attempted to form five-piece electric group which, legend has it, failed when hire purchase company repossessed their equipment. Out of wreckage, surviving members Bolan and percussionist Steve Peregrine Took started gigging as acoustic duo 1968 under name Tyrannosaurus Rex.

First and second albums were purely acoustic and featured Bolan compositions heavy with his own private mythologies. By the third album, **Prophets Seers And Sages** etc, in 1969, Bolan had expanded instrumentation and was writing some of his best songs.

Steve Took quit soon after, mainly through disenchantment with inability to stamp his own personality on duo's work, and he was replaced by Micky Finn, who met Bolan in health-food restaurant.

Finn made debut on 1970 **Beard Of Stars** album, which was transitional collection in that Bolan introduced electric guitar on several tracks. Up to this point Rex were minority appeal outfit on fringes of what British press termed at time "progressive" boom, in competition for audiences with far more successful contemporaries like of Ten Years After, Jethro Tull and Fleetwood Mac.

Then, in late 1970, Bolan and Finn, now operating under abbreviated name of T. Rex, had surprise U.K. No. 2 single with **Ride A White Swan** – which was issued simultaneously with T. Rex album as their debut release on now defunct Fly label.

Bolan's audience changed dramatically within a period of months. With addition of bassist Steve Currie and later drummer Bill Legend, consolidated new position as fast-growing teenybopper and chart attraction with **Hot Love**, which topped U.K. charts for six weeks in early 1971, and **Get It On** which enjoyed comparable success later same year. (Latter is closest Bolan ever got to breaking U.S. singles charts, retitled as **Bang A Gong**.)

By this time, totally on strength of Bolan's charismatic personality and penchant for commercial songs, T. Rex were drawing from their increasingly younger audiences the kind of hysteria previously not seen since golden days in U.K. of Stones, Beatles and The Monkees.

In mid-1971 **Electric Warrior** completed transition from gentle folkiness of early Rex to full-blown rock 'n' roll attack. It was an entertaining if flawed collection, and Fly pulled **Jeepster** track off album to release as single. It made U.K. No. 2 but Bolan, upset at not being consulted, started his own T. Rex label.

My people were fair and had sky in their hair...
But now they're content to wear stars on their brows

Right: From 1969 Steve Took and Marc Bolan, the original Tyrannosaurus Rex. Was Marc really the skinny hippy? Was he just holding his stomach in?

Through 1972 Bolan was at peak of his popularity. **The Slider** was great commercial success, and **Telegram Sam, Metal Guru,** re-issued oldie **Debora, Children Of The Revolution** and **Solid Gold Easy Action** continued stream of U.K. hits.

In 1973 Ringo Starr (♦) turned film-maker and directed movie about the T. Rex phenomenon "Born To Boogie", which, despite the participation of Elton John, satisfied only the faithful.

Critically however, his output came in for increasing hammering, and Bolan himself was obviously decidedly frustrated by total inability to open U.S. market with same ease. Albums from **Tanx** onwards failed to match U.K. sales of immediate predecessors, and by 1973 T. Rex fever started to abate as Bolan fans began to switch loyalties to U.S. bopper exports David Cassidy and Osmonds.

In 1976, after spending year or so in U.S. to avoid full weight of tax laws at home, Bolan charisma at low ebb – though the T. Rex fans who remain tend to be as strident in their support almost as much as those of Elvis Presley and were sufficient in number to ensure at least a couple of sellouts on low-profile spring '76 comeback tour of U.K.

Having left wife June Child, now lives with U.S. singer Gloria Jones with whom he also works on stage.

Over the years there has been considerable repackaging of Bolan/T. Rex material with first/second and third/fourth Tyrannosaurus Rex albums reissued as double album couplings in 1972.

Recordings:
Marc Bolan:
Beginning Of Doves (—/Track)
Tyrannosaurus Rex:
My People Were Fair And Had Sky In Their Hair But Now They're Content To Wear Stars On Their Brows (—/Regal Zonophone)
Prophets Seers And Sages, The Angels Of The Ages (Blue Thumb/Regal Zonophone)
Unicorn (Blue Thumb/Regal Zonophone)
Beard Of Stars (Blue Thumb/Regal Zonophone)
T. Rex:
T. Rex (Reprise/Fly)
Electric Warrior (Reprise/Fly)
The Slider (Reprise/T. Rex)
Tanx (Reprise/T. Rex)
Marc Bolan and T. Rex:
Zinc Alloy And The Hidden Riders Of Tomorrow (Reprise/T. Rex)
Zip Gun Boogie (Reprise/T. Rex)
Futuristic Dragon (Reprise/T. Rex)

Compilations:
A Beginning (A&M/—)
Best Of T. Rex (—/Fly)
Light Of Love (Casablanca/—)

Tommy Bolin

American guitar virtuoso and prolific composer, originally from Sioux City, Iowa. Played with U.S. groups Zephyr and Energy before joining James Gang (♦) in 1973 on recommendation of group's former axeman Joe Walsh (♦). Cut two albums with James Gang, supplying material for both, before quitting group summer 1974. Set to work on solo album **Teaser** which features Tubes drummer Prairie Prince and keyboarder Jan Hammer.

In summer 1975 joined U.K. rock group Deep Purple (♦) to fill guitar spot left vacant by Ritchie Blackmore. Release of **Teaser** in winter 1975 coincided with Bolin's first Purple album **Come Taste The Band,** for which he wrote or co-wrote no less than seven of ten tracks. Also featured heavily on Billy Cobham (♦) album, **Spectrum.**

Recordings:
Teaser (Nemperor/Atlantic)

Graham Bond

A 'founding father' of British R&B (♦) boom of '60s, Bond's story is one of the greatest tragedies of U.K. rock. Already an established jazz saxophonist, having played with Don Rendell Quintet, Bond led succession of line-ups through '60s which included at various times many of instrumental superheroes of years to follow: Ginger Baker, John McLaughlin, Jack Bruce, Jon Hiseman, Dick Heck-

Right: Graham Bond, a founding father of British R&B. Obsessed with the occult in later years, he died under the wheels of a London train in May 1974.

stall-Smith. In a sense Bond was catalyst in formation of both Cream (♦) and Colosseum (♦).

His first band in 1963 formed out of Alexis Korner (♦) Blues Incorporated with McLaughlin, Baker and Bruce (then on double bass) stayed close to jazz and blues roots. Later, when blues and R&B scenes erupted on U.K. gig circuit, the Graham Bond Organization became known for playing the most evil-sounding, dirty R&B heard on home shores.

Technologically as well as musically, Bond was an innovator: the first British musician to use the Hammond organ and Leslie speaker combination (in an R&B context), the first to "split" the instru-

ment for portability, the first to build an electronic keyboard and the first to use a Mellotron, which can be heard on first two albums.

After break-up of last Organization line-up circa 1969, Bond did some solo recording and session work and eventually turned up in Ginger Baker's muscle-bound Air Force (♦ Ginger Baker). He went to the U.S. to record and do session work, marrying singer Diane Stewart on his return to U.K. Later the couple teamed up with Pete Brown (♦) to form Bond And Brown and record **Two Heads Are Better Than One** in 1972.

Bond and his wife shared an interest in magick (sic) and together subsequently formed and disbanded several groups, including Holy Magick which recorded **We Put Our Magick On You** (released 1974).

After the near-simultaneous collapse of the band and his marriage, Bond formed Magus with British folk singer Carolanne Pegg. However, mainly for financial reasons, the group disbanded around Christmas 1973 without recording.

The following year found Bond at his lowest ebb. His financial affairs were in chaos, and the demise of Magus had badly hurt his pride. Throughout his career he had been hampered by severe bouts of drug addiction and, in Jan '73, had spent a month in hospital with a nervous breakdown.

He seemed on course again in early '74, however, until on May 8 of that year, in mysterious circumstances, Bond died under wheels of train at Finsbury Park Station, London. He was 37. Friends agree that he was off drugs, although he was becoming increasingly possessed by his interest in the occult (he believed he was Aleister Crowley's son). The day before his death he had phoned the "New Musical Express" offices saying he was "clean" and "looking forward to getting back to work again".

Along with John Mayall and Alexis Korner, one of the great catalytic figures of '60s rock in U.K. Arguably more gifted than both, has claim to title "Father of British Blues".

Recordings:
The Sound Of '65 (—/Columbia)
There's A Bond Between Us (—/Columbia)
Bond and Brown:
Two Heads Are Better Than One (—/Chapter One)
Holy Magick:
We Put Our Magick On You (—/Philips)
Compilations:
This Is Graham Bond (—/Philips)
Solid Bond (Warner Bros)

Bonzo Dog (Doo Dah) Band

Viv Stanshall vocals, trumpet
Neil Innes keyboards, guitar, bass, vocals
Roger Ruskin Spear saxes, devices
Rodney Slater saxes
"Legs" Larry Smith percussion

College group formed London 1966 (flexible early line-up also featured Vernon Dudley Bohay Nowell and Sam Spoons) as out-

crop of brief movement back towards Temperance Seven/Alberts-style very English mixture of trad jazz and surrealism inspired by contemporary commercial success of New Vaudeville Band. Attracted small but cult live following and cut two flop singles for Parlophone before moving to Liberty and expanding into burgeoning album market.

First album, **Gorilla**, in 1967, while reflecting the in-bred eccentricity of this genre, also showed Bonzos to be gifted beyond all competition. Spear providing authenticity with his thorough knowledge of '20s style, Innes contributing distinctive compositional ability, and Stanshall demonstrating genuine comic inspiration.

With second album (1968), group broadened musical base to encompass rock parodies and stepped up direct satire that had originally distinguished them, only Mothers Of Invention operating in this field at the time. In 1968 group had U.K. Top 10 hit **I'm The Urban Spaceman**, written by Innes and produced by Apollo C. Vermouth, a bombastic pseudonym for Paul McCartney.

Keynsham. Courtesy United Artists Records.

The 1969 **Tadpoles** album was temporary return to their point of origin dictated by Spear who was unhappy with new developments and – after **Keynsham** in 1969 had confirmed direction of second album – the band split up.

An attempt by Innes and Stanshall to revive group – **Let's Make Up And Be Friendly** (1972) – only partially successful, but it did provide link with personnel of likewise disbanded outfits operating in same territory (i.e. Scaffold, Liverpool Scene) which went on to result in Grimms musical-satirical revue.

Viv Stanshall has since worked solo – recording his own **Men Opening Umbrellas Ahead** album for Warner Bros in 1974 – with little success; Larry Smith appeared with Elton John and Eric Clapton on '74 U.S. tours; Ruskin Spear appears occasionally with his Kinetic Wardrobe; Rodney Slater became local government officer; Neil Innes since associated with former Monty Python personnel, notably Eric Idle's BBC-TV "Rutland Weekend Television" programme.

Recordings:
Bonzo Dog Band: Gorilla (Imperial/Sunset)
The Doughnut In Granny's Greenhouse (Imperial/Sunset)
Tadpoles (Imperial/Sunset)

Right: The Bonzos. Vintage rock lunacy.

Keynsham (Imperial/Liberty)
Let's Make Up And Be Friendly (United Artists)
Compilations:
History Of The Bonzos (United Artists)

Booker T. & The M.G.s

Booker T. Jones keyboards
Steve Cropper guitar
Al Jackson drums
Don "Duck" Dunn bass

Stax Records' house rhythm section, who almost inadvertently formed themselves into permanent group after one-off single release, **Green Onions**, had become a worldwide hit. Booker T. & The M.G.s (M.G. stood for Memphis Group) existed only as an occasional ensemble, though they regularly made records of their own, as well as intermittent live appearances.

Best-known line-up of the group was Booker T. Jones (keyboards), Steve Cropper (guitar), Al Jackson (drums) and Don 'Duck' Dunn (bass), though Dunn had replaced original member Lewis Steinberg. Jones, born Memphis, Nov 12, 1944, had been raised in middle-class area of the ghetto, while Cropper had had an entirely different rural upbringing. Jones and Jackson were black, Cropper and Dunn white; a truly integrated group. Despite success of **Green Onions**, Booker T. completed his studies at Indiana University until 1966.

Their own records notwithstanding, the band became best-known for their clean, tasteful work as session musicians in Memphis, working behind all major Stax label artists – Rufus and Carla Thomas, Otis Redding and Wilson Pickett. Their music, and that of Willie Mitchell (♦) came to represent the renowned Memphis sound in its quintessential form – a tight, disciplined, spare sound which had a profound influence on the development of soul and rock music.

Right: Bowie 1976, return of the thin white duke.

Despite continuing to produce hit singles and albums into the late '60s, the group began to phase out personal appearances, concentrating on studio work, until they disbanded in the early '70s. Jones married Rita Coolidge's sister, Priscilla, and embarked on a joint recording career with her. He also had other projects to sort out – for example, he produced **Just As I Am** for Bill Withers.

In 1975 Al Jackson was murdered by an intruder at his Memphis home (♦ Steve Cropper).

Recordings:
Green Onions (Stax/Atlantic)
Uptight (Stax)
Soul Limbo (Stax)
McLemore Avenue (Stax)
Booker T. Set (Stax)
Meltin' Pot (Stax)
Compilations:
The Best Of . . . (Stax/Atlantic)
Greatest Hits (Stax)
Booker T. & Priscilla:
Booker T. & Priscilla (A&M)
Home Grown (A&M)
Evergreen (Epic)

Bootlegs

Illicit recordings: **Bob Dylan – The Great White Wonder** being the album that in 1969 first brought bootlegs to public notice. It wasn't by any means the first however. For years, jazz fans had been transferring recordings of artists like Charlie Parker and obscure blues records on to limited edition albums. Most modern bootlegs are either recorded direct from concerts or are fourth-generation copy tapes. An illegal practice which infringes law of copyright, bootlegs continue to appear (virtually every major rock artist is in this unofficial "catalogue") despite increasing government pressures in U.S. and U.K. It is estimated that the Great White Wonder double set has sold in excess of 350,000 copies world-wide, thus qualifying for gold record status.

ing pop singer, fronted 12-piece U.K. jazz-rock outfit Dada which metamorphosed into Vinegar Joe (♦). It was when V. Joe split in late 1973 that Ms Brooks embarked on new solo career with A&M, the 1975-released album below being first fruits of that partnership.

Recording:
Rich Man's Woman (A&M)

Arthur Brown

A product of the U.K.'s psychedelic summer of 1967 – when he began working at London's UFO club with original Crazy World Of Arthur Brown group, which included keyboardist Vincent Crane – later of Atomic Rooster (♦) – and drummer Drachen Theaker. Born Whitby, Yorkshire June 1944 and an ex-Reading University philosophy student, Brown was a pioneer of theatre of shock-rock – appearing on stage with bizarre facial make-up and metal helmet which would be set on fire during finale of act.

In 1968 smashed into U.K. singles charts with Crane-composed Fire. Success was repeated in U.S. charts, but subsequent Crazy World tour there was near-disaster. Earlier audiences began to drift away, and Brown failed to capitalise on success of Fire. Before Crazy World eventually split, Carl Palmer (♦ Emerson Lake And Palmer) had spell in drum seat.

Brown re-emerged after lengthy lay-off in 1970 fronting the similarly theatrical but none too successful Kingdom Come, from whom he split in late '73 after band had produced three albums, Galactic Zoo Dossier, Kingdom Come, and The Journey.

Ever the eccentric, Brown took himself off on mid-Eastern trek which culminated with him playing guitar for Israeli troops, before returning to U.K. and six-month course in meditation. In 1975 signed to British Gull Records. Had small role in "Tommy" movie.

Recordings:
The Crazy World Of Arthur Brown (Track)
Galactic Zoo Dossier (—/Polydor)
Kingdom Come (—/Polydor)
The Journey (Passport/Polydor)
Dance (Gull)

James Brown

Born May 3, 1928 at Pulaski, Tennessee (though Brown has often disputed both his birth-date and -place) and raised in Augusta, Georgia, where he still lives, Brown rose from an early life of extreme povery to become a most potent symbol of successful black America. He began recording in 1948 and, before signing for King in 1955, made several records of the basic, contagious dance rhythms for which he later became renowned. His first record for King, Please Please Please (as usual, recording with his backing group, the Famous Flames) established him as a name in the black R&B market.

Over next decade, he issued a string of top-selling records, all of which utilized the same techniques. What made him so popular to a black audience was his intense, emotional involvement with each song; the passionate intensity of his delivery was quite unmatched, and this was accompanied by a stage show of total overkill, using a succession of dramatic effects. Brown went coast-to-coast, breaking box office records all over America. He became Soul Brother Number One, and even before Muhammed Ali, Brown was the personification of the spiritual liberation of black America. Rich and successful, he did it by taking care of business himself.

Nevertheless, Brown, supreme in the black market, wanted to extend his audience, and he did it without compromise. Disgruntled with King's lack of success in obtaining media promotion for him, he ignored his contract and made an album and single for Smash Records. Out Of Sight (1964) demonstrated the Brown technique par excellence, and it did indeed help widen his audience, but King subsequently re-claimed him. However the breach had now been made, and King now got him radio exposure, turning numbers like It's A Man's Man's Man's World into million-sellers. Although this song employed strings, it was nevertheless delivered in Brown's frenzied and distinctive gospel-

styled singing.

Say It Loud, I'm Black And I'm Proud was one of the first affirmative statements of the new black American consciousness, though Brown eschewed politics. He was personally thanked by the U.S. President for his part in calming down racial tensions during the riots of late '60s, by putting on a marathon television show to help keep people off the streets.

He has possibly been the most influential of all soul artists. Certainly, he is the one who made least concessions himself. His music has always been ideal dance music, and his use of jazz influences and Afro-rhythms helped pave the way for the prevalent street-funk music of the mid-'70s – something at which his new backing group, Fred Wesley and the J.B.s, who provide a complex rhythmic accompaniment, have particularly excelled.

In recent years he has tended to become a parody of himself. His records and stage act have a somewhat dated ambience. His bands are liveried retainers, totally regimented in style and movement; but while his own performance necessarily lacks something of the former athleticism (he is, after all, getting old) his persona still retains the chutzpah of earlier days, and he continues to add outrageous appellations like campaign medals. He has lately been referring to himself as the Minister of New New Super Heavy Funk. He is irrepressible.

Since his recorded output is prodigious – and he adds to it weekly (or so it sometimes seems), the discography lists only recent albums.

Recordings:
Revolution Of The Mind (Polydor)
Get On The Good Foot (Polydor)
Soul Brother Number One (Polydor)
Slaughter's Big Rip-Off (Soundtrack) (Polydor)
The Payback (Polydor)
It's Hell (Polydor)
Reality (Polydor)
Sex Machine Today (Polydor)
Everybody's Doin' The Hustle And Dead On The Double Bump (Polydor)
Compilations:
Soul Classics, Vols. I-III (Polydor)

Pete Brown

Born London, 1940, and a veteran of British Underground, Brown helped promote cause of poetry and jazz in early '60s. reading and playing with occasional groups that included musicians like Dick Heckstall-Smith and Graham Bond, with whom he later formed Bond And Brown partnership for 1972 album Two Heads Are Better Than One (♦ Graham Bond).

Of interest to rock buffs primarily due to songwriting partnership with Jack Bruce (♦). Brown wrote lyrics for Bruce compositions which provided Cream (♦) with some of their finest material – e.g. White Room, Tales Of Brave Ulysses, Sunshine Of Your Love. Also worked in same capacity on Bruce solo albums.

Has also fronted own rock bands, The Battered Ornaments, which

Left: Arthur Brown, The Man Who Crazed The World. He set himself on fire in 1968, and further pioneered the Theatre Of The Absurd with the neglected, anarchic Kingdom Come. A former student of philosophy, Brown was ever outrageous. Notice how one trouser leg doesn't match the other.

JACKSON BROWNE

Late For The Sky

Left: Late For The Sky. Courtesy Asylum Records/ WEA. Browne's concept for the cover photo was executed after the style of Magritte.

1970 **Things We Like** project with John McLaughlin, Dick Heckstall-Smith and Jon Hiseman.

During this time, also played with Tony Williams Lifetime and formed group with American jazzers Larry Coryell, Mike Mandel, and former Jimi Hendrix drummer Mitch Mitchell to present live the material from **Harmony Row** (1971), his second solo album.

Diversifying even further, collaborated with Paul Haines and Carla Bley on acclaimed jazz-rock album **Escalator Over The Hill,** and subsequently returned to rock to join sub-Cream trio West Bruce And Laing (◆) 1972-73. In November 1974 released third solo album **Out Of The Storm,** after which he formed short-lived group featuring ex-Stone Mick Taylor on guitar and previously-mentioned Carla Bley on keyboards. This band fell to pieces after handful of gigs when Taylor and Bley walked out.

Erratic nature of later work may have dampened reputation as musician which was at peak during Cream, but Bruce remains one of prime bass stylists in rock.

Recordings:
Songs For A Taylor (Atco/ Polydor)
Harmony Row (Atco/Polydor)
Out Of The Storm (RSO)
With John McLaughlin, Dick Heckstall-Smith, Jon Hiseman: Things We Like (Atco/Polydor)
Compilations:
Best Of (RSO)

Roy Buchanan

Virtuoso American guitarist, born Arkansas. Son of a preacher, raised in Californian farm community where travelling revivalists and their gospel music led him into abiding interest in blues. Backed rock legend Dale Hawkins (**Suzie Q**) for three years, during which time he struck up friendship with Robbie Robertson later of The Band (◆). Of Buchanan, Robertson has said: "He was the first great rock guitarist I ever heard . . . wonderful, just wonderful."

From 1959, when he married, Buchanan worked out of Washington D.C. recording with likes of Freddy Cannon and for ace producers/writers Lieber and Stoller (◆). In his time claims to have employed his battered Telecaster in more than 100 different bands in clubs the length and breadth of the U.S. Solo albums date from 1972.

Recordings:
Roy Buchanan (Polydor)
Second Album (Polydor)
That's What I Am Here For (Polydor)
Rescue Me (Polydor)
Live Stock (Polydor)
A Street Called Straight (Atlantic)

Lord Buckley

Born Richard M. Buckley in Stockton, California in 1905, he

---

included Chris Spedding (◆), and Piblokto. Both recorded for Harvest label in U.K.

Jackson Browne

Emerging out of Los Angeles music scene, went to New York as a 17-year-old where he played back-up guitar for Nico (◆) at the Electric Circus; three Browne songs were later featured on Nico's debut album, **Chelsea Girl.**

Browne's talents are quite formidable and, excepting Joni Mitchell (◆), he is certainly the most literate of singer/songwriters to emerge so far; but news of his talents was initially disseminated by colleagues as he was both too self-effacing and too suspicious of the business to promote his own affairs.

In the early days, the Nitty Gritty Dirt Band (◆) recorded several of his songs, and Tom Rush (◆) recorded **These Days** and **Jamaica Say You Will.** It was through people like Rush that Browne's name came to be known. Inevitably he found himself in David Geffen's L.A. stable of Asylum boy wonders. Though he recorded one album in demo form, it wasn't until 1972 (the same year he played some gigs in U.K. with Joni Mitchell) that **Jackson Browne** was released; it contained much material that had already been recorded by

other artists.

He has worked closely with The Eagles (◆), and **For Everyman** features a song co-written with Glenn Frey, **Take It Easy,** which had opened The Eagles' debut album; he also wrote, wholly or in part, **Nightingale, Doolin-Dalton** and **James Dean** for The Eagles. Basically, Browne had no need to further his own career as so many other people were doing it for him. **For Everyman,** in 1973 consolidated his fast-growing reputation, and **Late For The Sky** (1974) cemented it. He tends to work slowly and painstakingly, and hence his output is small;

Above: Jackson Browne.

but his songs continue to be recorded by a wide range of artists – **Doctor My Eyes** (the Jackson 5), **Jamaica Say You Will** (Joe Cocker), **Song For Adam** (Kiki Dee), **Fountain Of Sorrow** (Joan Baez), being just a few examples.

Again excepting Ms. Mitchell, he is most lyrically refined of new breed of singer/songwriters, and like her, tends to eschew the everyday superficialities of the rock-biz.

His brother, Severin Browne, has recorded one album, **Love Songs,** for Mowest.

Recordings:
Jackson Browne (Asylum)
For Everyman (Asylum)
Late For The Sky (Asylum)

Jack Bruce

Scottish bass virtuoso and singer/ songwriter. Born John Simon Asher Bruce in Bishopbriggs, Lanarkshire, May 14, 1943. Early musical exposures were to Scottish folk, jazz and Bach, all of which influences are evident on later recordings. At 17, won scholarship to Royal Scottish Academy of Music.

First gained attention playing R&B on double bass in Graham Bond Organization, subsequently appearing in John Mayall's Bluesbreakers and Manfred Mann before founding Cream with Ginger Baker and Eric Clapton (◆Bond, Mayall, Manfred Mann, Cream).

After Cream break-up 1969, Bruce was the odd-man-out in formation of Blind Faith (◆). Instead recorded much praised 1969 solo album **Songs For A Tailor,** followed by less-known began working night-clubs in Chicago during the depression. He adopted the language and mores of the urban streets, and in particular familiarised himself with the hip argot of the black jazz musicians. He used all this to develop an act of great originality, in which he employed unorthodox language to describe visions and allegories which would usually have been considered in an orthodox fashion – Jesus, for example, was referred to as "the Nazz".

A truly hip aristocrat, Buckley collapsed and died in New York in 1960, since when many lesser talents have earned a living just by repeating his patter wholesale. Most contemporary songwriters who aspire to humour owe at least something to him, from Bob Dylan, who loved Buckley's records, to Tom Waits (♦).

Tim Buckley

Born Feb 14, 1947 in Washington and bred in New York. Moved to California when he was 10, played with several country bands during his adolescence, and also developed an act with Jim Fielder (later a member of Blood, Sweat And Tears) for clubs in Los Angeles.

Buckley attracted attention as a solo performer and was signed by Frank Zappa's manager Herb Cohen, who was impressed by his striking voice, with its incredible range, and also his material. Cohen arranged Buckley a deal with Elektra Records. **Tim Buckley** was released in October 1966, when he was 19. It had been recorded in three days.

He was young, talented and versatile, ever the man most likely to. Even at the beginning, when he was essentially a folk-oriented performer, his music took in a wide variety of styles and Lilian Roxon, in "Rock Encyclopedia", wrote "There is no name yet for the places he and his voice go."

George Harrison thought highly of him and recommended him to Brian Epstein, who saw him in April '67, when Buckley was energetically playing clubs in New York; he stayed there to record his second album. **Goodbye And Hello** is generally considered to be his finest creative work. To a certain extent, it provided Buckley with his breakthrough as he came to the attention of a wide audience, both in the U.S. and U.K.

At this juncture, however, Buckley was probably too talented for his own good, too eager to explore different musical forms. He'd hardly established an audience for himself before he'd left it far behind. Nevertheless, his next albums, **Happy/Sad** and **Lorca** (recorded in 1969 and 1970) are highly effective in their jazz-tinged introspective melancholy. Buckley moved to Cohen's own company, Straight Records, and experimented further. **Starsailor** is notable for being a strange and unique voyage into the realms of avant-garde jazz.

Unfortunately this approach disaffected most of Buckley's audience. It was two years before his next album; he lived reclusively, devoting time to his family and working on a film script. He also acted in productions of Edward Albee's "Zoo Story" and Jean-Paul Sartre's "No Exit".

After his lay-off, his music became more conventional. **Greetings From L.A.** and **Sefronia** are both little more than exercises in commercial music-making and **Look At The Fool** was off-target altogether.

Goodbye And Hello. Courtesy Elektra Records/WEA.

Sadly it was to be his last album. He died June 29, 1975, of an overdose of heroin and morphine, leaving behind a mass of unfulfilled promises, but several albums that will appreciate and be appreciated with time.

Recordings:
Tim Buckley (Elektra)
Goodbye And Hello (Elektra)
Happy/Sad (Elektra)
Lorca (Elektra)
Blue Afternoon (Straight)
Starsailor (Straight)
Greetings From L.A. (Straight)
Sefronia (Discreet)
Look At The Fool (Discreet)

Budgie

Burke Shelley bass, vocals
Tony Bourge guitar, vocals
Steve Williams drums

Formed Cardiff, Wales, by Shelley in 1968, later joined by fellow Welshman Bourge and original drummer Ray Phillips. Released first album 1971. A somewhat pedestrian heavy-riffing outfit, Budgie had achieved little beyond small but solid U.K. gig circuit following until **In For The Kill**, fourth album (1974), gained certain measure of success in U.K. Ray Phillips had quit before release of that set, replaced by Pete Boot who in turn was replaced late in 1974 by current drummer, Welshman Steve Williams. Fifth album (1975) recorded at Welsh Rockfield Studios. Later same year signed to A&M.

Recordings:
Budgie (MCA)
Squawk (MCA)
Never Turn Your Back On A Friend (MCA)
In For The Kill (MCA)
Bandolier (MCA)
If I Was Brittania I'd Waive The Rules (A&M)

Buffalo Springfield

Neil Young vocals, guitar
Steve Stills vocals, guitar
Richie Furay vocals, guitar
Dewey Martin vocals, drums
Bruce Palmer bass

Seminal West Coast outfit, formed early 1966 with above line-up – initial inspiration stemmed from Stills (♦) who had previously been in New York-based vocal group The Au Go Go Singers with Richie Furay. When that band split, Stills made his way to Los Angeles, eventually phoning Furay to join him in formation of new group.

Stills had first met Neil Young (♦), then solo folk singer, during travels in Canada. Legend has it that while Stills and Furay were stuck in L.A. traffic jam they spotted hearse with Ontario number plates and had flash that it might be Young. It was.

True or no, Young was at time in company of bass-playing countryman Bruce Palmer. Dewey Martin brought number up to five and, in March 1966, Buffalo Springfield was born.

Thus constituted, they released **Buffalo Springfield** debut album in following year – re-issued by Atco/Atlantic and retitled **The Beginning** in 1973. Featuring all originals by Stills and Young, it was remarkable debut and set pattern for Springfield sound – highly melodic, poignant songs using up to four vocal parts against acoustic backing. Still's **For What It's Worth** was U.S. hit.

Buffalo Springfield Again, released 1968, saw a number of personnel changes. After playing on half album, Bruce Palmer was deported during sessions and two musicians Jim Fielder (bs), later of Blood Sweat & Tears, and Doug Hastings (gtr), later of Rhinoceros, came in for short stays until Jim Messina (bs, vcls) established himself as Palmer's replacement. (Palmer subsequently cut solo album, as did Dewey Martin.)

By this time, however, band was beginning to tear itself apart, largely it is said due to embittered personal squabbles between Stills and Young. Towards end of 1968 Springfield broke up, their third album, **Last Time Around**, being released posthumously the following year.

Young returned to solo work; Stills joined Dave Crosby and Graham Nash in CS&N (♦ Crosby Stills Nash & Young); Messina and Furay formed Poco (♦); Dewey Martin made short-lived attempt to keep Springfield name alive with three new members, then turned to sessionwork.

Real commercial success eluded band during their short lifespan, and the near-legendary status Springfield enjoyed in later years came only after CSN&Y achieved supergroup status. As a result of this posthumous interest, Springfield material has been re-issued and re-packaged a number of times on both sides of the Atlantic (Neil Young's 1973 retrospective double-album **Journey Through The Past** contained a couple of Springfield selections).

Recordings:
Buffalo Springfield (Atco/Atlantic)
Buffalo Springfield Again (Atco/Atlantic)
Last Time Around (Atco/Atlantic)
Compilations:
Retrospective (Atco/Atlantic)
Expecting To Fly (Atco/Atlantic)
Buffalo Springfield (Atco/Atlantic)

Jimmy Buffett

Born in 1948, Buffett grew up in Mobile, Alabama, and after dropping out from college went to New Orleans before settling in Nashville with ambitions to become a country singer.

He was shortly offered a contract by Andy Williams' Barnaby Records. He cut one album, **Down To Earth**, which wasn't particularly successful, and severed his associations with the company when they misplaced the master tape of his second album.

In any case Buffett's talent was hardly the sort that could be straight-jacketed by Nashville's orthodox music establishment. He moved to Key West, Florida, where he has resided ever since. After signing with ABC-Dunhill, he recorded his second debut album, ironically again in Nashville, though this time with greater artistic freedom. Released in 1973, **A White Sports Coat And A Pink Crustacean** helped to establish him, and it was a reputation he was able to enhance with his next album, **Living And Dying In 3/4 Time**, which received good reviews, and contained the moderately-successful single, **Come Monday**.

Buffett's subsequent releases have confirmed his talent without increasing the size of his audience. He is an original and talented tunesmith, able to handle anything from schlocky ballads to a facsimile of Lord Buckley's **God's Own Drunk**. His lyrics are wry, and his songs bear titles like **My Head Hurts, My Feet Stink And I Don't Love Jesus**. He used to perform alone, but in 1975 put together a backing group, the Coral Reefer Band with a line-up of: Roger Bartlett (gtr); Greg "Fingers" Taylor (hmnca, pno); Harry Dailey (bs); Phillip Fajardo (drms).

Recordings:
Down To Earth (Barnaby/—)
A White Sports Coat And A Pink Crustacean (ABC-Dunhill)
Living And Dying In 3/4 Time (ABC-Dunhill)
A1A (ABC)
Havana Daydreamin' (ABC)

Eric Burdon

Born May 11, 1941, in Walker-on-Tyne, England, Burdon grew up in Newcastle and went to art school there. He first heard black R&B records from a merchant seaman who lived in the flat below his, and decided that he too had to sing like that; he was to succeed better than most of his contemporaries in this ambition.

As vocalist with the highly successful Animals (♦) he soon distinguished himself by his powerful delivery and manic stage act. He also established a reputation as a hard-drinking, hard-talking Geordie, often speaking out against racism.

When the original Animals split in 1966, Burdon formed a new group, Eric Burdon And The Animals, with Danny McCulloch (gtr), Barry Jenkins (drms), Vic Briggs (kybds), John Weider (bs). With this line-up Burdon moved

Right: Early Byrds circa '65. But haven't we seen that pose before? With The Beatles? Uhmm. L to r (clockwise): Gene Clark, Hillman, McGuinn, Crosby, Mike Clarke.

away from R&B and into more straightforward rock. He experimented with acid rock and in the psychedelic summer of '67 began a complete change of image and style. Gone was the tough boozer – instead a new gentle Eric issued declarations of love for all. His records became increasingly pre-occupied with direct social comment and personal confessions of faith. **Good Times** encapsulated this new attitude – "Instead of just drinking/I should have been thinking". By now he was concentrating his activities in the U.S., where he was by now more successful. **San Franciscan Nights** and **Sky Pilot** were both Top 10 singles there.

The albums released in this period – **Winds Of Change, The Twain Shall Meet** and **Every One Of Us** – all made more impact in the U.S. (the latter was not even issued in the U.K.). At the end of 1968, Burdon put out **Love Is** (a double album in the U.S., a single in Britain) which he said would be his last record.

He then disappeared on the West Coast for a couple of years, amid rumours of a broken marriage and drug problems. In 1970 he resurfaced with War (➧), a black progressive band. Though Burdon's message songs still dominated the material, it was musically a great improvement, and the debut album of the partnership – **Eric Burdon Declares War** – produced a No. 1 U.S. single, **Spill The Wine.** Nevertheless, there was only one other album, **Black Man's Burdon,** before the two factions separated and War went on to bigger things.

In 1971 Burdon fulfilled a personal ambition by working with a long-time Blues hero of his, Jimmy Witherspoon, when the two collaborated on the album, **Guilty** – though it was evident the vocalists had too much respect for each other.

Above: Eric as boozer.

Burdon broke cover again in 1973 when he played three dates in the U.K. and some gigs in the U.S. with a three-piece hard-rock outfit – Aaron Butler (gtr), Randy Rice (bs), Alvin Taylor (drms). Burdon was looking and behaving as he had in the middle '60s, an image the album **Sun Secrets** consolidated, for it included new versions of old Animals' songs. Unfortunately it hardly provided him with a bona-fide come-back. The '70s have been a lean period for him, and in 1975 **Stop** showed that. Never-

theless, though sales of his albums in the U.S. have dropped off, he still has a loyal following there.

Recordings:
With Eric Burdon And The Animals:
Eric Is Here (MGM/—)
Winds Of Change (MGM)
The Twain Shall Meet (MGM)
Every One Of Us (MGM/—)
Love Is (MGM)
Compilations:
Best Of Eric Burdon And The Animals, Vol. II (MGM/—)
Eric Burdon: Star Portrait (MGM/—)
Mad Man Eric Burdon (MGM/—)
With War:
Eric Burdon Declares War (Polydor)
Black Man's Burdon (Liberty)
With Jimmy Witherspoon:
Guilty (United Artists)
With The Eric Burdon Band:
Sun Secrets (Capitol)
Stop (Capitol)

Burning Spear
➧ Reggae

James Burton

One of bona-fide guitar heroes, Burton first appeared on record in 1957 when, at the age of 16, he played solo on Dale Hawkins'

Suzie Q. Subsequently developed own style and, despite the prodigious amount of licks he put down, avoided becoming stereotyped by being continuously inventive. In 1958 he had moved to Hollywood – and most of his recording was consequently done on the West Coast – and joined Ricky Nelson's band with whom he remained into the '60s.

Moved on to work with the new breed of country stars, including Gram Parsons and Mike Nesmith, and also, like a close colleague Glen D. Hardin, was recruited to Elvis Presley's permanent stage band. By 1971 his name was sufficiently magnetic for him to be persuaded into making a solo album, **The Guitar Sounds Of James Burton** – but it was hardly distinguished, and he has not cared to repeat the experience.

He continued to work regularly in country-rock circles, and in 1975 he and Hardin came together to form the backbone of The Hot Band, backing band for Emmylou Harris (➧) in live concert and on record.

Recordings:
The Guitar Sounds Of James Burton (A&M)

Paul Butterfield

Central figure in U.S. white blues scene of the 1960s. Butterfield (b. Dec 17, 1942) grew up on the streets of Chicago, playing along-

side and learning from the black artists of Chicago's South side clubs – men like Muddy Waters, Little Walter, Buddy Guy and Junior Wells, perfecting his craft before forming his own band, the nucleus of which was himself (vcls, harmonica) and Elvin Bishop (gtr), with Jerome Arnold (bs) and Sam Lay (drms).

It All Comes Back. Courtesy Bearsville Records/WEA.

The band gained a huge local following in Chicago, before signing with the Elektra label, and producing **Butterfield Blues Band,** with the line-up by now extended to include Mike Bloomfield (lead gtr) and Mark Naftalin (kybds); Billy Davenport had replaced Lay on drums. It was this line-up which caused furore at the 1965 Newport Folk Festival – partly through their own performance, which offended the purists (they were the first electric band to play the festival) but

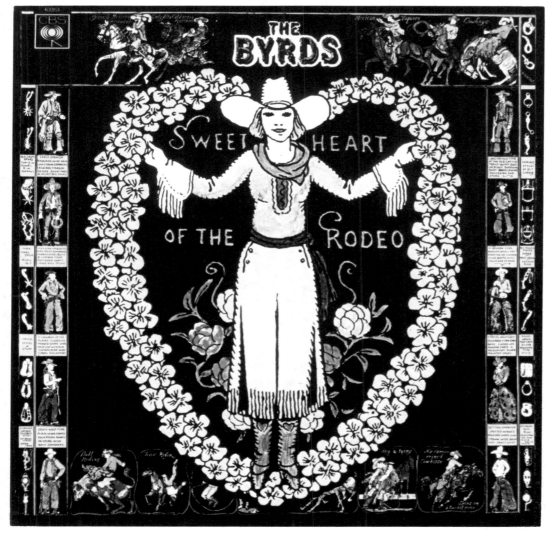

which went down a storm, and partly through their role in backing Bob Dylan's first electric performance.

In 1966 Butterfield Blues Band contributed four tracks to an Elektra collection, **What's Shakin'.** In a sense Butterfield was always too far ahead of his time for comfort. By 1967, when the world was spiritually prepared for high energy white electric blues, he'd already moved on to soul music, adding a brass section of Charles Dinwiddie (tenor sx), Keith Johnson (tpt) and David Sanborn (alto sx) for **The Resurrection Of Pigboy Crabshaw** and **In My Own Dream,** the album which also moved Bishop into the lead guitar chair, as Bloomfield had left to form Electric Flag (♦). In 1968 Bishop (♦ Elvin Bishop) too left to form his own band (he was replaced briefly by Buzzy Fieton), and Butterfield's subsequent albums were messy and showed a lack of direction, though **Live,** produced by Todd Rundgren (♦) struck a few sparks.

After one last album under the old Blues Band name, **Sometimes I Just Feel Like Smilin',** Butterfield switched to Albert Grossman's Bearsville label, and assembled new band Better Days, which consisted largely of local musicians – Billy Rich (bs), Christopher Parker (drms), Ronnie Barron (kybds), Amos Garrett (gtr) and Geoff Muldaur (vcls). Muldaur's then-wife Maria was an "ex officio" member, playing on most of the debut album **Better Days**

which was nevertheless disappointing; the band were well received on what few live gigs they did.

After a second album **It All Comes Back,** for which Butterfield added a horn section (and David Sanborn temporarily returned to the fold), the band just ground to a halt. Garrett went off to work with Maria Muldaur, and Parker with Aretha Franklin. Despite a solo album, **Put It In Your Ear,** Butterfield seemed to lack motivation at beginning of 1976.

Recordings:
Butterfield Blues Band (Elektra)
East-West (Elektra)
The Resurrection Of Pigboy Crabshaw (Elektra)
In My Own Dream (Elektra)
Keep On Movin' (Elektra)
Live (Elektra)
Sometimes I Just Feel Like Smilin' (Elektra)
Better Days (Bearsville)
It All Comes Back (Bearsville)
Put It In Your Ear (Bearsville)
Compilation:
Golden Butter (Best Of Paul Butterfield) (Elektra)

The Butts Band

After death of Jim Morrison in 1971, three remaining members of The Doors (♦) attempted to continue as recording act, but after **Other Voices** and **Full Circle** it became evident they needed new

vocalist. Considered Kevin Coyne (♦) and Howard Werth (♦) as replacements for Morrison, but finally engaged Jess Roden (♦); also Manzarek left after disagreements to make solo album, and others brought in Phillip Chen (kybds) and Roy Davies (bs), and new line-up called itself The Butts Band. Debut album recorded in Jamaica, somewhat reggae-influenced, but marginally promising, but band fell apart after short U.K. tour when Roden left. Chen has since worked with Chapman Whitney, and on Jeff Beck's **Blow By Blow,** and Davies with Gonzalez.

John Densmore and Robby Krieger reconstituted Butts Band 1975 for uninspired **Hear And Now** album, with Michael Stull (vcls/gtr), Alex Richman (kybds/vcls), Mike Berkowitz (drms) and Karl Ruckner (bs).

Recordings:
The Butts Band (Blue Thumb/Island)
Hear And Now (Blue Thumb/—)

The Byrds

Roger McGuinn guitar, vocals
Chris Hillman bass, vocals
Gene Clark vocals
David Crosby guitar, vocals
Michael Clarke drums

Like Buffalo Springfield, seminal West Coast group – at one time in early career, with Beatles pub-

licist Derek Taylor on Byrds payroll, they were being touted as U.S. answer to Liverpool Boom invasion.

Formed as Byrds (aka Jet Set aka Beefeaters) Los Angeles 1964 with above line-up. McGuinn at that time using birthname Jim – he changed to Roger in 1968 – formerly back-up musician for Bobby Darin and also Judy Collins. Crosby, who had spent five years as member of Les Baxter's Balladeers, joined him and Gene Clark (♦) to initiate the new group – personnel being completed by Beatle lookalike Michael Clarke and bluegrass mandolin player Chris Hillman, from The Hillmen.

Recorded first album, **Preflyte,** as demo before Bob Dylan "discovered" them and supplied their first hit single, **Mr Tambourine Man** (1965). This inaugurated category 'folk-rock', this period in group's career covered on **Mr Tambourine Man** album (1965) and **Turn! Turn! Turn!** (1966).

Gene Clark left during the recording of **Fifth Dimension** (1966), The Byrds continuing as quartet through their "space-rock" phase chronicled on **Younger Than Yesterday** (1967) and **The Notorious Byrd Brothers** (1968), the latter featuring a line-up reduced to trio by departure after disagreements of Dave Crosby (♦) to Crosby Stills & Nash (♦). Further light on Crosby departure under own entry.

Gram Parsons (♦) subsequently joined group, pushing McGuinn towards obsession with country genre evident on 1968 Nashville-produced **Sweetheart Of The Rodeo** LP. Though "country rock" went on to become formidable

Above: Roger McGuinn. His Dickensian shades and Rickenbacker guitar were early Byrds trademarks.

movement in own right, it was the start of a lingering deterioration for Byrds.

By following year, only McGuinn remained of previous members – Gram Parsons and Chris Hillman having quit to form Flying Burrito Bros (♦). McGuinn assembled new Byrds with Clarence White (gtr), John York (bs) and Gene Parsons (drms).

This line-up made **Dr Byrds And Mr Hyde** (1969) and **The Ballad Of Easy Rider** (1970). Skip Battin replaced John York on bass for the late 1970 double set **Untitled** which provided a slight – though temporary – upswing in group's downward progress. Byrds even returned to singles chart with early 1971 **Chestnut Mare**.

Byrdmaniax (1971) and **Farther Along** (1972), however, showed them at lowest ebb of creativity. A late attempt to re-establish Byrds myth with original line-up, on **Byrds'** album in 1973, misfired, resulting in final dissolution of group.

Byrds most productive and influential period is represented by the 1966-68 trilogy, **Fifth Dimension, Younger Than Yesterday** and **Notorious Byrd Brothers**, notably with songs like **So You Want To Be A Rock 'n' Roll Star** and **Eight Miles High** which had noticeable effect on Beatles' development.

Skip Battin now with New Riders Of The Purple Sage (♦); Gene Parsons with Flying Burritos; Clarence White killed by car in July 1973; Roger McGuinn working solo (♦ Roger McGuinn), though he retains rights to Byrds' name and has never ruled out possibility of re-formation.

Second and third albums packaged as double set in U.S.; sixth and seventh similarly coupled and recycled in U.K. 1976.

Fifth Dimension. Courtesy CBS Records.

Recordings:
Preflyte (Bumble/Asylum)
Mr Tambourine Man (Columbia/CBS)

Turn! Turn! Turn! (Columbia/CBS)
Fifth Dimension (Columbia/CBS)
Younger Than Yesterday (Columbia/CBS)
The Notorious Byrd Brothers (Columbia/CBS)
Sweetheart Of The Rodeo (Columbia/CBS)
Dr Byrds And Mr Hyde (Columbia/CBS)
The Ballad Of Easy Rider (Columbia/CBS)
Untitled (Columbia/CBS)
Byrdmaniax (Columbia/CBS)
Farther Along (Columbia/CBS)
Byrds (Asylum)

Compilations:
Greatest Hits (Columbia/CBS)
Greatest Hits Vol 2 (Columbia/CBS)
History Of The Byrds (Columbia/CBS)

Cactus

Tim Bogert bass
Carmine Appice drums
Rusty Day vocals, harmonica
Jim McCarty guitar

U.S. band, original line-up as above. Formed 1969 by Appice and Bogert, formerly of Vanilla Fudge (♦), after failure of plans to assemble group with Jeff Beck and Rod Stewart. Day previously with Mitch Ryder's Detroit Wheels and Amboy Dukes; McCarty with Mitch Ryder and Buddy Miles. Later included British vocalist Pete French and pianist Duane Hitchings.

Two founders quit 1972 to form Beck Bogert & Appice (♦) with Jeff Beck. A new group, without any of original members, later attempted gigs under name The New Cactus Band.

Recordings:
Cactus (Atco/Atlantic)
One Way . . . Or Another (Atco/Atlantic)
Restrictions (Atco/Atlantic)
'Ot And Sweaty (Atco/Atlantic)

J. J. Cale

Veteran of U.S. recording scene, although first album under own name didn't appear until 1972. Grew up in Tulsa, Oklahoma, with Leon Russell (♦). The pair played local clubs and dives. Cale later led band called Valentines and tried, unsuccessfully, to make it in Nashville as country singer.

Went to Los Angeles with Russell where he wrote and recorded **After Midnight**, which didn't come to notice until Eric Clapton's 1970 version made U.S. singles charts. Cale was first heard on album with 1967-released, little known **A Trip Down Sunset Strip** (Viva/Fontana), a quite atrocious piece of psychedelic opportunism credited to Leather Coated Mind, which he wrote songs for and co-produced.

Okie. Courtesy A&M Records.

Disillusioned with L.A., returned to Tulsa and built own small studio where he remained until fellow Tulsa musician Carl Radle (♦ Eric Clapton) took tapes of Cale to Nashville resulting in recording/management deal and his first real album, **Naturally** (1972).

With soft yet distinctive vocal phrasing, and haunting guitar style, above sparse instrumentation, Cale is epitome of 70's rock phrase 'laid back'.

Recordings:
Naturally (A&M)
Really (A&M)
Okie (A&M)

John Cale

Welsh-born and classically-trained, it was via Cale's interest in New York contemporary classical avant-garde that he became involved with Lou Reed and Velvet Underground (♦).

To Reed's startling mixture of musical primitivism and lyrical worldliness, Cale added authentic element of those experimental styles then in vogue in N.Y. – e.g., the influence of Lamonte Young, and Earle Brown's interest in the possibilities inherent in noise and monotony as embodied in Velvets cuts **Sister Ray** and **European Son To Delmore Schwartz**.

Velvets sound became markedly less extreme after Cale left in

Left: David Crosby and Roger McGuinn frolic foolishly in the grass for an early Byrds publicity pic. Crosby wrote many of the group's most memorable early songs, and was in the vanguard of The Byrds' whole raga-rock venture.

1968 to pursue multifold career as producer, arranger, composer, and performer.

Fruits of Cale's early cross-cultural associations can be found on 1971 album **Church Of Anthrax**, on which he collaborated only partially successfully with the experimental musician Terry Riley, and on **The Academy In Peril** the following year, a collection that allowed his classical background full rein.

Fourth album, in 1973, was second for Warner Brothers, for whom Cale worked as Staff producer and A&R man in California until approached by Britain's Island Records in early 1974.

Returned to U.K. under new contract to record **Fear** (1974) using services of Eno and Phil Manzanera (♦ Roxy Music). Produced **The End** album for former Velvets contemporary Nico (having worked in same capacity on her earlier records (♦) Nico), and appeared with her and other Island stablemates Kevin Ayers (♦) and Eno (♦) on album recorded live at London Rainbow Theatre, **June 1 1974**.

Slow Dazzle, his second solo album for Island, again used Eno and Manzanera, the latter sharing guitar duties with Chris Spedding (♦). From sessionmen for this LP – specifically Spedding (gtr), Timi Donald (drms), Pat Donaldson (bs), Chris Thomas (vln, kybds) – Cale formed road band for European tour spring 1975.

Towards end of 1975 returned to New York to produce stunning debut album for Patti Smith (♦), taking time out to record the somewhat poorly-received **Helen Of Troy** (1975). Has also produced albums for Iggy Pop (♦), Modern Lovers, Silverhead.

Recordings:
Vintage Violence (Columbia/CBS)
Church Of Anthrax (Columbia/CBS)
The Academy In Peril (Warner Bros)
Paris 1919 (Warner Bros)
Fear (Island)
June 1, 1974 (Island)
Slow Dazzle (Island)
Helen Of Troy (Island)

Church Of Anthrax. Courtesy CBS Records.

Robert Calvert

Born South Africa 1945, raised in Kent, England, from age of two. Had ambitions to be pilot foiled by defect of ear drum and attended Canterbury College of Technology studying to be surveyor. Joined Hawkwind (♦) as "resident poet/actor" 1973, leaving to work on first solo album – a satirical rock drama about deathtrap aero-

planes in German Air Force.

Recordings:
Captain Lockheed And The Starfighters (United Artists)
Lucky Lief And The Longships (United Artists)

Camel

Peter Bardens keyboards
Andy Latimer guitar
Doug Ferguson bass
Andy Ward drums

Veteran of U.K. R&B scene, Bardens served apprenticeship with Van Morrison's old band Them, Shotgun Express (which also included Rod Stewart and Peter Green) and Village before assembling Camel in 1972. Others had been together since 1968, first in band called Brew and later as back up musicians to Philip Goodhand-Tait.

Released first album 1973, second in following year. It wasn't until **Snow Goose** (1975), however, that Camel began to achieve recognition. A conceptual album inspired by Paul Gallico's novel "The Snow Goose" (the writer later served writ on band alleging copyright infringement), it put group into U.K. album charts for first time – also providing minor breakthrough in U.S.

Recordings:
Camel (MCA)
Mirage (Janus/Deram)
Snow Goose (Janus/Deram)
Moonmadness (Janus/Deram)

Glen Campbell

Born Delight, Arkansas, April 22, 1938, seventh son in family of 11. Rise to popularity in the late '60s coincided with the increasing commercial viability of country music.

Campbell moved to Los Angeles at beginning of '60s and worked clubs and occasional sessions, graduating to work with artists such as Johnny Cash, Dean Martin and the Mamas and Papas, and continually improving his skill at achieving a chunky, 12-string guitar sound. He was also a stand-in Beach Boy, filling the gap between the departure of Brian Wilson and the arrival of Bruce Johnston.

In the latter half of '60s, after modest success with **Turn Around, Look At Me** single, he was signed as solo artist to Capitol Records, and enjoyed major hits such as **Gentle On My Mind, Wichita Lineman** and **Galveston.**

By now he was big-business, and was given his own U.S. TV-show, which ran for the next four-and-a-half years, and a role in the John Wayne movie, "True Grit". He also worked temporarily in partnership with Bobbie Gentry (the two had a hit together with a revival of **All I Have To Do Is Dream**) and later with Anne Murray.

Success has been almost automatic in the '70s. Hits like **Rhinestone Cowboy** have continued to roll off the drawing-board. He now has 11 gold albums, though his style has changed not a jot since the beginning.

Recordings:
Glen Campbell Live (Capitol)
The Glen Campbell Album (Capitol)
Glen Campbell's Greatest Hits (Capitol)
Try A Little Kindness (Capitol)
The Last Time I Saw Her (Capitol)
Glen Travis Campbell (Capitol)
I Knew Jesus Before He Was A Star (Capitol)
I Remember Hank Williams (Capitol)
Glen (Capitol)
Reunion (Capitol)
Two Sides Of Glen Campbell (Capitol)
Rhinestone Cowboy (Capitol)
Bloodline (Capitol)
With Bobbie Gentry:
Bobbie Gentry & Glen Campbell (Capitol)
With Anne Murray:
Anne Murray & Glen Campbell (Capitol)

Left: Cookbook. Courtesy United Artists. This "best of" compilation includes a list of Heat's appearances up to Al Wilson's death.

With Tennessee Ernie Ford:
Glen Picks And Ernie Sings (Capitol)

Can

Michael Karoli guitar, vocals
Holger Czukay bass, vocals
Jaki Liebezeit percussion, wind instruments
Irmin Schmidt keyboards, vocals

Formed Cologne, Germany, 1968 with Malcolm Mooney on vocals, they recorded and privately distributed **Monster Movie** before Mooney was taken ill and replaced by Damo Suzuki, who had been discovered by the group singing for pfennigs on streets of Munich.

Their sparse style, based on repeated rhythmic figures and simple harmonies, was employed as basis of long, hypnotic improvisations, several of which can be found on **Tago Mago.**

The band can boast many classical and avant-garde influences; both Czukay and Schmidt have studied under Karlheinz Stockhausen. **Ege Bamyasi** is one of their most interesting releases, being less indulgent and patchy than the band have been in the past; however it is generally considered that they reached their peak with **Future Days.** In 1973 Suzuki left, and the others decided to handle the vocals themselves.

They are also known for their soundtrack music (some of which can be sampled on **Soundtracks**), and contributed some of the score for Skolimowski's "Deep End".

Along with Tangerine Dream (➡) they remain one of most important and creative of continental groups. They now live and work in Cologne, where they have built their own studio.

Unlimited Edition (1976) was double-album, one of which was a straight re-issue of **Limited Edition**; the other consisted of a selection of unreleased recordings.

Recordings:
Monster Movie (United Artists)
Soundtracks (United Artists)
Tago Mago (United Artists)
Ege Bamyasi (United Artists)
Future Days (United Artists)
Limited Edition (United Artists)
Soon Over Babaluma (United Artists)
Landed (Virgin)
Unlimited Edition (Virgin)

Canned Heat

Bob Hite vocals
Harvey Mandel guitar
Fito de la Parra drums
Richard Hite bass, tuba
Gene Taylor keyboards

Formed 1966 in California, nucleus of original band comprised the gargantuan Hite – hence nickname "The Bear" – (b. Torrance, California, Feb 26, 1945), a one-time record store manager, and guitarist, singer and harmonica player Al "Blind Owl" Wilson (b.

Boston, Massachusetts, July 4, 1943). Wilson had majored in music at Boston University, was a skilled arranger and shared with Hite an abiding interest in the collection and assimilation of old blues recordings. By time of his death, in September 1970, Wilson had, in fact, become recognized as one of world's leading authorities on the blues.

In 1965 he and Hite – along with drummer Frank Cook – put together first outfit, a jug band, in Los Angeles. By 1966, their music had drifted further towards blues, and the white blues band Canned Heat came into being with addition of Henry Vestine (b. Dec 25, 1944, Washington D.C.), late of Mothers Of Invention, and Larry Taylor to line-up.

First album, **Canned Heat** (1967), enjoyed moderate sales, but act really broke big with appearance at Monterey Festival. By the second album, Cook had been replaced by Mexican Fito de la Parra, and in 1968 a single from that album – **On The Road Again** (composed by Wilson) – became huge international hit. Vestine left in summer following year to launch own band. He was replaced by Detroit guitarist Harvey Mandel (➡).

A re-make of Wilbert Harrison's **Let's Work Together** provided further singles success in 1970 but, later that year, death of Al Wilson took band hard.

Various confusing personnel changes occurred between 1970–75. Larry Taylor had left in May 1970; Vestine had returned. Joel Scott Hill came in for Al Wilson, and later in the year Mandel left to pursue solo career, including spell with John Mayall (➡). Mexican-born bass player Antonio De La Barreda came in for a spell; Larry Taylor returned, then quit again; Joel Scott Hill departed;

Above: Bob Hite (left) and Al Wilson (right), at the time of the Heat's On The Road Again hit. Wilson died in Hite's back yard Sept 3, 1970.

49

and Vestine quit for second time late '75 – by which time Hite's brother Richard had joined band. Other personnel who came and went in later years include James Shane, Chris Morgan and Ed Beyer. Mandel completed this farcical cycle by rejoining Heat summer '76.

Since Wilson's death, output had been significantly inferior to earlier work, although quality picked up towards later years.

In 1971 group recorded set with blues legend John Lee Hooker. Other discographical notes: first album comprises tracks prior to Liberty signing not released until 1971; second listed album was later re-issued in U.K. under title **Rollin' And Tumblin'**.

Recordings:
Live At Topanga Corral (Scepter/DJM)
Canned Heat (Liberty)
Boogie With Canned Heat (Liberty)
Livin' The Blues (Liberty)
Hallelujah (Liberty)
Future Blues (Liberty)
Canned Heat Live In Europe (Liberty)
Historical Figures And Ancient Heads (Liberty)
New Age (Liberty)
One More River To Cross (Atlantic)
Compilations:
Cookbook (Liberty)
With John Lee Hooker:
Hooker 'n' Heat (Liberty)

Jim Capaldi

Of Italian descent, founder member U.K. group Traffic (➧), for whom he supplied lyrics as well as drums. Recorded first two solo albums 1972 and 1974 while still member of Traffic, and since demise of that band at end of U.S. tour 1974 has pursued full-time solo career. Made surprise appearance in U.K. singles charts December 1975 with reworking of Roy Orbison's **Love Hurts**. Third album part-recorded in Alabama with Muscle Shoals sessioners (Roger Hawkins, Barry Beckett etc – who had worked with Traffic in past), and rest in London with likes of Steve Winwood, Chris Spedding and Paul Kossoff.

Recordings:
Oh How We Danced (Island)
Whale Meat Again (Island)
Short Cut Draw Blood (Island)

Caravan

Pye Hastings guitar, vocals
Richard Coughlan drums
Geoff Richardson violin, guitar
Mike Wedgwood bass
Jan Schelhaas keyboards

Although not named as such until 1968, Caravan had been in existence in various forms as The Wilde Flowers since 1964 – this Canterbury, Kent, England, outfit also being the origin of Soft Machine (➧).

With line-up of Hastings and Coughlan plus the Sinclair cousins David (kybds) and Richard (bs, vcls), Caravan cut first three albums between 1968 and 1971 – the best being the second, **If I Could Do It All Over Again I'd Do It All Over You** – without ever achieving popular success

critics forecast for them.

David Sinclair left late 1971 to eventually join Robert Wyatt's Matching Mole, his place being taken by Steve Miller (not U.S. axeman of same name) for the 1972 set, **Waterloo Lily**. Sinclair re-enlisted with band 1973, until he quite again in 1975, his place taken this time by Jan Schelhaas.

In between these changes, bassist Wedgwood joined band June '74, replacing John Perry.

Sixth, "live" album recorded with New Symphonia Orchestra.

Recordings:
Caravan (—/MGM)
If I Could Do It All Over Again I'd Do It All Over You (London/Decca)
In The Land Of Grey And Pink (London/Deram)
Waterloo Lily (London/Deram)
For Girls Who Grow Plump In The Night (London/Deram)
Recorded Live At The Theatre Royal, Drury Lane, On The 28th Of October 1973 (London/Deram)
Cunning Stunts (BTM/Decca)
Blind Dog At St. Dunstans (BTM)

Eric Carmen

Born Cleveland, Ohio, Aug 11, 1949, formerly lead singer/creative force behind Raspberries – others were Wallace Bryson (gtr), David Smalley (rhy gtr), Jim Bonfanti (drums). Group began out of Cleveland early 1970, though their first album **Raspberries** for Capitol wasn't released until 1972.

Group's appeal from start was as premier U.S. "British" band (sic). Carmen had made close study of the compositional ability of groups such as Beatles, Who and Stones (as well as the Beach Boys) which he and Raspberries were able to duplicate with uncanny precision. The format brought band a string of U.S. hits (**Go All The Way, I Wanna Be With You, Let's Pretend, Overnight Sensation**). Raspberries and Carmen recorded four albums for Capitol 1972–74 before latter quit to launch solo career.

Signed by Clive Davis' remarkably successful Arista label, scored No. 1 U.S. hit with debut release **All By Myself** (February 1976) from solo album **Eric Carmen**. At same time started gigging with Eric Carmen Band featuring himself on vocals, keyboards, guitar plus Richard Reising (gtr, kybds, vcls), George Sipl (kybds, vocals), Dan Hrdlicka (gtr), Steve Knill (bs), and two drummers D. Dwight Kreuger and Michael McBride.
Raspberries Best Featuring Eric Carmen released by Capitol 1976.

Recordings:
Eric Carmen (Arista)

The Carpenters

Richard Carpenter vocals, keyboards
Karen Carpenter vocals, drums

Brother-sister vocal duo who have become major U.S. singles export of '70s with their wholesome image and interpretations of contemporary material.

From New Haven, Connecticut,

Richard (b. Oct 15, 1945) began playing piano at 12, later studying instrument at Yale. In 1963 Carpenter family moved to Downey, California, and Richard continued musical education at Cal State University at Long Beach. Younger sister Karen (b. Mar 2, 1950), meanwhile, developed interest in drums and the pair of them, plus a bass-playing friend, Wes Jacobs, formed first of three Carpenters aggregations, a jazz instrumental trio that managed a first place in Hollywood Bowl Battle Of The Bands talent contest.

Soon after, though, Richard disbanded trio in favour of group that would enable he and Karen to pursue growing interest in vocal harmonies. This band, Spectrum, brought in four other Cal State students alongside Carpenters, and went out gigging to somewhat desultory response.

Eventually Spectrum fell away to leave Carpenters on own, the pair employing overdubbing to achieve the harmonic blend long sought-after. They cut demo tapes of experimental new sound in friend's garage and, after a year hustling various companies, A&M Records co-founder Herb Alpert gave them a listen and signed pair to record contract.

Now And Then. Courtesy A&M Records.

In 1970 had million-seller with Bacharach-David song **Close To You**, which also broke them in U.K. Since then, The Carpenters have been virtually unstoppable on both sides of Atlantic: ten U.S. million-selling singles (including **We've Only Just Begun, For All We Know, Rainy Days And Mondays, Superstar, Yesterday Once More, Please Mr. Postman**); international sales of singles and albums in region of 25 million; three Grammy Awards; and sellout concerts around the world. The 1973 album, **The Singles 1969–73**, is among biggest-selling albums of all time.

Recordings:
Offering (A&M) – later re-issued as **Ticket To Ride**
Close To You (A&M)
The Carpenters (A&M)
A Song For You (A&M)
Now And Then (A&M)
The Singles 1969–73 (A&M)
Horizon (A&M)
A Kind Of Hush (A&M)
Compilations:
The Carpenters Collection (A&M)

Johnny Cash

Born Dyess, Arkansas, Feb 26, 1932 and raised in strict Baptist share-cropping family, Cash is country music's biggest-selling artist – without being strictly

country himself.

As a youth, Cash worked in Detroit, then joined U.S. Air Force, serving as radio operator in Germany where he started to play guitar and write songs. On discharge, married Vivien Liberto of San Antonio, moved to Memphis and worked as salesman in electricity business, attending radio announcers' school part-time.

In 1955 Cash signed to Sun Records, and thus was part of the first wave of rock performers that also included Elvis Presley, Jerry Lee Lewis, Roy Orbison and Carl Perkins. His debut recordings, two self-penned rockabilly numbers **Cry Cry Cry/Hey Porter**, sold well, before his 1956 recording of **I Walk The Line** became his first million-seller. This was succeeded by hits such as **Orange Blossom Special, Folsom Prison Blues** and **Ballad Of A Teenage Queen**, before in 1958 Cash moved his family to southern California to try his hand at movies, and also switched to Columbia Records.

At this point, Cash began to encounter personal problems; he became moody and depressed, left his family to go to New York, and started taking amphetamines. By 1963, at the same time as he had a big hit with **Ring Of Fire**, his career reached crisis point. With addiction affecting his work, he was arrested crossing the Mexican border with a guitarcase full of pep pills. His health deteriorated, and he almost died of an overdose following a car crash in Nashville. His wife divorced him.

At this point Cash was rescued by June Carter (daughter of Mother Maybelle Carter, of the famous Carter family, and an important singer in her own right – she had written **Ring Of Fire**). She acted as a steadying influence on Cash, helped him kick drink and drugs, and married him in 1967. They worked regularly together, and had a hit in 1967 with **Jackson**.

Cash's career was also abetted by an invitation to appear on Bob Dylan's **Nashville Skyline**. They duetted uncertainly on **Girl From The North Country**, and Cash also contributed fulsome sleeve notes (in verse), but this nevertheless helped widen his appeal to rock circles.

He also worked briefly with Dylan's producer, Bob Johnston (➧), a partnership which gave Cash one of his biggest-selling singles (which he had first performed on his ABC-TV show) **A Boy Named Sue**. It went gold in U.S. and was taken from album **At San Quentin** – he has regularly given concerts in prisons, and also featured prison songs in his act.

His career was thus fully restored by late '60s. In recent years has turned whole-heartedly to religion, and is a member of Evangelical Temple in Nashville (run by Pastor Jimmy Snow, son of country singer Hank Snow), and in 1971 went with his wife to Israel to make film about modernday life in the Holy Land. Also appeared in 1973 on concert platforms with leading U.S. evangelist, Billy Graham.

Cash is very prolific recording artist, normally issuing at least two albums a year, though he records his own material (which usually reflects all facets of American life) infrequently. His gtr/bs/drms supporting group play almost mechanically, a formula involving a one-two bass skip beat and little else, over which Cash projects his hard, masculine voice.

In recent years famous television documentary made about him – "The Man, His World, His Music"; his biography published 1974, written by Christopher S. Wren, and entitled "Winners Got Scars Too".

Discography is necessarily selective.

Recordings:
Original Golden Hits, Vols. I & II (Sun)
Greatest Hits, Vol. I (Columbia/CBS)
At Folsom Prison (Columbia/CBS)
At San Quentin (Columbia/CBS)
The World Of Johnny Cash, Vols. I & II (Columbia/CBS)
I Walk The Line (Columbia/CBS)
The Man In Black (Columbia/CBS)
That Ragged Old Flag (Columbia/CBS)
One Piece At A Time (Columbia/CBS)

David Cassidy

Born New York April 12, 1950, the son of actor Jack Cassidy and actress Evelyn Ward. After divorce of parents, moved to Hollywood when he was seven, returning to New York in teens after spell with Los Angeles Theatre Group. Acted in U.S. TV shows such as "Marcus Welby M.D." and "Bonanza" before landing part as Keith Partridge in "The Partridge Family", a weekly soap opera concerning exploits of pop-singing family. Even before series made its TV debut, first Partridge Family single **I Think I Love You**, featuring Cassidy's lead vocal, sold in excess of five million copies.

Continuing to appear weekly in "Partridge Family", by then being simultaneously shown on British TV, Cassidy shot to teenybop stardom with string of gold singles, albums and sell-out tours. In U.K., where his popularity was greater than in native U.S., between 1972–73 (along with Osmonds) created unparalleled wave of boppermania previously stirred by Marc Bolan (➧) and later tapped by Bay City Rollers (➧).

Then, in spring '74, after a fan died during hysterical London concert, Cassidy began to rethink direction of career. He quit "Partridge Family" series after four years. In February 1975 signed long-term contract with RCA, attempting to forsake earlier bopper image (although he still tries to "censor" unfavourable photographs).

First release in new stage was 1975 album **The Higher They Climb**, which Cassidy co-produced with ex-Beach Boy Bruce Johnston, using participation of likes of Harry Nilsson, Richie Furay, America's Gerry Beckley and Dewey Bunnell, and Flo & Eddie.

Returned to charts late '75 with singles **I Write The Songs**, written by Bruce Johnston, and subsequently the Beach Boys composition **Darlin'**.

Recordings:
Cherish (Bell)
Rock Me Baby (Bell)
Dreams Are Nuthin' More Than Wishes (Bell)
Cassidy Live (Bell)
The Higher They Climb The Harder They Fall (RCA)
Home Is Where The Heart Is (RCA)
Compilations:
Greatest Hits (Bell)

Cat Mother & The All Night Newsboys

Bob Smith keyboards, vocals
Roy Michaels guitar, bass, vocals
Michael Equine percussion, vocals
Charlie Chin guitar, banjo
Larry Packer guitar, violin, mandolin

New York rock 'n' roll band, with line-up as above recorded first album 1969 with Jimi Hendrix as producer. On second album, 1971, Chin replaced by Jay Ungar. For 1972 **Cat Mother** set, Ungar and Larry Packer replaced by Charlie Prichard (gtr) and Steve Davidson (percussion). By **Last Chance Dance** (1973), Charlie Harcourt (later of Lindisfarne) had taken over guitar spot from Prichard. Founder member Michaels one time in Au Go Go Singers with Steve Stills (➧) and Richie Furay.

Recordings:
The Street Giveth And The Street Taketh Away (Polydor)
Albion Doo-Wah (Polydor)
Cat Mother (United Artists)
Last Chance Dance (United Artists)

Cate Brothers

Born Dec 26, 1942, near Fayetteville, Arkansas, twin brothers Ernie and Earl Cate grew up with Grand Old Opry and southern R&B songs and were playing together by the time they were in high school.

They formed a band together in the mid-'60s (Ernie, kybds, vcls; Earl, gtr), which included Terry Cagle (drms), nephew of The Band's Levon Helm, who also worked with them on occasion.

When they signed with Asylum in late '74, they had been writing their own material for some time, and were playing energetic southern rock-soul. Widely-touted, they were able to acquire services of Steve Cropper as producer for their debut album, **Cate Brothers**, which was enthusiastically received.

Recordings:
Cate Brothers (Asylum)

Philip Catherine
➧ Focus

Right: a rare, Sun label photograph of Johnny Cash, circa '55. Not a line or bag in sight.

Felix Cavaliere
➧ The Rascals

CCS
➧ Alexis Korner

Chas Chandler

Former docker and founder-member of Newcastle, England, mid-'60s hit group The Animals (➧). Chandler has said that when he left that group he had just £1,400, two bass guitars and a share in a London flat! New career as manager began when he "discovered" Jimi Hendrix (➧) in New York Greenwich Village club.

In partnership with one Mike Jeffrey, Chandler took Hendrix to U.K. and constructed The Experience around him. It was Chandler who encouraged Jimi's flamboyant showmanship. Eventually, he and Jeffrey disagreed over the handling of Hendrix' career, and Chandler took up new job as talent scout and booker for Robert Stigwood Organisation. One of the acts he booked, later managed, was Slade (➧); under his guidance they became one of major U.K. pop-rock attractions of the time.

Harry Chapin

Born Dec 7, 1942 into a family of strong musical interests, Chapin was raised in Greenwich Village. When the family moved across the river, Chapin joined the Brooklyn Heights Boys Choir, where his adolescent colleagues included Robert Lamm (later to join Chicago, ➧).

After studying at Cornell University, entered film industry, and with Jim Jacobs made movie, "Legendary Champions", that won Academy Award nomination. In summer 1964 reunited with his two brothers and father to play in a group around Greenwich Village.

When that group disbanded (his brothers needed to avoid the draft) he formed his own with John Wallace (vcls), Ron Palmer (gtr) and Tim Scott (cllo); band became successful locally and signed to Elektra Records. Debut album, **Heads And Tales**, reproduced band's complex live sound, and single taken from it, **Taxi**, attracted considerable attention. Chapin's audience increased with his subsequent albums, as his largely narrative songs became popular; the heavily sentimental **W.O.L.D.**, taken from **Short Stories**, became a major U.S. hit 1973, and a minor hit in U.K. **Verities And Balderdash** became Chapin's first gold album in 1974, and again the single from it, **Cat's In The Cradle**, fared well. His recording success was paralleled by his success live – by this time Michael Masters had replaced Scott.

Also Chapin appeared in experimental musical revue, "The Night That Made America Famous", which contained several of his own songs.

By mid-'70s Chapin had firmly established himself with American audiences, but had not had much international acclaim.

Recordings:
Heads And Tales (Elektra)
Sniper And Other Love Songs (Elektra)
Short Stories (Elektra)
Verities And Balderdash (Elektra)
Portrait Gallery (Elektra)
Greatest Stories Live (Elektra)

Michael Chapman

Born in Leeds, U.K., Jan 24, 1941, Chapman is a singer, guitarist and songwriter whose powerful, idiosyncratic work has never achieved the popularity its merit has warranted. Funkier, bluesier and less indulgent than most of his contemporaries, his thrashing

guitar provides a simultaneously sparse and sensual backdrop for his terse, melancholy songs and quietly bitter voice.

In 1967, he quit his job as an art and photography teacher to tread the itinerant folkie path, eventually snaring a contract with Harvest Records. His early albums juxtaposed solo performances and guitar instrumentals with rock songs featuring top session musicians and friends from Hull.

Foremost among the latter were bassist Rick Kemp, who worked regularly with Chapman until 1972, and Mick Ronson, whose work on **Fully Qualified Survivor** led indirectly to his meeting with David Bowie, and drummer Ritchie Dharma, who worked alongside Chapman and Kemp for some time, subsequently surfaced on Lou Reed's **Transformer** album and then worked on Ronson's solo U.K. tour.
Wrecked Again was Chapman's last album for Harvest, after which he and Kemp toured the U.S. as a duo; on their return Kemp joined Steeleye Span, and Chapman signed to Deram where he got into electric guitar and the rock 'n' roll ramifications thereof. He released **Millstone Grit** (featuring Kemp and drummer Keef Hartley) in 1973 and **Deal Gone Down** surfaced in 1974. During the final months of '73, he had undertaken a short promotional tour for the latter album, with a band of Professor Sutton (gtr), Hartley (drms) and Rod Clements (bs).

Chapman has achieved his greatest popularity in Europe where his live album **Pleasures Of The Street** (as yet unreleased in U.K.) was recorded. **Savage Amusements**, released in 1976, was produced by Memphis studio man Don Nix, Chapman now lives on a farm in Cumberland, in the U.K.

Recordings:
Rainmaker (—/Harvest)
Fully Qualified Survivor (Harvest)
Windows (—/Harvest)
Wrecked Again (—/Harvest)
Millstone Grit (—/Deram)
Deal Gone Down (—/Deram)
Pleasures Of The Street (Nova – released in Europe only)
Savage Amusements (London/Deram)

Chapman Whitney (Streetwalkers)

Roger Chapman vocals
Charlie Whitney guitars
Bob Tench rhythm guitar, vocals
Jon Plotel bass
Nicko drums

From Leicester, England, Chapman and Whitney were songwriting, creative backbone of now defunct Family (♦). First album, credited to Chapman Whitney and entitled **Streetwalkers** was released in spring 1974, after which the duo appeared in U.K. with pick-up band including Philip Chen (bs), Tim Hinckley (pno), and Bobby Tench, latter from Jeff Beck (♦) Group.

Line-up eventually settled as Chapman, Whitney, Tench, plus Jon Plotel (bs) and Nicko (drms) –

these five being billed as Streetwalkers in concert and on **Downtown Flyers** (1975). Group's **Red Card** (1976) broke into U.K. charts, but Plotel and Nicko quit line-up summer '76 and, at time of writing replacements were being sought.

Recordings:
Streetwalkers (Mercury/Raft)
Downtown Flyers (Mercury/Vertigo)
Red Card (Mercury/Vertigo)

Bobby Charles

Louisiana-born Charles first came to public attention as an artist with the Chess label in the late '50s, although his most famous compositions, **See You Later Alligator**, **Walkin' To New Orleans** and **But I Do,** were all successful because they were covered by major artists (Bill Haley, Fats Domino and Clarence 'Frogman' Henry respectively).

He recorded for a variety of companies in the '60s, including the New Orleans-based Imperial Records. By the early '70s he was living in Woodstock, and signed to Albert Grossman's Bearsville Records. He made the richly-acclaimed album **Bobby Charles**, with the assistance of such respected sidemen as members of The Band, Amos Garett, Geoff Muldaur and Dr. John. The album contained the superb single **Small Town Talk**, as well as several compositions that were covered by other artists.

Though Charles is a proficient composer and a versatile musician, his own career has somehow never happened. That pattern seems likely to be maintained, as he has now been dropped by Bearsville.

Recordings:
Bobby Charles (Bearsville)

Ray Charles

So many people have called him genius so frequently, the hard thing to remember is that he certainly is. In the way he fused gospel music with the blues he has proved one of most influential forces on soul, and rock music, as we know it today. Many British vocalists of the '60s – in particular Eric Burdon (♦) and Joe Cocker (♦) owed a particular debt to him.

Born Albany, Georgia, Sept 23, 1930, Charles became permanently blind at age of six, and was orphaned at 15. His greatest early influence was Nat King Cole. Formed own band at 17, working regularly both on the West Coast and in Washington, and made a number of recordings for independent companies, before coming to the attention of Atlantic Records' Ahmet Ertegun, who bought up his contract.

Charles made his decisive contribution to modern music in the following years, using knowledge he had picked up in New Orleans and the south of gospel-styled singing and chordal piano play-

Right: Ray Charles. He became blind at the age of six, was orphaned at age 15. He would become one of the seminal figures in popular music.

ing. His performances in those years helped make possible the emergence of soul music; he was a regular chart artist, and his hit singles culminated with electrifying **What'd I Say?** which illustrated perfectly his gospel style, with prominent use of call-and-response antiphonies he'd developed.

Shortly afterwards, moved to ABC/Paramount, where his chart success continued with classic records such as **Georgia On My Mind** and **Hit The Road Jack.** In 1962 he astonished the music world at large, and alienated much of his hard-core R&B following, with album **Modern Sounds In Country And Western**, which suggested he had abandoned his gritty style and gone commercial. He was merely expanding his musical horizons still further, however, and that album too proved a seminal influence, selling millions of copies and providing the massive hit single, Hank Williams' **I Can't Stop Loving You.** In 1962 alone, Charles sold in excess of $8 millions' worth of records.

Towards middle-'60s, Charles demonstrated he was still the supreme interpretative singer with a powerfully emotional version of Paul McCartney's **Yesterday.**

Charles meanwhile had assembled round him all the luxuries that money could buy, and his stage show took on grandiose proportions with his own orchestra and girl backing group, The Raelettes. But the monumental extravagence of Charles' public persona was unfortunately mirrored by the despair and sordidness of his private life. In the late '60s his career was punctuated by a prison sentence for possession of heroin.

He kicked the habit in prison, but emerged a chastened, almost pathetic figure; while the luxuriousness of his stage show remains, and his vocals have lost only a little of their coruscating brilliance, his material has become leadenly unambitious, and liberally sprinkled with paeans to America and professions of faith to his God. Nevertheless, he will

always remain one of the most compelling and seminal personalities in popular music.

Now has own label, Crossover, and has bought up all his old tapes. Discography includes only recent albums, and his major early releases.

Recordings:
What'd I Say (Atlantic)
Ray Charles Live – The Great Concerts (Atlantic)
Genius Of Ray Charles (Atlantic)
Soul Meeting (with Milt Jackson) (Atlantic)
Modern Sounds In Country And Western (ABC)
Sweet And Sour Tears (ABC)
A 25th Anniversary Show Business Salute To Ray Charles (Atlantic)
Message To The People (Probe)
Renaissance (Crossover/London)
Focus On Ray Charles (—/London)

Cheech & Chong

Mexican-American Richard 'Cheech' Marin from California (son of policeman) and Chinese-Canadian Thomas Chong from Edmonton, Alberta, first joined forces in Canada with improvisational group City Lights, which besides comedy of Cheech & Chong also featured topless dancers and a mime artist (in fact, Chong had begun career more conventionally as guitarist for Motown outfit Bobby Taylor and the Vancouvers).

When City Lights fell apart, Cheech & Chong worked West Canadian clubs as duo before switching operations to Los Angeles where they were discovered working Hollywood Troubadour unpaid by producer Lou Adler (♦). Adler signed them to his Ode Records, and set about promoting them as rock culture's first real hard-rock comedy act.

First album 1971 set tone of their heavily drug-oriented style of humour, and that and the 1972 **Big Bambu** quickly went gold. 1973 **Los Cochinos** similarly went gold, on advance orders alone, but by this time the duo's interminable routines about stoned hippies were beginning to pall. The 1974 **The Wedding Album**, though still a big U.S. seller, milked the idiom to point of redundancy.

Recordings:
Cheech & Chong (Ode/A&M)
Big Bambu (Ode/A&M)
Los Cochinos (Ode)
The Wedding Album (Ode)
Sleeping Beauty (Ode)

Big Bambu.
Courtesy A&M Records.

Cher

After the personal and professional demise of Sonny and Cher (◆), Cher herself was hardly starved of public attention. She had already reasserted her status as a recording artists with hits like **Gypsies, Tramps And Thieves** and **Dark Lady**, moved into modelling (with "Vogue") to become a fashion queen, and established her own TV show, which was little more than a showcase for her, her wardrobe and her cosmetics.

In 1975 she married again, this time Gregg Allman (◆ Allman Brothers), and within nine days had claimed it was all a horrible mistake. She filed divorce proceedings, but then the couple were reconciled, and are now trying again. Meanwhile, she switched to Warner Bros label and engaged Jim Webb (◆) to produce **Stars,** an album of extravagance and bombast that was a brilliantly conceived reflection of her public persona.

Recordings:
Golden Hits (Sunset/Liberty)
Dark Lady (MCA)
Half Breed (MCA)
Greatest Hits (MCA)
Stars (Warner Bros)

Chicago

Robert Lamm keyboards, vocals
Terry Kath guitar, vocals
Pete Cetera bass, vocals
James Pankow trombone
Lee Loughnane trumpet
Walter Parazaider reeds
Daniel Seraphine drums
Laudir De Oliveira percussion

First came together Chicago 1968 as the Big Thing. Changed name to Chicago Transit Authority (since abridged) when they went to Los Angeles to work with producer James William Guercio (◆)

where they first accrued local following. First album in 1969, a double set, received with a degree of critical acclaim shown, by subsequent work, to have been premature.

A combination of white "soul" four-piece rhythm section with brass trio playing (initially) fairly original Kentonesque harmonies, their trademarks were mid-tempo urban blues, disrupted by jazz sequences and long solos, spiced with aggressive vocals and enormous chords played by entire group.

On the 1970 **Chicago II**, also a double set, this earthiness gave way to smooth, mechanical jazz-rock excursions that were not mitigated by self-parodic arrangements and gauche lyrics for which Chicago have become infamous. All releases from that point on compounded errors of taste and misplaced belief in their cultural significance that the band lapsed into on **Chicago II**, the quality of music trending sharply downwards into vapid gradiosity. Nevertheless, their commercial appeal was enormous – all albums were massive U.S. sellers. Live album, **At Carnegie Hall** (1971), was a quadruple set.

Cetera, Kath and Parazaider all make cameo acting appearances in Guercio's movie production "Electra Glide In Blue" (1973).

De Oliveira a later addition to line-up. Lamm solo LP released autumn 1974.

Recordings:
Chicago (Columbia/CBS)
Chicago II (Columbia/CBS)
Chicago III (Columbia/CBS)
At Carnegie Hall (Columbia/CBS)
Chicago V (Columbia/CBS)
Chicago VI (Columbia/CBS)
Chicago VII (Columbia/CBS)
Chicago VIII (Columbia/CBS)
Chicago X (Columbia/CBS)

Compilations:
Chicago IX – Greatest Hits (Columbia/CBS)
Robert Lamm solo:
Skinny Boy (Columbia/CBS)

Chicago IX. Courtesy CBS Records.

Chicken Shack

Stan Webb vocals, guitar
Christine Perfect vocals, keyboards
Andy Sylvester bass
Dave Bidwell drums

Formed by Webb in Birmingham, England, 1965. At peak during commercial break out of British Blues boom 1968–69 with above line-up, featuring Christine Perfect who, at time, was considered leading female U.K. blues singer.

Above: Stan "The Man" Webb.

Shack made British charts with Ms Perfect's interpretation of Etta James R&B classic **I'd Rather Go Blind** in summer '69.

Later same year Christine quit to join husband John McVie in re-shaped Fleetwood Mac (◆). Replaced by Paul Raymond (kybds). Then followed bad patch for group who, although they never stopped gigging, went through more line-up changes: Sylvester and Bidwell left and Webb held band together with new personnel.

In 1972-73 achieved something of minor renaissance on U.K. club circuit but finally came to an end winter '73 after internal friction during German tour. Webb joined re-organised Savoy Brown (◆) – he's since left – which also currently included Raymond and Bidwell in line-up.

Recordings:
40 Blue Fingers Freshly Packed And Ready To Serve (Epic/Blue Horizon)
O.K. Ken (Epic/Blue Horizon)
100 Ton Chicken (Epic/Blue Horizon)
Accept! Chicken Shack (Epic/Blue Horizon)
Imagination Lady (London/Deram)
Unlucky Boy (London/Deram)

The Chieftains

Paddy Moloney uilleann pipes, tin whistle
Sean Potts tin whistle
Sean Keane fiddle
Martin Fay fiddle
Michael Tubridy flute, concertina
Peadar Mercier bodhran, bones
Derek Bell harp

Group originally came together in late '50s with intention of preserving purity of Celtic music. The Chieftains emerged from Sean O'Raida's folk orchestra, Ceolteoiri Chaulann, of which Moloney, Potts, Tubridy and Fay were members. Those four played on **Chieftains 1,** recorded in 1962, but group made albums only rarely, concentrating on pursuing their individual careers (Moloney worked as administrator for Gareth Brown's Claddagh Records, but others all had jobs outside the music business) and working semi-professionally for The Chieftains.

Soon reinforced by additions of Keane (born 1946 and youngest member of the band) and Mercier, (born 1912, the oldest), band built up impeccable reputation in Ireland as main custodians of national folk heritage. Derek Bell, principal harpist with BBC orchestra, was

last to join in 1972.

By **Chieftains 4,** Moloney, musical arranger for the group, had moved beyond mere creative interpretation and gone into composition, while still remaining within the framework of Irish traditional music.

In 1975 their career was taken in hand by Jo Lustig (formerly manager of Steeleye Span and Pentangle), and with sell-out concert at London's Albert Hall in March 1975, proved that appreciation of their music extended far beyond Eire. Shortly afterwards band turned fully professional, being received with great enthusiasm both in U.S. and Europe.

Band have not adapted their style at all to meet commercial demands, and are popular primarily because of their ethnic skills. Although their acoustic music has nothing to do with rock, they are enthusiastically appreciated by a rock audience; Mick Jagger, Eric Clapton and Paul McCartney are reported to be numbered amongst the band's most fervent fans and Emmylou Harris plays their music all the time. Moloney composed score for Kubrick's "Barry Lyndon" (1975), and was also featured on Mike Oldfield's **Ommadawn** album. The Chief-

The Chieftains 5.
Courtesy Island Records.

tains also composed music for U.K.s National Theatre production of "Playboy Of The Western World", and are providing score for another movie – Joseph Strick's film of James Joyce's "Portrait Of The Artist As A Young Man".

As evidence of current success, **Chieftains 5** – first album under new recording contract – nudged bottom of U.K. album chart, and **Chieftains 1–4.** previously available only in Eire, were all issued simultaneously in U.K., Europe and U.S.

Recordings:
The Chieftains (Polydor/Island)
The Chieftains 2 (Polydor/Island)
The Chieftains 3 (Polydor/Island)
The Chieftains 4 (Polydor/Island)
The Chieftains 5 (Polydor/Island)
Contributions to:
Barry Lyndon (Original Soundtrack) (Warner Bros)
Paddy Moloney and Sean Potts:
Tin Whistles (Claddagh)

The Chi-Lites

Marshall Thompson vocals
Creadel Jones vocals
Eugene Record vocals
Robert 'Squirrel' Lester vocals

Above: Eric as reluctant axe hero. Ever since Layla, Clapton has seemed to be hiding in his own shadow.

Eric Clapton

United Kingdom's premier guitar hero, born March 30, 1945, Ripley, Surrey, raised by foster parents. Studied stained glass design at Kingston Art School before picking up guitar at 17, having listened extensively to records by Muddy Waters, Chuck Berry, Big Bill Broonzy and Buddy Holly.

First group The Roosters Jan–Sept 1963, an early British R&B outfit, also featured Tom McGuinness (♦ Manfred Mann, McGuinness Flint). Also made occasional appearances with Blues Incorporated at Ealing, London, club mentioned in British R&B (♦) – as "stand in" for Mick Jagger.

With McGuinness, spent two weeks in October 1963 with Casey Jones And The Engineers before replacing Anthony "Top" Topham in Yardbirds (♦) as lead guitarist.

Was with Yardbirds up to group's March '65 **For Your Love** U.K. hit single but left soon after, disagreeing with band's freshly-acquired commercial approach. Worked short while on building site until offer to join John Mayall's Bluesbreakers spring '65.

It was during this period Clapton first accrued following as guitar hero; his reputation spurred by shouts of "Give God a solo" at gigs and the phrase "Clapton Is God" which became a favoured graffiti slogan on London walls.

Recorded on number of albums with Mayall (♦) before handing over guitar spot to Peter Green July 1966 and forming Cream (♦) with Jack Bruce and Ginger Baker. (While with Mayall, also cut three tracks for Elektra as Clapton And The Powerhouse – a studio band including Jack Bruce, Steve Winwood – which appear on 1966 Various Artists anthology, **What's Shakin'**.)

With Cream, enjoyed his first real commercial success and international recognition as rock's foremost guitar virtuoso. Also made guest appearances at time on Mothers Of Invention **We're Only In It For The Money** album (1967) and – uncredited – on the November 1968 Beatles **White Album** (Clapton solo on **While My Guitar Gently Weeps**).

On demise of Cream Nov 1968, formed ill-fated Blind Faith (♦) taking time out from the group's 1969 U.S. tour to play with the Plastic Ono Band – he appears on **Live Peace In Toronto** (♦ John Lennon) – and with U.S. white soul act Delaney And Bonnie (♦). When Blind Faith split at end of 1969, Clapton set up residence in New York where he started hanging out with Delaney Bramlett, eventually part-financing and joining the Delaney & Bonnie U.S. tour January–March 1970.

With Carl Radle (bs), Jim Gordon (drms) and Bobby Whitlock (kybds) – all to have subsequent Clapton associations in various groups – the guitarist appeared on **Delaney & Bonnie & Friends On Tour** (1970) live album.

Much of same personnel – including Delaney & Bonnie, plus addition of Leon Russell and Steve Stills – also appeared on the **Eric Clapton** solo album recorded in Los Angeles and released August 1970. Around same time, also put in guest appearances on 1970 **Leon Russell** album, Steve Stills' **Steve Stills I** and George Harrison's **All Things Must Pass** set.

By this point, Clapton had become obsessed with living down what he felt was overblown early reputation, his next way-stop being with aforementioned ex D&B sidekicks Carl Radle, Jim Gordon and Bobby Whitlock in new group he perversely dubbed Derek And The Dominos. First live appearance was at a Dr Spock Civil Liberties concert; first recording the Phil Spector-produced **Tell The Truth** single, released in U.S. only.

Then came what many consider Clapton's finest hour, the December 1970 **Layla** album credited to Derek and Dominos and using services extensively of Allman Bros guitarist-leader Duane Allman. A masterwork, the **Layla** track itself was dedicated to "the wife of my best friend" – Patti (Boyd) Harrison, who was later to separate from her ex-Beatle husband and set up with Clapton.

However, **Layla** initially fell on stony critical ground and, partly due to the new low-profile Clapton had been striving for, even more barren commercial pastures.

During 1972 U.S. tour, Dominos did record a (rather unsatisfactory) live album, **Derek And The Dominos In Concert**, but eventually fell apart half-way through recording of follow-up studio set.

(In this period Clapton also appeared on **Steve Stills II** and Dr John's **The Sun The Moon And Herbs,** both 1971, as well as appearing in August same year at Concert For Bangladesh organised by George Harrison.)

It is now public knowledge (Clapton didn't start giving press interviews again until 1974-75) that the guitarist suffered deep depression. after death of close friend Duane Allman (♦ Allman Bros) and from lack of public acceptance for **Layla**. As consequence, he went into hiding in Surrey home. There followed two wasted years during which Clapton fought heroin addiction, attempting to haul himself out of abyss with assistance of friends such as Pete Townshend of The Who.

It was Townshend who organised, and appeared at – along with Steve Winwood, Ron Wood and Jim Capaldi – Clapton's "come-back" concert at London Rainbow January 1973, an event recorded live on the somewhat disappointing **Eric Clapton's Rainbow Concert** album (Sept 1973).

However, the comeback was rather premature, and it wasn't until the winter of '73–74, in new awareness that his addiction was destroying him, that Clapton sought eventually-successful aid of London electro-acupuncture therapist, following treatment by same with period working as labourer on a friend's farm in Wales.

As Clapton himself later described it, one day he decided he was fit again and got on a train to London where he walked into manager

---

A highly successful vocal group from Chicago, the Chi-Lites originally came together in 1961 as the Hi Lites – a name they had to change because it had already been taken by another outfit.

In 1968 they signed for the Brunswick label – at that time part of the MCA organisation – and Eugene Record came to the fore as a songwriter/producer. It was on his ingenuity and flair that the group's success was based.

They made several incursions into the U.S. soul charts before hitting the national charts with **(For God's Sake) Give More Power To The People.** This proved the start of a long sequence of hit singles; in 1971 the band toured with Barbara Acklin, and she and Record co-wrote **Have You Seen Her?**, on which The Chi-Lites brilliantly merged doo-wop and soft-soul styles. It sold by the million, reaching No. 3 in both the U.S. and U.K. charts in 1972. (A feat it all but repeated in the U.K. on its re-release three years later.)

The next single, **Oh Girl,** also topped the U.S. charts, and the band have since perfected a mellow style that's been the basis of subsequent hits like **Homely Girl, I Found Sunshine** and **It's Time For Love**. Record has now established himself as one of the most creative songwriter/producers working in any field of contemporary music.

Half A Love was augmented for British release by the addition of four tracks from the unreleased album, **Give It Away.**

Recordings:
Give It Away (MCA/—)
(For God's Sake) Give More Power To The People (MCA/Brunswick)
A Lonely Man (MCA)
A Letter To Myself (Brunswick)
The Chi-Lites (Brunswick)
Toby (Brunswick)
Half A Love (Brunswick)
Compilation:
Greatest Hits (Brunswick)

Robert Stigwood's office and announced he was ready to record an album. Stigwood booked Clapton on plane to Florida where, with assistance of Carl Radle from Dominos, new band was formed featuring Radle (bs), George Terry (gtr), Dick Sims (kybds), Jamie Oldaker (drms) and Yvonne Elliman (vcls, gtr). This line-up cut the widely-

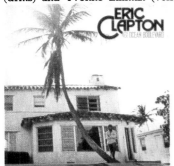

461 Ocean Boulevard.
Courtesy RSO Records.

Eric Clapton. Courtesy
Polydor Records.

acclaimed **461 Ocean Boulevard** album (released August 1974) in Miami, following with U.S. and European tours. From the album came Clapton's hit single version of Bob Marley's **I Shot The Sheriff**.

American singer Marcy Levy had augmented line-up by their second album, **There's One In Every Crowd** (1975), which disappointed in comparison to predecessor, and the live set **E.C. Was Here** later same year.

To describe Clapton's recorded output as erratic would be a truism. In many ways he's a chameleon-like figure, quality depending on the company he's keeping at the time. But in every other sense he is one of the great guitarists in rock – as well as one of the most imitated.

Recordings with Yardbirds, Mayall, Cream, Blind Faith, listed under those entries.

Recordings:
Eric Clapton (Polydor)
Delaney & Bonnie & Friends On Tour With Eric Clapton (Atlantic)
Layla & Other Assorted Love Songs (Polydor)
Derek And The Dominos In Concert (RSO)
Eric Clapton's Rainbow Concert (RSO)
No Reason To Cry (RSO)

461 Ocean Boulevard (RSO)
There's One In Every Crowd (RSO)
E.C. Was Here (RSO)
Compilations:
Eric Clapton And The Yardbirds (Springboard/—)
The Blues World Of Eric Clapton (London/Decca)
Eric Clapton At His Best (Polydor)
History of Eric Clapton (Polydor)

Gene Clark

Born Tipton, Missouri, 1941, Clark was a member of the New Christy Minstrels in early '60s. In 1964 he was in audience at Los Angeles Troubadour to see Jim (now Roger) McGuinn perform, and within 24 hours was part of a trio with McGuinn and David Crosby which ultimately led to formation of The Byrds.

With The Byrds, Clark was a prolific writer, but his apparent fear of flying led him to leave the group in April 1966, after he had made three albums with them (**Preflyte, Mr Tambourine Man, Turn! Turn! Turn!**) as well as appearing on some of **Fifth Dimension**, all as lead singer.

He later rejoined group for three weeks in October 1967, but subsequently embarked on erratic solo career. He made **Gene Clark With The Gosdin Brothers** (the latter had previously been with Chris Hillman, another original Byrd, in The Hillmen) which was remixed and re-released five years later in U.S. only as **Early L.A. Sessions**. Clark then joined Doug Dillard (➡ Dillards) for two memorable albums – **The Fantastic Expedition Of Dillard And Clark** and **Through The Morning - Through The Night**, a few tracks of which are excerpted on **Grass Roots**, and then resumed a solo career proper with **Gene Clark** and **Roadmaster**, the latter so far being unissued in Britain.

In the meantime he was involved

No Other. Courtesy
Asylum Records/WEA.

with unsuccessful Byrds reunion, instigated by David Geffen, to whose Asylum label he was by then signed, and for whom he put out the very creditable **No Other** in 1974 – reminding everyone that though he may have had a strange career, everything he does is always worthy of attention. (➡ The Byrds.)

Recordings:
Gene Clark With The Gosdin Brothers (Columbia/CBS)
The Fantastic Expedition Of Dillard And Clark (A&M)
Through The Morning - Through The Night (A&M)
Grass Roots (Dillard and Clark/ Flying Burrito Brothers) (A&M)
Gene Clark (A&M)
Collector's Series - Early L.A. Sessions (Columbia/—)
Roadmaster (A&M)
No Other (Asylum)

Jimmy Cliff

Born James Chambers in St. Catherine, Jamaica in 1948, Cliff quit college and moved to Kingston in 1962 in search of a career in the record business. First single was **Daisy Got Me Crazy**, for Count Boysie at Federal Studios, but it wasn't until he began to work with Chinese-Jamaican Leslie Kong that Cliff gained his first local hit, **Hurricane Hattie**.

Island Records boss Chris Blackwell persuaded him to move to U.K. in 1965, but it was not until the late '60s that he achieved more than moderate success, with, initially, **Wonderful World, Beautiful People**, a U.K. Top 10 hit, which he had written while touring Brazil, and in 1970 with Cat Stevens' **Wild World**. In this period too he also made the very successful **Jimmy Cliff** album back home in Jamaica, and boosted his reputation by writing hit singles for other artists – **Let Your Yeah Be Yeah** for The Pioneers and **You Can Get It If You Really Want** for Desmond Dekker.

But Cliff really wanted to become an international star, and things were moving a little too disjointedly as far as he was concerned. So he went to Muscle Shoals to make **Another Cycle**, a strictly non-reggae album. It was his first error of judgment.

His big moment seemed to have arrived when Perry Henzell, a friend of Blackwell's, offered him the leading role in a film he was making, "The Harder They Come". Both the movie itself and Cliff's central performance, received wide praise and the film – to this day, probably Jamaica's best – attracted a large cult following, but hardly gained widespread public acceptance. Also, the theme-song which Cliff had written failed to make the charts. He became dispirited, and broke with Island Records,· accepting a lucrative offer from EMI (Warner Bros in the U.S.).

Unlimited certainly has its moments, but his music has lost direction and drive since he swapped companies. In retrospect, Cliff's difficulties seem to have been born out of his own uncertainties. While most people thought of him as a reggae artist, he himself was greatly influenced by American soul music (one of his classic

The Harder They Come.
Courtesy Island Records.

and most widely-recorded compositions, **Many Rivers To Cross**, is a soul ballad), and he has often favoured hybrid musical forms, pitched somewhere between soul and reggae. This is a tendency that has been exacerbated by his

regular international touring and method of making albums (he often records half in Jamaica and half in Los Angeles), so that, unlike Bob Marley, he has divorced himself from his ethnic roots and not built a popular home base.

Nevertheless, he has amply shown his songwriting, singing, acting and even sleeve-designing abilities and just needs to put it all together in the right way at the right time. His day will surely come.

Recordings:
Hard Road To Travel (A&M/ Island)
Jimmy Cliff (A&M/Trojan)
Another Cycle (A&M/Island)
Unlimited (Reprise/EMI)
Struggling Man (Island)
House Of Exile (Reprise/EMI)
Brave Warrior (Reprise/EMI)
Follow My Mind (Reprise)
Contributions to:
The Harder They Come (Soundtrack) (Mango/Island)
Compilation:
The Best Of Jimmy Cliff (Island)

Climax Blues Band

Peter Haycock guitar, vocals
Colin Cooper vocals, saxes, guitar, harp
Derek Holt bass, vocals
John Cuffley drums
Richard Jones keyboards

Formed 1969 around Stafford area of England as six-piece Climax Chicago Blues Band, including all five members listed above. Came in towards latter part of British Blues Boom (➡) and, as name suggests, their material was strongly influenced by Chicago Blues.

Above: Peter Haycock.

This, with a few modifications, is largely what Climax still play. Since early '70s the band have concentrated their attentions towards the U.S. market – home from home for so many British blues bands (Savoy Brown, Fleetwood Mac, Foghat etc). There, they have been relatively successful, their albums invariably just making the album lists.

Founder-member Richard Jones, originally played bass, left after recording of their 1969 debut album to attend Cambridge University. Leaving with his degree, Jones played with Principal Edwards Magic Theatre up to that group's disbandment in 1974, rejoining Climax in keyboards role in 1975.

In the same year, the group's appearance in cross-Europe Startruckin' '75 package tour brought them back to attention of U.K. audiences.

Recordings:
Climax Chicago Blues Band
(—/Parlophone)
Climax Chicago Blues Band Plays On (—/Parlophone)
A Lot Of Bottle (—/Harvest)
Tightly Knit (Sire/Harvest)
Rich Man (Sire/Harvest)
FM/Live (Sire/Polydor)
Sense Of Direction (Sire/Polydor)
Stamp Album (Sire/BTM)
Compilation:
1969–72 (—/Harvest)

The Coasters

Among most important of U.S. black vocal groups, known as The Robins before contracted to Atlantic along with their production/writing team Jerry Leiber and Mike Stoller (➜ Leiber & Stoller) in 1956. First U.S. hit following year with **Searchin'.**

In States, consistent singles hit-makers into early '60s, owing innovative reputation to Leiber/Stoller compositions, bulk of which provided song goldmine for bands during U.K. R&B (➜) boom – **Poison Ivy, Little Egypt, Searchin'** etc. Material was half humorous (**Yakety Yak, Charlie Brown**), half quasi-documentary (**Shoppin' For Clothes, Riot On Cell Block 9**). All titles mentioned are on the 1973 compilation.

Recordings:
The Coasters – Early Years
(Atlantic)

Billy Cobham

Born May 16, 1944, Panama, raised in New York. Jazz/rock percussionist and composer/arranger. First gigged with Billy Taylor and New York Jazz Sextet 1967-68, then met up with and joined Miles Davis (➜) during European tour, returning to States to record with Davis on three albums.

Subsequently had spell with jazz/rock outfit Dreams before becoming part of John McLaughlin's Mahavishnu Orchestra (➜). During same period, much in demand as sessionman for likes of James Brown, Herbie Mann, Sam and Dave, Larry Coryell etc. **Spectrum,** his first solo album in 1974, featured Tommy Bolin (gtr) and Jan Hammer (kybds).

Recordings:
Spectrum (Atlantic)
Crosswinds (Atlantic)
Shabazz (Atlantic)
A Funky Thide Of Sings
(Atlantic)

Eddie Cochran

The years that have elapsed since Cochran's death in an automobile accident – in April 1960 at the age of 21 – haven't in any way diminished either the Cochran legend or his very real contribution to rock.

Not only was he an exceedingly fine stage performer (as witnessed by his role in "The Girl Can't Help It" and his performances on British TV) and guitarist (**Hallelujah, I Love Her So**) but his records encapsulated teenage lifestyle of late '50s America.

The singles **Summertime Blues** (1958), **C'Mon Everybody** (1959), and **Somethin' Else** (1959) are three of the greatest youth anthems ever recorded – something later recognised by The Who (➜) ten years later when they put their own stamp on **Summertime Blues.**

Born Oct 3, 1938, Cochran moved with his family from Minnesota to California, where he had the opportunity to launch into a record career in 1954 – first as a rockabilly singer, and then, influenced by Elvis Presley, as a raw rock 'n' roller. He became one of the more mature first-generation rockers, and certainly understood studio techniques. A pioneer of multi-dubbing, both **C'Mon Everybody** and **Summertime Blues** feature him singing and performing every part.

The Eddie Cochran Memorial Album. Courtesy United Artists.

Like Gene Vincent, he was more popular in the U.K. than the U.S. When he died he had just completed a British tour with Vincent; they were on their way to London airport. By a macabre coincidence, his current hit single was **Three Steps To Heaven.**

All after first album were posthumous releases.

Recordings:
Singin' To My Baby (Liberty)
Memorial Album (Liberty)
My Way (Liberty)
Cherished Memories (Liberty)
The Legendary Eddie Cochran (Liberty)
Legendary Masters, Vol. IV (Liberty)
On The Air (United Artists)
A Legend In Our Time (—/Union Pacific)
The Very Best Of Eddie Cochran (15th Anniversary Album) (United Artists)

Joe Cocker

Born John Robert Cocker May 20, 1944 in Sheffield, England, attended Sheffield Central Technical School, afterwards becoming gas fitter with East Midlands Gas Board.

At 14, discovered Ray Charles (➜) – an important influence – and at 15 joined local group The Cavaliers, for whom he played drums and harmonica, graduating to lead vocalist two years later when group were renamed Vance Arnold and the Avengers.

In 1964 Decca offered Cocker a contract and he was given six months leave of absence by gas board. First single, Lennon/McCartney's **I'll Cry Instead** was flop, earning ten shillings royalties, and after national tour on same bill as Manfred Mann he returned to gas-fitting.

Back in Sheffield he put together the definitive British funk outfit, the Grease Band, with original line-up of Kenny Slade (drums), Henry McCullough (gtr), Tommy Eyre (kybds) and, most importantly Chris Stainton (bs) who was to be Cocker's guiding musical intelligence in years to come.

Band gigged round pubs and clubs of the North, playing mostly Tamla and soul, and cutting a single for Sheffield University Rag live at local King Mojo Club.

Cocker was persuaded to move south again by offer from producer Denny Cordell, which Stainton had set up. Cocker cut Stainton's **Marjorine,** which aroused certain interest, before his appearance at Windsor Jazz and Blues Festival brought him to public prominence, and next single, again a Lennon/McCartney composition, **With A Little Help From My Friends,** soared to No. 1 in U.K. and made U.S. Top 40.

Early in 1969 he made album **With A Little Help From My Friends,** with such notable sessioneers as Jimmy Page, Stevie Winwood and Albert Lee – an early indication of the respect accorded him by his fellow-musicians.

With frequent comparisons to Ray Charles, Cocker was soon hailed as important and innovative white blues singer, while his stage style – resembling a flailing, epileptic human windmill – was, to say the least, distinctive, though some found his apparent spasticity offensive.

Mad Dogs And Englishmen. Courtesy A&M Records.

Grease Band's 1969 U.S. tour won Cocker many friends, among whom was Leon Russell (➜). Russell provided Cocker's next hit single, **Delta Lady,** and helped supervise recording of **Joe Cocker** in Los Angeles.

When Cocker arrived in States in 1970 wishing to cancel a Grease Band tour it was Russell who arranged instead a massive 40-plus entourage of musicians (including many Delaney & Bonnie sidemen), old ladies and dogs, collectively known as Mad Dogs And Englishmen, which ultimately furthered Russell's career more than Cocker's. A double live album, **Mad Dogs And Englishmen,** and an excellent full-length feature film of the same title resulted from the tour.

Chris Stainton had been the only one of Grease Band on the tour – meantime the Grease Band made a remarkable album (1970) before splitting up.

After Mad Dogs tour, Cocker seemed on verge of physical and mental disintegration, and there were rumours of drug problems. In any case, he disappeared for a while out on the West Coast,

later returning to stay with his parents in Sheffield. Made one fleeting live appearance in 1971 at Sheffield City Hall, coming on to sing with Rita Coolidge and the Dixie Flyers, who were supporting The Byrds.

In 1972 reteamed with Stainton and a 12-piece band and, after the briefest of British tours, went to Australia where he was busted for drugs. The Stainton band soon split, and he and Cocker put together **Something To Say,** a combination of live material and studio sessions which showed Cocker had lost none of his mastery.

Despite its quality, however, **Something To Say** had all the signs of acute labour pains, and it was clear Cocker was only holding his career together with considerable aid of Stainton.

Nevertheless they again parted company; Stainton went on to form short-lived Tundra, Cocker to return to Los Angeles, though clearly his career was in bad shape. His next mentor was Jim Price (trumpet-player with the Mad Dogs), and though he produced Cocker's next two albums, it was evident that he was unable to find sympathetic musical settings for Cocker's unique voice. **Stingray** (1976), produced by Rob Fraboni was a big improvement.

Cocker is now virtually a recluse; he has always been suspicious of the press, rarely gives interviews, and rarely performs live. He was easily the most convincing blues/soul singer to emanate from U.K., though he was virtually adopted by Americans, and has often seemed one of rock's saddest casualties.

Recordings:
With A Little Help From My Friends (A&M/Regal Zonophone)
Joe Cocker (A&M/Regal Zonophone)
(both now repackaged as double-album)
Mad Dogs And Englishmen (A&M)
Cocker Happy (A&M/Fly)
Something To Say (A&M/Cube)
I Can Stand A Little Rain (A&M/Cube)
Jamaica Say You Will (A&M/Cube)
Stingray (A&M)

Cockney Rebel

Steve Harley vocals
Jim Cregan guitar
George Ford keyboards
Duncan McKay keyboards
Stuart Elliott drums
Lindsay Elliott percussion

Formed 1973 by one-time journalist Harley (real name Steven Nice, b. South London Feb 27, 1951) who advertised for musicians resulting in line-up containing Stuart Elliott, Jean-Paul Crocker (vln), Paul Avron Jeffrys (bs) and Milton Reame-James (kybds).

Reworking elements of David Bowie, Bob Dylan and Roxy Music, Rebel were established early on as a vehicle for the forceful Harley personality. First hit U.K. charts with single **Judy Teen** (1974). Almost immediately Harley developed provocation as social style, keeping his name constantly in U.K. music press but bringing disintegration of original Rebel through internal friction.

New line-up – billed as Steve Harley and Cockney Rebel – made debut at Reading Festival in U.K. September '74, and in early '75 Harley's Dylanesque **Make Me Smile** single went on to become a U.K. No. 1.

From that point he remained fairly low-profile, seeing a fall '75 single **Black On White** shot flop disastrously, bearing more critical scorn in U.K., and ending that year supporting The Kinks none too successfully on a U.S. tour. Returned to U.K. for early 1976 tour and release of **Timeless Flight**.

Guitarist Jim Cregan previously with Family (♦).

Recordings:
The Human Menagerie (Capitol/EMI)
Psychomodo (Capitol/EMI)
The Best Years Of Our Lives (Capitol/EMI)
Timeless Flight (Capitol/EMI)
Compilations:
A Closer Look (Capitol/—)

Leonard Cohen

Canadian poet/novelist who subsequently embarked on successful singer/songwriter career. Born Montreal 1934, he has written several volumes of poetry, first four of which are available in collected form – "Poems 1956-68". Also two novels: "The Favorite Game" (1963) and "Beautiful Losers" (1966).

Began to set poems to music, and when Judy Collins recorded **Suzanne** in 1966 his solo career started to take shape. He was also assisted initially by a film, "Ladies And Gentlemen . . . Mr. Leonard Cohen", made by the National Film Board Of Canada.

The Songs Of Leonard Cohen was well received, full of haunting compositions which well suited his lugubrious, flat vocals. **Songs From A Room,** though it didn't have the impact of its predecessor, was similarly successful, and Cohen began to undertake a series of live appearances in U.S. and Europe. For his first European tour in 1970, he employed a backing group called The Army, which included Bob Johnston (♦), by now his producer.

Basically, however, Cohen lacked necessary stimulus to be a rock star – he was a reserved, slightly academic figure and was reportedly dismayed by the adulation fostered by live appearances.

Songs From A Room.
Courtesy CBS Records.

Songs Of Love And Hate gave the impression of being released with little enthusiasm; certainly it was received with little. The appeal of his droning, tuneless singing had momentarily worn thin. He suggested that he wanted to abandon his singing career, and as no new material was forthcoming **Live Songs** was released in 1973 – a collection of some of his most famous songs, performed in concert at least two years earlier. Tony Palmer (♦) directed movie about Cohen's 1971 European tour, "Bird On The Wire".

But Cohen's years of inactivity were not after all a prelude to his retirement. He put together an album of new material in 1974, **New Skin For The Old Ceremony,** and in 1976 went back on the road.

If Cohen's problem is that he is too self-consciously a poet ever to develop into a first-rate songwriter, equally it cannot be denied that he has brought to rock music an awareness of the more formal disciplines and classical themes of poetry.

Recordings:
The Songs Of Leonard Cohen (Columbia/CBS)
Songs From A Room (Columbia/CBS)
Songs Of Love And Hate (Columbia/CBS)
Live Songs (Columbia/CBS)
New Skin For The Old Ceremony (Columbia/CBS)
Compilation:
Greatest Hits (Columbia/CBS)

Judy Collins

Born Denver, Colorado, May 1, 1939. Like many after her a traditional folk-singer turned protest singer turned singer/songwriter; but she was better placed – being more talented – to ride on the crest of every successive wave of fashion.

Her father Chuck Collins, although blind, was well-known figure in radio in Denver and on West Coast. He died in 1967 (Judy writing **My Father** about him).

Hers was a thorough musical education. At age of six she began studying to be a classical pianist, often practising eight hours a day, and then playing with the Denver Businessmen's Symphony Orchestra. She made her first public performance at 13, playing Mozart.

She attended school in Jacksonville, Illinois, and University of Colorado. Interest in folk music developed, spending vacation summers at Rocky Mountain National Park, and she decided a career as concert pianist was not for her.

She began singing regularly at folk-clubs in Colorado, and then moving east to Chicago. **A Maid Of Constant Sorrow,** her debut album, was confined to traditional material, but by **Judy Collins No. 3** she was singing more contemporary material, including the protest songs of the day.

Her political consciousness thus stimulated, she was a regular performer on platforms at protest marches. By the time of her fourth album, **The Judy Collins Concert,** she was including much material of the angry young folk-singers – Tom Paxton, Phil Ochs and Bob Dylan.

With her good musical training, she soon began to find the voice/guitar formula too restrictive and developed musical ideas on **In My Life,** which was recorded in London. It included, for example, songs featured in Peter Brook's Aldwych Theatre production of Peter Weiss' "The Marat/Sade", with complete orchestral backing.

In My Life was not so much innovatory as revolutionary; it opened up new vistas for all her contemporaries. So did **Wildflowers,** which in its lush romanticism, was practically a musical companion piece to a film like "Elvira Madigan". It was also first album to feature any of her own compositions. **Who Knows Where The Time Goes** featured her own electric back-up group, which included Stephen Stills on guitar. They had brief affair, and he wrote **Suite: Judy Blue-Eyes** after she'd gone.

In My Life. Courtesy Elektra Records/WEA.

In 1969 she also tried her hand at acting, in Ibsen's "Peer Gynt".

Whales And Nightingales, in 1971, gave her a huge and unlikely hit on both sides of the Atlantic with her arrangement of the traditional hymn **Amazing Grace,** which subsequently became one of the most-performed songs of the '70s. The album also contained her version of **Farewell To Tarwathie,** an old Scottish whaling song used in conjunction with the so-called songs of the humpbacked whale, recorded by Roger Payne, of the New York Zoological Society, off the Bahamas.

Since the early '60s Judy Collins' musical vision has consistently outstripped everyone else's. She describes herself as an interpretative singer, and has been particularly successful in bringing to public attention the works of little-known songwriters. Joni Mitchell, Leonard Cohen, Randy Newman and Sandy Denny, among others, have good reason to be grateful to her. Possessed of an excellent voice, and a fine ability at arranging material; it was not until **True Stories And Other Dreams** that her own abilities as a songwriter were first made evident.

In 1972/73 she was involved with directing a documentary film about her former professor of music, Antonia Brico; the film was nominated for an Academy Award for best documentary.

She returned to the U.K. singles charts in 1975 with her version of **Send In The Clowns** (from the Stephen Sondheim musical "A Little Night Music"). The album from which it was taken, **Judith,** also sold very well. It also contained **Born To The Breed,** a song about her son, born in 1959; she was married to university lecturer Peter Taylor (the marriage was dissolved in 1966).

She has continued to tour both the U.S. and U.K. regularly, though infrequently, usually accompanied by a small ensemble.

Since the momentum of her career has not slackened since 1960, and since she tackles all her activities with care and thoroughness, it's safe to assume she will continue to be successful. **Judith** was produced by Jerry Wexler, and she has made a second one with him.

Recordings:
A Maid Of Constant Sorrow (Elektra)
Golden Apples Of The Sun (Elektra)
Judy Collins No. 3 (Elektra)
The Judy Collins Concert (Elektra)
Fifth Album (Elektra)
In My Life (Elektra)
Wildflowers (Elektra)
Who Knows Where The Time Goes (Elektra)
Whales And Nightingales (Elektra)
Living (Elektra)
True Stories And Other Dreams (Elektra)
Judith (Elektra)
Compilations:
Recollections (Elektra)
Colors Of The Day – The Best Of Judy Collins (U.K. title: **Amazing Grace – The Best Of Judy Collins**) (Elektra)

Judith. Courtesy Elektra Records/WEA.

Colosseum

Jon Hiseman drums
Dick Heckstall-Smith saxes
Dave Greenslade keyboards
Mark Clarke bass
Dave Clempson guitar
Chris Farlowe vocals

Formed 1968 from nucleus of musicians on John Mayall's (♦) **Barewires** album: Hiseman, R&B veteran Heckstall-Smith (ex Graham Bond etc) and founder bassist Tony Reeves. Music was fusion of jazz/rock, with Hiseman firmly at helm.

A child pianist, later drummer and jazz aficionado, first played in jazz-oriented outfit which also included Dave Greenslade and the aforementioned Reeves. Subsequently with Don Rendell Quintet (alongside Graham Bond (♦)), turning professional with Bond's newly-inaugurated Organization in 1966. In between that and appearance in Mayall's Bluesbreakers, had stints with Georgie Fame and New Jazz Orchestra, which he helped form.

Leading light behind Colosseum, Hiseman guided them towards considerable U.K. gig following while constantly having to overcome personnel changes possibly caused by rigid structure of eventually-too-complex music.

Best albums were the first and second, both 1969, particularly the latter's epic title-track. (Both albums noticeably influenced by Graham Bond.) Originals Reeves and Jimmy Litherland (gtr) left at this point.

Daughter Of Time (1970), the first album with Chris Farlowe (➧) on vocals, was also last studio album proper. Here, Hiseman's ambitious lyrics severely restricted band. The 1971 live set backed up group's high U.K. standing as stage band.

Disbanded autumn 1971: Hiseman formed Tempest (➧) with Mark Clarke; Dave Clempson joined Humble Pie (➧); Dave Greenslade re-united with Tony Reeves to form eponymous Greenslade (➧); Farlowe teamed up with Atomic Rooster (➧) for short spell and Heckstall-Smith went own way.

In summer 1975 group revived under name Colosseum II by Hiseman and Irish guitarist Gary Moore (ex-Skid Row, Gary Moore Band, Thin Lizzy) after pair had worked together on and off during previous year on various projects. Line-up completed by Mike Starrs (vcls), Neil Murray (bs) and Don Airey (kybds).

Colosseum II played first U.K. tour fall 1975, recording first album same period for 1976 release.

Recordings:
Those Who Are About To Die We Salute You (Dunhill/ Phillips)
Valentyne Suite (Dunhill/ Bronze)
Daughter Of Time (Dunhill/ Vertigo)
Colosseum Live (Dunhill/ Bronze)
Compilations:
The Collector's Colosseum (—/Bronze)
Colosseum II:
Strange New Flesh (—/Bronze)

Commander Cody And The Lost Planet Airmen

Commander Cody (George Frayne) vocals, piano
Andy Stein fiddle, saxophone, trombone
Bobby Black pedal steel
Bill Kirchen guitar, vocals
Bruce Barlow bass, vocals
Lance Dickerson drums, vocals
Norton Buffalo harp, vocals, trombone
Rick Higginbotham rhythm guitar

Formed by George Frayne (Cody) and John Tichy in Detroit, who had studied together at University of Michigan in Ann Arbor. Band was free assembly of musicians, largely country-based but playing a wide variety of styles, but all in a semi-anarchic manner, which has remained trademark ever since.

From 1968 this loose aggregation of students and freaks began to take on more permanent basis, with introduction of Stein, and then Billy C. Farlow (from Billy C. & The Sunshine, a white electric blues band, like Butterfield's) and Bill Kirchen and Higginbotham from another Ann Arbor band, The Seventh Seal.

Played gigs in and around Detroit, but in 1969 Kirchen recon-

noitred the West Coast, and band moved out to San Francisco, where their blend of C&W, rockabilly, cajun and truck-drivin' music soon gained them respectable following.

Group consistently went through personnel changes, but basic team of Cody, Stein and Kirchen have remained since the start, preserving their brand of musical mayhem.

In November '71 released first album, for Paramount, **Lost In The Ozone**, but it was their second, **Hot Licks, Cold Steel And Truckers' Favourites** – made on a four-track for a mere $5,000 that captured their vitality and looseness, and that many consider their most successful. When ABC bought out Paramount, Airmen switched to Warner Bros and though their first album was dreadful, their next, **Tales From The Ozone**, produced by Hoyt Axton (➧), showed the band at their versatile best.

Commander Cody has acted as session musician on albums by Poco, Link Wray and the New Riders Of The Purple Sage. Majority of the Airmen formed offshoot band, October '75, called The Moonlighters, to play occasional small club gigs; Billy C. Farlow left band at end of 1975 to form The Billy C. Farlow Band, in order to concentrate more on playing R&B music.

Recordings:
Lost In The Ozone (Paramount)
Hot Licks, Cold Steel And Truckers' Favourites (Paramount)
Country Casanova (Paramount)
Live From Deep In The Heart Of Texas (Paramount)
Commander Cody And His Lost Planet Airmen (Warner Bros)
Tales From The Ozone (Warner Bros)

Billy Connolly

Born Anderston, Glasgow, 1942, Connolly is a ribald Scottish comedian and erstwhile folk singer whose irreverent sense of humour was equally as important as the music of Bay City Rollers (➧) in bringing popular Scottish culture to the rest of the U.K.

Leaving school at 16, had a variety of occupations (messenger, welder, paratrooper, oilrig worker) before teaming up with Tam Harvey in late '60s to form Scottish folk duo The Humblebums, Harvey being replaced in 1968 by Gerry Rafferty, now of Stealers Wheel (➧). Humblebums had little immediate success, but a sizeable cult following.

Connolly, though, unable to take folk music seriously, embarked on solo career where his humour and on-stage charisma rapidly ousted his uncertain singing as "raison d'etre" of his live shows. With little media attention Connolly managed to become national institution in Scotland – colloquially referred to as The Big Yin – before anyone south of Hadrian's Wall had heard of him.

Towards end of '74, Connolly bandwagon began to reach rest of Britain, partly due to new record contract with Polydor, partly to remarkably successful appearances as guest on Michael Parkinson's BBC-TV "chat" show.

Cop Yer Whack For This, recorded live at Glasgow Kings Theatre, went gold in U.K., and in autumn '75 next album **Get RIGHT Intae Him** (recorded at Apollo Theatre, Glasgow) was similarly successful, though neither album captured essence of his stage act which by now ranged from the merely scurrilous to the unashamedly scatological.

Late in '75 Connolly's new status was confirmed by U.K. No. 1 single – a parody of Tammy Wynette's **D.I.V.O.R.C.E.**

Words And Music, issued in 1975, a compilation of material from his first two Transatlantic albums.

Recordings:
Billy Connolly Live (—/Transatlantic)
Solo Concert (—/Transatlantic)
Cop Yer Whack For This (Polydor)
Get RIGHT Intae Him (Polydor)

Ry Cooder

Born Los Angeles, March 15, 1947, Cooder had established first-class reputation as session-man by the end of '60s.

During adolescence, learned directly from people like Reverend Gary Davis, and as early as 1963 developed blues act with Jackie de Shannon – though it came to nothing. Listened to records of late delta blues singers to acquire expert knowledge of bottleneck guitar, and then in 1966 formed band with Taj Mahal (➧) called the Rising Sons which worked Hollywood area. After this, moved on to work with Captain Beefheart, playing slide-guitar on Beefheart's first two albums.

Above: Ry Cooder.

It was at this time he began to be offered session-work regularly. He met Jack Nitzsche (➧), and through him worked on the scores of "Candy", and the Mick Jagger movie "Performance"; he was also featured on the Rolling Stones' **Let It Bleed** album.

In the '70s he has continued his session-work, with people like Randy Newman and Maria Muldaur, and has initiated own recording career and undertaken rare live appearances as soloist. Albums have all been of high standard, and display an almost academic approach to his subject; his work is remarkable for its smooth blending of folk, rock, country and blues and for his comprehensive knowledge of American folk and blues of the '30s.

Recordings:
Ry Cooder (Reprise)
Into The Purple Valley (Reprise)
Boomer's Story (Reprise)
Paradise And Lunch (Reprise)

Sam Cooke

A pioneer soul singer, Cooke, like Ray Charles, put secular words in a gospel musical context and paved the way for modern soul music.

Born Chicago, Jan 22, 1935, one of eight sons of a local Baptist minister. In the first half of the '50s, sang with gospel group called Soul Stirrers (which also featured Johnny Taylor); he wanted to turn to pop music, but was afraid of effect this might have on both his gospel audiences and his father, so at first his early pop releases were issued under pseudonym Dale Cook. When truth came out, he was forced to leave Soul Stirrers, but he entered pop market with his father's blessing, and took his self-composed **You Send Me** to Keen Records. It became his first million-seller, and Cooke had many more hits for the label, including **Only Sixteen**.

By the time he moved to RCA in 1960 he was writing all his own material, and in next four years enjoyed unbroken succession of hits, including **Wonderful World, Twistin' The Night Away, Chain Gang** and **Bring It On Home To Me**.

Though Cooke's best was very good indeed, he did go too far into the pop market, and much of his RCA material (produced by Hugo & Luigi) veers into the excesses of supper-club schmaltz – but the superbly distinctive voice made even this eminently listenable.

On Dec 11, 1964, Cooke was shot dead in sordid circumstances in a Los Angeles motel. If he was influential while he lived, he was even more so after his death. His ballads became the raw material for soul music as it emerged in mid-'60s; Otis Redding recorded **Wonderful World, Shake, A Change Is Gonna Come** and **Chain Gang**. Aretha Franklin made **You Send Me** one of her earliest hits, while over in England The Animals recorded **Bring It On Home To Me**.

In recent years, Rod Stewart has frequently named Cooke as his favourite singer, and has recorded versions of **You Send Me, Bring It On Home To Me** and **Twistin' The Night Away** as tributes.

Meanwhile, the enduring legacy of Sam Cooke was demonstrated early in 1976 when two of his songs – **Cupid** and **Only Sixteen** – were simultaneously moving up the U.S. Top 20, in versions by Dawn and Dr. Hook respectively.

Recordings:
This Is Sam Cooke (RCA)

Priscilla Coolidge
➧ Booker T. & The M.G.s

Rita Coolidge

Born Nashville, Tennessee, 1944. Daughter of Baptist minister, she sang in church choirs from age of two. Attended Florida State University where she formed a band, RC & The Moonpies. When the family moved to Memphis, she and her sister, Priscilla, began doing radio spots and jingles; Priscilla started gaining more professional work, which brought her into contact with Booker T., whom she married in 1971. (➔ Booker T. & The M.G.s.)

Rita also cut a single in Memphis which became local hit, but by then she'd moved on to Los Angeles where she met up with Delaney & Bonnie (➔), beginning her career with them as a back-up singer and one of the Friends.

She recorded with them on **Down Home** and **Accept No Substitute** and toured with the famous Friends band three times, winning a first-class reputation with her fellow professionals. Leon Russell wrote Joe Cocker's hit **Delta Lady** as a tribute to her. When the Delaney & Bonnie & Friends operation was discontinued, she moved, as did most of the other Friends, to work on the notorious Cocker/Russell Mad Dogs And Englishmen tour.

For some time was a constant back-up performer on West Coast supersessions, working with Stephen Stills and Eric Clapton on their debut solo albums. Her own albums, **Rita Coolidge** and **Nice Feelin'** featured musicians of the same stable, but leant more towards country music.

Then in 1973 she married Kris Kristofferson, and settled down to a more subdued parallel career with him, appearing with him in Peckinpah's film, "Pat Garrett And Billy The Kid", and collaborating on two albums (➔ Kris Kristofferson).

She has a son, Casey, born in 1974.

Recordings:
Rita Coolidge (A&M)
Nice Feelin' (A&M)
The Lady's Not For Sale (A&M)
Fall Into Spring (A&M)
It's Only Love (A&M)

Alice Cooper

Born Vincent Furnier Feb 4, 1948, Detroit, Michigan, a preacher's son. Raised in Phoenix, Arizona, where he formed rock band with school-mates Glen Buxton (gtr), Michael Bruce (rhym gtr, kybds), Dennis Dunaway (bs) and Neal Smith (drms). In Beatle hats and yellow corduroy jackets, played mostly Rolling Stones material under names The Earwigs, Spiders and Nazz.

In 1968, after local hit in Phoenix, shifted operations to Los Angeles where they appeared under billing Alice Cooper. Eked living out of bars and clubs circuit before being discovered by manager Shep Gordon, who got them signed to Frank Zappa's newly-inaugurated Straight label. Garishly made-up, and with a burgeoning reputation as the worst band in L.A., they were certainly bizarre enough for Zappa, whose label released the undistinguished **Pretties For You** in 1969 and **Easy Action** the following year.

Neither did anything to suggest that Alice Cooper was much more than a rock 'n' roll freak show and, after a year of further scuffling around L.A., the outfit moved to Detroit $100,000 in debt (they lived there in a motel, five to a room) feeling that they could empathize with a city that had produced such similarly high-energy bands as The Stooges and MC5.

There they came under wing of iron-fisted producer Bob Ezrin, under whose direction they recorded the 1970 **Love It To Death** album which changed their artistic credibility and commercial fortunes almost overnight. From that album, **I'm 18** – America's equivalent to **My Generation** – smashed into the U.S. singles chart.

Killer enhanced growing record reputation, and utilizing Theatre Of The Absurd stage show – Alice chopping up dolls and employing props such as electric chairs, boa constrictors and gallows – were soon established as the top U.S. box office attraction.

Title track from 1972 **School's Out** collection became million-seller and broke band in U.K. However, early 1973 **Billion Dollar Babies** album (though American tour of same name was one of biggest money-making jaunts in history of rock) saw start of Alice Cooper's descent into self-parody and grossed-out theatricals evident in all subsequent activities.

In 1974 Cooper axed original members, replacing them with Dick Wagner and Steve Hunter (gtrs), Prakash John (bs), Whitey Glan (drms) and Josef Chirowsky (kybds), all of whom had played for Lou Reed.

Following year signed new recording contract with Atlantic in U.S., Anchor in U.K., for whom he recorded **Welcome To My Nightmare** (1975), touring both countries with stage revue of same name. Cooper's appeal has

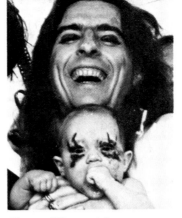

Above: Alice and fan.

abated (some critics have said it's redundant) since peak period of **Elected** and **School's Out** singles (1972), though he can still boast considerable following – a minor percentage of which is attracted through his activities as golfer, his other love after rock 'n' roll.

First two albums repackaged by Warner Bros 1973 as **Schooldays – The Early Recordings.**

Recordings:
Pretties For You (Straight)
Easy Action (Straight)
Love It To Death (Warner Bros)
Killer (Warner Bros)
School's Out (Warner Bros)
Billion Dollar Babies (Warner Bros)
Muscle Of Love (Warner Bros)
Welcome To My Nightmare (Atlantic/Anchor)
Alice Cooper Goes To Hell (Warner Bros)
Compilations:
Greatest Hits (Warner Bros)

Kevin Coyne

Born in Derby, England, Jan 27, 1944, Coyne attended local art college before taking a job in 1965 as social therapist in a psychiatric hospital in Preston. He stayed there until 1969 when he moved to London to advance his

Below: Alice Cooper, son of a preacher man.

singing career, which until then had been sporadically pursued in local clubs.

Since Coyne had a family to support, he took another job as social worker in the London borough of Camden, while he simultaneously joined Siren as vocalist; shortly afterwards the band was given a contract by Dandelion Records (owned by English DJ John Peel), and made two albums. Despite the promising start, little happened, and in 1972 Coyne took the plunge by quitting both his job and the band, and then made a solo album **Case History,** which is now very much a collector's item, undertook a European tour with his Dandelion stable-mates and co-wrote a revue which played at London's ICA.

In 1973 he signed a contract with Virgin Records, and his career began to assume more positive shape. **Marjory Razor Blade** was released to critical acclaim, though its mannered vocals and renouncement of conventional song formulae seemed almost wilfully anti-commercial. (A double set, **Marjory Razor Blade,** was reduced to just one album for U.S. release.)

Blame It On The Night was a more fluent and musically sophisticated album, and Coyne was developing a style of his own. He put together a band which played dates throughout U.K. and Europe but fell apart early in 1975, and was replaced by another line-up which made **Matching Head And Feet,** a disappointing album. Coyne then reconstituted his band again for **Heartburn** in 1976. The last line-up was: Zoot Money (kybds, vcls), Andy Summers (gtr), Steve Thompson (bs) and Peter Woolf (drms). This band was dissolved in summer 1976.

Recordings:
Case History (—/Dandelion)
Marjory Razor Blade (Virgin)
Blame It On The Night (Virgin)
Matching Head And Feet (—/Virgin)
Heartburn (Virgin)

Crabby Appleton
➔ Michael Fennelly

Crazy Horse

Best known for enduring association with Neil Young (➔) and for one brilliant album of their own. Story started with Billy Talbot (bass), Ralph Molina (drums), George Whitsell (guitar) and Danny Whitten (guitar and vocals) who formed a West Coast group called The Rockets.

Talbot, Molina and Whitten provided the entire backing for Young's second solo album, **Everybody Knows This Is Nowhere** (which contained the track **Running Dry – Requiem For The Rockets**) and then recruited keyboards session-man Jack Nitzsche (➔) to become Young's regular back-up group, both on record and stage.

Their own first album, for which they also added Nils Lofgren (➔) on guitar, was one of the strongest of 1971; it was full of strong compositions, including **Gone Dead**

Train from the film "Performance", and Whitten's **I Don't Want To Talk About It**, later recorded by Rod Stewart on **Atlantic Crossing**.

However, by the time they made **Loose** (1972), Whitten and Nitzsche had moved on, and only Talbot and Molina remained, though Whitsell, from The Rockets, returned, and John Blanton (keyboards) and Greg Leroy (guitar) had been added. **Loose** was an obvious anticlimax after **Crazy Horse**, but despite the band's rapidly diminishing status as a separate unit, Talbot and Molina, the constants in band, kept things going, replacing Whitsell and Blanton with Rick and Mike Curtis respectively, but **Crazy Horse At Crooked Lake** made little impact.

This brought about the band's temporary demise, and for his concert dates in 1972 and the **Harvest** album, Young formed a new backing group, the Stray Gators. (Ben Keith – steel guitar; Kenny Buttrey – drums; Tim Drummond – bass; Jack Nitzsche – piano). Then, in November of that year, Danny Whitten died of drug overdose.

Young retained all his side-men except Buttrey for **Time Fades Away**, though by then the team was no longer called the Stray Gators. Though the various personnel (perm any four from eight) were continuing to work with Young, it wasn't until 1975 that he resuscitated Crazy Horse. **Tonight's The Night** was an album dedicated to Whitten (and Bruce Berry, one of Crazy Horse's roadies, who had met a similarly tragic fate), and featured a picture of the band (Keith, Lofgren, Talbot and Molina) with an empty space where Whitten should have been. Then, on **Zuma**, for the first time since **Everybody Knows This Is Nowhere**, Young once again co-credited Crazy Horse on one of his albums. By this time, Crazy Horse were Talbot, Molina and Frank Sampedro on guitar. The story just goes on and on.

Recordings:
Crazy Horse (Reprise)
Loose (Reprise)
Crazy Horse At Crooked Lake (Epic)

Cream

Eric Clapton guitar, vocals
Jack Bruce bass, vocals
Ginger Baker drums

In theory Cream were first supergroup – pre-dating Blind Faith. In fact, when band formed only Clapton (♦) had any kind of sizeable reputation – and it took success in U.S. to get U.K. attention.

Bruce (♦) and Baker (♦) were previously in Graham Bond Organization, a group whose virtuoso "feature" format was inherited by Cream when they recruited Eric Clapton from John Mayall's Bluesbreakers in 1966.

According to Clapton, Cream was originally planned as blues trio, "like Buddy Guy with a rhythm section". However, first album – released after major debut appearance at 1966 Windsor Festival – revealed an outfit founded on strident blues-based numbers but with accent on improvisational technique, an un-

usual feature at this time. Also showed unexpected vocal and textural strength suggesting commercial potential in pop market – a side of band developed on **Disraeli Gears** (1967) second album.

Simple, riffed sequences were topped with slightly strange melody lines, a method epitomized in **Sunshine Of Your Love** and Cream's second U.K. hit single **Strange Brew** (1967).

However, group's first U.K. chart success was earlier same year with **I Feel Free** – the song that established Bruce and Pete Brown (♦) as writing team. Shortly after, group were feted in U.S. where they subsequently spent most of their time.

In fact, from 1967, through 1969, every Cream album exceeded one million sales mark in U.S. as group's reputation spread rapidly across country, backed up by SRO gigs wherever they appeared. **Sunshine Of Your Love**

single was also million-seller, and **Anyone For Tennis, White Room** (both 1968) and **Crossroads, Badge** (1969) kept band in U.S. singles charts.

Their third album, the double **Wheels Of Fire** set, was in fact recorded in New York and San Francisco, and its 1968 success enhanced Cream's position as world-wide act. With hindsight, it fails to convince: awkward contrasts between pure pop and straight blues on studio set, and somewhat suspect playing on much of live sides showed inherent cracks in facade – disparate aims and too much time on the road.

As 1968 wore on, group themselves began to share feeling that their progress as unit had run its course and in fall of that year they announced impending disbandment. On Nov 26, 1968, at Royal Albert Hall, London, group played emotional farewell concert.

They went on, however, to work

Left: Disraeli Gears. Polydor.

in studio for one final album, the 1969-released **Goodbye**, from which came Clapton's **Badge** U.S. and U.K. hit (co-written with George Harrison). **Goodbye**, in fact, suffered from same schizophrenic traits as **Wheels Of Fire** but does include Cream's best live cut after famous **Crossroads**, a half-crazed version of Skip James' **I'm So Glad**.

In retrospect, Cream were arguably over-rated as group. Nevertheless, they were responsible for opening up totally new areas in live performance, creating half a dozen classic tracks in process, and spawning whole wave of subsequent imitators.

Clapton and Baker re-appeared 1969 in Blind Faith (♦), while Bruce went own way.

Two more live albums were released posthumously, as well as several compilations some of which are listed below.

Recordings:
Fresh Cream (Atco/Polydor)
Disraeli Gears (Atco/Polydor)
Wheels Of Fire (Atco/Polydor) – later available as separate LPs.
Goodbye (Atco/Polydor)
Live Cream Vol I (Atco/Polydor)
Live Cream Vol II (Atco/Polydor)
Compilations:
Best Of Cream (Atco/Polydor)
Off The Top (Atco/—)
Heavy Cream (Atco/Polydor)

Creedence Clearwater Revival

John Fogerty guitar, vocals
Tom Fogerty rhythm guitar
Stu Cook bass
Doug 'Cosmo' Clifford drums

All born and bred in San Francisco Bay Area, it was while they were attending junior high school in El Cerrito that they first got together as a group – Tommy Fogerty & The Blue Velvets.

In 1964 the Blue Velvets auditioned with a local company, Fantasy Records, and were offered recording contract with proviso that they change name to The Golliwogs in an effort to cash in on current British beat boom. They reluctantly agreed, and a debut single was released 1965.

For next two years they worked continually around central California and, with exception of moderately-successful **Brown Eyed Girl**, cut a whole string of flop singles.

In make-or-break effort, Golliwogs turned fully professional in 1967 and on Christmas Eve of that year agreed with Saul Zaentz (by now boss of Fantasy Records) to become known as Creedence Clearwater Revival.

Following year, as San Francisco music explosion shook the industry, their debut album **Creedence Clearwater Revival**, containing a mixture of John Fogerty originals and rock standards, was released – partly as a result of public interest after tape had been previewed over local radio stations.

Left: Goodbye Cream. Polydor.

Two singles were simultaneously taken from album. The old Dale Hawkins' chestnut, **Suzie Q** was the first to register, and after it had enjoyed a lengthy chart spell, was replaced by Screamin' Jay Hawkins' **I Put A Spell On You.** With the release of **Bayou Country** it became evident that CCR were on point of emerging as first great U.S. singles band of late '60s; indeed, at a time when trend was towards conceptualised albums, CCR were virtually the only band to regard an album as a collection of potential singles. **Proud Mary/Born On The Bayou** was the single taken from **Bayou Country.** It immediately struck gold, and **Proud Mary** has become justly recognized as a classic 45.

All band's singles were products of John Fogerty's songwriting genius, and a tribute to his imagination. He had never lived in Bayou Country, had probably never hitched a ride on a river boat queen, yet his songs bore all the marks of verisimilitude.

Green River LP was to produce two million-selling singles, **Bad Moon Rising** and **Green River,** along with the magnificent **Lodi,** that clearly was based on personal experience.

By 1970, CCR were clearly established as the most successful-ever American rock band in terms of record sales and box-office returns. **Willy & The Poor Boys** further consolidated this (by now, Fogerty was writing material at a furious rate); a tour of Europe brought more fame and fresh acclaim.

Cosmo's Factory contained no less than three gold singles – **Travellin' Band, Up Around The Bend** and **Lookin' Out My Back Door,** but this was nevertheless the turning-point.

Internal stress points were beginning to be felt. Possibly Fogerty was seeking to break out of what he saw as artificial limitations imposed on band by their enormous commercial success (and, in **Willy & The Poor-Boys** had included a considerable amount of social comment). Certainly, **Pendulum** was an attempt to extend basic formula, but it fell far short of previous efforts. Also Tom Fogerty quit owing to a clash of personality; the other three carried on as a trio, and even undertook a world tour in this form (which resulted in **Creedence – Live In Europe**) but it was becoming evident that both Cook and Clifford now regarded the group as little more than a front for aspirations of John Fogerty.

Following successful single, **Sweet Hitch-Hiker** came the group's final album, **Mardi Gras,** maliciously referred to as Fogerty's Revenge, because he did evenly distribute creative functions between three group-members, and result was perhaps worst album ever recorded by a top-league band. CCR duly disbanded in October 1972, by which time most people had lost interest in them.

Tom Fogerty has since released three albums, which show him to be more than just a rhythm guitarist, as well as an interesting single, **Joyful Resurrection** – recorded with Cook and Clifford – which, he claimed, told the story of CCR.

Doug 'Cosmo' Clifford revealed only that he was a better drummer than singer.

Cook and Clifford have since been working regularly as a notable session rhythm team and have joined Don Harrison Band. (For John Fogerty's subsequent career, ♦ John Fogerty.)

Although friction in band possibly arose because Fogerty regarded himself as lynch-pin of whole operation, the fact remains that he was – it was his distinctive, hoarse 'n' wailing vocals and remarkable talent for writing hit singles that made CCR an unparalleled success. All the singles went gold, while all seven albums that contained their collected works went platinum. CCR's posi-

*Willy And The Poor Boys.
Courtesy Fantasy/EMI.*

tion as the finest '50s-oriented white rock 'n' roll band has never been challenged.

Recordings:
The Golliwogs (Fantasy/—)
Creedence Clearwater Revival (Fantasy)
Bayou Country (Fantasy)
Green River (Fantasy)
Willy & The Poor Boys (Fantasy)
Cosmo's Factory (Fantasy)
Pendulum (Fantasy)
Mardi Gras (Fantasy)
Creedence Gold (Fantasy)
More Creedence Gold (Fantasy)
Live In Europe (Fantasy)
Chronicle (Fantasy)
Tom Fogerty solo:
Tom Fogerty (Fantasy)
Excalibur (Fantasy)
Zephyr National (Fantasy)
Myopia (Fantasy)
Doug Clifford solo:
Doug 'Cosmo' Clifford (Fantasy)

The Crickets

Originally formed in Lubbock, Texas, by Buddy Holly (♦) and Jerry Allison, with original line-up of Holly (vcls, gtr), Allison (drms), Niki Sullivan (gtr) and Joe Mauldin (bs).

Holly had started off with an interest in country music, but, having been influenced by Elvis Presley, had moved into rock 'n' roll; his producer, Norman Petty, decided to use him both as lead singer of Crickets and as solo singer. Thus, Holly's first big hit, **That'll Be The Day,** was actually credited to The Crickets – as were **Oh Boy, Maybe Baby** and **Think It Over.**

Sullivan left the group early '58, and the others continued as a trio; after Holly's death in February '59, Allison kept group going through various personnel changes; most usual line-up was Allison, Sonny Curtis and Glenn D. Hardin. In this form they enjoyed two hits of their own in U.K. – **Don't Ever**

Change and **My Little Girl,** the latter from the British pop movie, "Just For Fun". (The Crickets also appeared with Lesley Gore in "The Girls On The Beach", a U.S. film made in wake of "A Hard Day's Night".) **My Little Girl** had been written by Curtis, but his most successful composition was **Walk Right Back,** for the Everly Brothers.

The band continued gigging together until 1973, when Hardin finally left, to play with Elvis Presley in Las Vegas, and to form The Hot Band to accompany Emmylou Harris (♦). The line-up that recorded the last Crickets album was Allison, Curtis, plus British musicians Rick Grech and Albert Lee – though that was obviously a studio band.

Recordings:
The Chirping Crickets (Coral)
Back In Style (MCA)
A Long Way From Lubbock (MCA)

Jim Croce

Born Philadelphia, 1942, Croce attended University of Villanova where he ran a folk and blues show on the local radio station, and formed a series of bands. He learned to play guitar at 18, and after graduating, took a series of manual jobs improving his musical abilities in his spare time.

In New York in 1967 he took the advice of an old college friend Tommy West (who worked with Terry Cashman), and began singing in local coffee houses. This led to a contract with Capitol and one unsuccessful album with his wife, Ingrid.

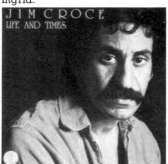

*Life And Times.
Courtesy Phonogram Ltd.*

After working as a truck driver, Croce came up with some compositions in 1971 which he submitted to Cashman and West, by now a production team in New York. He recorded them there with his close associate Maury Muehliesen – whose own debut album for Capitol, **Gingerbread,** had featured Croce as a backing musician – and the album, **You Don't Mess Around With Jim** (produced, as were all his albums, by Cashman and West) was issued in the spring of 1972. The album, and two singles from it, the title-track and **Operator,** all sold well, and in 1973 Croce's next album, **Life And Times** also became a best-seller, with the single taken from it, **Bad Bad Leroy Brown,** topping the U.S. charts.

Croce and Muehliesen were killed when their chartered private plane crashed on take-off at Natchitoches, Louisiana on Sept 20, 1973. It was particularly tragic as Croce seemed on the point of

becoming one of America's most successful singer/songwriters.

His whole career demonstrated great pertinacity. In one of his early labouring jobs, he had broken a finger with a sledgehammer, and adapted his guitar style accordingly to overcome that impediment. His songs, often closely-observed character studies or wry narratives, had carefully constructed lyrics supported by memorable melodies. The posthumous albums – **I Got A Name,** which he had completed before his death and was released late in '73, and the **Photographs And Memories** compilation – were both automatically best-sellers in the U.S.

Recordings:
Jim And Ingrid Croce (Capitol/—)
You Don't Mess Around With Jim (ABC/Vertigo)
Life And Times (ABC/Vertigo)
I Got A Name (ABC/Vertigo)
Compilations:
Photographs And Memories (Livesong/—)

Steve Cropper

Born Ozark Mountains, Missouri, Oct 21, 1942. Had rural upbringing, but after move to Memphis he discovered R&B and soul. After forming Mar-Keys at high school with 'Duck' Dunn, and having an early hit on Stax Records, he helped put together Booker T. & M.G.s (♦).

As guitarist, Cropper is unsurpassed, as evidenced by M.G.s' albums; also his fluid and memorable work on hit singles for a variety of other artists. As composer, he was responsible for two of most celebrated products of Stax studios, in Wilson Pickett's **In The Midnight Hour** and Otis Redding's **Sitting On The Dock Of The Bay.**

He was in fact closely involved with career of Redding, up until latter's death in 1967; he then graduated to role of producer, and in 1970 opened own studios, working for various companies including Stax. Has numerous production credits, including albums by Jeff Beck (♦) and Cate Brothers. In 1975, he was featured throughout on Rod Stewart's made-in-Memphis album, **Atlantic Crossing,** and co-wrote **Stone Cold Sober** with Stewart.

Less happy as featured solo artist playing extended lead, as on **With A Little Help From My Friends,** Cropper works best when his playing is used as a foil for others, as on **Jammed Together** (with Pop Staples and Albert King) or simply contributing these short tasteful guitar breaks.

Recordings:
With A Little Help From My Friends (Stax)
Jammed Together (Stax)

David Crosby

Born Los Angeles Aug 14, 1941, first musical venture was as one of Les Baxter's Balladeers, a clean-cut New Christy Minstrels type outfit. From there became solo folkie, until he met up with Roger McGuinn and Gene Clark, and the three formed nucleus of the Jet Set, later the Beefeaters and finally The Byrds (♦) in 1964.

Crosby's strongest characteristics during Byrds' **Mr Tambourine Man** era were his green cape and cute choir-boy features, but later his musical influence and high-voiced harmonies started to mesh together into overall Byrds sound.

Crosby's musical visions were wide. He was in vanguard of Byrds whole raga-rock venture and contributed some of their finest-ever songs, the jazz-tinged **Everybody's Been Burned** and **Renaissance Fair** on **Younger Than Yesterday** album (1967), the drug oriented **What's Happenin'** on **Fifth Dimension** (1966). McGuinn even used three Crosby songs on **Notorious Byrd Brothers** (1968), the first post-Crosby effort.

The Crosby/Byrds split was caused by inflated ego conflicts, and centred round Crosby's demands for Byrds to perform his **Triad** composition, a "risqué ménage à trois" song later to be recorded by Jefferson Airplane (**Crown Of Creation** album) and Crosby Stills Nash & Young on their **Four Way Street**.

Crosby was preparing solo album after split with Byrds when he teamed up with Steve Stills and Graham Nash (♦) to form Crosby Stills And Nash (♦) in 1968. This was his first real brush with superstardom and he became recognized for his intense minor-key love songs (**Guinevere**) and heavy political statements (**Long Time Gone** and the trite **Almost Cut My Hair**).

After CSN&Y disbandment, cut **If I Could Only Remember My Name** solo album, a somewhat self-indulgent collection employing services of all his West Coast frinds from Jerry Garcia through Grace Slick to Joni Mitchell.

The 1972 **Crosby & Nash** album, however, found Crosby back in control of his talents, if succumbing a little to the excessive "good vibes" feel of his on-stage raps. In 1974 took part in CSN&Y re-union tour, and in 1975 he and Graham Nash signed lucrative record deal with ABC.

Recordings:
If I Could Only Remember My Name (Atlantic)
With Graham Nash:
Crosby & Nash (Atlantic)
Wind On The Water (ABC/Polydor)
Whistling Down The Wire (ABC/Polydor)

Crosby Stills Nash & Young

David Crosby guitar, vocals
Stephen Stills guitar, bass, keyboards, vocals
Graham Nash guitar, vocals
Neil Young guitar, vocals

Formed summer 1968 by Crosby (♦), who was preparing solo album after quitting Byrds (♦), Steve Stills (♦) who had just left Buffalo Springfield (♦) and Graham Nash of U.K. pop outfit The Hollies (♦) who was then visiting California. The three sang together at John Sebastian's house in Laurel Canyon, were knocked out by Crosby and Nash vocal harmonies and decided to assemble as group.

Went to U.K. later that year for Nash to sever commitments with Hollies and then returned to Los Angeles to work on debut album released early 1969.

That first album, which won immediate critical acclaim, still stands as perfect example of contemporary acoustic music – powerful melodies, with harmony singing of Crosby and Nash to the fore. Stills at creative peak around this time – evidence his seven minute long **Suite: Jude Blue Eyes,** purportedly about old flame Judy Collins, which became group's first U.S. hit.

Nash's **Marrakesh Express,** from same album (by now a gold seller) followed it into U.S. singles charts and broke band into British lists same year.

Having previously played with Stills in Buffalo Springfield, Neil Young (♦) joined later that year at suggestion of Atlantic boss Ahmet Ertegun. Band were looking for keyboards player to fill out sound for live gigs. Ertegun suggested that Young should play guitar, allowing Stills to double on keyboards.

Second album, **Deja Vu** (1970) – further augmented by Greg Reeves (bs) and Dallas Taylor (drms), later replaced by Calvin Samuels and Johnny Barbata – was credited to Crosby Stills Nash & Young and more electric in its approach. Overall, though, it was a mixed bag, containing an electric version of Joni Mitchell's **Woodstock** (a U.S. hit), Nash's banal **Teach Your Children** and Dave Crosby's self-conscious song of hippie martyrdom **Almost Cut My Hair.** All were easily outclassed by the immensely-superior material of Young.

Their second gold record, **Deja Vu** was still on U.S. charts when the outfit's third album, the thoroughly-disappointing **Four Way Street** double live set was released early 1971. The title itself indicated different directions each member of the aggregation was taking prior even to release.

Young's brilliant **Ohio,** written in wake of Kent State University killings which outraged young America, provided another U.S. hit, but, shortly after, CSN&Y disintegrated to pursue individual paths. See under separate entries.

Throughout 1973 there were rumours of a re-union, and in the summer of that year they did in fact record together – with little success – and no release was forthcoming. Finally, a year later, the four joined forces again for series of massively-attended concerts across U.S., culminating in visit to U.K. summer that year to top huge outdoor festival at London's Wembley Stadium. Though there was further talk of an album together, group split again immediately after and have produced nothing as unit since.

Above: Crosby & Nash.

Recordings:
Crosby Stills And Nash (Atlantic)
Deja Vu (Atlantic)
Four Way Street (Atlantic)
Compilations:
So Far (Atlantic)

The Crusaders

Wilton Felder tenor saxophone, bass
Joe Sample keyboards
Larry Carlton guitars
Nesbert 'Stix' Hooper drums, percussion
Robert Popwell bass

Formerly known as the Jazz Crusaders, they are a highly-touted instrumental unit, playing a free-form jazz-rock. All the members come originally from Texas, though only Carlton, the newest recruit, is white. They are all respected session musicians whose services are regularly in demand, and have contributed to scores of West Coast recordings; their impressive instrumentation was one of the reasons why Joan Baez's rock album, **Diamonds And Rust,** was so successful.

In 1975 they released the widely-acclaimed **Chain Reaction,** and also recorded with Van Morrison.

They gave some highly-acclaimed concerts in Britain in 1976, just prior to which original member Wayne Henderson (trmbne) had left.

Recordings:
Crusaders I (ABC)
Second Crusade (ABC)
Unsung Heroes (ABC)

Left: Deja Vu. Courtesy Atlantic. Neil Young walks on – and walks away with the honours.

Scratch (ABC)
Southern Comfort (ABC)
Chain Reaction (ABC)
Those Southern Knights (ABC)

Crystals
◆ Phil Spector

Curved Air

Sonja Kristina vocals
Darryl Way violin, keyboards
Tony Reeves bass
Mick Jacques guitar
Stewart Copeland drums

Curved Air is an example of how lavish promotional budgets can often rebound on a band. The original line-up comprised Kristina and Way along with Florian Pilkington-Miksa (drums), Ian Eyre (bs) and Francis Monkman (synthesisers). From the start in winter 1970 they had all the hallmarks of a band carefully packaged and assembled to capitalise on prevailing rock trends, e.g. one attractive female focal point (Sonja Kristina, formerly of British "Hair" cast), quasi-classical trappings, and two instruments (violin and synthesiser) currently in vogue.

This in itself might have been suspect, but when Warner Bros then threw a mighty promotion budget behind a lavishly-gimmicky first album, the first pressings of which had track info printed on to coloured vinyl, the whole encased in a transparent sleeve, the U.K. public and rock press immediately smelled a "hype" – and reacted accordingly.

Unlike other "packaged" commodities, the Air could actually acquit themselves live as more than competent musicians – and in their short-lived original form, despite onerous tag as "gimmick band", they did manage to accrue a small but ardent British following. Their 1971 **Second Album** even managed to produce a U.K. Top Five hit in **Back Street Luv**, but it soon became obvious that the band were doomed to a short life-span, particularly when personality clashes ensued.

Ian Eyre was replaced by Mike Wedgwood (bs) before the re-recording of **Phantasmagoria** (1972) and, shortly after its release, Monkman, Way and Pilkington-Miksa quit band. (Darry Way formed own, equally short-lived, outfit, Wolf, before later returning to Air fold.)

With Sonja Kristina now the only surviving original member, Air re-grouped with drummer Jim Russell and two teenage instrumental prodigies, 19-year-old Kirby on guitar and 17-year-old Eddie Jobson on violin and synthesisers. This line-up recorded 1973 **Air Cut** but disbanded completely in July same year when Eddie Jobson was taken by Roxy Music (◆) to replace Brian Eno. Kirby later turned up in the "bogus" Fleetwood Mac (◆), and subsequently in Stretch, while Sonja Kristina attempted solo recording career before re-joining cast of "Hair" for three-month spell in summer 1974.

In autumn 1974, after originally coming together to sort out business affairs, Air founder-members Kristina, Way, Pilkington-Miksa

and Monkman decided to re-form the group for a one-off winter college tour of U.K. Phil Kohn was brought in as bassist.

Due to Pilkington-Miksa and Monkman having other commitments, this group itself disbanded after that one, relatively successful tour – out of which came the 1975 **Live** album – but Way and Kristina kept Air going with a new guitarist, drummer and bassist as listed above. Of these bass player Tony Reeves has longest pedigree, having previously played with Colosseum (◆), John Mayall (◆) and Greenslade (◆).

Recordings:
Air Conditioning (Warner Bros)
Second Album (Warner Bros)
Phantasmagoria (Warner Bros)
Air Cut (Warner Bros)
Curved Air Live (London/Deram)
Midnight Wire (RCA/BTM)
Airborne (BTM)
Compilation:
The Best Of (Warner Bros)

Roger Daltrey

As The Who moved towards their tenth anniversary as a front-line group, and they found both less necessity and less opportunity to work together quite as regularly, so the individual careers of the members of the band began to unfold.

For Daltrey, this meant the release of a solo album, **Daltrey**, in 1973, and a British Top 5 single, **Giving It All Away**. The album was produced by Adam Faith (◆) and David Courtney with songs by Leo Sayer (◆) and David Courtney, and such was the success of the album that it acted as a springboard for Sayer's own career.

It was hardly surprising that Daltrey was chosen in 1974 to take the eponymous role in Ken Russell's film of The Who's "Tommy"; what was, however, surprising was that Daltrey should so distinguish himself in the part that Russell selected him for the lead role in his next movie, "Lisztomania". Though this was less successful, both critically and commercially, it was evident that Daltrey's solo activities were taking better shape than most would have predicted. He amplified this by the release of a second solo album, **Ride A Rock Horse**, in 1975.
(◆ The Who.)

Recordings:
Daltrey (MCA/Track)
Ride A Rock Horse (MCA/Polydor)

one of the boys

Daltrey. Courtesy Polydor Records.

Nightrider. Courtesy Kama Sutra/Pye.

The Charlie Daniels Band

Charlie Daniels guitar, fiddle, vocals
Joel Di Gregorio keyboards, vocals
Freddie Edwards drums
Gary Allen drums
Barry Barnes guitar
Mark Fitzgerald bass

Like the Allmans, Lynyrd Skynyrd, Marshall Tucker and Z.Z. Top, The Charlie Daniels Band are one of the groups whose irrepressible brand of boogie has revitalised the rock scene in the American South.

Born in Wilmington, North Carolina, Daniels went to Nashville in 1967 at the invitation of Bob Johnston, and worked with him on the albums he subsequently produced for Bob Dylan – **Nashville Skyline, Self Portrait** and **New Morning**; Daniels played on Ringo's Nashville album **Beaucoups Of Blues,** as well as three Leonard Cohen albums and also produced four records for The Youngbloods.

At the turn of the '70s Daniels, a rather corpulent figure, started writing songs and branched out on a solo career, signing with Kama Sutra Records. In 1973 a talkin' country-blues anti-redneck song **Uneasy Rider** (from the album **Honey In The Rock**) became a U.S. Top 10 hit, and he then put together The Charlie Daniels Band, with the line-up as above. (As with the Allmans, two drummers were employed.)

The band moved from Nashville to set up house together in Mt. Juliet, Tennessee, at the beginning of '74 since when they have built up a reputation as a hard-working band. Sales of their albums have steadily increased so that they are now automatically Top 30 material. In 1975, they had another hit single **The South's Gonna Do It,** from the album **Nightrider**. Despite their success in the U.S., they are still virtually unknown in the U.K.

Recordings:
Te John Grease And Wolfman (Kama Sutra)
Honey In The Rock (Kama Sutra/—)
Way Down Yonder (Kama Sutra/—)
Fire On The Mountain (Kama Sutra)
Nightrider (Kama Sutra)
Saddle Tramp (Epic)

Cyril Davies

Born in England in 1932, Davies

played a key role in the growth of British R&B (◆) after early years in jazz bands and skiffle groups. A founder member with Alexis Korner (◆) of Blues Incorporated, which featured at various times Mick Jagger, Charlie Watts, Brian Jones, Jack Bruce and Ginger Baker, he left that group in late 1962 to lead his own even more ethnic R&B outfit, The Cyril Davies All Stars.

Long John Baldry (◆) came along as second vocalist, and the rest of the personnel were drawn basically from Screaming Lord Sutch's Savages: Nicky Hopkins (pno) (◆), Carlo Little (drms), Rick Barton (bs), Bernie Watson (gtr). Micky Waller – subsequently in Jeff Beck Group with Hopkins – later had a spell on drums.

Through 1963 this group established itself as one of the most popular and arguably the best of the early English R&B bands (the embryonic Rolling Stones used to support them regularly). Then, on Jan 7, 1964 Cyril Davies collapsed and died – a victim of leukaemia. He left scant recorded evidence of his talent.

Although 1964 was the year in which R&B found widespread acceptance, it's unlikely Davies would have enjoyed much of it himself – for his uncompromising attitude to his music as well as his unconventional personality were hardly conducive to commercialisation.

Recordings:
The Legendary Cyril Davies With Alexis Korner's Breakdown Group And The Roundhouse Jug Four (—/Folklore)

Clive Davis

Born Brooklyn, New York, Davis climbed executive ladder with rapid pace to become boss of the massive Columbia Records (CBS in U.K.) in 1965 where his remarkable business acumen and eye for talent multiplied profits ten-fold. Bob Dylan, Simon and Garfunkel, Janis Joplin and Blood Sweat & Tears are among acts whose careers owed much to Davis' ability. In 1974, after somewhat sordid intercompany powerplay and allegations over use of expenses and related matters, Davis was dismissed by Columbia. He went on to found his own Arista label (Patti Smith, Barry Manilow, Eric Carmen, Gil Scott-Heron, etc) where his every step has been paved with gold.

Miles Davis

By the end of the '50s, Miles Dewey Davis' trumpet was the most syndicated sound in jazz, his leadership and record for experimentation continuing through to late '60s when, on a trio of albums, **Miles In The Sky, Fillies De Kilimanjaro** and particularly **In A Silent Way,** he began to unite jazz with elements of rock. The last-named release in 1969, on which Davis picked up on the acid rock of the West Coast, sent a frisson of horror through the jazz establishment. As one critic has said, with hindsight: "It was like finding a raised lavatory seat in a nunnery."

It was the 1970 **Bitches Brew** set,

however, which first attracted the attention of rock audiences in a substantial way.

From that point on, and employing a pool of musicians rather than a regular group, Davis set out to disclose the African roots of both musical streams by utilizing the basic rhythmic and harmonic frames of rock in order to give his jazz-trained soloists maximum expressive freedom without straying into the anti-traditional anarchy of "free" music.

Predictably this experiment had variable success, later works like **On The Corner** and **In Concert** (both 1973) becoming too dense and introverted to triumph over the limited format.

Another reason may have been that, by then, Davis lacked the distinguished soloists he had been leading in the later '60s, many having left to form their own groups – e.g. Wayne Shorter and Joe Zawinul to Weather Report (♦), Tony Williams to Lifetime, Herbie Hancock (♦) and Keith Jarrett to their eponymous organizations, John McLaughlin (♦) to Mahavishnu Orchestra, Chick Corea to Return To Forever (♦). His recent releases have met with only a lukewarm response from jazz and rock reviewers alike.

Since The Birth Of The Cool in 1948, Davis has made upwards of 40 albums as a leader, of which the following is a selection. Most albums from 1967 onwards have been included.

Recordings:
Miles Ahead (Columbia/CBS)
Sketches Of Spain (Columbia/CBS)
Porgy And Bess (Columbia/CBS)
Milestones (Columbia/CBS)
Kind Of Blue (Columbia/CBS)
ESP (Columbia/CBS)
Miles Smiles (Columbia/CBS)
Sorcerer (Columbia/CBS)
Nefertiti (Columbia/CBS)
Miles In The Sky (Columbia/CBS)
Fillies De Kilimanjaro (Columbia/CBS)
In A Silent Way (Columbia/CBS)
Bitches Brew (Columbia/CBS)
Live At Fillmore (Columbia/CBS)
Jack Johnson (Soundtrack) (Columbia/CBS)
Live Evil (Columbia/CBS)
On The Corner (Columbia/CBS)
In Concert (Columbia/CBS)
Big Fun (Columbia/CBS)
Black Beauty (Columbia/CBS)
Get Up With It (Columbia/CBS)
Aqharta (Columbia/CBS)

Spencer Davis
♦ Spencer Davis Group

Kiki Dee

Born Pauline Matthews, Bradford 1947. Sang locally with dance bands in north before arrival in London 1964 where she met songwriter Mitch Murray who provided her with new name and first single, **Early Night**.

During five years with Philips Records in mid-'60s she recorded one album **I'm Kiki Dee** and a succession of singles, mostly in a sub-Motown vein, a couple of which clung to the bottom edges of U.K. charts. In 1970 she became the only white British girl singer to be signed to Tamla Motown, and she went to Detroit to make an album; but Motown was then engaged in moving to West Coast, and tracks she did cut there – in a very disorganised fashion – were not issued for over a year, by which time the album title of **Great Expectations** was sadly inappropriate.

With her career again in doldrums she played cabaret engagements in Australia and South Africa for seven months in 1972.

On her return she accepted offer from Elton John's manager John Reid to join the nascent Rocket Records. In 1976 she made the hit single **Don't Go Breaking My Heart** with Elton John.

The album she made in 1973 **Loving And Free** – sort of her third debut album – was co-produced by John. It was well received and at last provided her with a British hit, Veronique Sanson's **Amoureuse**. Her third single, and the title track of her next album, **I've Got The Music In Me** (1975), gave her another British hit, and, more importantly, the American breakthrough she needed – though the fact that she and her band had been touring the U.S. as support act to Elton John had helped in no small measure.

I've Got The Music In Me had been credited to The Kiki Dee Band, which at its height comprised: Bias Boshell (kybds), Jo Partridge (gtr), Roger Pope (drms) and Phil Curtis (bs). But after touring with the band for about a year, Kiki decided it wasn't quite the situation she was looking for. She thus disbanded them in summer 1975, and went to America to think out the next move.

Recordings:
I'm Kiki Dee (—/Philips)
Great Expectations (Tamla Motown)
Loving And Free (Rocket)
Patterns (—/Philips)
I've Got The Music In Me (Rocket)

Deep Purple

Jon Lord keyboards
Ian Paice drums
Glenn Hughes bass, vocals
David Coverdale vocals
Tommy Bolin guitar

British rock band, formed Feb 1968 by Lord, Paice and founder-guitarist Ritchie Blackmore while playing in Germany. Lord (b. Leicester, June 9, 1941) had early classical background, though his previous band had been the R&B outfit The Artwoods, led by Ron Wood's older brother Art.

Line-up of new band was completed by Nick Simper (bs) and Rod Evans (vcls) and, as Deep Purple, the five-piece cut a version of Joe South's **Hush** composition which made the U.S. Top 5 in summer 1968. First album also made American lists, as did second and third.

Two more pop hits in States followed before Purple attempted to attain heavier rock identity and break through in their native England. Ian Gillan (vcls) and Roger Glover (bs) from Episode Six replaced Simper and Evans. This new line-up first appeared on the 1970 **Concerto For Group And Orchestra** album, recorded at London's Albert Hall with Royal Philharmonic Orchestra.

Worked uphill to establish new image in U.K. and finally broke through in June 1970 with single **Black Night** and derivative yet million-selling **Deep Purple In Rock** album. The 1971 **Fireball** set was instant success, and the single **Strange Kind Of Woman** followed **Black Night** on to British singles charts.

By mid-1972, however, illness and internal friction were beginning to unsettle band. A year later vocalist Gillan left, citing Purple's "lack of progression", followed by bassist Glover, who went into production with Nazareth (♦).

Hughes, from Trapeze, was brought in as replacement bassist and, after auditions, completely-unknown Coverdale stepped into Gillan's old role.

In 1975 Ritchie Blackmore (♦)

also quit band after extensive speculation that the band would split. His place being taken by American Tommy Bolin (♦), who wrote or co-wrote seven of ten songs on his debut Purple album, the 1975 **Come Taste The Band**.

In July 1976 Hughes announced he was joining re-formed Trapeze for a "one-off" tour. Weeks later, amid mounting confusion, Purple finally split. At that point Jon Lord was planning new group with Tony Ashton, ex Family (♦).

Lord had previously cut solo product listed below, last of which was a collaboration with Ashton.

Recordings:
Shades Of Deep Purple (Tetragrammaton/Parlophone)
Book Of Taliesyn (Tetragrammaton/Harvest)
Deep Purple In Concert (Tetragrammaton/Harvest)
Concerto For Group And Orchestra (Tetragrammaton/Harvest)
Deep Purple In Rock (Warner Bros/Harvest)
Fireball (Warner Bros/Harvest)
Machine Head (Warner Bros/Purple)
Made In Japan (Warner Bros/Purple)
Who Do We Think We Are? (Warner Bros/Purple)
Burn (Purple)
Stormbringer (Purple)
Come Taste The Band (Purple)
Compilations:
24 Carat Purple (Purple)
Jon Lord solo:
Gemini Suite (Purple)
Windows (Purple)
First Of The Big Bands (Purple)

Delaney & Bonnie

Prior to Delaney Bramlett meeting Bonnie Lynn in 1967 and marrying her within seven days, he had been one-half of The Shindogs – a duo featuring Joey Cooper and resident on Jack Good's celebrated ABC show "Shindig".

Bonnie Lynn had been doing session work in Memphis with a number of Stax/Volt stars, and gigging with Fontella Bass and Albert King before she joined Ike & Tina Turner (♦) as one of The Ikettes.

The first white act to sign to Stax/Volt, Delaney & Bonnie cut **Down Home**, an album backed by Booker T & The MGs (♦) which remained unissued until after their rapid rise to fame. They had also cut earlier album, **Delaney & Bonnie** in 1968 for the Independence label.

By 1969 the Bramletts had formed the "Friends", a strictly casual grouping of whoever happened to be around at the time, and which included Leon Russell, Jerry McGee (ex-Ventures guitarist), Bobby Whitlock, Carl Radle, Jim Keltner, Bobby Keyes, Jim Price, Rita Coolidge, Dave Mason and Duane Allman – the nucleus of what was to become the over-exposed Los Angeles Blue-Eyed Soul School. However, **Accept No Substitute - The Original Delaney & Bonnie** still stands as a remarkable document – the

Left: Deep Purple In Rock. Courtesy EMI Harvest. Cut in 1970, it broke the group as a global heavy metal force.

quintessential fusion of gospel, country and soul influences that was easily the most exciting sound of its time.

When Eric Clapton joined the "Friends" for a British tour during which George Harrison also made occasional guest appearances, success was instantaneous, but relatively short-lived. **On Tour (With Eric Clapton)** was the album that came out of all that, and Clapton returned the favour by featuring both on **Eric Clapton**. The Delaney & Bonnie noise subsided as suddenly as it had erupted. Their band became foundation for 1970 Mad Dogs & Englishmen tour. After that, Whitlock, Radle and Jim Gordon became Clapton's Dominos (♦ Eric Clapton), Keyes and Price toured with the Rolling Stones.

Above: Bonnie Bramlett. Met and married Delaney in 7 days.

They both continued recording with all-star backing musicians, and made **To Bonnie From Delaney, Motel Shot** and **Country Life** for Atlantic, but the energy and style had become stagnant. In 1972 they signed with Columbia and made **Together,** but their personal and professional life together ended in divorce.

Undoubtedly Delaney and Bonnie had been victims of their own success when pushed into the big league. They have since recorded solo albums, though to little effect. In 1974 Bonnie, who had come to know Phil Walden and the Allman Brothers Band through working with Duane, signed with Capricorn Records, but the chemistry still wasn't right, and **It's Time** was not a successful venture.

Recordings:
Down Home (Stax)
Accept No Substitute – The Original Delaney & Bonnie (Elektra)
On Tour (With Eric Clapton) (Atlantic)
To Bonnie From Delaney (Atlantic)
Motel Shot (Atlantic)
Country Life (Atlantic)
Together (CBS)
Best Of . . . (Atlantic)
Delaney:
Delaney (CBS)
Something's Coming (CBS)
Bonnie:
Sweet Bonnie Bramlett (CBS)
It's Time (Capricorn)

Sandy Denny

A student at Kensington Art College, London, at the same time as Jimmy Page, Eric Clapton and John Renbourn, she initially gained a reputation as a folk-singer on the club circuit, before joining The Strawbs (♦) with whom she

recorded one album. In May 1968 she joined Fairport Convention (♦), recorded three albums with them, and established herself as top British female vocalist, while also gaining name as songwriter – Judy Collins used Denny's **Who Knows Where The Time Goes** as the title track of one of her albums. In Dec 1969 Sandy quit Fairport at the time of their greatest national popularity.

Formed her own band Fotheringay, Mar 1970 – Trevor Lucas (gtr), Jerry Donahue (gtr), Pat Donaldson (bs), Gerry Conway (drms) – but despite individual reputations of members and partial commercial success of **Fotheringay** debut album the line-up didn't work out, and band was dissolved in throes of recording a second album.

Sandy's personal standing remained high in Britain, and each of her subsequent solo albums met with critical, and some commercial, success – the lushly orchestrated **Like An Old Fashioned Waltz** took her right away from her folk origins. She also participated with other folk/rock musicians (known collectively as The Bunch) in strictly rock 'n' roll venture that resulted in **Rock On.**

In 1973 she married the aforementioned Trevor Lucas (both he and Donahue had by now been drafted into Fairport) which invited speculation that she would rejoin the band. After assisting them on a world tour, 1973-74, she finally stepped back into her

The North Star Grassman And The Ravens. Courtesy Island.

old role in spring 1974. Appeared with Fairport on one studio album, **Rising For The Moon,** but the reunion never did work out, and in Feb 1976 she and her husband left together to pursue their own separate careers.

Recordings:
Fotheringay (A&M/Island)
The North Star Grassman And The Ravens (A&M/Island)
Sandy (A&M/Island)
Like An Old Fashioned Waltz (A&M/Island)

John Denver

Singer/songwriter/guitarist, born John Henry Deutschendorf in Roswell, New Mexico, on Dec 31, 1943. His father an air force pilot who held three world aviation records, the young Denver travelled U.S. as his parents moved from one base to another. First performed as folk singer in Lubbock, Texas, where he attended college – majoring in architecture – in early '60s.

Performed in Los Angeles from 1964 and successfully auditioned for gig with Chad Mitchell Trio,

replacing the departing Mitchell. Toured with Trio between 1965-69 before embarking on solo career performing much of own material, notably **Leaving On A Jet Plane** which Peter Paul & Mary recorded in 1969 for huge hit.

Denver's version of song was included on his first solo album **Rhymes & Reasons,** released in U.S. Sept 1969 (Denver albums issued in different order in U.K.). By 1970 and two more albums, **Take Me To Tomorrow** and **Whose Garden Was This?,** Denver was still seeking widespread acceptance although the tenor of subsequent recordings had by then been established – sacharrine acoustic melodies topped off with lyrics which plumbed the depths of naiveté.

Ideal Easy Listening fodder, in fact, for those who felt urge to empathise with the "youth movement" (Denver has also milked ecology dry as a source for material) but couldn't handle the incisiveness of a Bob Dylan, Neil Young or even Paul Simon – and in 1971 America eventually took country-boy Denver to its heart with the gold single **Take Me Home Country Roads** and the similarly million-selling **Poems Prayers & Promises** album.

Friends With You also made singles lists later same year, and Denver's buck-toothed grin and homespun banalities have dominated U.S. AM airwaves and charts ever since.

Aerie and **Rocky Mountain High** became gold albums in 1972, the title track from the latter becoming his second million-seller. In 1973 **Farewell Andromeda** similarly went gold, as did **Annie's Song** single following year which saw Denver enter U.K. charts for first time.

In 1975, the Denver bandwagon accelerated into new gear with a series of U.S. TV specials and Lake Tahoe cabaret appearances back to back with Frank Sinatra. His album **Windsong** racked up a million in advance orders alone, while **Thank God I'm A Country Boy** and **I'm Sorry** kept him at top of singles charts. Backed by coast-to-coast John Denver TV Special "Rocky Mountain Christmas" watched by some 30 million viewers, Dec 1975 album of same name was guaranteed gold virtually on announcement of its release.

A measure of Denver's phenomenal commercial appeal is the fact that his **Greatest Hits** collection had, by the end of 1975, racked up two consecutive years on the U.S. album charts.

Live In London (U.K. only) was recorded during spring 1976 concerts in the city and – in what is probably record time – rush-released within some ten days of Denver's last gig. In addition to list below, Mercury have issued **Beginnings,** an album from Chad Mitchell Trio days.

Recordings:
Rhymes & Reasons (RCA)
Take Me To Tomorrow (RCA)
Whose Garden Was This? (RCA)
Poems Prayers & Promises (RCA)
Aerie (RCA)
Rocky Mountain High (RCA)
Farewell Andromeda (RCA)
Back Home Again (RCA)
An Evening With John Denver (RCA)

Windsong (RCA)
Rocky Mountain Christmas (RCA)
Live In London (—/RCA)
Spirit (RCA)
Compilations:
Greatest Hits (RCA)
Best Of John Denver (RCA)

Derek And The Dominos
♦ Eric Clapton

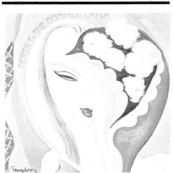

Layla And Other Assorted Love Songs, Courtesy Polydor.

Rick Derringer

In Union City, Indiana, 1962, the 15-year-old Derringer (ne Zehringer) and his brother Randy, plus next-door neighbour Randy Hobbs, started group The McCoys (taking name from Ventures' track **The McCoy**).

With addition of Bobby Petersen (kybds) played gigs around Dayton, Ohio, opening shows for the Beach Boys and Four Seasons, backing Chuck Berry, Drifters and other rock legends, before New York producer Bert Berns took them to the Big Apple to record an R&B song he'd written, **Hang On Sloopy.** A month after release, the single was a smash hit around the world – with Rick still only 18.

Other Top 10 hits followed until the group – by now minus Petersen – switched to the Mercury label and attempted to progress out of their initial bubblegum image. Recorded a couple of psychedelic albums for that label, **Human Ball** (1968) and **Infinite McCoys** (1969), which flopped disastrously, and ended-up as virtual house band at Steve Paul's Scene Club in New York. (Two aforementioned albums re-released 1974 as double set **Outside Stuff** – U.S. only.)

In 1969 Steve Paul took over their management and a short time later they resurfaced as Johnny Winter's back-up band on his 1971 **Johnny Winter And.** The album was produced by Rick Derringer (he changed name at this point), who also wrote several tracks including hit **Rock And Roll Hoochie Coo.**

Subsequently Derringers and Hobbs toured as Winter's back-up band, Rick sharing vocal/guitar chores with the Texan guitar star, and when, later that year, Johnny Winter quit performing Derringer joined Edgar's White Trash (♦ Edgar Winter).

Derringer produced Edgar Winter's **They Only Come Out At Night** album (1973), a U.S. No. 1. Also played on Edgar's "live" **Roadwork** album (1972), and produced **Still Alive And Well** (1973) for brother Johnny.

Other credits include appearances on three Alice Cooper albums, and on sets by Richie Havens, Todd Rundgren and Steely Dan.

He released his first solo album, **All American Boy** (1974), on Steve Paul's Blue Sky label, following with **Spring Fever** set (1975). Also appeared, late 1975, on Blue Sky release **The Edgar Winter Group With Rick Derringer**, but in early 1976 was planning his own road band.

Recordings:
All American Boy (Blue Sky)
Spring Fever (Blue Sky)
Derringer (Blue Sky)

Neil Diamond

Born in Brooklyn, New York, Jan 24, 1941. In the early '60s he began to take what jobs he could with New York-based record companies in order to further his songwriting ambitions. After hawking around his material, he was hired as staff writer by Sunbeam Music, where he turned out songs to order for particular artists – the most successful of which were **I'm A Believer** and **A Little Bit Me, A Little Bit You** recorded by The Monkees (♦) 1966–67.

It was the boost Diamond needed to strike out on his own, and first single for Bang Records, **Solitary Man** was, in May 1966, the first of a series of U.S. hit singles. If Diamond's vocals were rather limited, he did have the swarthy good looks of a clean-cut entertainer, and the ability to produce hit material seemingly at will. His career burgeoned, and his fame grew wider when he moved to Uni Records at close of '60s. Records like **Cherry, Cherry, Sweet Caroline** and **Cracklin' Rosie** provided him with hits throughout the world.

In 1970 began to write more lyrically ambitious (some would say pretentious) material, and **Tap Root Manuscript** was noteworthy for a six-part composition,

The African Trilogy, which illustrated the three stages of Man's development – birth, maturity and death – through such musical devices as primeval jungle rhythms and gospel singing.

During this period Diamond attempted to abandon smooth, easy listening image, grew his hair, and seemed to court the approval of the intelligentsia; though he didn't get it, his audience continued to expand anyway, and in 1973 he was offered one of biggest deals in record industry history by CBS – reputed to be five million dollars. His first album for them was the extremely successful original score for **Jonathan Livingstone Seagull**. CBS seemed to have backed a winner, but Diamond has not been overly productive in recent years, issuing only **Serenade** in 1974 and **Beautiful Noise** in 1976, the latter with Robbie Robertson (♦ The Band) as producer.

Recordings:
Feel Of Neil Diamond (Bang/London)
Just For You (Bang/London)
Velvet Gloves And Spit (Uni/MCA)
Brother Love's Travelling Salvation Show (Uni/MCA)
Touching You . . . Touching Me (Uni/MCA)
Tap Root Manuscript (Uni/MCA)
Stones (Uni/MCA)
Moods (Uni/MCA)
Hot August Night (Uni/MCA)
Rainbow (Uni/MCA)
Jonathan Livingstone Seagull (Original Score) (Columbia/CBS)
Serenade (Columbia/CBS)
Beautiful Noise (Columbia/CBS)
Compilations:
Neil Diamond's Greatest Hits (Bang/London)
Gold (Uni/MCA)
Double Gold (Uni/—)
Focus On Neil Diamond (—/London)
Diamonds (—/MCA)

Below: Jonathan Livingston Seagull. Courtesy CBS. Diamond scored the film adaptation of Richard Bach's book.

NEIL DIAMOND
THE HALL BARTLETT FILM
Jonathan Livingston Seagull
ORIGINAL MOTION PICTURE SOUND TRACK

Bo Diddley

One of the key figures in development of rock music; a stable-mate of Chuck Berry (♦) with whom he frequently recorded; the reputations of the two ripened side by side.

Born Elias McDaniel in McComb, Mississippi on Dec 30, 1928, his family moved to Chicago when he was five. He began to study violin at seven, and soon taught himself guitar.

Exposed to post-war blues sounds of Chicago, he had his first group at high school. Later formed close-knit ensemble with Frank Kirkland (drms), Otis Spann (pno), Jerome Green (maraccas), and Billy Boy Arnold (hrmnca); with his half-sister, "The Duchess", these played on many of his records.

During the early '50s Diddley got his first real gig at 708 Club in Chicago, playing either with his band or solo. With the advent of rock 'n' roll in mid-'50s he began writing material in that vein, and signed contract with Checker Records (sister label to Chess). His first single, **Bo Diddley**, a self-composed anthem to himself, released at same time as Chuck Berry's **Maybellene**, was a major U.S. hit in 1955 and introduced one of most basic and famous riffs in rock music.

Diddley was among first of the R&B artists to explore the potential of a purely electric sound, and he experimented with a bewildering variety of custom-made axes, his favourites being distinctively square or oblong. His music was always powerfully charged, with a pounding, jungle rhythm and very hypnotic.

Bo Diddley was first of a series of successes which quickly established him as major attraction with U.S. rock audiences. Other singles included **I'm A Man, Mona, Who Do You Love** and, in the '60s, **You Can't Judge A Book By Its Cover** and **Road Runner**; but he seemed to dry up at this point, and has written virtually no new songs for a decade or more.

This body of material was fully enough to sustain his reputation, however. Both his songs and sound were covered extensively, and in British beat boom, with many going to R&B sources for their material, his work was extensively plundered. The Rolling Stones put **Mona** on their first album, The Yardbirds recorded **I'm A Man,** and Eric Burdon & The Animals revived **The Story Of Bo Diddley**; The Pretty Things even took their name from one of his songs.

However his own personal career was in decline in later '60s until, like so many other early rock acts, he was revitalised through appearances in Richard Nader's rock 'n' roll revival shows, and he gave a characteristically electrifying performance in "Let The Good Times Roll" movie.

Golden Decade is a compilation containing all his well-known material. Other releases listed are only his recent ones.

Recordings:
Bo Diddley London Sessions (Checker)

Got Another Bag Of Tricks (Checker)
20th Anniversary Of Rock 'n' Roll (Checker)
Another Dimension (Checker)
Compilation:
Golden Decade (Checker)

The Dillards

Rodney Dillard vocals, guitar, synthesiser
Dean Webb mandolin
Billy Ray Latham guitar, banjo
Paul York drums

In early '60s two natives of Salem, Missouri, Rodney and Doug Dillard (bnjo) met up with Mitchell Jayne (bs), a local radio announcer, and Dean Webb from Independence, Missouri, and formed The Dillards. Their essentially lighthearted form of bluegrass quickly attracted attention of then still ethnic Elektra label, who were looking towards rock 'n' roll at the time, and regarded The Dillards as a move in a more commercial direction.

Back Porch Bluegrass and the often hilarious **Live! Almost!** were issued, and then the band met Byron Berline, at the time a national fiddle champion, but not yet a notable recording musician. **Pickin' And Fiddlin'** was thus made with him as tribute to old-time country, particularly fiddle, music, and remains an in-demand item to connoisseurs of the genre.

Shortly afterwards Doug Dillard left, to make two albums with Gene Clark (♦), and more recently two solo albums and a reputation as a first-class session musician. His replacement was Herb Pedersen, from San Francisco, whose stronger vocals moved Dillards in even more commercial direction on **Wheatstraw Suite** and **Copperfields** in 1969 and 1970 Pedersen himself left early 1972 to join Country Gazette, while his predecessor in Gazette, Billy Ray Latham, joined Dillards. With the addition also of Paul York, the band made the disappointing **Roots And Branches** for the now-defunct Anthem label.

Their last album, released in 1973, was **Tribute To The American Duck**, since when group's direction has changed yet again, with Rodney Dillard now playing synthesisers. But Jayne has left so band are again a four-piece, and without regular bass player.

Recordings:
Back Porch Bluegrass (Elektra)
Live! Almost! (Elektra)
Pickin' And Fiddlin' (Elektra)
Wheatstraw Suite (Elektra)
Copperfields (Elektra)
Roots And Branches (Anthem/United Artists)
Tribute To The American Duck (Poppy/United Artists)
Compilation:
Country Tracks, The Best Of The Dillards (—/Elektra)

Dion

Born in The Bronx on July 18, 1939 Dion Dimucci first recorded in mid-'50s as lead singer of Dion and the Tamberlanes, one of the countless New York-based teenage vocal groups (most of which were of Italian or black origins); the group issued one disc, **The Chosen Few**, before Dion re-appeared as leader of a new outfit Dion And The Belmonts, who took their name from a street in The Bronx. The other three group members were Fred Milano, Carlo Mastangelo and Angelo D'Aleo.

In May 1958 their first single **I Wonder Why** made an impression on the U.S. charts, and the line-up subsequently established themselves as the most successful of their type with songs like **A Teenager In Love** and **Where Or When?**, both of which were million-sellers. (In 1959 Dion And The Belmonts had been touring the States with Buddy Holly; Dion had declined an invitation to fly by the plane that subsequently crashed killing all the passengers, including Holly.)

Though the group separated in 1960, Dion, whose personal charisma had arguably been the reason for the group's consistency, continued recording for the same company, Laurie Records, and his success rate was maintained with **Runaround Sue** and **The Wanderer.** Even when he moved to Columbia in 1963, he was still having hits, with **Ruby Baby** and **Drip Drop,** but then the advent of Beatlemania, coupled with his own by now considerable drug problems, temporarily halt-ed his career.

By 1968 he was ready for a come-back, having kicked his drug habit and reshaped his act. He was now a folk-styled balladeer, accompanying himself on guitar. Still with Laurie, he had a U.S. Top 10 hit with **Abraham, Martin And John,** a song composed by Dick Holler about the assassinations of Martin Luther King and John and Bobby Kennedy.

Dion's second career in the van-guard of the acoustic folk/rock movement blossomed; by now with Warner Bros, his albums like **Sit Down Old Friend,** released in 1970, mostly composed of original material written in col-laboration with Tony Fasce, sold encouragingly. In 1972 **Sanctuary** contained some tracks recorded live at The Bitter End in Green-wich Village.

Finally Warner Bros persuaded him, in the wake of the rock 'n' roll revival, to bring the Belmonts together again for a live concert at Madison Square Garden which resulted in the bestselling album, **Reunion.**

When Phil Spector's Philles label was acquired for distribution by Warner Bros, Dion met Spector, and was invited to record for him, and thus Dion's third career was begun. His first single on Philles Records, **Born To Be With You,** dramatically employed all the familiar devices of the Spector 'Wall Of Sound', though the album of the same title was less successful.

Dion is one of rock's survivors, both in so far as he's twice been close to death, and also in that he's proved versatile enough to meet the challenge of changing musical fashions.

Recordings:
Sit Down Old Friend (Warner Bros)
You're Not Alone (Warner Bros)
Sanctuary (Warner Bros)

Suite For Late Summer (Warner Bros)
Born To Be With You (Philles)
Streetheart (Warner Bros)
With The Belmonts:
Reunion (Warner Bros)

Dog Soldier
◆ Keef Hartley

Dr Ray Dolby

American inventor who, around 1965, came up with noise reduc-tion system for tapes and records which has subsequently made his name a (hi-fi) household word.

Fats Domino

Born Antoine Domino on Feb 26, 1928 in New Orleans, and thus raised in the same environment that produced Little Richard (◆), Professor Longhair and Dr John (◆). His first professional appear-ance was at age of 10; after that he just pounded away at the piano, until in 1949 he was given a regular engagement by band-leader and trumpeter Dave Bar-tholomew – and thus began a professional partnership that sur-vived and flourished through the years, Bartholomew being Domi-no's musical arranger and co-writer.

In 1949 Domino signed to Im-perial Records, his debut single becoming his first million-seller, **The Fat Man.** (Given his re-markably rotund frame, he had only one possible appellation from the beginning.)

Play It Again, Fats.
Courtesy United Artists.

By 1955 he'd made a name for himself, produced some of his finest material and stockpiled a number of hit singles. But then his pounding, up-tempo piano style made him a natural rock 'n' roller (he never had to adapt at all) and Domino established himself with this new audience, both in terms of his concert appearances, and with a panoply of rock classics that were uniquely his own – **Ain't That A Shame, I'm Walkin',** **Blueberry Hill** and **Margie.** He also appeared in two early rock 'n' roll movies – "The Girl Can't Help It", and "Shake, Rattle And Roll".

He earned his last gold disc – his twentieth – in 1960 with **Walkin' To New Orleans,** and the '60s then proved a fallow period. In 1967 Brian Epstein (◆) persuaded

Right: Donovan as flower child. He cut a series of semi-classic singles in the '60s. Unfortunately, he can't get into the '70s.

him to play his first British con-cert, at the Savile Theatre. He subsequently made further U.K. visits, and also found his career re-activated by the rock 'n' roll re-vival boom – he was given small part in "Let The Good Times Roll".

Nevertheless, he is now semi-retired, living in luxury in New Orleans with his wife and eight children, but still playing regular dates in Las Vegas. His inventive-ness has been running low in later '60s and the '70s. His records have often been composed merely of different versions of his stan-dard repertoire; certainly his concert performances have be-come ritualised retreads of the same old songs.

Recordings:
Fats Domino Million Sellers, Vols I, II & III (Liberty)
Rare Dominoes, Vols I & II (Liberty)
Legendary Masters (United Artists)
Fats (Warner Bros)
Play It Again, Fats; The Very Best Of Fats Domino (United Artists)
Live At Montreux – Hello Josephine (Atlantic)

Tom Donahue

American DJ, born 1928, Donahue virtually invented the format of FM rock radio now crucial to the existence of U.S. rock. Working at San Francisco's KSAN station during the mid-'60s, Donahue came up with his new radio concept after listening to the then-emergent Bay Area bands and realising that there was a burgeon-ing audience not catered for by the then-prevailing DJ hierarchy. There are now hundreds of such FM rock stations across the U.S. Donahue died in 1975.

Donovan

Born Glasgow, Scotland, May 10, 1946 as Donovan Leitch. Projected to instant stardom in U.K. early 1965 when he was booked as first-ever resident on British TV's best, but long since defunct, rock programme "Ready Steady Go". The blue denim cap, harmonica stand, sloganised acoustic, and nasal inflection at first drew criticism that Donovan was ersatz Dylan.

Fairy Tale. Courtesy Pye Records.

Same year saw first two self-composed singles, **Catch The Wind** and **Colours,** go into British singles chart, before involve-ment with golden-touch U.K. pop impresario/producer Mickie Most (◆) produced a series of quasi-psychedelic, semi-classic singles **Sunshine Superman, Mellow Yellow** and **There Is A Moun-tain** through 1966-67.

Third album, **Sunshine Super-man** (1967), produced by Most and John Cameron, became some-thing of early acid-head bible. Then came double set, **A Gift From A Flower To A Garden** (1968), with its cover pin-up of guru Maharishi Yogi and flower

power trimmings, which, along with **Sgt Pepper**, summed up that particularly whimsical period of pop "progression". (Both halves of set subsequently re-released as single albums.)

Almost inevitably from that point (although there were further interesting singles – **Jennifer Juniper, Hurdy Gurdy Man, Goo Goo Barabajagal,** the last named a 1969 collaboration with Jeff Beck Group), he slipped from fashion.

Experiments with "Celtic rock" on 1970 **Open Road** set have since been surpassed by likes of Alan Stivell, and his dream visions outdistanced in invention by the Incredible String Band.

In fact, 1970 saw Donovan drop almost completely out of sight when for various reasons, the punitive British tax laws among them, he retired to his home in Ireland for a full year. Having engaged in an (unsuccessful) attempt to switch labels, recordings dried up at this point, although Donovan made the first of his excursions into movie-scoring via soundtrack for "If It's Tuesday It Must Be Belgium" and subsequently "The Pied Piper", released in 1972, in which he also had starring role. (Also scored 1973 "Brother Sun Sister Moon".)

Returned to record scene with 1971 **H.M.S. Donovan** set and to U.S. singles chart with the eco-logically-flavoured **Celia Of The Seals,** though his concert appearances remained sporadic.

There was a further lull in recording until late 1972 **Cosmic Wheels** set, produced by Mickie Most, which was followed in 1973 by **Essence to Essence,** production credit going to Andrew Loog Oldham. Donovan then spent a year working on late 1974 conceptual album **7-Tease,** recorded in Nashville with Norbert Putnam producing, which he followed with an international tour.

Since April 1974, Donovan has based activities in America (though he retains home in Scotland). Has two daughters Astella and Oriole by wife Linda, who also has a son Julian fathered by late Stones guitarist Brian Jones before her marriage to Donovan.

Recordings:
What's Bin Did And What's Bin Hid (Epic/Pye)
Fairy Tale (Epic/Pye)
Sunshine Superman (Epic/Pye)
A Gift From A Flower To A Garden (Epic/Pye)
Mellow Yellow (Epic/—)
Donovan In Concert (Epic/Pye)
Hurdy Gurdy Man (Epic/—)
Barabajagal (Epic/—)
Open Road (Epic/Dawn)
H.M.S. Donovan (Epic/Dawn)
Cosmic Wheels (Epic)
Essence To Essence (Epic)
7-Tease (Epic)
Slow Down World (Epic)
Compilation:
Greatest Hits (Epic/Pye)

The Doobie Brothers

Pat Simmons guitar, vocals
Tom Johnston guitar, keyboards, vocals
Jeff 'Skunk' Baxter guitar, vocals
Tiran Porter bass
John Hartmann percussion
Keith Knudsen drums

Michael McDonald keyboards

Though none of them were related, The Doobie Brothers were originally a trio called Pud formed in California in 1970 and comprising Johnston, Hartmann and bassist Greg Murph, the latter quickly replaced by Dave Shogren. Started out as a hard rock band, toyed for a spell with gospel-oriented material using horns before return to rock roots. Expanded to four-piece with addition of Pat Simmons, a native of San Jose.

Signed to Warner Bros, this line-up appeared on 1971 debut album although Shogren left soon after. Tiran Porter and Mike Hossack (percussion) were enlisted to bring Doobies up to quintet. This use of two guitarists and two percussionists was later to draw comparisons with similarly boogie-oriented Allman Brothers, although Doobies have always professed a closer affinity to San Francisco band Moby Grape. Indeed, the Grape's Skip Spence had been instrumental in bringing original Doobies together.

Above: Jeff 'Skunk' Baxter.

Their second album, the gold-seller **Toulouse Street** (1972) found the band experimenting with horns on certain tracks and moving further in direction of hard rock, results being a high placing on U.S. album lists and a hit single **Listen To The Music.**

1973 set, **The Captain And Me,** repeated the process with gold status and a hit single, **Long Train Running** – and by now the Doobies were a substantial concert attraction in the U.S. Attracting cult attention in U.K., they managed to sell-out two London Rainbow gigs on British debut early 1974 with very little pre-publicity.

Later that year the group's instrumental prowess was boosted by the talents of former Steely Dan (➡) slide guitarist Jeff 'Skunk' Baxter (though many critics interpreted the move as a backward one on Baxter's part). The guitarist had, however, already appeared in session role on earlier Doobies albums.

More personnel changes occurred in the following year: Hossack departed to be replaced by Keith Knudsen, formerly with Lee Michaels (➡), with line-up boosted to six by addition of keyboards player Michael McDonald – like Baxter before him, a recruit from Steely Dan.

Stampede certified as Doobies' third gold album 1975; also yield-

Right: Strange Days. Courtesy Elektra/Asylum. Released in 1968, its design displayed remarkable confidence and inventiveness for the time.

ed U.S. hit single **Take Me In Your Arms.**

Recordings:
The Doobie Brothers (Warner Bros)
Toulouse Street (Warner Bros)
The Captain And Me (Warner Bros)
What Were Once Vices Are Now Habits (Warner Bros)
Stampede (Warner Bros)
Takin' It To The Streets (Warner Bros)

The Doors

Jim Morrison vocals
Ray Manzarek keyboards
Robby Krieger guitar
John Densmore drums

James Douglas Morrison was born Dec 8, 1943 in Melbourne, Florida, the son of a Rear-Admiral, in a family that had a long history of career militarists. (During his early career, Morrison, the arch-rebel, claimed his parents were both dead.)

He graduated from George Washington High School in 1961, spent a year at St Petersburg Junior College in Florida, and then switched to Florida State University. He enrolled in the theatre arts department of UCLA in 1964 and majored in film technique. In 1965 he met Manzarek in Los Angeles, having previously known him at UCLA. They agreed to put a group together.

Manzarek was born Chicago on Feb 12, 1935. He had studied piano from an early age, before becoming interested in R&B music when he was 12. Though he showed considerable talent as a classical pianist, he continued to spend time at the blues clubs in Chicago's south side, and took a degree in economics before moving to UCLA. It was while studying in the film department there that he got acquainted with Morrison. In between times, Manzarek had developed his own blues-oriented group, Rick and the Ravens.

It was Manzarek who discovered Krieger and Densmore (of a band called The Psychedelic Rangers)

Above: Jim Morrison's final resting place.

in a Los Angeles meditation centre. Krieger was born Jan 8, 1946 and Densmore Dec 1, 1945, both in Los Angeles. The Doors were now assembled.

After rehearsing for some time together, the band made their professional debut at the London Fog Club on Sunset Boulevard, and after some hard, discouraging, dues-paying months, were signed to Elektra Records. **The Doors** was released at the beginning of 1967. The band had their original roots and support in the underground, but this debut album blew such considerations sky-high, and made them one of the top U.S. rock bands almost immediately. A breathtaking introduction, it had a very theatrical atmosphere (and included one Bertolt Brecht/Kurt Weill song), and Morrison's songs established straightaway his sex and death motifs that became of fundamental importance in the group's image. **The End** evoked his mystical and eschatological preoccupations, while Krieger's composition **Light My Fire** was a stone-classic song, and an abbreviated version issued as a single went to No. 1 in the U.S. charts.

Arguably the band played too many cards too soon, but they managed to emulate their initial success. **Strange Days** showed them at their most imaginative, if not at their most powerful, and their third album **Waiting For The Sun** (which was the only Doors album, prior to **L.A.**

Woman, on which they used an outside bassist, Doug Lubahn; usually Manzarek played a bass foot-pedal) contained on the inside-sleeve the full libretto of "The Celebration Of The Lizard King", a diffuse narrative poem based on the beliefs of The Shaman and other oriental philosophies, which was given its only musical expression on the album in "Not To Touch The Earth". Plans for presenting "The Celebration" in the theatre didn't reach fruition, but Morrison did make the film "A Feast Of Friends" with two colleagues from UCLA. (He also made two promotional films for **Break On Through** and **The Unknown Soldier,** and by the time of his death had also completed another film screenplay with the novelist Michael McClure.)

Waiting For The Sun also contained another song that became a No. 1 single, **Hello I Love You** (which seemed to be derivative of The Kinks' **All Day And All Of The Night**). Certainly, The Doors now had such a vast following, it was absurd to consider them an underground group. Morrison's extravagant, sensual style of singing, and the pyrotechnics of his every performance were attracting widespread attention. He was obsessed with the notion of rock star as performer, and seemed to live on a permanent stage. He became the Lizard-King himself.

Factoids about him were commonplace. He always seemed to be living on the edge, and it wasn't surprising that once or twice he went over it. He had several skirmishes with the law; he was arrested in New Haven, Connecticut in Dec 1967 for using obscene language and starting a riot, and again in Mar 1969 in Miami for alleged indecent exposure on stage.

Though their album release of 1969, **The Soft Parade,** suffered from a lack of direction and a surfeit of pop content, **Morrison Hotel/Hard Rock Cafe** (1970), a carnival of crude delights, showed the band again in excellent form, with Morrison's writing attaining a new economy. One of the songs, **Queen Of The Highway,** was dedicated to his new wife, Pamela.

Absolutely Live finally contained a version of Morrison's reptilian drama, **The Celebration Of The Lizard.**

L.A. Woman was released in 1971. This was a tour de force, still the most potent kind of rock 'n' roll, combined with lyrics that retained the forcefulness, imagination and bleakness of the band's best work. **The Wasp (Texas Radio And The Big Beat)** was laced with striking images, and **Riders On The Storm** became their most successful latterday song.

Shortly afterwards Morrison, wearied and disillusioned, particularly as a consequence of the Miami charge, announced he was quitting the band to take a lengthy rest, and went to live in Paris. For four years he had over-indulged in alcohol and life, and was in a bad way. The band were trying to persuade him back, but on July 3, 1971 he died of a heart attack in his bath. His widow died of a heroin overdose in May 1974.

Morrison is a quintessential rock figure. Like Eddie Cochran, Jimi Hendrix, Janis Joplin and also James Dean, he was an incorrigible rebel who seemed ineluctably committed to a course of self-destruction. He played every show like Marlon Brando in "On The Waterfront". He had studied Nietzsche and William Blake (from whose writings he had taken the name "The Doors") and was one of the most erudite and widely-read of rock stars; though perhaps not a genius, he was one of the few commanding talents the genre had thrown up. He quite literally lived and died for his Art. His poems were published in 1971 as "The Lords" and "The New Creatures".

L.A. Woman. Courtesy Elektra/Asylum Records.

The three other Doors bravely carried on, and **Other Voices** was a good deal better than anyone had any right to expect. **Full Circle,** however, indicated their inspiration was exhausted, and they went their separate ways. At one point Manzarek wanted to reform The Doors with Iggy Stooge (who dyed his hair black in anticipation of such a move), but nothing came of it. Manzarek himself went on to make a dizzily pretentious solo album, **The Golden Scarab** in 1974, and in May 1975 released his follow-up, entitled **The Whole Thing Started With Rock 'n' Roll, Now It's Out Of Control** (both on Mercury Records).

Krieger and Densmore produced an album called **The Comfortable Chair** by the group of the same name, and then went on to form the Butts Band (◆).

Mike Jahn has written "The Doors: An Unauthorised Biography", and there is a second book, "Jim Morrison: Au Dela De La Doors" by Herve Muller, which has so far been published only in French.

Recordings:
The Doors (Elektra)
Strange Days (Elektra)
Waiting For The Sun (Elektra)
The Soft Parade (Elektra)
Morrison Hotel/Hard Rock Cafe (Elektra)
Absolutely Live (Elektra)
L.A. Woman (Elektra)
Other Voices (Elektra)
Full Circle (Elektra)
Compilations:
13 (Elektra)
Weird Scenes Inside The Gold Mine (Elektra)

Tom Dowd

As a distinguished engineer/producer who raised his technical functions to the level of an art form, Dowd engineered almost everything for Atlantic Records from the time he first worked for them in 1948 until he left the company to go freelance a quarter of a century later.

The exceptional clarity of his work earned him wide respect in the industry in the early '50s, and in the mid-'50s he was one of the first people to work on stereo recordings.

As Atlantic's staff engineer, he worked on all their celebrated sessions, including Otis Redding's live album **Saturday Night At The Apollo,** and all of Aretha Franklin's records, on which he was regularly credited as co-producer with Jerry Wexler, Arif Mardin, and often Aretha herself. (In fact, Atlantic's regular use of all its heavyweight staff on sessions for Aretha, its star performer, often backfired.)

Since Dowd left the staff of Atlantic, his services have been in demand by many top rock acts, and recent assignments have included Eric Clapton's **461 Ocean Boulevard,** Rod Stewart's **Atlantic Crossing** and Wishbone Ash's **Locked In.**

Dr Feelgood

Lee Brilleaux vocals, harmonica
Wilko Johnson guitar, vocals
John Sparks bass
Figure Martin drums

Formed 1971 in Canvey Island, Essex – a small, eyesore oil-refinery community in Thames estuary that might be described as the "arm-pit" of South East England. Indeed, the most unlikely background for a band that set the pace through 1975 as one of the U.K.'s brightest rock hopes.

Down By The Jetty

Down By The Jetty. Courtesy United Artists.

Figure and Johnson played together in first group The Roamers 1964 both as 16-year olds. Wilko went off on own into group The Heap, playing Canvey weddings and working men's clubs for £2 a night, employing his dervish-like Telecaster after the style of his idol, the semi-legendary Mick Green of Johnny Kidd & The Pirates (◆).

The band broke up, however, when the guitarist left Canvey for Newcastle University in 1967. Meanwhile Figure Martin, John Sparks and Lee Brilleaux – whose family had moved to Canvey from Ealing, London, when he was 13 – played in various groups around London.

After Newcastle University and abortive attempt to join band there, Wilko took hippy trail to Nepal, finally returning to a Canvey Island which still remembered his early reputation. It was summer 1971 when he ran into Lee Brilleaux, and Dr Feelgood came into being.

For a time they backed the then faded former '50s U.K. rock star Heinz (ex of Tornadoes) before working again in own right. As such, they quickly established a second-to-none reputation on London and South East England pub/club circuit. In some ways a throwback – they've been compared to early Stones, and mode of dress certainly recalls '60s – Feelgoods base their appeal on a mix of old R&B standards and band originals, working a dynamic stage show out of menacing interplay between vocalist Brilleaux and ace guitarist Johnson.

In 1975, after considerable press acclaim and cult following, Feelgood were signed by United Artists in U.K. and released somewhat disappointing debut **Down By The Jetty,** in mono! – a group obsession of time. In the same year they completed their first major British tour and recorded the much-improved **Malpractice.** Though few doubts remain about "live" ability (except what America will make of them!), there are still some question marks as to whether Feelgoods can pull it off on record. Still based in Canvey.

Recordings:
Down By The Jetty (—/United Artists)
Malpractice (Columbia/United Artists)

Dr Hook & The Medicine Show

Ray Sawyer vocals, guitar
Dennis Locorriere vocals, guitar
Rik Elswit guitar
Billy Francis keyboards
Jance Garfat bass
John Wolters drums

American group, assembled over a gradual period in late '60s around a nucleus of Locorriere and Southerners Sawyer, George Cummings and Francis. Sawyer, an eye-patched, ex-soul singer from Chicksaw, Alabama, and Locorriere, a New Jersey folkie, were vocalist-leaders of the group which played bars and dives around New Jersey area until their "discovery" by "Playboy" cartoonist/songwriter Shel Silverstein.

Silverstein got them gig of appearing in, and performing soundtrack music for, a Dustin Hoffman movie he had scored, "Who Is Harry Kellerman And Why Is He Saying These Terrible Things About Me?"

This led to CBS recording contract for the band, at that time a five-piece. From 1972 debut album came U.S. and U.K. hit single with Silverstein-written **Sylvia's Mother.** The Hook added Garfat and Elswit to fill out their stage sound and record **Sloppy Seconds** (1972), from which Silverstein's **The Cover Of Rolling Stone** single was an American smash.

In fact all the material on the first two albums was Silverstein-composed (among his earlier credits was **A Boy Named Sue** for Johnny Cash), and the group returned the compliment by playing back-up on the songwriter's **Freakin' At The Freakers Ball** solo album (1973).

Belly Up (1973) introduced Dr Hook's own compositions, but follow-up **Fried Face** (not released U.K.) caused friction between band and label resulting in switch to Capitol. Though chart placings have since then been infrequent – 1976 version of Sam Cooke's **Only Sixteen** took them high in U.S. lists – they remain one of the most eccentrically entertaining live outfits in rock.

Founder-member George Cummings (gtr, steel gtr) quit band autumn 1975 suffering nervous problems.

Recordings:
Dr Hook (Columbia/CBS)
Sloppy Seconds (Columbia/CBS)
Belly Up (Columbia/CBS)
Fried Face (Columbia/—)
Bankrupt (Capitol)
A Little Bit More (Capitol)
Compilations:
The Ballad of Lucy Jordan (—/CBS)
The Best of Dr Hook (Columbia/—)

Dr John

Born Malcolm John ("Mac") Rebennack in New Orleans 1941. His mother a professional model, the baby Dr John himself once appeared in soap company ads. A stronger influence was his father, who owned a record store. From an early age, Rebennack grew up listening to likes of Big Bill Broonzy, later playing guitar and piano in school bands.

As a teenager he hung out around New Orleans recording studios, befriending and learning from likes of local legends Professor Longhair, Huey Piano Smith, and Walter Nelson and Roy Montrell of Fats Domino's band.

By 1956, on strength of this unique grounding, Rebennack had graduated as far as backing Longhair, Frankie Ford (of **Sea Cruise** fame), Joe Tex, Leonard James, and in the following year he made his own (though unreleased) instrumental album.

Later in the '50s he worked as a producer/session player with Minit label in New Orleans and ABC in Baton Rouge, and was instrumental in formation of AFO (All For One) black artists cooperative label, signing with same. (Latter is indicative of respect the white "Mac" Rebennack had by then achieved within black New Orleans music community.) AFO also boasted one Prince Lala (since deceased), whose mystical voodoo trappings Rebennack would later re-work for Dr John persona.

The mid-'60s found him working as a sessionman in Los Angeles (for the likes of Phil Spector, Sam Cooke, Sonny & Cher), and, through his growing interest in voodoo, gradually metamorphosing into Dr John The Night Tripper (latter part of name is said to be answer to Beatles' **Day Tripper**).

First-released Dr John album, **Gris Gris** (1968), in fact comprised a number of songs written during pre-Los Angeles period, as did the second set **Babylon** the following year. Both were startlingly original recordings, combining traditional Creole chants and New Orleans influences with trimmings of emergent psychedelia.

Like The Band (◆) before him, Dr John's reputation spread at first largely by word of mouth, his name constantly appearing in interviews with major rock celebrities. Two of these, Mick Jagger and Eric Clapton, later appeared on his 1971 **Sun, Moon And Herbs** album, by which time Dr John was firmly established as cult attraction, appearing onstage in garish beaded robes and feathered head-dress with similarly-attired carnival-type retinue of dancing girls and musicians.

Voodoo-orientation was continued on 1972 **Gumbo** set, though following year's **In The Right Place** marked shift of emphasis towards more conventional rock paths, becoming one of Dr John's biggest sellers. From that album, the stand-out cut **Right Time Wrong Place** made the U.S. singles charts.

First two albums listed below, both not issued until after **Gris Gris**, are difficult to date, though probably the first predates move to Los Angeles while second comprises material recorded around same time as first release. Though there are differences, mainly that the British release contains 12 tracks to America's nine, **Dr John** album is basically the same as the 1975 U.K. release on DJM Records, **Cut Me While I'm Hot**.

Last listed album was one-off 1973 collaboration, on which Dr John and Bloomfield play secondary roles to John Hammond.

Recordings:
Dr John (Springboard/—)
Anytime Anyplace (Barometer/—)
Gris Gris (Atco/Atlantic)
Babylon (Atco/Atlantic)
Remedies (Atco/Atlantic)
Sun, Moon And Herbs (Atco/Atlantic)
Gumbo (Atco/Atlantic)
In The Right Place (Atco/Atlantic)
Desitively Bonnaroo (Atco/Atlantic)
Hollywood Be Thy Name (United Artists)
With John Hammond, Mike Bloomfield:
Triumvirate (Columbia/CBS)

Nick Drake

Born 1948 in Burma while his parents were stationed there, Drake came to England when he was six, and in 1967 took up a place at Fitzwilliam College, Cambridge to study English literature. He devoted more time, however, to writing songs and developing his guitar technique; when he started giving public performances in Cambridge, he was discovered by Ashley Hutchings, who recommended him for Joe Boyd's Witchseason Company. Drake threw over the academic life, and recorded his first album **Five Leaves Left**, a sometimes brilliant, always assured debut with a uniformity of mood that made it comparable to Van Morrison's **Astral Weeks**.

In 1970 his second album **Bryter Later** was recorded with the assistance of Richard Thompson, sundry other Fairports, and Chris McGregor; Drake was beginning to attract attention, and the album was his most commercially successful (even so its sales were merely adequate). After **Pink Moon**, which showed his guitar playing at its most accomplished, Drake became disillusioned and depressed, and sought psychiatric treatment.

In the summer of 1974 he announced he was ready to record again, and laid down – and scrapped – four tracks; he was ever the perfectionist. He tragically died of a drug overdose on Oct 25, 1974.

Recordings:
Five Leaves Left (—/Island)
Bryter Later (—/Island)
Pink Moon (—/Island)

The Drifters

Not so much a group of identifiable personnel, more a name for one of the world's most successful hit-making operations.

The group originally had a gospel sound in 1953 when they first went professional – they were a New York act from Harlem with Clyde McPhatter as lead singer and George Treadwell (husband of Sarah Vaughan at the time) as manager.

After initial American success, McPhatter left to go solo, and in 1955 Johnny Moore joined as lead, but was immediately drafted. The period 1955-58 saw more personnel changes than hit records.

At the end of this time group disbanded, but Treadwell determined to continue using the name, and a group called The Five Crowns (also from Harlem) were selected to become the new Drifters, which made Ben E. King the new lead singer.

One of their first recordings, **There Goes My Baby**, became a huge hit. This was, for the time, innovatory music, using an orchestral section in an unconventional way for a pop/R&B record. The group were by now aimed exclusively at a white teenage market, performing R&B pop songs with a semi-Latin American ambience, which became their trademark. Hits followed one another unfailingly – **Save The Last Dance For Me** being probably the most successful. Their success in fact mirrored the rise to prominence of the Atlantic label, for whom they were recording.

After **Spanish Harlem**, Ben E. King left to go solo, and was replaced by Rudy Lewis, who sang lead on **Sweets For My Sweet**, **On Broadway** and **Up On the Roof**, this being arguably The Drifters' real golden era; most of the songs were written by the hit factory of the Brill Building (◆ Don Kirshner).

When Lewis died in summer 1964, Moore again took over as lead, and **Under The Boardwalk**, recorded the very same day, was tinged with especial sadness. The hits continued unabated though – **At The Club, Saturday Night At The Movies** – but the group, though still performing regularly in cabaret, seemed to get buried in the psychedelic upheaval at the end of the '60s.

By this time the group had been subject to so many personnel changes that many line-ups, such as The Original Drifters, traded on their name and reputation.

Successful re-issues of **At The Club** and **Come On Over To My Place** reactivated their career in Britain in 1972. By now managed by George Treadwell's widow, Fay, and contracted to Bell Records, The Drifters, still indisputably a singles band, began to enjoy a fresh spell of success with a series of records written and produced by British writers Roger Cook and Roger Greenaway, even though the new hits – **Kissin' In The Back Row, Down On The Beach Tonight** – seemed bland and unconvincing remakes of their classics. Certainly, they are now aimed more at an easy-listening market, something which has completed the emasculation process evident over the last decade.

Recent popularity in Britain emphasised by extraordinary success of double-album, **24 Original Hits**, which collected together the best of the Atlantic output, and the best of the Bell material.

In 1975 The Drifters became first black act to perform in South Africa with white back-up musicians and before integrated audiences.

Of current line-up, Johnny Moore, lead singer, has been present off and on since 1955, while the other three, Billy Lewis, Clyde Brown and Jo Blunt joined at various times during 1975.

Discography is selective.

Recordings:
Golden Hits (Atlantic)
The Drifters' Story/20 All-Time Hits (—/Atlantic)
The Drifters Now (Bell)
There Goes My First Love (Bell)
24 Original Hits (—/Atlantic & Bell)

Lesley Duncan

British born, initially a songwriter and unsuccessful pop singer. However, she was far more successful in session field where she sang back-up on numerous U.K. '60s pop hits (Dusty Springfield etc.). Married to producer Jimmy Horowitz, she retired to home and motherhood until Elton John recorded her **Love Song** composition on his **Tumbleweed Connection** album (1970).

On strength of new interest she signed to CBS and recorded her debut album as singer/songwriter, **Sing Children Sing**, in 1971. Her reluctance to tour dissipated appeal engendered by artistically more successful **Earth Mother** album (1972) – at which point she was on brink of discovery as "British Carole King" – and subsequent releases have appeared as only small ripples on the surface of singer/songwriter scene. She toured U.S. in 1976.

Recordings:
Sing Children Sing (Columbia/CBS)
Earth Mother (Columbia/CBS)
Everything Changes (—/GM)
Moonbathing (MCA/GM)

Bob Dylan

Born Robert Allen Zimmerman May 24, 1941 in Duluth, Minnesota, Dylan's family moved to Hibbing when he was six. When he was 12 he started playing guitar and formed several groups in high school before going to Minnesota University in 1959, where he first adopted the surname Dylan, probably in imitation of the poet Dylan Thomas. He dropped out the following year and by 1961 had made his way to New York.

Of the rumours and myths with which Dylan has constantly shrouded his career – indeed, whole life – one thing is not open to doubt: he was determined to make it. He began singing in folk clubs as soon as he arrived in New York in Jan 1961, and regularly visited Woody Guthrie (➧) in hospital. Dylan had a strong desire to emulate the itinerant folk-minstrel, and boasted about his acquaintance with his hero. He also assimilated himself into New York folk circles, getting to know Ramblin' Jack Elliott and Cisco Houston, as well as the younger singers like Dave Van Ronk and Tom Paxton.

He had a personal magnetism, an unpolished but effective singing style, and was good at hustling. He had been there only a couple of months before he began to win wide attention, and in spring 1961 was given second billing to John Lee Hooker at Gerde's Folk City in Greenwich Village.

He was impatient for success, and got an isolated opportunity to play harmonica on a Harry Belafonte album (though he quit the session prematurely and appears on just one track) and performed the same duties on a Carolyn Hester album. A "New York Times" review, written by Robert Shelton, of one of his by now frequent gigs at Gerde's, boosted his early career and John Hammond of Columbia Records – who had just signed Peter Seeger in an attempt to capitalise on the youth market – saw him play and signed him. At this time Albert Grossman (♦) began acting unofficially as Dylan's manager.

Dylan cut his first album late in 1961 and it was released in Mar 1962. **Bob Dylan,** with its traditional blues songs and Dylan's earthily urgent instrumental style, caused a mild tremor, though the record company was not overly impressed. Grossman too insisted that Hammond no longer work with Dylan, and Tom Wilson acted as producer on the next four albums.

Meanwhile a single – **Mixed Up Confusion/Corrina Corrina** – was issued, but it was a strange hybrid of folk and rock, enjoyed no contemporary success and was withdrawn almost immediately. It is now of interest, however, as it anticipated the recordings that Dylan made some years later with an electric backing group.

The Freewheelin' Bob Dylan was the album that established him. It was a total departure from **Bob Dylan,** containing all his own material; the compositions showed that Dylan had discovered the folk-protest movement and dived into it with characteristic commitment. Songs like **A Hard Rain's A-Gonna Fall, Blowin' In The Wind** and **Masters Of War** became classics of the genre, while **Oxford Town** showed his excellence as a commentator on contemporary social/political events.

The Times They Are A-Changin' (with a sleeve picture of Dylan as dust-bowl hero, indicating his infatuation with the image of Guthrie

and his concerts – like that at Newport – were receiving mixed receptions; despite chart successes with both **Subterranean Homesick Blues** (his first U.S. hit) and **Like A Rolling Stone,** his change in style had polarised his audience, and his tour received rough treatment both in America and Britain with outraged folk purists barracking Dylan. A fascinating record of one such appearance can be heard on **Live At The Royal Albert Hall 1966,** one of the most famous of the hundreds of bootleg Dylan albums that became available in the late '60s as the myth grew, and he proved reluctant to release much vital recorded material.

By the time he recorded the epic **Blonde On Blonde** most of the opposition had died down. The album is a milestone in contemporary music. Again, the sustained standard of performance and lyrical invention over a lengthy double album was quite unprecedented. A single taken from it, **Rainy Day Women Nos 12 & 35,** reached No. 2 in the U.S. charts despite a widespread ban by radio stations because of the song's drugs connotations. Another track **Sad-Eyed Lady Of The Lowlands** – which he later declared had been written for his wife Sarah, whom he married in Nassau on Nov 22, 1965 – clocked in at a massive 12 minutes.

A mysterious retirement followed. The official explanation – now generally accepted – is that Dylan had a serious motorcycle accident which almost killed him. There are, however, reasons for doubting the truth of this story (mainly the desultory way in which information filtered through); what can be said is that if Dylan had not had a motorcycle accident it would have been necessary to invent one. The pace at which he was living threatened to kill him anyway, and he was certainly oppressed by fears of dying, since he had to face the fact that he had a following of Messianic proportions (an Australian girl had told him he was like a Christ offering himself for sacrifice). Also, his close friend Richard Farina had been killed in a motorcycle accident a few months previously.

Another Side Of Bob Dylan.
Courtesy CBS Records.

Blonde On Blonde.
Courtesy CBS Records.

Desire. Courtesy
CBS Records.

Above: An early shot of
Zimmerman.

lingered still) featured more mature political statements, particularly about the treatment of Negroes in America **(The Lonesome Death Of Hattie Carroll, Only A Pawn In Their Game)** as well as a powerful anti-war song **(With God On Our Side)** and the title track, which became an all-purpose anthem for youth movements (and later, in 1965, his first hit single in Britain).

A more obviously personal style was apparent in the transitional **Another Side Of Bob Dylan;** it was accordingly greeted by the American Left-wing folk movement with disapproval, but Dylan's central period was well under way and it was too late to stop now. **Bringing It All Back Home** featured a solo Dylan on one side, and, on the other, tracks with him and a small ensemble of musicians. Of the songs, **Mr Tambourine Man** was evidence of his increasing interest in drugs, while others – **Gates Of Eden** and **Subterranean Homesick Blues** – were fully-developed exercises in allusive surrealism for which Dylan became best known.

By now he was already more of an international phenomenon than a recording star. His albums sold in large quantities, his shows were sell-outs. He was a familiar figure in his denim cap and suede jacket, and his semi-beatnik lifestyle and penchant for unpredictable utterances made for good newspaper copy. He was seen as the spokesman of a disillusioned, alienated, but nevertheless articulate generation.

His songs also advanced the careers of less gifted rock stars. Peter, Paul & Mary had an international hit with **Blowin' In The Wind,** and The Byrds inaugurated their own legend with versions of two Dylan songs, **Mr Tambourine Man** and **All I Really Wanna Do.**

Though Joan Baez had helped him enormously in his early career – by introducing him at her concerts, for example – their relationship cooled in 1965 and she walked out on him in a scene recorded in Don Pennebaker's film of the 1965 British tour, "Don't Look Back". The documentary captures vividly Dylan's lifestyle at the time, and the mounting pressures that were surrounding him. At this time he also had a cameo appearance in a BBC-TV Wednesday Play, and also wrote a theme-song **Jack O'Diamonds** for another, titled "The Man Without Papers".

Back in the U.S., Dylan, always at least two steps ahead of his vast audience, caused a furore at the 1965 Newport Folk Festival by appearing backed by the Paul Butterfield Blues Band.

Highway 61 Revisited (the first Dylan album to be produced by Bob Johnston), recorded in New York that same year, was a quite remarkable album with a sustained level of extraordinary creative lyricism, containing what is arguably Dylan's quintessential performance, **Like A Rolling Stone,** and also the tour de force **Desolation Row.**

By now Dylan was touring with The Band (♦), then known as the Hawks,

During his convalescence and/or period of withdrawal Dylan cut the legendary **Basement Tapes** at Big Pink in Woodstock with The Band. Though the tapes, not issued until Dylan re-signed with Columbia in 1975, only helped swell the mythology at the time (who else would record a double album of stunningly inventive material, and then refuse to sanction its commercial release?), the songs began to be circulated freely in Britain and America and cover versions were soon appearing. Peter, Paul & Mary recorded **Too Much Of Nothing,** Brian Auger and Julie Driscoll had a U.K. hit with **This Wheel's On Fire,** and Manfred Mann's **The Mighty Quinn** was a No. 1 in Britain in 1968. (In 1972 Coulson, Dean, McGuinness & Flint recorded **Lo And Behold,** an entire album of unissued Dylan material, much of which was from the Basement Tapes.)

When Dylan finally broke his silence, there was again a surprise awaiting his public. His voice had lost its gritty huskiness and mellowed; his songs were of austere understatement, many permeated with religious imagery. The album, **John Wesley Harding,** introduced songs such as **All Along The Watchtower,** which Hendrix later rendered in his own inimitable fashion. Hindsight shows the album to be one of Dylan's best – though the sequel **Nashville Skyline,** on which Dylan retreated into homely sentimentality, duetting with Johnny Cash on one track, was over-estimated at the time.

It almost seemed as though Dylan was determined to smash the myth; to do it he had to issue the teasingly-titled **Self Portrait,** a diary-like record of Dylan's musical roots containing much country material and his interpretations of contemporary songs by Paul Simon and Gordon Lightfoot. It was released to universally bad reviews and possibly Dylan himself felt he'd gone over the edge, for his next album was issued with some haste. **New Morning** was hailed as such at the time, but, though it was funkier and more positive than Dylan's recent work had been, it was fatally flawed and showed him to be obviously lacking in inspiration.

In 1969 Dylan had appeared at the British Isle of Wight Festival before a crowd of over 250,000 – his first major public engagement since his accident. But after **New Morning** Dylan again became reclusive and took care of his family life – as **Sign On The Window,** from **New Morning,** had predicted. He made two singles – the vacuous **Watching The River Flow** with in-demand producer Leon Russell, and **George Jackson** which marked a return to overt political sentiments.

Though relatively inactive, there were occasional signs that he was keen to return to work. He accepted George Harrison's invitation to play at the Concert for Bangla Desh, and also recorded five new tracks for the compilation, **More Greatest Hits.** In 1972 he appeared on the title-track of Steve Goodman's **Somebody Else's Troubles,** and also made selected appearances with John Prine. In 1973 he worked on Doug Sahm sessions for **Wallflower** and **Doug Sahm And Band.**

Surprisingly he agreed to play a supporting role as a character called Alias (it was a part he seemed to have written for himself) in Sam Peckinpah's movie "Pat Garrett And Billy The Kid", starring Kris Kristofferson. Dylan wrote a score and the title-theme **Knockin' On Heaven's Door** became one of his largest latterday hits.

His Columbia contract expired in 1973, and he signed with David Geffen's fast-rising Asylum label, and also agreed to do a comeback tour with The Band which took place, amid great publicity, in Jan-Feb 1974. (The tour is extensively chronicled in the "Rolling Stone" book, "Knockin' On Dylan's Door").

Though his much-heralded comeback album, **Planet Waves,** was hardly the real McCoy, his double live-album of the tour, **Before The Flood,** finally showed Dylan again at his magnetic and exuberant best.

After co-producing an album for Barry Goldberg on Atco that summer, Dylan announced that he was returning to Columbia. Though his ability to produce more-than-adequate new material was by now open to question, his next album, **Blood On The Tracks** (1975), triumphantly reasserted his genius; an album obviously borne out of pain – he had just separated from his wife – it reminded everyone that no one could be as compelling as Dylan. No one at all.

He celebrated his return to public esteem by sanctioning, finally, the celebrated **Basement Tapes** and then again toured the U.S. – this time on a more informal basis with a show called the Rolling Thunder Revue, which utilized the services of many leading rock performers, including Joan Baez, Roger McGuinn, Ronee Blakley, Mick Ronson and Joni Mitchell. The tour was an unqualified success.

At the beginning of 1976 Dylan, who now seemed to be working as enthusiastically and prolifically as he had 10 years earlier, produced another new album **Desire** (for which he employed Emmylou Harris as second lead vocalist) which emphasised his re-emergence by simultaneously topping the album charts in Britain and the U.S. The single taken from it, **Hurricane,** about the wrongful imprisonment of boxer Hurricane Carter, showed that Dylan's political sensibilities were as sharp as ever.

Bob Dylan's importance to the development of rock is rivalled only by that of The Beatles. His influence went much further than the innovative qualities of his lyrics, his semi-visionary songs effecting a change in the consciousness of an entire generation, and opening up a general awareness of attitudes, both personal and political, that, without him, might still be stifled and denied today.

There is a growing pile of literature about Dylan. Anthony Scaduto's "Bob Dylan" is an informative biography that is particularly illuminating about the early days in Greenwich Village; "Bob Dylan: A Retrospective", edited by Craig McGregor, collects together many of the most famous articles about Dylan, including Nat Hentoff's justly celebrated and quite electric "Playboy" interview. Dylan's own stream-of-consciousness novel, "Tarantula", which he never completed to his satisfaction, was published by Macmillan in 1970.

Recordings:
Bob Dylan (Columbia/CBS)
The Freewheelin' Bob Dylan (Columbia/CBS)
The Times They Are A-Changin' (Columbia/CBS)
Another Side Of Bob Dylan (Columbia/CBS)
Bringing It All Back Home (Columbia/CBS)
Highway 61 Revisited (Columbia/CBS)
Blonde On Blonde (Columbia/CBS)
John Wesley Harding (Columbia/CBS)
Nashville Skyline (Columbia/CBS)
Self Portrait (Columbia/CBS)
New Morning (Columbia/CBS)
Pat Garrett And Billy The Kid (Soundtrack) (Columbia/CBS)
Dylan (Columbia/CBS)
Planet Waves (Asylum/Island)
Before The Flood (Asylum/Island)
Blood On The Tracks (Columbia/CBS)
The Basement Tapes (Columbia/CBS)
Desire (Columbia/CBS)
Compilations:
Greatest Hits (Columbia/CBS)
More Bob Dylan Greatest Hits (Columbia/CBS)

The Eagles

Glenn Frey guitar, piano, vocals
Randy Meisner bass, vocals
Don Henley drums, vocals
Don Felder guitar, vocals
Joe Walsh guitar, vocals

Through the period 1972-76 The Eagles graduated to a position as one of America's most successful albums and singles bands, having taken up the all-pervasive West Coast country-rock mantle pioneered by the likes of The Byrds, Poco and Flying Burritos. In fact, two of the original Eagles had roots in the last-named bands.

Meisner (b. Nebraska Mar 8, 1947) was previously in Poco (♦) and Rick Nelson's Stone Canyon Band (♦) – he also played on James Taylor's **Sweet Baby James** album – while the since-departed Bernie Leadon (b. Minneapolis, Minnesota July 19, 1947) sang and played guitar with the Flying Burrito Bros (♦) and Dillard & Clark Expedition (♦ Dillards), also completing a stint in Linda Ronstadt's backing band.

Of the other founder-members, Glenn Frey (b. Detroit Nov 6, 1948) had backed Bo Diddley and also Linda Ronstadt and, with John David Souther, had been half of the duo Longbranch Pennywhistle; Don Henley (b. Texas July, 1947) was with the band Shiloh alongside guitarist Al Perkins.

Frey and Henley first met up in Los Angeles where they assembled the original Eagles with Leadon and Meisner. The new group travelled to England to record their debut album (1972) with British producer Glyn Johns at London's Olympic Studios. The resulting collection went into the U.S. bestseller lists, and the group really made up with the stand-out cut **Take It Easy,** co-written by Frey and Asylum label stablemate Jackson Browne, which became a massive American hit in the same year.

Their second album **Desperado** (1973) was again recorded with Johns at Olympic, and it was on the subsequent American tour that The Eagles first drew considerable acclaim as a stage band. **On The Border,** part recorded in England with Johns, the rest in Hollywood with Bill Szymcyzk, provided another bestselling album and a No. 1 U.S. single, **The Best Of My Love.**

Above: Bernie Leadon, who quit band in early '76.

Guitarist Don Felder, from Florida, augmented the line-up as fifth Eagle after adding slide guitar on sessions for the **Border** album. His previous credits included playing with David Blue (♦).

Having built a steady cult following, The Eagles broke into the British market in mid-1975 with the singles **Lyin' Eyes** and **One Of These Nights,** also making the albums list on both sides of the Atlantic with the 1975 **Nights** collection (produced again by Szymcyzk). This album, however, appeared to presage a more avidly commercial approach to their music, and marginally reduced their early press support among certain critics.

Also in 1975, the band's U.K. reputation was boosted by their appearance with Elton John and the Beach Boys on the former's midsummer open-air bash at London's vast Wembley soccer stadium.

In early 1976, however, The Eagles were rocked by the departure after disagreements of founder-member/composer Bernie Leadon (♦), who shares the same management and has a substantial reputation as an artist in his own right, was announced as replacement. However, it seems likely that his stay will be only a temporary one.

Recordings:
Eagles (Asylum)
Desperado (Asylum)
On The Border (Asylum)
One Of These Nights (Asylum)
Compilations:
Their Greatest Hits (Asylum)

Earth, Wind & Fire

Maurice White vocals, kalimba, drums
Verdine White vocals, bass percussion
Philip Bailey vocals, congas, percussion
Larry Dunn piano, organ, moog
Al McKay guitars, percussion
Ralph Johnson drums, percussion
Johnny Graham guitars
Andrew Woolfolk flute, tenor and soprano saxophone
Fred White drums, percussion

Earth, Wind and Fire are a cooperative musical ensemble, formed in Chicago in 1971 by Maurice White. After two early albums, they moved to Columbia Records, and they have since become one of America's top-selling bands.

All of their Columbia albums have gone gold; their third and fourth, **Open Your Eyes** and **That's The Way Of The World,** were recorded at James Guercio's Caribou studios, and the latter was the soundtrack of the film of the same name, in which Earth, Wind & Fire starred, unsurprisingly, as a rock 'n' soul band.

With their shifting rhythms and superb dynamics, allied to their joyous and positive philosophy of universal happiness and spiritual brotherhood, they are an exuberant band whose purpose has usually been better conveyed by their live performance, for they have a shrewd grasp of theatre, and use their own sound and light crew, dress very visually and employ arresting devices like a drummer on a revolving, levitated rostrum. The live double-album **Gratitude** was the first one on which they successfully captured the exuberance of their live performance.

Recordings:
Last Days And Time (Columbia/CBS)
Head To The Sky (Columbia/CBS)
Open Our Eyes (Columbia/CBS)
That's The Way Of The World (Columbia/CBS)
Gratitude (Columbia/CBS)

Edgar Broughton Band

Edgar Broughton guitar, vocals
Steve Broughton drums
Arthur Grant bass, vocals

Along with original member Victor Unitt (gtr, vcls), all are from Warwick, England, where they started performing together at school. In a sense, the Broughton brothers, (Robert) Edgar and Steve, were black sheep freaks of a black sheep family. Up until 1970 the band was managed by Ma Broughton herself.

Having built loyal local following, they moved to London in 1968 where they signed to Harvest Records for first album, **Wasa Wasa,** released the same year. Playing British underground circuit, Broughtons remained true to ideals of the new social/musical liberation while contemporaries went on to superstar status. Their speciality was free concerts, the Broughtons sometimes footing the bills themselves. On one notable occasion, when thwarted by Warwick Council from playing in local park, they played instead free from the back of moving lorry.

As one of few groups openly committed politically, their material has always included satirical and political comment on issues such as Vietnam War (viz. **American Boy Soldier**), while their anthem **Out Demons Out,** borrowed from Fugs, remained in the repertoire for a lengthy period.

Live music has always been their forte, and records have at times been disappointing. Aforementioned early founder, Victor Unitt, rejoined group at a time when they were beginning to explore new musical territories, e.g. acoustic. 1973 album **Oora** includes effects humour reminiscent of Bonzo Dog Band.

After **Oora,** Unitt left band again and Broughtons switched record labels to WWA where they encountered acute managerial hassles resulting in court action. Main point of contention was album **Bandages,** tapes of which Broughton Band claimed were illegally witheld from them by record company – along with their equipment.

Broughtons survived bitter, and sometimes ugly, squabble but neither **Bandages** nor any other new recordings were forthcoming for three years. However, they continued to slog the British club circuit with remarkable tenacity and perseverance.

Last listed album comprises collection of singles tracks, released 1975; and in spring 1976 **Bandages** finally made its appearance on market.

Recordings:
Wasa Wasa (Harvest)
Sing Brothers Sing (Harvest)
The Edgar Broughton Band (Capitol/Harvest)
Inside Out (Harvest)
Oora (Harvest)
Bandages (NEMS)
Compilations:
A Bunch of 45s (Harvest)

Dave Edmunds

Born Cardiff, Wales, April 15, 1944, first came to public notice in 1967 as guitarist on British group Love Sculpture's rock version of Khatchaturian's **Sabre Dance,** which made No. 1 in British singles lists. (Recordings of time are contained on 1974 **Dave Edmunds And Love Sculpture – The Classic Tracks 1968/72,** U.K. only, on One Stop label).

After a six-week American tour, the band split and Edmunds returned to Cardiff, his home town, where he decided to work solo. He spent the next couple of years working at his own Rockfield Studios in Monmouthshire, Wales, mastering recording techniques.

In 1970 Edmunds released a solo single, his remake of the old Smiley Lewis blues number **I Hear You Knocking,** which was a British No. 1 selling in excess of three million copies. His first solo album **Rockpile** (1972) featured Andy Fairweather Low (◆) and

John Williams, ex-Love Sculpture.

Since then Edmunds has released infrequent singles, remarkable re-creations of Spector sound of early '60s playing virtually all instruments himself, to varying degrees of success, while also producing at Rockfield for acts including Brinsley Schwarz and Flamin' Groovies. 1975 **Subtle As A Flying Mallet** second solo album was released on his own Rockfield label (RCA in U.S.).

Edmunds also appeared in David Essex movie "Stardust", writing several songs for soundtrack of same. In 1976 he signed to Led Zeppelin's Swan Song label.

Recordings:
Rockpile (MAM-London/ Regal Zonophone)
Subtle As A Flying Mallet (RCA/Rockfield)

Electric Flag

Mike Bloomfield guitar
Nick Gravenites vocals
Buddy Miles drums
Barry Goldberg organ
Harvey Brooks bass
Peter Strazza tenor saxophone
Marcus Doubleday trumpet
Herbie Rich guitar

Formed 1967 with above personnel by Mike Bloomfield (◆) after his departure from Butterfield Blues Band. Goldberg had previously played with Steve Miller (◆), Miles had done sessions with Otis Redding and Wilson Pickett, and Doubleday with Dylan, Al Kooper and The Doors.

Electric Flag made their debut at the famous 1967 Monterey Festival, and had a short but illustrious career, mainly because of the standards of instrumental virtuosity the eight musicians set themselves. Bloomfield's use of a brass section was also a pointer to the future, and the device played an important part in formation of bands like Blood, Sweat & Tears.

After just two albums **A Long Time Comin'** and **An American Music Band,** and work on the

soundtrack of the Peter Fonda – Roger Corman movie "The Trip", the band split up, having worked together no more than 18 months; with its composition of eight highly skilled individuals, they just fell apart under internal stresses.

Buddy Miles (◆) went on to form the Buddy Miles Express, and Brooks to play with the Fabulous Rhinestones. Goldberg made several solo albums, including one co-produced by Jerry Wexler and Bob Dylan, and also wrote **I've Got To Use My Imagination** with Gerry Goffin – which became a U.S. No. 1 for Gladys Knight and the Pips.

In 1974 the nucleus of the Electric Flag (Bloomfield, Gravenites, Goldberg and Miles) reformed, with Roger Troy replacing Harvey Brooks on bass. The reunion, like so many others, didn't really work out, because the magic had long since gone. Bloomfield and Goldberg have since moved on to the newest supergroup of them all, KGB (◆).

Recordings:
A Long Time Comin' (Columbia/CBS)
An American Music Band (Columbia/CBS)
The Band Kept Playing (Atco/Atlantic)
Compilations:
The Best Of The Electric Flag (Columbia/CBS)

Elephant's Memory
◆ John Lennon

Yvonne Elliman

Hawaii-born, arrived penniless in England, circa 1969, where her first musical experience was busking in London streets. Graduated to club dates, as singer/guitarist, where she was "discovered" by Tim Rice who, with Andrew

Lloyd Webber, wrote the smash hit "Jesus Christ Superstar" musical. Rice cast her as Mary Magdelene in London and Broadway productions of show, but she meant little to rock audience until her association with Eric Clapton.

That came about when Ms Elliman, who had married RSO Records president Bill Oakes, was hanging out at the same Miami, Florida, studios where the guitar star went to record his **461 Ocean Boulevard** album. Yvonne sang on the sessions, and later joined Clapton's band on a permanent basis (◆ Eric Clapton).

She recorded her first two solo albums before joining Clapton band.

Recordings:
I Don't Know How To Love Him (Polydor)
Food Of Love (Purple Records)
Rising Sun (RSO)

Electric Light Orchestra

Jeff Lynne guitar, vocals
Bev Bevan drums
Richard Tandy keyboards
Mik Kaminski violin
Hugh McDowell cello
Melvyn Gale cello
Kelly Groucutt bass

Jeff Lynne (born Birmingham, England, Dec 30, 1947) originally played in local band called The Nightriders, which became the highly-touted semi-underground band, the Idle Race. He was invited to join The Move (◆) on two occasions, and accepted the second time in 1971, by which the band solely comprised Roy Wood and Bev Bevan; Lynne joined because of the possibilities of ELO, then in its planning stages, though while with The Move he wrote **Do Ya** (the B side of **California Man**) which became his bestselling U.S. single, and hence an indication to things to come.

The Electric Light Orchestra was originally conceived by Wood as a parallel outfit to The Move which would take up the baton of orchestral rock music from where The Beatles had left it with **Strawberry Fields Forever** and **I Am The Walrus.** Due to The Move's contractual obligations, however, by the time he could devote time to ELO, he had already begun to lose interest in the project; **Electric Light Orchestra** issued in 1971, had been recorded over a very lengthy period; an experimental album on the experimental Harvest label, it nevertheless had some commercial success, and produced the U.K. hit single, **10538 Overture.** In 1972, however Roy Wood (◆) left to form Wizzard taking Rick Price and Hugh McDowell with him, and that looked like the end of ELO, but Lynne and Bevan built it up from there, assembling a group composed of a strange collection of musicians with a background in either rock or classical music, though rarely both. Three of the nine-man line-up who played on **ELO II** were former members of the London Symphony Orchestra.

Left: Dave Edmunds. In summer '76 the Welsh hermit signed a new contract with Swan Song.

ELO II was issued in Feb 1973 to largely indifferent reviews, but once again the album contained a hit single, this time an ambitiously orchestrated reworking of Chuck Berry's **Roll Over Beethoven.**

In the summer of 1973 the band made their first U.S. tour and by the time the third album was released later in the year, their line-up, after considerable teething troubles, was becoming stabilised, Kaminski having by then joined, and McDowell returning to the fold from Wizzard. **On The Third Day** again produced a hit single, **Showdown,** which could have been passed off as a black American soul production, and was the first real hint of the creative potential and versatility

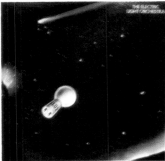

ELO 2. Courtesy EMI/Harvest.

within the band.

With regular tours (six in just under three years) and a succession of hit singles, they have built up a strong following in the States. **Eldorado** (1974) went gold, a feat that its successor, **Face The Music** (1975) easily emulated. In Britain, however, their following has been based largely around hit singles, such as **Ma-Ma-Ma Belle** and **Evil Woman,** and their blend of rock music and the classics has yet to break through to a large audience.

Ironically, however, ELO are at least fulfilling Wood's original hopes for the band – they have become a highly versatile and thoroughly imaginative unit, and, most importantly, able to function on stage equally as effectively as in the studio.

Recordings:
The Electric Light Orchestra (United Artists/Harvest)
ELO II (United Artists/Harvest)
On The Third Day (United Artists/Harvest)
Eldorado (United Artists/Warner Bros)
Face The Music (United Artists/Jet)
Compilation:
Showdown (—/Harvest)
Ole ELO! (United Artists/—)

Cass Elliott
◆ The Mamas And Papas

Emerson, Lake And Palmer

Keith Emerson keyboards
Greg Lake bass, guitar, vocals
Carl Palmer drums

Foremost architects of British

"techno-rock" school. Formed late 1969 after chance meeting in San Francisco between Emerson, then with Nice (◆), and Lake, at that time bassist-vocalist with King Crimson (◆).

An early plan to link up with Jimi Hendrix and Mitch Mitchell proved abortive (in fact Emerson, Lake aborted it themselves when a "wigged-out" Mitchell came to see them with two bodyguards) and Carl Palmer, ex of Atomic Rooster, completed the trio. As such, they made debut at Isle of Wight Festival 1970.

Emerson had already established unique reputation as organist supreme, coupling natural ability with daring acrobatics involving flung daggers, organ-vaulting, Hammond-raping and general musical sadism towards his equipment – all of which made him the most spectacular rock showman since Hendrix.

Lake, from Bournemouth, a sedate South England coastal resort, had cut his vocal teeth with Crimson, while Palmer had played with Chris Farlowe's Thunderbirds at the age of 16, subsequently joining Crazy World Of Arthur Brown (◆) and Atomic Rooster (◆).

All were beginning to stagnate in previous roles and the new partnership gelled immediately into a unique and dynamic trio, firmly dedicated to musical finesse and showmanship. From beginning, they established a reputation as furiously active trio of unsurpassed technical ability – though some critics felt their music as

Above: Keith Emerson, formerly of Nice.

evidenced on debut 1970 album didn't compensate for a certain lack of feeling exacerbated on successive collections.

Their first album met with immediate success in U.S. and U.K., as did 1971 gold seller **Tarkus. Pictures At An Exhibition** (also 1971) was a live album based on long-standing stage version of the Moussorgsky classical composition.

There were signs that a change of style was necessary, however, when the 1972 set **Trilogy** failed to equal success of predecessors (though, like **Pictures,** it did eventually go gold in U.S.). Experiments with effects machinery, including trial of a fully-portable stage, failed to lift group out of musical rut which – with hindsight – was inevitable from beginnings of band. The trio inaugurated their own label for release of the 1973 collection **Brain Salad Surgery** which kept ELP at top of bestseller lists but did little to dissipate critical theory that band had evolved into ego-inflated dinosaur. 1974 **Welcome Back My Friends To The Show**

That Never Ends was live-set. All three had been virtuoso-winners of various poll awards since time of inception, though by late 1975 there were signs that their popularity was beginning to ebb (at least on home-front). The trio began to work on solo projects, first of which was Lake's out-of-character Christmas 1975 U.K. hit single, **I Believe In Father Christmas.**

For earlier details of Keith Emerson (◆) Nice.

Recordings:
Emerson Lake And Palmer (Cotillion/Island)
Tarkus (Cotillion/Island)
Pictures At An Exhibition (Cotillion/Island)
Trilogy (Cotillion/Island)
Brain Salad Surgery (Manticore)
Welcome Back My Friends To The Show That Never Ends (Manticore)

Eno

A founder-member of Roxy Music (◆) along with Bryan Ferry, with whom he clashed during recording of the group's **For Your Pleasure** second album, Brian Eno quit for solo career in summer 1973. An early focal point of Roxy – one of reasons for ego conflicts with Ferry – Eno was band's synthesiser player, although he has always described himself as a "non-musician".

First post-Roxy project was the **No Pussyfootin'** collaboration with King Crimson's Robert Fripp, which was an avant-garde experimentation influenced by the work of Terry Riley. Eno's first real solo album, **Here Come The Warm Jets,** later in 1974, fell well short artistically and commercially of what many critics had regarded as an interesting potential new force in rock. (In June 1974 he played London Rainbow with John Cale, Nico, Kevin Ayers – an event recorded on **June 1, 1974.**)

Early 1975 **Taking Tiger Mountain By Strategy** fared little better with critics and public alike, and the same year's **Another Green World** only marginally improved that status. In retrospect, however, last two mentioned albums were arguably unfairly dismissed – probably a result of disappointment engendered.

No Pussyfooting. Courtesy E.G. Management.

dered by **Jets** set.

Diversifying in other fields in 1975, he guested on **Diamond Head** solo album by Roxy guitarist Phil Manzanera, worked on John Cale's **Slow Dazzle** and **Helen Of Troy** sets (also playing with Cale in concert), played on Robert Wyatt's **Ruth Is Stranger**

Than Richard album and produced own Oblique Strategies box-set of writings.

Also produced **Lucky Lief And The Longships** album for Bob Calvert, completed lecture tour of English universities, and recorded **Evening Star,** second album with Robert Fripp (released Jan 1976), following with European tour with same.

At end of year started work on building own studio with Robert Wyatt and Phil Manzanera, and launched own Obscure Records label (distributed through Island), on which was released his Nov 1975 set **Discreet Music.**

Recordings:
Here Come The Warm Jets (Island)
Taking Tiger Mountain By Strategy (Island)
Another Green World (Island)
Discreet Music (Island/Obscure)
With Robert Fripp:
No Pussyfootin' (Island/Help)
Evening Star (Island/Help)
With John Cale, Nico, Kevin Ayers:
June 1, 1974 (Island)

John Entwistle

Nicknamed The Ox, Entwistle might be the most taciturn member of The Who (◆), but he is also the most industrious in individual projects, and has been the only one to take a band of his own on the road.

Though his own compositions (**Boris The Spider, My Wife, Heaven And Hell,** etc.) were infrequently recorded by The Who, he never tried to assume a more prominent role, and in the main reserved his own ideas for solo albums. The first of these, **Smash Your Head Against The Wall** (a title that was a relic of The Who's days of ultra-violence) attracted reviews that were largely unencouraging, but he was undaunted, and his sequel, **Wistle Rhymes** was better received. In 1973 his album **Rigor Mortis Sets In** – for which he had assembled his own studio band, Rigor Mortis – was a vehicle for some straightforward, lusty rock 'n' roll.

In 1974 Entwistle patiently sifted the detritus of The Who's recording career to put together an album, **Odds 'n' Sods,** at a time when none of the other three could muster the necessary interest in the project. It turned out to be a rather fine album.

Then in 1975 he assembled his own band, which he called John Entwistle's Ox, which made one album, **Mad Dog,** and a tour of Britain and America which Entwistle financed out of his own pocket. The band featured highly-touted young axeman Robert A. Johnson.

Recordings:
Smash Your Head Against The Wall (MCA/Track)
Wistle Rhymes (MCA/Track)
Rigor Mortis Sets In (MCA/Track)
Mad Dog (MCA/Decca)

Brian Epstein

Born Sept 19, 1934; while managing one of his father's record shops in Liverpool in Nov 1961 was asked by customer for **My Bonnie,** an early German Beatles recording. He discovered group was a local one and, intrigued, went to hear them play at Cavern Club. Became their manager, changed their leather jackets for smart suits and worked diligently to get them more gigs and a recording contract. The rest really is history (→ The Beatles).

Although this was his first experience as a pop manager, he subsequently began to handle other local acts from Liverpool, among them Cilla Black, Gerry & The Pacemakers and Billy J. Kramer, all of whom he guided to international success.

As his role as Beatles' manager became apparently redundant, so he began to diversify his interests – e.g. buying the Savile Theatre in London to promote rock concerts there.

On Aug 27, 1967, while The Beatles were in Bangor, Wales, with the Maharishi, Epstein died in London from accidental overdose of drugs. Four years later John Lennon said: "The Beatles broke up after Brian died. We'd never have made it without him, and vice versa."

David Essex

Born East End of London July 23, 1947, Essex, unsuccessfully attempted a singing career before landing the lead acting part in the London stage production of "Godspell" musical 1971, following that with central role of Jim McLaine in immensely-successful "That'll Be The Day" movie.

The McLaine character was clearly earmarked as a future rock star and, on the strength of the film's success, Essex attempted a re-launch of his singing career – with remarkable results. His million-selling **Rock On** single almost made top of U.S. and U.K. charts, followed into U.K. lists by **Lamplight** and **America.** But it was not until he played McLaine again – by now, the script called for superstar status – in the sequel movie "Stardust", that Essex's career began to assume gigantic proportions in teenybopper field.

Toured U.K. Nov 1974 to hysterical response, achieving his first British No. 1 with **Gonna Make You A Star,** and shrugging aside rock press criticism that his mannered performances and often plagiaristic material (of Dr John) evidenced a "contrived" product. Most of this criticism derives from Essex's inability, either on stage or on record, to eschew his acting background – he always appears to be acting the part of a rock star rather than performing with spontaneity.

His uneasy relationship with British rock press has probably not been helped by his long-time manager Derek Bowman, a one-time Fleet Street show business journalist, who has achieved a certain notoriety for his zealous guardianship of the Essex image. Bowman and Essex have hotly denied any "manufacturing" on their part, while both were at one point striving hard to play down the star's teenybopper appeal and instead caught the attentions of the rock audience.

Against that background, the release of Essex's 1975 single, the unashamedly teen-oriented **Hold**

Right: Don and Phil of the bionic harmonies. Their unique sound remains one of the most enduring in rock.

Me Close, couldn't fail but to bewilder press pundits. It gave Essex his second British No. 1, and anchored him even further in the hearts of U.K. boppers.

Quite where he wants his career to go next is anybody's guess, though the gold records will probably continue to pile up.

Recordings:
Rock On (Columbia/CBS)
David Essex (Columbia/CBS)
All The Fun Of The Fair (Columbia/CBS)
In Concert (Columbia/CBS)

Everly Brothers

Country rock harmony duo, one of most important acts in the evolution of rock music.

Don Everly, b. Feb 1, 1937, Phil Everly, b. Jan 19, 1938, both in Brownie Kentucky. Parents Ike & Margaret Everly were well-known country singers, and it was inevitable their sons should appear in shows with them from an early age, touring the South as well as

The Golden Hits Of The Everly Brothers. Courtesy Warner Bros.

appearing on local radio shows.

Signed with Columbia Records 1956, and cut one unsuccessful single; then signed management deal with Wesley Rose in Nashville and joined Cadence Records.

With Cadence, they turned into rockers – their fine harmonies were given rich acoustic guitar accompaniment and a pronounced beat. Chet Atkins (→) produced many of their records, and the success formula was completed by the composing talents of Boudleaux and Felice Bryant (a husband-and-wife partnership), who wrote nearly all of Everlys' early material.

Bye Bye Love and **Wake Up Little Susie** were recorded 1957, and both were million-sellers. Brothers rapidly became nationally famous and gave regular TV appearances. Ike and Margaret could afford to step aside.

While Don and Phil visited U.K. for the first time in 1958, their sequence of hit records continued unabated – **All I Have To Do Is Dream** (their first single to make No. 1 in America and Britain), **Bird Dog** and **Problems.** In 1960 they left Cadence for a lucrative deal with Warner Bros.

Right: The bionic duo, Don and Phil – Phil and Don? Who's to tell with those haircuts? – go on parade in the Marines.

Though their popularity was not immediately affected, the new deal put them ultimately at a disadvantage as they lost the services of the Nashville production team and, more importantly, the Bryants. This was hardly apparent initially – the self-composed **Cathy's Clown** was a No. 1 on both sides of the Atlantic, as was **Ebony Eyes** in the U.S., and its B side **Walk Right Back,** in Britain. Nevertheless, they did a stint in the Marines, and their career began to lose momentum.

On tour of England 1963 Don had nervous breakdown and Phil performed alone; but it was a real turning point. From then on they were hindered by misfortune and personal disagreement, and despite a further No. 1 in U.K. 1965, **The Price Of Love,** they never regained earlier status.

In late '60s made partial come-back with **Roots,** an album produced by Lenny Waronker, but even that didn't do as well as it deserved. Signed with RCA in early '70s with intentions to make records both together and separately, but the quarrels persisted and on July 14, 1973 they told the world that they were playing their last concert together – time will tell if that was indeed the case.

Despite their fall from grace, they remained consistently popular in U.K. and toured to full houses in both 1971 and 1972. In 1976 **Walk Right Back With The Everly Brothers,** a compilation of Warner Bros material, put them back in the U.K. charts.

Their unique sound will remain one of the most enduring in rock music, as well as one of the most influential. The Beatles, Dylan, The Byrds, Mamas And Papas,

Lovin' Spoonful, Simon & Garfunkel and many other important '60s acts all acknowledged their debt to the Everly Brothers.

Recordings:
The Everly Brothers (Cadence/London)
Songs Our Daddy Taught Us (Cadence/London)
Fabulous Style Of The Everly Brothers (Cadence/London)
It's Everly Time (Warner Bros)
Date With The Everly Brothers (Warner Bros)
Both Sides Of An Evening (Warner Bros)
Instant Party (Warner Bros)
Everly Brothers Sing Great Country Hits (Warner Bros)
Gone Gone Gone (Warner Bros)
Two Yanks In England (Warner Bros)
Rock 'n' Soul (Warner Bros)
Beat 'n' Soul (Warner Bros)
In Our Image (Warner Bros)
Hit Sounds Of The Everly Brothers (Warner Bros)
Everly Brothers Sing (Warner Bros)
Roots (Warner Bros)
The Everly Brothers Show (Warner Bros)
Stories We Could Tell (RCA)
Pass The Chicken And Listen (RCA)
Compilations:
The Very Best Of The Everly Brothers (Warner Bros)
Golden Hits Of The Everly Brothers (Warner Bros)
Everly Brothers Original Greatest Hits (Barnaby/CBS)
End Of An Era (Barnaby/CBS)
Don & Phil's Fabulous '50s Treasury (—/Janus)
Walk Right Back With The Everly Brothers (—/Warner Bros)
Songs Our Daddy Taught Us (—/Philips Int.)
(a reissue of album on Cadence, plus four extra tracks)
Don Everly solo:
Don Everly (Ode)
Sunset Towers (Ode)
Phil Everly solo:
Star-Spangled Springer (RCA)
There's Nothing Too Good For My Baby (Pye)
Mystic Line (Pye)
Phil's Diner (Pye)

The Faces

Rod Stewart vocals
Ron Wood guitar
Kenny Jones drums
Ian MacLagan keyboards
Ronnie Lane bass

When Steve Marriott left Small Faces (➡), remaining members Lane, MacLagan and Jones dropped the "Small" and after period of disillusionment and aimlessness were joined by Stewart and Wood from Jeff Beck Group (➡) early 1969. Legend has it that Stewart met others in Hampstead, London, pub which aptly set seal on image of boozing, carefree camaraderie associated with band.

Started out on British club and university circuit, and toured States with release of **First Step**, a rather hesitant album but one that gave indication of what was to follow.

Stewart meanwhile continued parallel solo career; as his personal popularity increased (at first strongest in States through Beck Group associations) so, proportionally, did that of The Faces.

Despite inability to make completely satisfactory albums (both **Long Player**, 1971, and **A Nod's As Good As A Wink**, 1972, were flawed, though latter was fairly ballsy and contained full-scale work-out on Chuck Berry's **Memphis Tennessee**) they became one of most popular live bands in Britain and States during period 1972–75.

Their credibility as recording outfit took a real dive with low-key **Ooh La La**; Stewart claimed he didn't like the album and, though he quickly retracted remarks, the damage was done. Faces never again made an album of fresh material together, and also rumours about Stewart's commitment to band (or lack of it) circulated more freely.

In 1973 Lane left, and was replaced by ex-Free Japanese bassist Tetsu Yamauchi. Others carried on in their shambling, inebriated way, and released **Overtures And Beginners,** a live album, to show just how sloppy they could get.

A Nod Is As Good As A Wink.
Courtesy Warner Bros Records.

In 1974 Wood released solo album **I've Got My Own Album To Do** (co-writing one track, **Far East Man,** with George Harrison; song subsequently also appeared on Harrison's **Dark Horse**), and played a couple of London dates with famous friends Keith Richard, Willie Weeks, Andy Newmark, et al. From 1975 Wood began gigging with the Rolling Stones (reduced to one guitarist after departure of Mick Taylor), and that summer played consecutive tours of the States with the Stones and Faces. Also released second solo album **Now Look** (1975) again with assistance of distinguished company, this time including Bobby Womack.

With Faces in disarray and somewhat inactive, Stewart finally put others out of their misery in Dec 1975 by announcing he was quitting, and opened way for strongly-rumoured reunion of Small Faces occasioned by successful re-issue of that band's 1967 **Itchycoo Park** single. Wood now permanent member of Stones. (➡ Rod Stewart, Ronnie Lane, Rolling Stones.)

Recordings:

First Step (Warner Bros)
Long Player (Warner Bros)
A Nod's As Good As A Wink To A Blind Horse (Warner Bros)
Ooh La La (Warner Bros)
Coast To Coast: Overture And Beginners (Warner Bros/Mercury)
Ron Wood solo:
I've Got My Own Album To Do (Warner Bros)
Now Look (Warner Bros)

John Fahey

Born Feb 28, 1939 in Takoma Park, Maryland, Fahey is an acoustic guitar pioneer, who has studied folklore and the techniques of the bluesmen, being particularly influenced by Bukka White and Skip James; he has written one biography, "Charley Patton".

His records are blues-based, and he employs idiosyncratic tunings, but is intensely rhythmic. He fervently believes in the use of the steel-string guitar, and in the roots of American music. He also thinks that if an audience demand exists for something, however small, then he should try to meet it, and it was with these aims in mind that he set up his own Takoma Records, to release a variety of ethnic albums, of which his own **The Transfiguration Of Blind Joe Death** became the most prestigious. Takoma also issued a Leo Kottke record, **Six And Twelve String Guitar** in 1971.

He signed with Vanguard in 1967, before moving to Reprise, though he has shown little interest in commercial success. In 1969 his **Dance Of Death** was used on the soundtrack of Antonioni's "Zabriskie Point". He remains a reclusive figure, pertinaceously advancing his own ideals, and giving the outside

Below: The Faces, circa 1974. Ian MacLagan, Rod Stewart, Ron Wood, Kenny Jones, Tetsu Yamauchi. Notice how Rod's the only one drinking shorts.

world little around which they can construct a personality, beyond the fact that he is a passionate collector of turtles.

Discography is selective due to size of record output.

Recordings:
Blind Joe Death (Takoma/ Sonet)
Death Chants, Vol. I (Takoma/ Sonet)
The Transfiguration Of Blind Joe Death, Vol. II (Takoma/ Sonet)
John Fahey (Vanguard)
Yellow Princess (Vanguard)
After The Ball (Reprise)
Of Rivers And Religion (Reprise)
Old Fashioned Love (Takoma/—)
Fare Foreward Voyagers (Takoma/Sonet)
Voice Of The Turtle (Takoma/—)

Fairport (Convention)

Dave Swarbrick violin, vocals
Dave Pegg bass
Bruce Rowlands drums
Roger Burridge violin
Bob Brady keyboards
Dan Ar Bras guitar

The band, formed in Muswell Hill, London 1967 as an English equivalent to Jefferson Airplane (♦), were in their early days closely associated with burgeoning London underground, with appearances at clubs such as the UFO and Middle Earth.

Original line-up was Judy Dyble (vcls), Ian Matthews (vcls), Richard Thompson (gtr), Simon Nicol (gtr), Ashley Hutchings (bs), Martin Lamble (drms). In this form they made partially successful **Fairport Convention** (1968) before changing labels and bringing in Sandy Denny to replace Judy Dyble, who went on to form band called Trader Horne.

What We Did On Our Holidays (1969), an album of wide-ranging contemporary material, began the process of establishing their reputation, but before **Unhalfbricking** (1969) Ian Matthews left to form his own group, and a month before album was released band's van was involved in motorway accident after a gig. Lamble was killed, the others emotionally scarred by the experience, but determined to carry on. Since then their luck has been doggedly cruel, but equally doggedly they have recovered from multitude of setbacks.

Unhalfbricking was transitional album, which provided the band with U.K. Top 10 hit, **Si Tu Dois Partir** (a version of Dylan's **If You Gotta Go, Go Now,** and one of three of his songs on the album); it also included the ambitious **A Sailor's Life**, which turned the band in the direction of English traditional music, as did their growing association with Dave Swarbrick (vln, vcls) who first accompanied Fairport on this album, and shortly afterwards joined them on a permanent basis; Dave Mattacks (drms) was recruited to replace Lamble.

Thus by time of **Liege And Lief** (also 1969) the band had been virtually reconstituted, and certainly redirected. They toured

Britain continuously, and **Liege And Lief** was commercially successful; they seemed on the verge of a positive breakthrough, but then band had to survive second major crisis.

Denny and Hutchings quit simultaneously in 1969 – the former to found Fotheringay, the latter to form Steeleye Span (♦) – and Fairport looked doomed. However, Dave Pegg was brought in to replace Hutchings, and **Full House** was cut without a recognised vocalist.

Despite high standards of this middle-period work, band seemed cursed. Thompson also quit, and then lorry hurtled into their communal home. As a quartet, still concentrating on traditionally-based music, they then made **Angel Delight** (the title-track of which was autobiographical) and **Babbacombe Lee**, a concept album, based on an idea of Swarbrick's, and largely composed by him, and in 1975 made into a documentary for BBC2, "The Man They Could Not Hang".

Band again seemed at the end of the road when Nicol and Mattacks quit before sessions for the next album. There were now no surviving original members. Tom Farnell (drms) and Roger Hill (gtr) joined briefly, but line-up did not work out, and original tapes for **Rosie** were scrapped. Personnel again reshuffled, with Swarbrick and Pegg bringing in former Fotheringay members Trevor Lucas and Jerry Donahue,

not expanding their British audience.

They needed another album as fresh and exciting as **Liege And Lief.** Problem was exacerbated by departure for the second time of Mattacks, this time for good. He was replaced by Bruce Rowlands (ex-Grease Band).

Rising For The Moon (1975) was a long time in preparation. It was well received, though failed to make necessary impact; Lucas and Denny opted to concentrate on forging a career separately, and Donahue decided to stay playing sessions on the West Coast of America.

Nevertheless, they kept coming back for more, and band was reconstructed April 1976 with personnel as above, working under abbreviated billing Fairport. This line-up recorded 1976 set, **Gottle O' Geer.**

Almost singlehandedly, Fairport Convention initiated the English wing of folk/rock, but their influence was otherwise circumscribed. It would be difficult to name a band that's paid more dues and been rewarded with as much wretched luck.

(♦ Sandy Denny, Ian Matthews, Richard and Linda Thompson.)

Recordings:
Fairport Convention (Polydor)
What We Did On Our Holidays (Polydor/Island)
Unhalfbricking (Polydor/Island)
Liege And Lief (A&M/Island)
Full House (A&M/Island)

Above: Unhalfbricking. Courtesy Island. The couple are Sandy Denny's parents; the group are in their garden.

and persuading Mattacks to rejoin. **Rosie** was re-recorded with Lucas as producer; end result was charming but quite uncharacteristic album. **Fairport Nine** (1973) displayed the band's new instrumental virtuosity to good effect, before Sandy Denny (now married to Lucas) rejoined, and was featured on some tracks on **Live Convention** (1974).

But the band were now facing heavy debts and struggling. They had a name and a first-rate reputation, but had never achieved anything in America, and were

Angel Delight (A&M/Island)
Babbacombe Lee (A&M/Island)
Rosie (A&M/Island)
Fairport Nine (A&M/Island)
Live Convention (Island)
Rising For The Moon (Island)
Gottle O' Geer (Island)
Compilations:
History Of . . . (—/Island)
Fairport Chronicles (A&M/—)

Andy Fairweather Low

Welsh-born, achieved his first taste of fame as vocalist for the late '60s British teenybopper band Amen Corner, which also contained Dennis Byron (drms), Alan Jones and Mike Smith (sxs), Neil Jones (gtr), Clive Taylor (bs) and Blue Weaver (kybds). Originating from Cardiff area, Amen Corner shot to national prominence in U.K. with the 1967 smash **Gin House** and continued with a string of British Top 10 hits – **Bend Me Shape Me** (1968), **High In The Sky** (1968), **Half As Nice** (1969) and **Hello Susie** (1969).

Group's disbandment in 1970 coincided with bopper slump in U.K. and simultaneous "progressive" boom. (Blue Weaver was later with Strawbs, Mott, and finally Bee Gees back-up band, where he rejoined Dennis Byron.)

Fairweather Low first attempted to change fortunes by forming eponymous "progressive" band Fairweather, which managed one U.K. hit **Natural Sinner** (1970), before itself disbanding. After three years of inactivity, Low resurfaced as a singer/guitarist with A&M label on his first solo album **Spider Jiving** (1974), produced by Eliot Mazer. From that set came a U.S. hit with the title track, and British success with cut, **Reggae Tune.**

In 1975 he had a follow-up U.K. success with **Wide Eyed And Legless,** released **La Booga Rooga** album and toured with a band comprising B. J. Cole (pedal stl gtr), John David (bs), ex-Fairport drummer Dave Mattacks and ex-Free keyboards player "Rabbitt" Bundrick.

Recordings:
Spider Jiving (A&M)
La Booga Rooga (A&M)

Adam Faith

Born Terence Nelhams in Acton, London, June 23, 1940, Faith rivalled Cliff Richard as Britain's top teen idol for a short time in the early '60s.

He began as vocalist with Working Men skiffle group in 1957 and made his first record a year later while working in a film processing lab; he moonlighted between singing and his day job until late in 1959 he recorded **What Do You Want?,** backed by nine pizzicato violins, over which Faith hiccoughed the lyrics in a soft emasculated fashion. This style made him a star overnight – **What Do You Want?** reaching U.K. No. 1 spot in Nov 1959, and 16 hits followed in the next five years.

Faith was no singer, but he made a virtue of his failings and aroused the protective instincts of girl fans of that era with song-titles like **Poor Me** and **Lonely Pup.**

He was probably the shrewdest of his contemporaries, and managed to follow a parallel acting career (which was probably his first love), and made films – "Beat Girl", "What A Whopper!" (about the Loch Ness monster), neither of which were very impressive, and "Mix Me A Person", which was a more dramatically-conceived role and a much better film; Faith played a man awaiting execution for murder. With this experience behind him, he opted out of his flagging singing career in 1965 and spent two years in provincial repertory theatre.

He came back into the public eye in 1971 with a convincing portrayal of the small-time villain Budgie, in the British television series of the same name. He then returned to the music business, through his involvement with Leo Sayer (♠), whom he managed and produced.

After an excellent performance in the movie "Stardust", Faith relaunched his own singing career with considerable fanfare. Despite all the publicity, and photographs by Snowdon, **I Survive** failed, however, to cut the ice with the consumers of the '70s.

Recordings:
The Best Of Adam Faith
(—/EMI Starline)
I Survive (Warner Bros)

Marianne Faithfull

Better remembered for her turbulent relationship with Rolling Stone Mick Jagger, chronicled in detail at time by a rapacious international press, than for her previous lightweight career as a pop singer.

English born, the daughter of an Austrian baroness, Marianne was attending St Joseph's Convent School, Reading, when she went to a London party and was discovered by then Stones manager Andrew Loog Oldham (♠). Oldham was immediately enchanted by her peaches and cream complexion and a personality poles apart from that which he was nurturing for the Stones. He launched her on her pop career in 1964 with the Jagger/Richard composition **As Tears Go By**. She was 17 at time, and still at school when the record made the charts.

More hits followed in 1965, **Come And Stay With Me, This Little Bird** and **Summer Nights**, and at the end of that year she supported the Rolling Stones on tour. By this time her marriage to artist John Dunbar – by whom she had a son, Nicholas – was falling apart, and Marianne was living with Jagger.

In a famous interview with Andrew Tyler in "New Musical Express" 1974, Marianne recounted her ambitions of time thus: "My first move was to get a Rolling Stone as a boyfriend. I slept with three and decided the lead singer was the best bet."

Her pop career was in limbo by the turn of 1966, but Marianne nevertheless had ensured her place in the headlines that followed the Stones wherever they went: a semi-clad Marianne busted for drug possession along with Jagger and Richard when police raided latter's home; Mick and Marianne making heavily-publicised visit to Maharishi Yogi; the couple busted again in 1969; Marianne achieving acting ambitions taking lead role in "Girl On A Motorcycle" movie and appearing in London production of

"Hamlet" alongside Nicol Williamson; Marianne rocking the "establishment" preaching free love in TV interviews; Mick and Marianne flying out to Australia shortly after Brian Jones' death for Jagger to film eponymous role in "Ned Kelly" movie.

Marianne Faithfull.
Courtesy Decca Records.

However, theirs was never the easiest of relationships, and in late 1969 it all began to fall apart. In Australia, depressed by Jones' death and still feeling the strain of her arduous season in "Hamlet", Marianne lived on pills and on her nerve ends. Finally she made the first of her suicide bids, resulting in a period of hospitalisation, the whole tragedy enacted in the full glare of international publicity. Other suicide bids were rumoured, as was a heroin addiction, and suddenly Jagger left her.

Various other courtiers helped Marianne pick up the pieces of her life (though an air of fatality has always enshrouded her) and she has been subsequently relatively successful in her acting career. However, the drugs problem persisted.

Then in Jan 1976, admitting to having spent the previous four years on a drug recovery programme, Marianne signed a new record deal with NEMS/Immediate, re-uniting her with producer Andrew Oldham, for whom she cut an unsuccessful singles shot – her version of Waylon Jennings' **Dreamin' My Dreams**. Jagger is said to have written the poignant Stones cut **Wild Horses** with Marianne in mind.

Compilation:
Greatest Hits (London/Decca)

Georgie Fame

Born Clive Powell, June 26, 1943, in Leigh, Lancashire, England. While playing piano and singing in London ballroom Powell came to the attention of Larry Parnes, an English pop impresario who in the mid-'50s groomed his own stable of derivative rock 'n' rollers, each one modelled on an American original, each reborn with a name to match the image (e.g. Billy Fury, Marty Wilde, Duffy Power). Parnes first used Powell as a back-up pianist, including a semi-regular stint behind Billy Fury, before the impresario renamed him Georgie Fame – assembled the Blues Flames as his backing band – and attempted to launch him as teen idol in his own right. Despite the fact that Fame had more intuitive talent than any of the others, the bid failed. Instead, 1961 found Fame and Blue Flames parted from Parnes

and working as the semi-resident attraction at London's Flamingo Club, subsequently to become one of the breeding grounds of British R&B (♠). Fame's music, influenced heavily by a predominantly black audience, developed into its own unique form of R&B – blending together about equal amounts of Mose Allison, American R&B and soul, Jimmy Smith, Lambert Hendricks & Ross, and the West Indian ska rhythm.

Between 1962 and 1965, several sets a week, Georgie Fame and the Blue Flames – nucleus of Colin Green (gtr), Tex Makins (bs), Red Reece (drms), Mick Eve (sx) – held court at the Flamingo as kings of that particular strand of British R&B. (Other Blue Flames during that period included John McLaughlin and Mitch Mitchell, latter subsequently of Jimi Hendrix Experience.)

Fame cut two albums, both 1964, before his single **Yeh Yeh** toppled The Beatles from British No. 1 spot in Jan 1965.

By mid-1966 he had enjoyed a second U.K. No. 1 with **Get Away**, following with Top 10 version of Bobby Hebb's **Sunny**. By this time, however, Fame had disbanded Blue Flames to fulfil longstanding ambition to sing with big band, working with both Harry South and Count Basie.

In the following year he pursued a two-fold career – continuing his excursions into jazz and big band territories but continuing to release pop singles, one of which, **The Ballad Of Bonnie And Clyde** (late 1967/early 1968), brought him his third British chart-topper.

From that point, however, Fame's fortunes went into decline. He formed a somewhat uneasy musical partnership with former Animals organist Alan Price (♠), who had also tired of leading own band, and together they assembled an unashamedly MOR act for TV and cabaret. From that alliance also came the 1971 album **Fame And Price, Price And Fame Together.**

The pair parted company late 1973, and in mid-1974 Fame made an attempt to re-form Blue Flames and rediscover R&B roots under patronage and backing of Island label founder Chris Blackwell. He played a series of gigs (with Colin Green only surviving Blue Flame original) and cut one album for Island, the 1974 **Georgie Fame.**

However, in 1976, Fame is ironically probably best known in U.K. for his appearances in TV coffee commercials.

Recordings:
R&B At The Flamingo
(—/Columbia)
Fame At Last (—/Columbia)
Sweet Thing (—/Columbia)
Sound Venture (—/Columbia)
Hall of Fame (—/Columbia)
Two Faces Of Fame
(Columbia/CBS)
Third Face Of Fame
(Columbia/CBS)
Seventh Son (Columbia/CBS)
Georgie Does His Thing With Strings (Columbia/CBS)
Going Home (Columbia/CBS)
All Me Own Work (Reprise)
Georgie Fame (Island)
With Alan Price:
Fame And Price, Price And Fame Together (Columbia/CBS)

Family

Roger Chapman vocals
Charlie Whitney guitar, vocals
Rob Townsend drums
Tony Ashton keyboards, vocals
Jim Cregan bass, guitar

Formed Leicester, England in 1966 through an amalgamation of two local bands. Above was last line-up when band broke up in 1973. Constant factors during those seven years were firstly the personnel nucleus of Chapman, Whitney, Townsend; secondly the prolific composing partnership of Chapman/Whitney which produced more than 90 per cent of group's material.

Previously known as Roaring Sixties and Farinas, the first Family line-up comprised Chapman, Whitney, Townsend plus Jim King (sx, flt) and Rick Grech (bs, vln, vcls).

The group went to London in 1968 to cut their **Music In A Doll's House** album with producers Jimmy Miller and Dave Mason. Bar one Mason song, the set comprised all originals and was a startlingly successful debut – immediately establishing them as one of the half dozen most original bands on Britain's embryonic "progressive" rock scene.

Bandstand. Courtesy Warner Bros Records.

Family were subsequently to join the London "underground" circuit (contemporaries of Pink Floyd, Nice) where the demented aggression of the Chapman stage persona heightened their reputation as a considerable live attraction. Their lifestyle of the time was later the subject of Jenny Fabian's "Groupie" novel.

Though inconsistent, **Family Entertainment** (1969) confirmed burgeoning talent, particularly Side 1 where cuts like **Hung Up Down, Observations From A Hill** and the evergreen **Weaver's Answer** blitzed the senses with hurricane-force rhythms and manic vocals. Mix and programming however (both undertaken without group supervision) left much to be desired.

Shortly after, the band suffered the first of several line-up changes. In April 1969, midway through a disastrous U.S. tour (there were other incidents, notably bust-up with promoter Bill Graham, which made return visits difficult), Ric Grech (♠) quit to join Blind Faith (♠) supergroup. Replaced by John Weider (bs, vln), ex of New Animals, then working U.S. as sessionman.

Later that same year, Jim King also left, Family losing a good deal of aural/visual impact as a

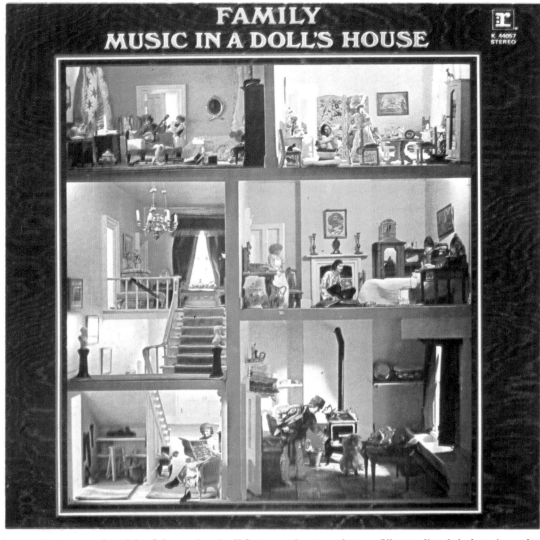

FAMILY
MUSIC IN A DOLL'S HOUSE

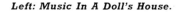
K. 44057
STEREO

Left: Music In A Doll's House.

result. He was replaced by John "Poli" Palmer (kybds, vbs) from Blossom Toes.

This line-up survived three years of steady if not trailblazing success but cut relatively unmemorable albums. Fourth, **Anyway** (1970), was half live/half studio set which provided U.K. hit single debut **Strange Band.** Following year, **Weaver's Answer** followed it into singles lists, taken from the 1971 compilation album **Old Songs New Songs** which band issued primarily as an excuse to remix tracks they felt had been mistreated on aforementioned **Family Entertainment.**

Weider quit June 1971 to be replaced by the altogether more powerful bass of John Wetton, formerly of Mogul Thrash. This line-up cut peerless 1971 album **Fearless,** their best since **Entertainment. Bandstand** following year was similarly a statement of group's striving for perfection and progression, and from this **Burlesque** made British singles charts.

Both albums were lavishly packaged and promoted but failed to accrue deserved commercial success.

In 1972 came two more changes: in September, Wetton left to join King Crimson (♦) and subsequently Uriah Heep (♦) – and was replaced by Jim Cregan (ex-Blossom Toes, Stud); in November "Poli" Palmer was replaced by Tony Ashton (ex of jazz/rock trio Ashton Gardner & Dyke and Remo Four).

Thus reorganised, Family com-

pleted a U.S. tour and returned to the U.K. with refreshed, more good-time approach at the expense of Chapman's vocalist-as-schizophrenic stance – and cut their last album, **It's Only A Movie** (1973), after announcement of imminent break-up.

As sessionmen and producers (Linda Lewis and Medicine Head respectively), Cregan and Ashton had outside commitments which made overseas tours impractical; and opportunity to achieve major British success – let alone break stubborn America – was by now receding further into horizon.

Family's insistence on pursuing own unique path probably more than anything kept them from very top of Rock's Premier League – and, while American success could have supplied that status and impetus, the problems of setting up U.S. tours were becoming progressively more difficult to overcome.

The end came in Oct 1973, ironically, after an immensely successful British farewell tour. If that first revolutionary album had been released some years later, when public might have been more ready to accept it, there might have been a wholly different story to tell.

Chapman and Whitney went off to work together as Streetwalkers (♦ Chapman Whitney); Rob Townsend joined since-defunct Medicine Head (♦); Cregan continued to produce Linda Lewis (♦) and is currently with Cockney Rebel (♦).

Albums listed below in order they were made and released in U.K. American release order differed greatly.

Recordings:
Music In A Dolls House (Reprise)
Family Entertainment (Reprise)
A Song For Me (Reprise)
Anyway (Reprise)
Fearless (United Artists/Reprise)
Bandstand (United Artists/ Reprise)
It's Only A Movie (United Artists/Raft)
Compilations:
Old Songs New Songs (Reprise)
Best Of Family (Reprise)

Fanny

Jean Millington bass, vocals
June Millington guitar, vocals
Nicole Barclay keyboards
Alice De Buhr drums

Billed early on as rock's first all-female group, Fanny was founded by the Millington sisters June and Jean with original line-up as above. A year apart in age, the Millingtons were born in Manilla, Philippines, where their father was at U.S. Navy base. Growing up in Sacramento, California, they first performed as a duo, later as part of a quartet The Sveltes before they met drummer Alice De Buhr, who had left home state of Iowa for California at age of 17. They signed to Warner Bros in 1969, then under name Wild

Honey.

Fourth original member, Nicole "Nicky" Barclay, a native of Washington D.C., joined band during recording of first album **Fanny** (1970), leaving spring 1970 to tour as part of Joe Cocker's Mad Dogs revue but returning to the fold later the same year.

First three albums all produced by Richard Perry to certain degree of critical acclaim, the last of them being cut at Apple Studios in London. **Mother's Pride** (1973) was also recorded in London, at Olympic Studios, under production of Todd Rundgren. (Millington sisters also played behind Barbra Streisand on her 1970 album **Stoney End.**)

After fourth album, however, the group went through period of personnel strife. June Millington quit band early 1974, followed by Alice De Buhr. Patti Quatro, Detroit-born sister of Suzi Quatro (♦), was brought in as bassist, Jean Millington switching to lead guitar, and Brie Howard recruited on drums.

With this line-up, Fanny toured U.K. summer 1974 with Jethro Tull, at the end of which their principal songwriter "Nicky" Barclay and newcomers Howard also announced their imminent departures.

Late 1974 album, **Rock 'n' Roll Survivors,** which features line-up of Jean Millington, Quatro, Barclay and Howard, was an ironically-titled lacklustre set which cost them their early critical support, reflecting as it did the group's ongoing personnel traumas.

American Cam Davies, a press officer's assistant with ABC, was recruited to drumstool towards the end of 1974 and in spring 1975, as a trio, Fanny enjoyed a largish American singles hit with **Butter Boy.** However, this success only made matters worse. Personality clashes got out of hand and Patti Quatro and Cam Davies departed in far from harmonious circumstances. June Millington and Brie Howard returned in their places but this final incarnation survived only a matter of weeks before total disintegration of the band.

Patti Quatro was last heard of attempting to form band; Nicky Barclay leading own group Good News (she released 1976 **Diamond In A Junk Yard** album on Ariola America). Future of Millingtons, at time of writing, uncertain.

Recordings:
Fanny (Reprise)
Charity Ball (Reprise)
Fanny Hill (Reprise)
Mother's Pride (Reprise)
Rock 'n' Roll Survivors (Casablanca)

Richard And Mimi Farina

American folk duo; Richard Farina was fascinating figure; born in 1937 of Cuban father and Irish mother, both of whom emigrated to States in the '20s, and he had to divide his childhood between Brooklyn, Cuba and Northern Ireland.

In the mid-'50s he fought with the IRA in Ireland, and was forced to leave the country; then also espoused revolutionary cause in Cuba while Castro was fighting in the mountains, and left Cuba as rebel forces were entering Havana.

Returned to New York in 1959 where, for a while, he was prominent on the booming Greenwich Village folk scene; youthful, and studious-looking, he was briefly married to Carolyn Hester.

In 1963 he married for a second time, to Mimi (b. May 1, 1945) sister of Joan Baez (♦), and they went to live in California.

They performed together as a duo at many festivals, and often on stage with Joan – singing some traditional material, but, increasingly, Farina's own compositions. He'd been one of earliest protest singers to have a keen lyrical ear, and one of his first songs, **Pack Up Your Troubles,** was widely recorded.

In 1965 and 1966 they made **Celebrations For A Grey Day** and **Reflections In A Crystal Wind,** the latter being a wild, poetic album, beautifully sung, with many imaginative songs, including **Hard Lovin' Loser.**

In addition, Farina had parallel literary career from 1963–66 and wrote for several magazines, as well as having a few plays performed. He wrote a classic underground novel "Been Down So Long It Looks Like Up To Me", and was tragically killed in motorcycle accident after a party to launch its publication, April 1966. He had been prodigiously talented, and was an exceptionally witty writer.

Mimi, who has a voice almost the equal of her sister's, withdrew for a few years, but then began composing herself (several of her songs are on Joan's later albums) and also undertook some gigs in partnership with Tom Jans – they toured the U.K. in 1971, appearing on gigs with Cat Stevens, and also made one album together, **Take Heart.** In Dec 1971 Mimi also appeared at one of Joan's English concerts. She has made no albums in recent years, preferring to devote her time to organising charitable ventures on the West Coast.

The Best Of Richard And Mimi Farina is a compilation that serves to illustrate what a great loss Richard Farina was.

Recordings:
Celebrations For A Grey Day (Vanguard)
Reflections In A Crystal Wind (Vanguard)
Memories (Vanguard)
The Best Of Richard And Mimi Farina (Vanguard)
Mimi Farina And Tom Jans: Take Heart (A&M)

Chris Farlowe

Born John Deighton, London 1940, Farlowe started his career during the British skiffle era, then joined the R&B movement that took that earlier phenomenon's place on the U.K. club circuit. His band, Chris Farlowe and the Thunderbirds, played a minor supporting role in British R&B (♦) boom, appearing mainly at the London Flamingo Club from 1962 onwards. Backing Farlowe's bravura vocals as members of the Thunderbirds were Albert Lee

(gtr) and Dave Greenslade (org), 1970's leaders of their own bands Head Hands & Feet and the eponymous Greenslade (♦).

Farlowe enjoyed little commercial success, however, until under Mick Jagger's patronage he made a U.K. singles No. 1 with the Jagger/Richard composition **Out Of Time** (1966). Follow-ups flopped, and his solo career led to the break-up of the Thunderbirds until Farlowe revived band as trio 1967 with Albert Lee, Pete Shelley and Carl Palmer (♦ Emerson Lake And Palmer).

On demise of this band, Farlowe sang with Colosseum (♦), and later Atomic Rooster (♦) on two albums – Palmer had also had earlier spell with Rooster – before retiring from music business 1972 to concentrate on shop he owns in Islington, North London, which specialises in the sale of Second World War German memorabilia.

Came out of retirement late 1975 to tour with new band (once again with Albert Lee), promote a re-issue of **Out Of Time,** and record album for Polydor, **The Chris Farlowe Band Live.**

Leo Fender

Born 1907, Fender is famous for designing a series of guitars that were of paramount importance in the evolution of rock music. They were used at one time by virtually all the seminal musicians, and proved capable of adaptation to virtually every form of electric music.

Fender started developing his original models in his garage in California in the '40s. They utilized all the latest electronics, and had solid bodies to eliminate screech and feedback. They stayed in tune whatever, had sharpness and attack, and were easy to handle.

The Telecaster and Stratocaster were the two most famous models. Steve Cropper was Telecaster Man for almost 10 years, before Jeff Beck saw more possibilities for the instrument, by using the bass pick-up and boosting it with studio electronics; somehow Beck coaxed feedback from a guitar that was specifically designed to eliminate it.

Hendrix became the most famous owner of a Stratocaster, a guitar which had previously been notable for the use to which Buddy Holly and Hank Marvin, of The Shadows, had put it; but Hendrix's unique style boosted the instrument to its peak of popularity.

Fender's approach has always been to construct a guitar from basics. The result has been an unparalleled series of futuristic, well-designed and superbly-engineered instruments – as the sales proved. Fender's company was taken over by CBS in 1965.

Michael Fennelly

Born New Jersey 1948, Fennelly took classical guitar lessons at age of 10, but became more interested in rock music, and while in his teens moved to Los Angeles, where he became a minor league protest singer.

In 1967 he became involved with Mee Moo Music, a publishing company run by Curt Boetcher,

who had previously produced The Association's biggest hits, and now was able, with Fennelly, to put together a studio group called The Millennium, whose one solitary album is now a rare collectors' item, as are the two albums released by Sagittarius, a later version of the same group, of which Fennelly was also a member.

After these groups achieved little commercial success, in 1970 Fennelly met up with a group called Stonehenge – Phil Jones (drms), Casey Foutz (kybds), Felix Falcon (prcsn), Hank Harvey (bs) – and together they formed a new band, Crabby Appleton (taking their name from a TV cartoon character).

They signed to Elektra, and seemed set for a bright future. Both their albums – **Crabby Appleton** and **Rotten To The Core** – received good reviews, and a Fennelly-composed single, **Go Back,** from the first album sold encouragingly, but in 1972 Fennelly opted to pursue a solo career, and the band broke up.

In 1973 Fennelly made his debut solo album in England, using members of Argent (♦) as backing musicians; **Lane Changer** showed for the first time his extraordinary vocals and instrumental capabilities; **Stranger's Bed** was issued in 1975.

Recordings:
With The Millennium:
Begin (Columbia/—)
With Sagittarius:
Present Tense (Columbia/—)
Blue Marble (Columbia/—)
With Crabby Appleton:
Crabby Appleton (Elektra)
Rotten To The Core (Elektra/—)
Solo:
Lane Changer (Epic)
Stranger's Bed (Mercury/—)

Bryan Ferry
♦ Roxy Music

The Fifth Dimension

Marilyn McCoo vocals
Florence LaRue Gordon vocals
Billy Davis Jnr vocals
Lamonte McLemore vocals
Ron Townson vocals

Florence Gordon and Marilyn McCoo grew up in Los Angeles, while the three male members of the group knew each other from Louisiana; in the '60s they came together as a unit, basing their appeal on their strong harmonies.

They worked initially as The Versatiles, and then as The Hi-Fi's, before meeting Marc Gordon while touring in the Ray Charles Revue. Gordon became their manager, and introduced them to Johnny Rivers (♦), who signed them to his Soul City Records (which was distributed through Liberty) and suggested the change of name.

As the Fifth Dimension, they almost automatically found heady success. Their first single, **Go Where You Wanna Go,** became a U.S. Top 10 single, before their second release, written by the then unknown Jim Webb (♦), **Up Up And Away,** earned them a

gold disc. In line with their new quasi-psychedelic image, they made a concept album with Webb, **The Magic Garden,** which was distinguished by lively tunes, ingenious arrangements, and spirited vocals, and which earned the band another gold disc.

Over the next few years, they were to amass a total of eight gold albums, and six gold singles, as they made a series of widely-acclaimed albums, and selected their material from impeccable sources – Laura Nyro (♦), for example, provided **Stoned Soul Picnic** and **Wedding Bell Blues.** The secret of their success was probably the production and arrangements of Bones Howe, with the assistance of musical director Rene De Knight and Webb.

In 1969 the band made it a family affair – Davis marrying McCoo, and LaRue marrying the manager, Gordon.

Earthbound.
Courtesy A&M Records.

However their style, ever sophisticated, became full of cliches and somewhat mannered at the turn of the '70s, and the level of their success eased off. In 1975, in an attempt to rekindle old triumphs, they made another concept album with Jim Webb, **Earthbound,** but the reunion produced little more than lethargy.

Recordings:
Up, Up And Away (Soul City/Liberty)
The Magic Garden (Soul City/Liberty)
Stoned Soul Picnic (Soul City/Liberty)
Age Of Aquarius (Soul City/Liberty)
Fantastic (Soul City/Liberty)
Portrait (Bell)
Love's Lines, Angles And Rhymes (Bell)
Individually And Collectively (Bell)
Live! (Bell)
Earthbound (ABC)

Fillmore
♦ Bill Graham

Roberta Flack

Born Ashville, North Carolina Feb 10, 1939 into a musical family, Roberta Flack was trained in piano from an early age and also developed an excellent voice; she was well-placed to handle diverse styles of music. She left high school to enter Harvard University in Washington, where she took degrees in music and education before settling down in early '60s to a teaching job in segregated black school in North Carolina. She returned to Washington and took several teaching positions, while she also worked part-time accompanying opera singers at the Tivoli Restaurant and directed an amateur production of "Aida".

In May 1967 she started residency at Mr Henry's Pub in Washington, and by taking other engagements at late-night clubs was able to quit teaching for a full-time musical career and became widely-known and respected locally. In 1969 she was signed by Atlantic Records.

Her debut album **First Take** was released towards end of the year, and immediately aroused interest. It gradually picked up sales as the single taken from it, **First Time Ever I Saw Your Face,** moved to the top of U.S. charts 1972, largely as a result of being featured on soundtrack of movie "Play Misty For Me".

Chapter 2 consolidated her reputation; this time the single taken from it was **Killing Me Softly With His Song,** written by Norman Gimbel and Charles Fox for Lori Leiberman after watching a Don McLean concert. **Killing Me Softly** was another U.S. No. 1.

Her American success has eased off slightly in recent years, but she is a performer who spends months perfecting her act and releases product infrequently. She collaborated with Atlantic stablemate Donny Hathaway for an album which produced the 1972 hit single **Where Is The Love?;** **Feel Like Makin' Love** provided her with another hit single and the album of the same name, released in 1975, featured a composition Stevie Wonder had written for her, **I Can See The Sun In Late December.**

Though generally regarded as a soul singer, there are strong classical and jazz influences in her often slow-paced piano playing and singing. Like Hathaway, she has brought an awareness of classical form to popular music.

Recordings:
First Take (Atlantic)
Chapter 2 (Atlantic)
Quiet Fire (Atlantic)
Killing Me Softly (Atlantic)
Feel Like Makin' Love (Atlantic)
With Donny Hathaway:
Roberta Flack And Donny Hathaway (Atlantic)

The Flamin' Groovies

Cyril Jordan guitar, vocals
James Farell rhythm guitar, vocals
Chris Wilson vocals, guitar, harp
David Wright drums
George Alexander bass, vocals, harp

Began 1965 as Bay Area High School Band, The Chosen Few, then featuring legendary Cyril Jordan, original vocalist and lyricist, Roy A. Loney, George Alexander and Tim Lynch on rhythm guitar. Drummer Ron Greco completed line-up. Changed name to Lost And Found, which they touted in local Battle Of The Bands contests.

After a sojourn in Holland, Jordan and Lynch returned in summer 1966 to join Whistling Shrimp drummer Danny Mihm and form Flamin' Groovies.

While the mid-'60s was noted for explosion of Haight-Ashbury drug-oriented psychedelia, Groovies remained faithful to a brand of high energy rock and a white R&B tradition which seemed an anachronism to the then San Franciscan scene.

Bypassed by record companies on look-out for anything in kaftan and beads that moved, the Groovies customised their own record label, Snazz, and released a 10-inch album, **Sneakers** (1969).

Epic, impressed by band's ability to sell over 2,000 copies by word of mouth, signed the group and released **Supersnazz** (1970). Produced by Steve Goldman this was a much better indication of their potential, fitting comfortably into the niches of punk rock history occupied by Detroit's MC5 (♦) and The Stooges (♦). Despite its excellence, Epic gave the Groovies inadequate promotion and their contract was severed.

When local impresario Bill Graham (♦) moved business from the Fillmore West to the more respectably situated Carousel Ballroom the Groovies took over the lease on vacated venue and began promoting their own concerts; as house band they hosted to Grateful Dead, Pink Floyd, Alice Cooper, MC5 and Iggy Pop but legal wrangling again, this time with manager Alfred Kramer, a former employee of Graham's, forced a closure and further travelling.

In New York the band met up with punk rock aficionado Richard Robinson who secured them a deal on Buddah Records' Kama Sutra label. In this year, 1971, the Flamin' Groovies released their most important works, the Robinson-produced **Flamingo** (Commander Cody on piano) and **Teenage Head** – both of which are definitive additions to the catalogue of manic rockin' rock. The Jordan-Loney team was at a peak to match Jagger and Richard while Jordan's uniquely powerful guitar style was a logical extension from Scotty Moore, Cliff Gallup and James Burton.

Yet another setback prevented the band reaping their true reward when second guitarist, Tim Lynch, was busted for drug abuse and draft evasion. He was replaced by James Farrell while Jordan laid down the overdubs on **Teenage Head** himself. As so often happens critical acclaim was high and sales low; both albums were soon cut out.

Roy A. Loney left after musical disputes based around his inexplicably ballad oriented new material, Chris Wilson stepping in as vocalist, third guitarist and writer with Jordan. Meanwhile European interest in the band was greater than at home and under the enterprising auspices of Andrew Lauder, United Artists financed an English and French tour which included over 200 gigs. United Artists released two singles, **Slow Death** – produced by Dave Edmunds (♦) at Rockfield – and the Frankie Lee Sims number **Married Woman.**

Success was not forthcoming. Though the Groovies were a star attraction at the rain-sodden Bickershaw Festival, they failed to impress at their vitally important London Roundhouse date.

Mixed critical response and financial disagreement led to Mihm being replaced for a time by Terry Rae, the vacated seat then filled by David Wright to complete the current line-up.

For three years the band was again without a contract or label until Dutch independent company Skydog put out a live EP and single (1974) in Europe, while in the States, lifelong fan and friend Greg Shaw (editor, "Who Put The Bomp" fanzine), released a classic single **You Tore Me Down** on his Bomp label.

Encouraging sales revealed the Groovies were not a spent force and a new Sire album, **Shake Some Action** (1976), produced by Dave Edmunds (♦), heralded a return to their vintage years.

Long plagued by ill luck, personnel changes and personal inability to shine at the right time, the Flamin' Groovies remain steadfast, hoping for a brighter future.

Both Kama Sutra albums released in U.K. a double-package by Buddah.

Recordings:
Sneakers (Snazz/—)
Supersnazz (Epic/—)
Flamingo (Kama Sutra/—)
Teenage Head (Kama Sutra/—)
Shake Some Action (Sire)

Fleetwood Mac

Christine McVie keyboards, vocals
Mick Fleetwood drums
John McVie bass
Stevie Nicks vocals
Lindsey Buckingham guitar

In 1967, guitarist Peter Green left John Mayall's Bluesbreakers – where he had replaced Eric Clapton – and took Mayall bass player John McVie with him to form his own group. The line-up was completed by the diminutive vocalist and Elmore James-influenced slide guitarist Jeremy Spencer, and the stringy, six-foot-plus drummer Mick Fleetwood, who had also had a brief spell with John Mayall (♦).

The group first appeared under the billing Peter Green's Fleetwood Mac, the latter part of name deriving from the bass player, and as such made their debut at British National Jazz & Blues Festival on Aug 12, 1967. Shortly after, they signed contract with blues impresario/producer Mike Vernon's Blue Horizon label.

Green already boasted an impressive reputation as a blues singer and guitarist from spell with Mayall, and Fleetwood Mac – as they became known after a few months – rapidly established a large U.K. following as leaders of the nascent British Blues (♦) movement. Their first album – appearing early 1968 at a time when, aside of Beatles, Stones and Cream, the British albums Top 30 was monopolised by MOR material – stunned the music industry by staying among the best-sellers for some 13 months.

Late in 1968, Green added his young protege, Danny Kirwan, to the group's line-up – Fleetwood Mac at this point featuring a unique three-guitar front-line, all of whom could compose and perform their own material.

However, Peter Green's direction was by now beginning to shift away from straight blues – this trend being evidenced in its experimental stage on the surprise hit single **Albatross,** a U.K. No. 1 in Dec 1968, which was a low-key Green-composed instrumental reminiscent of Santo & Johnny's 1959 **Sleep Walk** hit. Other outstanding Green numbers, **Man Of The World** and **Oh Well** (both 1969) kept Fleetwood Mac in the British Top 5, while the group worked on the culmination of Green's new direction; the inconsistent but largely under-rated **Then Play On** album, which contained composing contributions from Green, Spencer and Kirwan.

Left: Fleetwood Mac, 1976 variant. John McVie foreground, Mick Fleetwood background. L to r: Lindsey Buckingham, Stevie Nicks, Christine McVie.

Above, colour: Spencer, Green, Fleetwood, McVie – original Fleetwood Mac. Inset: The earlier Peter B's – Dave Ambrose, Green, Fleetwood, Peter Bardens.

By this time, although American success was proving hard to attain (on their first U.S. tour the Mac opened on the Jethro Tull/Joe Cocker package tour even though they were bigger than both acts on home turf), Fleetwood Mac were at their peak – to all intents and purposes, Britain's hottest rock property.

Then in May 1970, in a spell of self-doubt raddled by his burgeoning interest in religion, Peter Green announced his decision to leave the Mac and retire from the music business (➧ Peter Green). The guitarist's **Green Manalishi** composition was issued shortly after his split announcement and, apart from a re-release of **Albatross** in 1973, was to be the Mac's last appearance in the British singles charts.

Shaken and confused, the group retired to their country retreat for several months, finally emerging with the late 1970 album **Kiln House** (named after their home) on which Spencer and Kirwan, somewhat shakily, shared leadership duties. Ironically, however, this was to be the album that provided a springboard to future U.S. success.

John McVie's singer and keyboards-playing wife Christine, then still working under maiden name Christine Perfect, ex of blues contemporaries Chicken Shack (➧), augmented the Mac during the sessions for **Kiln House** (as she had on previous albums) and as "guest" on the subsequent American tour. (However, due to contractual obligations, Ms McVie didn't officially join the band until **Future Games.**

In Feb 1971 came a second blow to a group still recovering from the traumas caused by Green's shock withdrawal. While in Los Angeles during that U.S. tour, Jeremy Spencer "walked out" on the group and was posted missing with local police for several days until he was discovered in the Los Angeles headquarters of the religious cult, the Children Of God. The eccentric guitarist – who on stage mixed his Elmore James-influenced blues work with remarkable comic parodies of the likes of Elvis Presley and Buddy Holly – had been approached in the street by a member of the cult and, like Green before him, had taken an on-the-spot decision to renounce his former existence.

(Spencer's solo album listed over, an often brilliant collection of his best-loved parodies, had been released in 1970. In 1972 he made his second solo appearance on record, this time backed by fellow Children Of God musicians, and in 1974–75 he toured U.S. and Europe with a band drawn from members of the cult.)

Peter Green returned temporarily to help Fleetwood Mac finish their U.S. commitments before, once again, the group staggered back to the English countryside for a lengthy spell of recuperation.

Out of this came the recruitment of Californian singer/guitarist/composer Bob Welch, whose influence was immediately felt on the 1971 **Future Games** album which, as one (British) critic remarked at the time, could almost have been the product of a West Coast band. The album made healthy inroads into the American lists, while the Mac oldie **Black Magic Woman** – featuring its composer, Peter Green – took them high in the U.S. singles charts in the same year.

Bare Trees (1972) retained the same line-up, and the same feel, but musically reflected the group's ongoing identity crisis. However, the new-look Mac continued to push further into the American consciousness, their fortunes in the States from that point on rising almost in ratio to their decline from public attention in Britain.

Later in 1972 Kirwan was ousted, to be replaced by Americans Bob Weston and Dave Walker for the much-improved **Penguin** set in 1973. In the same year, the aforementioned re-release of **Albatross** took the Mac to No. 2 in the British singles lists, though its success only marginally aided U.K. sales for **Penguin.**

By the disappointing **Mystery To Me** set, later that same year, Walker had also departed, with Weston following him soon after release. In all, 1973 was a traumatic year, largely due to personality clashes within the band. At one point they almost disbanded altogether – and it was out of this confused situation that Mac manager Clifford Davis assembled a new band which opened a tour of the U.S. under billing "Fleetwood Mac" even though it contained none of the original members.

Founder-members Fleetwood and McVie immediately took out a court injunction forcing the ersatz Mac off the road, and eventually won their way through protracted court proceedings. (Historical footnote: members of the bogus "Mac" turned up in a group called Stretch with a 1975 U.K. hit single **Why Did You Do It?**, the lyrics of which purportedly concerned that legal dispute.)

These court hassles, though, meant that the band were unable to work for over a year, and it wasn't until late 1974, by which time they had also resolved their own internal personal problems, that Fleetwood Mac resumed normal service. From their new, now-permanent base in Los Angeles, they returned to the U.S. concert circuit and to the charts with the album **Heroes Are Hard To Find.**

Fleetwood Mac's turbulent, often tragic story, is essentially one of survival, and of pertinacity paying rewards – showing a recent phenomenal upswing in the band's fortunes. In February 1975 Bob Welch left to form new band Paris (with Glenn Cornick, ex Jethro Tull) and the Mac regrouped with American husband and wife team Buckingham-Nicks. With this new line-up, **Fleetwood Mac** exceeded platinum sales status in the U.S., also two monster-selling American singles, **Rhiannon** (written by Nicks) and **Over My Head** (Christine McVie).

Album notes: **Fleetwood Mac In Chicago** – British title **Blues Jam At Chess** (first released 1969) – was double-set featuring various American blues veterans alongside guitars of Peter Green and Jeremy Spencer; **The Original Fleetwood Mac** (not released in U.K. until 1971 and in U.S. until 1976) comprises previously unissued material cut around time of first album, **English Rose** was released as group's second U.S. album but is in fact a specially-made compilation featuring the early singles plus cuts from the British second album **Mr Wonderful**; Danny Kirwan's solo album was released in 1975.

Recordings:
Fleetwood Mac (Epic/Blue Horizon)
Mr Wonderful (—/Blue Horizon)
The Original Fleetwood Mac (Sire/CBS)
Fleetwood Mac In Chicago (Sire/Blue Horizon)
Then Play On (Reprise)
Kiln House (Reprise)
Future Games (Reprise)
Bare Trees (Reprise)
Penguin (Reprise)
Mystery To Me (Reprise)

Heroes Are Hard To Find (Reprise)
Fleetwood Mac (Warner Bros)
Compilations:
English Rose (Epic/—)
Greatest Hits (Epic/CBS)
Black Magic Woman (Epic/—)
The Best Of Fleetwood Mac (Sire/—)
Jeremy Spencer:
Jeremy Spencer (Epic/CBS)
Jeremy Spencer And The Children Of God (Epic/CBS)
Danny Kirwan:
Second Chapter (DJM)

Flo & Eddie

Flo And Eddie, aka The Phlorescent Leech And Eddie, are respectively Marc Volman and Howard Kaylan, founder-members and creative force behind the late '60s American hit group The Turtles, which is the only logical point from which to unfold their history.

With a line-up of Volman, Kaylan, Chuck Portz and Al Nichol, The Turtles began life in 1963 as a surfing band out of Inglewood, California, first as The Nightriders and later as The Crossfires. Changed name to Turtles when they came under management of DJ Reb Foster and signed with new U.S. label White Whale.

The year was 1965, and folk/rock was breaking out all over the West Coast. The Turtles – with Jim Tucker (gtrs) and Don Murray (drms) added to line-up – took Bob Dylan's **It Ain't Me Babe** and smashed into the American singles charts, consolidating their success with **Let Me Be** and **Grim Reaper Of Love** in the same year.

Soon after the last-named single, Murray was replaced by Johnny Barbata (later with CSN&Y, Steve Stills, Jefferson Starship).

Throughout the mid- to end-'60s – with Volman and Kaylan leaders of the band – the hits kept on coming. The platinum single **Happy Together** (1967) broke band in Britain, and subsequent singles **She'd Rather Be With Me** and **Elenore** maintained Turtles status as international hit band.

The infectious yet vacuously-poppy **Elenore** came, in fact, from the Turtles' 1968 satirical **Battle Of The Bands** album, which was hailed at time by "Rolling Stone" as one of that year's most "significant" releases, and has since achieved status of collectors' item.

The end of the '60s, however, found The Turtles beginning to forsake their earlier pop-oriented approach in favour of trappings of psychedelia – massed sitars, 14-minute space improvisations etc. which confused not only the group's audience but also their record label. By this time founder-member Portz and early members Tucker and Barbata had departed, their places being taken by bassist Jim Pons, from The Leaves, and John Seiter, formerly of Spanky And Our Gang, on drums.

In 1970, The Turtles broke up amidst a messy tangle of lawsuits and allegations – the end result of which was that Volman and Kaylan were left with rights to group's name (there's been talk since of a re-union tour) and all their original tapes.

After a farewell Turtles U.S. tour, Volman and Kaylan picked up threads of a new career in the company of an old friend, Frank Zappa, becoming fully-fledged Mothers Of Invention at which time they first adopted the billing The Phlorescent Leech And Eddie. Volman and Kaylan had their own "feature" spot with The Mothers, as well as providing back-up vocals, and toured Europe and U.S. extensively with Zappa in the early '70s. During this time they appeared on four Zappa albums,

Chunga's Revenge, Fillmore East, Just Another Band From L.A. and the soundtrack album **200 Motels**, also taking prominent parts in the movie of the same name.

In late 1972, having broken from Zappa, the pair released their first solo album, **The Phlorescent Leech & Eddie,** following with a tour for which they enlisted the back-up group support of ex-Turtle Jim Pons, English drummer Aynsley Dunbar, guitarist Gary Rowles and keyboardsman Don Preston. Apart from Rowles, ex-Love, all had put in spells with Mothers.

After tours of the U.S. and Europe supporting Alice Cooper, the group disbanded and Kaylan and Volman once again struck out in new directions: writing musical soundtrack and dialogue for X-rated animated movie, "Cheap"; contributing satirical columns and articles to U.S. rock press; and hosting own radio show.

It is for the last-named activity that Flo & Eddie are best known in America in mid-'70s. Their "Flo & Eddie By The Fireside", a weekly three-hour show which originated on Radio KROQ in Los Angeles, was an immediate success and, by 1976, in various edited forms, was being run on radio stations all over the U.S.

A second solo album – produced by Bob Ezrin – was released in 1974. Kaylan and Volman, as back-up vocalists, also appear on three Marc Bolan/T. Rex albums, **The Slider, T. Rex** and **Electric Warrior.**

A double Turtles hits collection – containing one side of previously unissued material – was released on Sire 1974. **Happy Together Again,** a similarly retrospective double set, was released on Philips in U.K. 1975.

Recordings:
The Phlorescent Leech & Eddie (Reprise)
Immoral Illegal And Fattening (Columbia/—)

Flying Burrito Brothers

Sneaky Pete Kleinow pedal steel
Gram Parsons vocals, guitar
Chris Hillman guitar, vocals
Chris Ethridge bass

The original Flying Burritos – accept no substitute – were formed at the end of 1968, with line-up as above. Parsons and Hillman had graduated from The Byrds (➧), while both Kleinow and Ethridge were well known for session activities.

Musical direction of band – as envisaged by Parsons – was to introduce country music to rock audiences and vice versa; this would develop the work he had been undertaking with The Byrds on **Sweetheart Of The Rodeo,** and which he had originally initiated with the International Submarine Band, who recorded **Safe At Home,** an album that many people consider to be the very first example of country rock, in 1967.

With addition of various session drummers, the Burritos released **The Gilded Palace Of Sin** in Mar

1969, at which point band engaged another alumni of The Byrds, Michael Clarke, as permanent drummer.

Later that year, Ethridge left the band to return to session work, and with Hillman moving to bass, Bernie Leadon (ex-Hearts And Flowers, Dillard & Clark) came in on guitar and vocals. This combination produced **Burrito Deluxe,** released in May 1970, just prior to which Parsons left group, though it isn't clear whether he jumped or was pushed; whatever, it was while he was in line-up and band were recording his compositions that they accomplished his best work.

His replacement was Rick Roberts, that line-up lasting a full year before Sneaky Pete left, to be replaced by Al Perkins (formerly of a group called Foxx); after only a further three months, Bernie Leadon left to join The Eagles (➧), during which time a third album, **The Flying Burrito Brothers,** was released, containing contributions by both the recently departed members.

The death knell of Burritos was by now clearly sounding, but the band limped on until Oct 1971, with addition of three members from Country Gazette – Byron Berline (fdl), Roger Bush (bs) and Kenny Wertz (gtr), and managed to complete **Last Of The Red Hot Burritos.** As a European tour was

Close Up The Honky Tonks. Courtesy A&M Records.

then scheduled, it was arranged that this should be undertaken by a hybrid titled the Hot Burrito Revue with Country Gazette.

However, before this could take place the Burrito band virtually folded, since both Hillman and Perkins joined Manassas and Michael Clarke had returned to his "pied a terre" in Hawaii; so the final member of Country Gazette, Alan Munde, was added on banjo and guitar, together with Don Beck, who'd played with Dillard & Clark, on pedal steel and guitar; Erik Dalton, formerly of Southwind, as drums. Thus the only longstanding Burritos member was Roberts, and he'd only been in the line-up for 18 months. It was no surprise at all that the group ceased to exist altogether after the European tour, though several live albums did emanate from Europe afterwards.

After such a troubled history, it might have been more sensible to let it be, but at the end of 1974 two original members of band, Kleinow and Ethridge, decided to try again. Together with Floyd "Gib" Guilbeau, a vastly experienced cajun musician who had already played on several Byrds offshoots, Joel Scott Hill, a veteran of Canned Heat and hundreds of sessions, and Gene Parsons, the longest serving Byrds drummer, they reformed and cut **Flying Again** in 1975. The critics were not amused.

Nevertheless the farce – for such it is becoming – continues; Ethridge quit early in 1976, and almost inevitably was replaced by another ex-Byrd, Skip Battin.

Recordings:
The Gilded Palace Of Sin
(A&M)
Burrito Deluxe (A&M)
The Flying Burrito Brothers
(A&M)
Last Of The Red Hot Burritos
(A&M)
Live In Amsterdam (—/Bumble)
Flying Again (Columbia/CBS)
Airborne (Columbia/CBS)
Compilations:
Close Up The Honky Tonks
(A&M)
Gram Parsons with the Flying
Burrito Brothers:
Sleepless Nights (A&M)

Focus

Thijs van Leer keyboards, flute, vocals
Bert Ruiter bass, vocals
David Kemper drums
Philip Catherine guitar

Focus originated in Holland from a trio formed by van Leer (who studied classical music at Amsterdam Conservatoire) with Martin Dresden (bs) and Hans Clever (drms). They became back-up band for Dutch stage version of "Hair" musical 1969, guitar virtuoso Jan Akkerman joining the line-up during recording of an album issued in U.K. in 1971 as **In And Out Of Focus**.

After a year of only moderate success, Akkerman quit to link up with drummer Pierre van der Linden, with whom he had played in renowned Dutch rock bands The Hunters and Brainbox. The pair formed a new outfit, inviting Thijs van Leer to join along with bassist Cyril Havermans. This line-up recorded **Moving Waves** (1971) under the name Focus, which set style for band's reworkings of classical themes in rock context, leaning heavily on improvisational abilities of Akkerman and van Leer.

In Sept 1971, Havermans departed (working solo he later released own album, **Cyril**). With Bert Ruiter as replacement, the band set about extensive touring schedule of U.K. achieving almost instant recognition as headlining attraction, their success assisted by 1973 U.K. instrumental hit singles **Sylvia** (from album **Focus 3**) and **Hocus Pocus** (from earlier **Moving Waves**). Subsequently both albums – **Focus 3** a 1973-released double set – made British album lists.

Later same year Focus toured U.S. and received unprecedented acclaim for a support act, with first three albums and both singles repeating U.K. success in U.S. charts. Of these, **Moving Waves** and **Focus 3** certified gold sellers. **Focus At The Rainbow**, recorded at London Rainbow Theatre 1973, was a live set of material from second and third albums.

In winter of same year, Pierre van der Linden was replaced by ex-Stone The Crows (◆) drummer

Colin Allen. Allen, in turn, quit mid-'75, van der Linden returning for brief period before permanent recruitment of American David Kemper.

Both Thijs van Leer and Jan Akkerman have released solo albums. The former's are listed below while Akkerman's work appears under his own name, as he quit band in shock departure early 1976 on eve of sell-out British tour.

There's little doubt that from 1974 onwards Focus lost much of their early impetus, though as noted in previous paragraph, they are still capable of sell-out tours. However, the loss of guitar virtuoso Akkerman must cast considerable questions over their future, despite replacement by talented London-born (of Belgian father) Philip Catherine, who has played with Jean Luc Ponty, Mike Gibbs and John McLaughlin. Catherine had also previously recorded solo releases.

Recordings:
In And Out Of Focus (Sire/Polydor)
Moving Waves (Sire/Polydor)
Focus 3 (Sire/Polydor)
Focus At The Rainbow (Sire/Polydor)
Hamburger Concerto (Atco/Polydor)
Mother Focus (Atco/Polydor)
Compilations:
Dutch Masters (Sire/—)
Focus (Atco/Polydor)
Thijs van Leer solo:
Introspection (Columbia/CBS)
Introspection II (Columbia/CBS)
O My Love (—/Philips)
Philip Catherine:
September Man (Atlantic)
Guitars (Atlantic)

Dan Fogelberg

American singer/songwriter with roots in country and western, Fogelberg dropped out from studying to be painter at University of Illinois to start working folk circuit. Accompanied Van Morrison on tour before switching base from Los Angeles to Nashville

where he met Norbert Putnam, who produced first album **Homefree** (not released in U.K.).

The record met with little commercial success (although Putnam is said to regard it as one of his best productions), and the next couple of years found Fogelberg hanging out in Nashville working as sessionman. Eventually he came under the astute management of Irv Azoff, handler of The Eagles and Joe Walsh, the latter of whom produced Fogelberg's critically-hailed second album, **Souvenirs**, in 1974. Walsh also played on this set, along with Graham Nash and members of The Eagles.

Fogelberg subsequently toured the U.S. with Eagles and carried out own production work on third album, **Captured Angel**. (He also appears on Jackson Browne's **Late For The Sky** album.)

In 1976 Fogelberg's regular backing group, Fools Gold, embarked on a parallel recording career. They had a hit single with **Rain, Oh Rain** and placed their eponymous debut album (both on Morning Sky/Arista) on the U.S. lists, subsequently touring as a group in their own right.

Recordings:
Homefree (Epic/—)
Souvenirs (Epic)
Captured Angel (Epic)

John Fogerty

Born Berkeley, California May 28, 1945. Fogerty enjoyed an illustrious career as pivotal figure of Creedence Clearwater Revival (◆); when the group finally disbanded in Oct 1972, Fogerty's was the name that mattered, but he strangely maintained a low profile – to the extent of implying that his debut solo album **Blue Ridge Rangers** had been made by the group of that name.

In fact, the album was Fogerty's own from start to finish – he played everything, sang everything, arranged and produced, etc. The album marked a departure for him, being composed mostly of

country material; nevertheless the set provided two U.S. hit singles – **Jambalaya** and **Hearts Of Stone**.

Blue Ridge Rangers.
Courtesy Fantasy, EMI.

Fogerty's next album, **John Fogerty,** was likewise all his own work, but it didn't appear until late 1975, by which time he had a new U.S. record contract with Asylum Records. **John Fogerty** sold well in the U.S., though, no doubt because of his long periods of inactivity, less well than might have been expected, considering that the songs were of a high quality indeed. The album absolutely demonstrated Fogerty's continuing creativity as a frontline rock performer.

Recordings:
Blue Ridge Rangers (Fantasy)
John Fogerty (Asylum/Fantasy)

Foghat

Lonesome Dave Peverett
guitar, vocals
Roger Earl drums
Rod Price slide guitar
Nick Jameson bass, keyboards

Like the latter-day Fleetwood Mac and Savoy Brown, Foghat are that phenomenon: a British band virtually unknown at home but very popular in the U.S. They have taken up permanent residency in New York.

Originally Foghat was a breakaway from the aforementioned and similarly boogie-minded Savoy Brown (◆), of which Lonesome Dave, Roger Earl and bassist Tony Stevens had all been members. These three, together with Price, built on Savoy Brown's reputation in States as driving, blues-oriented boogie outfit, producing three albums between 1972 to early 1975 when founder-bassist Stevens gave way to Missouri-born Nick Jameson.

Jameson had previously added synthesiser and piano to group's first album, mixed their U.S. hit single **What A Shame** from **Rock & Roll,** and as a member of band produced the late 1975 **Rock And Roll Outlaws** and Jan 1976 **Fool For The City** sets. Their **Energized** album was certified a U.S. gold seller in 1975.

Recordings:
Foghat (Bearsville)
Foghat: Rock & Roll
(Bearsville)
Energized (Bearsville)
Rock And Roll Outlaws
(Bearsville)
Fool For The City (Bearsville)

Left: Dan Fogelberg. Dropped out of University and into Nashville.

Four Seasons

Frankie Valli vocals
Gerry Polci vocals, drums
Don Ciccone bass
Lee Shapiro keyboards
John Paiva guitar

The Four Seasons have been the most successful American recording act of the rock era, with a remarkable story of success that spans 14 years. At the last count, they had sold in excess of 80 million records.

They emanated from the Italian community of New Jersey, and hence it's perhaps not surprising that the dramatis personae of this particular piece of rock history reads like the cast-list of "The Godfather".

In 1953, Valli (b. Francis Castelluccio in Newark, May 3, 1937) joined Variatone Trio, which comprised Tommy and Nick DeVito and Hank Magenski. In 1956 they changed their name to Four Lovers, signed to RCA, and had a minor hit with **Apple Of My Eye,** written for them by Otis Blackwell. After achieving nothing in the next three years, they were dropped by RCA in 1959, at which point Valli met Bob Crewe.

Crewe was an independent producer, who had already had some success in Philadelphia with his partner Frank Slay on their Swan label, which had launched careers of Freddy Cannon, The Toys and Mitch Ryder. Crewe employed the Four Lovers initially as back-up singers and musicians, and the group went through several changes in personnel – Nick DeVito left to be replaced by Charles Callello, who in turn was

Below: Francis Castelluccio – Frankie Valli to you bud! – whose manic falsetto is the group's trademark.

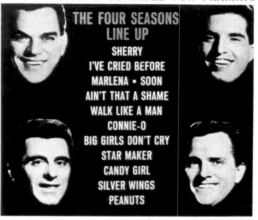

replaced by Bob Gaudio (b. The Bronx, New York, Nov 17, 1942) and Magenski also quit and was replaced by Nick Massi.

Crewe had deliberately brought in Gaudio, who was a promising songwriter, and once the Lovers had become the Four Seasons, Crewe felt ready to launch them as a major act, with the settled line-up of Valli, Gaudio, Massi and Tommy DeVito.

Their second single, **Sherry,** was placed with Chicago's Vee-Jay label. Gaudio, the composer, persuaded Valli to sing it in a manic falsetto; the song was a quick-fire No. 1 in States 1962, and reached No. 8 in Britain, and the Seasons immediately established a formula that they were effortlessly able to follow with **Big Girls Don't Cry** and **Walk Like A Man.** While their style originated in black doo-wop vocals of the '50s, the Seasons made it special through the songwriting talents of Gaudio and Crewe, who wrote most of the hits, and the unique range of lead singer Valli, especially his distinctive falsetto. They rapidly became the hottest chart act of all.

However, contractual problems arose with Vee-Jay, and they negotiated a new deal with Philips, though by the time of release of their debut on the new label, **Dawn (Go Away),** the composition of the U.S. charts had been metamorphosised by the arrival of The Beatles. The Seasons were resolute; **Dawn** reached No. 3, and for a time they and the Beach Boys were the only

U.S. acts able to hold their own in the face of British competition. (Since Vee-Jay held the rights to early Beatles as well as early Seasons material, in 1964 they issued a lavish two-record set, **The Beatles vs The Four Seasons,** and promoted it as "The international battle of the century.")

Throughout '64 the Seasons' run of success was uninterrupted; one of their biggest hits, **Rag Doll,** is arguably their quintessential song, even if the dramatic introduction owed much to the one Phil Spector had conceived for The Ronettes' **Be My Baby.**

Meanwhile, the Rolling Stones toured America that year, and proclaimed the Seasons to be the only home-grown act worthy of attention; this kind of endorsement undoubtedly helped them to survive a period of considerable upheaval.

Massi departed in 1965, and was replaced by Joey Long, but the group's success continued, if on a marginally diminished scale. There were hits like **Let's Hang On** and **Workin' My Way Back To You;** Valli had a couple of solo successes with **The Proud One** and **Can't Take My Eyes Off You.** In addition, the Seasons recorded Bob Dylan's **Don't Think Twice, It's All Right** under the nom de disque The Wonder Who; it seems they wanted to pride themselves on the fact that their records were hits on the strength of the music, rather than just the name of the group – **Don't Think Twice** gave them another Top 5 U.S. single.

Probably the reason for the Seasons' consistency was that they held to their own distinctive style, while others were slavishly trying to copy The Beatles; the Seasons were to the East Coast what the Beach Boys (◆) were to the West Coast, but their prestige in Britain was never particularly high in the second half of '60s.

By 1969, the Seasons finally felt obliged to eschew the simple demands of pop music for something of more gravity. **Genuine Imitation Life Gazette** was one of the most expensive albums ever produced – an expense which was justified neither by the sales, which were minimal, nor by the quality of socio-economic dialectics.

After this, they fell out with both Crewe, their producer, and Philips, their company. Though Valli had a solo hit in Britain 1971 with **You're Ready Now,** the song had originally been recorded in 1968, and the band spent a couple of years in limbo, a situation which was finally relieved when Berry Gordy offered them a contract on Mowest, Motown's new West Coast label. They recorded one album, **Chameleon,** and several singles, none of which made any contemporary impact, and it was during these lean years that the group underwent a series of personnel changes, before they arrived at the current line-up (as above).

Even so, it is a measure of their status, that they continued to be an enormous box-office draw, especially on East Coast, where

Left: Vintage Four Seasons (Frankie Valli far left) strike a vintage doo-wop pose, and do their tailors proud.

they filled Madison Square Garden eight times. Also a quadruple album of their best material – **The Greatest Hits Of Frankie Valli And The Four Seasons,** which had been leased to the Longines Symphonette Society – met with considerable commercial success.

The band left Motown after a dispute over Valli's **My Eyes Adored You,** which Motown considered to have little commercial potential. Valli backed his judgement, took the song to Private Stock, and was rewarded with a Top 5 hit in Britain and America in late 1974.

So the many contractual hassles revolving round the band finally seemed to be resolved. Valli signed as a solo artist to Private Stock, who also gained the rights, from mid-1975, to all the old material (which, of course, automatically entered the album charts again in Britain and America when it was all re-packaged as **The Four Seasons Story**), and the group signed to Warner Bros.

The Four Seasons Story.
Courtesy Private Stock Records.

The spade-work for a Seasons come-back had already been done. In 1975 revivals of **Bye Bye Baby** (the Bay City Rollers), **The Proud One** (The Osmonds) and **Sherry** (Adrian Baker) filled the U.K. charts, while **The Night,** a Seasons' Motown recording that had been changing hands for £10 a time in the esoteric British 'Northern Soul' circles, was re-issued and became a Top 3 hit.

With the release of their debut Warners' album, **Who Loves You,** the Seasons themselves were suddenly big business again; the title-track became a large hit in Britain and America, probably because of its disco popularity, and the next single from the album, **December '63,** gave the band their first-ever U.K. No. 1. A third, **Silver Star,** also reached Top 5, and a successful tour demonstrated that the Seasons were now more popular in Britain than they had ever been, while in America they were turning on the magic as if it was still December '63.

All the songs of the **Who Loves You** album were written by Bob Gaudio and Judy Parker; though Gaudio still records with the band, he doesn't tour with them because of producing and songwriting commitments.

The enduring success of the Seasons can probably be ascribed to the fact that as a band they have never been known to court a particular audience, and have always maintained the widest possible appeal, through their impeccably-produced, quality material.

Discography is selective.

Recordings:
Inside You (Mowest)
Who Loves You (Warner Bros)
Compilation:
The Four Seasons Story (Private Stock)
Frankie Valli Solo:
Our Day Will Come (Private Stock)
Compilation:
Gold (Private Stock)

Four Tops

Levi Stubbs vocals
Abdul "Duke" Fakir vocals
Renaldo Benson vocals
Lawrence Payton vocals

Originally known as the Four Aims, the Tops have retained the same line-up since their formation in 1954 in Detroit. They recorded one single for Chess in 1956, before recording for Singular and Riverside and Columbia. In 1964 Berry Gordy signed them to Motown, and they became one of Motown's most consistent hit-making acts.

Their first record, **Baby I Need Your Loving,** was a hit, and they began to be highly sucessful in 1965 with **I Can't Help Myself** – a U.S. No. 1 and their first million-seller, and **It's The Same Old Song.** Their material was all composed by the prolific songwriting team of Holland-Dozier-Holland, and together they produced some classic songs, but undoubtedly their best was **Reach Out I'll Be There,** which was distinguished by the powerful vocals and the clever arrangement, and was a No. 1 on both sides of the Atlantic.

After 1967, the Tops lost the services of their songwriters, though they continued to have hits on both sides of the Atlantic with **Walk Away Renee, Do What You Gotta Do** and **It's All In The Game.** With a narrower range than other vocal outfits like The Temptations, the Tops' style has remained basically the same, concentrating on love-lorn ballads in which the straining, dramatic vocals of Stubbs have been predominant.

By 1972, however, disappointed with their diminishing returns at Motown, they signed to ABC-Dunhill. Though this temporarily abated their declining popularity, and they returned with a few minor hits like **Keeper Of The Castle,** they achieved no lasting success, and at the beginning of 1976 were thought to be ready to re-sign to Motown.

Few of their albums retain any interest today.

Recordings:
The Four Tops Story (Motown/ Tamla Motown)

Kim Fowley

One of the true eccentrics of West Coast rock – which might unkindly be said to be his only current claim to fame – Fowley nonetheless has been a prolific contributor to the genre for more than a decade in a variety of roles: singer, composer, producer, poet, actor, manager and impresario to name just a few.

Fowley is also unquestionably an incorrigible boaster and showman; even admirers have described him as one of rock's greatest liars, which makes it often difficult to be specific about his career. He claims, for instance, to have discovered British acts Slade and Soft Machine (he certainly produced latter's first single), while even reports of his birthplace vary.

One source maintains that Fowley was born in New Zealand; another in Manilla, in the Philippines, July 21, 1942, where his parents were interned by the Japanese during the Second World War. More certain is that Fowley's ancestry is rooted in entertainment. His father, Douglas Fowley, was an actor (he appeared as Doc Holliday in TV's "Wyatt Earp" cowboy soap opera), while his grandfather, Rudolph Friml, had a substantial reputation as a composer of musical comedies.

Either way, Fowley spent the latter part of his youth in California where he worked as a singer and composer in his teens. In 1960 he instigated the Hollywood Argyles outfit which had a million-selling U.S. hit with the novelty song **Alley Oop.** He diversified in the early '60s, writing poetry, acting, dancing on an exhibition basis in Los Angeles clubs, while continuing as writer/producer in the music business. Two of his best-known production credits from the period are B. Bumble And The Stingers' **Nut Rocker** smash, and the Murmaids' **Popsicles And Icicles,** which was a U.S. No. 1.

He continued as a writer through the '60s, selling his material to some of America's best-known acts of the day, but enjoyed his greatest spell in the public eye during San Francisco's flower power period. One of the leading figures behind that movement's break-out as an international trend, Fowley organized a series of "love-ins" in San Francisco which first earned him notoriety as a creature of excess and eccentricity. It was on the strength of this that Tower Records signed him for his first solo album, the 1967 **Love Is Alive And Well.**

Fowley's career – he's acted, written film scripts for cartoon movies, put out something in the region of a hundred singles – has since then gone in fits and starts. A new contract with Capitol resulted in two more solo albums, **I'm Bad** and **International Heroes.** His most recent, **Animal God Of The Street,** on the Skydog label, while not exactly altering the course of rock, was possibly the best of his album releases, while he also took a co-production credit with John Cale on Jonathan Richman's **Modern Lovers** album.

In 1976, as producer/entrepreneur, Fowley unveiled his latest 'find', The Runaways, all-girl, all-teen five piece whose eponymous debut album was released on Mercury.

Peter Frampton

Born Beckenham, Kent, England, Apr 22, 1950, Frampton first came to attention as baby-faced singer/ guitarist with the late '60s U.K. bopper attraction The Herd, who had hit singles **From The Underworld** (1967), **Paradise Lost** (1968) and **I Don't Want Our Loving To Die** (1968). The group included other mildly charismatic personalities in Gary Taylor and Andy Bown, but it was Frampton who was singled out as the pin-up boy of British bopper press.

Like so many bopper outfits before and after them, the band folded when individual members decided they wanted to pursue paths which might bring them some artistic credibility.

Frampton, in fact, had better reason than most, because behind the 10 x 8 features lay a highly talented guitar player, a fact that attracted the attention of a number of rock contemporaries, among them Steve Marriott (♦). Frampton and the erstwhile Small Faces vocalist got together with Greg Ridley (bs) and Jerry Shirley (drms) to launch the now-defunct Humble Pie (♦) in 1968. But it was always an uneasy alliance and, after a series of mostly disappointing albums with the group, Frampton quit in 1971 to develop writing and multi-instrumental potential outside Pie confines.

His first solo album, featuring the most tasteful playing from a U.K. rock guitarist for some time, was recorded in 1972 with assistance from Ringo Starr, Billy Preston, Klaus Voormann and ex-Herd sidekick Andy Bown. Also on sessions were Mike Kellie, ex-Spooky Tooth, and Rick Wills,

Frampton Comes Alive.
Courtesy A&M Records.

formerly with Cochise – both were subsequently recruited for Frampton's Camel group along with Mick Gallagher, ex of Bell 'n' Arc. When Kellie quit to join yet another reincarnation of Spooky Tooth, his place was taken by John Siomos, an American drummer formerly with Voices Of East Harlem and Mitch Ryder.

This line-up cut second album listed below and toured U.S. (Frampton had by this time virtually turned his attention full-time to the more amenable Stateside market) until disbandment in 1974.

Somethin's Happening was basically another solo album, as was **Frampton**, recorded in Wales with Camel drummer Siomos and the aforementioned Andy Bown, these two musicians by this time forming nucleus of Frampton road band.

Since second album, Frampton had worked extensively on road in States in a concerted attempt to establish a reputation which has, in fact, grown with each successive release. His major U.S. breakthrough was achieved when **Frampton Comes Alive**, an in-concert double set featuring Siomos plus Stanley Sheldon (bs) and Bob Mayo (gtr), topped American charts and was certified platinum seller late 1975. Both that and **Show Me The Way** made U.K. lists early 1976, bringing

long-overdue recognition in U.K.

Recordings:
Wind Of Change (A&M)
Frampton's Camel (A&M)
Somethin's Happening (A&M)
Frampton (A&M)
Frampton Comes Alive (A&M)

Aretha Franklin

Born 1942 in Detroit, Aretha was one of five children of Reverend C. L. Franklin, himself a well-known figure in gospel music whose recorded sermons (he has had over 70 albums issued on the Chess label) have had regular sales.

From an early age Aretha was used to singing with her brothers and sisters in the choir of New Bethal Baptist Church, her father's church in Detroit. At 14 she joined her father on his inter-state evangelistic tours, and gained a reputation as a remarkable soloist with his choir.

When she was 18, she was encouraged to broaden her musical horizons by singing blues, and then like Sam Cooke moved East to try the pop market. John Hammond (♦) at Columbia Records was impressed, and gave her a contract.

Though Aretha always seemed a star in the making, her career was frustrated rather than assisted by her spell at Columbia; no one seemed to know how to produce her, or what kind of material she was best equipped to handle.

In winter of 1966 she signed with Atlantic, a company far better placed to deal with blues and soul singers. For her first session, producer Jerry Wexler took her to Muscle Shoals studios, and all the fire and passion of her voice was, incredibly, unleashed straightaway on a song called **I Never Loved A Man (The Way I Loved You)**, which was a classic by any standards, and well merited its gold record. The song practically changed the course of soul music – it was that emotionally powerful. Aretha was immediately dubbed Lady Soul, a title she's never since needed to relinquish or even contest.

She had a string of million-sellers in the closing years of the '60s – **Respect, Baby I Love You,** and **I Say A Little Prayer** etc; her albums sold equally as consistently, though her heady success in America was never equalled in Europe, but a 1968 tour was accounted a complete triumph, and produced the album **Aretha In Paris.**

In 1969 **Think** became her first self-composed million-seller, and she began to start both writing and producing her own material – though in the main production duties continued to be allocated to the tried and trusted Atlantic team of Wexler, Tom Dowd and Arif Mardin.

At the turn of the decade, personal problems forced her into temporary semi-retirement; Aretha's diffidence about recording and her apparently lukewarm interest in her career was an open secret, but within 18 months, she had been coaxed back into the old routine, recording and playing gigs, though rarely outside U.S. Al Jackson, the drummer with Booker T & The MGs remarked that "Aretha carries you back to

church in everything that she does", and she has remained a gospel-oriented performer, more popular with the black communities in America; the live double-album **Amazing Grace,** recorded with her father, addressing the congregation, and James Cleveland, playing piano and conducting the Southern California Community Choir, was a much-heralded return to pure gospel music.

Though her albums in the '70s have possibly sacrificed some of the dynamic earthiness of her early music for greater orchestration and sophistication, they have nevertheless been compelling listening; it seems like she has never made a bad album. **Hey Now Hey (The Other Side Of The Sky)** was an interesting experimental album, co-produced by her and Quincy Jones, that burred the edges of soul and jazz. It contained the stand-out track, **Angel,** written by Aretha's sister Carolyn; another of her sisters, Erma, has also established a career for herself, having recorded the powerful **Piece Of My Heart** in 1967.

Recordings:
Today I Sing The Blues (Columbia/CBS)
I Never Loved A Man (The Way I Loved You) (Atlantic)
Aretha Arrives (Atlantic)
Lady Soul (Atlantic)
Aretha In Paris (Atlantic)
Aretha Now (Atlantic)
Soul '69 (Atlantic)
This Girl's In Love With You (Atlantic)
Spirit In The Dark (Atlantic)
Don't Play That Song (Atlantic)
Live At Fillmore West (Atlantic)
Young, Gifted And Black (Atlantic)
Amazing Grace (Atlantic)
Hey Now Hey (The Other Side Of The Sky (Atlantic)
Let Me In Your Life (Atlantic)
With Everything I Feel In Me (Atlantic)
You (Atlantic)
Compilations:
Greatest Hits, Vol. I (Columbia/CBS)
Greatest Hits, Vol. II (Columbia/CBS)
Aretha's Gold (Atlantic)
Aretha's Greatest Hits (Atlantic)

Above: Aretha Franklin.

Free

Paul Rodgers vocals
Paul Kossoff guitar
Andy Fraser bass
Simon Kirke drums

Now defunct British group which had a somewhat turbulent history. Above is their original, and best-known, line-up; founded by Rodgers (b. Middlesborough, Dec 12, 1949), Kirke (b. Chelsea, London, July 28, 1948) and Kossoff (b. Hampstead, London, Sept 14, 1950 – d. Mar 19, 1976).

Kirke and Kossoff were playing together in a blues group, Black Cat Bones, when they saw Rodgers singing with the outfit Brown Sugar in a North London pub, The Fickle Pickle.

The three assembled their new band with the addition of Andy Fraser, 16-year old bass player from John Mayall's Bluesbreakers.

While still in their embryonic stage, they came to the attention of Alexis Korner (♦), one of "founding fathers" of British blues, who suggested the name "Free", introduced them to Island Records boss Chris Blackwell (who wanted to call them The Heavy Metal Kids), provided early musical "coaching", and even arranged group's debut gig in spring 1968.

Above: Rodgers, Kossoff of Free.

Though the subject of some initial criticism – they were dubbed as ersatz Cream in certain quarters of British rock press – the band established a strong club following within a year of formation, playing a mix of original material and blues standards.

Early albums (first in 1969) were only moderately received by press and public alike, until in 1970 their original composition, **All Right Now,** went to No. 1 in British singles lists, and into American Top 5 in autumn of that year. Free followed up with **My Brother Jake.**

In early 1971, however, for a variety of reasons never fully explained, one of them being possibly their immaturity, the band split – for the first time.

Each member pursued various, though largely unsuccessful projects. Rodgers and Fraser formed own bands, Peace and Toby respectively; Kirke and Kossoff recorded own band (**Kossoff Kirke Tetsu Rabbit** – Island, 1971) with Texan keyboards player John "Rabbit" Bundrick and Japanese bassist Tetsu Yamauchi.

Then in early 1972, the band regrouped with their original line-up to cut disappointing **Free At Last,** plus the hit single **A Little Bit Of Love,** and for a reunion tour.

Fraser departed towards end of that year, however, and Tetsu and "Rabbit" – from aforementioned album – came in to make Free a five-piece for only a short period of time before Paul Kossoff (➧), suffering from drug addiction, also quit. Nevertheless, Kossoff appears on parts of the final Free album **Heartbreaker** (1973).

Wendell Richardson, then with Osibisa (➧), was brought in as a temporary replacement for Free's early 1973 American tour, after which Tetsu quit to join The Faces (➧).

Free disintegrated for second and last time in late 1973, allowing Rodgers and Kirke to form instantly successful Bad Company (➧). Original bassist Fraser subsequently led own eponymous Andy Fraser Band with relatively little commercial success.

Compilation listed below was 1973-issued, limited edition double set.

Recordings:
Tons Of Sobs (A&M/Island)
Free (A&M/Island)
Fire And Water (A&M/Island)
Highway (A&M/Island)
Free Live (A&M/Island)
Free At Last (A&M/Island)
Heartbreaker (Island)
Compilations:
The Free Story (Island)

Alan Freed

American DJ, born Pennsylvania 1922, and credited with first use of the term "rock 'n' roll" – in 1952. Freed was working for Cleveland radio station WJW when a local record-shop owner persuaded him to visit his store and see the phenomenon of white kids buying what were then called "race records" (i.e. R&B, blues). Later switching activities to New York, as DJ and MC of own rock 'n' roll concerts, Freed was a major figure in the spread of new music. Also a songwriter (collaborated with Harvey Fuqua on '50s Moonglows hits and takes co-credit for Chuck Berry's **Maybelline**), and moviemaker ("Rock Around The Clock" and "Don't Knock The Rock"). In 1960, how-

ever, Freed's career was blown to pieces when he was indicted on payola charges. He died January 1965 in Palm Springs, California.

Kinky Friedman

Kinky Friedman is the extreme type of new-wave country star, with an irreverent and charmingly lunatic approach to his work; he is that ethnic rarity – a Jewish country singer, and as such formed a backing band called the Texas Jew-Boys. His forte often seems to lie in his sheer offensiveness, but he is also a capable and exceptionally witty composer.

Sold American.
Courtesy Pye Records.

Most of his best material (**High On Jesus, Top Ten Commandments**) appeared on **Sold American,** which was a remarkably mature debut album. His second, recorded partly in Nashville and partly in Los Angeles, was disappointing, and his ritual slaughter of various sacred cows has possibly left him temporarily up a commercial cul-de-sac.

Recordings:
Sold American (Vanguard)
Kinky Friedman (ABC)

Edgar Froese
➧ Tangerine Dream

Fruupp

Vince McCusker guitar, vocals
Peter Farrelly vocals, bass
John Mason keyboards
Martin Foye drums

From Belfast, Northern Ireland, formed early '70s by McCusker whose roots lie in same mid-'60s Belfast R&B circuit that produced Van Morrison's Them. Now based in London, Frupp have released four albums but as of 1976 hadn't succeeded in rising above level of minor club/college attraction. Music is on fringes of Yes, Genesis techno-rock school – with quasi-mystical trappings. John Mason replaced Stephen Houston on keyboards 1974.

Recordings:
Future Legends (—/Dawn)
Seven Secrets (—/Dawn)
Prince Of Heaven's Eyes (—/Dawn)

Right Free. Courtesy Island Records. The group's second album, released 1969, found them still seeking mass acceptance.

Modern Masquerades (—/Dawn)

Fugs

Ed Sanders vocals
Ken Weaver vocals, drums
Tuli Kupferberg vocals
Ken Pine guitar, vocals
Charles Larkey bass
Bob Mason drums

The Fugs began life in the mid-'60s at the small MacDougall Street Theatre in Greenwich Village, New York, as a random collection of poets, some of whom decided to sing. From start, their intention was to shock audiences with poetry, satire, and what respectable society considered gross obscenity.

Sanders, Weaver and Kupferberg were prime movers behind the unit which developed small but loyal following among New York Lower East Side hip community. Then the unheard-of happened: poets had turned themselves into a rock band. But not quite like any other.

The Fugs debut album, released 1965 on small jazz-oriented ESP label, contained 10 of their less offensive songs and was effectively first of what would later be called "underground" music. A second set of material for ESP was rejected as too crude for contemporary public taste and instead, a slightly less offensive package, **The Fugs,** was substituted.

The group subsequently signed to Reprise, the resulting 1968 **Tenderness Junction** album containing **Out Demons Out** peace junket anthem later adopted by English outfit Edgar Broughton Band (➧). **Junction** never exactly made any waves outside of New York, but it did provoke ESP to finally issue that originally banned second set as **Virgin Fugs** – the group's finest hour. Two more Reprise albums followed, the last in 1969, after which the Fugs folded. A 1968 compilation **Golden Filth** comprises material from the three ESP albums.

Through his book "The Family" on Charles Manson, Ed Sanders has since gone on to become one of luminaries of new U.S. journalism. Kupferberg also appears occasionally in print; Charlie Larkey later married Carole King (➧), playing bass for his missus.

Fugs historical importance is that – though no great shakes musically – they made offensiveness a fashionable and acceptable commodity in rock, a direction subsequently pursued by Stooges, MC5 and Zappa's Mothers Of Invention.

Recordings:
First Album (ESP)
Virgin Fugs (ESP)
The Fugs (ESP)
Tenderness Junction (Reprise/Transatlantic)
It Crawled Into My Hand Honest (Reprise/Transatlantic)
The Belle Of Avenue A (Reprise)
Compilations:
Golden Filth (Reprise)

Gallagher & Lyle

Benny Gallagher and Graham Lyle, both of whom play guitar, piano, mandolin, accordion, banjo and sing, first came to prominence in U.K. as songwriting members of McGuinness Flint outfit, for whom they composed most of that group's album and singles material including British hits **When I'm Dead And Gone** (1970) and **Malt And Barley Blues** (1971).

Both born in Largs, Scotland, they originally teamed-up in the early '60s in various local bands. Arrived in London 1966 where they were signed to Beatles' Apple Corps as contract songwriters, providing material for Mary Hopkin among others.

In summer 1970, on expiry of Apple contract, both were recruited by Tom McGuinness, the former Manfred Mann bass player, to join McGuinness Flint (➧). However, after some 18 months

with group, the pair opted out in favour of less restrictive independent career.

Released first four albums through A&M basically as acoustic duo (performing live as same) to certain degree of critical acclaim but little public acceptance. After well-received fifth album, the 1976 **Breakaway,** the title song of which has been recorded by Art Garfunkel, Gallagher & Lyle assembled road group to present new material: this comprising Jimmy Jewell (sax), John Mumford (trom, euphonium), Ian Rae (kybds), Alan Hornall (bs) and Ray Duffy (drums).

Shortly after, Gallagher & Lyle enjoyed spell of huge success in British singles chart with **I Wanna Stay With You** and **Heart On My Sleeve,** both tracks from **Breakaway.**

First album originally released by Capitol.

Recordings:
Gallagher & Lyle (A&M)
Willie And The Lapdog (A&M)
Seeds (A&M)
The Last Cowboy (A&M)
Breakaway (A&M)

Rory Gallagher

Durable Irish guitar virtuoso. Gallagher was born in Ballyshannon, County Donegal, but was raised from an early age in Cork, South East Eire, which he regards as his home town. He had toyed around with guitars as a child – his first "real" instrument cost £4.50 and was gifted to him at nine – and he played with and formed various bands up to leaving school at 15.

Gallagher's roots even then were firmly into blues and rock – but the Irish music scene being dominated as it is by that particularly Irish phenomenon, the showband, his first post-school gig was with The Fontana Showband (later renamed The Impact).

Against the Grain.
Courtesy Chrysalis Records.

The guitarist has recalled: "I wasn't fond of showbands, but promoters thought you had to have 15 members before you were a proper group, which meant that my own groups didn't get any work."

Gallagher played with the showband for two and a half years until their disbandment in 1965, at which point he recruited the bass player, Charlie McCracken, and the drummer, John Wilson, to form the blues trio Taste. This outfit commuted between Hamburg and Ireland, working up a solidly blues-based repertoire, until they came to London in an attempt to break into the U.K. market in 1969.

Right: Peter Gabriel demonstrates his unique stage charisma. A bad skin problem need be no barrier to success. See Genesis.

Outside of Jimi Hendrix Experience and Cream, though they never climbed similar heights of virtuosity and mass acclaim, Taste were one of the pioneering, blues-based power trios, specialising in interpretations of blues standards such as **Sugar Mama.** But Taste were strictly Rory Gallagher's band, with McCracken and Wilson often relegated to roles of back-up musicians, and it was the internal friction over this arrangement that precipitated break-up of the band in early 1971. (McCracken and Wilson went on to form short-lived Stud with guitarist Jim Cregan, later of Family.)

By this time, Taste had accrued a steady U.K. following – their four albums racked up healthy sales without denting the Top 30 lists – and Gallagher was able to retain the group's audience when he subsequently formed his own new band with fellow Irishmen Wilgar Cambell (drms) and Gerry McAvoy (bs). This time, with a working name of The Rory Gallagher Band, there would be no doubts as to who was the boss.

This line-up played on **Rory Gallagher** (1971), which also had Atomic Rooster's Vincent Crane guesting on piano, **Deuce** (1971) and **Live In Europe** (1972), the last-named giving Gallagher his first major bite at the U.K. albums charts.

The same year saw a personnel reshuffle: Wilgar Cambell was replaced by Rod de'Ath and, just before an American tour, keyboards player Lou Martin was recruited to boost line-up to present four-piece. Both new members were previously with Irish outfit Killing Floor.

With Martin's keyboards giving the band a wider range, **Blueprint** was released early 1973, following which album Gallagher completed his most successful British and American tours.

At Christmas 1973 the band returned to Ireland to play a series of sell-out gigs in Belfast, Cork and Dublin, the results being recorded on the double-set live album **Irish Tour '74** and in the 90-minute documentary movie "Rory Gallagher – Irish Tour '74", directed by Tony Palmer (♦), which was premiered at the Cork Film Festival in June 1974.

A soft-spoken, gentle-mannered Irishman (despite a reputation for toughness acquired in stormy last days of Taste), Gallagher is one of the most accomplished guitarists in rock. His playing is heavily influenced by B.B., Freddie and Albert King, and his band's music is a mixture of urban blues and Gallagher's own material.

The very antithesis of glitter rock, he has been described variously as "the hardest gigging musician in the business" and as "the people's guitarist" – the latter tag deriving from Gallagher's shunning of show business trappings. Hanging on to his battered guitars and equally battered Levis, always seemingly attired in the same checked lumberjack shirt, Gallagher has long been the butt of cynicism and jokes. Nevertheless he has survived all

trends – the aforementioned glitter/rock, the decline of the guitar hero as a rock force – and now that the latter is showing signs of going into reverse, he could be on the brink of a major breakthrough in the U.S.

To this end, he should be helped by his 1975 signing to Chrysalis Records, whose roster of acts also includes that other nascent guitar hero Robin Trower.

Album notes: the first listing below was not released until 1974 but comprises tracks recorded in Ireland circa 1967, around time of Taste's embryonic period.

Recordings:
In The Beginning (—/Emerald Gem)
Rory Gallagher (Polydor)
Deuce (Polydor)
Live In Europe (Polydor)
Blueprint (Polydor)
Tattoo (Polydor)
Irish Tour '74 (Polydor)
Against The Grain (Chrysalis)
With Taste:
Taste (Polydor)
On The Boards (Polydor)
Live Taste (Polydor)
Taste At The Isle Of Wight (Polydor)

Kenny Gamble and Leon Huff
♦ Philadelphia Soul

Art Garfunkel

Born New York, Oct 13, 1941, Garfunkel met Paul Simon at school where the two initiated a partnership that was ultimately to lead to the prodigious success of Simon and Garfunkel (♦).

Since Simon had been the dominant creative partner, it was uncertain how much Garfunkel would achieve as a solo artist when the duo split up in 1970.

He had already been attracted to the film industry, and having appeared in "Catch-22" in 1969, he made "Carnal Knowledge" in

1970 for the same director, Mike Nichols (who had used Simon & Garfunkel's music as the score of "The Graduate").

Garfunkel's first solo album, **Angel Clare,** was issued in 1973 and showed his penchant for exquisitely-produced, lavishly-orchestrated MOR material. It was praised for its overall perfection and scorned for its lack of incisiveness. The next solo album, **Breakaway,** produced by Richard Perry (♦), was released in 1975. This was more commercially successful; it included **I Only Have Eyes For You,** a No. 1 single in Britain in Oct 1975, and also **My Little Town,** which Simon had written for him to counterbalance the preponderance of saccharine material on his albums.

Recordings:
Angel Clare (Columbia/CBS)
Breakaway (Columbia/CBS)

David Gates

Born Dec 11, 1940 in Tulsa, Oklahoma, Gates was given a thorough musical education, which he found useful background when he came to work in Hollywood as a musical arranger, and then when he helped to found Bread (♦).

After leaving Bread, he, as the one who had composed most of the material and sung lead vocals was in the best position to make it alone, and his solo albums **David Gates** and **Never Let Her Go** have both been successful, though his activities have been somewhat circumspect since the demise of Bread, encouraging widespread speculation that the group would be re-formed.

Recordings:
David Gates (Elektra)
Never Let Her Go (Elektra)

Marvin Gaye

Born in Washington Apr 2, 1939, the son of a minister, Gaye began his musical career playing organ in his father's church. He was a member of the orchestra at high school, had a short and troubled spell of military service, and attached himself to street corner doowop groups.

He sang with The Rainbows, at one time Washington's premier vocal group. Don Covay was lead vocalist, though his functions would occasionally be filled by Billy Stewart or Gaye. In 1957 Gaye formed a group with two other Rainbows, and they called themselves the Marquees; under the sponsorship of Bo Diddley, they recorded **Wyat Earp** for the Okeh label, as well as backing Diddley on his own **I'm Sorry** for the Checker label. The Marquees stayed with Diddley until 1958 when Harvey Fuqua, leader of The Moonglows, arrived in Washington to put a new line-up together; he selected the Marquees to become the new Moonglows, and they made two records for Chess in 1959.

It was when The Moonglows played in Detroit that Berry Gordy heard the band, and signed-up Gaye; Fuqua, married Gwen Gordy, and became a Motown producer himself.

For some time Gaye was just a session drummer at Motown – he was on all the early records of Smokey Robinson & The Miracles, and toured with them on the road for six months. He also started making his own solo singles, and it was his fourth, **Stubborn Kind Of Fellow** (which featured backing vocals by Martha and the Vandellas) which gave him his first taste of success.

During 1963 he consolidated this with further hits – from now on every record he made went on to the U.S. R&B charts. In Britain, his most important early record was **Can I Get A Witness?**, because it brought him to the attention of the white rock audience through the cover version on the Rolling Stones' debut album, and also because it became a sort of anthem with the British "Mod" movement.

I'll Be Doggone, Ain't That Peculiar and **How Sweet It Is** provided Gaye with more hits. Motown began to use him both as a solo artist, and also in tandem with a succession of girl singers, Mary Wells, Kim Weston, Tammi Terrell, and finally Diana Ross.

Let's Get It On. Courtesy Tamla Motown Records.

He was thus already established as a reliable hitmaker when, in 1968, his popularity reached fresh heights after he recorded Gladys Knight's **I Heard It Through The Grapevine**. The song had already been a U.S. No. 1 hit for Gladys in 1967; Gaye improved on this feat by taking the song to No. 1 on both sides of the Atlantic (it was in fact his first

British hit); his version has now become accepted as one of the classic rock singles. His follow-up, **Too Busy Thinking 'Bout My Baby,** was another huge success.

Nevertheless, this marked a turning point in Gaye's career. He ceased touring altogether, and went into seclusion shortly afterwards. It is uncertain how much this was due to the traumatic effects of the death of Tammi Terrell, who collapsed in his arms on stage of a brain tumour; she died some months later.

Certainly, after a decade of being the company's most faithful retainer, he now demanded more independence of the Motown machine. In practical terms, this meant his recordings moved away from the classic three-minute dance disc to more lavish, sophisticated material.

Ironically, this only enhanced his commercial success. **What's Going On** was a song cycle that ran the gamut of contemporary American social ailments, and was scored in a lavishly orchestral manner. He claims that Motown were sceptical of its commercial potential, but they released it anyway. It became one of the company's largest-selling albums, and provided three million-selling singles – the title-track, **Mercy Mercy Me** and **Inner City Blues**. He had won his spurs as an independent writer, and now started producing and arranging his own albums as well.

His next assignment was the soundtrack of "Trouble Man", and, as with Curtis Mayfield's score for "Superfly", the quality of the music transcended that of the film itself. In 1973 he released another magnum opus – **Let's Get It On,** which again was a complete departure. It was one of the most joyous celebrations of sex ever recorded.

In 1974 Gaye returned to live performance, and his first concert for almost six years, at the Oakland Coliseum, was recorded for the album **Marvin Gaye Live.** His next album of new material was not issued for two years, and **I Want You** showed him disappointingly treading water.

He is painstaking in his work, and hence releases product less often than Motown would no doubt wish. But he and Stevie Wonder are the only two Motown artists to have really forged an identity for themselves separate from the corporate one. He now lives with his family just outside Detroit in a house formerly owned by Berry Gordy, his brother-in-law. He has behaved idiosyncratically in recent years, and has apparently become increasingly religious.

Discography lists only recent albums.

Recordings:
What's Going On (Tamla/ Tamla Motown)
Trouble Man (Tamla/ Tamla Motown)
Let's Get It On (Tamla/ Tamla Motown)
Marvin Gaye Live (Tamla/ Tamla Motown)
I Want You (Tamla/ Tamla Motown)
With Diana Ross:
Diana And Marvin (Tamla/ Tamla Motown)
Compilation:
Anthology (Tamla/ Tamla Motown)

David Geffen

Born in 1944, Geffen is one of the most important and most powerful managerial figures in the rock industry. Though renowned for never entering into contractual agreements with his clients, he nevertheless manages to persuade them to meet rigorous obligations.

He started at the William Morris Agency as a television booker for comedians before setting-up his own operation with Elliott Roberts after discovering first Laura Nyro (♦) and then Joni Mitchell (♦).

The Geffen Roberts Co. managed both Ms Mitchell and Crosby, Stills, Nash & Young (♦), before in 1971 Geffen set-up his own label, Asylum Records. His first signing was Jackson Browne; David Blue agreed to join the label, before Geffen acquired some chart success via the ministrations of Jo Jo Gunne.

Joni Mitchell completed her contract with Reprise before moving to Asylum herself; but the label became increasingly identified with West Coast country rock, partly through Browne, but primarily through the label's most commercially viable acts, The Eagles and Linda Ronstadt. In 1973 Asylum merged with Elektra and Geffen became chairman of the new company.

He also pulled off the most celebrated record industry coup of the '70s by persuading Bob Dylan to undertake his first major tour for eight years in 1974, and also signing him to Asylum for two albums (**Planet Waves** and **Before The Flood**), before Dylan quickly reverted to Columbia.

Geffen also got CSN&Y back on the road, though he was less successful in other areas. He got the original Byrds (♦) together for a reunion album they'd all rather forget, and in between times gained some personal notoriety through a much-publicised but short-lived liason with Cher.

He has been less conspicuously manipulative in recent years, but Asylum Records continues to prosper. His newest signings to the label include Tom Waits, Andrew Gold and the Cate Brothers.

Genesis

Phil Collins drums, vocals
Steve Hackett guitar
Tony Banks keyboards
Michael Rutherford bass

Formed by Peter Gabriel, Genesis' singer/leader and theatrically visual front man up to his shock departure from the band in autumn 1975, from among schoolfriends at England's famous Charterhouse Public School – a background which didn't assist their acceptance in a rock culture which prefers its heroes, if not genuinely working class, at least superficially so.

Of original four – Gabriel, Banks, guitarist Anthony Phillips and Rutherford – the first three (with Gabriel then playing drums) performed in the school group Garden Wall, although they have said that they came together initially through mutual interests in songwriting.

In a 1974 interview, Gabriel insisted that unlike other British groups with whom they have been compared – notably Yes – Genesis always considered themselves primarily as song-oriented rather than music-oriented; hence, they felt less desire than others to show off musical technique.

In fact, it was primarily as a vehicle to publicise and sell their songs that Genesis came into being post-Charterhouse and art school/university, a fifth member, John Mayhew (drms), having by this time augmented the line-up. However, they were notably unsuccessful in this aim until they came to the attention of producer, singer and all-round pop entrepreneur Jonathan King (♦) in the late '60s. King, it transpired, was also an ex-Charterhouse schoolboy, though not a contemporary.

Selling England By The Pound. Courtesy Charisma Records.

King produced their first album, **From Genesis To Revelation** (1969), also suggesting the group's name. The public showed little interest. Neither did King or Decca Records subsequently and, after a year with the company, their contract was allowed to lapse. (This debut album has since been re-issued under title **In The Beginning** – London/ Decca, 1974.)

At this point the group were on the verge of splitting, but determined to soldier on. There followed a period when several people showed interest – including Guy Stevens, then producing Mott The Hoople with whom Genesis struck up an early friendship, and the Moody Blues, who toyed with the idea of signing them to their newly inaugurated Threshold label – but nobody came up with a firm offer until Tony Stratton-Smith, boss of the small Charisma company, took out an option.

The group cut **Trespass** for Charisma in 1970 before Mayhew and Phillips quit the line-up. Phil Collins, ex of Flaming Youth and who, like Steve Marriott, had as a child actor played the Artful Dodger in a stage production of "Oliver Twist", took over on drums. A guitarist however, proved harder to come by, and Genesis played gigs for some six months as a four-piece before the arrival of Steve Hackett.

Both new members made their recording debut on the altogether more adventurous **Nursery Cryme** (1971), which reflected embryonic period of what was to become Genesis' distinctive style. At around the same time the band began to experiment on stage with the visuals and theatrics on which they would subsequently found their reputation. It was here that Peter Gabriel, bedecked in an ever more outrageous wardrobe of theatrical costumes, came into his own as the focal point of the group.

The 1972 set **Foxtrot** contained two of the band's best-known numbers **Watcher Of The Skies** and **Supper's Ready**, and marked their debut in U.K. albums lists. Their British tour in the winter of 1972–73 enhanced their growing reputation, evidenced by the chart success of the 1973 **Genesis Live** collection.

In autumn of the same year came the remarkably successful **Selling England By The Pound** album, which supplied the band's first British hit single **I Know What I Like.** By the time of the ambitious, conceptual double-set **The Lamb Lies Down On Broadway** (1974), Genesis' reputation as a major British band was already secured. They followed the album's release with their most adventurously-produced tour presentation, Gabriel acting out the story of the album's lead character, which drew sell-out audiences in Britain and considerable public attention in American concert halls.

However, in late 1975 after a spate of music business rumours, Peter Gabriel – who **was** Genesis in the minds of many of the group's fans in the same way that Paul McCartney is Wings – announced that he was leaving to work solo.

Most observers were at that point ready to write off the group's future – Gabriel looked irreplaceable. However, the band confused pundits by declining to bring in a new face; instead, drummer Phil Collins stepped forward from the drum stool to take lead vocals with quite remarkable self-confidence. The resulting album **A Trick Of The Tail** (1976) won almost unanimously excellent reviews, when it had seemed just a few months earlier that Genesis were all washed up.

To enable Collins to sing on stage, group then augmented with ex Yes, King Crimson drummer Bill Bruford. In 1975 the industrious Collins formed "offshoot" group Brand X, which cut debut album **Unorthodox Behaviour** 1976.

Steve Hackett's solo album below was released in 1975. The second and third, and fourth and sixth albums have subsequently been re-issued as two double-package couplings, both in 1975.

Recordings:
From Genesis To Revelation (London/Decca)
Trespass (ABC/Charisma)
Nursery Cryme (Charisma)
Foxtrot (Charisma)
Genesis Live (Charisma)
Selling England By The Pound (Charisma)
The Lamb Lies Down On Broadway (Atco/Charisma)
A Trick Of The Tail (Atco/Charisma)
Steve Hackett:
Voyage Of The Acolyte (Atco/Charisma)

Gentle Giant

Derek Shulman vocals, guitar
Ray Shulman bass, violin, guitar
Kerry Minnear keyboards
Gary Green guitar

John Weathers drums

Gentle Giant emerged 1970 from the ashes of Simon Dupree and the Big Sound, an undistinguished British pop group fronted by the Shulman brothers Derek (Simon Dupree), Ray and Phil, whose father was a jazz musician. Their group had slogged British pop circuit for several years, making the U.K. Top 10 in 1967 with the single **Kites** but failing to produce a follow-up.

The Giant was the brothers' way of dropping out of the then-declining pop market and making play for the burgeoning rock audience. To this end, their first album – in 1971 – made use of elements of jazz, classics and rock in a manner which nodded in direction of King Crimson (➡). However, neither of first two releases garnered much in the way of critical or public support on home-front, and in initial stages the Giant had to rely on a small but ardent European following to keep them off the breadline.

The third set, **Three Friends**, in 1972, aroused a certain degree of interest, and by the following year's **Octopus** the group were able to boast a minor following in Britain and North America, particularly in Canada.

The band themselves were never satisfied with the fifth album, **In A Glass House** (1973), however. Recorded under pressure in the wake of Phil Shulman's departure from the band, this set was never released in the U.S.

They were happier with the results of the sixth, **The Power And The Glory** (1974), which went on to become the group's biggest-selling American release. The follow-up set, **Free Hand** (1975), which was more melodic in content than its conceptual, epic-constructed predecessor, has also sold well in the U.S.

Despite overseas success, however, Gentle Giant remain critically unfavoured in their home country – where their commercial showing has also been relatively poor.

Keyboards player Kerry Minnear is a graduate of the Royal College of Music, formerly of the group Rust; guitarist Gary Green was with a blues group prior to joining Gentle Giant, though his roots are in jazz; John Weathers, who joined after **Three Friends**, had previously worked with Graham Bond and is third drummer to occupy this position in line-up.

Recordings:
Gentle Giant (Vertigo)
Acquiring The Taste (Vertigo)
Three Friends (Columbia/Vertigo)
Octopus (Columbia/Vertigo)
In A Glass House (—/Vertigo)
The Power And The Glory (Capitol/Vertigo)
Free Hand (Capitol/Chrysalis)
Interview (Chrysalis)
Compilation:
Giant Steps (Columbia/Vertigo)

Dana Gillespie

Singer and actress, b. Woking, Surrey, and a contemporary of David Bowie. British water skiing champion when she was 15 – at which age she made the first of several attempts to break into music business.

Over subsequent years she achieved marginally more success along other chosen path as an actress – appearing in Hammer production "The Lost Continent" and the British stage musical "Liz". In 1970 she was cast in the London production of "Catch My Soul", following this with a spell as Mary Magdelene in "Jesus Christ Superstar", a return to movies in Ken Russell's "Mahler", and a part in National Theatre production of Shakespeare's "The Tempest".

Meanwhile, under the aegis of David Bowie and his then-manager Tony DeFries, Ms Gillespie made most concerted attempt to date to break into rock as a singer. Unfortunate, DeFries' MainMan organisation opted to package her as some kind of ersatz Bowie, with similar bisexual undertones – viz title of her first RCA album **Weren't Born A Man** – the publicity from which probably caused more harm than good.

The "supervamp" persona, however, stopped short at the promotion and packaging of her records – on the actual grooves of both RCA releases, Ms Gillespie turned in relatively understated performances in an area which might be loosely described as blue-eyed soul. Public and critical acclaim has thus far eluded her, though reports improved via 1975 gigs with a pick-up band. As actress, she picked up some excellent reviews for her part in the British stage musical "Mardi Gras" (1976).

Recordings:
Box Of Surprises (London/Decca)
Weren't Born A Man (RCA)
Ain't Gonna Play No Second Fiddle (RCA)

Charlie Gillett

Born Feb 20, 1942 in Morecambe, Lancashire, Charlie Gillett published "The Sound Of The City" in 1970, a book which was written as an extension of his MA thesis which he took at Columbia University, New York, and which has since become recognised as the definitive account of the evolution of rock 'n' roll.

In 1975 he completed his second book, "Making Tracks", a history of Atlantic Records, and he has also compiled "Rock Files", Vols I–IV (published in the U.S. as "Rock Almanac" in 1976), a collection of subjective articles and hard info about British and American chart placings.

After a spell managing Kilburn And The High Roads (➡) 1973–74, he formed his own record company Oval with Gordon Nelki, and in 1974 issued **Another Saturday Night,** a superb collection of late '60s cajun-style material licensed from the Jin and Swallow labels in Louisiana.

Since Mar 1972, he has also hosted his own radio programme on BBC Radio London, "Honky Tonk", which has a relatively small but totally devoted audience.

Gary Glitter

Born Paul Gadd in Banbury, Oxfordshire, England, on – according to his record company biography – May 8, 1944, although

sceptics have suggested this date errs greatly in Glitter's favour.

Using stage name Paul Raven, Gadd spent a lengthy early period in virtual anonymity, pushing out a string of unsuccessful solo pop singles for first Decca and later Parlophone labels (for the latter he did manage to rack up a hit in the Middle East 1961 with his version of **Walk On By**). In 1965, he worked for a spell as a programme assistant on the British TV pop show "Ready Steady Go", and in this same year made his first contact with Mike Leander, the man who would become his manager and co-writer in Gadd's later reincarnation as Gary Glitter.

Leander was at that time forming a band to support Irish MOR trio The Bachelors on a tour. Gadd became vocalist with the band which, after the Bachelors' engagement, metamorphosed into Paul Raven And The Boston Show Band.

In 1967, back as Paul Raven, solo-pop-star-hopeful, Gadd signed to MCA Records – in fact he appears on that label's million-selling **Jesus Christ Superstar** album. Out of this period also came a flop version of Beatles cut **Here Comes The Sun,** this time under a new alias Paul Monday.

It was his signing to Bell Records in 1971 and renewed acquaintance with Mike Leander which reversed Gadd's up-to-then abysmally undistinguished career. Shamelessly jumping on the "glitter-rock" bandwagon set in motion by the likes of Rod Stewart, Elton John and Marc Bolan's T. Rex, Gadd and Leander produced from their drawing board the startling specimen Gary Glitter, in which was embodied the ultimate of every element of the new "glamour" fad.

Gadd/Glitter was suddenly all over British TV screens, his far-from-svelte figure squeezed into silver lurex jump suits, the whole spectacle atop of stacked platform heels, with a backing group – The Glitter Band – similarly attired. His first single, **Rock And Roll Parts 1 And Two,** in fact, took some four months to make the British charts – but, when it did, it opened the floodgates for a whole string of similar one-riff U.K. smashes: **Didn't Know I Loved You (Till I Saw You Rock 'n' Roll), Do You Wanna Touch Me?, Hello Hello I'm Back Again, I'm The Leader Of The Gang, I Love You Love Me Love** and so on and so forth. (Later, The Glitter Band were to issue their own singles and albums concurrently with Gadd's, and now exist as separate entity, although minus original lead singer John Rossall.)

Glitter's unabashed commerciality at first fired the rock press into fierce denunciations of everything he stood for. However, though many still today regard him as a freak out-take from an equally freak period, criticisms became muted in latter stages. Most observers acknowledge Glitter and Leander's shrewd use of showmanship, also their simple yet highly effective compositional ability, if not exactly endorsing same.

Certainly Glitter managed to prove he was more than just a passing fad, lasting the course much better than other teenybopper contemporaries. The hits were still coming, the Glitter concert spectaculars still selling out when, at the turn of 1976, he announced his retirement from the music business for "personal reasons", he has, to date, kept to himself. His departure leaves no great loss to mourn over – then again, it must remain a possibility that his retirement is only stage one of a lucrative come-back plan.

Recordings:
Glitter (Bell)
Touch Me (Bell)
Remember Me This Way (Bell)
G.G. (Bell)
Compilation:
Greatest Hits (Bell)

Andrew Gold

Born Burbank, California Aug 2, 1951, of famous parents. His father, Ernest Gold, is a veteran composer of film scores (including that for "Exodus"), while his mother, Marni Nixon, has also worked in films, as the off-screen singing voice of actresses like Audrey Hepburn and Natalie Wood in many of Hollywood's most outstanding musicals, including "West Side Story", "My Fair Lady" and "The King And I".

Andrew became musically accomplished, learning to play guitar and piano, and in his mid-teens formed a band called Bryndle, which also included Wendy Waldman (♦) and former Stone Poney Kenny Edwards; the band provided Gold with studio experience, and also associations that were to prove lasting – particularly with Edwards, and producer Chuck Plotkin.

After Bryndle collapsed, Gold became seasoned as a session musician before he and Edwards joined a band called The Rangers; when Linda Ronstadt (♦) heard tapes of the band, she invited the two of them to work with her, both on stage and in the studio.

Gold has since become virtually Ronstadt's right-hand man, bringing his instrumental versatility to her sessions, and also working out many of her arrangements. In between times, he continued his work as a sessioneer, playing on Wendy Waldman's first two albums as well as recordings by Art Garfunkel, Carly Simon and Loudon Wainwright.

In 1975 he signed with Asylum Records, and his debut solo album, produced by Plotkin, was issued later that year. The songs, mainly sophisticated pop material, were all self-composed; much of the instrumentation was similarly all his own work.

Recordings:
Andrew Gold (Asylum)

Golden Earring

George Kooymans guitar, vocals
Rinus Gerritsen bass, keyboards
Barry Hay vocals, flute, sax
Cesar Zuiderwijk drums
Robert Jan Stips keyboards

Dutch rock band, first came to attention of American and British audiences in early '70s after nearly a decade as Holland's top group. Earring, in fact, first hit the Dutch Top 10 with their debut single **Please Go** in 1964, since which time every one of their 19 singles and 10 albums have entered home charts. Kooymans and Gerritsen are the survivors of that original line-up – although the band is still produced by the man who "discovered" them, Freddy Haayen, now managing director of Polydor Limited.

It was in 1968, after overturning early quasi-bubblegum image in favour of hard rock approach, that the group attempted to broaden their appeal into American and British markets. For next three/four years they made occasional forays into both areas, picking up creditable reviews but minimal record sales. The group recognized that their material wasn't yet sufficiently sophisticated for the new audiences, and set about creating new repertoire heavy on visuals and rock theatrics.

In 1972, Golden Earring were hired by The Who to support them on a European tour (the two bands had been friendly since

Above: Angel's Egg. Courtesy Virgin. Cut in the woods near Gong's French home, this was the second part of their Radio Gnome's Invisible Trilogy.

meeting in Holland in 1965) and it was out of this pairing that the Dutchmen were signed to Track Records by Who managers Kit Lambert and Chris Stamp. The first release on Track, **Hearring Earring** in 1973, was a compilation album featuring the best cuts from previous two albums, and was designed to fill void until release of **Moontan** later that same year.

With fellow Dutchmen Focus having proved by this time that it was possible to break native stranglehold on "foreign" territories, **Moontan** drew considerable interest and sales in both America and Britain – as did the major hit single from the album, **Radar Love**. At this point, the Earring looked set for a gold-plated commercial future but, for reasons that are hard to define, they have since then failed to fulfil that potential.

Recordings:
Hearring Earring (Track)
Moontan (Track)
Switch (Track)
To The Hilt (Track)

Gong

Mike Howlett bass, vocals
Didier Malherbe saxes, flute
Pierre Moerlen drums
Mireille Bauer xylophone, glockenspiel, percussion
Patrice Lemoine keyboards
Jorge Pinchevsky violin

Gong's tortuously confused history – only Malherbe survives from original line-up, while Moerlen has split from and rejoined the group twice – evolves from the activities of composer/guitarist/poet Daevid Allen. An Australian beatnik who first arrived in U.K. 1961, Allen was a founder-member with Mike Ratledge, Robert Wyatt (♦) and Kevin Ayers (♦) of the British avant-garde outfit Soft Machine (♦).

Allen was with the Softs on their first European tour. However, on return, his passport was claimed to be invalid and the Australian was consequently denied re-entry to the U.K.

Instead, Allen drifted back to Paris (where prior to the Softs he had written poetry and fraternised with the literary cognoscenti) and along with vocalist Gillie Smyth began to play with various itinerant musicians. Out of this came two solo albums for Byg Records, **Magick Brother, Mystic Sister** and **Banana Moon**, and eventually Gong circa 1970.

Camembert Electrique and **Continental Circus** were credited to this flexible new group – which included Gillie Smyth, plus Christian Tritsch and Didier Malherbe, and drummer Pip Pyle on the first set. Pyle, later of Hatfield And The North (♦), quit during Gong's first U.K. tour and was replaced by jazz-based Laurie Allen.

Bassist was Francis Mose, ex of Magma.

By this time, Gong were among the most popular of avant-garde bands operating in France – accruing small cult following in Britain through import shop sales and occasional concerts. (An example of how they sounded then can be heard on the 1973-released Revelation live album **Glastonbury Fayre** – various artists.)

However, in early 1972 Daevid Allen disbanded the group to concentrate on his writing, only re-forming Gong towards the end of that year upon offer of new recording deal from Britain's Virgin Records. Malherbe, Smyth, Laurie Allen, Tritsch and Mose were retained from original incarnation, with additions of British guitarist Steve Hillage and synthesiser player Tim Blake.

This group recorded **The Flying Teapot** for Virgin in early 1973, after which Daevid Allen and Gillie Smyth split for Spain. A group calling itself Paragong (mostly billed as "Gong") and comprising Hillage, Blake, Malherbe plus newcomers Pierre Moerlen and Fiji-born Mike Howlett toured France through the spring until Daevid Allen and Gillie Smyth's return in June.

Thus constituted, Gong cut **Angel's Egg** (1973), recorded in the woods near their French home, and **You** (1974), at Virgin's Manor Studios in England. With the earlier **Flying Teapot**, these completed Allen's Radio Gnome Invisible trilogy, concerned with the activities of the imaginary planet Gong, and Allen then left the group once more to write, an activity he has since pursued at a leisurely pace at his Majorcan home.

It was after **You** that Pierre Moerlen left the band twice, replaced once extensively by Bill Bruford, fresh from the demise of King Crimson (♦), on the second occasion by Brian Davison, ex of Nice and Refugee.

Steve Hillage recorded a solo album **Fish Rising**, which was released in 1975 and included most of Gong personnel, but by the end of that year he too had departed. The group re-formed for the 1976 set **Shamal**, produced by Nick Mason of Pink Floyd and backed by heavy Virgin promotion. All three new members, however, already had previous associations with Gong: French-born Mireille Bauer having played sessions for **Angel's Egg** and **You**; Argentinian Jorge Pinchevsky having supported the group on their 1975 U.K. tour; Patrice Lemoine, also French-born, having jammed with the band in Strasbourg circa 1973.

Apart from the aforementioned **Glastonbury Fayre** set, Gong also appear on one side of the double-album **Greasy Truckers: Live At Dingwalls Dance Hall** (1974) and on Dashiell Hedayat's **Obsolete** album (1971). Other album notes: **Camembert Electrique**, after being strong import seller on original Continental label Byg, was issued in U.K. on Virgin's Caroline label in 1974; similarly, Allen's **Banana Moon** solo album was re-issued on Caroline 1975.

Allen's third, belated solo project, **Good Morning**, was released in 1976, featuring accompaniment by the Spanish group Euterpe with whom he toured U.K.

Recordings:
Camembert Electrique
(—/Caroline)
Continental Circus
(—/Phonogram)
The Flying Teapot (—/Virgin)
Angel's Egg (Virgin)
You (Virgin)
Shamel (Virgin)
Daevid Allen:
Magick Brother, Mystic Sister
(Byg – Europe only)
Banana Moon (—/Caroline)
Good Morning (Virgin)
Steve Hillage:
Fish Rising (Virgin)

Steve Goodman

Born Chicago, July 25, 1948, Goodman attended the University of Illinois, and by late '60s was performing regularly at folk festivals, while still living in Chicago; he supplemented his irregular income by writing advertising jingles.

In 1971 he was discovered – along with John Prine (➧) – by the unlikely combination of Paul Anka and Kris Kristofferson, and signed to Buddah Records.

Debut album **Steve Goodman** was released 1972; it included **City Of New Orleans**, which has since become recognized as a classic train song and been widely recorded, the most famous cover versions being by Arlo Guthrie (who took the song into the U.S. Top 20) and Judy Collins. Thus by the time he was making his second album **Somebody Else's Troubles**, Goodman's eclectic talents were already being widely appreciated, so that he was able to enlist the services of Bob Dylan, Maria Muldaur and various Rascals.

Despite such distinguished support, the album was received with an evident lack of enthusiasm, not least from Goodman himself, who devoted more time to live performance. He switched to Asylum Records, and carefully planned his debut for them, **Jessie's Jig And Other Favourites**. It was a mixture of folk and rag tunes, and compositions by himself and other welterweight songwriters, such as Prine and Jimmy Buffett. Nevertheless, the album still failed to reach a mass audience.

Recordings:
Steve Goodman (Buddah)
Somebody Else's Troubles
(Buddah)
Jessie's Jig And Other Favourites (Asylum)
Words We Can Dance To
(Asylum)

Berry Gordy Jnr
➧ Tamla Motown

Bill Graham

American promoter and rock entrepreneur, variously regarded as the founding father and/or undertaker of West Coast rock. An aggressive, hot-blooded yet thoroughly astute businessman, Graham rose in flamboyant style to become the single most important promoter and booking

agent in North America.

The tough, often bullying side of his character – which brought him into several head-on clashes with major rock figures, most of which Graham won – was unquestionably a reflection of a remarkably hard upbringing. Born Wolfgang Grajonca to Russian parents in Berlin 1931, his father died in an accident two days after his birth. The young Graham grew up in orphanages in Germany and France before, fleeing from the invading Nazis, his arrival in New York. He spent the latter part of his youth in a Jewish foster home in The Bronx. In 1949 he changed his name legally to Bill Graham, as which he was drafted into the U.S. Army for the Korean War.

Back in New York, he worked as a cab driver to finance his way through a course in business management, moving West in 1955 when he received his degree.

In the rock field, Graham first came to notice in 1965 as business manager of the San Francisco Mime Troupe. Looking for a venue in which to hold a benefit gig for the Troupe, Graham came across a decrepit skating rink in the black ghetto – his first concert there was so successful that Graham was soon leasing the rink permanently and, having renamed it The Fillmore Auditorium, was taking bookings for the Bay Area bands comprising the nascent San Francisco rock movement. The place rapidly achieved the status of a local, thence a national, legend.

In late 1967 Graham's and the Fillmore's reputations spread even further afield when the Carousel Ballroom in San Francisco was acquired to become the new Fillmore West, and a Fillmore East opened at the Village Theatre in New York the following year. Over the next three years, until the closures of the venues in 1971, the name Fillmore became synonymous internationally with the rock explosion – just as Bill Graham accrued unparalleled reputation as an ebullient entrepreneur whose wily fledgling rock acts and their managements crossed at their own risk.

By time of their closures – Graham said it was because of the over-commercialization of the music, his detractors countercharged that Graham was a direct cause of same – the Fillmores had played host to virtually all of America's top bands, as well as being regarded by British acts as the launching pad to U.S. success.

After the Fillmores, Graham's influence abated only marginally; he remains a powerful force, particularly on the West Coast. Among his credits are the Bob Dylan and The Band U.S. tour (1974); the world's biggest-ever rock festival (600,000 people) at Watkins Glen, New York, in July 1973; the 1974 CSN&Y re-union tour; and the star-studded 1975 SNACK benefit bonanza. His attempt to form his own record label was, however, not so successful.

One-time manager of Jefferson Airplane, more recently he has assumed management of Santana and Montrose.

Graham Central Station

Larry Graham bass, vocals
Patrice Banks drums, vocals
Herschel Kennedy clarinet, vocals
Willie Sparks drums
David Vega guitar
Robert Sam vocals, organ

Larry Graham, born in Beaumont, Texas Aug 14, 1946, grew-up in Oakland, California, and attended Cabot College for 18 months. He learned bass and organ and accompanied his mother, a professional pianist, in local clubs for four years, before meeting Sylvester Stewart, then a record producer and DJ. When the latter put together Sly & The Family Stone (➧) in 1967, he invited Graham to be bass player.

Graham remained in Family Stone until the end of 1972, playing on all the band's albums up to and including **Fresh**. At the time he left was producing an American band called Hot Chocolate, which consisted of Banks, Kennedy, Sparks and Vega; Kennedy and Sparks had previously been working in the backing band of Little Sister, the spin-off group from Sly & The Family Stone.

Instead of producing an album for Hot Chocolate, Graham combined with them, and Robert Sam, who'd previously been in Billy Preston's backing band, to form Graham Central Station. They played their first concert on Jan 28, 1973, soon gained a contract with Warner Bros, since when they have released albums that retained the poly-rhythmic funk of the Family Stone but not apparently moved on from it.

Recordings:
Graham Central Station
(Warner Bros)
Release Yourself (Warner Bros)
Ain't No Bout Adout It
(Warner Bros)
Mirror (Warner Bros)

Grand Funk (Railroad)

Mark Farner guitar, vocals
Mel Schacher bass
Don Brewer drums
Craig Frost organ

The all-time loud white noise (as Rod Stewart has so cogently described them), loathed and reviled with virtual unanimity by rock critics in America and Britain, Grand Funk nonetheless have racked-up a whole string of instant-gold albums, singles and sell-out concerts throughout the Western hemisphere to make them America's foremost exponents of heavy metal thrash.

Their story starts in Flint, Michigan, hometown of Farner (b. Sep 29, 1948) and Brewer (b. Sep 3, 1948). Schacher, the third founder-Funk, is from Owosso, Michigan (b. Apr 8, 1951). The three crossed paths several times in various rock groups during their teens, but the turning point came when drummer Don Brewer joined a group called The Pack and first came into contact with Terry Knight, the man who was to play a leading role in Grand Funk's stake for rock fame.

Knight was also from Flint (b. Apr 9, 1943) and had become a popular radio DJ in Detroit by the

time he was 20 – until his head-strong personality forced the station to dispense with his services. Knight then joined The Pack (later Terry Knight and the Pack) as lead singer, assisting them towards a series of local hits. However, Knight's aggressive nature eventually led him to fall out with the rest of the band, and the singer struck out for New York in an attempt to make out in the Big Apple.

Don Brewer, meanwhile, played on with The Pack until late 1968 when, with schoolfriend Mark Farner, he determined to form his own group. The pair brought in Schacher on bass, and Brewer called Terry Knight back from New York to advise the trio, Grand Funk Railroad.

Knight listened, was impressed with the potential he saw, and agreed to help band – on the condition that he was allowed complete control. As manager he organised their debut gig in Buffalo, New York, spring 1969 and subsequently handled their career in characteristically rigorous style: acting as press spokesman in interviews, musical mentor, producer, and supervising promotion of group's image (rumour has it that Capitol Records destroyed 30,000 covers planned for first Funk album because Knight wasn't satisfied with aspects of the design).

Born To Die.
Courtesy Capitol Records.

His first breakthrough was to secure Grank Funk a spot at the Atlanta Pop Festival in July 1969 – waiving a fee to do so – at which the group's "loud white noise" went down to a phenomenal audience response.

On the strength of this, although Knight had several rejects before finding a taker, Grand Funk signed to Capitol. The first album set the pattern for all successive releases. Tuneless heavy metal at its most crass, it received a unanimous thumbs-down from rock critics, achieved little or no radio airplay, yet went to the top of the U.S. albums charts and ended 1969 a gold seller. In the same year came the first of the band's singles smashes, **Time Machine** and **Mr Limousine Driver**.

In 1970 further hostile reviews were countered by colossal sales: this time thrice-fold in the albums market with **Grand Funk, Closer To Home** and the double in-concert set **Live Album**. With more singles success to ice America's most lucrative-ever heavy metal cake, five million dollars worth of sales were racked-up in that one year.

By 1971, Grand Funk albums (the Railroad appendage had been dropped the previous year) were guaranteed gold status prior to release, Terry Knight's business brain had made them a sell-out attraction across the States (reaching its peak with two house-full concerts at New York's massive Shea Stadium), and it looked as if the band's metallic thrashings would go on to conquer the globe. (In fact, while other areas have succumbed, Britain has to date kept the Funk at arm's length; it could be argued that with its own, marginally-better heavy metal exports such as Black Sabbath and Status Quo, the U.K. has little need of imported heavyweight noise.)

However, after the **E Pluribus Funk** album in December 1971 and three years of Terry Knight's all-pervasive influence, Grand Funk decided to off their Svengali-like manager in favour of John Eastman, a New York lawyer who is also business representative and brother-in-law of Paul McCartney.

Knight responded by charging Eastman with "deliberate, wrongful and malicious interference" in a five million dollar damages suit, and his erstwhile act with breach of contract. For a time, writs pursued the Funk around the States, although Knight emerged the loser in the legal battle that ensued. The band are now managed by Andy Cavaliere.

Craig Frost (b. Apr 20, 1948) and a long-time friend of the Funk from Flint, Michigan, augmented group as keyboards player during sessions for the 1972 Funk-produced **Phoenix** set, joining them as fourth member for the follow-up **We're An American Band** (1973). This last was produced by Todd Rundgren (♦).

Shinin' On was released in early 1974, followed later same year by **All The Girls In The World Beware** on which the Funk attempted to introduce soul influences into the dark world of heavy metal, utilizing a horn section on certain tracks. They followed this with major world-wide tour in 1975.

The band still live in Michigan, where Mark Farner has a 110-acre farm on which he rears horses, one of which has won him major awards in national shows.

All albums listed below have achieved American gold status, although the rock press has remained entrenched in its view that Grand Funk possess nothing to single them out from hundreds of other (unknown) riff-happy bands.

Recordings:

On Time (Capitol)
Grand Funk (Capitol)
Closer To Home (Capitol)
Live Album (Capitol)
Survival (Capitol)
E Pluribus Funk (Capitol)
Phoenix (Capitol)
We're An American Band (Capitol)
Shinin' On (Capitol)
All The Girls In The World Beward (Capitol)
Born To Die (Capitol)
Compilation:
Mark, Don & Mel – 1969-1971 (Capitol)

Peter Grant
➧ Led Zeppelin

Below: Jerry Garcia.

The Grateful Dead

Jerry Garcia guitar
Phil Lesh bass
Bob Weir rhythm guitar
Keith Godchaux piano

Donna Godchaux vocals
Mickey Hart percussion
Bill Kreutzmann drums

One of San Francisco's best-loved bands, the Grateful Dead had an ethos that was a product of the hippie/drug environment from which they sprang, and are one of the few community bands to have attained some commercial success.

The Dead started with Jerry Garcia (b. San Francisco, Aug 1, 1942). In 1959 he joined the army, though he came out after nine months and met Robert Hunter, who was to become the Dead's non-performing songwriter. They attended San Mateo Jnr College together, and Garcia started playing the coffee-house circuit in the San Francisco Bay Area (at the same time as people like Country Joe McDonald and Jim McGuinn), and it was there he met both Bob Weir and Ron McKernan, nicknamed Pigpen, who played harp and piano.

Garcia took a job at a music store, and became acquainted with Bill Kreutzmann. While Kreutzmann and Pigpen formed a rock band called The Zodiacs, Garcia, who was at this time into ethnic music – folk, blues and country – formed a bluegrass band with Hunter (who was then participating in LSD tests at Stanford University) called The Wildwood Boys – the other members of the group being David Nelson, who turned-up later in the New Riders Of The Purple Sage (➧) and Pete Albin, who became one of the founder members of Big Brother And The Holding Company (➧ Janis Joplin). They subsequently changed their name to the Hart Valley Drifters, and in this guise won the 1963 Monterey Folk Festival.

This was the background to the group, with the leading protagonists already assembled; it provided a hint of the cross-fertilisation to follow, which would help to create the thriving San Franciscan music scene.

The direct antecedents of the Grateful Dead can be traced back to Garcia's next inspiration, Mother McCree's Uptown Jug Champions, which included Hank Harrison's, "A Social History Of The Grateful Dead", Pigpen had spent some time playing in small blues clubs, accompanying Janis Joplin.)

Unfortunately, nobody wanted a West Coast jug-band at the time, so at Pigpen's insistence they became an electric blues band and changed their name to The Warlocks. Dawson had left by now, so Kreutzmann was brought in as drummer, and when they started playing gigs in San Francisco in July 1965, Garcia offered the job of bass player to Phil Lesh.

Lesh had known Garcia five years earlier. He had a background in classical music, having been trained in violin, trumpet and composition. He worked for a radio hootenanny show, and knew Ken Kesey. Garcia wanted him in the band, and the fact that he had never before played bass was irrelevant. In any case, Lesh was such a prodigiously talented musician that he learned in two weeks.

So The Warlocks were assembled with a line-up of: Garcia, (gtr, vcls), Weir (rhym gtr), Pigpen (kybds), Lesh (bs, vcls), and Bill Kreutzmann (aka Bill Sommers) (drms). Initially they played rock 'n' roll, but gradually, under the influence of a consciousness-expanding chemical called LSD their music took on less conventional forms. This was the period when the whole Dead gestalt was unfurled. They became the house-band for the Acid Freaks and Merry Pranksters who hung out at the Ken Kesey corral in La Honda, because Kesey liked them if no one else did.

This was the period documented in Tom Wolfe's book, "The Electric Kool-Aid Acid Test". The Acid Tests of 1965, in fact, were seminal events, as they were multi-media electronic entertainments, possibly the only successful ones ever to have been arranged. With all these freaks surrounding them, the Dead's music rapidly became a vast and colourful tapestry of hybrid influences, as all kinds of musical form were assimilated by the band.

Acid was legal in California until ~~August~~ *Sept.* 1966, so all this was a licit background for the group. Such events helped develop the band's identiy as a community group – they often played for free, for example, and didn't really start making money until the '70s.

In 1966 they chose their name; in keeping with the band's image, it was a decision made under the influence of various drugs. Grateful Dead is a kind of folk ballad collected by Francis Child. The band thought it seemed vaguely appropriate, and certainly it had trippy connotations.

In 1967 their growing reputation as a live band won them a contract with Warner Bros, and they recorded their debut album **The Grateful Dead** over three days. It set out the basics of the band's music, though not particularly successful, and, going to the opposite extreme, they took six months to record their follow-up **Anthem Of The Sun** (released summer 1968), which left them heavily in debt to their record company – as they were way over schedule – but at least the painstaking nature of the Dead's music was better conveyed; it was a critical, though not a commercial, success.

Even so, for a band with one good album under their belt, and a first-class reputation in live performance, they were securing very little media attention, possibly because the band, with their almost studious approach, lacked a charismatic personality. They had however recruited two new members – Mickey Hart, on percussion, and Tom Constanten (an old friend of Lesh's), who had written a symphony at the age of 13 and reputedly had an IQ of 170 on keyboards.

By the time of their third album, with the palindromic title **Aoxomoxoa**, they were seriously in debt to Warners. However, things began to turn upward. At the beginning of 1970 they did the logical thing and made a live double album (since so much of their appeal was based on their live performance, and anyway how could they resist the title **Live Dead**?)

The album illustrated perfectly the musical stance of the band; songs like **Dark Star** and **St Stephen** were lengthy extemporisations, but fully conceived mood music. No one knew more about music-to-get-stoned-by than the Dead.

They issued two more albums in 1970; this was undoubtedly their most creative period. **Workingman's Dead** was their first fully successful studio album (and also the first one that Warners had regarded as marketable). It reached back to Garcia's love of country music, and contained short, well-constructed songs and had an overall mellowness, with much acoustic guitar work, and some fine harmonies, which had been inspired by Crosby, Stills and Nash. The lyrics were by Hunter, the music by Lesh and Garcia.

American Beauty, released towards the end of the year, was in many ways their crowning achievement, with tracks that were tightly-constructed observant pieces, and included the autobiographical **Truckin',** a song that recounted their adventures and mishaps of that year.

It had indeed been an eventful year; they had had to file a charge of embezzlement against their manager, Lenny Hart, Mickey's father. Mickey was naturally upset, and left the band after **American Beauty** (though he did later re-join). They had been busted for a second time in New Orleans, and the threat of prison sentences was hanging over them. In addition, Constanten left the band to devote more time to

scientology.

On the more positive side, they had played their first European date, at a festival in England just outside Newcastle-under-Lyme, and had performed to enthusiastic audiences throughout America in a series of concerts with an off-shoot band, the New Riders Of The Purple Sage (➧), in a promotion called "An Evening With The Grateful Dead".

This was the peak of the Dead's in-concert gestalt. They played marathon sets of two to five hours' duration, with a repertoire as varied as any band has managed. Not that what they played mattered, since the ~~audience was usually too stoned to notice and/or care~~; the Dead were the first band from the underground to become a massive institution, and they did it on their own terms. Each concert was more than a concert, it was a total experience; and it was more than a total experience, it was a whole way of life.

In 1971 they released their second live double album – called simply **The Grateful Dead,** even though they'd used the title before, since Warners had nixed their original title, Skullfuck. Despite Warners' objections, it became the band's first gold album. By now, they were definitely in the black as a recording act.

Nevertheless, these four albums formed a pinnacle of achievement they have not been able to repeat. In 1971 they played at the Fillmore East with the Beach Boys (an event which led to totally spurious rumours about the two bands going into the studios together). By the end of the year, Pigpen was becoming seriously ill with a liver disease, and Keith Godchaux was brought into the band to play keyboards. He had previously played with the Dave Mason band; he also recruited his wife, Donna, who had formerly been a session singer in Nashville and Muscle Shoals.

American Beauty.
Courtesy Warner Bros Records.

Live Dead. Courtesy
Warner Bros Records.

In April and May of 1972 the band made an extremely successful tour of Europe, though when they released another live album that this time wasn't merely a double, but a triple, **Europe '72** (the band had wanted to call it Europe On Five Thousand Dollars A Day) it all began to seem too much. As the Dead's concerts got longer, so their music began to display signs of flatulent circumlocution.

On Mar 8, 1973 Pigpen, who had accompanied the band on their 1972 Euro tour, against doctor's advice, died of a stomach haemorrhage.

The Dead carried on, though from this point solo projects were being worked out by members of the band – Garcia's own debut solo album having been released in 1972, beating Bob Weir's infinitely superior **Ace** by only a few months. The Dead issued another live album – **History Of The Grateful Dead, Vol. I, Bear's Choice,** which had been recorded live at the Fillmore East in February 1970, and was an eclectic selection of material.

In 1973 the Dead appeared with The Band and the Allman Brothers at the largest latterday festival, at Watkins Glen, but then in 1974 they stopped full-time touring, partly it seems because they were in danger of becoming an anachronism (as the last of the species that functioned on the belief that rock music could change the world) and partly because it gave the band's members time to concentrate on their various solo projects, which inevitably were becoming more creative than those of the band itself – though the Dead maintain that they will continue to play as occasion sees fit.

The band's later albums – **Wake Of The Flood** and **Mars Hotel** have not been entirely convincing, but **Blues For Allah** showed them moving into a quiet, introspective phase and a jazz-oriented direction.

Wake Of The Flood was the initial release on Grateful Dead Records which had been set up in July 1973 to handle solely albums by the band, and in the following January Round Records was established to handle solo project by the band's members. Though distribution was originally undertaken by themselves, in 1975 they arranged a deal through United Artists.

Meanwhile, the members of the band did their own individual thing. Garcia rehearsed with a line-up of John Kahn (bs), Ronnie Tutt (drms), and Nicky Hopkins (kybds). Bill Kreutzmann joined Keith and Donna Godchaux's jazz and R&B band; Lesh teamed up with composer Ned Lagin to form Seastones, a venture into bio-electric music. Mickey Hart was in the Diga Rhythm Band, a percussion ensemble featuring tabla-player Zakir Hassain. Bob Weir looked to be on to the best bet with Kingfish, a Californian band that featured ex-New Riders bass player David Torbert, and whose 1976 debut album was more than impressive.

The Dead have also set up a film production company, Round Reels, and have financed two feature-length documentaries. One is a film about New York Hell's Angels and is called "Angel Forever, Forever Angel"; the other is a film of the Dead's five days in concert at the Winterland, San Francisco in October 1974. It is inevitably accompanied by a double-album soundtrack.

There are two books about the Dead – Hank Harrison's "A Social

History Of The Grateful Dead'' (Links/Star) and a lengthy ''Rolling Stone'' interview, credited to Jerry Garcia, Charles Reich and Jann Wenner, ''Garcia – A Signpost to New Space'' (Straight Arrow).

Recordings:

The Grateful Dead (Warner Bros)	**Hotel** (Grateful Dead)
Anthem Of The Sun (Warner Bros)	**Blues For Allah** (Grateful Dead)
Aoxomoxoa (Warner Bros)	**Steal Your Face** (Grateful Dead)
Live/Dead (Warner Bros)	**Jerry Garcia solo:**
Workingman's Dead (Warner Bros)	**Garcia** (Warner Bros)
American Beauty (Warner Bros)	**Reflections** (Round)
The Grateful Dead (Warner Bros)	**Jerry Garcia with Howard Wales:**
Europe '72 (Warner Bros)	**Hooteroll** (Douglas)
History Of The Grateful Dead, Vol. I, Bear's Choice (Warner Bros)	**Bob Weir solo:**
	Ace (Warner Bros)
Wake Of The Flood (Grateful Dead Records)	**Kingfish:**
	Kingfish (Round)
Grateful Dead From The Mars	**Seastones:**
	Seastones (Round)
	Diga Rhythm Band:
	Diga Rhythm Band (Round)

Dobie Gray

Drift Away

Drift Away. Courtesy MCA. Give the beat, boys, and Free my soul . . . Gray notches up a winner.

Dobie Gray

Born Brookshire, Texas in 1942, one of eight children, Gray had a poor upbringing – his parents were share-croppers. In 1964 he went West looking for work as a singer, and answered an ad. which put him in touch with Sonny Bono, then at Specialty Records in Los Angeles. In no time at all, Gray had had two hit singles – **Look At Me** and **The In Crowd,** the latter being a major hit in America and Britain; it was later covered by The Mamas and Papas (♦) though, as Gray's own career soon went into eclipse, the song survived better than he did.

For a time he went to law school, and he also enjoyed some success as an actor. He appeared as Billy the Kid in the New York production of ''The Beard'', was in Jean Genet's ''The Balcony'', and also spent two years in the cast of ''Hair''.

He didn't break his ties with the music business, and worked both with a group called Pollution, and also cutting demos for Paul Williams (♦). His luck really turned again through his associa-

tion with Paul's brother, Mentor, whom he had met when they were both staff writers for A&M. Once Gray had severed his contractual links with Pollution, he secured a contract with MCA Records.

His first album release, **Drift Away** (1973) was produced by Mentor Williams in Nashville with the aid of many distinguished sidemen, including David Briggs, Reggie Young, Kenny Malone and Troy Seals. At the time, it was still unusual for a black singer to be recording in Nashville with country musicians, but the album was an unqualified success, and the single, **Drift Away,** written by Williams, became No. 1 in the U.S. charts, and has since become recognized as a rock classic, even in the U.K. where the song has yet to gain a chart placing.

Gray's subsequent albums for MCA were equally professional and widely admired. They became a source of material for other artists – apart from all the cover versions of **Drift Away** (of which Rod Stewart's on **Atlantic Crossing,** is probably the best-known), Seals' **We Had It All** and **There's A Honky Tonk Angel** have both become standard fare for country artists, Tom Jans' **Loving Arms** did well for Millie

Jackson, and **Cado Queen** was included on Maggie Bell's debut solo album.

Meanwhile, Gray moved on to Capricorn Records, and his first album for the label, **New Ray Of Sunshine,** was issued towards the end of 1975.

Recordings:
Drift Away (MCA)
Loving Arms (MCA)
Hey Dixie (MCA)
New Ray Of Sunshine (Capricorn)
Compilation:
Greatest Hits (MCA)

Great Society

♦ Jefferson Airplane

Ric(k) Grech

Born in Bordeaux, France, on Nov 1, 1945 but raised from the age of eight in Leicester, England, where he played violin in that town's Youth Symphony Orchestra. As bassist/violinist/singer/composer, Grech was later a founder member of Family (♦), leaving them abruptly in 1969 during an American tour to return to England and take up an offer to join the newly-formed supergroup Blind Faith (♦).

Grech was the unknown in Blind Faith alongside rock heavyweights Eric Clapton, Stevie Winwood and Ginger Baker, but his sudden projection into the public eye was to be as short-lived as that group's traumatic history.

Subsequently, Grech virtually found himself an itinerant sideman. He joined Ginger Baker's Air Force at the turn of 1969 until an offer to become a member of Traffic (♦) a few months later. Leaving them in December 1971, Grech turned to session work, playing during this time with Gram Parsons (♦).

He next confounded rock pundits by turning up as a backing musician for veteran rock 'n' rollers The Crickets (♦), playing with them for two hours and two albums **Bubblegum Bop, Ballad And Boogies** and **A Long Way From Lubbock.** In January 1973 he was reunited briefly with Clapton as a member of backing group for the guitarist's ''comeback'' gig at London Rainbow.

Over the next couple of years he worked extensively as a session-man, before turning up in late 1975 as a member of the newly-formed American ''supergroup'' KGB (♦). However, Grech split after their first album and formed his own band, the Square Dancing Machine. Playing music described as ''pure country in the Gram Parsons style'' this comprises, apart from Grech, John Cusack (bs mndln), Mick Fleming (accordion, vcls), Alan Sansome (gtr, vcls), Dave Siddons (stl gtr), Scott Gibson (kybds) and singer Claire Hamill (♦).

In 1973 RSO Records released an album collecting some of Grech's work for the aforementioned bands (excluding Crickets, KGB) with songs of his which have been recorded by other acts.

Recording:
The Last Five Years (RSO)

Al Green

Born Apr 13, 1946 in Forrest City, Arkansas, Al Green moved with his family to Grand Rapids, Michigan when he was nine, and pressed his elder brothers, Walter, William and Robert to include him in their gospel group.

He performed with the quartet until he was 16, when he got together with two friends, Palmer James and Curtis Rogers to form The Creations, a soul group which played the mid-West chitlin' circuit. In 1967 James started his own Hot Line Music Journal label, and persuaded Green to record a song he (James) had written, **Back Up Train,** for the company. The song was a national hit, and Green had an early taste of stardom, with appearances at the Apollo in New York; however though he cut a follow-up, **Lover's Hideaway,** and an album, it proved an isolated hit, and he was soon back in the old routine.

While playing a gig in Midland, Texas in 1969, however, he met respected producer and bandleader Willie Mitchell (♦), who invited him to record in Memphis and arranged a contract for him with Hi Records. He also promised to make Green a star within 18 months.

Though Green's initial work was not immediately successful, in 1970 he recorded a cover version of The Temptations' **I Can't Get Next To You,** which again brought him to public attention, but it was his next two singles – **Tired Of Being Alone** and **Let's Stay Together** that catapulted him straight into the top echelon of American male singers.

Green was composing virtually all his own material by now, either independently or with Mitchell, or Al Jackson, the famed Memphis drummer, who played a valuable supporting role in Green's career until his death in 1975. The next two albums from Green – **Let's Stay Together** in 1971, and **I'm Still In Love With You** in 1972 were both million-sellers, as were the two singles from the latter, **Look What You Done To Me,** and the title-track – though in Britain, **Love And Happiness,** which became an important ingredient of his stage show, was the hit single.

By now Green and Mitchell had evolved a style which they have not yet abandoned. The gritty nature of the material on **Gets Next To You** was replaced by an altogether more lush approach, which utilized the splendidly spare techniques of Mitchell's Memphis band, as well as a subdued horn section and a prominent string section. It was a sound that made Mitchell's work instantly recognisable, since he also employed the same ideas on sessions for his other artists.

By early 1973 Green had sold an incredible 20 million units, but as his albums rapidly became more stereotyped and less experimental, the law of diminishing returns began to operate, for all the albums' intrinsic beauty and perfection of production.

Green probably reached his peak of popularity in 1973, when

he was one of the major attractions in U.S. – partly because of his huge record success, and partly because he is a dynamic and original stage performer; he also worked hard, gigging for at least 40 weeks a year. In 1973 he also made a successful tour of Britain.

His subsequent albums, **Call Me** (1973), **Living For You** (1974), **Explores Your Mind** (1974), **Al Green Is Love** (1975) and **Full Of Fire** (1976), all evinced little development and were released with production-line frequency. In 1975 he also issued **Greatest Hits.**

In 1974 a rather sordid incident at his home – when his girlfriend poured boiling grits over him, causing second-degree burns to his back, and then shot herself – apparently resulted in an awakening of his religious consciousness. He has certainly given financial aid to charitable foundations in recent years.

*I'm Still In Love With You.
Courtesy Decca Records.*

He also starred in a film in 1974 – "Mimi", which also featured Melba Moore. The film – a kind of twentieth-century secular version of "La Boheme" – was not noticeably successful.

Though critics have poured scorn on Green and Mitchell for their refusal to forsake the formula that has served them so well, it is nevertheless true that no Green record on Hi has yet been a commercial flop. The only hypothetical question is whether Green might have been ever bigger had he chosen to broaden his musical base. His singing is consistently brilliant and his range, should he ever feel the need to extend himself, is impressive.

Recordings:
Back Up Train (Action/—)
Green Is Blues (Hi/—)
Al Green Gets Next To You
(Hi/London)
Let's Stay Together (Hi/London)
I'm Still In Love With You
(Hi/London)
Call Me (Hi/London)
Living For You (Hi/London)
Al Green Explores Your Mind
(Hi/London)
All Green Is Love (Hi/London)
Full Of Fire (Hi/London)
Compilation:
Greatest Hits (Hi/London)

Peter Green

Born Peter Greenbaum of Jewish parentage in tough Bethnal Green section of London's East End, his first professional gig was as a bass player with Peter Bees, an outfit led by Peter Bardens, now of Camel (♦). Green stayed with

Bardens, switching to guitar, for latter's Shotgun Express R&B group which also included Mick Fleetwood (drms) and, for a time, Rod Stewart (vcls).

However, Green's forte was as a blues guitarist, and he received the first big break of his career when John Mayall asked him to join the Bluesbreakers in 1966 on Eric Clapton's departure to form Cream. Green rapidly blossomed as an outstanding axeman for Mayall (he appears on the Bluesbreakers 1966 **A Hard Road** set) before he took his burgeoning reputation, along with Mayall's bassist John McVie, to form his own group Fleetwood Mac (♦) in 1967.

With Green's singing, guitar playing and composing their main strength, the Mac raced to a position as Britain's leading blues group. When they broke into British singles lists, again it was down to Green's multi-faceted ability – the singles **Albatross, Man Of The World, Oh Well** and **The Green Manalishi,** all outstanding cuts, were Green compositions, as was the Mac "standard" **Black Magic Woman.**

Then, in 1970, after becoming obsessed with religion and raddled with doubts about his life, Green rocked Fleetwood Mac and the rock world at large with his decision to quit the band and drop out of the music business altogether. At the same time, he also announced that he would give all his royalty monies away to charities.

Green's activities got cloudy after this point, but remained decidedly low-key: he pursued his connections with a commune in Germany, played a handful of unpublicised solo gigs in London pubs (shunning the rock press who sought him out), before dropping out of sight for a lengthy spell.

There was a half-hearted solo single and album, **The End Of Of The Game.** in late 1970 – a lacklustre, badly-produced collection of jam tracks which captured little of his former magic – and then, in 1971, Green made a temporary return to the stage, helping Fleetwood Mac complete an American tour when Jeremy Spencer similarly dropped out of rock and into religion.

Since then Green has maintained such a low profile that aficionados who long for his return – and there are still many – hane been dependent on half-rumours as to his whereabouts: these have had him working as a grave-digger (true), as a barman in Cornwall (unverified), joining a commune in Israel (true), playing guitar (uncredited) on **Night Watch** track on Mac's **Penguin** album (unverified), and, more recently, working as a hospital orderly in Southend (true).

The nearest he came to a comeback was when Stone The Crows (♦) vocalist Maggie Bell tried valiantly to persuade him to stand in for the then recently-deceased Les Harvey for a one-off appearance at the 1972 Lincoln Festival – it could have led to a regular gig. Green at one point said a tentative yes, but changed his mind. He's hardly been heard of since – and his loss as an abundantly talented musician is one of the great rock tragedies of our time.

Recordings:
The End Of The Game
(Reprise)

Greenslade

Dave Greenslade keyboards, vibes
Tony Reeves bass
Dave Lawson vocals, keyboards, clarinet, flute
Andrew McCulloch drums

British group now defunct, personnel listed above were original line-up on formation in November 1972 by Dave Greenslade and Tony Reeves. Both were original members of the musically similar Colosseum (♦), R&B scene veteran Dave Greenslade having composed some of that band's best known material, including **Valentyne Suite** and **Lost Angeles.**

The group's first two albums (both released in 1973) illustrated a complexity of arrangements and marriage of various musical styles with the emphasis on the keyboard work and were critically well received.

By the third album, **Spyglass Guest** (1974), Greenslade had grown to six-piece by addition of Dave Clempson (gtr), ex of Humble Pie (♦), and Graham Smith (fiddle). However, within a few months, founder-member Reeves quit to return to production work, his place taken by Martin Briley for U.S. tour. (Reeves later with Curved Air (♦).)

Fourth album, **Time And Tide,** was released in mid-1975, racking-up moderate but healthy sales as had its predecessors. Greenslade hadn't yet joined the premier league of rock attractions, but they did have a steady sales graph, were able to headline U.K. concert tours and looked capable of further progress.

Nevertheless, in January 1976, the band announced its dissolution – giving as a reason the complicated managerial hassles which had troubled them from the outset. Disbandment, they announced, was the only way out of a business impasse, and this they had reluctantly decided to accept.

Recordings:
Greenslade (Warner Bros)
Bedside Manners Are Extra
(Warner Bros)
Spyglass Guest (Warner Bros)
Time And Tide (Warner Bros)

Grin
♦ Nils Lofgren

Albert Grossman

Born in 1926, and originally from Chicago where he ran the Gate Of Horn Club and established audiences for Big Bill Broonzy and Odetta, Grossman also ran the early Newport Folk Festivals, but is best known as the manager of Bob Dylan.

After making his reputation as starmaker with Peter, Paul & Mary, he began to look after the interests of Dylan in the early '60s; Grossman was familiar with the folk scene, and seems to have handled Dylan clandestinely initially so as

not to alienate Dylan's groundswell of support. (Grossman, known as "the floating Buddha" was a big man both literally and metaphorically and had a somewhat sinister reputation.) Dylan checked out Grossman thoroughly (his producer, John Hammond, advised him to sign) before putting his name to a seven-year contract. It expired in 1969 and Dylan has been without a manager since (♦ Bob Dylan).

In the early days, Grossman managed to get Dylan exposure through his other acts – Peter, Paul & Mary took **Blowin' In The Wind** to No. 2 in the U.S. charts and Odetta recorded a complete album of Dylan songs. Like most successful managers, Grossman worked industriously for his artist, had utter faith in his abilities, and probably over-protected him. But he did assist Dylan's rise to a position of prominence enjoyed by no other contemporary artist; he was featured, and well remembered, for his hard-talking role in the documentary movie "Don't Look Back".

In the later '60s he handled The Band (♦), and then signed Janis Joplin (♦) after seeing her perform at Monterey in 1967. By 1970 he had build one of the toughest and most successful organisations in the field; but since then he has maintained a low profile, having set up his own record label, Bearsville Records, in Woodstock, where he seems to have become the local maharajah. Artists on Bearsville's roster include Todd Rundgren, Jesse Winchester and Paul Butterfield.

Stefan Grossman

New York ragtime guitarist, Grossman was a member of the Even Dozen Jug Band in the '60s. He is well known for having put on record some classic performances by blues guitarist Rev. Gary Davis, preserving them for academic reasons. He has also written many excellent guitar tutor books, and recorded albums to accompany them.

Grossman's own recording career has been somewhat low-key, since he releases albums erratically, and though few have made much impact, most have been professionally put together. He now has his own record label – Kicking Mule – and has recorded an album with Danny Kalb, formerly of the Blues Project (♦). He is a witty and articulate live performer, though apparently unable to vary his act.

The discography is selective.

Recordings:
Ragtime Cowboy Jew
(Kicking Mule/Transatlantic)
Hot Dogs (Kicking Mule/ Transatlantic)
Stefan Grossman with Danny Kalb:
Crosscurrents (Atlantic/—)

Groundhogs

Tony (T.S.) McPhee guitar, keyboards, vocals
Dave Wellbelove guitar
Martin Kent bass
Mick Cook drums

An out-take from the British blues boom, The Groundhogs have endured two splits and several line-up changes in their history, the one constant factor through these changes being balding guitarist Tony McPhee, a one-time telephone engineer.

The origins of the band lie in a 1963-formed aggregation which comprised McPhee, Pete Cruickshank (bs), John Cruickshank (vcls, harp), Bob Hall (pno) and David Boorman (drms). This group made living as backing musicians for visiting American bluesmen, notable among whom was John Lee Hooker, whom they accompanied on a number of tours under the billing John Lee's Groundhogs. In fact it was Hooker who gave the group their first recording break, introducing them to his producer Calvin Carter for whom the 'Hogs cut a single, **Shake It** – released in the U.S. only – on the Interphon label. There also exists an album from this period – see list below.

That aside, the group had to content itself with gigs as a pick-up outfit which is how they remained until the first wave of British interest in the blues petered out (homegrown blues bands were to be a thing of the future) and the band dissolved in 1965.

By 1968, however, the blues had returned to favour, and The Groundhogs were reconstituted by McPhee and Cruickshank, from the original line-up, as a group in their own right – the new four-piece being brought up to strength by Ken Pustelnik (drms) and Steve Rye (vcls, harp). It was this line-up which signed to Liberty for the first Groundhogs album, **Scratching The Surface**, a 1968 production by Mike Batt (♦).

Steve Rye departed shortly after, leaving McPhee, Cruickshank and Pustelnik as the best-remembered incarnation of the group. The trio cut **Blues Obituary** (1969), closing a chapter on their blues period before turning towards the more rock-oriented approach of successive releases. The third set, **Thank Christ For The Bomb** (1970), was in fact writer McPhee's attempt at sociopolitical observation, and saw The Groundhogs make their debut in British album lists.

Split (1971) was another "conceptual" album, this time Tony McPhee turning his attention to the psychological ills of the world, and **Who Will Save The World?** (1972) continued to offer similar naive panaceas against an aggressive rock backdrop. Both maintained 'Hogs status among top-sellers, a position backed-up by consistent U.K. gigging.

By **Hogwash** (1972), Ken Pustelnik had been replaced by Clive Brooks (drms), from Egg, and the newly-reconstituted trio set off on their first and only American tour brought to an abrupt end when McPhee suffered a riding accident in the Pocono Mountains.

Back in England the following year, the guitarist recorded a solo album **The Two Sides Of T.S. McPhee** for a new company, WWA; a new Groundhogs album **Solid** appearing on the same label the following year. Shortly after, confirming rumours rife in music circles since his solo project, McPhee confirmed that he was dissatisfied with the band's pro-

gress and that they had disbanded.

The guitarist went into "semi-retirement", working from his home in Suffolk, England – where he has constructed his own 16-track studio – for some 10 months, until his return to United Artists and a new incarnation of the Groundhogs in late 1975 (line-up as under heading).

McPhee also recorded two albums with British blues singer/folkie Jo-Ann Kelly, and has produced albums for Big Joe Williams and Andy Fernbach as well as all 'Hogs product.

Recordings:
John Lee Hooker With The Groundhogs (Xtra)
Scratching The Surface (World Pacific/Liberty)
Blues Obituary (Imperial/Liberty)
Thank Christ For The Bomb (Liberty)
Split (United Artists/Liberty)
Who Will Save The World? The Mighty Groundhogs (United Artists)
Hogwash (United Artists)
Solid (WWA)
Tony McPhee:
The Two Sides Of Tony (T.S.) McPhee (—/WWA)
Tony McPhee and Jo-Ann Kelly:
Me & The Devil (Imperial/Liberty)
I Asked For Water, She Gave Me Gasoline (Imperial/Liberty)

Gryphon

Richard Harvey recorders, crumhorns, glockenspiel
Brian Gulland bassoon, crumhorns
David Oberle percussion, vocals
Bob Foster guitar
John Davie bass
Alex Baird drums

Gryphon was formed 1972 around multi-instrumental talents of Gulland and Harvey, both former

Above: Producer James William Guercio in his role as occasional bassist for the Beach Boys. Photograph from group's 1975 concert at Wembley Soccer Stadium.

students at Royal College of Music, with raison d'etre of bringing together the gutsy, bright, rhythmic qualities of early, pre-classical music with a folk-rock approach. Harvey is a first-class recorder virtuoso and Gulland blows crumhorns of all sizes in a suitably frenetic manner. The strength of band's repertoire is in their immaculate command of intricate uptempo instrumentals.

Gryphon, released in 1973, attained brief chart success. Since then however the band have eschewed much of medieval folksiness of origins to launch into more extended instrumental compositions – the second side of **Midnight Mushrumps** (1974) is one whole piece commissioned by Peter Hall for a National Theatre production of "The Tempest". Since then they have toured with Yes (with whom they share the same management) in Britain and America, and lost much of their early distinctiveness. At one time the appeal of their music was wide enough to earn them the (probably unique) distinction of appearing on all four BBC radio channels in one week.

They have played the score for "Pope Joan" and "Brother Sun, Sister Moon", and arranged and played the title-theme for "Glastonbury Fayre". Harvey has also written music for television plays, jingles for commercials, and has issued his own solo album of classical recorder music, **Divisions On A Ground**.

In 1975 Graeme Taylor, original bassist and guitarist left, and a new line-up (above) was put together. Alex Baird previously played in Scottish folk-rock group, Contraband.

Gryphon have had no product released in U.S. as yet, but they have tied up a record deal with Arista.

Recordings:
Gryphon (—/Transatlantic)
Midnight Mushrumps (—/Transatlantic)

Red Queen To Gryphon Three (—/Transatlantic)
Raindance (—/Transatlantic)
Richard Harvey: Divisions On A Ground (—/Transatlantic)

James William Guercio

Though best known for his production credits with Chicago (♦) and Blood Sweat & Tears (♦), American Guercio (b. 1945) first paid his dues as a bass player on highly successful Dick Clark Road Shows in States, backing the likes of Tommy Roe, Del Shannon and The Shangri-Las.

In studio during '60s, he was closely involved with British pop duo Chad & Jeremy and instrumental in producing a string of U.S. hits for The Buckinghams.

However, it was in his role as mentor and producer of Chicago – he took them to Los Angeles to launch their career – that Guercio first attracted international recognition. His reputation was further enhanced (though the whole U.S. jazz-rock movement has been subject to critical ridicule now for several years) when Columbia/CBS brought him in to produce the second, million-selling Blood Sweat & Tears album.

More recently Guercio has opened his own Caribou ranch studios – where Elton John cut his 1974 album of the same name – and has taken over management of the Beach Boys, with whom he frequently appears on stage as bassist. In 1973 Guercio added a further facet to his career by producing and directing the highly-acclaimed movie, "Electra Glide In Blue", in which three members of Chicago were cast in supporting roles.

The Guess Who

Burton Cummings vocals, keyboards
Billy Wallace bass
Domenic Troiano guitar
Garry Paterson drums
Don McDougall guitar

Over a lengthy period Canada's top singles band, The Guess Who originated out of the Winnipeg area and a 1959-formed outfit called Al and the Silvertones led by singer Chad Allan with Randy Bachman on guitar. In the early '60s the pair set about forming the first Guess Who line-up, Bachman taking over as leader when Allan quit in 1965 to attend university. Other personnel at this time comprised Cummings, Peterson and bassist Jim Kale.

With Cummings adopting Jim Morrison vocal mannerisms and Bachman playing derivative but highly effective guitar riffs, the reorganised group first established a local, then a national, following over the next two years, culminating in their own weekly show on Canadian TV, "Where It's At". The group released upwards of more than a dozen singles during 1967-68, first major success coming with **These Eyes.**
Signed to RCA for U.S. distribution in 1969, their first American album **Wheatfield Soul** became a million-seller, and was followed

by a string of North American hits, including the double-sided gold **Laughing/Undun** and Randy Bachman's chauvinistic **American Woman** (1970). This last brought the group their one and only U.K. hit, while the album of the same name became their second U.S. million-seller.

However, in the summer of 1970 Randy Bachman, sick and in need of hospitalisation and a rest from touring, quit the group. A converted Mormon (no alcohol, tea, coffee, dope, immorality) he had always had difficulty in stomaching his band's on-tour lifestyle.

Bachman went on to form Brave Belt with the forementioned Chad Allan, out of which emerged the enormously-successful Bachman Turner Overdrive (♦). Although the parting was at first amicable, it became less so with the passing of time – and in the early '70s there existed considerable animosity between BTO and The Guess Who.

Two more Canadians, guitarists Kurt Winter and Greg Leskiw, came in to replace Bachman and, despite the loss of latter's compositional ability, The Guess Who continued to dominate the albums and singles markets. **Share The Land** (1970) and the compilation, **Best Of The Guess Who** (1971) both went gold, while the title track from the former made the U.S. singles lists along with **Raindance** and **Hang On To Your Life**.

Further personnel changes followed in 1972 when Leskiw and original bass player Kale quit line-up to be replaced respectively by Don McDougall and Billy Wallace, both from Winnipeg. Winter stayed around longer but was eventually replaced by Domenic Troiano, ex of James Gang (♦).

From 1973 onwards, the fortunes of The Guess Who drifted gradually into decline as Bachman's BTO took over their former position as Canada's hottest commercial rock group.

In late 1975 Billy Wallace left the band and, as the year ended, The Guess Who ended industry speculation by announcing their final dissolution. After a 75-concert North American tour, they had played their last date in Montreal on Sept 7. At the height of their popularity, in 1970, Guess Who record sales had grossed an estimated five million dollars. In early 1976, Burton Cummings was planning a solo career.

Albums listed below include only those released outside of Canada.

Recordings:
Wheatfield Soul (RCA)
Canned Wheat (RCA)
American Woman (RCA)
Share The Land (RCA)
So Long Bannatyne (RCA)
Rockin' (RCA)
Live At The Paramount (RCA)
10 (RCA)
Road Food (RCA)
Artificial Paradise (RCA)
Flavours (RCA)
Power In The Music (RCA)
Compilations:
Best Of The Guess Who (RCA)
Best Of . . . Vol. II (RCA)

Arlo Guthrie

Born Coney Island, New York,

Jan 12, 1947 Arlo is the son of Woody Guthrie (♦) and grew up in a houseful of folk music and inevitably developed musical ambitions. He was, however, in the awkward position of having not only a famous father, but one whose work had been directly continued by one artist (Jack Elliott) and developed by another (Bob Dylan) into a universally influential style.

It is therefore to Arlo's credit that he made a totally individual mark with his epic **Alice's Restaurant** at the 1967 Newport Folk Festival, the song being based on actual events which had taken place during 1965-66. (In which Arlo had been refused induction into the U.S. Army on the grounds of a criminal conviction, which had been for the dumping of garbage.) His singing and delivery is similar to that of both his father and Dylan, but his humour is unique: a gleeful, stoned celebration of the lifestyle of an alternative, but more rational society.

Although he has remained an established artist, he has never opped his first masterstroke – even though songs like **Comin' Into Los Angeles** and his version of Steve Goodman's **City Of New Orleans** are classic performances. **Alice's Restaurant** also inspired the film of the same title (in which Arlo himself starred), directed by Arthur Penn. Released in 1970, it remains perhaps the most intelligent film analysis of the U.S. alternative society.

He has also contributed to a U.S. television documentary propaganda health film called "VD Blues". He now lives with his family in rural Massachusetts; his music continues to be uniquely his own, and quite independent of all prevailing trends.

Recordings:
Alice's Restaurant (Reprise)
Arlo (Reprise)
Running Down The Road (Reprise)
Washington County (Reprise)

Alice's Restaurant (Soundtrack) (United Artists)
Hoboes' Lullaby (Reprise)
The Last Of The Brooklyn Cowboys (Reprise)
Arlo Guthrie (Reprise)
Arlo Guthrie and Pete Seeger: Live Together In Concert (Reprise)

Woody Guthrie

Born Woodrow Wilson Guthrie in Okema, Oklahoma in 1912; natural disasters such as storms and droughts played a part in splitting up his family. He spent his early life working as a merchant seaman, then throughout the depression he was a drifter and jack-of-all-trades, putting together and singing songs which altogether form an important chronicle of America in the '30s; he made his

Above: Alice's Restaurant. Guthrie's anecdotal title track, based on events which took place during 1965–66, inspired the 1970-released Arthur Penn movie, in which the singer himself starred.

heroes the hoboes and bums and forgotten rural poor (as on **Dust Bowl Ballads**), or victims of injustice like the two Italian fish-peddlars Sacco and Vanzetti, falsely accused of anarchy and murder (as on **Sacco & Vanzetti**).

His ability to formulate complex political arguments in very simple terms (as Pete Seeger once said, "Any damn fool can get complicated; it takes genius to attain simplicity") within the framework of traditional folk/country tunes made him the absolute archetype of all American singer/songwriters. His accusatory, righteous stance as the guitar-pickin' blue-jeaned People's Sage was adopted lock, stock and cracker-barrel (even down to the harmonica stand) in Dylan's formative work – except that Dylan identified adolescent alienation with the displaced hobo figure.

It wasn't only Dylan, though; Guthrie (who had joined the merchant marine in 1943 with Cisco Houston, and after the war briefly played with the Almanac Singers, which also included Seeger and Lee Hays) influenced a whole generation of folk min-

strels – Tom Paxton and Phil Ochs are obvious examples. Donovan adapted Guthrie's slogan on his guitar ("This machine kills fascists") for himself. Today, Ry Cooder maintains the dust-bowl tradition.

As well as his many now-classic songs (e.g. **So Long It's Been Good To Know You, This Land Is Your Land, Pastures Of Plenty**), Guthrie wrote many children's songs – as on **Songs To Grow On/Poor Boy** – and perfected the ironic style of delivery known as "talking blues".

But no irony could compete with the fact that his rise from obscurity to the status of a national hero took place during the years he lay slowly and agonisingly dying of a rare heriditary disease, Huntingdon's Chorea (which had also killed his mother); Guthrie entered hospital in 1954, (Bob Dylan visited him several times in the early '60s), and died on Oct 3, 1967; he was survived by five children.

Two memorial concerts (the first of which took place at Carnegie Hall in 1968, the second at the Hollywood Bowl in 1970) were issued as albums, with contributions from Dylan, Paxton, Seeger, Joan Baez, Judy Collins, Ritchie Havens, Odetta, and Country Joe McDonald, which testified to his stature and influence. Royalties from the concert were donated to a research centre to find a cure for Huntingdon's Disease.

Guthrie was also a first-class author. His autobiography "Bound For Glory", with his own illustrations, was published in 1943; a second book of songs and sketches was called "American Folksong", and in 1965 Robert Shelton edited "Born To Win", a collection of Guthrie's prose and poems.

Only selected recordings are listed.

Recordings:
Dust Bowl Ballads (Folkways/—)
Sacco & Vanzetti (Folkways/—)
Songs To Grow On/Poor Boy (Xtra)
Library Of Congress, Boxed Set (Elektra)
Tribute Album:
Woody Guthrie Memorial Concert, Vol. I (Columbia/CBS)
Vol. II (Warner Bros)

Bill Haley

Born Detroit, March 1927, began playing C&W music in bands while a teenager, doing rounds of mid-West like a hundred other groups. While working for six years on Pennsylvania radio station he realised attraction of black music to some young whites who found big bands and country schmaltz boring.

Impressed by energy of kids he met while playing school dances, he introduced his version of black R&B into his act; Haley and his band The Saddlemen released a series of unimpressive singles on small labels before ditching country image altogether and changing name to The Comets. Haley realised what he needed was a steady beat the audience could clap their hands to, as well as dance to, and this he created by

Right: The man whose music incited riots across the globe – Bill Haley tells it like it was in 1956. Was it really like that in 1956?

fusing elements of black R&B and white C&W, writing songs from high-school phrases he heard kids use, like **Crazy Man Crazy.**

In 1951 he had some success with **Rock The Joint,** and did better in 1953 with **Crazy Man Crazy,** the first rock 'n' roll record to enter U.S. charts. In 1954 he left the small Essex company, and joined Decca, taking for his first release the initially unsuccessful **Rock Around The Clock.** His follow-up, **Shake Rattle And Roll** (a diluted version of the Joe Turner original) made the U.S. Top 20 for 12 weeks, and entered the U.K. charts in 1956.

But Haley's star was really in the ascendent when **Rock Around The Clock** was used as the theme song for the film "Blackboard Jungle", and the single, re-issued, became a world-wide hit; it has sold well on the several occasions it has since been revived. It last had a spell in U.K. Top 20 in 1974 and has become one of the top two or three selling singles of all time.

From that point, the chubby singer with the kiss-curl found himself elevated to the highest ranks of stardom. Rock had arrived, and Haley had helped create it.

When his movie "Rock Around The Clock" was released, cinema seats were ripped up from San Francisco to Scunthorpe. Slightly bewildered by it all, Haley made more records to the same formula, including Bobby Charles' **See You Later Alligator,** and **Don't Knock The Rock.**

Even so, Haley's success rate in his native America didn't compare with that in Britain, where the kids did not have access to the real thing. It wasn't until a European tour that they realised he was rather too fat to be a rock 'n' roll hero and he was deserted for the man who could provide the sex appeal he couldn't, Elvis Presley.

After those early days of heady success, Haley's fortunes fell sharply, though it is to his credit that he simply made way for those who were better equipped to handle the new music; he never tried to be hipper than he was, and just stuck with the style that had made him famous, even though it quickly became rather effete and outmoded.

Like most of the other early rock stars, Haley made a comeback with Richard Nader's Rock 'n' Roll revival shows, and was particularly well received in the film "Let the Good Times Roll".

Recordings:
Golden Hits (MCA)

Hall & Oates

Daryl Hall and John Oates met in Philadelphia 1967, while Oates was at college majoring in journalism and Hall working as studio musician at Sigma Sound. They started writing songs together, and joined a band called Gulliver which recorded one album for Elektra.

When the band broke up, Hall and Oates began working seriously together in Philadelphia area, and in 1972 signed with Atlantic, for whom they cut debut album, **Whole Oates,** in New York with Arif Mardin producing.

Mardin produced the second album as well, **Abandoned Luncheonette** (1973), which yielded the U.S. hit single, **She's Gone.**

Their third album, **War Babies,** was produced and engineered by Todd Rundgren who also played lead guitar. In 1975 they issued their first album for RCA, simply titled **Hall And Oates.** The single taken from this, **Sara Smile,** became a U.S. Top 10 single in May 1976, as Hall and Oates set out for their second European visit inside 12 months, as their smooth blend of rock and R&B music began to win admirers.

Recordings:
Whole Oates (Atlantic)
Abandoned Luncheonette (Atlantic)
War Babies (Atlantic)
Hall And Oates (RCA)

Claire Hamill

Born in Middlesbrough, England, 1955, eldest of seven children, she began her career playing in local clubs, and then, as something of a teenage prodigy, won a record contract with Island. She had a clear, pure voice, bags of confidence, and wrote her own material. Two albums were released, **One House Left Standing** (1972) and **October** (1973), and she also played a headlining gig at London's Royal Festival Hall.

Despite the faith placed in her by many people in the business, and despite encouraging reviews, it never seemed to happen for her, and she went to America where she worked regularly on the West Coast.

In 1974 she became the first artist to be signed to Ray Davies' newly-formed Konk Records. Davies produced her third album, **Stage Door Johnnies,** a mixture of her own songs and more

Above: Claire Hamill.

familiar material like Michael Murphy's **Geronimo's Cadillac.** Her range had broadened considerably since her start as an acoustic folk-guitarist.

In 1975 she released her fourth album, **Abracadabra,** which included mostly her own songs, though out of deference to her boss she covered his **Celluloid Heroes.** It now began to seem that she was having some difficulty establishing an individual style, and public reaction was again indifferent.

If her material has often seemed over-sensitive, she has an extrovert personality, and in 1975 bared a breast for "Penthouse" (a British equivalent to "Playboy") and explained in an accompanying interview how it was easier for a girl to get laid in America than Britain.

One advantage of Claire's early entry to the record business is that she still has considerable time in which to allow her undoubted talent to mature.

In April 1976 she became lead vocalist of Rick Grech's S.D.M.

Recordings:
One House Left Standing
(—/Island)
October (—/Island)
Stage Door Johnnies (Konk)
Abracadabra (Konk)

John Hammond

Born Dec 15, 1910, Hammond studied classical music at the Juilliard, and has had a long association with Columbia Records, after supervising jazz sessions in the '30s and '40s, and helping careers of many jazz and blues singers; Billie Holiday was one of the people he brought to the company.

In the '60s he persuaded Columbia to sign Pete Seeger (➤) while he was still under indictment for contempt of Congress, and also brought in Aretha Franklin (➤) before losing her to other producers. He discovered and signed Bob Dylan (➤) in 1961; even though Dylan was known for a time within the company as "Hammond's Folly", Hammond maintained faith, and produced Dylan's debut album. It is known that Dylan respects Hammond absolutely.

His "scouting" potential continued into '70s and, in 1973, he took Bruce Springsteen (♦) to Columbia.

His son, John Hammond Jnr (b. 1943), now known as John Paul Hammond, is a blues guitarist and singer. In 1964 he was responsible for bringing The Band (♦) – or The Hawks as they were then known – from Toronto to New York. In 1973 he made **Triumvirate** with Mike Bloomfield and Dr John.

Herbie Hancock

In the middle '70s one of America's biggest album sellers in any field, Hancock's foundations lie, like his contemporaries Wayne Shorter and Joe Zawinul (Weather Report), Chick Corea (Return To Forever) and John McLaughlin, in the late '60s experimentations of Miles Davis (♦). All the afore-named were, like Hancock, members of Davis' various ensembles during Miles' most inventive jazz-rock period.

Hancock, however, already had a substantial reputation as a jazz piano prodigy before his association with Miles. Born Herbert Jeffrey Hancock on Chicago's south side Apr 12, 1940, he formed his first band – 17-strong! – while attending Iowa's Grinnel College in late '50s, firstly studying engineering and later majoring in music composition (he was made an honorary Doctor Of Fine Arts in 1972).

Hancock was still only 20 when, back in Chicago, nascent jazz trumpet ace Donald Byrd came to town and recruited the youngster to deputise for his regular but blizzard-stranded pianist. This initially one-off gig turned into a residency in Byrd's band.

In fact, it was Byrd's persuasion that gave Hancock the chance to record his first solo album, for Blue Note. This set, **Takin' Off**, yielded a surprise U.S. hit in the shape of the pianist's **Watermelon Man** composition.

Hancock's reputation burgeoned rapidly at that point, and he was asked to join the Miles Davis band after Miles had gone out of his way to catch Hancock playing with Clark Terry at the New York Village Gate.

From 1963–68 Hancock was an integral part of what some regard as the greatest jazz band ever, filling out the solos of Miles and Wayne Shorter in an inspired style, while also making a considerable contribution to the band as composer.

Meanwhile, Hancock continued to record separately for Blue Note on albums such as **Maiden Voyage, Succotash, Inventions And Dimensions,** and **The Prisoner;** at the same time doing session-work for likes of Freddie Hubbard and Wes Montgomery and composing advertising jingles for Chevrolet, Pillsbury Bakeries and Standard Oil. Further recognition came when the director Antonioni asked Hancock to score his seminal "Blow Up" movie (starring David Hemmings, Jane

Birkin, Vanessa Redgrave).

On leaving Miles in 1968, he formed his own Herbie Hancock Sextet and recorded **Mwandishi**, which marked the pianist's exploration of the improvisational possibilities inherent in electronic keyboards. His reputation spread: **Mwandishi** was placed by "Time" magazine among 10 best albums of 1971; he was voted top pianist in the "Downbeat" and "Playboy" polls; and subsequently, almost overnight, he changed his audience from the jazz circuit to rock halls and colleges.

Signing to Columbia Records, Hancock recorded **Sextant** (1972) and, after a shift of home base to Los Angeles, the phenomenally-successful **Headhunters** (1973), and album which easily outstripped total combined sales of all his previous output. **Thrust, Death Wish** and **Man Child,** the last in late 1975, consolidated his new eminence as an across-the-board commercial property.

A convert to Nicherin Shoshu Buddhism, one of the many sects of the faith, Hancock has said that his hybrid sound is rooted in "soul funk", rhythmically-rich and embellished with various facets of modern jazz.

The other five members of the Sextet are Bernie Maupin (reeds), also an ex-Miles sideman, Paul Jackson (bs), Blackbird McKnight (gtr) and drummers Mike Clark and Bill Summers. These five have latterly had own support spot on Hancock concerts, and have recorded one album **Survival Of The Fittest** (1975) as Headhunters on Arista label.

Discography below, apart from compilation on Blue Note, lists product since **Mwandishi.**

Recordings:
Mwandishi (Warner Bros)
Sextant (Columbia/CBS)
Headhunters (Columbia/CBS)
Thrust (Columbia/CBS)
Death Wish (Columbia/CBS)
Man Child (Columbia/CBS)
Compilation:
The Best Of Herbie Hancock (Blue Note)

Tim Hardin

Born Eugene, Oregon, 1940, into a famous musical family (his mother was a well-known violinist), Hardin was a direct descendent of the nineteenth-century outlaw John Wesley Hardin. After a spell in U.S. Marines in late '50s, he went to Cambridge, Massachusetts on discharge in 1961, where he began performing, and he developed a strong following in Boston folk-clubs.

After success at 1966 Newport Folk Festival, he signed recording contract with Verve, but though he released albums regularly, he became more widely known for other artists' interpretations of his compositions. His most successful song was **If I Were A Carpenter,** which became an international hit for Bobby Darin in 1966 and for the Four Tops in 1968, though songs like **The Lady Came From Baltimore, Black Sheep Boy** and

Right: Tim Hardin. In recent years his writing has declined with his health. He is currently resident in Britain.

Reason To Believe were also widely recorded, the latter by Rod Stewart on **Every Picture Tells A Story.**

In September 1967 Atco released an album Hardin had recorded in 1962, which showed his feeling for jazz and blues. In later '60s he moved to Woodstock, where he became acquainted with Bob Dylan and The Band and is thought to have provided the incentive for Dylan's **John Wesley Harding** album (Dylan adding a "g").

Hardin moved to Columbia Records in 1969, for whom he issued the very ambitious **Suite For Susan Moore And Damion – We Are One, One, All In One** (a thematic work dedicated to his wife and son). However, both commercial success and general critical respectability continued to elude him, and his writing began to decline with his health. Now resident in Britain, he performs occasionally, and has a contract with GM Records, for whom he issued **Nine** in 1974.

Tim Hardin I & II were repackaged as double album in 1974.

Recordings:
Tim Hardin I (Verve)
Tim Hardin II (Verve)
This Is Tim Hardin (Atco/—)
Live In Concert (Verve)
Tim Hardin IV (Verve)
Suite For Susan Moore And Damion - We are One, One, All In One (Columbia/CBS)
Bird On A Wire (Columbia/CBS)
Painted Head (Columbia/CBS)
Nine (Antillis/GM)
Compilation:
Best Of Tim Hardin (Verve)

Steve Harley
♦ Cockney Rebel

Roy Harper

Born June 12, 1941 in Manchester, England, Harper's initiation into music came at 13 when he played

skiffle in a group with his brother David. He joined the Royal Air Force as a teenager, playing Big Bill Broonzy and Leadbelly folk–blues material at camp concerts and, also during this time, started writing poetry.

The apochryphal story is that Harper faked a mental illness to secure his release from the R.A.F., resulting in a 15-week spell of hospitalisation during which time he underwent his first ECT treatment (an experience recounted in the song **Committed** on his debut album). Subsequent sessions of group therapy were followed by a spell in Lancaster Moor Mental Institution and a year of imprisonment in Liverpool.

Arriving in London 1964, Harper busked on the streets for more than a year before cutting **The Sophisticated Beggar** (later re-issued as **The Return Of The Sophisticated Beggar**) on a modest revox machine in 1966. A spell on the London folkie circuit preceded his second album, **Come Out Fighting Genghis Smith,** in 1967.

Both recordings provided early evidence of a distinctive guitar style and often aggressive lyrical talent. However, they also displayed hints of faults to be found in his later work; Harper has always stretched his ideas to their limits, gaining something of a reputation for megalomania in the process.

In 1968 he was a regular on the series of free concerts in London's Hyde Park, carving his own small but unique niche as Britain's paramount stoned freak poet. **Folkjokeopus** was cut for Liberty in 1969, and the much-improved **Flat Baroque** (1970), featuring members of The Nice (♦) uncredited on one track, for Harvest Records.

For his highly-acclaimed 1971 **Stormcock** set Harper was well served by producer Peter Jenner and arranger David Bedford (♦). His close friend, Jimmy Page of Led Zeppelin, put in a session appearance on guitar, and has since played on all subsequent Harper releases.

Roy Harper

Ironically, Harper is perhaps still best known in certain quarters for Page and Zeppelin's touting of his talents. **Hats Off To Harper,** a track on the third Zeppelin album, was a sign of the high regard in which the singer/guitarist was held not just by Page, Plant, etc., but by a number of his contemporaries, including another long-time friend Ian Anderson of Jethro Tull. Harper had first met Zeppelin at Britain's 1970 Bath Festival, and has on occasion toured the States with them at their request.

In 1972 Harper made a disappointing appearance as an actor in the British movie "Made", completing a debilitating British tour in March of that year after which he was taken gravely ill; hospitalised with a circulation complaint which gave rise to rumours that he had been given a limited period to live, and that the cut, **The Lord's Prayer,** on the much-delayed early 1973 **Lifemask** album, was written as a kind of last will and testament.

However, Harper recovered from his illness and went on to fill London's Albert Hall on his "comeback" concert.

His next album didn't appear for a full year. Entitled **Valentine** it was, in fact, released on St Valentine's Day – Feb 14, 1974 – on which date Harper played an over-publicised concert at London's Rainbow Theatre backed by an orchestra conducted by David Bedford and a group which included some of his many friends and admirers – Jimmy Page (gtr), Ronnie Lane (bs), Keith Moon (drms). Dave Gilmour of Pink Floyd and Zeppelin bassist John Paul Jones turned out to support him at a Hyde Park gig in August of that year.

The late-1974 **Flashes From The Archives Of Oblivion** was a double live album containing material from the Rainbow gig.

In April 1975 Harper released his ninth album **HQ**, and toured the U.K. with a specially-formed back-up band Trigger comprising Chris Spedding (♦), Bill Bruford (ex-King Crimson and Yes), and Dave Cochran, disbanding same

in July 1975.

Pink Floyd having guested on **HQ**, the band reciprocated by inviting Harper to handle lead vocals on the **Have A Cigar** cut on their 1975 **Wish You Were Here** album.

HQ – re-titled **When An Old Cricketer Leaves The Crease** – belatedly released in America February 1976 and, having made dark statements about quitting Britain due to public apathy, Harper crossed the Atlantic to promote the U.S. issue. He extended his stay, re-formed Trigger with Andy Roberts replacing Chris Spedding, and completed a six-week U.S. tour.

America may yet give him the attention he craves, but it seems more likely that Harper is doomed to play out only a supporting role in rock – despite all claims made on his behalf to the contrary.

Above: Roy Harper.

Recordings:
The Sophisticated Beggar (—/Strike, re-issued on Youngblood)
Come Out Fighting Genghis Smith (Columbia/CBS)
Folkjokeopus (Liberty)
Flat, Baroque And Berserk (—/Harvest)
Stormcock (—/Harvest)
Lifemask (—/Harvest)
Valentine (—/Harvest)
Flashes From The Archives Of Oblivion (—/Harvest)
HQ – When An Old Cricketer Leaves The Crease (Chrysalis/Harvest)

Left: Lifemask. Courtesy EMI/Harvest. The mask lifts up to uncover the direct stare of Harper's face.

Emmylou Harris

Born Birmingham, Alabama 1949, she developed an interest in country music, and when her family moved to Washington, tried her hand in clubs there and in New York. She got as far as making an album, in 1969, on the small Jubilee label, but it sank without trace. There was a fruitless sojourn in Nashville before she was back in Washington living with her parents, and all she had to show for her early experience of the music business was a broken marriage and a newly-born daughter, Hallie.

She continued to work in clubs, singing country material, and her big break came through meeting Gram Parsons (♦), who at that time was a member of the Flying Burrito Brothers (Emmylou herself was on the point of joining when they split up). Instead, Parsons invited her to work with him in Los Angeles on his solo album, **G.P.** The partnership worked, and Emmylou virtually shared vocal duties with him the next time on **Grievous Angel;**

Above: Ms Emmylou.

she also became a regular member of Parsons' band, and toured with him until Parson's death later that year.

To assuage her grief, Emmylou returned to Washington, where she worked feverishly, forming the Angelband to back her; she returned to the West Coast when Reprise Records offered her her own contract. **Pieces Of The Sky** was a finely executed, and surprisingly successful album, and on the strength of it she was able to put together a band comprising many well-known figures in country music circles, who had previously worked on **G.P.** and **Grievous Angel.** It was called simply but accurately The Hot Band, and toured the States and Europe with her. Personnel were: James Burton (gtr), Glen D. Hardin (pno), Hank De Vito (pdl stl), Rodney Crowell (rhm gtr, harmony vcls), Emory Gordy (bs), John Ware (drms). This line-up also worked on **Elite Hotel,** which enhanced her reputation and was a bestselling album in U.K.

After her association with Parsons, her harmony vocals were widely admired, and she worked on albums for Linda Ronstadt,

Little Feat and John Sebastian. But her big opportunity came when Bob Dylan asked her to contribute vocals to **Desire.**

Emmylou Harris has a warm personality and a mature self-confidence to set alongside her natural attributes – her voice and her attractiveness. There seems little to prevent her rapidly increasing popularity from burgeoning further.

Recordings:
Pieces Of The Sky (Reprise)
Elite Hotel (Reprise)

George Harrison

Even before final split of The Beatles (♦), Harrison had been involved with pet projects of his own – **Wonderwall,** for example (the first release on the Apple label), a mostly oriental soundtrack to accompany a mostly psychedelic film, and **Electronic Sounds,** an experimental album of radio static and other examples of musical technology – one of the few works actually to appear on the short-lived Zapple label, which was intended to provide a commercial outlet for avant-garde music.

His first post-split solo album proper, **All Things Must Pass,** with producer Phil Spector (♦), was a huge surprise, both because much of it was of an exceptionally high standard and because it became one of the bestselling albums of all time. The single, **My Sweet Lord,** sold by the juggernaut-load, even though it seemed more than a little derivative of The Chiffons' **He's So Fine.**

Primarily an affirmation of Harrison's spiritual affinities, **All Things Must Pass,** was a triple-album – four sides of songs, and two of an extended jam session with talented and famous friends; although inevitably too long, the album nevertheless demonstrated that as a songwriter Harrison had

All Things Must Pass. Courtesy Apple, EMI.

latent resources – much was perfectly acceptable, some highly commendable.

Harrison's primary concerns remained All Things Eastern, and as a result of a famine in Bangla Desh, he organised a concert at Madison Square Garden in August 1971 which involved many leading rock personalities, including Bob Dylan and Eric Clapton, as well as Ravi Shankar. Proceeds from concert itself, the subsequent live triple-album and the film of the event ran into millions – it was easily the most profitable charitable venture ever promoted in rock field. Harrison himself had put together the whole affair, his stature being enhanced as a result.

Nevertheless, his own career ran into difficulties. **Living In The Material World** was clearly uninspired and a thoroughly inadequate sequel to **All Things Must Pass**. But if that was bad, **Dark Horse**, was far worse. The singing was dreadful, the melodies dreary, the lyrics full of sickening self-righteousness; **Bye Bye Love** was rewritten as a maladroit attack on his erstwhile best friend, Eric Clapton, who'd just relieved Harrison of his wife.

In the meantime, Harrison had launched his own Dark Horse label in June 1974, and produced its first single, Splinter's **Costafine Town**, which became a moderate hit in Britain. Later in the year, he toured the States (with guest star, also Dark Horse's first signing, Ravi Shankar), but it was not a critical success.

After rock-bottom reception to **Dark Horse**, Harrison tried to repair the damage by quickly releasing **Extra Texture – Read All About It**. Though inevitably an improvement, it displayed no indication that Harrison really had anything genuinely creative left to offer.

His commercial success has been relatively unimpaired in the U.S., but in the U.K. **Ding Dong**, the single taken from **Dark Horse**, became the first single by any of The Beatles, either as a unit or separately, to fail to make the U.K. Top 30.

At beginning of 1976, he signed himself to his own record label; it would be unfair to suggest this was because no one else would have him.

Recordings:
Wonderwall Soundtrack (Apple)
Electronic Sounds (Zapple)
All Things Must Pass (Apple)
Living In The Material World (Apple)
Dark Horse (Apple)
Extra Texture – Read All About It (Apple)
With guest artists:
Concert For Bangla Desh (Apple)

Mike Harrison
➡ Spooky Tooth

Keef Hartley

Born Preston, Lancashire, England in 1944, Hartley left home for Liverpool in 1962 where he took over the drum stool in Rory Storme and the Hurricanes left vacant by the departing Ringo Starr. After demise of Mersey Boom – Rory Storme's was one of the acts that missed the boat – Hartley stayed in the north playing various gigs before his arrival in London 1964.

He took his drum kit into the R&B band The Artwoods (led by Ron Wood's brother Art, they also included Deep Purple key-boardsman Jon Lord), where he stayed for three years until an offer to join John Mayall's Blues-breakers in April 1967. Hartley had known Mayall on and off for several years as session player, in which role he had also played with Eric Clapton on Champion Jack Dupree recordings.

Hartley played on two albums for Mayall (➡) before forming his own band in 1968 at the latter's suggestion.

Throughout its three years together, the line-up of The Keef Hartley Band fluctuated around a nucleus of Scots-born Miller Anderson (gtr, vcls), Mick Weaver (kybds) – who later worked under pseudonym Wynder K. Frogg – and Gary Thain (bs), subsequently of Uriah Heep (➡). Various hornmen – including Henry Lowther and Johnny Almond – augmented this foursome, whose material ranged from blues standards to composer Miller Anderson's more melodic contributions.

In 1971 Hartley took on an enlarged brass section to form The Keef Hartley Big Band, the **Little Big Band** album (1971) being recorded live at London's Marquee Club (which had always been the ebullient Hartley's happiest stomping ground).

From this point, however, the band started to fall to pieces – there was always a certain friction between Anderson and Hartley – and the 1972 albums **Seventy Second Brave** and **Lancashire Hustler** were essentially solo albums, Hartley using session

support.

After 1972 Hartley worked inter-mittently with Mayall (again) and Michael Chapman (➡), spending most of his time in the former's adopted Los Angeles home. Miller Anderson, meanwhile, was also primarily based in the U.S., touring as member of Savoy Brown (➡). (Anderson was once offered a gig with Blood Sweat & Tears but declined.)

Back in England, Hartley and Anderson – having settled their old differences – formed a new band, Dog Soldier, in late 1974, completing the line-up with Derek Griffiths (gtr), Mel Simpson (kybds) and Paul Bliss (bs). Griffiths, like Hartley, had also had a spell in The Artwoods.

Naturally the new band made its debut at the Marquee, releasing their first album **Dog Soldier** in 1975, on release of which Hartley announced his decision to quit (Eric Dillon temporarily took his place). Since then, largely inactive.

Recordings:
Halfbreed (London/Deram)
Battle Of NW6 (London/Deram)
The Time Is Near (London/Deram)
Overdog (London/Deram)
Little Big Band (London/Deram)
Seventy Second Brave (London/Deram)
Lancashire Hustler (London/Deram)
Dog Soldier (United Artists)
Compilation:
Best Of Keef Hartley (London/Deram)

Alex Harvey
➡ Sensational Alex Harvey Band

Hatfield And The North

Richard Sinclair bass, vocals
Dave Stewart keyboards
Phil Miller guitar
Pip Pyle drums

Formed November 1972, taking their name from road sign directions which greet motorists heading north out of London on the A1 artery (a subtle witticism which ensured considerable publicity at the expense of the Ministry Of Transport!).

Original line-up comprised Sinclair, ex of Caravan (➡) and its progenitor Wilde Flowers (➡); Pip Pyle, ex Delivery and briefly Gong (➡); and the brothers Steve and Phil Miller (ex Matching Mole), the first of whom supplied Hatfield keyboards until his replacement by Dave Sinclair (brother of Richard) who in turn gave way to Dave Stewart, ex of Uriel and Egg.

The group played the kind of rock avant-garde suggested by their pedigrees on numerous radio and concert appearances before their first record contract, with Virgin, in 1973. Cut **Hatfield**

Left: George and Patti, Sept 1969. When Patti left him for Eric Clapton, George turned Bye Bye Love into an attack on the guitarist.

And The North for March 1974 release, following with The Rotters Club in January 1975. Devoid of the kind of success necessary to stimulate their experimentations, Hatfields disbanded mid-1975.

Recordings:
Hatfield And The North (Virgin)
The Rotters Club (Virgin)

Richie Havens

Born in the Bedford-Stuyvesant area of New York, Havens was the eldest of nine children. His father was a pianist, and Richie himself showed signs of musical talent at the age of six, but his family were too poor to help develop it. Eventually Havens begun as a street-corner singer, and when he was 14 formed the McCrea Gospel Singers.

At beginning of '60s he moved to Greenwich Village, where he painted portraits of tourists, and in 1962, at the height of folk revival, he began playing guitar professionally. He used an E-chord open tuning which enabled him to manipulate chords which would not have been possible with a standard tuning; this unique style still characterises both his performance and his recordings.

He gained an underground following in the Village, and made two early records – **The Richie Havens Record** and **Electric Havens**. When he signed to Verve, his popularity began to increase, and **Mixed Bag**, which contained numbers like **Eleanor Rigby**, indicated the rhythmic qualities of his work. After he played an outstanding set at Woodstock in 1969, everyone had heard of him, and most could describe his music, and it was to this background of popular interest that **Richard P. Havens, 1983** was released.

Havens never quite made it, however, beyond the respectable cult figure stage; partly this was because he relied on outside material, and one Havens treatment of a Lennon/McCartney composition began to sound very much like another. Though he did have a hit with Harrison's **Here Comes The Sun**, recent albums have proved rather uninteresting – though he remains a popular live performer. Apart from Woodstock, he took part in Woody Guthrie Memorial Concert in New York in 1968, and the 1972 stage production of Tommy.

Recordings:
The Richie Havens Record (Douglas Int/Transatlantic)
Electric Havens (Douglas Int/Transatlantic)
Mixed Bag (Verve)
Something Else Again (Verve)
Richard P. Havens 1983 (Verve)
Stonehenge (Stormy Forest/Polydor)
Alarm Clock (Stormy Forest/Polydor)
A State Of Mind (Stormy Forest/Polydor)
Great Blind Degree (Stormy Forest/Polydor)

Right: Space Ritual. Courtesy United Artists. On which the group collaborated with science fiction writer Michael Moorcock.

Richie Havens Live On Stage (Stormy Forest/Polydor)
Portfolio (Stormy Forest/Polydor)
Mixed Bag II (Stormy Forest/Polydor)
Compilation:
Richie Havens (—/Polydor)

Ronnie Hawkins

Sometimes regarded as the very last of the original breed of American rock 'n' rollers, Hawkins was born Jan 10, 1935 in Huntsville, Arkansas.

In 1952 he formed his first backing group, The Hawks, while at the University of Arkansas, and also gigged with his friend Harold Jenkins, who eventually gained international fame as Conway Twitty.

He took his Hawks – which by then included Levon Helm – to Canada with him in 1957, and from then on used that as his base, though he signed a contract with an American company, Roulette Records, and achieved a measure of success with aggressive reworkings of **Forty Days** and **Mary Lou**. In 1963 he recorded a version of Bo Diddley's **Who Do You Love?** which featured a guitar solo by Robbie Robertson that was five years ahead of its time. His following in Canada was by this time sufficient for him to establish his own club, the Hawks' Nest, on Yonge Street. Meanwhile, his backing group split to the States, helped out Bob Dylan and became better known as The Band (➧).

Hawkins is perhaps best known for the musicians he employed – a later incarnation of The Hawks went on to become Crowbar at the beginning of the '70s – though he is notorious as a hard-living womaniser. In 1969 Hawkins' contract was picked up by Cotillion Records, and he made a couple of comeback albums in Muscle Shoals, though with little visible success.

Discography is selective.

Recordings:
Ronnie Hawkins With The Band (Roulette/—)
Ronnie Hawkins (Cotillion/—)
Hawk (Cotillion/—)

Hawkwind

Dave Brock guitar, vocals, synthesiser
Nik Turner flute, sax, vocals
Paul Rudolph bass, vocals
Simon House mellotron, synthesiser, violin
Robert Calvert vocals
Simon King drums
Alan Powell drums

Founded by Dave Brock and Nik Turner, Hawkwind began life as a loose collection of freaks from the Notting Hill area of London who specialised in acid-oriented improvisations around a basic riff. For a time they were known as Group X, having close associations with the loosely-termed alternative society.

By the time of their first album **Hawkwind** in 1970, the had attracted a small but fanatical following – most of it in London and south – as Britain's premier stoned freak band. In that year they appeared at the star-studded, Bob Dylan-topped Isle Of Wight Festival. Not that Hawkwind were on the bill – they just turned-up and played for free outside the festival fence, Nik Turner painting himself silver much to the amusement of the national press who'd gone along to watch the freaks at play and look for bared nipples with which to titillate their readers.

Basically however, Hawkwind's early reputation was centred around their willingness to play anywhere anytime – for free – for any charity or cause with which they felt sympathy. A couple of drug busts, which again made the Fleet Street papers, helped cement the mini-legend; the band's early following being attracted as much by their philosophy/life-style as their music, which has never been adventurous.

Thus it was that they accrued the tags "people's band" and "the last of the true underground bands," while the archetypal **In Search Of Space** second album managed to make the British 1971 album charts.

In 1972 Hawkwind played what was to be one of their most significant gigs – at the London

Above: Nik Turner, co-founder of Hawkwind, auditions for a horror movie.

Roundhouse for an "alternative music" organisation The Greasy Truckers. A live album was recorded, **Greasy Truckers' Party** (Hawkwind on one side only), and from the out-takes came the band's million-selling **Silver Machine** single (1972).

Their interest in science fiction developing rapidly (SF writer Michael Moorcock was an early associate and aficionado of the band) they used the money from **Silver Machine** to fund their most ambitious project to date, The Space Ritual Road Show. By now they were playing much larger venues, and the album **Space Ritual Live** was recorded at the Brixton Sundown and Liverpool Stadium.

Dancer Stacia and poet/writer Robert Calvert (◆) augmented the band during this period.

Subsequent months, however, brought a series of baffling personnel changes; they had remained a loosely-organised outfit since inception, with people constantly leaving, returning, then leaving again – various other musicians often standing in when one or more members went sick or "missing".

In early 1973 the long-serving Dik Mik (kybds) left the band, and in 1974 the aforementioned Calvert quit to work solo (he has since rejoined them on an occasional basis). Two other longtime Hawkwinds, synthesiser player Del Dettmar and bassist Ian "Lemmy" Kilminster subsequently left the group, the latter being fired during 1975 U.S. tour. He has since formed Motorhead.

Simon House, previously with Third Ear Band, replaced Dettmar after "jamming" with the band on their spring 1974 U.S. tour, and Paul Rudolph, formerly of the Pink Fairies (◆), came in to replace Lemmy. Rudolph had previously often "depped" for both Lemmy and Dave Brock – he had also worked on Robert Calvert's solo projects.

Second drummer Alan Powell, ex Chicken Shack, Vinegar Joe, Pacific Gas And Electric, augmented the band as permanent member after filling in for Simon King when latter suffered an accident playing soccer.

In recent times, Hawkwind have been moderately successful in the U.S. and have become virtually an institution in British rock, though their status hasn't really displayed growth since peaking with **Silver Machine.**

Most of the early aficionados have stayed true to the band; new converts being similarly attracted primarily by the Hawkwind lifestyle. Musically, claims made on their behalf vary between "sonic warriors exploring the outer limits of sci-fi rock" (sic) to hamfisted chord bashers who camouflage their limitations behind strobe lights and a wall of noise – which view is held seems to depend on the constitution of the recipient's brain cells. One critic has described a typical Hawkwind set as "four hours of 4/4 with an occasional trot in 8/8"; others have suggested the band is long overdue to add a fourth chord to the three they already know! However, one feels that even their detractors find it hard to consider this bizarre freak collective without a certain fondness, and an admiration for their durability.

The 1976-released **Roadhawks** includes **Silver Machine** and chronicles group's history from 1970–75.

Recordings:
Hawkwind (United Artists)
In Search Of Space (United Artists)
Greasy Truckers' Party (—/Greasy Truckers)
Doremi Fasol Latido (United Artists)
Space Ritual Live (United Artists)
Hall Of The Mountain Grill (United Artists)
Warrior On The Edge Of Time (Atco/United Artists)
Compilation:
Roadhawks (Atco/United Artists)

Hot Buttered Soul.
Courtesy Pye Records.

Issac Hayes

Born Covington, Tennessee, Aug 20, 1943, Hayes became first black superstar in the field of music, mainly because of his extravagant public persona as the richest, fattest, most arrogant black cat of them all. His music was indubitably of secondary importance.

Brought-up in conditions of poverty, an orphan on his grandparents' sharecropper farm near Memphis, Hayes took several manual jobs in his adolescence while trying to further a musical career with a part-time group, Sir Isaac and the Doodads; he eventually accomplished this ambition by integrating himself into the famed circles of the Stax session musicians in Memphis, and becoming one of the leading names there. Hayes was proficient on saxophone and keyboards, and he played piano on most of the Otis Redding sessions. He also came to attention as co-writer, with David Porter, of the classic material that Sam and Dave recorded in the mid-'60s – **You Don't Know Like I Know, Soul Man** and **Hold On, I'm Comin'.**

Becoming a fully-fledged producer, he inaugurated his own recording career with **Presenting Isaac Hayes** in 1967, recording some tracks after a drunken party. Though the album achieved little, Hayes had now got the bit between his teeth, and in 1969, when Stax needed 30 albums for a promotional campaign, he recorded **Hot Buttered Soul** to make up the quota.

This was the album that catapulted Hayes to fame and fortune. It proved to be a model for his future output, and showcased his own bombastic interpretations of familiar songs. He turned innocuous pop songs like **By The Time I Get To Phoenix** into elaborately-scored 15-minute mini-symphonies; but while he practically invented orchestral soul, he also took the genre to its wildest, most self-parodying, extremes.

Hot Buttered Soul turned platinum by end of 1970, a feat that, incredibly, his five next albums were to repeat. **To Be Continued** and **The Isaac Hayes Movement** were constructed along similar lines, but his stature was further increased when he was asked to score "Shaft", the archetype of '70s Black movies. Hayes' theme tune became the first piece of seminal music in the '70s. It was the prototype of all the chuckawucka sounds that became omnipresent over next few years. (To the extent that, in Britain, a piece of Shaft-type music was used with a Metropolitan Police television recruiting advertisement.) **Shaft** topped the U.S. charts and reached No. 4 in the U.K. in 1971, and deservedly won Hayes an Academy Award.

He flaunted his success. His stage shows were celebrations of opulence that had much in common with the decadence of imperial Rome. Hayes appeared accompanied by a 40-piece orchestra, dressed in gold and black, in gold chains, shaven-headed, supported by an entourage of beautiful girls; it was pure theatrics, and entirely successful. He was known as Black Moses, and accordingly used that as the title of his 1971 album release.

Hayes, rampant, released nine albums in the four years from 1969–73 (including the early **In The Beginning**), gaining as much mileage as possible out of his musical ideas which at their best were very inventive, and at their worst crassly self-indulgent.

His success, however, was beginning to wane. In 1974 he released two film soundtracks almost simultaneously – **Tough Guys** and **Truck Turner,** and had a starring role in the latter film, but by now it was the end of the golden era. In 1975 he moved to ABC Records, though his first release for them, **Chocolate Chip,** just indicated the extent to which his own extravagances had become mere self-parody.

tain Beefheart on a European jaunt and producing a second album **Unrest,** by now minus the services of Geoff Leigh.

Fred Frith also cut his own critically-acclaimed album **Guitar Solos,** having contributed a learned series of articles on guitar technique to the "New Musical Express". Towards the end of that year the group began to work closely with Virgin stablemates, Slapp Happy(→), comprised of Peter Blegvad, Anthony Moore and German vocalist Dagmar.

With the two outfits outwardly stylistically dissimilar, it appeared a bizarre "marriage", although the resulting merger album **Desperate Straights** (1975) drew certain critical approval. Plans for a second collaboration were laid and both bands worked on **In Praise Of Learning,** released in late 1975. However, Blegvad and Moore left shortly after, though Dagmar opted to remain with the Cow.

Sixth member Lindsay Cooper is ex Royal Academy and the group Comus.

Musically, Henry Cow have proved notoriously difficult to describe – they have often crossed swords with British critics, one of whom termed their music "determinedly unapproachable" – though they would hardly argue with the statement that they are one of the few genuinely progressive outfits currently in operation, extending the boundaries of the rock avant-garde with rigorous disregard for critics and, if necessary, their audiences. Perhaps their influences offer more insight: these include Frank Zappa, John Coltrane, Stockhausen, Varese, Kurt Weill (Dagmar's contribution?) and various strains of avant-garde jazz.

Rock would have to take a virtual somersault to accommodate Henry Cow in its present conception, which makes major commercial success – even if desired on their part – a virtual nonstarter. Lesser talents have been nurtured by smaller cults, however.

Recordings:
Legend (Virgin)
Unrest (Virgin)
Slapp Happy/Henry Cow:
Desperate Straights (Virgin)
In Praise Of Learning (Virgin)
Fred Frith solo:
Guitar Solos (—/Caroline)

Mike Heron's Reputation
→ Incredible String Band

Dan Hicks And His Hot Licks

Hicks formed his Hot Licks in San Francisco 1968, at a time when he was still playing drums in a band called The Charlatans; for a time he combined the two activities.

Original line-up of the Hot Licks was: David Laflamme (vln), Bill Douglas (bs) and his wife Misty (vcls), Patti Urban (vcls), with Hicks himself on vocals and guitar.

Laflamme left to form It's A Beautiful Day (→), and Hicks put together a new line-up: Jaime Leopold (bs), John Weber (gtr), Sid Page (vln), Sherry Snow (vcls) and Tina Gancher (vcls). This line-up made the debut album, **The Original Recordings,** produced by Bob Johnston (→) for Epic in August 1969.

Snow, Gancher and Weber then departed, and Hicks recruited Naomi Eisenberg and Maryann Price, on vocals, to complete the band, which then produced **Where's The Money?,** a live album.

This line-up was supplemented by John Girton for **Strikin' It Rich,** and **Last Train To Hicksville,** and a drummer was also added to the line-up for the first time for the latter album.

The Hot Licks play jug-band material, Hicks describing their music as "a cross between The Andrews Sisters and the Jim Kweskin Jug Band". One of Hicks' songs, **Walkin' One And Only,** appears on the album **Maria Muldaur.**

The band have recently concluded a new record deal with Warner Bros.

Recordings:
The Original Recordings (Epic/—)
Where's The Money? (Blue Thumb/—)
Strikin' It Rich (Blue Thumb/ Island)
Last Train To Hicksville (Blue Thumb/—)

Steve Hillage
→ Gong

Holland-Dozier-Holland
→ Tamla-Motown

The Hollies

Allan Clarke vocals
Tony Hicks lead guitar
Terry Sylvester guitar
Bobby Elliott drums
Bernie Calvert bass

Formed Manchester 1963 at beginning of so-called British beat boom, from nucleus of a group called The Deltas. Original Hollies line-up was Clarke, Hicks, Graham Nash (gtr), Eric Haydock (bs) and Don Rathbone (drms), though later that year Rathbone left to be replaced by Elliott. This line-up established band as Britain's most consistently successful chart act, with sole exception of The Beatles. From **Searchin'** in 1963 to **Gasoline Alley Bred** in 1970 they had an unbroken sequence of 21 Top 20 hits.

This is a feat for which there seems no more explanation than that they chose each successive single with the greatest care, and had in Clarke a vocalist as strong and distinctive as any the "beat boom" unearthed, and in Nash an inimitable harmony vocalist.

Like most other major bands of the time (including Beatles and Stones) The Hollies took their early material from impeccable sources

Above: The Beat Boom beckons, and Graham Nash's molars lead the way. Others, from left, are: Bobby Elliott, Eric Haydock, Tony Hicks, Allan Clarke.

– the vast U.S. R&B catalogue. So they initially offered bastardised versions of The Coasters' **(Ain't That) Just Like Me** and **Searchin',** Maurice Williams And The Zodiacs' **Stay** and Doris Troy's **Just One Look.**

After that, as they became established, so top songwriters would offer them first refusal on their songs. Hits like **Here I Go Again, Yes I Will** and **Bus Stop** – written by Graham Gouldman, now of 10cc (→) – just kept on comin', though **I'm Alive** was to prove their only British No. 1.

In 1966 Haydock left to be replaced by Bernie Calvert, and then the band moved uneasily into 1967's Summer Of Love. Their problem was simple: they had tapped a massive singles market they could hardly ignore, while they openly yearned for the more lasting critical approbation that groups like The Beatles were receiving via the albums market. It was a dilemma never resolved. Their albums of this period, **For Certain Because, Evolution** and **Butterfly,** became more self-consciously ambitious, and certainly they were creditable; equally their singles improved in quality as they concentrated on writing their own material. But the singles continued to be successful, while they failed to crack the albums market to any significant degree.

Graham Nash took this failure particularly hard, and left the group in 1968, partly because he wanted to record more substantial material, and partly because he was upset at The Hollies' plans to record an album of Dylan songs. He had also been disenchanted with relative failure of his **King Midas In Reverse** single. He joined forces with Crosby and Stills and became a superstar, though whether he recorded weightier material is a matter of opinion. (→ Graham Nash; Crosby Stills Nash & Young.)

Nash's replacement was former Swinging Blue Jeans singer Terry Sylvester, who came from Liverpool, and from this moment on the band grimly resumed wooing the singles market, as hits like **He Ain't Heavy, He's My Brother** were created.

In 1971, with the band apparently at a low ebb, Clarke announced his departure to pursue a solo career, and the band selected Swedish singer Michael Rickfors as his replacement, but then a strange thing happened. A single recorded with Clarke as lead vocalist, **Long Cool Woman In A Black Dress,** inexplicably failed to score in Britain. It was, however, a U.S. No. 1. The unfortunate Rickfors was despatched whence he came, and Clarke resumed his old striker's position, and the band, with a fresh lease of life, signed a contract with Polydor, and were soon back to their old ways with a No. 2 U.K. hit in 1974 with the million-selling **The Air That I Breathe.** The band remain one of the most professional outfits in business.

Discography is not entirely complete, though British and American releases have differed so much it is necessary to provide separate listings.

Another Night.
Courtesy Polydor Records.

Recordings:
U.K. Releases:
Stay With The Hollies
(Parlophone)
In The Hollies Style
(Parlophone)
Would You Believe?
(Parlophone)
For Certain Because
(Parlophone)
Evolution (Parlophone)
Butterfly (Parlophone)
Hollies Sing Dylan (Parlophone)
Hollies Sing Hollies
(Parlophone)
Confessions Of The Mind
(Parlophone)
Distant Light (Parlophone)
Romany (Polydor)
The Hollies (Polydor)
Another Night (Polydor)
Write On (Polydor)
Compilation:
The History Of The Hollies
(EMI)
U.S. Releases:
Hear Here (Imperial)
Here I Go Again (Imperial)
Beat Group (Imperial)
Bus Stop (Imperial)
Stop, Stop, Stop (Imperial)
Evolution (Epic)
Dear Eloise/King Midas In
Reverse (Epic)
Hollies Sing Dylan (Epic)
He Ain't Heavy, He's My
Brother (Epic)
Distant Light (Epic)
Romany (Epic)
Another Night (Epic)
Compilations:
Very Best (United Artists)
Greatest Hits (Epic)
Allan Clarke solo:
My Real Name Is 'Arnold
(Epic/RCA)
Headroom (Epic/EMI)

Buddy Holly

In just over two years, Buddy Holly wrote one of the most important chapters in the history of rock music, and created a legend which survives to this day.

Born Charles Harden Holley (he dropped the "E" for professional use) in Lubbock, Texas Sept 7, 1936, his early interests, like so many other early rockers, were in C&W music. With his partner Bob Montgomery, played high-school hops, started a regular "Buddy & Bob" show over KDAV local radio station and in 1954–55 cut 11 demo songs which were not issued until after his death.

As a solo performer he cut further 16 tracks, this time in rock-

abilly vein, for Decca in Nashville in 1956, having been given a contract after appearing as support act when an Elvis Presley/Marty Robbins package tour visited Lubbock. His first release was **Love Me/Blue Days Black Nights,** issued July 2, 1956. He soon returned to Nashville to record with his own group Three Tunes, comprising Don Guess (bs), Jerry Allison (drms), Sonny Curtis (gtr); under the influence of Presley, they cut more fully-fledged rock 'n' roll songs.

It was when Holly's Decca contract terminated and he travelled to Clovis, New Mexico, and the studio of Norman Petty that things began to happen. With his new group The Crickets – only Allison was retained – and Petty as producer, Holly re-recorded **That'll Be The Day** from the earlier Nashville session. With this line-up of Holly (gtr, vcls), Allison (drms), Niki Sullivan (gtr), Joe Mauldin (bs), the song, a Holly-Allison composition, was very successful, reaching No. 3 in U.S. and No. 1 in the U.K., in 1957. Like all the early hits, it was credited simply to The Crickets.

To gain double mileage out of the commercial potential of the group, Petty had the idea of issuing Crickets' records, with Holly singing lead and the group playing and providing back-up harmonies, on the Brunswick label, while also issuing Holly solo records on the companion Coral label; later Petty would use ambitious multi-tracking techniques and allow Holly to stretch out with his guitar playing – which was highly advanced for the time.

The result was a string of million-sellers, including **Maybe Baby** for The Crickets and **Peggy Sue** for Holly. Songs like **Oh Boy** and **Think It Over** have a relaxed yet insistent sound which has remained contemporary for almost 20 years.

With Allison and Mauldin supporting, Holly toured Britain in 1958 very successfully; on returning to the States married Maria

Elena Santiago and moved to Greenwich Village. At this point Holly split from The Crickets, as Petty wanted to record him with strings, and some tracks were cut with Dick Jacobs' orchestra and chorus. Forming a new three-man backing group, Holly also recorded with guitarist Tommy Allsup and black saxophonist King Curtis in September 1958, the sessions resulting in **Reminiscing.**

By now, Holly was second in popularity only to Presley. He joined the Biggest Show Of Stars For 1959 package and after concert at Clear Lake the chartered light plane took-off from nearby Mason City airport and crashed minutes after at 1.50 a.m. on Feb 2, 1959 killing all the passengers, which included, as well as Holly, Big Bopper and Ritchie Valens. Holly was 22.

With his death Holly's popularity soared to new heights, particularly in Britain, where **It Doesn't Matter Anymore** topped the charts for six weeks. Holly releases continued to pour forth, Petty constantly unearthing old tracks and dubbing on strings and other instrumentation to beef them up, while the issue of compilation albums was unabated for a decade. For their part, The Crickets continued recording without Holly – **Love's Made A Fool Of You** was their first single without him – and they later cut a tribute album with Bobby Vee.

Holly's sound has often been termed Tex-Mex (i.e. from the Texas-New Mexico area), but though he was a product of his musical environment, Holly's style was certainly unique; it has been lastingly influential.

Virtually every major rock singer has admitted his debt to Holly. The Hollies took their name from him, and The Beatles just thought of an alternative insect name to The Crickets. In 1974 Bob Dylan said that Holly's music was still as valid then as it had been at the time. Don McLean's **American**

Below: Charles Harden Holley straightens his bow tie before going out and profoundly influencing the course of rock 'n' roll.

Pie album was dedicated to Holly, and the title track, an American cultural Odyssey, traced the beginning of the decline of rock 'n' roll – and by extension everything else the American teenager

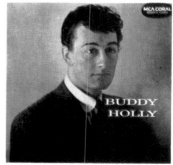

Buddy Holly.
Courtesy MCA Records.

held dear – from the death of Holly.

Recordings:
The Chirping Crickets
(Brunswick/Coral)
Buddy Holly (Coral)
That'll Be The Day (Decca/Ace Of Hearts)
The Buddy Holly Story (Coral)
The Buddy Holly Story, Vol. II
(Coral)
Reminiscing (Coral)
Showcase (Coral)
Holly In The Hills (Coral)
The Best Of Buddy Holly
(Coral/—)
Buddy Holly's Greatest Hits
(Coral)
Buddy Holly's Greatest Hits,
Vol. II (—/Coral)
Giant (Coral/MCA Coral)
Good Rockin' (Vocalion/—)
Remember (—/Coral)
Buddy Holly: A Rock 'n' Roll
Collection (Decca/—)
Legend (—/MCA Coral)
Nashville Sessions (MCA Coral)
The Complete Buddy Holly
Story (9-album set) (MCA Coral)

John Lee Hooker

♦ Blues – American

Nicky Hopkins

Though even the most dedicated rock aficionado would have difficulty putting a name to the face, Nicky Hopkins is arguably rock's most proficient sessionman, as well as one of the finest piano-players in the genre.

Born South London Feb 24, 1944 and a former student at the Royal Academy Of Music, Hopkins' first name band was Screamin' Lord Sutch's Savages, the personnel of which later supplied the nucleus of Cyril Davies' All Stars (♦ Cyril Davies). This was Britain's best early R&B group (the embryonic Rolling Stones used to play as support gigs to them), and Hopkins reserves his fondest memories for that particular semi-legendary outfit.

However, the frail young pianist was always prone to illness, and in mid-1963 he was forced to leave the All Stars to undergo hospital treatment for a serious internal disorder. When he came out on Christmas Eve 1964, Cyril Davies had only a matter of days to live before his sudden death from leukaemia.

Instead, Hopkins turned to session-work – a physically less demanding occupation than gigging musician. His first experience, however, was a shambolic affair featuring Jeff Beck under the production supervision of Jimmy Page. These studio "jams" have subsequently turned-up credited to Jeff Beck And The All Stars on various British rock anthologies.

After a lengthy spell as one of the most in-demand session-men of his day – he appears on The Who's **My Generation** album and single, and The Beatles' single **Revolution** – Hopkins reunited with Jeff Beck for the latter's excellent **Truth** album (1968). Beck subsequently persuaded Hopkins to join his first Jeff Beck Group, the pianist staying with that musically illustrious but shambolically organised outfit up until June 4, 1969 when he decided he had had enough of Beck's foibles. Within days the rest of the band similarly left, and Beck's group dissolved within a week (♦ Jeff Beck; Faces).

During his U.S. visits with Beck, Hopkins had guested on the Jefferson Airplane (♦) album **Volunteers**, and post-Beck he was approached by Steve Miller (♦) to play on his **Your Saving Grace** set. Hopkins' reputation was spreading rapidly on the West Coast by now, and in 1969 he took up an offer to join the legendary Quicksilver Messenger Service (♦), staying for a lengthy spell.

His session-work continued in tandem with Quicksilver, however. Hopkins set up home in Mill Valley, near San Francisco, commuting regularly between the U.S. and the U.K.

Despite his impressive track record, it is perhaps for his work with the Rolling Stones (♦) that Hopkins is best known. He first played for them on the **Satanic Majesties** set (1967) and appeared on successive releases right through to the early '70s. It's a little-known fact that at one time Hopkins was asked to join the Stones as a fully-fledged member. The occasion was shortly after Brian Jones' death; Hopkins was asked to play the Stones' London Hyde Park gig in summer 1969 and subsequently stick around. He said a tentative yes, fell ill, returned to Mill Valley, hesitated about flying back for the gig and let the opportunity slide. However, he did later join them in a "guest" capacity on the Stones 1972 U.S. tour.

In 1973 Hopkins made his first solo album **The Tin Man Was A Dreamer** for Columbia/CBS, for which he had the session support of George Harrison, Mick Taylor and Klaus Voorman. In fact he recorded a second one, **Long Journey Home**, but grew disillusioned with Columbia when they offed managing director Clive Davis (♦) in a shoddy manner. Hopkins and Columbia mutually lost interest in the album which was left to gather dust in the company's vaults.

In 1974 Hopkins left Mill Valley to set up home in Egham, Surrey. He remains as frail as ever, a man who has lived with constant illness but who has led perhaps the most celebrated uncelebrated career in rock.

Recordings:
The Tin Man Was A Dreamer (Columbia/CBS)

Horslips

Charles O'Connor fiddle, mandolin, vocals
Jim Lochart flute, pipes
Barry Devlin bass, vocals
Eamon Carr drums
Johnny Fean guitar, banjo, flute

Dublin band formed 1970, Horslips turned professional on St Patrick's Day (Mar 17) 1972. They leavened their traditional Irish jigs and reels with a strong undertow of rock. Original guitarist, Declan Sinnott was replaced by Gus Guiest, who in turn was replaced by Fean.

Unlike many other Irish bands – Thin Lizzy, for example – they decided to popularise themselves on the native gig circuit before attempting to crack the English market.

In March 1972 they had a hit single in Ireland with **Johnny's Wedding**, and in July followed this with a song called **Green Gravel**. Despite their increasing success, they refused offers from major recording companies and formed their own, entirely independent, Oats company. They recorded an album on the Stones mobile, mixed it, pressed it, and distributed it themselves; the result, in early 1973, was the fastest-selling album of all time in Ireland, and one which dominated the Irish charts for over two months.

After a solid base of support, the band signed a distribution deal with RCA Records and went to England. In autumn 1973, they supported Steeleye Span on a nationwide British tour, and released second album, **The Tain** (which was a concept based on an ancient Irish myth), again to an enthusiastic press.

However, the band have not yet succeeded in building on this remarkably successful opening to their career, possibly because they have abandoned their Celtic music influences in favour of a rock-based approach.

Recordings:
Happy To Meet . . . Sorry To Part (Atco/Oats)
The Tain (Atco/Oats)
Dancehall Sweethearts (RCA)
The Unfortunate Cup Of Tea (RCA)

Hot Chocolate

Errol Brown vocals
Patrice Olive bass
Larry Ferguson keyboards
Tony Connor drums
Harvey Hinsley guitar

Formed by Errol Brown 1970, they were initially contracted to Apple label, for whom they recorded a version of John Lennon's **Give Peace A Chance** as their only single. In 1970 the band signed to Mickie Most's RAK Records, since when many of their releases have been British hits, though they are not a prolific band, and tend to release material only when fully satisfied with quality.

Of personnel, Olive, Ferguson and Hinsley have been there more or less since the beginning. In 1973 Hinsley invited Connor (who had previously played in Audience for thee years) to join. Tony Wilson, who played bass and sang, and composed most of material with Brown, was a long-serving member of band who left in November 1975 to concentrate on independent songwriting and producing.

Hot Chocolate.
Courtesy RAK Records.

Love Is Life and **I Believe In Love** provided group with early hits, and then in 1973 their song **Brother Louie** was covered in the U.S. by Stories, for whom the song became a No. 1 Hot Chocolate's U.K. follow-up **Rumours**, was also covered by a home-grown act in the U.S., but eventually this proved to be just a foot in the back door of the U.S. charts for H.C. themselves, and their recent singles – **Emma, You Sexy Thing** and **Don't Stop It Now** have been as successful in the U.S. as in British charts.

Although their first British chart entry was in 1970, the band concentrated on producing quality material for the singles market, and did not issue their first album (**Cicero Park**) until 1974.

Recordings:
Cicero Park (Victory/RAK)
Hot Chocolate (Victory/RAK)
Man To Man (Victory/RAK)
Compilation:
The Best Of Hot Chocolate (Victory/RAK)

Hot Tuna

Jorma Kaukonen guitar, vocals
Jack Casady bass
Bob Steeler drums

Formed circa 1969–70 by Jefferson Airplane (♦) founder members Kaukonen and Casady to jam and record as means of keeping themselves occupied while other Airplaners were busy procreating babies and solo albums. Kaukonen, Casady first started jamming as acoustic duo at folk clubs augmented by mouth-harp player Will Scarlett. They called themselves Hot Shit but reached compromise name when RCA baulked at first choice appearing on albums.

Aforementioned trio appeared on eponymous Tuna debut 1970, subsequently regrouping with drummer Joey Covington when they went electric. Veteran fiddler Papa John Creach later recruited to Hot Tuna which, when Airplane resumed gigging, used to appear as support act – Kaukonen and Casady then joined with parent band for main set. Covington, Creach also became fully-fledged members of Airplane.

Kaukonen, Casady regrouped with drummer Steeler (though line-up has always contained a certain flexibility) and pursued Hot Tuna as full-time career on demise of Airplane in 1973.

Casady was perhaps best instrumentalist Airplane ever had, but Tuna have been hampered by Kaukonen's limited ability as singer and composer and recent albums have met with little critical enthusiasm.

Recordings:
Hot Tuna (RCA)
First Pull Up Then Pull Down (RCA)
Electric-Live (RCA)
Burgers (Grunt)
The Phosphorescent Rat (Grunt)
America's Choice (Grunt)
Yellow Fever (Grunt)

Hudson-Ford

Singers and songwriters Richard Hudson and John Ford first came to prominence as drummer and bassist respectively of the chameleon-like British group The Strawbs (♦). For that band, Hudson and Ford wrote the January 1973 U.K. No. 2 **Part Of The Union** which, quite disproportionate to its import, caused a minor political row fleetingly stirred by British national press. Nevertheless it was a fair, catchy pop hit, and ended the year taking an Ivor Novello Award as best composition.

However, by then Hudson and Ford had fallen out with Strawbs leader Dave Cousins and left to pursue their own career, quickly picking up another U.K. hit (September 1973) – this time in their own right – with **Pick Up The Pieces** (unrelated to Average Whites' hit of same name).

Subsequent success has proved somewhat harder to come by, although the duo has released three albums, the 1975 **World Collide** set being recorded at Ringo Starr's Ascot studios with the support of Ken Laws (drms) and Chris Parren (kybds), plus sax player Dick Morrisey and arranger John Mealing, the last two former members of If.

Richard Hudson switched to lead guitar for this set, playing same in the duo's touring band which features John Ford's bass and the aforementioned Parren and Laws.

Recordings:
Nickelodeon (A&M)
Free Spirit (A&M)
Worlds Collide (A&M)

Alan Hull
♦ Lindisfarne

Humble Pie

Steve Marriott guitar, vocals
Greg Ridley bass, vocals
Jerry Shirley drums
Dave Clempson guitar, vocals

Formed 1968 as a somewhat lightweight rock band centred around Marriott, ex Small Faces (♦), and Peter Frampton (gtr, vcls), ex

Right: Original Humble Pie, from 1971. From left: Jerry Shirley, Peter Frampton, Steve Marriott, Greg Ridley.

pretty boy "face" with the pop group Herd. Jerry Shirley and Greg Ridley, the latter from Spooky Tooth (♦), completed the line-up and the group rehearsed for some considerable time at Marriott's Essex home before release of their 1969 debut album **As Safe As Yesterday** on Andrew Loog Oldham's Immediate label.

Both Marriott, as gut-bucket singer and writer, and Frampton, as writer/guitar prodigy, were not inconsiderable talents; however, both had become infatuated, along with many of their contemporaries, with the innovative music being produced by The Band (♦), and the first and second Humble Pie albums came across as somewhat limp pastiches of the American group.

Subsequently, their early label of "supergroup" became a millstone around their necks, and hoped-for acceptance in the albums market proved hard to come by. They did however, crack the U.K. singles market charts in 1969 with the Top 5 hit **Natural Born Bugie.**

American success also, initially, proved elusive, and matters weren't helped when the group returned from their first U.S. visit to find that Immediate Records had gone into liquidation. The Pie almost disbanded, but persisted and found an aggressive new manager in America lawyer Dee Anthony, a man with impressive credentials in the U.S. rock arena.

With Anthony and, by now, with A&M, their 1970 **Humble Pie** set enjoyed minor success in the States, but the follow-up **Rock On** (1971) was one of the topsellers of its year. An American tour in early 1971, the Pie by now leaning towards a heavy rock orientation, drew ecstatic reviews – their new success reflected in the bestselling **Performance – Rockin' At The Fillmore.**

Somewhat predictably, however, Frampton (♦) left shortly after,

Marriott bringing in Dave Clempson from the disbanded Colosseum (♦) and steering the Pie towards an even heavier rock identity. In early 1972 **Smokin'** was a U.S. topseller, joined on the charts by a repackage of the two

Below: Janis Ian.

Immediate albums under the title **Lost And Found.**

Eat It, in 1973, was a double-set comprising part-live, part-studio, work. In that same year the band had experimented briefly with a soul revue-type stage show, augmenting with the three-girl singing group The Blackberries.

By now, however, the rot had long since set in musically. Marriott had always displayed a lamentable tendency to ape black vocal mannerisms, which became virtually parodic in the Pie's later stages. Partly as a result of this, partly because of the rut they had run themselves into, Humble Pie staggered amidst countless rumours towards a final break-up in 1975, Dave Clempson having left to join Greenslade (♦) in the preceding year.

In late 1975 to early 1976 Marriott was working gigs with his own Steve Marriott All Stars, and recorded a solo album in New York. His name was also linked frequently in the rock press with a possible reunion of the Small Faces. ♦ Steve Marriott.

Recordings:
As Safe As Yesterday (Immediate)
Town And Country (Immediate)
Humble Pie (A&M)
Rock On (A&M)
Performance – Rockin' At The Fillmore (A&M)
Smokin' (A&M)
Eat It (A&M)
Thunderbox (A&M)
Street Rats (A&M)

Ian Hunter (Hunter-Ronson)

Founder member of Mott The Hoople (♦), Ian Hunter was born in Shrewsbury, England, on a date given in "official" biographies as June 3, 1946 – though he is probably (perhaps considerably) older. With his characteristic curly hair and omnipresent dark glasses, Hunter was leader, vocalist and focal point of Mott up to his far from harmonious departure in late 1974. He had endured a period in a New Jersey hospital suffering nervous and physical collapse, although the prime reason for his exit was internal friction in the band.

Former David Bowie guitar sideman Mick Ronson (♦), who had had a fleeting spell with Mott, left at the same time; he and Hunter proposing to collaborate on various projects while pursuing their own solo activities.

Ronson produced and played on Hunter's first solo album **Ian Hunter** (1975) from which came the U.K. hit **Once Bitten Twice Shy.** In the same year, as The Hunter Ronson Show – line-up completed by Peter Arnesen (kybds), Jeff Appleby (bs), Dennis Elliott (drms) – the pair played gigs in U.S. and U.K. but later separated. Hunter's second solo album, **All American Alien Boy,**

was released spring 1976.

With his American wife Trudi, Hunter is now semi-resident in the U.S. partly for tax reasons. A one-time would-be journalist, Hunter set out his experiences as a rock star in the 1973-published "Diary Of A Rock 'n' Roll Star", re-published 1976 as "Reflections Of A Rock 'n' Roll Star".

Recordings:
Ian Hunter (Columbia/CBS)
All American Alien Boy (Columbia/CBS)

Janis Ian

By time she was 15, Janis Ian was a well-known name in the U.S. as a result of her hit single **Society's Child,** not merely because it was very successful, but because of its ethical bias – it dealt with the love of a white girl and a black guy and the hypocritical attitudes of society.

Janis Ian was born New York, May 7, 1951 though her parents regularly moved around the Eastern seaboard. In 1965 she

started singing at Village Gate and was signed by Elektra Records, though the company dropped their option when they discovered she wanted to be a singer as well as songwriter. Her family moved from New Jersey to New York where she met the Reverend Gary Davis, and sang at the Gaslight, prior to receiving a contract from MGM Records. She recorded **Society's Child,** along with a whole album of angry, generation-gap material that was issued in 1967 as **Janis Ian.**

At age of 16, she had her first album in charts, Murray the K filled his airwaves with the tracks nightly, and she continued living with her parents and doing countless college concerts all over the U.S. After her initial releases, however, she became disillusioned with the pop market-place and retired to get married and live in Philadelphia.

By 1970 she felt more assured; she recorded one album for Capitol in 1971, **Present Company,** and began to make live appearances again. However, it was not until 1974 that she was

Left: Ian Hunter. He left Mott
The Hoople to work with
Mick Ronson, though it was a
short-lived alliance.

Left: Ian Hunter. He left Mott The Hoople to work with Mick Ronson, though it was a short-lived alliance.

restored to widespread public esteem. With a new Columbia contract, she made an album, **Stars,** that fully realised the potential of all the talent of which her previous work had merely scratched the surface. The title track of **Stars** was an almost harrowing exposition of the illusions of success; **Between The Lines,** released in 1975, included **At Seventeen,** which became a U.S. No. 1 single, an achievement which illustrated the efficacy of her comeback.

Her later, more mature work has been suffused with both folk and jazz influences; her skilfully crafted songs have something of the nature of the confessional, being intensely personal. Sensitivity had become almost a dirty word for

Aftertones.
Courtesy CBS Records.

singer/songwriters, but Janis Ian again showed that it could be a potent attribute for a lyricist.

Her present status is testimony to the careful and patient way she's been nurtured to maturity by a sympathetic management since her success with **Society's Child.**

Her songs have been recorded recently by many other artists – **Jesse,** for example, has been covered regularly, and was included on Joan Baez's **Diamonds And Rust.** In 1976 she released **Aftertones,** to the same kind of instant critical acclaim and the same kind of chart success.

Because of her fresh popularity, most of her early work has been re-issued in 1976.

Recordings:
Janis Ian (Verve-Folkways)
For All The Seasons Of The Mind (Verve-Folkways)
The Secret Life Of J. Eddy Fink (Verve-Folkways)
Present Company (Capitol)
Stars (Columbia/CBS)
Between The Lines (Columbia/CBS)
Aftertones (Columbia/CBS)

If

Dick Morrissey saxophones, flute
Terry Smith guitar
John Mealing keyboards
J. W. Hodkinson vocals
Dennis Elliott drums
Dave Quincy alto sax
Jim Richardson bass

If were formed by Morrissey and Smith in late '60s. The former had

been a member of a jazz quartet in the early '60s which also included Ginger Baker, Harry South and Phil Seamen. Later on, he worked with The Animals and Georgie Fame, both of whom were then experimenting with jazz-blues music; an attempt was also made to get something together with Graham Bond, but nothing came of it.

The line-up above is the most celebrated one, which played on **If III** and **If IV**; they were a hard-gigging jazz-rock combo who never made the breakthrough they consistently threatened – possibly because they left hungry their staunch British following in order to spend several months of each year touring in the U.S.; a corollary of this was that towards the end they were subject to regular personnel changes – life on the road being tough. Mealing, Elliott and Richardson left the band, to be replaced by Dave Greenslade (kybds), Cliff Davies (drms) and Dave Wintour (bs).

However, this aggregation merely rehearsed together, and before they either went on the road or recorded another album Greenslade and Wintour had both left again.

Final line-up of the band when they eventually folded in 1975 was Morrissey, Davies, Geoff Whitehorn (gtr, vcls), Gabriel Magno (kybds, clarinet) and Walt Monaghan (bs, vcls).

Davies had joined If from The Roy Young Band, the personnel of which also included Onnie McIntyre (later of the Average White Band (➧)) and Rick Dod, who went on to play with Kevin Coyne. Monaghan played with the Mick Abrahams Band for three years.

Despite their demise, If are fondly remembered in Britain; Morrissey and Smith were gigging in Sweden at beginning of 1976.

If IV was re-titled **Waterfall** for U.S. release.

Recordings:
If I (Capitol/Island)
If II (Capitol/Island)
If III (Capitol/United Artists)
If IV (Capitol/United Artists)
Not Just Another Bunch Of Pretty Faces (Capitol/Gull)
Tea Break Over, Back On Your Heads (Capitol/Gull)

The Impressions

Sam Gooden
Fred Cash
Ralph Johnson
Reggie Torian

The Impressions have a long and distinguished history as one of America's most successful black vocal groups. In 1956 Curtis Mayfield and Jerry Butler, who already knew each other from a church choir, were neighbours in Chicago's north side; a group called The Roosters had just moved into the area. There were three in the group – Sam Gooden, and Arthur and Richard Brooks, though a fourth, Fred Cash, had opted to remain at home in Chattanooga, Tennessee.

Butler and Mayfield joined forces with the other three, and they became The Impressions. Their first break came in 1958 when **For Your Precious Love** became a local and then a national hit; though unfortunately the success of this record had a divisive effect, as the record company, without consulting the group, had credited the record to Jerry Butler & The Impressions; this created ill feeling, and Butler duly left to go solo, leaving the others back at square one.

The Impressions Big Sixteen. Courtesy ABC Records.

The group was thus dormant for a time, and Mayfield made out as Butler's guitar player, and wrote Butler's first solo hit, **He Will Break Your Heart.** With this boost, the other Impressions (by now Cash had moved up from the South to replace Butler) followed Mayfield to New York and recommenced recording themselves; with Mayfield's **Gypsy Woman,** in 1961, they became big business.

The Brooks brothers quit in 1963, while the other three – Mayfield, Cash and Gooden – went on to become an institution in soul music, as Mayfield penned a score of superlative R&B songs: **People Get Ready, I'm So Proud, Keep On Pushing,** etc., **The Impressions' Big 16,** which is a compilation of these singles, is rightly adjudged to contain a uniquely impressive body of work. Certainly, the high-pitched harmonies of the trio influenced the vocal style of many black groups in mid-'60s.

The songs also showed Mayfield's lyrical strength, at a time when such a quality was hardly expected of black musicians; songs like **People Get Ready** were true songs of inspiration, and showed the stirrings of a black consciousness.

Mayfield took this a stage further when he formed his own Curtom label in 1968, and he introduced The Impressions to less ambivalent social consciousness songs via material on **This Is My Country** and **The Young Mods' Forgotten Story** – in particular, **Mighty Mighty Spade And Whitey,** which became a U.S. No. 1.

In 1970 Mayfield left to concentrate on his solo career, and his by now considerable outside activities, though he continued to be involved with the group through his roles of mentor, producer and label-owner.

He was replaced by Leroy Hutson, a songwriter and graduate of Howard University in Washington, who stayed in the line-up for little more than two years before himself undertaking a solo career. At this point, Cash and Gooden slightly changed the group's format, and made it a four-piece, bringing in Torian and

Johnson.

This was a sign for the group to resume their former level of success, and the first release of the new line-up, **Finally Got Myself Together** (1974), re-established them in America as a top vocal group (the title track became a U.S. No. 1 when issued as a single); in the U.K., they had to wait a little longer for chart success, which came in 1975 when the title track of **First Impressions** gave them a Top 20 hit single.

Now produced by Ed Townsend, there seems little doubt of their ability to survive without the guiding hand of Curtis Mayfield (➡).

Discography is selective.

Recordings:
This Is My Country (Curtom/Buddah)
The Young Mods' Forgotten Story (Curtom/Buddah)
Finally Got Myself Together (Curtom)
First Impressions (Curtom)
Loving Power (Curtom)
Compilations:
The Impressions' Big 16,
The Impressions' Big 16, Vol. II (ABC)

Incredible String Band

Robin Williamson vocals, guitar, assorted instruments
Mike Heron vocals, guitar, assorted instruments

Although the Incredibles contained several different members during their lifespan, and were a five-piece when they disbanded in November 1974, the rest were always essentially mere supporting players to the songwriting nucleus of Williamson and Heron.

Initially, however, they were a trio, Scottish folk artists Robin Williamson and Clive Palmer first forming a loose association in their home country during 1965 before adding fellow Scot Mike Heron and adopting the name Incredible String Band. Their debut album for Elektra in 1966 caused a sensation in folk circles, though it took the following year's **The 5000 Spirits Or The Layers Of The Onion** to bring them wider recognition, before which Palmer had left.

The Hangman's Beautiful Daughter. (Reverse). Elektra.

By now working extensively outside of Scotland (Heron and Williamson made their major London concert debut on a bill with Judy Collins and Tom Paxton, and subsequently played the 1967 Newport Folk Festival in the U.S.), their music had taken on a com-

plexity of various influences and equally exotic instrumentation – both in part culled from the pair's earlier world travels investigating indigenous music cultures.

Their own music was deeply rooted in the "alternative" British youth culture of the day; that second ISB album becoming virtually the bible of the burgeoning acid generation. In-concert appearances cemented a growing legend.

The third album, **The Hangman's Beautiful Daughter,** appearing in 1968, still stands as something of a masterwork. Critically acclaimed not only in the "underground press" but also in the "quality" Fleet Street papers, it further revealed the compositional abilities of Heron and Williamson as unique in structure and variety. "Folk" had long since become a redundant description for a music so eclectic and rich in texture. The majestic **Hangman's Daughter** set its own standards; defined its own territories.

Unfortunately those standards weren't maintained; and those territories became cul-de-sacs. After **Hangman,** group policy was reviewed and two girlfriends, Licorice McKenzie (vln) and Rose Simpson (bs), were brought in to augment the line-up. Concert appearances became ever more parodic, the berobed Williamson and Heron seemingly intent on proving beyond all else that they could not only play every instrument in conventional use but also some that hadn't yet been invented.

Wee Tam And The Big Huge (1968), a double-set, while evidencing flashes of their earlier genius, was over-ambitious and largely self-indulgent – and the ISB never regained their initial mastery and poise. In retrospect they had been born of and fed from the drug culture; once Williamson and Heron began to eschew the drugs, if not the culture, they saw themselves en route to creative decline.

Between 1969–70 there appeared a sequence of mostly disappointing albums, the 1970 releases **U** and **Be Glad For The Song Has No Ending** being written for stage and film shows respectively. Rose Simpson left in 1971. Malcolm LeMaistre (bs, vcls, dance) joined in 1972 and Gerald Dott (kybds, reeds) in 1973.

Reaching a peak so early in their career the Incredibles were in decline ever since, although solo ventures by Heron – **Smiling Men With Bad Reputations** (1971) – and Williamson – **Myrrh** (1972) – did go some way to recapturing what the group had forfeited after **Wee Tam** in 1968.

However, it would be unfair to dismiss the ISB's latter period without mentioning that they maintained a small but devoted following as a live attraction. In the early '70s they were a regular feature of open-air festivals, often stealing honours from headline acts, many times converting initially-sceptical audiences with their intrinsically naive but infectiously exuberant approach.

Looking back on the Incredibles in an interview in late 1974, Mike Heron acknowledged that records had been the group's Achilles heel in their later years, though he himself maintained that live support had remained buoyant.

The inevitable dignified break-up came in Nov. 1974, provoking a sense of relief rather than mourning, particularly from critics who had acclaimed them at the beginning and watched their decline with growing dismay.

Robin Williamson took off for Los Angeles; Mike Heron (a convert to Scientology) stayed in Britain to do session-work, write and eventually form a new band. As Mike Heron's Reputation this retained three members from final ISB line-up – LeMaistre, John Gilston (drms) and Graham Forbes (gtr) – with newcomers David Barker, ex Magna Carta and Mike Tomich, ex If. They toured U.K. with Andy Fraser Band and made one album **Mike Heron's Reputation** (1975) without overmuch success.

Recordings:
The Incredible String Band (Elektra)
The 5000 Spirits Or The Layers Of The Onion (Elektra)
The Hangman's Beautiful Daughter (Elektra)
Wee Tam And The Big Huge (Elektra)
Changing Horses (Elektra)
I Looked Up (Elektra)
U (Elektra)
Be Glad For The Song Has No Ending (Reprise/Island)
Liquid Acrobat As Regards The Air (Reprise/Island)
Earthspan (Reprise/Island)
No Ruinous Feud (Reprise/Island)
Hard Rope And Silken Twine (Reprise/Island)
Compilation:
Relics Of The Incredible String Band (Elektra)
Robin Williamson:
Myrrh (Reprise/Help)
Mike Heron:
Smiling Men With Bad Reputations (Elektra/Island)
Mike Heron's Reputation (Neighbourhood)

Iron Butterfly

Erik Braunn guitar, vocals
Ron Bushy drums
Phil Kramer bass
Bill De Martines keyboards

Archetypal American heavy metal outfit, originated out of San Diego, California, with founder member keyboards man Doug Ingle plus drummer Bushy and fellow San Diegan Jerry Penrod, Danny Weis and Darryl DeLoach. This five cut the debut album **Heavy** in early 1968 but group friction caused Penrod, Weis and DeLoach to quit shortly after.

In their places Ingle and Bushy recruited Boston-born guitarist Erik Braunn and multi-instrumentalist Lee Dorman.

As four-piece, the group cut the monster-selling **In A-Gadda-Da-Vida** set later in 1968, that album staying on the U.S. album charts for more than two years, and becoming one of the largest-grossing rock albums of all time. It was also reputedly the first ever rock group album to achieve platinum status.

Predictably, however, the disproportionate acclaim garnered by **In-A-Gadda-Da-Vida** (title came from 17-minute composition by Doug Ingle) became something of a millstone around their necks. Braunn left in late 1969, to be replaced by the twin guitars of Mike Pinera and Larry Reinhardt (a former associate of Duane Allman).

Thus reorganised they recorded **Iron Butterfly Live** and **Metamorphosis** (both in 1970). However, the rot had long since set in. Butterfly were typical)although more explosively popular) of the run-of-the-mill West Coast heavy groups, and they were always on the decline from their 1968 peak; their pulling power dropping at an alarming rate.

In-A-Gadda-Da-Vida.
Courtesy Atlantic Records.

After a farewell American tour they dissolved in May 1971.

However, after relatively unsuccessful alternative careers, Bushy and Braunn reunited to form a second incarnation of Iron Butterfly in 1974 with Phil Kramer (bs) and Howard Reitzes (kybds). They cut **Scorching Beauty** (1975), then Bill DeMartines replaced Reitzes.

Recordings:
Heavy (Atco/Atlantic)
In-A-Gadda-Da-Vida (Atco/Atlantic)
Ball (Atco/Atlantic)
Iron Butterfly Live (Atco/Atlantic)
Metamorphosis (Atco/Atlantic)
Scorching Beauty (MCA)
Sun And Steel (MCA)
Compilation:
Best Of The Iron Butterfly (Atco/—)

The Isley Brothers

Ronald Isley lead vocals
Rudolph Isley vocals
Kelly Isley vocals
Ernie Isley guitar, drums
Marvin Isley bass
Chris Jasper keyboards, ARP

Over the past 20 years, the Isleys have proved one of the most versatile and redoubtable of American soul-rock acts.

Originally there were the three brothers – Ronald (b. May 21, 1941), O'Kelly (b. Dec 25, 1937 – he later dropped the "O") and Rudolph (b. Apr 1, 1939), who left home in Cincinnati, Ohio, to make their first recordings in New York 1957. They recorded for the Teenage and Gone labels, material ranging through both doowop ballads and raucous rock 'n' roll. By 1959 they'd signed for RCA, with producers Hugo and Luigi – who now own the Avco label, from where they guide The Stylistics (◆).

They recorded **Shout**, a song that was almost pure energy; it took

elements of gospel music, particularly its call-and-response features, and practically opened door for '60s soul music. It was deservedly a hit, making the U.S. Top 50 (though it was actually more successful in cover versions, by Joey Dee and the Starlighters in U.S., and Lulu and the Luvvers in Britain).

But the Isleys had no run of consistency, and changed companies as frequently as they changed styles. For a time they were produced by Leiber and Stoller at Atlantic; but in 1962, by now aboard the Twist bandwagon, they had a hit on the Wand label – **Twist And Shout,** under the tutelage of Bert Berns; it was actually a cover of an original by The Topnotes, but the intensity of the Isleys' interpretation carried the song into history (though once again, they were trumped, this time by The Beatles).

There followed a fresh period in the wilderness, during which they formed their own T-Neck production company, one of the first black acts to do so, though to little immediate effect. During 1964 they employed a young left-handed guitarist named Jimi Hendrix; his recordings with them indicate that even then he was more than an average sessionman, and it was a relationship that was to have a profound effect later on.

In December 1965 the Isleys accepted an invitation from Berry Gordy to join Motown label. Their first release, **This Old Heart Of Mine,** produced by Brian Holland and Lamont Dozier was an immediate U.S. hit, and a chart success in Britain when it was re-released two years later; **Behind A Painted Smile** and **I Guess I'll Always Love You** were further Motown successes; but still lacking consistency, they were allowed to move on towards the end of '60s.

After 12 years in business, the Isleys were still in starting blocks, but they had survived this far on an energetic stage act, and the strength of Ronald's vocal performances. In 1969 they reacti-

This Old Heart Of Mine.
Tamla Motown Records.

vated T-Neck and almost immediately earned a gold disc with the brash up-front funk of **It's Your Thing,** which was far removed from their soft-soul style at Motown.

Following the success of **It's Your Thing,** Ernie, Marvin and their cousin Chris Jasper joined the other Isleys to form a self-sufficient family unit that rapidly moved away from conventional soul music. The Isleys were one of the first bands to pick up on both what Stevie Wonder was achieving with synthesisers, and also what rock could offer soul

music. Not unnaturally the Isleys were also influenced by Hendrix – especially Ernie, who became one of the first popular guitarists to make intelligent and creative use of the Hendrix legacy. The Isleys became more adventurous, their repertoire expanded in all directions.

In 1973, through a new distribution contract with Columbia, they issued the superb **3 + 3,** which was full of exciting new rhythms, and won honours in all departments. The stand-out tracks, their own **That Lady,** and Seals and Crofts' **Summer Breeze,** both climaxed in soaring guitar solos from Ernie. The album was a major success, and broke the band with a mass audience.

Their albums since – **Live It Up** and **The Heat Is On** – were merely refinements of the themes, but after 20 years the Isleys have finally created something of their own that is exciting, fresh and durable. In 1975 **The Heat Is On** provided them with another No. 1 U.S. album, and the single **Fight The Power,** achieved no less.

Discography lists only recent albums.

Recordings:
This Old Heart Of Mine (Tamla Motown)
Brother Brother Brother (T-Neck/—)
Live (T-Neck/—)
Giving It Back (T-Neck/—)
3 + 3 (T-Neck/Epic)
Live It Up (T-Neck/Epic)
The Heat Is On (T-Neck/Epic)
Harvest To The World (T-Neck/Epic)
Compilation:
Super Hits (—/Tamla Motown)

Isotope

Gary Boyle guitar
Nigel Morris drums
Zoe Kronberger bass
Dan K. Brown keyboards

British jazz-rock outfit founded 1973 by India-born guitarist Boyle, formerly with Julie Driscoll/Brian Auger Trinity. London-born Morris was also original member, along with Jeff Clyne (bs) and Brian Miller (kybds) who left the band in May 1974.

Latter pair were replaced by bass player Hugh Hopper, ex Soft Machine (◆) musician with impressive credentials, and by Laurence Scott on keyboards. The 1974 **Illusion** collection was produced by John "Poli" Palmer, former keyboards player with Family.

Having achieved little in the way of commercial success, Isotope again re-organised for the 1976 album **Deep End,** producing personnel as listed above.

Recordings:
Isotope (—/Gull)
Illusion (Mowest/Gull)
Deep End (Gull)

It's A Beautiful Day

David Laflamme electric violin
Val Fuentes drums
Pattie Santos vocals
Bill Gregory guitar
Tom Fowler bass

It's A Beautiful Day were a San Francisco band, based around the extraordinary violin-playing of Laflamme, formerly a classical musician. The band almost literally exploded on to the scene with their debut album **It's A Beautiful Day** (1969), and especially one stand-out instrumental **White Bird.**

Marrying Maiden.
Courtesy CBS Records.

However, they couldn't sustain this impact. Since it was apparent that the other members were virtually redundant, they were subject to frequent personnel changes; by the time of their second album **Marrying Maiden** (1970), Gregory and Fowler had been replaced by Hal Wagenet and Mitchell Holman respectively, and Fred Webb had been introduced on keyboards; even so, **Marrying Maiden** had its moments – particularly the opening track, **Don And Dewey,** a tribute to the rock duo of the '50s, written by Laflamme. Also of interest was the I Ching hexagram on the cover.

After their electrifying beginning, however, the band just became less and less interesting until they faded away altogether.

Recordings:
It's A Beautiful Day (Columbia/CBS)
Marrying Maiden (Columbia/CBS)
Choice Quality Stuff (Columbia/CBS)
Live At Carnegie Hall (Columbia/CBS)

Jack The Lad
◆ Lindisfarne

Lee Jackson

Born Newcastle Jan 8, 1943 he first came to attention as the dapper bass player and vocalist in The Nice (◆), having worked previously with Keith Emerson in Gary Farr's T-Bones. On demise of The Nice due to the departure of keyboards virtuoso Emerson, the bassist formed his own band Jackson Heights – initially Jackson (bs, vcls), John McBurnie (gtr), Brian Chatton (pno), later augmented by Charlie Harcourt and Tony Connor.

Jackson sank a great deal of his own money into the band which, despite releasing four albums and gigging extensively, never really got off the ground. Then, in 1973, he ran into keyboards player Patrick Moraz and saw in him the person to put some new life into his ailing band.

However, it quickly became obvious that Moraz's particular talents weren't suited to the essentially-acoustic Jackson Heights. Jackson opted to leave his group (they carried on for a time as Heights without him) and instead set about forming a new band to feature Moraz prominently. Former Nice drummer Brian "Blinky" Davison, who'd also been unsuccessfully leading his own band Every Which Way, completed the new trio, Refugee, launched in a burst of publicity in summer 1974.

They cut one moderately successful album, **Refugee** (Charisma 1974), played concerts, and then in summer 1975 Yes (➡) came looking for a keyboards virtuoso to replace Rick Wakeman. Moraz took the job – dumping Jackson and Davison just as Emerson had done some five years earlier. Refugee, consequently, ground to a halt – leaving Jackson and Davison to lick their wounds and ponder the ironies of life.

The Jackson 5

Jackie Jackson lead vocals, guitar
Tito Jackson guitar, vocals
Jermaine Jackson bass, vocals
Marlon Jackson vocals
Michael Jackson lead vocals

The Jackson 5 are the male children of Joe and Kathy Jackson, and were all born in Gary, Indiana: Jackie on May 4, 1951; Tito on Oct 15, 1953; Jermaine, Dec 11, 1954; Marlon, Mar 12, 1957 and Michael, Aug 29, 1958. A sixth son, Randy (b. Oct 29, 1962), who plays bongos and sings, is still too young to join the others permanently. There are also three Jackson daughters.

In early '50s, Joe Jackson was a guitarist with a Chicago group called The Falcons. He fervently encouraged his sons' musical interests, by buying secondhand instruments for them to practise on – he insisted that each should become proficient on at least one.

Tito was determined that there should be a formal group, and they began singing in neighbouring Chicago gig circuit, mainly material borrowed from Temptations or Miracles. They won a talent show at local school, Roosevelt High, and several regional competitions.

The five eldest brothers turned professional in 1967, and after winning a contest in presence of Mayor Richard Hatcher of Gary, they did a campaign benefit for him in 1969, which led directly to their being offered a contract by Tamla Motown boss, Berry Gordy. They were supposedly discovered by Diana Ross (➡), but that is probably just a piece of Motown folklore.

At start of their association with Motown, their affairs were taken out of the hands of their father and they were placed under control of Gordy and "The Corporation", which probably referred to Fonso Mizell, Freddy Perren and Deke Richards, who composed all the J5's early material.

From beginning, the group proved phenomenally successful. All their early singles were million-sellers – **I Want You Back**, **ABC**, **The Love You Save** and **I'll Be There** sold four million. They

quickly established themselves as the bestselling act in Motown's history.

There was nothing fabricated about the Jacksons themselves – they were pure talent, and their stage show (for which they were augmented by two cousins, Ronnie Rancifer on electric piano and Johnny Jackson on drums, making it entirely a family affair) was pure electricity.

Practically everything they did in the early '70s turned gold, at least; and Motown, astutely making hay in the sunshine, supplemented the group's output with solo product from Michael and Jermaine; Michael had a string of hits of his own, with **Ben** (the theme-song of the film) reaching No. 7 in the U.K. and No. 1 in U.S. late 1972.

Get It Together. Courtesy Tamla Motown Records.

Despite all this success, things began to turn sour. There was a suspicion, when The Osmonds (➡) were cleaning-up with the teeny-bopper market, that the J5 were being modelled as the hip alternative. An animated TV series was built around them.

So, notwithstanding another No. 1 U.S. single in 1974, **Dancing Machine,** the feeling persisted that they were unnecessarily restricted at Motown – both in terms of the type of audience they were being aimed at, and also in type of material they were being given to record, which was just mainstream Motown funk. Certainly, they found it hard to re-capture the frenetic intensity of their early songs.

Consequently they made a highly-publicised change of company, moving to Epic Records in 1975. This resulted in a family rift, since Jermaine, who had married Berry Gordy's daughter in 1973, opted to remain at Motown. Because of this, and also because of the contractual arguments surrounding the ownership of the group name, the Jackson 5 became the Jackson Family and young Randy became a more regular member of the team. Solo albums not included in discography. **Anthology** issued 1976 as triple in U.S., double in U.K.

Recordings:
Diana Ross Presents The Jackson 5 (Motown)
ABC (Motown)
Third Album (Motown)
Jackson 5 Christmas Album (Motown)
Maybe Tomorrow (Motown)
Lookin' Through The Windows (Motown)
Skywriter (Motown)
Get It Together (Motown)
Dancing Machine (Motown)
Moving Violation (Motown)

Compilation:
Jackson 5 Greatest Hits (Motown)
Anthology (Motown)

The James Gang

Dale Peters bass, vocals
Jimmy Fox drums, vocals
Bubba Keith guitar, vocals
Richard Shack guitar

Founded Cleveland, Ohio, by Jimmy Fox as hard rock trio featuring Joe Walsh (gtr) plus Tom Kriss (bs). Took name from legendary outlaws, accrued reputation in mid-West 1968–69 before release of debut set **Yer Album** (1969). Kriss replaced by Dale Peters January 1970.

Achieved most of early attention via nascent guitar star Walsh, a former student at Kent State University, Ohio. Walsh's guitar ability was highly lauded by Britain's Pete Townshend, and under Townshend's patronage group toured extensively as support to The Who.

After **Yer Album,** three best-selling U.S. albums were cut with Walsh – the gold status **Rides Again** (1970), **Thirds** (1971) and **Live In Concert** (released 1972) – before he quit November 1971 to form own group and subsequently pursue solo career (➡ Joe Walsh).

Peters and Fox reorganised band, bringing in Canadians Dom (Domenic) Troiano (gtr, vcls) and Roy Kenner (vcls). Thus constituted, group cut two albums, **Straight Shooter** (1972) and **Passin' Thru'** (1973), before departure – August 1973 of Troiano, who later turned up with Guess Who (➡). In his place, James Gang recruited Tommy Bolin, formerly of band Energy, who came to group on recommendation of their former axeman Joe Walsh. This line-up produced two albums, **Bang** (1973) and **Miami** (1974), the latter with producer Tom Dowd at Criteria Studios, both featuring composing contributions by Bolin. However, in late 1974, both Bolin and Kenner quit band and James Gang folded. Bolin then joined Deep Purple. (➡ Tommy Bolin, Deep Purple.)

Peters and Fox re-formed the band January 1975 with Keith and Shack, this line-up cutting **Newborn** for release in June that year. However, group is prime example of deterioration following departure of star member – Joe Walsh – and recent albums have sold in fewer and fewer quantities. Present position of band uncertain at time of writing, though they remain contracted to Atco/Atlantic.

Recordings:
Yer Album (ABC/Probe)
James Gang Rides Again (ABC/Probe)
Thirds (ABC/Probe)
Live In Concert (ABC/Probe)
Straight Shooter (ABC/Probe)
Passin' Thru' (ABC/Probe)
Bang (Atco/Atlantic)
Miami (Atco/Atlantic)
Newborn (Atco/Atlantic)
Compilations:
The Best Of The James Gang (ABC)
16 Greatest Hits (ABC/—)

Jan And Dean

In the early '60s second only to The Beach Boys (➡) as America's prime exponents of "surf music", Jan Berry (b. Los Angeles Apr 3, 1941) and Dean Torrance (b. Los Angeles Mar 10, 1940) first met as members of their high-school football team and, after a first success with **Jennie Lee** (credited to Jan And Arnie) for Arwin Records in 1958, cut a series of hits for the Dove and Challenge labels while still at college.

Linda was another hit for them in 1961 when they switched to Liberty, but their fortunes really went on an upswing with the 1963 **Surf City,** a U.S. No. 1 within two weeks after release. The song had been given to them by Brian Wilson of The Beach Boys and epitomised the surf genre perhaps better than any other of its kind – eulogising, as it did, a 'teen Utopia where perfect waves crashed on sun-soaked beaches and there were "two girls for ev-e-ry boy".

It was the start of a close association between the two acts – they often sang on each other's records, to the chagrin of their respective labels – which resulted in a string of surf and hot rod classics: **Honolulu Lulu, Drag City, Dead Man's Curve** (on which Brian Wilson reputedly sings lead), **Ride The Wild Surf, The Little Old Lady From Pasadena,** etc.

Then in April 1966 Jan Berry – who'd been studying to be a doctor throughout the duo's run of hits – smashed-up his Corvette automobile in Whittier Boulevard, Los Angeles. He was dragged from the wreckage physically and mentally damaged, nearly died, and was totally paralysed for over a year.

Dean Torrance tried to keep going on his own but eventually cut his losses and moved towards a new career as graphic artist with his own sleeve design company, Kittyhawk. Under the duo's early producer Lou Adler, Jan Berry cut a handful of singles as a form of therapy – but his speech and physical co-ordination had been so seriously impaired he found it near-impossible to re-adjust.

The pair attempted one comeback, at a Surfer's Stomp reunion in 1973, but the result was a fiasco. These days Dean Torrance continues to run his graphics firm, never missing the chance, even now, to get down on the beach and catch the perfect wave.

The best of their '60s hits can be heard on the 1975 United Artists collection **Gotta Take That One Last Ride,** which Dean himself supervised.

Bert Jansch

Born Glasgow Nov 3, 1943, Jansch worked in Edinburgh as a nurseryman before moving to London where his innovatory guitar technique quickly helped to establish him as one of the most talented artists on the folk-club scene.

Though originally influenced by bluesmen like Big Bill Broonzy, Jansch, following the lead of Davy Graham, became a leading exponent of folk baroque style, which he applied very successfully to his own songs like **Needle Of Death,** and to Davy Graham's **Anji,** and then to traditional material on **Jack Orion.** Donovan was particularly impressed by Jansch, and dedicated two songs to him.

After **Nicola,** an unsuccessful experiment with an orchestra, he joined Pentangle (♦) 1967.

Since break-up of that band, he has been coaxed back to work by Tony Stratton-Smith, at Charisma Records, for whom Jansch has now made two albums – **L.A. Turnaround,** which was recorded in Sussex and Los Angeles and produced by Mike Nesmith (♦) and **Santa Barbara Honeymoon,** recorded in California. Though the results are generally felt to have been tasteful and to have revitalised Jansch's stylistic individuality, neither album has made much impact; Jansch has now, however, returned to live concerts, and performs occasionally in Britain and America.

Recordings:
Bert Jansch (Vanguard/ Transatlantic)
It Don't Bother Me (—/Transatlantic)
Jack Orion (Vanguard/ Transatlantic)
Nicola (—/Transatlantic)

Birthday Blues (—/Transatlantic)
Rosemary Lane (—/ Transatlantic)
Moonshine (—/Warner Bros)
L.A. Turnaround (—/Charisma)
Santa Barbara Honeymoon (—/Charisma)

Below left: Grace Slick takes off. Below: Marty Balin — a shot from Woodstock. Bottom right: Papa John Creach busts a gut.

Jefferson Airplane (Starship)

Grace Slick vocals
Paul Kantner vocals, guitar
Marty Balin vocals
Jorma Kaukonen guitar
Jack Casady bass
Spencer Dryden drums

Above is best-remembered though not original incarnation of Airplane which evolved into Jefferson Starship in 1974. The Airplane were San Francisco's first and finest, emerging in the mid-'60s initially as a rallying point for the S.F.-Haight Ashbury freak community, subsequently as national standard-bearers of Young America's new-found politico/druggie consciousness.

They were to San Francisco what Beatles had been to Liverpool – though, ironically, none of above personnel, with exception of Kantner (b. Mar 12, 1942) were San Franciscans by birth. In fact, very few of those involved in various Airplane/Starship incarnations were locally born.

Balin was from Cincinnati, Ohio (b. Jan 30, 1943) though he'd grown-up in California; Slick originated from Chicago (b. Oct 30, 1943); Dryden from New York (b. Apr 7, 1943); and Casady (b. Apr 13, 1944) and Kaukonen (b. Dec 23, 1940) were friends from Washington D.C.

The group began in early 1965, formed by Balin and folk guitar/banjoist Kantner, who were joined by singer Signe Anderson (also originally from Washington D.C.) and later Kaukonen. The latter recommended Casady to come West and enlist with new band. Skip Spence was last to join mid-1965. He was the drummer but not particularly at ease in that role, as evidenced by his later decision to quit band and start Moby Grape (♦) as rhythm guitarist.

They were instrumentally shaky at start, but the nascent Bay Area hippie community called for enthusiasm first, finesse later, and the group began to accrue considerable local status. When Bill Graham (♦) – who managed them for short period – opened his legendary Fillmore Auditorium, Airplane were one of first bookings; the first of 'Frisco bands to become a legend, first to secure a major record contract.

Jefferson Airplane Takes Off was released on RCA in August 1966. Though the band was still feeling its way, and this quasi-folk rock debut was only marginally representative of later work, it nevertheless spread the legend nationally and brought them their first gold album. The result was a flood of record company executives pouring into San Francisco, proffering contracts to virtually anything that moved.

Before long, however, Signe Anderson had left to have a baby and Skip Spence had quit to procreate Moby Grape. Former jazzer Dryden took Spence's gig, while Anderson's went to Grace Slick. Slick had been in another early 'Frisco band The Great Society, alongside her husband Jerry and brother-in-law Darby, which was on verge of breaking up when Airplane offer came through (they had recorded two albums for Columbia not released until after Grace's new-found fame). Great Society often supported the Airplane on Bay Area gigs – on the occasions when they didn't, legend has it that Grace's beau-to-be Paul Kantner used to follow them around just to hear her singing.

When she joined the Airplane in late 1966, Slick not only brought with her a voice that was virtually unique in rock but also two killer songs from her old band's repertoire. These were **Somebody To Love** (written by Grace, Jerry and Darby Slick) and **White Rabbit**, a drug-oriented song which developed Lewis Carroll's "Alice Through The Looking Glass" via its acid connotations. Both were considerable American singles hits in 1967, the Airplane's first.

With these two pieces finally in place, producing line-up as above, the band proceeded to record **Surrealistic Pillow** (1967) which, apart from the two aforementioned singles, contained two more killer cuts in **Plastic Fantastic Lover** and the brilliant **Today.** Slick's vocal contribution was immediately felt. With Kantner and Balin the three combined to create strange keening harmonies, while the band provided a backdrop of unpredictable musical interludes and unusual and disturbing guitar lines. It was a quite dazzling pot-pourri of jazz folk and blues idioms, duly laced with drug-oriented textures and lyrics.

By December 1967 and the third album, **After Bathing At Baxters,** the Airplane really were something special. This found them taking chances and developing earlier format into even stranger territories: i.e. the enthusiastically daring if possibly over-rated nine-minute long Kaukonen-Casady-Dryden jam **Spayre Change** and Grace Slick's mammoth **Rejoyce,** an ambitious interpretation of James Joyce's "Ulysses" literary classic.

Yet signs of impending rifts were evident on both these albums. Control of the group was gradually swinging from founder Balin – the first album had been basically his progeny – towards the sexually and musically-allied Slick/Kantner axis. On **Baxters,** Balin managed only one half-credit as songwriter, while Kantner composed three quarters of material. The latter was to explain that he was the only one who could write while on the road, the Airplane touring U.S. extensively at this point.

In 1968 came their magnum opus, **Crown Of Creation.** It contained some really weird band material (i.e. Slick's **Lather**) plus the David Crosby (♦) composition **Triad,** a somewhat risque ménage-a-trois song which had been rejected by The Byrds (♦), then Crosby's band. The Slick-Kantner material here was superior to Balin's, though signs of this teaming's subsequent heavy handedness were hinted at. Yet here, without doubt, was some of the group's most vital material to date, with the title track containing some quite breathtaking ensemble vocalising.

Then came 1969, the year the Haight Ashbury peace-love vibe met its Waterloo. The Chicago riots had gone down the year before, conspiracy trials and drug busts proliferated, hippie panaceas were manifestly redundant.

The Airplane cut a live album **Bless Its Pointed Little Head,** and then went into the studio to record the heavily political **Volunteers.** This contained the battle-cry "Tear down the walls, Motherfuckers!" (ironically, a track on first album had been rejected by RCA because of word "trip"), though its aggressively propagandist tone hasn't worn well. Nevertheless this was one hell of a gutsy album, their most potent pure rock collection to date, containing something of a piece de resistance in **Wooden Ships,** written by Kantner, Crosby and Steve Stills (♦), which also cropped up on **Crosby, Stills And Nash.**

Stills, Crosby were among West Coast heavyweight cohorts who weighed-in with session support, along with Jerry Garcia, Nicky Hopkins, and Joey Covington, the latter subsequently to replace Dryden as Airplane drummer.

Restricted again to half a song credit, this was to be Marty Balin's last album with group he founded.

At this point, after a string of arduous U.S. tours and free festivals – including the horrendous nerve-shattering event at Altamont (♦) where the Airplane played as one of support acts to Stones – other schisms began to appear, precipitated primarily by Grace Slick's pregnancy (bearing Kantner's child).

This precluded further Airplane gigging, and Kaukonen and Casady – for whom performing was still of prime importance – threw themselves (along with Covington) into their own pet project Hot Tuna. This was originally an "offshoot" of the parent band; they used to open for the Airplane proper. Hot Tuna was also notable for introducing veteran fiddle player Papa John Creach (b. May 1917) into Airplane/Starship "family". (♦ Hot Tuna.)

Slick and Kantner, meanwhile, concerned themselves with session work. Utilizing usual West Coast studio gang – Garcia, Crosby, Graham Nash, et al. – in 1970 they produced **Blows Against The Empire.** Credited to Paul Kantner And The Jefferson Starship (the first use of latter name), this was a "space opera" of soap-opera standards, a mish-mash of hippie mysticism and platitudes which, whatever its intentions, represented a retreat from the outfront approach of **Volunteers.**

Apart from a Best Of compilation, perversely entitled **The Worst Of Jefferson Airplane** (1970) and an excellent collection of their finest moments, this was their last album for RCA.

For **Bark,** the next Airplane-proper studio set, they created their own label Grunt. As noted, Balin had gone – but Creach and Covington arrived on scene. **Bark** appeared almost simultaneously with Slick and Kantner's **Sunfighter** album and perhaps all that needs to be said

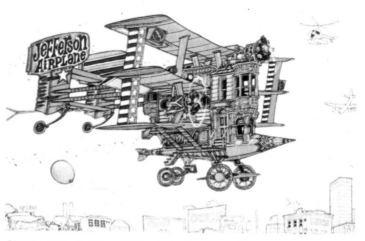

Above: After Bathing At Baxter's. Courtesy RCA Records.

Above: Manhole. Courtesy RCA Records.

regarding the first-named release is that Slick and Kantner gave the appearance of saving their best material for their own collection.

In fact **Sunfighter,** appearing after birth of Slick's daughter China, was an excellent set, able to withstand comparison with any of early seminal Airplane work. Again the usual session heavies strutted their stuff, plus most of Airplane alumni and the Edwin Hawkins Singers.

But from then on deterioration occurred at a rapid pace. The next Airplane album, **Long John Silver** (1972), though better than **Bark,** evinced similar degrees of flaccidity and self-indulgence. Kantner and Slick gave impression they would be happier soloing, while Kaukonen and Casady appeared to have their minds more on Hot Tuna.

At this point band was augmented by former Quicksilver Messenger Service (♦) singer/bassist David Frieberg, who could be regarded as much-belated replacement for missing Balin. Frieberg played on Airplane's second live album, **Thirty Seconds Over Winterland** (1973), comprising material from **Bark** and **Long John Silver,** subsequent to which the Airplane activated self-destruct button they had threatened to push for so long.

Casady, Kaukonen poured energies full-time into Hot Tuna, while Slick, Kantner and Frieberg (the album is credited to all three) worked on studio set **Baron Von Tollbooth And The Chrome Nun** (1973). The Von Tollbooth bit came, reputedly, from Dave Crosby joke about Kantner. It was better than recent Airplane efforts, but largely dispensable, subsequent to which Grace Slick produced her much-maligned **Manhole** solo album.

Fully fragmented by now, it was an ignominious end to band which at peak of creativity had laid down some of the finest rock music of their time.

However, even Slick and Kantner were not totally satisfied with their solo work and in early 1974 decided to tour again – the first time in two years. Kaukonen and Casady were in Europe, unavailable for call-up, so instead they assembled a band out of latter-day Airplane personnel Frieberg, Creach and drummer John Barbata (ex Turtles, CSN&Y back-up band) with addition of newcomers, British bassist Peter Sears and teenage guitarist Craig Chaquico. Both last-named had played on Slick/Kantner solo sessions.

They called the new band Jefferson Starship (though Kantner insisted it bore no relation to **Blows Against The Empire** aggregation) and did a try-out tour using repertoire from early Airplane material and Slick/Kantner solo work. The tour went so well that the Starship booked for another, and went into studio to record **Dragon Fly.** They still couldn't rid themselves of the dumb polemics which marred solo outings, but the album managed to shift some 450,000 copies in U.S., and was notable for fact that it contained one song, **Caroline,** which reunited them with long-estranged Marty Balin. Balin, in fact, wrote lyrics to Kantner's original composition.

By second Starship album, the phenomenally-successful **Red Octopus,** which went to No. 1 in U.S. on more than one occasion through summer 1975, Balin had to all intents and purposes rejoined the Jefferson fold. Albeit somewhat shakily at first, he turned-up on American concerts that year on which the Starship were acclaimed with almost Messianic fervour.

It may not prove to be the Second Coming but there's enough fresh enthusiasm and purpose behind this new incarnation of San Francisco's counter-culture flag-wavers of the late '60s to suggest that an artistic renaissance (as well as commercial one) may be at hand.

Though in the U.K. the Airplane never enjoyed commercial success comparative to that in the U.S., they accrued a smaller but equally devoted following despite minimal appearances (they played first-ever Isle Of Wight Festival, and infamous London Roundhouse gig sharing bill with The Doors).

Album notes: **Early Flight,** released 1974, comprises tracks circa 1966–67 never before released on album; British version of **Surrealistic Pillow** omits **White Rabbit, Plastic Fantastic Lover** and instead includes three cuts from **Jefferson Airplane Takes Off,** that last not being released in U.K. until 1970; Airplane also appear on **Woodstock** album (which includes better than studio version of **Wooden Ships**) and in Maysles Brothers' 1970 "Gimme Shelter" film of Stones at Altamont Festival.

Recordings:
Jefferson Airplane Takes Off (RCA)	**Paul Kantner and Grace Slick: Sunfighter** (Grunt)
Surrealistic Pillow (RCA)	**Baron Von Tollbooth And The Chrome Nun** (with Frieberg) (Grunt)
After Bathing At Baxters (RCA)	
Crown Of Creation (RCA)	**Grace Slick:**
Bless Its Pointed Little Head (RCA)	**Manhole** (Grunt)
Volunteers (RCA)	
Bark (Grunt)	**Jefferson Starship:**
Long John Silver (Grunt)	**Dragon Fly** (Grunt)
Thirty Seconds Over Winterland (Grunt)	**Red Octopus** (Grunt)
Compilations:	**Spitfire** (Grunt)
Early Flight (Grunt/RCA)	**Jorma Kaukonen:**
The Worst Of Jefferson Airplane (RCA)	**Quah!** (Grunt)
Paul Kantner and Jefferson Starship:	**Papa John Creach: Papa John Creach** (Grunt)
Blows Against The Empire (RCA).	**Filthy!** (Grunt)
	Playing My Fiddle For You (Grunt)

Waylon Jennings

Alongside Willie Nelson (➧), Jennings was the prime mover in the "outlaw" country-music movement.

He already had cult status from back in '50s when he was, for a time, one of Buddy Holly's Crickets. From Littlefield, Texas, both he and Holly at one time sang country music on Lubbock radio station. In 1959, when Holly's chartered plane crashed killing the three stars aboard, Waylon had originally been scheduled for the flight, The Big Bopper (J. P. Richardson) asking to take his place at the last moment.

Jennings went back to singing country and wrote several standards, all delivered in his distinctive macho, deep-brown voice. But, finding Nashville's assembly-line producers and businessmen too constricting, he negotiated a new deal which included personal production rights.

In 1972, Jennings' heavier, contemporary country direction became apparent with **Ladies Love Outlaws,** and by the time of **Honky Tonk Heroes** (1973), the mould was firmly set with a collection of lonesome and intensely gritty songs, most of them written by young Nashville songwriter Billy Joe Shaver.

Although Jennings has often pitched his live performances to rock crowds (gigs with the Grateful Dead and others) he insists that he is not part of a "country-rock" movement but simply a country boy who has taken his chosen music in new and adventurous directions.

His music is now an accepted part of Nashville and he scores regularly in country charts; more recently he hit U.S. national charts with a duet with Willie Nelson (the double-sided singles hit **Are You Sure Hank Done It This Way?/Bob Wills Is Still The King**).

In 1976 Jennings was one of the four artists who appeared on the compilation set **The Outlaws,** which became a Top 20 album in the U.S. The other three were Nelson, Tompall Glaser, and Jessi Colter, Jennings' wife.

Discography is selective.

Recordings:
Ladies Love Outlaws (RCA)
Honky Tonk Heroes (RCA)
The Ramblin' Man (RCA)

Jethro Tull

Ian Anderson flute, guitar, vocals
Martin Barre guitar
John Evan keyboards
Barriemore Barlow drums
John Glascock bass

During 1966–67 Ian Anderson, John Evan, Barrie Barlow and former Jethro bassists Glenn Cornick and Jeffrey Hammond-Hammond were all involved at various times with The John Evan Band, a semi-pro outfit operating around their home town of Blackpool in the North of England. At the time seven strong, the band travelled south to London in the winter of 1967 to record and attempt to break London gig circuit.

As it transpired only Anderson (b. Aug 10, 1947), a Scots-born ex art student, and Glenn Cornick stuck it out in the city as the other five gradually drifted back home. The pair met with Mick Abrahams (gtr) and Clive Bunker (drms) from Luton area and conceived Jethro Tull in early 1968 taking their name from an 18th-century English agriculturalist, one of whose books was spotted by Anderson in the home of their manager-to-be Terry Ellis.

Aqualung. Courtesy Jethro Tull.

Their early music was a naive but interesting hybrid of jazz and blues quite unique in rock circles at the time, and the group rapidly accrued a devoted following on the British "progressive" rock circuit alongside such contemporaries as Ten Years After, Fleetwood Mac, Pink Floyd and The Nice. From the start, Ian Anderson cut a startlingly eccentric figure; his rat's-tails hair hanging over an over-sized, dirty overcoat and a pair of moth-eaten bumpers. To cap it all, he evinced a caustic line in wit and again unique – was a frontman who played flute. Not very well at first, mind – he'd only picked it up by listening to a Roland Kirk album – but what he lacked initially in expertise he made up for in infectious enthusiasm.

An unexpected ovation at the 1968 National Jazz And Blues Festival boosted their burgeoning reputation immensely, and when the debut Tull album **This Was** was released later that year it shot almost immediately into the U.K. charts – taking the musical "establishment" completely by surprise.

However, the uneasy alliance between the conflicting musical ideals of Anderson and Abrahams came to a head at the close of 1968, and the guitarist left to form his own band Blodwyn Pig (➧). Tony Iommi, now with Black Sabbath, was recruited for a matter of weeks (he was with band when they guested on the Rolling Stones Rock 'n' Roll Circus TV special) until Martin Barre emerged from auditions as Abrahams' permanent replacement.

Ian Anderson now took over as unchallenged leader of the group – a role he's strengthened over the years to the point where he is

A Passion Play.
Courtesy Chrysalis.

virtually Jethro Tull – and pulled them into one of their most productive phases. In 1969 they produced the U.K. Top 5 single **Living In The Past** and the brilliant **Stand Up** album, which many regard as Tull's classic contribution to rock.

This showed Anderson moving well away from Abrahams' excursions into blues (a popular form of the time); instead producing a series of tight, riffy little songs strong on melody lines and ripe with lyrical wit. The album went to No. 1, staying there for several weeks.

A series of sell-out concerts followed, Anderson extending his early eccentricities into a whole gallery of postures and poses, playing up to his tramp-as-rock-star persona until his cross-legged stance, at the same time blowing flute as ferociously as others played guitar, became as much a trademark for the Tull as was the equipment-smashing of The Who. The "mad dog Fagin", as he was once described, was the antithesis of the later glitter movement in British rock but no less a showman for it.

Meanwhile **Sweet Dream** and **The Witches Promise** kept the Tull in the singles charts, forcing a complacent music industry to sit-up and take note. Indeed, it should be noted that Jethro Tull, along with Fleetwood Mac, played a major part in opening up hitherto blocked avenues in British music for the emergence of a whole wave of what were at

Above: '68 Ian Anderson.

the time dubbed "progressive" bands.

Success in the U.S. was equally instantaneous, with the Tull headlining there virtually from the first of several subsequent visits. **Benefit,** which appeared in 1970, was a massive seller in the States but in the U.K. failed somewhat to equal the success of its predecessor – an early sign that Jethro's increasing concentration on the American market might cost them in terms of home following.

Musically, however, it wasn't far short of **Stand Up,** presenting as it did some of Ian Anderson's finest melodic compositions with augmentation on keyboards by John Evan – he of the previously-mentioned John Evan Band who, on return to Blackpool, had pursued studies to become a pharmacist.

By **Aqualung** (1971) Evan had joined Jethro as a fully-fledged member, and bassist Cornick had left to form own band Wild Turkey (in 1975 he turned-up in new group Paris with ex Fleetwood Mac guitarist Bob Welch). Jeffrey Hammond-Hammond, from the original John Evan Band and Blackpool origins, was brought in as replacement, his name being already familiar to Tull aficionados through Anderson material like **A Song For Jeffrey** (their first single), **Jeffrey Goes To Leicester Square,** etc. Up to joining Tull he had been studying as an artist, and legend has it Anderson had to teach him the rudiments of bass.

Aqualung, with lyrics of the title song by Anderson's wife Jennie (they have since separated), was Jethro Tull's first excursion into concept albums, with one whole side devoted to the group leader's views on organised religion. Through some of the gentler, wittier side of the band remained, this was in large measure bombastic and pretentious. Perhaps in response to the demands of American audiences, the riffs rose at times to the point of overkill, Anderson's stage gestures simultaneously veering to the brink of self-parody. In retrospect it marked a turning-point; an omen of things to come. Nevertheless it met with considerable commercial success on both sides of the Atlantic.

Later that year Clive Bunker also quit the band – leaving Anderson the only surviving founder member. Out went a call to Blackpool and in came another former John Evan Band alumni Barriemore Barlow, whose first studio gig with the Tull was on the **Life Is A**

Long Song British maxi-single.

Through 1971–72, extensive overseas touring (particularly in the U.S.) continued unabated, with Jethro by now learning to live with a barrage of criticism about deserting their U.K. following.

Then came **Thick As A Brick,** the band's first full-blown concept album – one continuous piece of music elaborately constructed and flawlessly played, yet critically received as obscure and lacking in feel. **A Passion Play** (1973) was ditto, only more so, and received a virtually unanimous thumbs-down from the rock press. The 1973 concerts also met a hostile press reaction in the U.K., backed-up with comparatively poor sales for the album (although the American lists still succumbed at will).

A few months later, in August 1973, citing disillusionment over "press abuse" as the major factor, Jethro Tull announced their "retirement" from the concert circuit. It was a fatuous gesture.

What had happened, as Ian Anderson told reporters in 1975 when the group started giving interviews again, was that he had simply grown tired of the constant touring and had other things on his mind, such as a projected movie starring the band. Explaining this to his management, Anderson found himself foolishly going along with the specious "retirement" announcement (though it was true that he hadn't enjoyed the critical brickbats). With hindsight he admitted that their "retirement" was mishandled and a mistake.

Nonetheless, the band took themselves off the road, hired homes in Montreux, Switzerland, and set to work in the studio on the **War Child** album originally conceived as the soundtrack for the (aforementioned) movie of the same name. Over-budgeted, the latter was eventually shelved – though the album appeared in 1974.

A retreat from the concept formula, though Anderson vehemently denied that he had succumbed to critical pressure, this went some way to recapturing the group's early magic. Subsequently the group played sell-out "comeback" tours of the U.S. and U.K. from late 1974 to early 1975, while the **Bungle In The Jungle** track re-established Tull in the American singles lists.

Minstrel In The Gallery (1975) was similarly a "song" collection, moderately well received by the press, but like its predecessor

it sold far better in the States than in the U.K. In December 1975 Hammond-Hammond returned to his art studies and was replaced by John Glascock.

Since **This Was** in 1968 Jethro Tull has, as previously mentioned, been quintessentially Ian Anderson's band – though the contribution of normally astute young manager Terry Ellis (co-founder of Chrysalis Records) has been equally influential. One of rock's more intelligent and articulate recruits, there are those who think Anderson has squandered his talents in wasteful areas – however much eight U.S. gold albums and a horde of fanatical followers might argue to the contrary.

Of the two compilation albums listed below, the double-set **Living In The Past** is by far superior to the 1976-released **M.U.** compilation. Among his outside activities, Ian Anderson produced the 1974 **Now We Are Six** album for Steeleye Span (➧).

Recordings:
This Was (Reprise/Island)
Stand Up (Reprise/Island)
Benefit (Reprise/Chrysalis)
Aqualung (Reprise/Chrysalis)
Thick As A Brick (Reprise/Chrysalis)
A Passion Play (Chrysalis)
War Child (Chrysalis)
Minstrel In The Gallery (Chrysalis)
Too Old To Rock 'n' Roll: Too Young To Die (Chrysalis)
Compilations:
Living In The Past (Reprise/Chrysalis)
M.U. – The Best Of Jethro Tull (Chrysalis)

J. Geils Band

J. Geils guitar
Peter Wolf vocals
Magic Dick mouth harp
Seth Justman keyboards
Stephen Bladd drums
Danny Klein bass

Formed Boston, Massachusetts, area in 1969 as J. Geils Blues Band (Wolf and Bladd formerly in The Hallucinations). First accrued devoted local following – discovered by Atlantic Records on bill with Dr John – from which point they developed into one of America's premier live acts with high energy fusion of rock 'n' roll, blues, and R&B. Band contains two excellent musicians in Magic Dick and J. Geils himself who, despite band's name, adopts a comparatively low profile on stage.

Frontman proper is vocalist Peter Wolf, whose much-publicised long-running courtship of movie actress Faye Dunaway resulted in their marriage in 1974.

Despite consistent U.S. chart placings, albums have not always been their forte. **J. Geils Band** (1971) and **The Morning After** (1972), although good debut sets, hinted at more than they actually delivered, and it wasn't until **Bloodshot** (1973), which went gold in the U.S., that the band turned in a really convincing studio album. Its successor, however, **Ladies Invited** (1974), lost them a certain amount of critical support retrieved by the same year's **Nightmares And Other Takes From The Vinyl Jungle.** As a studio outfit, they're that kind of

Live Full House.
Courtesy Atlantic Records.

band.

The live third album (1972), however, illustrates J. Geils at their best – in front of an audience.

Recordings:
J. Geils Band (Atlantic)
The Morning After (Atlantic)
Full House (Atlantic)
Bloodshot (Atlantic)
Ladies Invited (Atlantic)
Nightmares And Other Takes From The Vinyl Jungle (Atlantic)
Hotline (Atlantic)
Blow Your Face Out (Atlantic)

Jo Jo Gunne

Jay Ferguson vocals, keyboards
Matthew Andes vocals, guitar
Mark Andes bass, vocals
Curly Smith drums, vocals

Los Angeles band, formed 1971 by Ferguson and Mark Andes, both of whom had just left Spirit (➧). They were instantly recognisable by their highly photogenic appearance, the epitome of a young Californian group, which was enhanced by the fact that they were among the earliest signings to Asylum label.

Jo Jo Gunne, released 1972, is generally reckoned to be peak of group's achievement, as it contains the excellent **Run, Run, Run,** which reached No. 6 in U.K. and No. 27 in U.S. After this, Mark Andes was replaced by Jimmie Randell, for the next two albums, **Bite Down Hard** (1972) and **Jumpin' The Gunne** (1973), the latter of which has a quite unnecessarily tasteless sleeve.

So . . . Where's The Show? (1974) is apparently the group's final epitaph, on which Texan John Staehely (coincidentally also a member of Spirit after Ferguson and Andes had left) substituted for Matthew Andes. Both Andes brothers joined re-formed Spirit 1976 while Ferguson released solo album **All Alone In The End Zone** (Asylum).

Recordings:
Jo Jo Gunne (Asylum)
Bite Down Hard (Asylum)
Jumpin' The Gunne (Asylum)
So . . . Where's The Show? (Asylum)

Jo Mama
➧ Carole King

Elton John

On Mar 7, 1976, after countless gold records, pairs of spectacles, sell-out tours, costume changes, hairs lost, and total disc sales in the region of 80 million worldwide, Elton Hercules John added a further honour to his celebrated career – on that date the singer/composer/tennis player/soccer director's effigy joined the monarchs and other historical giants on display at London's famous Madame Tussaud's waxworks museum; the first celebrity from the "world of popular music" to pass the rigorous Tussaud's selection procedure since The Beatles in 1964.

A mighty long way to rock 'n' roll for the boy born Reginald Kenneth Dwight in the anonymous town of Pinner, Middlesex, England on Mar 25, 1947.

The schoolboy Dwight was a chubby, ungainly figure even then, but his mother and stepfather (his parents had separated when Reg was 14) encouraged his yearnings for show business as a youth. At 16, having left school, he was at times simultaneously pursuing three jobs: by day working as a messenger/tea-boy for a music publishing company, at nights playing alternatively with the group Bluesology and thumping-out public bar piano at the Northwood Hills Hotel.

This last, for which he earned £1 a night (boosted by whatever collected in the hat he passed round), involved entertaining the drinkers with such standard British public house fare as **Roll Out The Barrel** and **When Irish Eyes Are Smiling.**

Meanwhile, the band Bluesology used to rehearse at the Northwood Hills, and once Dwight had saved enough bread to equip himself with a Hohner electric piano and an amp he quit the public bar to devote his evenings full-time to the group.

Essentially, though their ambitions lay in other directions, Bluesology was a semi-pro backing act for visiting soul musicians. Most of their engagements came through impresario Roy Tempest, whose agency was notorious for (among other things) squeezing maximum mileage out of the acts they handled: Elton remembers, for instance, an occasion when Tempest booked soul singer Billy Stewart and Bluesology into four different clubs through the course of one solitary evening!

Patti Labelle and the Bluebelles (aka Labelle) and Major Lance were among other U.S. stars they supported (Tempest once offered them to Wilson Pickett who rejected them out of hand) – though it was the aforementioned Stewart, whom they backed extensively, who gave Bluesology most in the way of musical guidance and support.

Times were hard, though. Bluesology earned approximately £15 a week each, out of which they had to pay all their own expenses, hotel bills, petrol, hire purchase instalments, repairs. Roadies were out of the question – John's calling for keyboards making his chores the most onerous of them all. However, when near London, he still lived at home, so his £15 went somewhat further than most, and his memories of the period are only fond ones.

One of the clubs where they frequently appeared was The Cromwellian, London's premier pop star hang-out of its day. When he wasn't playing, John used to go there often – simply as a fan. An early hero, Stevie Wonder, put in an appearance there once, the future Elton John watching in a wash of reflected glory as Wonder channelled his genius through Reginald Dwight's humble Vox Continental amp. Mike Bloomfield was another who borrowed Bluesology's equipment for a Cromwellian gig.

It was at that self-same club that R&B singer Long John Baldry (♦) first saw Bluesology perform, subsequently reorganising them as his regular backing group.

(Elton John was strictly a keyboards player at this time. Before Baldry, Stuart A. Brown had been Bluesology vocalist. After all, the dumpy bespectacled Dwight was hardly anybody's idea of a charismatic front-man, though he did get to sing on one Bluesology single – cut in three hours – because the song was out of Brown's range.)

Elton stayed with Bluesology and Baldry, who remains one of his closest friends, right up to the period when the latter mistakenly chose to forsake his R&B roots in a "last ditch" stab for pop stardom. As Baldry's drek-laden **Let The Heartaches Begin** single soared to No. 1 in the U.K., October 1967, the Bluesology line-up, the last, then comprised Reg Dwight (kybds), Neil Hubbard (gtr), Pete Gavin (drms), Marc Charig (tpt), Freddy Gand (bs) and a saxophonist called Elton Dean.

Later, when looking for a new name to replace the uncharismatic Reginald Dwight for his own stab for stardom, he found it by uniting the first names of Dean and Baldry. Elton Hercules John, the middle part an early nickname, would some years on become his name in law via a deed poll change.

By now, with Baldry fully committed to the cabaret circuit, Bluesology had disbanded. Desperate for work, Elton applied for a job as a record plugger with Philips and was waiting on the outcome when he saw an ad in "New Musical Express", placed by a subsidiary of Liberty Records looking for "new talent".

The audition took place in a studio. Unfortunately, Elton hadn't as previously mentioned sang in Bluesology, and was forced to draw his repertoire from his days back at the Northwood Hills. Jim Reeves' **I Love You Because** was one of the five songs he performed, to the horror of watching executives. However, someone present remembered the name of Bernie Taupin, similarly unknown, a lyricist from the wilds of Lincolnshire who had also answered the "NME" ad.

Elton went away with a pile of Taupin's lyrics, around which he attempted to compose. He and Taupin didn't actually meet until some six months later, by which time Elton had prepared 20 songs.

Liberty's interest had waned, however, and the pair drifted into the publishing house of Dick James, one of the old breed of cigar-puffing

Tin Pan Alley moguls. James offered John and Taupin a three-year songwriting contract at £10 a week, at which point they figured they had finally arrived.

However, Dick James had a conflicting view of which direction their writing should take, insisting that they write Top 40 material which he could sell to the easy listening topsellers of the day, artists like Cilla Black and Engelbert Humperdinck.

Around this time, John worked to supplement his income with one of the many peripheral British record companies which specialise in budget-priced collections of contemporary hits performed by unknown (and uncredited) artists. John appeared anonymously on a number of these collections, sometimes alongside Dana Gillespie (♦) and David Byron, later of Uriah Heep. He also did occasional session work proper (e.g. piano on Hollies **He Ain't Heavy, He's My Brother**).

Meanwhile, he and Taupin wasted away in Dick James' Denmark Street offices for some two years before the arrival there as a song plugger of one Steve Brown. It was Brown who advised them in no uncertain terms – "Fuck Dick!" was the exact phrase – to disregard James and follow their own course.

Determined to do just that, John and Taupin set to work on a whole new batch of material, the first of which was **Skyline Pigeon.** Another was **Lady Samantha**, which was issued as Elton John's first single in 1969.

It failed to chart but did draw considerable air-play to assist promotion of the first album **Empty Sky** (June 1969), produced on a four-track machine by Steve Brown. It was a promising but ineffectual debut, following which Steve Brown bowed gracefully out of the picture, John and Taupin instead recruiting the talents of producer Gus Dudgeon and arranger Paul Buckmaster.

By this time, the writers had enough material stockpiled for three albums. Some were selected for **Elton John** (April 1970), his second album, the rest put aside for **Tumbleweed Connection.**

On **Elton John,** all the early faults were rectified. Dudgeon and Buckmaster had served him well, as they have ever since. **Border Song** was released as a single, causing much interest but flopping nonetheless. The song has since been widely covered – and Elton John names Aretha Franklin's version as one of his favourite "covers" of his compositions.

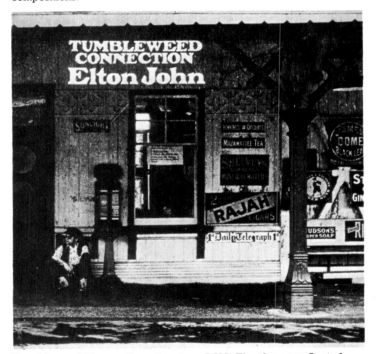

Tumbleweed Connection. Courtesy DJM. The theme reflected Taupin's preoccupation with the mythology of the Old West.

Tumbleweed Connection (October 1970) followed within a few months of **Elton John**. A less ornate, more energetic album displaying Taupin's affection for the American Old West mythology and Elton John's increasingly personalised vocal style, it found critical and public favour and marked his debut in the U.K. albums Top 20. Similarly, **Your Song** became his first major success in the singles chart, and, on the strength of both, the earlier **Elton John** album joined **Tumbleweed** in the U.K. bestseller lists.

Meanwhile, the pace had been even hotter in America. MCA Records having secured distribution rights in the U.S., the publicity machine was put into top gear for Elton John's August 1970 appearances at the Troubadour Club in Los Angeles. The house-full signs went up, crowds clamoured around the block, and the reviews were almost universally ecstatic. From there, **Your Song** hit charts and became one of the biggest U.S. sellers of its year. **Elton John** similarly charted (**Empty Sky** wasn't released in America until 1975) as did **Tumbleweed Connection.**

Although at this time using regular accompanists in Dee Murray (bs) and Nigel Olsson (drms), both former members of Spencer Davis Group (♦), there was little evidence of them on record until the **17-11-70** collection, a recording of a live radio broadcast spotlighting John's

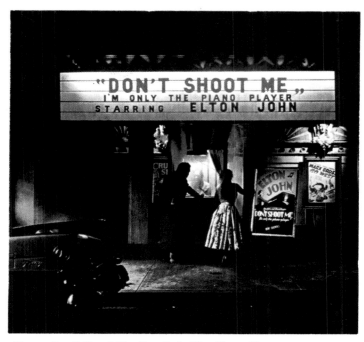

Above: Don't Shoot Me, I'm Only The Piano Player.
Courtesy DJM Records. Released January 1973.

growing dexterity but also a certain self-indulgence.

Unfortunately its release, in mid-1971, coincided with **Friends,** a soundtrack album written by John/Taupin some time before their climb to fame. (Ironically, despite Elton's and reviewers' low opinion of it, that set earned him his first U.S. gold record). However, his next "official" release, **Madman Across The Water,** appeared on the market only a few months later in October 1971, leaving the artists in serious danger of over-exposure. Not surprisingly he was widely criticised for spreading his talents too thinly.

Ex Magna Carta guitarist Davey Johnstone (gtr), who had contributed to **Madman,** was recruited full-time in the line-up in February 1972 and **Honky Chateau** (May 1972), the first studio album as The Elton John Group, indicated a return to form and even wider popularity consolidated by the enormous sales of **Don't Shoot Me, I'm Only The Piano Player** (January 1973) and the double-set **Goodbye Yellow Brick Road** (October 1973).

A full list of every Elton John hit single around the world would probably fill a page, but since **Your Song** smashed into the U.S. and U.K. charts, **Rocket Man, Honky Cat, Crocodile Rock, Daniel, Saturday Night's Alright For Fighting, Goodbye Yellow Brick Road, Candle In The Wind** and **Bennie And The Jets** (to name but a few) have all followed suit.

However, the pace was by now beginning to tell. The **Yellow Brick Road** album had been widely acclaimed as Elton John's finest hour, but with a contract that stipulated two albums a year there had to be

doubts about whether he could maintain quality. On **Caribou** (June 1974) he certainly didn't.

Although all his albums had been recorded in a comparatively short space of time (up to **Captain Fantastic** the record stood at 15 days – for **Yellow Brick Road**), **Caribou** was recorded in America in a matter of only three/four days between arduous international touring commitments. Elton himself has since expressed his own dissatisfaction with the album, particularly with his vocals. Ironically, one of the tracks he at one time desperately wanted to withdraw because of the weak vocal, **Don't Let The Sun Go Down On Me,** was nominated for a Grammy Award as best vocal performance of its year!

Elton promised better on his next release, the epic-like double set **Captain Fantastic And The Brown Dirt Cowboy** (June 1975), an autobiographical account-in-song of his and Bernie Taupin's early hardships, which some critics felt indicated an inflated sense of the duo's own importance. Expensively packaged, with sleeve artwork by artist Alan Aldridge, it nevertheless took the artist's sales potential to a new peak – going to No. 1 in the U.S. albums chart in the first week of its release (and staying there right through the summer).

Shortly after, and just before his massive June 1975 gig at London's Wembley Stadium, Elton terminated his long association with Nigel Olsson and Dee Murray. He currently works with a bigger, more flexible unit (which at Wembley included Caleb Quaye, Kenny Passarelli and Doobies' Jeff Baxter).

A track off the album, **Someone Saved My Life Tonight,** which purported to tell of a suicide bid the singer had made during his days living in an Islington, London, apartment with a girlfriend who detested his music, went to No. 1 in the U.S. singles charts later in the year – while **Captain Fantastic** was still holding down the top albums slot.

Since then, although **Rock Of The Westies** (October 1975) and the live **Here And There** (April 1976), were guaranteed goldsellers even before release, Elton John's record output has been the subject of mixed reviews. Some critics suggested that the artist was only "marking time" until expiry of his contract with Dick James' DJM – although Elton John has refuted this emphatically.

Nevertheless, he remains one of the world's most celebrated and highest-paid rock performers – MCA Records (his U.S. label) are said to have taken out a 25 million dollar insurance policy on his life after signing him to one of the most lucrative record deals ever.

Aside of his recordings, Elton John has numerous other interests. He launched his own Rocket Records with youthful manager John Reid in 1973 which, after an indifferent start – they pruned acts and staff extensively in 1974 – has enjoyed considerable success with main signings Kiki Dee (♦) and Neil Sedaka (♦). In 1975 he appeared as the Pinball Wizard in Ken Russell's "Tommy" (♦) movie. An avid sports fan, John is a director of Los Angeles Aztecs and chairman of English soccer club Watford F.C., whom he has supported since his youth (his cousin, Roy Dwight, was a professional soccer player with Nottingham Forest F.C.).

Indeed, Elton John's disposition to be unashamed of his wealth (in marked contrast to some of his contemporaries), and to enjoy to the hilt the opportunities that fame has brought him, is arguably one of his endearing qualities. Essentially he is still as much a fan as he was in the days of The Cromwellian – constantly appearing on stage with other acts (Faces, Doobie Bros, John Lennon, etc.), playing tennis with Billie Jean King, acting as host to Hollywood idols like Groucho Marx and Mae West, whom he idolised as a kid.

He maintains three wildly expensive homes, in England, America and France, all furnished in unbelievable comfort, but has resisted the temptation to join other British rock stars who have fled the U.K. to escape punitive tax laws. His generosity is legend; he gives Rembrandts and Rolls Royces to his friends as birthday presents, and in 1975, in his most magnanimous gesture yet, he flew his family, friends, fellow directors and fans of Watford F.C., and the entire London staff of Rocket Records to America, putting them up at his expense for a week in which he performed two sell-out concerts at the massive Hollywood Bowl. The trip was chronicled in a subsequent British TV documentary.

Ostensibly, only the worry of his ever-thinning pate remains to disturb an existence in which he can (and does) indulge his every whim and fancy. The Liberace of the '70s looks like being around for a considerable time to come, making the Madame Tussaud's pronouncement that they select only those celebrities who are "likely to have an exhibition life of at least three years" seem somewhat on the conservative side!

Bernie Taupin – The Brown Dirt Cowboy of the album title – has collaborated an all Elton John albums. His solo album was released 1971. In 1976 he published "The One Who Writes The Words For Elton John".

Recordings:

Empty Sky (MCA/DJM)	**Caribou** (MCA/DJM)
Elton John (MCA/DJM)	**Captain Fantastic And The**
Tumbleweed Connection	**Brown Dirt Cowboy** (MCA/
(MCA/DJM)	DJM)
17-11-70 (MCA/DJM)	**Rock Of The Westies** (MCA/
Friends (Paramount)	DJM)
Madman Across The Water	**Here And There** (MCA/DJM)
(MCA/DJM)	**Bernie Taupin:**
Honky Chateau (MCA/DJM)	**Bernie Taupin** (MCA/DJM)
Don't Shoot Me, I'm Only The	
Piano Player (MCA/DJM)	**Compilation:**
Goodbye Yellow Brick Road	**Elton John's Greatest Hits**
(MCA/DJM)	(MCA/DJM)

Left: Captain Fantastic And The Brown Dirt Cowbody.
Courtesy DJM Records. Sleeve designed by Alan Aldridge.

Robert Johnson
➡ Blues – American

Bob Johnston

Regarded as the first of the super-producers, initially through his work as a Columbia/CBS staff producer with Bob Dylan, Simon & Garfunkel and Leonard Cohen. He produced every Bob Dylan album from **Highway 61 Revisited** to **New Morning**, as well as the tracks that ultimately surfaced as **Dylan**. He is also a close personal friend of Cohen's, and was a member of his touring backing band, The Army; he played guitar and keyboards.

He specialises in fussy, low-key productions, which is quite the reverse of his work in the '50s when he concentrated on straight chart-oriented material like Patti Page's **How Much Is That Doggie In The Window?**

In recent years, he has worked as an independent producer, and has fallen from the public eye, though he did work in the U.K. for a time, and produced two albums for Lindisfarne (➡), **Fog On The Tyne** and **Dingley Dell**, though the group themselves were dissatisfied with latter.

Janis Joplin

Born Jan 19, 1943, Port Arthur, Texas, where she grew up in passable comfort and developed into something of a loner, Janis said in later life: "Texas is O.K. if you want to settle down, but it's not for outrageous people, and I was always outrageous."

She acquired an ear for Bessie Smith and Leadbelly records, and in early '60s began singing country and blues music with a bluegrass band. In 1961 she worked in Austin, Texas, and in 1962 in San Francisco; she was briefly enrolled at University of Texas.

In 1966 she returned to San Francisco to become lead vocalist of a local band with a growing reputation, Big Brother And The Holding Company. The line-up was: Sam Andrew (gtr), James Gurley (gtr), Pete Albin (bs), David Getz (drms). The band were good, and with Joplin as vocalist they were something special; their rising stock was further swelled by an early album on Mainstream Records, **Big Brother And The Holding Company** (which was re-issued by Columbia in 1971). But the moment when Janis Joplin Superstar was born can probably be dated from the band's appearance at Monterey Festival August 1967, where Janis drew ecstatic audience reaction and rave reviews.

Her voice was big and rough as a steam engine; she was hoarse, insistent and hortatory, idolized Otis Redding (she shared the Monterey limelight with him and Jimi Hendrix; coincidentally, all three were dead within three years) and could sing the blues like few other white singers. On stage she was particularly powerful, giving a frantic, passionately sexual performance.

After this her standing increased rapidly, and in January 1968 she signed a managerial contract with Albert Grossman (➡). Big Brother recorded **Cheap Thrills** in New York, and it sold a million on release in September 1968 (though the response was lukewarm in Britain, where she never enjoyed commercial success).

By the end of the year, her star status far outweighed that of the rest of the band and she inevitably went solo (though the split was not without some bitterness). She performed with irregular back-up groups, and **I Got Dem Ol' Kozmic Blues Again Mama!** was released in 1969 to favourable reviews.

Ever outrageous, she was perhaps elevated to star status too quickly – after all her recorded output had been small - and she seemed to overdo everything trying to live up to her reputation. She drank heavily and was a mercurial performer; one minute she could look old and used, the next young and vulnerable. In March 1970 she was fined for using profane language at a concert.

She put together a new backing group, The Full Tilt Boogie Band, with a line-up of John Till (gtr), Ken Pearson (org), Richard Bell (pno), Brad Campbell (bs), Clark Pierson (drms). She had finished recording 11 songs with them for **Pearl** when she was found dead in her Hollywood hotel room on Oct 4, 1970. A rock 'n' roll victim, she died of a heroin overdose; most of her short, comet-like career had been marred by overdoses of some sort.

Cheap Thrills.
Courtesy CBS Records.

Pearl (which was the appellation by which her friends knew her) was issued posthumously, was obviously unfinished, with two backing tracks. (Nick Gravenites had been asked if he wanted to put on vocals as a tribute, but he declined.) It nevertheless included some of her finest singing, and **Me And Bobby McGee** (the Kris Kristofferson song) became a U.S. No. 1 single.

A double live set was issued 1972, and **Greatest Hits** in 1973. A movie documentary, "Janis", was completed towards the end of 1974, and inevitably that too had its double-album soundtrack. Already there had been more Joplin product released after her death than before it. There are also two biographies – "Buried Alive" by Myra Friedman, her friend and associate who had worked in Grossman's New York office; and "Going Down With Janis", by Peggy Caserta, an altogether more sordid account of her life and death.

Big Brother And The Holding Company, meanwhile, hadn't ceased operations, and after acquiring the services of Gravenites as lead vocalist issued **Be A Brother** in 1972.

Recordings:
Big Brother And The Holding Company (Mainstream/—)
Cheap Thrills (Columbia/CBS)
I Got Dem Ol' Kozmic Blues Again Mama! (Columbia/CBS)
Pearl (Columbia/CBS)
In Concert (Columbia/CBS)
Greatest Hits (Columbia/CBS)
Janis (Soundtrack) (Columbia/CBS)

Pearl. Courtesy CBS Records.

Journey

Gregg Rolie vocals, keyboards, guitar
Neal Schon guitar
George Tickner rhythm guitar
Aynsley Dunbar drums

Formed in late 1973, Journey made their debut at San Francisco Winterland on New Year's Eve that year, followed by New Year's Day second gig before 100,000 audience at annual Sunshine Festival at Diamond Head Crater, Hawaii. Not that such sizeable gatherings were strange territory to at least three members of this minor-supergroup.

Rolie and Schon were both members of San Francisco's massively successful Santana (➡); indeed Rolie was co-founder of that group with guitarist Carlos Santana in 1967. He played on four platinum-selling albums and was primarily responsible for band arrangements and vocals before Carlos' moves towards jazz caused conflict of opinions.

Schon was something of teenage guitar protégé, encouraged by Carlos Santana after declining Eric Clapton's offer of gig in his Derek and Dominos group at age 16. He cut two albums with Santana band, as well as appearing on **Carlos Santana And Buddy Miles** live album. Before Journey, played briefly, with Graham Central Station (➡).

Drummer Aynsley Dunbar, born in Liverpool, England, has similarly illustrious credits. He first came to attention as highly accomplished drummer with John Mayall's Bluesbreakers, subsequently forming own band Retaliation and later the ambitious Blue Whale, using large brass section. Arrived in America to join Mothers Of Invention (➡), cutting four albums and touring extensively with same. When Flo & Eddie (➡) left Mothers to gig on own, Dunbar accompanied them. Numerous session credits include work for Jeff Beck, Bonzo Dog Doo Dah Band, Lou Reed, David Bowie.

Fourth member Tickner was session-man of four years experience, having previously played in Fruminous Bandersnatch outfit with original Journey bassist Ross Valory who left band after first album.

Journey released 1975; second set in 1976.

Recordings:
Journey (Columbia/CBS)
Looking Into The Future (Columbia/CBS)

Joy Of Cooking

Toni Brown vocals, keyboards
Terry Garthwaite vocals, guitar
Ron Wilson congas, harmonica
Fritz Kasten drums
David Garthwaite bass

Founded 1967 in California, with above line-up, which was unusual in that it included two girl lead vocalists – whether this aspect was an advantage or a disadvantage was a matter of some press speculation.

Musically, the band were rock-oriented, with strong jazz and country overtones. The character of the band was projected on their 1970 debut album, **Joy Of Cooking,** which attracted rave reviews and critical acclaim from Womens Lib-oriented critics. However, this did not seem to be enough to win them mass acclaim, and their next albums **Closer To The Ground** and **Castles** retained a cult status.

In 1971 Jeff Neighbor replaced David Garthwaite (Terry's brother) on bass, but the band split up altogether in 1973 when Toni and Terry opted to go their own way, making **Cross Country** together in 1973. Again, the album attracted good notices, but little in the way of positive sales, a fate that was to overtake Toni Brown's own solo album, **Good For You Too**, in 1974. In 1976 both girls working clubs in North California (separately).

Recordings:
Joy Of Cooking (Capitol)
Closer To The Ground (Capitol)
Castles (Capitol)
Toni Brown & Terry Garthwaite:
Cross Country (Capitol)
Toni Brown:
Good For You Too (Capitol)
Terry Garthwaite:
Terry (Arista)

KGB

Ray Kennedy vocals
Mike Bloomfield guitar
Barry Goldberg keyboards
Carmine Appice drums
Rick Grech bass

KGB, formed in 1975, are probably the world's most recent supergroup, certainly the world's most redundant one. Brought together by the bottomless coffers of MCA, they cut one remarkably uninteresting debut album, after which Rick Grech (➡) and Mike Bloomfield (➡) both immediately left, publicly claiming they never had any faith in the band anyway. For the record, they were replaced by Greg Sutton and Ben Schultz respectively.

Recording:
KGB (MCA)

Doug Kershaw

Born Tiel Ridge in a French-speaking area of Louisiana, Doug Kershaw was weaned on the local folk music – cajun music; by the age of eight, he was playing fiddle professionally, and in the '50s he teamed-up in a duo with his brother Rusty. By 1957 he was regular on the Grand Ole Opry, and in 1961 his song **Louisiana Man** became a huge success; it has since become a quasi-anthem for him.

However, he spent most of the '60s in the shadows, and it wasn't until he met his producer Buddy Killen and moved to Warner Bros that he began to acquire a viable national reputation; he was also assisted by an appearance on the Johnny Cash TV show, since a fellow guest was Bob Dylan.

Though he has enjoyed no tangible success in chart terms, his career has revived in the last five years, through his effervescent fiddling at gigs across the States. He has some film experience; he had an impressive cameo role in "Zachariah", and appeared in "Medicine Ball Caravan", and also had the misfortune to be involved with an appalling rock movie called "We Have Come For Your Daughters".

Nevertheless, he remains the one cajun musician who has broken through – in reputation if nothing else – to a mass rock audience. In 1975 he paid a brief visit to Britain, and played a solitary gig at Dingwall's in North London.

Recordings:
The Cajun Way (Warner Bros/—)
Spanish Moss (Warner Bros)
Doug Kershaw (Warner Bros)
Swamp Grass (Warner Bros)
Devil's Elbow (Warner Bros)
Douglas James Kershaw (Warner Bros)
Mama Kershaw's Boy (Warner Bros)

Johnny Kidd

Born Frederick Heath, Willesden, London, Dec 23, 1939. Kidd and his group, the Pirates, came to attention in U.K. June 1959 with self-penned **Please Don't Touch.** Adopting swashbuckling leather gear and black patch over left eye, Kidd consolidated his position with co-written **Shakin' All Over.**

With Pirates – the semi-legendary Mick Green on guitar, Johnny Spencer (bs), Frank Farley (drms) – Kidd's claim to posthumous fame is that he originated prototype for heavy-metal guitar-dominated trios, pre-dating same by several years. Wilko Johnson of Dr Feelgood (➧) is probably the most ardent extant admirer of Mick Green's axe playing, though several other present-day guitar greats have acknowledged his influence.

A prolific recording artist, Kidd never really enjoyed the sustained success he deserved. Overshadowed by the Merseybeat explosion, he gained not even a slender foothold on the American rock consciousness. However, Johnny Kidd And The Pirates had the distinction of being the only authentic rock act Britain produced prior to 1962. **Shakin' All Over** has since become a rock 'n' roll classic.

Kidd was killed in an auto smash Oct 7, 1966, while struggling for another much-needed hit. Primarily a singles and live act, his albums are long-since deleted, and unfortunately there has been no attempt by his British record company to issue a definitive compilation of his work. Recommended listening but difficult to obtain: **Johnny Kidd Memorial Album** and **Your Cheating Heart**, both on French Odeon/Columbia. There is however a budget-priced album available in Britain on EMI Starline, **Shakin' All Over.**

After lengthy period of anonymity as session-man, Mick Green emerged with new band Shanghai (signed to Warner Bros U.K.) in 1975.

Kilburn And The High Roads

Ian Dury vocals
Ted Speight guitar
George Dynysiuk bass
Malcolm Mortimore Mortgage drums
John Earle horns

Formed 1973 in Canterbury, England, by former East London art student, painter and illustrator Dury, who was working at time as art lecturer. Original guitarist Keith Lucas was one of his students. Rest of early line-up comprised Russel Hardy (pno), Davey Payne (sx), Charlie Sinclaire (bs) and Tony Richards (drms).

One of the first of the London pub-rock circuit groups to achieve wider attention, the original (brilliantly-named) Kilburns featured quite the most motley assembly of characters rock is ever likely to produce. Leaving aside the crippled drummer, who had to be lowered on to his drum stool, and the seven-foot tall bass player called Humphrey Ocean, focal point was vocalist and songwriter Dury. With a withered hand encased in a black leather glove Dury was a squat, crop-haired Runyonesque figure of menace and unsurpassed ugliness who spat rather than sang inspired lyrics which drew heavily on what was, for once, a genuinely working-class (Cockney) background.

They began to develop a devoted cult following, were signed to management by noted rock writer Charlie Gillett (➧), and were widely-acclaimed in the rock press as the most amazing unknown act then treading British rock boards. Comparisons were made to early Stones and Who, both in terms of imagery and aggression.

All the signs pointed to imminent stardom, but just as suddenly it all fell to pieces. Quite why is something of an enigma. Perhaps the early acclaim was premature. What happened was that Dr Feelgood (➧) came along and captured a great deal of the Kilburns' critical and public support, traumatic personnel changes occurred in the band, Gillett bowed gracefully out of the picture, and then the straw that broke the camel's back: after much in the way of offers, the band had finally got a deal with Raft, a newly-formed offshoot of Warner Bros; they had got as far as recording an album with producer Tony Ashton when Raft was axed just as speedily as it had been inaugurated. The album, reportedly unsatisfactory, was never released.

Somewhat disenchanted, the Kilburns continued to play the pubs and clubs and in 1975, after six months of hawking their tapes around town, they finally got a new record contract with Dawn, resulting in the poorly-produced and disappointing **Handsome.**

Since then the Kilburns have re-organised again – line-up in 1976 as above, leaving Dury the only surviving member – and have introduced neo-jazz undertones into what is, on its night, still one of the best acts currently on show. The shame is that it is such a limited showing. Now signed to Blackhill Enterprises and gigging under billing "Ian Dury And The Kilburns", their time may yet come.

One point of interest is that Humphrey Ocean was employed as a cartoonist by Paul McCartney on the Wings 1976 American tour.

Recordings:
Handsome (—/Dawn)

Albert King

Born Apr 25, 1923, King was inspired by T-Bone Walker, and moved to Chicago where he made his first recordings in the early '50s, though he was then inactive until signed by the St Louis-based Bobbin Records in 1959. Subsequently King again slipped into obscurity, until after a few singles for the small Count-Tree label in Tennessee, he signed to Stax Records in Memphis, in a move that proved to be the turning-point of his career.

On those recordings, he was backed by resident musicians, Booker T & The MGs. Though he retained his own pure, earthy blues sound, he hit both the pop and R&B charts with **Crosscut Saw** and also recorded powerful compositions like **Laundromat Blues,** from **Born Under A Bad Sign,** which became seminal material for the emerging breed of white blues guitarists.

King, in fact, was one of the most rock-influenced of the great blues singers; he has a distinctive guitar style, playing his V-shaped custom-built Gibson in a way that complements his raw vocals. He is a massive figure anyway, standing 6ft 4in.

With guitarists like Eric Clapton creating an interest in blues innovators, King benefited from the new-found young white rock audience, and recorded **Live Wire/Blues Power** at Fillmore West. His albums since have been both critically and commercially successful, and **I Wanna Get Funky** is particularly dynamic. Discography is selective.

Recordings:
Born Under A Bad Sign (Stax/Atlantic)
King Of The Blues Guitar (Stax/Atlantic)
Live Wire/Blues Power (Stax/Atlantic)
Years Gone By (Stax)
Albert King Does The King's Things (Stax)
Lovejoy (Stax)
I'll Play The Blues For You (Stax)
I Wanna Get Funky (Stax)

B. B. King

Born Riley King on Sep 16, 1925, in Itta Bena, Mississippi, King was raised by a foster family, before moving to Memphis, Tennessee, where he met Sonny Boy Williamson II (Rice Miller), who was running the King Biscuit Boy radio show. Williamson gave him a 10-minute spot as DJ, and it was there he was nicknamed Blues Boy, which he abbreviated to B.B. In between radio shows, he just played with jazz and blues artists, whoever was around at the time.

His first record, **Miss Martha King**, was released by Bullet Records in 1949; immediately afterwards he went to Modern Records, appearing on their RPM label up to the time he signed for ABC-Paramount in 1961. **Three O'Clock Blues,** was a major national R&B hit in 1950, and King went on to turn out a succession of blues classics. **Woke Up This Morning, Sweet Little Angel, Eyesight To The Blind** and others established him as a leading exponent of the blues idiom. He had listened to his cousin, country blues artist Bukka White, but had also been influenced by Charlie Christian, and his clean-cut, almost jazzy style contrasted with the raw earthiness of blues artists like Muddy Waters and Elmore James,

To Know You Is To Love You. Courtesy ABC Records.

making it easy for King to attract white as well as black audiences.

Live At The Regal, sometimes regarded as his finest album, was recorded in Chicago in the early '60s; but the most significant move for King came in 1969 when he was teamed with Rock producer Bill Szymczyk for **Live And Well**; one side was cut with his own band during a show at New York's Village Gate, and the other in the studio in Los Angeles with a small combo of white rock musicians and top black sessionmen; Al Kooper, Hugh McCracken, Herbie Lovelle, Paul Harris and Jerry Jemmott all participated. The same team, minus Kooper, was used for **Completely Well,** a thoroughly modern, feverishly swinging album, which included several extended jams, and closed with the sensational **The Thrill Is Gone,** on which King made the radical move of using strings in a pure blues setting. The result was a U.S. hit single, King's second million-seller.

From then on, King, long acclaimed by white rock and blues musicians as a formative influence, found himself booked increasingly into rock venues. He adjusted his material accordingly, using Joe Walsh, Leon Russell and Carole King as musicians on **Indianola Mississippi Seeds.**

Like his white country counterpart, Johnny Cash, King became interested in prison welfare, and cut **Live In Cook County Jail;** he also followed the lead of other bluesmen by coming to London to work. For **B.B. King In London** he acquired the services of Peter Green, Alexis Korner, Steve Marriott and Ringo Starr.

A superb showman, King is one of the world's greatest guitar soloists, and is certainly the best-known and most influential bluesman of them all; he confesses, however, that he cannot play rhythm, nor sing while playing.

Discography is selective.

Recordings:
Live At The Regal (ABC/HMV)
Live And Well (ABC/Stateside)
Completely Well (ABC/ Stateside)
Live In Cook County Jail (ABC-Probe)
Indianola Mississippi Seeds (ABC-Probe)
B.B. King In London (ABC-Probe)
Guess Who (ABC-Probe)
To Know You Is To Love You (ABC-Probe)
Friends (ABC)
Lucille Talks Back (ABC)
Compilations:
The B.B. King Story (—/Blue Horizon)
The B.B. King Story, Chapter Two (—/Blue Horizon)
The Best of B.B. King (ABC)
With Bobby Bland:
Together, Live . . . For The First Time (ABC)

Carole King

Born Carole Klein in Sheepshead Bay, Brooklyn, New York on Feb 9, 1942 she was able to play piano from the age of four. When she was 14 she used to hang around stage doors and dance in the aisles at Alan Freed's Brooklyn rock 'n' roll shows.

At high school, she started a rock group herself, called The Cosines, and began writing bad lyrics. The first time the public heard of her was when her friend Neil Sedaka had a hit in October 1959 with a song dedicated to her called **Oh! Carol.** She wrote a reply called **Oh! Neil,** which went nowhere, and the same happened to her other early singles, **Goin' Wild, Baby Sittin'** and **Queen Of The Beach.**

She graduated from high school, moved to Queens and went to Queens College where, in later 1958, she had met Gerry Goffin. He had written a play which had song lyrics in it, but which needed music, and she had lots of rock 'n' roll songs which needed

Above: Carole King. With husband Gerry Goffin, she wrote a whole string of '60s pop classics; in the '70s she was in the vanguard of the singer songwriter boom.

lyrics. They worked well together. Initially their main concern was to make money; Carole was pregnant, and they were getting married.

One day Goffin came home from work and Carole played him a melody she had just written. He immediately wrote a set of lyrics, and they had their first hit when **Will You Love Me Tomorrow?** was recorded by The Shirelles and reached No. 1 in the U.S. in 1960, and No. 3 in the U.K. the following year.

Goffin and King signed with Al Nevins' and Don Kirshner's Aldon Music, and became part of the "cubicle syndrome" at the Brill Building, 1650 Broadway. Ultimately, they composed more hits than anyone except Lennon/McCartney, writing **Up On The Roof** and **When My Little Girl Is Smiling** for The Drifters, **Go Away Little Girl** and **I Want To Stay Here** for Steve Lawrence and Eydie Gorme, **Take Good Care Of My Baby, Sharing You** and **How Many Tears** for Bobby Vee, **Don't Bring Me Down** for The Animals, **Goin' Back** for Dusty Springfield, **Wasn't Born To Follow** for The Byrds. The list is endless . . . .

They first worked with Phil Spector (♦) when they wrote **Every Breath I Take** for Gene Pitney in 1961; Carole played piano on **Uptown** for The Crystals, and she and Goffin also wrote **Hurt Me** and **He Hit Me (And It Felt Like A Kiss)** for them. With Spector they co-wrote **Just Once In My Life** and **Hung On You** for the Righteous Brothers (♦).

In 1962 they wrote, arranged, conducted and produced a song for their baby-sitter, Little Eva (Boyd). **The Locomotion** was a No. 1 in the U.S. and a No. 2 in the U.K. in June 1962. A few months later the three unknown singers they'd used for backing vocals named themselves The Cookies, and had a hit themselves with **Chains,** a Goffin/King com-

position that was later recorded by The Beatles.

Lou Adler (♦) formed The Dimension Record Company to produce demos for the Kirshner-Nevins publishing group; he took one demo Carole had made, which was originally written for Bobby Vee, and released it commercially. **It Might As Well Rain Until September** was a hit (No. 3 in the U.K.), but Carole did no promotion or concerts, and her follow-ups, **School Bells Are Ringing** and **He's A Bad Boy,** flopped.

In mid-'60s, Goffin and King, plus columnist Al Aronowitz started the ill-fated Tommow label, releasing Carole's own version of **Road To Nowhere,** and a couple of records by The Myddle Class. The bass-player with the latter was Charlie Larkey, and it wasn't too long before Carole and Gerry were divorced (Carole taking custody of the two children, Sherry, for whom Goffin had written **Child Of Mine,** and Louise) and Carole and Charlie married.

Playing on same New York circuit as The Myddle Class was The Flying Machine, featuring vocalist James Taylor and guitarist Danny Kortchmar, aka Kootch. When these two groups split-up, Larkey and Kootch initially joined The Fugs, playing on three of their albums, and then in 1968 were joined by Carole to form the group known as The City.

Plans to take the group on the road were abandoned when Carole's shyness got the better of her, but the group did make one superb album, **Now That Everything's Been Said.** Among the tracks were **That Old Sweet Roll, (Hi-Di-Ho)** which became a hit for Blood, Sweat And Tears, Carole's own version of **Wasn't Born To Follow,** and **You've Got A Friend,** which later reappeared on two bestselling albums – her own **Tapestry,** and **Mud Slide Slim And The Blue**

Horizon by James Taylor, who had a huge hit single with the song.

Carole moved to Los Angeles, and began to make guest appearances on her friends' albums, playing on Taylor's **Sweet Baby James** and John Stewart's **Willard.** This built-up her confidence, and in 1970 she recorded her first solo album, **Writer,** using a line-up of Kootch (gtr), Larkey (bs), Ralph Shuckett (kybds), Joel O'Brien (drms). With the addition of Abigail Harness on vocals, this line-up became Jo Mama, and made two albums for Atco/Atlantic, **Jo Mama** and **J Is For Jump,** on both of which Carole plays piano.

Writer set the trend for singer/songwriter albums. It was not a total success – Lou Adler's production is thin, and Carole sings flat much of the time; it sounds like a demo album. But her audience was intrigued to hear how Carole herself would handle **Up On The Roof,** and it received a quite favourable press.

James Taylor persuaded her to join him on a tour and they used Jo Mama as their musicians. In 1971 she used the same team again, including Taylor, to cut the **Tapestry** album, which was again produced by Adler.

She clicked. The album caught the mood of the country just right, and it became a huge hit. A single from it, **It's Too Late,** made No. 1, as did the album itself. To date it has sold in excess of 13 million copies and registered over 250 consecutive weeks in the U.S. album charts. It is the second-biggest-selling album ever. The songs represented a great change from the adolescent melodramas; they were mature and sophisticated and appealed to almost every side of the record-buying market.

Tapestry was followed by **Carole King Music** which, though a good album, didn't have quite that magic quality which had made **Tapestry** so right for its time. She used a larger orchestration and one track, **Music,** featured Curtis Amy on tenor sax.

Rhymes And Reasons (1972) was unremarkable and reflected a pleasant uneventful life in Los Angeles surrounded by friends and children. In 1973 **Fantasy** was the complete opposite, an album concerning itself with social unrest, drug addiction, women's liberation, and the ghetto; the music she wrote was fittingly characterised by tough trumpet riffs and Isaac Hayes-flavoured arrangements.

In late 1974 she had another U.S. No. 1 single with **Jazzman** (featuring a sax break by Tom Scott, who had assimilated himself into Hollywood session circles), taken from **Wrap Around Joy,** a wide-ranging album of pop and jazz influences.

She wrote the music for a children's TV programme, **Really Rosie** in 1975; it was released as an album and features her own children singing background vocals.

When David Crosby and Graham Nash went on tour in October 1975, Carole joined them on stage for some of the shows, singing new material she'd written with Gerry Goffin. These turned-up on her next album, **Thoroughbred** on which Crosby, Nash and the inevitable Taylor sang background vocals.

1976 saw her cutting loose in New York City, and one can assume that, rather than sitting back and becoming a musical institution she will continue to change and grow.

Recordings:
Writer (Ode)
Tapestry (Ode)
Carole King Music (Ode)
Rhymes And Reasons (Ode)
Fantasy (Ode)
Wrap Around Joy (Ode)
Really Rosie (Ode/—)
Thoroughbred (Ode)
With The City:
Now That Everything's Been Said (Ode/—)

Thoroughbred.
Courtesy A&M Records.

Freddie King

Freddie King was born Sep 30, 1934 in Longview, Texas, and was heavily influenced by both T-Bone Walker and B.B. King (no relation). At 19, he began playing professionally in the band of Little Sonny Copper, and by 1954 had switched to Earl Payton's Blues Cats. First recorded under his own name for El-Bee label in 1956.

By now living in Chicago, and part of the important blues scene there, he was leading his own band by 1960 when he was signed to the Cincinatti-based Federal Records; he recorded prolifically in following years, cutting many impressive tracks, particularly, **Have You Ever Loved A Woman?** and **Hide Away.**

The waning black interest in blues left him without a contract by the middle of the '60s, but ironically he achieved wider recognition by abandoning commercial R&B in favour of a more biting, ethnic style, similar to that of B.B. King, as the white rock audiences were turned on to pure blues. After an appearance in Britain at the Savile Theatre in London, he became involved with the white blues revival scene, and recorded **Freddie King Is A Blues Master** and **My Feeling For The Blues** for Atlantic's subsidiary label, Cotillion. The albums were produced by King Curtis.

After this, he signed for Leon Russell's Shelter label, and found himself working regularly with white rock musicians, especially those who had formed Clapton's Derek & The Dominos (who had included **Have You Ever Loved A Woman?** on **Layla And Other**

Right: The 1974 King Crimson. L to r: Robert Fripp, David Cross, Bill Bruford, John Wetton. Cross quit and band folded a few months later.

Assorted Love Songs); Freddie's albums for Shelter were **Gettin' Ready, Texas Cannonball** and **Woman Across The River.** In 1974, however, he was persuaded by Mike Vernon to join RSO Records, for whom he recorded **Burglar,** with the assistance of Eric Clapton.
Discography is selective.

Recordings:
Freddie King Is A Blues Master (Cotillion/Atlantic)
My Feeling For The Blues (Cotillion/Atlantic)
Gettin' Ready (Shelter)
Texas Cannonball (Shelter)
Woman Across The River (Shelter)
Burglar (RSO)
Larger Than Life (RSO)
Compilations:
King Of Rhythm And Blues, Vol. II (—/Polydor)
The Best Of Freddie King (Shelter)

Jonathan King

Born in London, Dec 6, 1948, King first came to public attention 1965 by writing and recording **Everyone's Gone To The Moon** while still a university student. The song reached No. 4 in the U.K., and No. 17 in U.S.

He followed this initial success by writing and producing **It's Good News Week** for Hedgehoppers Anonymous, which made the Top 5 in Britain and the Top 50 in the States.

It's Good News Week was a sort of gaumless protest song, and since then King has made a living out of reducing pop/rock formulae to their most cretinous — and ergo most commercial level. It's difficult to respect someone who has so cynically demonstrated the commercial advantages of pandering to the lowest

common denominator in public taste, and who has practically made a virtue out of his lack of moral fibre. In his defence it can be said that he is disarmingly honest about the value of his material, that he can unfailingly spot a commercial tune, and that he has sometimes debunked self-consciously worthy musical poses; e.g. he recorded the ultimate bubblegum anthem, The Archies' **Sugar Sugar,** in heavy-metal style, said it was by a group called Sakkharin, and the song was a hit.

King came down from Trinity College, Cambridge, with an English degree in 1966. Almost immediately he received his own ATV show on British television; called "Good Evening", it ran for six months.

He became assistant to Sir Edward Lewis, Chairman of Decca Records, and discovered and initially produced Genesis (➧), while continuing to pursue his own idiosyncratic recording activities. He left Decca at the end of 1970 and produced several minor British hits by groups (The Weathermen, St Cecilia, The Piglets) which were either operating under his aegis, or actually were him under a pseudonym. He also says he was the man responsible for putting the Bay City Rollers (➧) in the Top 10 with **Keep On Dancing,** though whether he considers this a proud boast or an admission of guilt is not clear.

In 1972 he formed his own label, UK Records. Though he'd always been assumed to be at home within a bubblegum format, one of his first signings was the very excellent 10cc (➧), and he was also astute in securing the British rights to Kevin Johnson's **Rock 'n' Roll I Gave You The Best Years Of My Life,** a song that deserved to be a bigger hit than it was. He also signed the Kursaal

Flyers (➧) to UK in 1975.

He had another major hit in Britain that same year with **Una Paloma Blanca,** and has continued to issue records under his own name. **Greatest Hits Past, Present And Future** is a good example of his irrepressible vanity.

Recordings:
Or Then Again (London/Decca)
Bubblerock Is Here To Stay (—/UK)
Try Something Different (London/UK)
Pandora's Box (London/UK)
A Rose In A Fisted Glove (London/UK)
Greatest Hits Past, Present And Future (—/UK)

King Crimson

Robert Fripp guitar, mellotron
Ian McDonald reeds, keyboards
Greg Lake bass, vocals
Mike Giles drums
Pete Sinfield lyrics, lights, VCS3 synthesiser

Above was original line-up on conception January 1969, though Robert Fripp (b. Wimbourne, Dorset, 1946) was only surviving founder member when group finally split in September 1974.

The origins of King Crimson, however, pre-date January 1969 by some 15 months. First there was the mildly humorous, light-weight pop-oriented trio Giles Giles And Fripp which emerged out of the sedate South of England coastal resort of Bournemouth circa 1967 and comprised the aforementioned Fripp plus the brothers Mike (drms) and Pete Giles (bs). Signed to Deram label, this band made two singles and one album **The Cheerful Insanity Of Giles Giles And Fripp** (1968), all of which were dis-

mally received. The album racked up world sales of 600 and the group had failed to secure even one gig when it wound-up in November 1968. Pete Giles left to become a computer operator and finally a solicitor's clerk while Mike Giles and Robert Fripp conceived King Crimson.

Two of the other originals had already had associations with the earlier group. One-time army bandsman Ian McDonald had joined them at one point (**I Talk To The Wind,** from the debut Crimson album, was made as a home demo during the GG&F period) and McDonald in turn introduced lyric writer Pete Sinfield. (The first Fairport Convention vocalist, Judy Dyble, was also briefly a member of GG&F.)

Greg Lake, also from the Bournemouth area and newly arrived in London, was roped in as bassist/vocalist, and the new group began rehearsing in the basement of a cafe in the Fulham Palace Road. Pete Sinfield was elected road manager, and also given the job of preparing a light show. Justin Hayward and Graeme Edge of the Moody Blues were among many who listened in at this time, and briefly considered signing them to their newly-inaugurated Threshold label.

Even before their first real gig – at the London Speakeasy Club Apr 9, 1969 – word was beginning to spread of the amazing new sounds being produced in the cafe basement. Friends would drop by, listen and pass the word on through the "underground" press.

When the gigs did start to come through, small ones at first, the word spread even faster. But the band really made their mark – and their reputation – when they secured a spot on the Rolling Stones' July 5 free concert in Hyde Park. King Crimson stunned the estimated 650,000 audience with their quite devastating use of mellotrons and classical influences in a rock format.

A few months later, in October 1969, came release of their debut album, **In The Court Of The Crimson King,** received on a wave of near-unanimous acclaim. Considered a classic at the time – Pete Townshend went into print calling it "an uncanny masterpiece" – it established the band as the most fashionable of its day both in the U.K. and the U.S., though it hasn't worn so well with time.

What happened next was symptomatic of the band's subsequent career. During their first American tour, in December, Mike Giles, drummer extraordinaire, and Ian McDonald, a shy, retiring character whose contribution to the first album was never fully recognised, decided to leave. Both somewhat eccentric talents, they chose to reject what they considered as the "plasticity" of rock and/or the U.S.

(The pair later collaborated on the eponymous **McDonald And Giles** album – Atlantic/Island 1970 – which was critically well received but a commercial flop.)

In debt and disillusioned, and now down to a trio, King Crimson returned to the U.K. to work on their second album, during the sessions for which Greg Lake left to join Keith Emerson in formation of Emerson Lake And

Above: In The Court Of The Crimson King. Courtesy EG Records. Stunning artwork for a stunning debut.

Palmer (➧). Lake and Emerson had first met in the States during that aforementioned tour. Meanwhile Fripp turned down offers to replace Pete Banks in Yes, and join Aynsley Dunbar's Blue Whale.

A friend of Fripp's, Gordon Haskell, came in to complete the new album's vocals, while Pete Giles made a brief return as bassist. Mel Collins "guested" on reeds and Mike Giles stayed on while Crimso looked for a new drummer. In the midst of all this turmoil perhaps it is not surprising that their second album, **In The Wake Of Poseidon** (1970) came across as a somewhat poor duplication of its predecessor.

(An interesting historical sidenote here is that the then unknown Elton John was originally booked to sing on **Poseidon** for a session fee of £250. However, Fripp decided Elton's style was wrong for the band and cancelled the arrangement.)

By later 1970 Fripp was pronouncing his new Crimso personnel as Haskell (bs, vcls), Collins (reeds), Andy McCulloch (drms) plus Pete Sinfield, whose lyrics for the most part were a constant source of embarrassment to Crimso aficionados. This group, augmented by jazzers Keith Tippett (pno) and Marc Charig (cornet), went into the studios to cut the much-improved **Lizard.** Jon Anderson of Yes also made a guest vocal appearance.

However, even before the album's release in December 1970 (two days after its completion in fact) Gordon Haskell had been edged out of the band.

King Crimson returned again to their cafe basement, where Sinfield started to toy around with the VCS3 synthesiser and Fripp started auditioning for a new band. Bryan Ferry was one of the vocalists who didn't meet his requirements. Mel Collins who, by now, had left and rejoined some three or four times was re-

tained; Ian Wallace came in on drums. Bass was more of a problem: Rick Kemp (who later joined Steeleye Span) rehearsed for a short while, but Fripp with typical perversity eventually settled on an unknown singer Boz Burrell who couldn't even play the instrument. "Don't worry," said Fripp, "I'll teach you how" – and he did.

This band cut **Islands** (late 1971), and returned to the U.S. for another King Crimson tour early in 1972 – meeting a similar fate to the first. The problem here was that Wallace, Collins and Burrell were essentially of a totally different nature to the reserved, intelligent Fripp. They were looners – he most certainly was not.

Whatever the reasons this band, like the first, fell apart in the U.S. Collins (now with Kokomo), Wallace (subsequently with Chapman-Whitney Streetwalkers and Alvin Lee), and Burrell (now with the commercially huge Bad Company) went off to form a short-lived group Snape with Alexis Korner (➧).

Pete Sinfield had also disappeared from the Crimson fold. In fact, he'd been the first to go, leaving in a flurry of ill feeling late 1971. He subsequently turned-up as producer on the debut Roxy Music (➧) album.

Band morale – or, more specifically, Fripp's – hadn't been helped either by U.S. audiences' constant baying for early Crimso material such as **Epitaph** and **21st Century Schizoid Man.** However, the band hadn't acquitted itself that badly on tour – as the subsequent "live" album **Earthbound** (1972), however poorly recorded, was to show.

So now that left only one surviving member of the original band; one more-than-disillusioned musician who was always too idiosyncratic, always perhaps too much a perfectionist for his own good. Fripp returned to England for a

lengthy spell hiding out in his Dorset cottage, until in late 1972 emerging with what some regard as the best-ever incarnation of King Crimson.

This featured former Yes drummer Bill Bruford; John Wetton, ex of Family and Mogul Thrash, an excellent bassist and powerful vocalist; the brilliantly-anarchic percussionist Jamie Muir, hitherto unknown; and the equally unknown and inexperienced young violin and mellotron player David Cross. Bruford's arrival, spurning a lucrative gig with Yes, was testimony indeed to Fripp's standing. One Robert Palmer-Jones was by now supplying whatever lyrics this essentially instrument-oriented outfit required, though in this department there was little improvement on the outgoing Sinfield.

The resulting album, **Lark's Tongue In Aspic** (1973), was undoubtedly Crimson's finest so far, evincing a discernable new style of compositional activity, making full use of the group's greatest assets – Fripp's guitar, Wetton's vocals and the Muir/Bruford combination. Concert appearances were unanimously acclaimed.

Then, disappointingly, Jamie Muir made an enigmatic announcement about "leaving the music business" and vanished, reportedly, into a monastery.

As a four-piece they made another interesting album, **Starless And Bible Black** (1974), after which David Cross similarly quit and returned to obscurity. On July 1 King Crimson ended the U.S. tour which produced their second live album **USA** (1975) with a concert in New York's Central Park. It was to be their last-ever gig. Back in England in September, Fripp announced the final dissolution of King Crimson. At that point founder member Ian McDonald was on the verge of rejoining the group, and in fact appears on King Crimson's posthumously-released **Red** album (1974) along with other alumni Mel Collins and Marc Charig. It was an excellent valedictory set, making Fripp's decision to disband all the more puzzling.

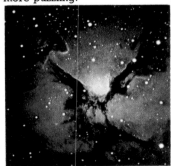

Islands. Courtesy E.G. Records Ltd.

John Wetton was subsequently with Roxy Music for a spell before joining Uriah Heep (➧); Bill Bruford has had short stints with Gong and Pavlov's Dog.

Fripp, meanwhile, has latterly restrained his activities to two esoteric albums in collaboration with Brian Eno (➧), touring Europe with same, and the preparation of the double-album compilation **A Young Person's Guide To King Crimson** which contains an exhaustive account of the band's turbulent history, and includes numerous press clippings. These last show that for every Crimso aficionado there was one who loathed their every essence, the same holding true for each album. A controversial band throughout its several incarnations, perhaps a few years of hindsight will present a clearer picture.

Recordings:
In The Court Of The Crimson King (Atlantic/Island)
In The Wake Of Poseidon (Atlantic/Island)
Lizard (Atlantic/Island)
Islands (Atlantic/Island)
Earthbound (—/Island)
Lark's Tongues In Aspic (Atlantic/Island)
Starless And Bible Black (Atlantic/Island)
Red (Atlantic/Island)
USA (Atlantic/Island)
Compilation:
A Young Person's Guide To King Crimson (Atlantic/Island)
Fripp and Eno:
No Pussyfootin' (Island/Help)
Evening Star (Island/Help)

The Kinks

Ray Davies vocals, guitar
Dave Davies guitar, vocals
Mick Avory drums
John Dalton bass
John Gosling keyboards
Laurie Brown trumpet
Alan Holmes saxophone
John Beecham trombone

The Kinks were formed in London 1964, as a four-piece – Ray Davies (b. Jun 21, 1944), Dave Davies (b. Feb 3, 1947), Mick Avory (b. Feb 15, 1944) and Peter Quaife (b. Dec 27, 1943); only Quaife, born in Tavistock, Devon, was not a native Londoner.

Ray Davies was an art college student at the time, and after playing clubs in London, the band won a recording contract with Pye. Their first single, **Long Tall Sally,** was virtually a cover version of The Beatles' cover version of the song, and it flopped anyway, as did second single, **You Do Something To Me,** which

Above: Vintage Kinks.

apparently amassed a sale of 127 copies. The third, **You Really Got Me,** reached No. 1 in the British charts in 1964 and No. 7 in the States.

You Really Got Me had a driving, raw beat, with a riff that had been (probably unconsciously) lifted from The Kingsmen's **Louie Louie.** It served to establish the basic image and sound of the band at the beginning, as well as indicating the strengths of Ray Davies as a songwriter. The song

The Kinks Are The Village Green Preservation Society. Courtesy WEA. The Kinks on ecology on Ray Davies' first concept LP.

had been produced by Shel Talmy, as were all the band's hits over the next 18 months – **All Day And All Of The Night, Tired Of Waiting For You, Everybody's Gonna Be Happy, Set Me Free, See My Friends** and **Till The End Of The Day.**

However an EP, **Kwyet Kinks,** released in late 1965 suddenly gave notice that Davies had songwriting qualities his hit singles had not begun to explore. **A Well Respected Man,** one of the four songs on the EP, was a character sketch ridiculing the prototype conservative, and it went on to become one of the most famous rock songs never to have been a British hit. Davies was so encouraged by the response that he followed it with a single, **Dedicated Follower Of Fashion,** which was cast in a similar mould, though this time it was the prototype Swinging London dandy who was being satirised; what was strange was that it was one of the rock groups (supposedly an integral part of the whole scene) who could see through it all so clearly. The song reached No. 4 in the U.K. in 1966, and Davies has never looked back. Henceforth, his songwriting was tailored to his own satisfaction and commercial considerations were strictly secondary.

The style of tragi-comic observation matured through **Sunny Afternoon, Dead End Street, Waterloo Sunset, Autumn Almanac** and **Days,** and Davies applied it in a specifically English context, self-consciously tapping music-hall traditions.

This was in other ways a turning-point for the band, who began to tour less regularly; Ray became involved with certain solo projects (e.g. providing the score for "The Virgin Soldiers"), and his brother, Dave, accordingly did the same, issuing a solo single in 1967, **Death Of A Clown,** which was so successful he was encouraged to follow it with **Susan-**

nah's Still Alive and **Lincoln County.** Of The Kinks' albums of this period, the 1967 **Live At Kelvin Hall** (in Glasgow) is remarkable for the raucous atmosphere, and **Something Else By The Kinks** was the last album produced for them by Shel Talmy (Davies going on to handle his own productions); other material they recorded at this time was only issued in the '70s in America as **The Kink Kronicles** and **The Great Lost Kinks Album.**

So The Kinks began expanding their horizons, and **The Kinks Are The Village Green Preservation Society** is their first album amounting to more than just a collection of songs. It represents the continuous evocation of the passing of time, a sepia photograph of old England, which was expanded into terms both more specific and more cynical on **Arthur (Or The Decline And Fall Of The British Empire),** a highly acclaimed album that was originally commissioned as a TV soundtrack. Before **Arthur** was recorded, however, Quaife, whose departure had been long since rumoured, finally quit. His place was taken by John Dalton.

The band had exhausted their need to come up with regular hit singles after **Days,** and since their new concept albums initially frightened-off audiences, they were to enjoy little more chart success until 1970 when the excellent **Lola,** with its mildly controversial transvestite theme, reached No. 2 in the U.K. and No. 9 in the U.S., and was quickly followed by **Apeman,** and an album, **Lola Versus Powerman And The Moneygoround,** which had some acid comments on the operation of power in the pop-music industry; The Kinks themselves had been victims of most of the corporate ills that the record business is heir to.

Meanwhile, Davies had completed the soundtrack for "Percy",

though the film was dreadful and the music aroused little interest. He also signified his burgeoning thespian interest by taking the lead role in a television play, "The Long Distance Piano Player".

The group finally overcame their substantial hassles with both their management and their record company, by negotiating a new deal for themselves with RCA, and their first release (for which they had introduced a keyboards player, Gosling, and also recruited the Mike Cotton Sound on brass, after which Brown, Holmes and Beecham became regular members of the band) was **Muswell Hillbillies,** one of their most satisfying albums, with songs that have become inextricably associated with the band – **Skin And Bone** and **Alcohol.**

It sold disappointingly; but just as the band were going through a commercially lean period in Britain, their following in America began to pick up, probably because of Davies' skills in live performance (by this time the others were practically acting as his support band) and his use of elements of English music-hall. **Everybody's In Showbiz-Everybody's A Star** consolidated this new success, even though it was an uneasy mixture of American tour impressionism and live crowd-pleasing. Over in Britain, the comparative failure of **Supersonic Rocketship** and **Celluloid Heroes,** both of which were first-class, emphasised that The Kinks no longer had a significant groundswell of support there.

Encouraged by the American plaudits, Davies embarked on a series of grandoise projects to exploit fully the possibilities of stage theatre. He returned to the **Village Green** album for the character of Mr Flash, and re-thought the plot as a triple-album concept (**Preservation** was released in two parts: **Part I** in 1973 was a double album, and **Part II,** in 1974, a single), which almost inevitably showed Davies stretching his ideas too thinly.

Schoolboys In Disgrace illustrated the nefarious adolescence of Mr Flash, and it was scheduled for American release a full three months ahead of the U.K. date, something which perfectly illustrates the current standing of the band on each side of the Atlantic.

For the stage act, The Kinks were augmented by three girl singers, who also played occasional roles in the narrative. While **Schoolboys In Disgrace** made for some quite well-conceived theatrics, it was thematically very thin gruel, and the music was old hat.

But while their output has been (to English audiences, at least) disappointing of late, The Kinks do represent a continuing musical tradition of old England. It is all Ray Davies would wish.

Partly to let other artists benefit from their own unpleasant experiences, The Kinks formed their own label, Konk Records, in 1974. One of first signings was Claire Hamill, (➡), whose **Stage Door Johnnies** was produced by Ray Davies, as was the debut album of Cafe Society, also on Konk.

Discography lists all the Kinks' recordings; as they have been victims of the most merciless, unintelligent recycling most of the many compilations have been omitted.

Right: Ray Davies. His
unique writing style
mixes tragi-comic
observation with English
music-hall traditions.

Recordings:
The Kinks (Reprise/Pye)
Kinks – Size (Reprise/—)
Kinda Kinks (Reprise/Pye)
Kinks Kinkdom (Reprise/—)
The Kink Kontroversy
   (Reprise/Pye)
Face To Face (Reprise/Pye)
Live At The Kelvin Hall
   (Reprise/Pye)
Something Else By The Kinks
   (Reprise/Pye)
**The Kinks Are The Village
   Green Preservation Society**
   (Reprise/Pye)
**Arthur (Or The Decline And
   Fall Of The British Empire)**
   (Reprise/Pye)
**Lola Versus Powerman And
   The Moneygoround** (Reprise/
   Pye)
Percy (Soundtrack) (Reprise/
   Pye)
Muswell Hillbillies (RCA)
The Kink Kronikles (Reprise/—)
The Great Lost Kinks Album
   (Reprise/—)
**Everybody's In Showbiz –
   Everybody's A Star** (RCA)
Preservation, Act I (RCA)
Preservation, Act II (RCA)
Soap Opera (RCA)
Schoolboys In Disgrace (RCA)
Compilations:
Golden Hour Of The Kinks
   (—/Pye)
All The Good Times (—/Pye)
Celluloid Heroes (RCA)

Don Kirshner

Regarded as pop music's most
successful publisher, he first
made his reputation in New York
music circles in '50s, and went on
to set up Aldon Music, with his
partner Al Nevins, which created
production-line product for the
mass teenage market; some of it
was very good, but that was
almost accidental.

In New York's Brill Building,
Kirshner and Nevins created a
professional organisation which
discovered and nurtured the
songwriting talents of Gerry
Goffin and Carole King (➧), Barry
Mann and Cynthia Weil, Neil
Sedaka (➧) and Howard Greenfield, and many others. Playing-off
one songwriting team against
another, Kirshner had his contracted writers working in claustrophobic cubicles, often with
just a piano at which to work.
Nevertheless, they created an
enormous number of hits for the
company, which was later sold
off to Screen Gems.

Kirshner's greatest success, however, came with the manufacturing of The Monkees (➧), a teenage
pop group designed to be
America's answer to The Beatles,
but who had the added advantage
of a weekly TV series through
which to promote their records.

Within months, The Monkees
were the biggest recording act
in the world, with their material
written by Aldon staff writers,
often Tommy Boyce and Bobby
Hart, sometimes Goffin and King,
and sometimes other regulars
such as Neil Diamond.

Following a dispute with the
group, Kirshner left and started
all over again, equally successfully, with The Archies; this time,

however, the group were literally
cartoon characters, so there could
be no personality clashes. The
Archies unleashed the international bubblegum anthem,
Sugar Sugar, in 1969; it reached
No. 1 on both sides of the Atlantic,
and became one of the largest-
selling singles of all time.

After helping to reunite Howard
Greenfield and Neil Sedaka –
which paved the way for Sedaka's
successful comeback, Kirshner
moved directly into television in
1972 with a syndicated live show,
"Don Kirshner's Rock Concert".

Kiss

Ace Frehley guitar
Paul Stanley guitar
Gene Simmons bass, vocals
Pete Criss drums

Originating out of New York 1973,
at the tail end of androgynous
cycle set in motion by likes of
David Bowie and Lou Reed, Kiss
were initially received with quite
unprecedented bile in most quarters as representing the very
nadir of the then long played-out
glam-rock era.

What could have been more suspicious than a hitherto unknown
band, who had taken stage make-
up to the extreme by completely
obliterating their features behind
garish grease paint, and who
blitzkrieged audiences with an
arsenal of explosive devices,
snow machines, police lights,
sirens, rocket-firing guitars, levi-

tating drumkits and, as if all that
wasn't sufficient to disguise their
apparent ineptitude, a fire-eating
bass player?

That this same outfit went on to
rise meteorically in three years to
become one of America's hottest
in-concert and album-shifting
bands still remains, to some, not
only one of rock's all-time mysteries but also one of the most dis-
tressing symptoms of the genre's
decline in the '70s.

Such at any rate was the hostility
that faced the group when they
set out to interest the youth of
America in 1973–74 on a touring
schedule which had them gigging
virtually seven nights a week. It
was an arduous initiation but, first

Destroyer.
Courtesy Casablanca/EMI.

as a support band, they gradually
got through to a new generation
of American rock fans: to the point
where the first two albums, **Kiss**
and **Hotter Than Hell** (the last

not released in the U.K.), were
able to rack up healthy sales
around the quarter-million mark.

Still, however, the press remained almost unanimously hostile –
though gradually some cracks of
recognition began to appear.
Even certain initial detractors
found themselves acknowledging
that behind the make-up and unashamedly derivative style, there
lurked a high-energy macho
presence and a genuine, if not
much more than musically competent, grasp of the niceties (sic)
of heavy metal rock 'n' roll.

Not that Kiss needed critical
support overmuch by then. In
May 1975, at Detroit's 12,500-
capacity Cobo Hall, the band headlined for the first time ever – and
sold out. Meanwhile the fourth
album, **Alive!,** was on its way to
platinum status in the U.S. album
charts, hotly pursued by box-
office records.

Few new bands have had to face
such a vitriolic initial critical reception; that Kiss not only survived it but flourished in no uncertain terms is either a credit to
the band's faith and perseverance
or a monument to the power of
hype – take your choice. One of
the few bands for which the cliche
"love them or hate them" is apt.

Recordings:
Kiss (Casablanca)
Hotter Than Hell
   (Casablanca/—)
Dressed To Kill (Casablanca)
Alive! (Casablanca)
Destroyer (Casablanca)

Allen Klein

American accountant who heads his own ABKCO industries in New York, and has negotiated rock deals in excess of 30 million dollars. He gained control of the Cameo-Parkway Philadelphia operation, and has recently leased their tapes to Decca for release in Britain.

He began to work with British acts by handling U.S. affairs of Herman's Hermits, Chad & Jeremy and Donovan, but he made no secret of his desire to purchase controlling interests in the affairs of both the Rolling Stones and The Beatles.

He achieved both, even though he parted company from the Stones in very rancorous circumstances and he had a business reputation not so much for shrewdness as for total ruthlessness. His involvement with The Beatles led indirectly to their break-up, as it was against McCartney's wishes to bring him in; his affairs with both bands ended in lengthy litigation.

Gladys Knight and the Pips

Gladys Knight vocals
Merald (Bubba) Knight vocals
William Guest vocals
Edward Patten vocals

Like the Isley Brothers, Gladys Knight and the Pips are a family group who have survived the vicissitudes of over 20 years in show business, and in that period have consistently increased both their stature and their audience, and become much more than simply a soul act.

All four of them are originally from Atlanta, Georgia; Gladys was born in 1944, and as a child performed in the Mount Mariah Baptist Church, sang with the Morris Brown Choir throughout the South, won a national talent contest and, like both her parents before her, joined Atlanta's Wings Over Jordan Choir; all this by the time she was 10.

A birthday party for her elder brother, Merald Jnr, accidentally brought about the birth of the Pips in 1952; she formed a group with Merald, her sister Brenda, and her cousins William and Elenor Guest. The group were soon playing local clubs, and made their first national tour with Sam Cooke and Jackie Wilson when Gladys was 12.

They had a first stab at recording in 1957 for the Brunswick label; it was unsuccessful, and after this Elenor and Brenda left to get married, and were replaced by Patten, another cousin, and Langston George. It was not until they cut a single for a local Atlanta label, **Every Beat Of My Heart** (written by Johnny Otis) that they gained their first national hit, and also their first million-seller in 1961. In the next year they had further success on the New York-based Fury label, with **Letter Full Of Tears** (written by Don Covay); after **Operator,** a less than convincing follow-up, George left the group and they have continued ever since as a quartet.

At this point, the group's affairs ebbed; Gladys, who was pregnant, went back home to her husband in Atlanta, while the Pips did sessions as back-up singers.

Gladys returned to the fold in 1963, and in the summer of that year the group had another hit with Van McCoy's **Giving Up,** but after this their fortunes were handicapped by the financial insolvency of their record company; nevertheless, they had by now developed their stage set into something special, and were one of the most sought-after acts on the R&B circuit; after being booked on a Motown tour package, they were offered a contract by Berry Gordy at Motown. They voted three to one to accept it.

It was their stint at Motown (where they recorded for the subsidiary Soul label) that really established them with a wide audience. Their initial releases – **Just Walk In My Shoes** and **Take Me In Your Arms And Love Me** – evoked murmurs of approval from critics, though without commensurate commercial success, before Gladys' powerhouse vocalising on Norman Whitfield/Barrett Strong composition **I Heard It Through The Grapevine,** took them right to top of U.S. charts; their follow-up, **The End Of Our Road,** was equally torrid and equally successful.

After her years of experience as a gospel singer, Gladys was establishing herself as one of the most fervent female vocalists in contemporary music – though she was aided by her instinctive rapport with the Pips, who were no redundant back-up group (a role to which, say, the other Supremes were often relegated when Diana Ross was singing), but had developed a keen appreciation of supporting harmonies. In addition, their choreography on stage was never less than absolutely sharp. Other million-sellers for the group while at Motown included **Friendship Train** and **If I Were Your Woman.**

*Second Anniversary.
Courtesy Pye Records.
The fourth gold for Buddah.*

In 1972 her version of Kris Kristofferson's **Help Me Make It Through The Night** (with a spoken intro, a gambit she was to employ quite regularly) reached No. 33 in U.S., and made the Top 10 in the U.K.; despite this consistent recording success, and the status of the band as a live act, she and the Pips were itching to leave Motown, where they claimed they'd always been treated as second-string artists. Even the memory of their major success, **I Heard It Through The Grapevine,** had been expunged when the song had been even more

successfully recorded by one of Motown's favourite sons, Marvin Gaye (♦).

Ironically, they had another major chart success, with Jim Weatherley's **Neither One Of Us,** just as they were leaving the company; but their decision to move has nevertheless been retrospectively justified by their phenomenal success at Buddah Records.

Their first album, **Imagination,** probably lacked the technical proficiency of the Motown production team, but it more than compensated for this by the strength of the material and the quality of Gladys' vocals. The album went platinum some months after its release and spawned three gold singles – **Midnight Train To Georgia, I've Got To Use My Imagination** and **Best Thing That Ever Happened To Me.** It had been a long, 20-year haul, but finally, in 1973, they were just about the most commercially successful vocal group in America.

Strangely, Motown ran Buddah neck and neck initially; they issued an album with **Neither One Of Us** as the title track, and also extracted a further single in **Daddy Could Swear, I Declare** (written by the group with Johnny Bristol); that went gold, too, but Motown's releases of Pips' material since, **A Little Knight Music** and **All I Need Is Time,** have hardly shown the group to their best advantage.

In 1974 they joined forces with Curtis Mayfield (♦) on the soundtrack to the movie "Claudine"; though the venture was not as successful as the sum of their talents would have led one to expect, the album nevertheless went gold, as did the single **On And On.**

Success has continued to be virtually automatic. Another major hit was **The Way We Were,** recorded live in a Detroit club. It showed that Gladys has been able to ride two horses. Though some of the group's material is obviously suited to the lucrative supper-club circuit, equally her vocals can still be wonderfully gutsy, to provide some of the most exhilarating moments in contemporary music – as numbers like **I Feel A Song** demonstrate.

Now married for a second time, Gladys lives in Detroit with her three children. Her husband, a social-worker turned film-producer, has produced "Pipe Dreams", the film in which Gladys makes her acting debut; she and the Pips – who do not appear in the film – also recorded the soundtrack.

All the group's albums on Buddah have gone gold (at least); they have also received two Grammy awards.

Discography is selective.

Recordings:
Neither One Of Us (Soul/Tamla Motown)
Imagination (Buddah)
Claudine (Soundtrack) (Buddah)
I Feel A Song (Buddah)
Second Anniversary (Buddah)
Compilations:
Gladys Knight And The Pips (Springboard/DJM)
Anthology (Soul/Tamla Motown)
The Best Of Gladys Knight And The Pips (Buddah)

Kokomo

Alan Spenner bass, vocals
Neil Hubbard guitar, vocals
Mel Collins saxes
John Sussewell drums
Frank Collins vocals
Paddy McHugh vocals
Dyan Birch vocals
Tony O'Malley piano, vocals

Along with Average White Band (♦), prime exponents of British soul. Originally a 10-piece, included all the above with the exception of American-born Sussewell who replaced founder-drummer Terry Stannard. Other founders who departed after first album are Jim Mullen (gtr) and Jody Linscott (congas).

*Kokomo. Courtesy
CBS Records.*

In its original formation, in May 1973, Kokomo drew its personnel from a number of now-defunct U.K. bands – viz. Hubbard and Spenner from the Grease Band, McHugh, Birch, O'Malley and Frank Collins from pop outfit Arrival (they had two U.K. hits in 1970 with **Friends** and **I Will Survive**). Mel Collins had been working sessions prior to Kokomo, but was previously with King Crimson and Chapman-Whitney Streetwalkers.

Signed to Pink Floyd manager Steve O'Rourke, built early reputation playing small venues until release of first album in 1975, hailed by U.K. rock press as best debut by a British band for several years. Inspired by the tight, disciplined playing of Spenner and Hubbard, Kokomo is unusual (among white soul bands anyway) for its use of four featured vocalists, i.e. the ex-Arrival foursome. Band also contains in-depth compositional strength. Second album released January 1976.

Recordings:
Kokomo (Columbia/CBS)
Rise And Shine (Columbia/CBS)

Al Kooper

To one generation probably best known for his super-sessioning and as the man who played the influential organ parts on the seminal Bob Dylan works **Like A Rolling Stone** and **Blonde On Blonde**; to another for his production credits with '70s bands such as Lynyrd Skynyrd and The Tubes.

Born Brooklyn, New York, Feb 5, 1944 he had learned piano and guitar by the age of 13 when he turned-up as a member of the group The Royal Teens, who had a U.S. smash 1958 with the novelty song **Short Shorts.** Subsequently moved towards session-work, record-engineering and song-writing. He took third of the composition credit on the Gary Lewis And The Playboys 1965 million-seller **This Diamond Ring.**

Still, there was nothing there yet to suggest that he would next emerge in the company of Bob Dylan. Legend has it that Kooper somehow inveigled his way into Dylan's studio circle during re-cording of what many regard as the best single of all time, **Like A Rolling Stone** (1965). Kooper apparently turned up with his guitar but found that Mike Bloom-field (♦) had already copped that gig; instead Kooper persuaded producer Tom Wilson to let him play an organ that was languish-ing in one corner of the studio. It was arranged that Kooper's playing did not come over the intercoms to the other musicians. However, when Dylan listened to the playback he insisted that the organ be brought from the back of the mix to the fore, and Kooper was asked to stay around for the rest of the **Highway 61** sessions.

During this same period Kooper was among backing musicans at Dylan's controversial 1965 New-port Folk Festival appearance. (He also worked on Dylan's **Blonde On Blonde** in 1966 and **New Morning** in 1970.)

His work with Dylan thus en-hancing reputation, Kooper next formed seminal New York outfit Blues Project (♦) with Steve Katz, before both left to similarly assist formation of Blood Sweat & Tears (♦). The apochryphal story here is that Kooper originally assembl-ed them to play a gig to fund a projected but aborted trip to U.K. That notwithstanding, he helped select musicians for BS&T, played on and produced their highly-acclaimed **Child Is Father To The Man** (1968) debut album before going own way to join Columbia as a producer.

One of his first projects was **Super Session** (1968), a jam album featuring himself with guitarists Mike Bloomfield and Steve Stills (♦). This became one of bestselling American albums of that year, resulting in a series of concert appearances, and a "fol-low-up" with Bloomfield, **The Live Adventures Of Al Kooper And Mike Bloomfield** (1969).

Aside from these activities and his continuing session-work on keyboards and guitar for likes of Dylan, Stones (**Let It Bleed**), Jimi Hendrix (**Electric Ladyland**), B.B. King and Taj Mahal, Kooper acted as producer for Don Ellis Band and recorded a string of largely mediocre solo albums, of which the 1970 **Easy Does It** is generally regarded as the best. (The 1969 **Kooper Session** found him introducing the guitar talents of 15-year old Shuggie Otis, son of R&B vet Johnny Otis.)

Of late, through his own Sounds Of The South label, Kooper has been primarily based in Atlanta acting as producer to various Southern acts, e.g. Lynyrd Sky-nyrd (♦). Also produced The Tubes' (♦) 1975 debut album and Nils Lofgren's 1976 set **Cry Tough.**

It is largely through his associa-tions with Dylan, Blues Project, and early BS&T that the contro-versial, often heavily-criticised Kooper earns his place in rock's hall of fame. That aside, he re-mains one of the most gifted (if thoroughly inconsistent) minor talents in rock.

Recordings:
Al Kooper And Steve Katz (Verve)
Super Session (With Bloomfield, Stills) (Columbia/CBS)
I Stand Alone (Columbia/CBS)
The Live Adventures Of Al Kooper And Mike Bloomfield (Columbia/CBS)
You Never Know Who Your Friends Are (Columbia/CBS)
Kooper Session (Columbia/CBS)
Easy Does It (Columbia/CBS)
The Landlord (Soundtrack) (United Artists)
New York City (Columbia/CBS)
A Possible Projection Of The Future/Childhood's End (Columbia/CBS)
Naked Songs (Columbia/CBS)
Compilation:
Al's Big Deal/Unclaimed Freight (Columbia/CBS)

Alexis Korner

One of the "founding fathers" of British rock, Korner was born in Paris 1928 of an Austrian father and Greek/Turkish mother. Much of his early childhood was spent on the move throughout Europe before the family settled in England in the mid-'30s. Alexis had started learning piano and musical theory from the age of five.

Towards the end of the '40s, Korner found work in various roles within the music business, while playing semi-pro as a musician in the evenings. His interests were in jazz, which led to the first of his associations with bandleader Chris Barber. He subsequently attempted to form his own jazz band, returned for another stint with Barber, follow-ing which he met up with har-monica player Cyril Davies.

Korner's interests were by now veering towards the blues, a form at that time almost totally ignored outside of black ghettos in the States, and in Davies he found a like-minded spirit.

At the close of the '50s the pair of them attempted to create an audience for their music, opening the London Blues And Barrelhouse Club for Thursday night sessions at the Roundhouse pub in Soho. But largely because London wasn't yet ready for this "new" music – a mix of blues, jazz and R&B – Korner (with Davies in tow) found himself back again with Barber by the end of the decade.

Barber, though, was by now making his own excursions into R&B; specifically a "set-within-a-set" in which Korner and Davies backed singer Ottilie Paterson. Featured as the finale to Barber's act, it showed signs of growing popularity . . .so much so that in 1961 Korner and Davies decided to form an R&B group of their own: the legendary Blues Incorporated.

There remained one problem, however. At that time, the British club circuit was still dominated by traditional ("trad") jazz, and

Top right: Alexis Korner, a founding father of U.K. rock.

Right: Back Street Crawler. Courtesy Island Records.

KOSSOFF

Back Street Crawler

Korner and Davies found strong opposition to their amplified music – just as Muddy Waters had when he first played electric blues in 1958.

Their solution, once again, was to create their own venue. This time, though the circuit may not have been ready, the audiences certainly were. The Ealing Rhythm & Blues Club was opened Mar 17, 1962, in a basement beneath a tea-shop near the local underground station. Blues Incorporated's line-up on that first night, apart from Korner and Davies, comprised Keith Scott (pno), Andy Hoogenboom (bs), Charlie Watts (drms) and Art Wood (vcls).

Of these only Charlie Watts went on to achieve lasting fame (with the Rolling Stones), but before long Jack Bruce had come in on bass, Dick Heckstall-Smith was playing tenor sax and Ginger Baker (replacing Watts) was on drums. Davies left in November 1962 to start his own Cyril Davies All Stars (♦ Cyril Davies).

One of the first white electric blues bands in the world, their reputation spread rapidly. Soon the Ealing basement had given way to the more central Marquee Club, and a host of aspirant musicians were jostling with the punters eager to discover and learn from this new musical hybrid.

Korner was leader and guitarist, leaving most of the vocals to future stars such as Mick Jagger, Eric Burdon, Paul Jones and Long John Baldry while the constantly flexible line-up also introduced the embryonic instrumental expertise of Graham Bond, Keith Richard, Brian Jones, Lee Jackson, Phil Seaman, John McLaughlin, John Surman, Davy Graham and dozens more. All were influenced by Korner's faith in R&B – the original Rolling Stones (♦) first came together to "dep" for Blues Incorporated at The Marquee when the rest of the parent band were doing a radio broadcast.

For further details of this period ♦ British R&B.

However, as acknowledged in that entry, few of the founders of British R&B enjoyed success comparative to that of those who learned from them. Although it's true that Korner never put himself out to make commercial records, the boom that produced the Stones, The Yardbirds, The Animals, Cream, Manfred Mann, etc., largely passed him by.

For a time in the mid-'60s Korner puzzled aficionados by withdrawing from performing to work in children's TV along with Danny Thompson (bs) and Terry Cox (drms) – these two later of Pentangle (♦). When he did return to gigs in 1967 it was with the short-lived Free At Last – the line-up included Marsha Hunt and Victor Brox – and was significant only in that it featured Korner stepping out for the first time as featured vocalist. The rest of 1967–68 saw him working in duos with first Victor Brox and subsequently Robert Plant, later of Led Zeppelin.

During 1968 Korner toured Scandinavia with Danish singer Peter Thorup and Danish band The Beefeaters. On return to England in 1969 he formed New Church in which he shared vocals with Thorup and his teenage daughter Sappho Korner, bassist Colin Hodgkinson (later of Back Door) being among the back-up musicians. Though popular in Europe, the outfit's only memorable British gig was as one of support acts to the Rolling Stones on the 1969 Hyde Park concert.

On disbandment of New Church late 1970, Korner continued his association with Thorup, the pair of them linking with producer Mickie Most (♦) and musical director/composer John Cameron to create the studio big band CCS (Collective Consciousness Society). In late 1970, CCS had a sizeable British hit with their version of the Led Zeppelin monster **Whole Lotta Love** (the track has since become the theme music for BBC-TV's "Top Of The Pops"). Suddenly, at the age of 42, Alexis Korner had got himself on the charts, his first real commercial success. Follow-up CCS singles, **Walking** and **Tap Turns On The Water** (both 1971), were even more successful – but after that the project slowly disintegrated.

In 1972, during American tour, Korner formed yet another group Snape with Thorup and former members of King Crimson, Mel Collins (sx), Ian Wallace (drms) and Boz Burrell (bs), the last-named now with Bad Company. They backed him on the 1973-released **Accidentally Born In New Orleans** album, but the group disbanded after only a few months together.

Since the late '60s, Korner's bear-growl of a voice had made him much in demand for TV commercials, and his earnings from this source have allowed his musical philosophy to remain comparatively free of financial imperatives – while also probably providing him with a lucrative source of income for years to come.

In addition to aforementioned activities, Korner was also directly involved in the formation of Free (♦).

His most recent release, **Get Off My Cloud** (1975), features back-up from Keith Richard, Steve Marriott, Peter Frampton, Kokomo, Nicky Hopkins and Colin Hodgkinson.

The following is a selective discography.

Recordings:
The Legendary Cyril Davies With Alexis Korner's Breakdown Group And The Roundhouse Jug Four (—/Folklore)
R&B From The Marquee (—/Ace of Clubs)
Alexis Korner's Blues Incorporated (—/Ace of Clubs)
Alexis Korner And New Church – Both Sides (Metronome – Continental release only)
Alexis (—/RAK)
Accidentally Born In New Orleans (—/Transatlantic)
Get Off My Cloud (Columbia/CBS)
Compilation:
Bootleg Him (RAK)

Paul Kossoff

The son of British character actor David Kossoff, he was born Hampstead, London, Sep 14, 1950 and was guitarist for Free (♦) from formation in 1968 to his departure prior to that now-defunct band's final 1973 album. It was in last years of Free that Kossoff first began a protracted battle against personal problems – serious drug addiction and a series of related illnesses.

These took him completely out of the rock business for two years after recording of first solo album **Back Street Crawler** (1973). He didn't return to public eye until spring 1975 British tour accompanying singer/songwriter John Martyn, after which he set about assembling his own band – using name of debut album – with Newcastle-born Terry Wilson-Slesser (vcls), New Yorker Mike Montgomery (kybds) and Texans Tony Braunagel (drms) and Terry Wilson (bs).

Above: Paul Kossoff.

Second album, credited to Back Street Crawler, released mid-1975. However, a projected autumn tour was postponed when Kossoff suffered a serious heart attack which almost cost him his life. After spending a week on the critical list he made a swift recovery (aided by the devoted attentions of his father) and was able to play three gigs in late November.

Doctors would not allow him to play any more dates at that time, but in early 1976 he was given the all-clear to set-up a full-scale spring U.K. tour for the band (due to begin Apr 25). However, on Mar 19, 1976, Kossoff died in his sleep on a 'plane taking him to New York for discussions with Atlantic Records' executives. He had apparently suffered a recurrence of his heart ailment.

Kossoff was a talented guitarist and composer, and his was a major contribution to Free. However, more than anything else, his death was a tragedy for his father, who had coaxed him through four or five years of addiction and illness and seemed to the last to have saved his son from drugs and himself.

2nd Street (1976), group's second album, dedicated to Kossoff.

Recordings:
Back Street Crawler (Island)
The Band Plays On (Atco/Atlantic)

Leo Kottke

Born Athens, Georgia, into a musical family, (his mother had a Master's degree in music) Kottke moved around the U.S. in his adolescence, and now regards St Cloud, Minnesota, as his home. Started playing guitar in his 'teens, and was influenced by blues singers like Mississippi John Hurt; he also supported people like Son House at gigs. After completing high school, he joined the Submarine Service of U.S. Navy, and during training in Atlantic Ocean his hearing was permanently impaired.

On his discharge, he played clubs in Minneapolis, and in 1970 recorded **Circle Round The Sun,** a thousand copies of which were pressed for a local label, Oblivion, the record being subsequently reissued later that year on Symposium. Meanwhile, Kottke sent some of his tapes to John Fahey (♦) who was favourably impressed, and invited Kottke to record an album for his company, Takoma Records. **Six And Twelve String Guitar** was issued in 1971. In the meantime, Fahey gave Kottke a job as a record-packer so that he could eke out his meagre living from gigs.

Although Kottke lived with Fahey for a time and was considerably influenced by him, he needed to work out a more lucrative record deal, and eventually got one from Capitol Records, for whom he has since recorded, whilst earning a reputation as one of America's leading acoustic guitarists through both his regular live work (in 1975 he played the Cambridge Folk Festival in Britain) and his recordings.

Recordings:
Circle Round The Sun (Symposium/—)
Six And Twelve String Guitar (Takoma/Sonet)
Mudlark (Capitol)
Greenhouse (Capitol)
My Feet Are Smiling (Capitol)
Ice Water (Capitol/—)
Dreams And All That Stuff (Capitol)
Chewing Pine (Capitol)

Kraftwerk

Ralf Hutter vocals, keyboards, string and wind instruments, drums, electronics
Florian Schneider as above

Kraftwerk began as one of Connie Plank's German groups, recording in his studio in middle of an oil refinery in Dusseldorf, surrounded by hissing, smoke and fire.

They reflect this heavy industrial environment in long production-line tracks which characterise their work. As Organisation, Hutter and Schneider were part of five-piece band, heavily influenced by Pink Floyd and early Tangerine Dream. In 1970 RCA released **Tone Float** by Organisation which, though not electronic, shows by its long percussion tracks which direction group was to take.

Ralf and Florian broke away and formed Kraftwerk – it means Powerplant. In 1972 came double-set **Kraftwerk** composed of their first two German albums, and it is here that the huge influence of John Cage, Terry Riley, Karl-heinz Stockhausen, as well as continuing influence of Floyd, can be seen. The albums are filled with harsh, mechanised sounds of heavy industry, the eaeryday reality of modern German life: sudden noises, unidentifiable bangings. They use the studio to make phase-shifts, speed-up tapes and treat their sounds. Both albums are highly experimental and show group finding their feet among new electronic elements at their disposal.

Ralf And Florian (1973) was produced by them, though with Connie Plank still engineering. This was much more exuberant, enthusiastic album with fresh surface texture and strong beat. It led straight to their most commercially successful realisation: **Autobahn** established group in U.S. and U.K. A single cut down from 22-minute original track made charts and group enjoyed both FM avant-garde sponsorship and AM ''easy listening'' audiences in U.S., a cross-over feat only matched by Mike Oldfield's **Tubular Bells**. Unfortunately Kraftwerk did not benefit directly from this success, having sold complete rights on album to Phonogram for two thousand dollars in 1971.

For **Autobahn** they added two members to line-up: Klaus Roeder (violin, gtr) and Wolfgang Flur (pcsn). Flur remained for their follow-up **Radio Activity** but Roeder was replaced by Karl Bartos, the two of them playing ''electronic pads'' rather than conventional percussion instruments.

Radio Activity is a curious album, being at first ''concept'' follow-up of straightforward commercial nature with lots of references to their successful **Autobahn**, and loaded with puns and easy-listening electronics, but by Side 2 the album breaks down into more obscurantist use of radio call signals, overlapping tapes and celestial interference patterns. The precise clean beat of the electronic pads simulates gadget-ridden advanced technological environment that their fans presumably live in.

Recordings:
Kraftwerk (Vertigo)
Ralf And Florian (Vertigo)
Autobahn (Vertigo)
Radio Activity (Capitol)
Compilation:
Exceller 8 (Vertigo)

Kris Kristofferson

Born Brownsville Texas on Jun 22, 1936, Kristofferson moved to California while he was at high school, and seemed all set for an academic career when he received a Ph.D. from Pomona College, and went to England to attend Oxford University on a Rhodes scholarship in 1958. He was studying English literature, and had ambitions to be a writer himself, but his early manuscripts were rejected. While at university, though, he began writing songs, and was signed by Tommy Steele's manager and became Kris Carson.

After Oxford, he joined the army, went to jump school, ranger school, flight school, and became a pilot, settling in Germany flying helicopters. He stayed in the army for five years.

During his third year in Germany, Kristofferson played army clubs and resumed songwriting. He sent some material to a friend's relative, songwriter/publisher Marijohn Wilkin in Nashville, and on returning to

America, turned down the opportunity to teach literature at West Point (the American military training college) after meeting Johnny Cash and deciding to concentrate on his songwriting career.

Above: Kris Kristofferson.

To this end, he moved to Nashville in 1965, where his first professional job for Columbia Records was cleaning their local studios. (It was a job in which he was succeeded by Billy Swan (➧).) For years he took temporary jobs while trying to get his songs accepted. Short of money and living in a Nashville tenement, he was about to take a job as a construction worker when Roger Miller decided to record one of his songs, **Me And Bobby McGee**. Miller helped to bring the song to some attention, though it was not until Janis Joplin's version posthumously went to No. 1 in the U.S. charts that the song became indelibly printed on the public consciousness.

Kristofferson finally received a recording contract from Monument and in 1970 released his debut album, **Me And Bobby McGee**, and also brought his touring band to Britain to play the Isle of Wight festival. Though virtually unknown then, his fame spread quickly, partly through his own album releases, partly through the success of his songs

Me And Bobby McGee and **Help Me Make It Through The Night**, both of which were recorded by a variety of artists. (The latter was creatively used as the theme song for the movie ''Fat City''.) In 1973, Kristofferson was reportedly selling more records for Columbia than Bob Dylan.

In 1973 he also married Rita Coolidge (➧) in Los Angeles, and the two ran parallel careers as solo artists and in tandem. They pooled their bands for touring purposes, and made two albums together – **Full Moon** and **Breakaway**. They also appeared together in Sam Peckinpah's film ''Pat Garratt And Billy The Kid''. Kristofferson's film career, in fact, burgeoned alongside his singing one. Apart from ''Pat Garrett'', he had starring roles in ''Cisco Pike'' and ''Alice Doesn't Live Here Anymore'', and also wrote the score for Dennis Hopper's ''The Last Movie''.

Recordings:
Me And Bobby McGee (Monument)
The Silver Tongued Devil And I (Monument)
Border Lord (Monument)
Jesus Was A Capricorn (Monument)
Spooky Lady's Sideshow (Monument)
Who's To Bless And Who's To Blame? (Monument)
With Rita Coolidge:
Full Moon (A&M)
Breakaway (Monument)

Kursaal Flyers

Paul Shuttleworth vocals
Richie Bull banjo, bass, vocals
Graeme Douglas guitar
Will Birch drums
Vic Collins steel guitar

An out-take of both the Southend/Canvey Island scene (Dr Feelgood, Mickey Jupp Band, etc.) and

Below: Jesus Was A Capricorn. Courtesy Monument, CBS. Kristofferson appears on the sleeve of this 1973 release with singer Rita Coolidge, whom he married later the same year.

the London and south-east pub-rock circuit, the Kursaal Flyers became such in early 1974 – taking name from one of the more daring ''rides'' in Southend's Kursaal amusement park. Shuttleworth, Birch and Douglas had first come together in 1970-formed Surly Bird.

As Kursaals, first broke through locally with residency at Southend's Blue Boar pub, following which their reputation and engagements spread through southeast and thence nationally, culminating in a signing to Jonathan King's (➧) UK Records.

Their music broadly rock 'n' roll with country and theatrical leanings also evinces a certain degree of wit and, by 1976, despite the somewhat disappointing debut album **Chocs Away** (1975) they had earned reputation as one of the brightest of the new British hopes.

Recordings:
Chocs Away (—/UK)
The Great Artiste (—/UK)

Jim Kweskin (Jug Band)

Jim Kweskin guitar, vocals
Geoff Muldaur washboard, guitar, kazoo, vocals
Maria d'Amato kazoo, vocals
Bill Keith banjo, pedal steel
Richard Greene fiddle
Fritz Richmond jug, washtub bass

The Jug Band were an assortment of folkies who got together in Cambridge, Massachusetts, at the suggestion of Albert Grossman (➧). Their essential character lay in the spontaneity and vitality of their live performance, as they banged, plucked or scraped anything that came to hand to entertain the masses with goodtime and ragtime music. Never successfully captured on record (though several attempts were made), the band fell apart in 1968 as haphazardly as it had come together.

Geoff and Maria got married, and ultimately became the most successful alumni (Geoff Muldaur, Maria Muldaur ➧), Greene, who had only joined towards the end, threw in his lot with the West Coast group Seatrain (➧) in 1969. Keith and Richmond both turned to sessions, while Kweskin himself became a convert to Mel Lyman's authoritarian religious sect (Lyman, a harmonica player, had briefly been involved with the band).

LaBelle

Patti Labelle vocals
Nona Hendryx vocals
Sarah Dash vocals

Originally Patti LaBelle and the Bluebelles – Patti coming from Philadelphia (the mother of two, she's married to a local schoolteacher), the others from New Jersey – they were an archtypal Atlantic soul outfit who had a run of American hits between 1963–66 with cuts such as **I Sold My Heart To The Junkman, Down The Aisle** and **Danny Boy**. The group was a quartet then, Cindy Birdsong leaving in 1967 to re-

Arthur Lee
◆ Love

Jerry Leiber & Mike Stoller

Leiber and Stoller were arguably the most important and influential songwriting/production team that flourished on the American R&B scene in the '50s and early '60s. Stoller supplied a whole string of instantly memorable tunes, while Leiber added the observant and witty lyrics. It was through their initial work for The Coasters (particularly **Riot In Cell Block No. 9**) that the pair became well known, and ultimately contracted to Atlantic, where they continued to work very successfully with The Coasters (◆), and also created some of The Drifters' (◆) most seminal work (notably **There Goes My Baby**) and Ben E. King's **Stand By Me**.

They also wrote **Hound Dog** for Willie Mae Thornton; the song was subsequently covered by Elvis Presley, which secured them a contract to write material for the Presley movies "Loving You" and "Jailhouse Rock".

After a period of relative inactivity, they revived their successful partnership in the '70s, with some work for Stealers Wheel (◆) which resulted in the worldwide hit, **Stuck In The Middle With You** (1973). They also restored Procol Harum to the U.K. singles charts with **Pandora's Box,** a track from the album **Procol's Ninth,** which had been produced by Leiber and Stoller, and to which they contributed only a solitary composition – **I Keep Forgetting.**

John Lennon

Although McCartney had been the first to positively leave The Beatles, Lennon had been the one who'd consistently issued commercial singles of his own (under the guise of the Plastic Ono Band) while the band were still officially functioning as a unit.

His first was **Give Peace A Chance,** recorded with Yoko Ono and assorted hangers-on in a Toronto hotel bedroom. Intended as a contemporary pacifist anthem – a function it perfectly fulfilled – it was the first indication on record of Lennon's post-**Revolution** volte-face.

No doubt this could be attributed to his increasing involvement with Japanese media-person Yoko Ono (whom he married in Gibraltar in 1969), as could his increasing interest in avant-garde musical forms, to which **Unfinished Music No. 1 – Two Virgins** (1968) (on the cover of which they both appeared stark naked), **Unfinished Music No. 2 – Life With The Lions** (1969) and **The Wedding Album** (1969) now bear witness. They developed along even more abstract lines the type of thinking

Right: John Lennon. His lengthy battle with U.S. immigration authorities ended in victory July 1976.

that Lennon had first applied to **Revolution No. 9** on the Beatles' White Album.

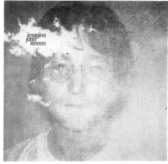

Imagine. Courtesy Apple/EMI Records.

By way of contrast, Lennon then formed a scratch group in September 1969 to play rock 'n' roll revival festival in Toronto. The line-up of himself, Yoko, Eric Clapton (gtr), Alan White (drms) and Klaus Voormann (bs) thus became the first incarnation proper of the Plastic Ono Band – though Lennon was to continue to use the name for whatever group of musicians were working for him at a particular time. **Plastic Ono Band – Live Peace In Toronto** (1969) offers recorded highlights of this gig; at least one side is excellent hardcore rock.

Nevertheless the 1970 **John Lennon/Plastic Ono Band** was the first real Lennon solo album, and many still consider it his best. It was quite stark musically (the Plastic Ono Band here referred to Voormann (bs), Ringo Starr (drms), and Yoko Ono (wind), and frighteningly intense – evidently Lennon's cathartic reaction to the years of Beatlemania – with audio-group therapy techniques and primal screams galore. Other writers have licked their emotional wounds in public before, but few have done it as harrowingly and compellingly as here.

Other contender for Lennon's best is **Imagine** (1971), which largely followed the highly personal approach used on **John Lennon/Plastic Ono Band,** but with less harshness and greater melodicism. The title track is outstanding and his most distinctive composition since break-up of Beatles. A contemporary hit single in the States at the time, it was not issued in Britain until November 1975 when it effortlessly made the Top 5.

Imagine also contained a controversial and acrimonious attack on McCartney, **How Do You Sleep?,** and this period marked the nadir of relationships between the two.

Production on **John Lennon/Plastic Ono Band, Imagine** and subsequent albums has largely followed devices of vast, intricate Phil Spector (◆) mixes and lavish reverb; to which, for **Some Time In New York City** (1972) Lennon added the use of orchestration in the shape of Elephant's Memory, the New York-based band led by Stan Bronstein whose

main claim to fame before that had been the music they contributed to the "Midnight Cowboy" soundtrack.

Musically **Some Time In New York City** has moments of magnificence, but it was received with hostility by critics who objected to its glib politicising and over-dependence on slogans, cliches and annoyingly insistent repetition. It was also handicapped by the frequent use of Yoko's vocals (this album represented the largest role she has ever taken on one of John's works) and failed to sell encouragingly.

Subsequent releases revealed a Lennon chastened not only by an adverse press, but also by his separation from his wife. **Mind Games** (1973) ditched the quasi-revolutionary fervour, and was an attempted return to melodicism of **Imagine,** but it was nevertheless lightweight and unconvincing. **Walls And Bridges** (1974) did something to restore his reputation, though it was hardly a vital contribution to contemporary music, and it was 1975 which saw Lennon in clover again.

Rock 'n' Roll was a pet project Lennon had worked on intermittently for the previous two years. It is illuminated by his fond memory and his evident enthusiasm, and is one of the most successful albums of its type. At the end of year, he collected his single releases together in **Shaved Fish** which showed that, in this area at least, he'd been the most productive of the four ex-Beatles. The

year 1975 brought him further good news, for he was reunited with Yoko Ono, who gave him a son, and, after a five-year legal battle, was finally granted a Green Card by the U.S. Supreme Court, which gave him the right of entry to the U.S.

Some Time In New York City. Courtesy Apple/EMI Records.

Though he has not managed to return to the sardonicism and surrealism of the past, his career now seems buoyant again. On past achievements alone, Lennon ranks as one of the two most important and influential modern composers of the last 20 years.

Recordings:
Unfinished Music No. 1 – Two Virgins (Apple)
Unfinished Music No. 2 – Life With The Lions (Zapple)
The Wedding Album (Apple)
Plastic Ono Band – Live Peace In Toronto (Apple)
John Lennon/Plastic Ono Band (Apple)
Imagine (Apple)
Some Time In New York City (Apple)
Mind Games (Apple)
Walls And Bridges (Apple)
Rock 'n' Roll (Apple)
Compilation:
Shaved Fish (Apple)

Deke Leonard
➡ Man

Jerry Lee Lewis

Born Ferriday, Louisiana, Sep 29, 1935, Lewis was taught piano by his father, Elmo. It is said that when Jerry Lee was eight his parents mortgaged their house to buy him a 900-dollar piano, and lost their home when they couldn't meet the repayments.

In his early 'teens, Lewis studied to be a minister at the Assembly of God Institute, Wazahatchie, Texas, but he became homesick and returned to Ferriday. He played in the school orchestra, then became a professional nightclub entertainer, specialising mainly in gospel material.

After the success of Elvis Presley at Sun Records, Lewis sought an audition there, and his audition tape became his first Sun release, **Crazy Arms.** His second release was **Whole Lotta Shakin' Goin' On** (1957), which reached No. 3 in the U.S. and No. 8 in the U.K., and earned him a gold disc.

His follow-up, **Great Balls Of Fire,** was even more successful (No. 2 in U.S., No. 1 in U.K.), and

he was firmly established as rock 'n' roll's most frenetic pianist. His guest spots in the films "Disc Jockey Jamboree" and "High School Confidential" spread his fame wider. If Presley was the sex symbol of rock 'n' roll, Lewis was without doubt the wildest white performer; blatantly arrogant, he hollered the lyrics while almost demolishing the piano with a sustained, boogie-styled assault.

At height of his success in 1958, Lewis visited Britain, having just married his 13-year old cousin, and was met with a barrage of criticism and not allowed to perform in the U.K. The incident virtually ruined his career; since the marriage lasted 13 years, Lewis probably had good reason to feel ill-treated.

Though Lewis continued to make the charts (and a 1961 version of **What'd I Say?** was especially good), his career was obviously on the decline. In 1963 he left Sun, and eventually signed for Smash, a subsidiary of Mercury, where he had some success as a contemporary country artist, though he never emulated his achievement at Sun.

His appearance at 1969 Toronto Rock 'n' Roll Revival Show restored him to some prominence as both concert star and recording artist, but he could not dispel the reputation he'd acquired for being a hard-drinking womaniser and an arrogant eccentric; even a starring role in Jack Good's Los Angeles stage production of "Catch My Soul" did little to redress the tarnished image.

Although Lewis did not manage to grow old gracefully, he does retain a cult following of rabidly loyal fans, who still believe that "rock 'n' roll's the thing, and Jerry Lee's the King". Certainly, Lewis has a piano style that was, and is, unique.

He has had his share of family tragedy: two of his children have been killed – one drowned, and one died in a car accident.

Discography is selective; all his greatest recordings were made for the Sun label. **The Best Of Jerry Lee Lewis** is merely the best of his later, country material. **Rare Jerry Lee Lewis, Vols I & II** were issued in Britain only in 1975, being tapes almost 20 years old that had never previously seen the light of day.

Recordings:
Original Golden Hits, Vols I-III (Sun)
Rare Jerry Lee Lewis, Vols I & II (—/Charly)
Rockin' Up A Storm (—/Sun)
The Greatest Live Show On Earth (Smash/Philips)
Country Songs For City Folks (Smash/Philips)
The Best Of Jerry Lee Lewis (Mercury)
The Killer Rocks On (Mercury)

Linda Lewis

Born in docklands area of London's East End, trained as actress from early age and had small cameo roles in number of British movies. Leaving convent school, she sang first with John Lee Hooker, then Herbie Goins And The Nightimers before two-year stint with Ferris Wheel.

In 1970 decided to go it alone as

singer/songwriter, in which role she was signed by Warner Bros who released debut solo album in 1971. Developed writing abilities on **Lark** (1972), produced by her boyfriend Jim Cregan, ex of Family and now with Cockney Rebel. In early 1973 she played extensive club tour of U.S., making debut in U.K. singles lists on return with **Rock-A-Doodle-Doo.** **Fathoms Deep** was released early 1974, produced again by Cregan, after which she went on exhaustive world tour as support to Cat Stevens. In 1975 signed to Clive Davis' Arista label and recorded **Not A Little Girl Any More** in London and New York. From latter sessions came remake of Betty Everett soul cut **It's In His Kiss,** her second U.K. hit in June that year.

Somewhat irritatingly coy vocal delivery has met with limited critical favour.

Recordings:
Say No More (Reprise/Warner Bros)
Lark (Reprise/Warner Bros)
Fathoms Deep (Reprise/Raft)
Not A Little Girl Any More (Arista)

Gordon Lightfoot

Canadian singer/songwriter, born circa 1939 in Orillia, Ontario. Emigrated to Los Angeles in 1958 to study orchestration at Westlake College which he left to work as demo singer, arranger, and writer and producer of commercial jingles.

Don Quixote. Courtesy Warner Bros Records.

After listening to Pete Seeger and Bob Gibson in 1960, took up guitar and interest in folk music encouraged by fellow Canadian Ian Tyson (of Ian And Sylvia, the first act to record a Lightfoot song).

His music had distinct country undertones when, in 1963, he worked in Britain, returning to Canadian bar and coffee-house circuit. Subsequently underwent change of compositional direction, like so many others, upon hearing nascent Bob Dylan. Career boosted by signing to management with Albert Grossman (➡), who placed Lightfoot songs **Early Morning Rain** and the U.S. hit single **For Lovin' Me** with one of his other acts, Peter, Paul & Mary.

Released his first album **Lightfoot** in 1966, being voted Canada's top folk-singer same year. Following year was voted Canada's top male vocalist.

He has always been a prolific songwriter (with in excess of 400 compositions to his credit), and

in mid- to late-'60s often forced his pace by locking himself away in hotel rooms for furiously-productive five or six day writing spells. Often these took him to England. In 1967, during one week in the U.K., he is said to have written 15 songs, most of which turned-up on his **Back Here On Earth** collection.

Lightfoot has also been a prolific in-concert performer in his time, working often to a schedule of 70 appearances a year, though in mid-'70s he had slackened off pace in both departments. Then, though he still "took off" specifically to write, he allowed himself lengthier stays and a more relaxed productivity level.

Though never rated in the front rank of contemporary singer/songwriters, and never a particularly fashionable artist, Lightfoot has always been able to shift albums in healthy quantities and has stayed the course better than many. His songs have been extensively covered by likes of Bob Dylan, Judy Collins, Johnny Cash, Glen Campbell, Barbra Streisand, Anne Murray, Richie Havens, Elvis Presley, Waylon Jennings and scores more. Of all his compositions, **Early Morning Rain** and the early '70s American smash **If You Could Read My Mind** probably remain his best known.

United Artists have released several Lightfoot compilations, two of which are listed below. The 1975 Reprise double-set compilation **Gord's Gold** includes **If You Could Read My Mind, Early Morning Rain** and **For Lovin' Me.**

Recordings:
Lightfoot (United Artists)
The Way I Feel (United Artists)
Did She Mention My Name (United Artists)
Back Here On Earth (United Artists)
Sunday Concert (United Artists)
Sit Down Young Stranger (Reprise)
If You Could Read My Mind (Reprise)
Summer Side Of Life (Reprise)
Don Quixote (Reprise)
Old Dan's Records (Reprise)
Sundown (Reprise)
Cold On The Shoulder (Reprise)
Summertime Dream (Reprise)
Compilations:
The Very Best Of Gordon Lightfoot Vols I & II (United Artists)
Gord's Gold (Reprise)

Lindisfarne

Alan Hull guitar, vocals
Ray Jackson harp, mandolin
Ray Laidlaw drums
Rod Clements bass, violin
Simon Cowe guitar

Formed in Newcastle in 1967 as the Downtown Faction; after two more temporary appellations – The Brethren, and Alan Hull and the Brethren – they became Lindisfarne when they signed to Charisma in 1968. Story goes that Charisma boss Tony Stratton-Smith signed the band because he liked Jackson's harmonica playing.

They established a strong following on college circuit, but it was playing at festivals in U.K. from 1969–70 that really broke the band into the big-time. Their brand of good time folk-rock was particularly suited to open-air events.

Nicely Out Of Tune, their debut album released 1969, was greeted with strong approval from the fans and critics alike, and is still commonly regarded as Lindisfarne's high-water mark. Hull had written many of the songs before the band was formed, while he was working as a nurse in a mental hospital.

However the band recruited Bob Johnston (➡) as their producer in 1970, and they recorded **Fog On The Tyne,** which reached No. 1 in the British albums chart and in addition became the largest-selling album of 1970. The single from the album **Meet Me On The Corner** climbed to No. 5 in the singles chart, after which Charisma re-issued the earlier unsuccessful **Lady Eleanor,** which this time held down the No. 3 spot; despite this formidable success in Britain, however, the band never really broke through in America – **Lady Eleanor** did reach No. 82 in the U.S. Top 100, but that can hardly be described as a breakthrough.

Fog On The Tyne.
Courtesy Charisma Records.

At this point, however, the group faltered, possibly because all the material on the first two albums had been written sometime before the band became a major act. **Dingley Dell** was comprised of fresh material, and, though it was again produced by Johnston, it met with critical disapproval. There had been other problems. Johnston is thought to have wanted to record Hull solo in Nashville, but nothing came of it; also the band were unhappy with Johnston's mix of **Dingley Dell,** and did it again themselves.

In 1973 the original unit split. Clements, Laidlaw and Cowe moved on to form Jack The Lad, a band which itself went through line-up changes (Clements split before the second album was recorded), before proving itself on the club circuit and attracting a staunch following; however after **It's Jack The Lad** (1974) and **The Old Straight Track** (1975), the band were dropped by their record company.

Meanwhile, Hull and Jackson retained the name Lindisfarne and brought in Paul Nichols (drms), Kenny Craddock (kybds), Tommy Duffy (bs) and later Charlie Harcourt (ld gtr); the magic had evaporated however, and though

Right: Little Feat; (left to right) Richard Hayward, Lowell George, Sam Clayton, Kenny Gradney and Bill Payne, (front) Paul Barrere.

the band issued **Happy Daze,** which was actually a promising album, on a new label, Warner Bros. But their spirit was broken. They decided to call it a day soon afterwards.

Hull had issued a solo album **Pipedream** in 1973 (complete with Magritte reproduction on the cover), which helped to enhance his reputation as a songwriter; his second solo album, **Squire,** released in 1975, was often ingenious and entertaining, but it failed to attract widespread attention. By then, the band's large audience of the early '70s had been quite dispelled. The rapid rise and equally rapid fall of Lindisfarne remains one of the mysteries of British rock.

Recordings:
Nicely Out Of Tune
(Elektra/Charisma)
Fog On The Tyne (Elektra/ Charisma)
Dingley Dell (Elektra/ Charisma)
Lindisfarne Live (—/Charisma)
Roll On Ruby (Elektra/ Charisma)
Happy Daze (Elektra/Warner Bros)
Compilation:
Lindisfarne's Finest Hour
(—/Charisma)
Alan Hull:
Pipedream (—/Warner Bros)
Squire (—/Warner Bros)

Little Feat

Lowell George guitar, vocals
Bill Payne keyboards, vocals
Richard Hayward drums, vocals
Paul Barrere guitar, vocals
Sam Clayton congas
Kenny Gradney bass

Formed mid-1970 by Hollywood-born Lowell George after comparatively undistinguished spell with Mothers Of Invention – he

Above: Alan Hull, founder member of Lindisfarne.

plays small supporting roles on **Reuben And The Jets** and **Weasels Ripped My Flesh.** The apochrypal story is that George played Frank Zappa a song he'd written, the truckers' anthem **Willin',** which Zappa liked but didn't think was suitable for the Mothers. Instead, he told George he was fired – and to go back to Los Angeles and form his own band.

George took Zappa's advice hitched-up with ex-Mothers bassist Roy Estrada and started auditioning. They first found Richie Hayward, recently departed from The Fraternity Of Man (George had guested on a couple of their album tracks), and then pianist Bill Payne. Zappa's manager Herb Cohen helped finance them on instructions from Uncle Frank, and they took their name, so legend has it, from an aside made by Mothers drummer Jimmy Carl Black.

Thus constituted they cut their debut album **Little Feat** for release in December 1969, which contains the first of band's two versions of **Willin'** – the second is on **Sailin' Shoes.** Producer Russ

Titelman also played piano, other guests including Ry Cooder and Sneaky Pete Kleinow. It was an interesting debut, acclaimed at the time, but the record company's pressing of only 10,000 copies didn't exactly evidence any great faith in the band.

The immeasurably better **Sailin' Shoes** (all bar three songs by Lowell George), in early 1972, again drew apparently little record label support, and made little impact. Produced by Ted Templeman from Harper's Bizarre, this featured the first of Neon Park's three successive, brilliantly-conceived album sleeves and a great deal of extremely inventive but largely ignored music. Not surprisingly it sold in no great quantity, and gave rise to the first of a series of "split" rumours. At one point there was talk of George teaming-up with John Sebastian but the only outcome was that the guitarist played sessions on Sebastian's **The Tarzana Kid.**

Then in 1973 Roy Estrada quit to reappear as Orejon in Captain Beefheart's Magic Band, and in his place came newcomers Paul Barrere, Sam Clayton (brôther of Merry) and Kenny Gradney – this line-up making the excellent **Dixie Chicken** (1973) with guest back-up vocals from Bonnie Bramlett.

Again good reviews but little impact. The Feats teetered for a while on the brink, then broke up; various members turning up on a variety of different albums: George and Hayward on John Cale's **Paris 1919** and Van Dyke Parks' **Discover America;** Payne on the Doobie Brothers **The Captain And Me** and **Toulouse Street;** various Feats on the Bonnie Raitt albums **Taking My Time** and **Streetlights;** George on Robert Palmer's **Sneaking Sally Through The Alley.**

Warner Bros had apparently lost

interest; to all intents and purposes Little Feat had ceased to exist, or might have if co-manager Bob Cavallo hadn't discovered a studio in Maryland cheap enough to support a Little Feat reunion album, the brilliant **Feats Don't Fail Me Now** which appeared at the end of 1974.

Any extra encouragement the band might have needed was supplied when they made their debut in the U.K. early 1975 as part of the Warner Bros European Music Package tour. Appearing second billed to the Doobie Brothers at the London Rainbow, Little Feat blew the headliners clean off-stage, received tumultuous applause, and an almost unprecedented (for a relatively unknown band) wave of press acclaim.

The majestic late 1975 set **The Last Record Album** was widely regarded as one of the finest albums of its year, and this time the Feats even managed to shift enough units in the U.K. and U.S. to scrape into both countries' charts.

All of them exemplary musicians, they are undoubtedly one of the best bands to emerge from the States in the '70s. All albums below, bar the first (which wasn't released in the U.K. until 1975), are highly recommended.

Recordings:
Little Feat (Warner Bros)
Sailin' Shoes (Warner Bros)
Dixie Chicken (Warner Bros)
Feats Don't Fail Me Now (Warner Bros)
The Last Record Album (Warner Bros)

Nils Lofgren

Of Swedish/Italian parentage, grew-up in Chicago and later Maryland, Washington D.C., where as a teenager he played in a succession of bands before forming Grin with Bob Berberich (drms, vcls) and Bob Gordon (bs, vcls). Lofgren himself had something of a whizz-kid reputation as pianist and guitarist (his skills on latter largely inspired by Jimi Hendrix visit to Maryland when Nils was 16) while his younger brother Tom also played guitar in later incarnation of the band.

Before Grin had got round to recording, Lofgren's instrumental expertise had come to the attention of Neil Young (➡) and Danny Whitten's Crazy Horse (➡), the result being a guest spot on the latter's brilliant 1971 debut album.

Lofgren might well have stayed as a permanent member of Crazy Horse had not Whitten's slump into junkiedom subsequently caused that band the first of its many traumas; however, Neil Young also took advantage of his prodigious talents and splashed them liberally over his (Young's) classic **After The Goldrush** album, giving Lofgren his first brief taste of public recognition. He was still just 17.

One result was that Grin did get to sign a record contract, with Columbia subsidiary Spindizzy, for whom they cut a highly-promising debut album in 1971. Then came **1 + 1** (1972), an album which many regard as one of the "lost" classics of rock, but which fell on stony ground at the time.

Thus were Grin plunged into a depressing cycle of playing third-billing on ceaseless tours, always missing out on the commercial breaks essential to their survival. Perhaps due to the frustration caused by apathetic audiences, the third album **All Out** (1972) disappointingly failed to match its predecessors.

Then in 1973 Neil Young came looking for musicians to join his "Tonight's The Night" tour (Nils plays on the album of the same name which appeared in 1975), and since there was virtually nothing happening for Grin, Lofgren had little hesitation in taking up the offer – though he could never have known what a monumentally-bizarre experience he was letting himself in for.

With Young, Lofgren played gigs in the U.S. and U.K. and on completion of the tour returned to Washington to resuscitate Grin. They got a new record deal, with A&M, for whom they recorded **Gone Crazy** at the end of 1973, but this was again comparatively disappointing and was not released outside the U.S. at the time.

By June 1974 Grin had split. Lofgren didn't re-surface again until his 1975 solo album **Nils Lofgren** for A&M, a powerful, widely-acclaimed set that featured Wornell Jones on bass and Aynsley Dunbar on drums. Among much fine material was Lofgren's **Keith Don't Go**, written for Keith Richard, one of his heroes and a prime influence; others, though, have pointed to Hendrix as a stronger source.

Nils Lofgren. Courtesy A&M. Lofgren's first solo LP, in 1975, was widely acclaimed.

Either way, Lofgren had at last produced something to stand beside **1 + 1** and this time looked like getting recognition for it too. Accompanied by brother Tom, 1975 concerts spread cult attention across to wider audience, his growing reputation enhanced by the 1976 **Cry Tough** set produced by Al Kooper.

Perhaps the archtypal punk guitarist, Lofgren's is high energy but disciplined rock 'n' roll, backed by a real flair for composition in the genre. If he'd had to wait a long time for recognition, he had one consolation – in 1976, when **Cry Tough** made the U.S. and U.K. album lists, he was still only 24.

Recordings:
Grin:
Grin (Spindizzy/Epic)
1 + 1 (Spindizzy/Epic)
All Out (Spindizzy/Epic)
Gone Crazy (A&M)
Nils Lofgren:
Nils Lofgren (A&M)
Cry Tough (A&M)

Loggins And Messina

Messina (b. Maywood, California, Dec 5, 1947) was a recording engineer in Hollywood when he met up with Buffalo Springfield (➡), and replaced Bruce Palmer for the band's final album. He was then a founder member of Poco (➡), playing bass and producing the band. He left to work as an independent producer.

*On Stage.
Courtesy CBS Records.*

Loggins (b. Everett, Washington, Jan 7, 1948) was in a band called Second Helping, and then wrote **House At Pooh Corner**, which became a sizeable hit for the Nitty Gritty Dirt Band (➡). He was offered a contract by Columbia, who assigned Messina to produce his debut solo album.

It was then the two joined forces, and Loggins' solo album became Kenny Loggins – with Jim Messina **Sittin' In**, which was released at the same time as the duo's very successful debut gig at the Los Angeles Troubadour, backed by a four-piece band that included Michael Omartian on keyboards. **Sittin' In** included **House At Pooh Corner**, and also **Danny's Song**, which became a U.S. Top 10 hit when it was covered by Anne Murray. The album sold a million, and the partnership has not gone off the gold standard since.

They had a bestselling single themselves in 1972 with **Your Mamma Don't Dance**, taken from their second album, and their strong brand of country-rock, though ultimately somewhat vapid, has become one of America's most commercial sounds. The band have yet to break through in Europe, where they are still virtually unknown.

On Stage, issued in 1974, is a live double album; **So Fine** (1975) is an album composed of their favourite old rock 'n' roll songs.

Recordings:
Sittin' In (Columbia/CBS)
Loggins And Messina (Columbia/CBS)
Full Sail (Columbia/CBS)
On Stage (Columbia/CBS)
Motherlode (Columbia/CBS)
So Fine (Columbia/CBS)
Native Sons (Columbia/CBS)

Love

Arthur Lee guitar, vocals
Bryan MacLean guitar, vocals
John Echols lead guitar
Ken Forssi bass
Alban "Snoopy" Pfisterer drums

Arthur Lee was born and raised in Memphis but moved to Los Angeles where he formed and disbanded a number of groups before Love. One of these was Arthur Lee & The LAGs – the name inspired by his home town band Booker T&The MGs (LAG stood for "Los Angeles Group".) They cut one single for Capitol.

Love were formed Los Angeles 1965 with first four of personnel above plus drummer Don Conka, who was reputedly fired, replaced by Swiss-born Snoopy before first recording. Of others, Echols, like Lee, was born in Memphis, MacLean, a one-time roadie for The Byrds, was a native of Los Angeles; Forssi, formerly with post-hits Surfaris, was from Cleveland.

They were originally known as The Grass Roots until another U.S. band simultaneously appeared with same name. As Love, they made their debut at Los Angeles diner Brave New World spring 1965, and in 1966 had residency at Bido Lito's in Hollywood. In between the two they became a cult attraction. Both Lee and MacLean wrote songs and sung lead, though the former's was always the greater contribution and Love would subsequently become synonymous with Arthur Lee.

They signed to Elektra Records and, in 1965, recorded **Love**, that label's first real excursion into rock, for release early 1966. Produced by Jac Holzman and Mark Abramson, **Love** was a superior debut album. Of the tracks, three were of particular interest. **Signed D.C.** was drug-oriented, the title referring to original drummer Conka. **My Little Red Book** was a Bacharach-David song the group had heard performed by Manfred Mann in "What's New Pussycat?" – in Love's hands, it became an altogether more potent, brooding slice of rock 'n' roll. Also included was their version of the traditional **Hey Joe**, and it has been suggested Love pilfered the idea from The Byrds who had it scheduled for their **Fifth Dimension** album. (The song would later be a huge U.S. hit for The Leaves, and a British smash for

Forever Changes. Courtesy Elektra Asylum Records.

Jimi Hendrix.) **Love** shifted some 150,000 copies which was a good start for an unknown act.

After this, Lee decided Snoopy didn't cut it on drums and switched him to keyboards, bringing in Michael Stuart from Los Angeles unknowns The Sons Of Adam as drummer and augmenting with horn player Tjay Cantrelli.

Then in early 1967 came the brilliant **Da Capo**, which included the classic **Seven And Seven Is** (their second U.S. hit single), **The Castle** and **Stephanie Knows Who** (covered by The Move). On the reverse of this well-programmed, exquisitely-crafted collection of outstanding songs was another "first" – at 20 minutes, **Revelation** took up the whole of Side 2. It was highly adventurous for its time – though not altogether a successful experiment.

However, by the end of the summer, Snoopy had gone altogether, as had Cantrelli.

Towards the end of 1967, the five remaining members then cut the masterful **Forever Changes**, which included **Along Again Or** and **Andmoreagain** and is justly regarded as one of the all-time rock classics. It was to have a considerable influence (Robert Plant, later of Led Zeppelin, was one of the impressionable young British fans of Love).

By the turn of the year Lee had broken the band up – "Those guys couldn't cut it any more", he told a reporter. Instead he pieced together a new Love in 1968 from long-time friend Frank Fayad (bs), George Suranovitch (drms) and Jay Donellan (gtr), plus recording assistance from Jim Hobson (kybds), Paul Martin (gtr), Gary Rowles (gtr) and Drachen Theaker (drms). The last-named was an Englishman, formerly of Crazy World of Arthur Brown (✦), then working sessions in Los Angeles.

This band made **Four Sail** and the patchy double-album **Out Here,** both released 1969 and recorded during same sessions. With Gary Rowles finally replacing Donellan, they toured Britain in 1970 having previously rarely left Los Angeles.

In England Lee teamed-up with an old friend, Jimi Hendrix (✦), and together they cut an album which for legal reasons has never been released. However, one track from this collaboration did "escape", **The Everlasting First,** and turned up on the 1971 **False Start** album. Yet there was a noticeable decline in standard of Love's work post-Elektra, and all of last three mentioned albums were disappointing after group's early substantial promise.

Love again split after **False Start** and, after a brief unproductive period with Columbia Records, Lee released his "solo" album **Vindicator** (1972). It was credited to Arthur Lee & Band Aid, the latter including Fayad from second incarnation of Love. Again there was a distinct deterioration in Lee's skills as writer and player; high on energy but low on ingenuity.

And then again there was a lull. There were reports of Lee living wild in the woods on the West Coast, but in late 1973 he signed for, and recorded an album for, Paul Rothchild's newly-inaugurated Buffalo Records. Unfortunately Buffalo ran straight into financial difficulties and this was another Lee album never released.

In 1974 he finally re-surfaced, with another version of Love: Melvan Whittington and John Sterling (gtrs), Sherwood Akuna/Robert Rozelle (bs) and Joe Blocker (drms). With Harvey Mandel (gtr) and Buzzy Feiten (gtr) guesting, they cut the disappointing **Reel To Real** for RSO Records and, in a somewhat modified form, visited the U.K.

Sadly, the precision-like song-crafting of the early Love had mutated into a comparatively lack-lustre form of heavy metal soul. At time of writing, Lee is without a record contract.

Of the two collection albums, **Love Masters,** compiled by John Tobler, is recommended – though not available in the U.S.

Recordings:
Love (Elektra)
Da Capo (Elektra)
Forever Changes (Elektra)
Four Sail (Elektra)
Out Here (Blue Thumb)
False Start (Blue Thumb)
Reel To Real (RSO)
Compilations:
Love Revisited (Elektra)
Love Masters (—/Elektra)
Arthur Lee & Band Aid:
Vindicator (A&M)

The Lovin' Spoonful

John Sebastian vocals, guitar, harmonica
Zalman Yanovsky vocals, guitar
Joe Butler drums
Steve Boone bass

Sebastian (b. New York, Mar 17, 1944) first came together with Yanovsky (b. Toronto, Dec 19, 1944) in the early '60s in a New York group, The Mugwumps, which also included Cass Elliott and Denny Doherty; in later years, when both The Lovin' Spoonful and The Mamas And The Papas (✦) had become famous, an album of this early material was issued – **An Historic Recording Of The Mugwumps** (Warner Bros/Valiant).

After the demise of this band Sebastian briefly trekked South, collecting folksongs and talking to bluesmen. Back in New York in 1965, and with the encouragement of producer Eric Jacobson, he put together The Lovin' Spoonful.

The band was composed of extrovert, zany personalities; after an initial residency at the Night Owl Cafe, they quickly established a following on the New York club circuit, and signed to Kama Sutra Records. With their combination of good-time music and Sebastian's ebullient compositions, they were instant karma in those heady days of 1966; **Do You Believe In Magic?**, their first hit, was a paean to rock 'n' roll, the music that can set you free. Their most noteworthy successes were **Daydream,** which broke the band in Britain, and **Summer In The City,** which gave them their only U.S. No. 1.

In 1966 they were popular right across the States, both with the rock audience, and with the so-called intelligentsia. After hits like **Nashville Cats** and **Darlin' Be Home Soon,** Sebastian composed film scores for Francis Ford Coppola's "You're A Big Boy Now", and Woody Allen's "What's Up Tiger Lily?" – though by then it was evident that Sebastian's compositional abilities were being strained.

After two years of exuberant success the band began to fall apart; after some unhappy circumstances surrounding a drugs bust, Yanovsky left the group and was replaced by Jerry Yester

(formerly producer of The Association) who appeared only on the band's fourth and final album, **Everything Playing.** The Spoonful were cracking under a series of arduous tours, and they ceased operations in 1968, after which Sebastian embarked on a solo career. (✦ John Sebastian.)

Butler made an abortive attempt to raise Spoonful flag again in 1969, and issued **Revelation – Revolution,** an album that was fairly dreadful, though Butler was the only original band member concerned. Jerry Yester, on the other hand, went on to record with his wife, Judy Henske, for Frank Zappa's Straight label. They made one wonderful artefact of psychedelia together, **Farewell Aldebaran** (co-produced, ironically, by Yester and Yanovsky) which is considered a classic album in some quarters, and a disaster in others.

The Spoonful made only four albums proper, although they also contributed some material to the Elektra compilation, **What's Shakin'?** Since their songs have been frequently re-packaged, the discography is selective.

Recordings:
Do You Believe In Magic? (Kama Sutra)
Daydreams (Kama Sutra)
Hums Of The Lovin' Spoonful (Kama Sutra)
Everything Playing (Kama Sutra)
What's Up Tiger Lily? (Soundtrack) (Kama Sutra)
You're A Big Boy Now (Soundtrack) (Kama Sutra)
Revelation – Revolution (Kama Sutra)
Compilations:
John Sebastian Song Book, Vol. I (Kama Sutra)
The Best Of The Lovin' Spoonful (Kama Sutra)
The Best Of The Lovin' Spoonful, Vol. II (Kama Sutra)

Lynyrd Skynyrd

Ronnie Van Zant vocals
Gary Rossington guitar
Allen Collins guitar
Billy Powell keyboards
Leon Wilkeson bass
Artimus Pyle drums

All above with exception of drummer Pyle (who replaced Bob Burns in January 1975) raised in Jacksonville, Florida, where most of them attended same high school. Group's name came from that school's gym coach, one Leonard Skinner, who made a habit of chastising his charges for the length of their hair.

Playing small club and bar gigs in the South, they were discovered one night in an Atlanta bar by New York super-sessioner Al Kooper (✦), who was scouting for talent for his newly-inaugurated Sounds Of The South label (distributed via MCA). First album, **Pronounced Leh-nerd Skin-nerd** (1973), was recorded at Kooper's Atlanta studio and featured session-man Ed King (ex of Strawberry Alarm Clock), who subsequently joined band as bassist then guitarist, until 1974.

First breakthrough was in support role to The Who on 1973

American tour, from which point band began to accrue fast-growing reputation as raunchy R&B-based outfit, making full use of three lead guitars and gut-bucket vocals of the ebullient Van Zant.

Second album, **Second Helping** (1974), again produced by Kooper, this time in Los Angeles, achieved U.S. gold status. Skynyrd by now ranked as one of the U.S.'s foremost in-concert rock attractions, their popularity boosted by success of **Sweet Home Alabama** as surprise U.S. singles smash.

This last-named was the group's proudly chauvinistic answer to the declamatory Neil Young (✦) opus **Southern Man;** some have suggested that Young got in the last word with his 1975 **Walk On** composition though that remains only supposition.

Second Helping.
Courtesy MCA Records.

An intrinsically Southern band, playing against backdrop of Confederate flag, Skynyrd's live aggression is freely matched by their off-stage reputation as hard-drinkin', fist-throwin' good ol' boys. The fact that fists are quite frequently thrown amongst each other – resulting in guitarists playing with bandaged hands, etc. – apparently just adds to their brotherly spirit (sic).

Managed by young English impresario Peter Rudge, tour co-ordinator extraordinaire for Rolling Stones and The Who. The 1976 **Gimme Back My Bullets** was produced by Tom Dowd (✦).

When they don't slide into excess, among the best of the crop of the '70s Southern bands.

Recordings:
Pronounced Leh-nerd Skin-nerd (MCA)
Second Helping (MCA)
Nuthin' Fancy (MCA)
Gimme Back My Bullets (MCA)

Lonnie Mack

Born Harrisburg, Indiana in 1941, Mack has a distinctive twangy guitar style. In 1963 his version of Chuck Berry's **Memphis,** which had been cut as an afterthought at the end of some sessions at King Studios in Cincinnati, Ohio, was released on Fraternity, and became a big hit, as was its follow-up **Wham;** they were both rockabilly-styled instrumentals, and an album **The Wham Of That Memphis Man,** of similar ilk ensued; after which Mack disappeared for five years, during which time he played one-night stands in South and mid-West.

A chance review of his album in "Rolling Stone" led to his re-emergence; Elektra bought the rights to his old material (reissuing **The Wham Of That Memphis Man** in 1970) and put him back in the studio again; he responded with the superb **Glad I'm In The Band** and **Whatever's Right,** both of which added funk to his previously raunchy style, and also leaned more heavily towards his gospel-tinged vocals.

By the time of **The Hills Of Indiana** in 1971, Mack had struck-up a creative friendship with former Mar-keys sax man Don Nix (♦), and they worked in a softer, more contemporary country style, recording in Nashville and Muscle Shoals.

After this, Mack again retired from the business, though he has made the occasional single.

Recordings:
The Wham Of That Memphis Man (Fraternity/—)
Glad I'm In The Band (Elektra)
Whatever's Right (Elektra)
The Hills Of Indiana (Elektra)

Magma

Christian Vander drums
Stella Vander vocals
Klaus Blasquiz vocals, percussion
Gabriel Federow guitar
Benoit Widemann keyboards
Didier Lockwood violin
Bernard Paganotti bass
Jean-Pol Asseline keyboards

For several years France's leading underground group, Magma were formed by Christian Vander – under heavy early influence of jazz saxophonist John Coltrane – to perform enormous oratorio concerning Earth's future.

Their eponymous debut, a double, portrays a vast interstellar journey; the second, **1001 Degrees Centigrade,** concerns rivalry between Earth and the imaginary planet Kobaia (Kobaia also being the name of a new language Vander invented, and which is used by his singers).

Released 1970 and 1971 respectively, these purported to be parts one and two of an eventual nine-album work known as **Theusz Hamtaahk.** However, by the third album, **Mekanik Destructiw Komandoh** (1973), Magma personnel had altered radically over policy disagreement and a choir had been drafted in to tell story of the end of the world.

Only Klaus Blasquiz was retained by Vander, a whole new crop of French musicians coming in for **Kohntarkosz,** released early 1975. However, even before release, personnel altered dramatically again – Blasquiz and, of course, Vander being only survivors. Newcomers included Vander's wife Stella. In June 1975, having switched from A&M to Giorgio Gomelsky's new Utopia label, group recorded **Magma Live** double set at The Taverne de l'Olympia in Paris, where they are based.

Musically complex, ambitious, but prone to repetition, Magma are open to criticism for the humourless and irredeemable pretentiousness of their overall concept. Since continuity of work is rigidly controlled by Vander – who cites Stravinsky, Bartok, Stockhausen and Ornette Coleman

among other influences – any of their albums can be taken as representative.

Recordings:
Magma (French Philips – import)
1001 Degrees Centigrade (French Philips import)
Mekanik Destruktiw Kommandoh (A&M)
Kohntarkosz (A&M)
Magma Live (Utopia)

Taj Mahal

Born New York May 17, 1942 Taj Mahal was raised in Springfield, Massachusetts in New England countryside, and took a degree in animal husbandry at University of Massachusetts.

He felt cut off from his own Negro culture and developed an interest in the blues, initially via big band music and the influence of his father, a noted jazz arranger. At university, Taj had been a member of the Pioneer Valley Folklore Society, studying the roots of American black music; he became an expert musicologist.

Meanwhile, he tried to make a career for himself in music, though a band he formed in the mid-'60s with Ry Cooder (♦) in Los Angeles called the Rising Sons broke up before anything had been recorded. Taj continued to augment his natural musical ability with his academic knowledge, and made sufficient impression to sign with Columbia Records.

He has since made 11 albums, of which both **Giant Step/De Ole Folks At Home** and **The Real Thing** have been double sets. In that time, he has moved from country blues on his early albums to West Indian roots music on **Music Keeps Me Together,** which was recorded with the Intergalactic Soul Messengers' Band.

Mo' Roots.
Courtesy CBS Records.

He usually accompanies himself on guitar and harmonica, though he is a multi-instrumentalist and also plays piano, banjo, bass and fife. He has recorded with Cooder and people such as Jesse Ed Davis; usually he produces and arranges the albums himself.

Mahal's strength is that although he is essentially an academic, he leaves behind such considerations when he is actually recording, and his albums have an exuberance and joyousness that few others know how to communicate – his attitude to his music is affectionate, rather than reverential.

Music Keeps Me Together includes a poem written and recited by his wife Inshirah Mahal.

Taj has also appeared in, and written the soundtrack for, "Sounder".

Recordings:
Taj Mahal (Columbia/Direction)
The Natch'l Blues (Columbia/Direction)
Giant Step/De Ole Folks At Home (Columbia/CBS)
The Real Thing (Columbia/CBS)
Happy Just To Be Like I Am (Columbia/CBS)
Recycling The Blues And Other Related Stuff (Columbia/CBS)
Ooh So Good 'n' Blues (Columbia/CBS)
Sounder (Soundtrack) (Columbia/CBS)
Mo' Roots (Columbia/CBS)
Music Keeps Me Together (Columbia/CBS)
Satisfied 'N Tickled Too (Columbia/CBS)

Mahavishnu Orchestra
♦ John McLaughlin

Birds Of Fire.
Courtesy CBS Records.

Mallard

Bill Harkleroad (Zoot Horn Rollo) guitar
Mark Boston (Rockette Morton) bass
Artie Tripp (Ed Marimba) marimba, drums
Sam Galpin vocals

Following the dissolution of the Captain Beefheart & The Magic Band partnership after Beefheart's **Blue Jeans And Moonbeams,** the three central members of the Magic Band, who had each won distinguished service medals for their part in Beefheart's superior middle-period work (**Trout Mask Replica, Lick My Decals Off Baby, The Spotlight Kid, Clear Spot**), formed themselves into a new band, with the addition of vocalist Sam Galpin.

Galpin was born Oct 19, 1940, and started playing piano when he was 18, and worked in a local group with Roy Estrada. He was a member of The Champs when they had their massive world-wide hit in 1958, **Tequila.** He subsequently played with The Coasters, before moving on to spend a decade or more playing in Las Vegas casinos. It was Winged Eel Fingerling who recommended him to Mallard; at the time Galpin had reputedly never heard of Beefheart or the Magic Band.

Since Beefheart held the copyright on both "the Magic Band" and also the individual members' noms de disque, the band resorted to calling themselves Mallard, after one of the tracks on their debut album, which was released in March 1976.

Recordings:
Mallard (Virgin)

The Mamas And The Papas

John Phillips vocals
Michelle Gilliam vocals
Cass Elliott vocals
Denny Doherty vocals

The Mamas And The Papas were put together in 1965 by Phillips (b. Parris Island, South Carolina, Aug 30, 1935), who had been working the Greenwich Village folk clubs since 1957, and was once a member of a folk trio, The Journeymen. In 1962 he married Michelle Gilliam (b. Long Beach, California, Apr 6, 1944).

Cass Elliott (b. Baltimore, Maryland Sep 19, 1943) had also worked the New York folk scene, and joined a formative band called The Mugwumps, which also included Doherty (b. Halifax, Nova Scotia, Nov 29, 1941) and Zal Yanovsky, who later became one of the founder members of Lovin' Spoonful (♦). Early history of Mamas and Papas is documented on one of their most endearing hits, **Creeque Alley.**

When the line-up had been settled, Phillips moved his base of operations to Hollywood and arranged a record deal with Lou Adler (♦), through the latter's newly-formed Dunhill label.

The Mamas And The Papas began to make live appearances in 1965, and made their first recordings in 1966. **California Dreamin'** was a moderate hit, and certainly brought them to public attention; their next single, **Monday, Monday,** was an instant smash, reaching No. 1 in the U.S. and No. 3 in the U.K., and it proved to

If You Can Believe Your Eyes And Ears. ABC Records.

be the start of a lengthy run of chart success through 1967 and 1968.

They purveyed a very slick folk-rock, but though the sound and their hippy image (they dressed the part on stage) was totally contrived, they had a lot going for them; their vocal harmonies were consistently impressive, Phillips' own compositions were first-rate, the group were always backed by the best session-men available, and on the whole 1965-67 were good years for optimism.

In 1967 they had three huge singles – **Dedicated To The One I Love, Creeque Alley** and **Twelve Thirty** (the latter, one of their very best songs, was strangely never a hit in Britain), and two gold albums, **If You Can Believe Your Eyes And Ears . . .** and **The Mamas And The Papas Deliver,** with a third, **The Papas And The Mamas** in 1968.

They appeared at the Monterey Festival, which Phillips himself had arranged, in 1967, and were naturally in the festival film, "Monterey Pop", also financed by Phillips and Adler.

After their peak years of 1966–67, they began to decline, and in any case the band were hit by internal friction. John and Michelle's marriage had been on the rocks once in 1966 (and Michelle had temporarily quit); by 1968 the various schisms were too great, and the group was dissolved.

Phillips made one excellent solo album, **The Wolfking Of L.A.** before going into film production; he financed Robert Altman's tragi-comedy "Brewster McCloud", which didn't have the commercial success it deserved; Michelle, meanwhile, tried her hand at an acting career. Papa Doherty and Mama Cass both went solo.

After group split up, the market was inundated with re-packaged material; in 1971 the four made an abortive reunion, the album **People Like Us** providing only uninspired facsimiles of their earlier work.

The subsequent career of Cass Elliott, who had had a solo hit in 1968 with **Dream A Little Dream Of Me,** was distressingly pathetic. Though her initial solo material was very bland, she appeared to be returning to her former direction when she teamed with Dave Mason (➧), but the partnership accomplished little beyond one unmemorable album, **Dave Mason And Cass Elliott.** Towards the end of her career she was working the cabaret circuit. Always overweight, she died of natural causes in London on Jul 29, 1974.

Recordings:
If You Can Believe Your Eyes And Ears . . . (Dunhill/RCA)
The Mamas And The Papas Deliver (Dunhill/RCA)
Cass, John, Michelle, Denny (Dunhill/RCA)
The Papas And The Mamas (Dunhill/RCA)
People Like Us (Dunhill/Probe)
Compilations:
Farewell To The First Golden Era (Dunhill/RCA)
A Gathering Of Flowers (Dunhill/Probe)
John Phillips solo:
The Wolfking Of L.A. (Dunhill/RCA)
Cass Elliott solo:
Dream A Little Dream (Dunhill/Stateside)
The Road Is No Place For A Lady (Dunhill/RCA)
Don't Call Me Mama Anymore (Dunhill/RCA)

Man

Mickey Jones guitar, vocals
Deke Leonard guitar, vocals
Terry Williams drums, vocals
Phil Ryan keyboards, vocals
John McKenzie bass, vocals

A biographer's nightmare, Man's tortuously-complicated history is confused not so much by the number of different line-ups (12 by 1976) but by the fact that everyone involved in the group since their inception appears to have left and rejoined at least twice.

The one constant factor through all these changes is guitarist Mickey Jones, who was playing in a Swansea, Wales, area group The Bystanders along with Clive John (kybds), Jeffrey Jones (drms) and Ray Williams (bs), when they recruited guitarist Deke Leonard from The Dream and became Man in 1968.

Thus constituted this all-Welsh line-up recorded their first album, **Revelation,** in the same year, evincing influences firmly anchored to U.S. West Coast which have survived to present day. The same line-up recorded the 1969 set **Two Ounces Of Plastic,** etc. But by third eponymous album for Liberty in 1971, Jeffrey Jones and Ray Williams had departed to be replaced respectively by Terry Williams and Martin Ace.

However, none of albums made much impact in U.K. (outside small Welsh following) and the band eked out their living on small-time club/college circuit. Some degree of success in Europe, particularly Germany, nevertheless provided encouragement – as well as enough bread to stop them splitting altogether – and the same line-up was still intact for the late 1971 set **Do You Like It Here Now? Are You Settling In?**

Gradually, a small but ardent British Man audience was beginning to form, and their next set, their limited edition **Live At The Padgett Rooms, Penarth,** scraped the lower rungs of U.K. album lists.

Martin Ace had, however, departed by now. Out too, shortly after the album's release, was Deke Leonard – to cut own **Iceberg** album (1972) and subsequently form touring band of same name.

Clive John was not around for the Padgett Rooms set either, but had returned for the next Man collection, **Be Good To Yourself At Least Once A Day** (1972) which introduced two new members Phil Ryan (kybds) and Will Youatt (bs). This set was probably group's finest achievement to date, but the real chart breakthrough came with the following year's double-set **Back Into The Future.** Naturally there was the obligatory line-up change, but only one this time: Tweke Lewis for Phil Ryan.

Deke Leonard's Iceberg supported Man on breakthrough 1973 British tour, and by the 1974 set **Rhinos Winos And Lunatics,** Leonard had re-joined the band. Other line-up changes: in – Malcolm Morley (kyds) and Ken Whaley (bs) from Help Yourself and Bees Make Honey respectively; out – Will Youatt and Tweke Lewis.

In spring 1974 this line-up played first U.S. tour supporting Hawkwind, returning to find the **Rhinos** album high in the U.K. charts but losing Malcolm Morley at end of successful British concert series.

As four-piece, Jones and Leonard writing all the material between them, Man cut **Slow Motion** for autumn 1974 release, and entered one of the most eventful periods of their career. After seeing **Slow Motion** make charts in four European countries at the end of 1974, early 1975 found them embarking on second American tour.

Their fortunes were mixed – Ken Whaley quit the band, the aforementioned Martin Ace (remember him?) suspending his career in Flying Aces to come in as temporary replacement; **Slow Motion** became one of most played albums in U.S. that year; and the group enjoyed considerable audience acclaim on last two dates of tour, at Bill Graham's Winterland in San Francisco. A Welsh band playing San Francisco music had taken that music back to its source, and had been received with unprecedented warmth.

Graham asked them to return for four more dates as headliners two weeks later, and during rehearsals for these gigs the group struck-up friendship with a West Coast musician who had been one of their earliest influences – and heroes. This was John Cippolina, ex of Quicksilver Messenger Service (➧) who subsequently joined Man on the Winterland concerts and returned to play a British tour with them in May 1975. From this came **Maximum Darkness** live album.

With Cippolina having returned to States and Martin Ace to previous work, Man re-grouped once more with return of Phil Ryan (kybds) and newcomer John McKenzie (bs). The result of this new formation and label switch to MCA was 1976 set **The Welsh Connection.**

Slow Motion. Courtesy United Artists Records.

Such a plethora of personnel changes would normally suggest a perpetually strife-torn band. However, that is not the case with Man – like the West Coast bands to whom their music owes a major debt, they are simply a collection of endearingly amiable, music and dope-loving Welsh freaks to whom flexibility has become a way of life.

Apart from albums below, Man also appears on the live albums **The Greasy Truckers Party** (United Artists) and **Christmas At The Patti** (United Artists) – both 1972. **Man** was re-released on Sunset as **Man 1970.**

Recordings:
Revelation (—/Pye)
Two Ounces Of Plastic With A Hole In The Middle (—/Dawn)
Man (—/Liberty)
Do You Like It Here Now? Are You Settling In? (United Artists)
Live At The Padgett Rooms, Penarth (—/United Artists)
Be Good To Yourself At Least Once A Day (United Artists)
Back Into The Future (United Artists)
Rhinos, Winos And Lunatics (United Artists)
Slow Motion (United Artists)
Maximum Darkness (United Artists)
The Welsh Connection (MCA)

Manassas
➧ Steve Stills

Melissa Manchester

Born in The Bronx, New York, Feb 15, 1951, her father David is long-established bassoonist with Metropolitan Opera Orchestra.

She graduated from the prestigious High School Of The Performing Arts in Manhattan, and between ages 16 and 18 was a staff writer for Chappel Music. Continued music studies at New York University School Of The Arts, being one of small group there who studied songwriting and record production under tutorship of Paul Simon (➧).

Displaying influences of Simon in writing style, cut debut album for Bell Records in 1973. Backed on second album **Bright Eyes** (not released in U.K.) by band comprising Cooker Lo Presti (bs), David Wolfert (gtrs), James Newton-Howard (kybds) and Kirk Bruner (drms).

Ms Manchester herself plays piano at in-concert appearances with band, as well as singing own material. Lyrically she was seen as a spokeswoman for feminists, but this was not always entirely intentional.

Third album **Melissa** (1975) produced by Vini Poncia and Richard Perry (➧), and yielded American hit single **Midnight Blue.**

Recordings:
Home To Myself (Bell)
Bright Eyes (Bell/—)
Melissa (Arista)
Better Days And Happy Endings (Arista)

Harvey Mandel

Detroit born, Mandel cut musical teeth on West Coast and accrued minor reputation as thoughtful, talented jazz-influenced guitarist through series of solo albums before he joined Canned Heat (➧) in 1970. He replaced Henry Vestine in that band, having – as Mandel tells it – walked into the Fillmore on the night Vestine quit.

He stayed with the Heat for a year, then played with British bluesman John Mayall (➧), during Mayall's jazz-blues period, for similar period before forming own purely instrumental band Pure Food And Drug Act.

A jazz-oriented outfit, Mandel was disappointed when they failed to make impact, reminiscing on break-up 1973 that they were "sophisticated rather than exciting" and that public couldn't seem to accept a group devoid of vocals. Formed new band, this time with vocalist, and toured U.K. and U.S. 1974 as support to Canned Heat.

He had thus far still failed to achieve commercial success, though his many albums show evidence of his talent as a musician – this latter opinion borne out by the calls for his services on numerous sessions, and the fact that in 1975 he was heavily tipped to replace Mick Taylor in Rolling Stones (➧). As everybody knows, Ronnie Wood eventually got that job, but Mandel did turn-up on session credits on 1976 Stones album **Black And Blue.**

Recordings:
Christo Redentor (Philips)
Righteous (Philips)
Games Guitars Play (Philips)
Get Off In Chicago (Ovation/ London)

Top: Down The Road. Right: Better Days And Happy Endings.

Baby Batter (Janus/Dawn)
The Snake (Janus)
Shangrenade (Janus)
Pure Food And Drug Act: Choice Cuts (Epic/—)
Compilations:
Feel The Sound Of Harvey Mandel (Janus/—)
Best Of (Janus/—)

Barry Manilow

Born Brooklyn, New York, worked in Columbia Records mailroom to pay rent while he studied at New York College Of Music and subsequently at the famous Juilliard Academy. In 1967 became music director of WCBS-TV talent series "Callback", going on to conduct/arrange for Ed Sullivan specials.

Manilow was filling in as pianist at New York's Continental Baths in 1972 when he first met Bette Midler (➧), subsequently becoming her music director, conductor and pianist. He co-produced and arranged Midler's first two albums, and joined her on her 1973 U.S. tour. In addition to aforementioned duties with Bette, Manilow performed his own songs as support act.

He did his own first U.S. tour in spring 1974, and really sprang to prominence in January 1975 when his **Mandy** composition went to No. 1 in U.S. singles charts only nine weeks after release. Followed up with **It's A Miracle** and **Could It Be Magic?**

During his career, Manilow has also been prolific writer/producer/singer of U.S. TV and radio commercial jingles.

Recordings:
Barry Manilow (Arista)

Barry Manilow II (Arista)
Flashy Ladies (Arista)
Trying To Get The Feeling
(Arista)

Manfred Mann

Manfred Mann keyboards
Paul Jones vocals, harmonica
Mike Vickers saxophone, flute,
guitar
Tom McGuinness bass
Mike Hugg drums, vibraphone

Manfred Mann was originally formed by Mann (b. Mike Lubowitz in Johannesburg, South Africa, Oct 21, 1940) and Mike Hugg (b. Andover, Hampshire, Aug 11, 1942) as a jazz-band called the Mann-Hugg Blues Brothers; in 1964 they started playing R&B, and consolidated themselves into a five-piece with the line-up as above though Dave Richmond was the group's original bassist. Jones (whose real name was Paul Pond) was still an undergraduate at Oxford University.

They signed to HMV and released an unsuccessful, but promising, instrumental called **Why Should We Not?**, and then found their style with a fast-moving **Cock-A-Hoop**. However, it was not until their third single **5-4-3-2-1**, with Jones' harmonica-playing prominently featured, that the band established themselves as a chart act.

5-4-3-2-1, which reached No. 5 in the U.K. charts in February 1964, was undoubtedly assisted by the fact that it was used as the theme tune to the TV programme, "Ready Steady Go", until it was replaced by the Manfreds' follow-up, **Hubble Bubble, Toil And Trouble**, also a major hit. Manfred Mann had 15 hits in the next few years, with what was often just high-class pop material, while they tried to show their more substantial skills on albums like their blues-oriented, debut **Five Faces Of Manfred Mann**. Their hits included **Doo Wah Diddy Diddy** (1964), which reached No. 1 on both sides of the Atlantic, despite the fact that it was

a cover of a record by The Exciters, **Come Tomorrow, Oh No Not My Baby** (both 1965) and **Pretty Flamingo** (1966). Meanwhile, Vickers left to pursue some solo projects, and McGuinness moved over to lead guitar, with Jack Bruce (♦) coming in on bass.

They also recorded a very popular EP which included Paul Jones' composition about the band (and himself) **The One In The Middle**, and also Dylan's **With God On Our Side**.

Within six months, Bruce had left to join Cream, and Paul Jones had similarly opted for a solo career (he had two hits, **High Time** and **I've Been A Bad Bad Boy**, the theme-tune from "Privilege", a movie in which he starred); their replacements were Klaus Voorman and Mike D'Abo respectively.

The band signed to Fontana label, and resumed their chart success with **Semi-Detached Suburban Mr James, Ha! Ha! Said The Clown** and **My Name Is Jack**.

The outfit always made capital out of covering Dylan songs, **With God On Our Side, If You Gotta Go, Go Now**, and later **Just Like A Woman** and **The Mighty Quinn**, which provided the band with their third British No. 1 in February 1968. Dylan himself was quoted as saying that he thought Manfred Mann came up with the best cover versions of his material.

Meanwhile, Manfred Mann were becoming increasingly jaded with what seemed the demeaning process of merely following hit single with hit single, and many members, like Vickers, had absorbed themselves in "heavier" pursuits – Hugg, for example, had written the score for "Up The Junction".

So in 1969, Mann broke up the band and he and Hugg formed the more ambitious Manfred Mann Chapter Three with a full brass section; although their debut album included a fine version of a Hugg song, **Shapes Of Things**, that had been a 1966 hit for The Yardbirds (♦), Manfred Mann

did not find true happiness and artistic credibility in an albums-oriented band, and Chapter Three was dissolved in 1971, only for Mann to try again with Manfred Mann's Earth Band (♦).
(♦ McGuinness Flint.)
Discography is selective.

Recordings:
Five Faces Of Manfred Mann
(Ascot/HMV)
Mann Made (Ascot/HMV)
Soul Of Mann (—/HMV)
As Is (—/Fontana)
Up The Junction (Soundtrack)
(—/Fontana)
Mighty Garvey (—/Fontana)
Compilations:
Mann Made Hits (—/HMV)
This Is Manfred Mann
(—/Philips International)
**Manfred Mann Chapter Three:
Manfred Mann Chapter Three**
(Polydor/Vertigo)
Chapter Three, Volume Two
(—/Vertigo)

Manfred Mann's Earth Band

Manfred Mann keyboards,
synthesisers
Colin Pattenden bass
Chris Slade drums, percussion
Chris Thompson guitar, vocals
Dave Flett guitar

Manfred Mann's Earth Band was formed in late 1971 with Mann, Pattenden, Slade and guitarist Mick Rogers, after Mann had dissolved his previous outfit, Chapter Three. The group pointed themselves in a heavy-rock direction, and gained a following through their ambitious instrumental approach, lengthy guitar solos of Rogers, and Mann's synthesiser work. Their standing increased with the regular release of albums, and in 1973 they had a hit single with **Joybringer**, which was based on the Jupiter theme from Holst's "The Planets".

Anyone who bought their fifth album, **The Good Earth**, re-

leased in October 1974, also acquired the rights to a minute plot of land in Wales.

After several tours of the U.S., the band have built up a following there.

In autumn 1975, Rogers left the band, and was replaced by Thompson and Flett, neither of whom had previous experience.

Messin' was re-titled **Get Your Rocks Off** for U.S. release.

Recordings:
Manfred Mann's Earth Band
(Polydor/Philips)
Glorified Magnified (Polydor/
Philips)
Messin' (Polydor/Vertigo)
Solar Fire (Polydor/Bronze)
The Good Earth (Warner Bros/
Bronze)
Nightingales And Bombers
(Warner Bros/Bronze)
The Roaring Silence (Warner
Bros/Bronze)

Manhattan Transfer

Tim Hauser vocals
Janis Siegel vocals
Alan Paul vocals
Laurel Masse vocals

Formed 1969, then signed to Capitol, veteran Tim Hauser was only survivor of original group when the Transfer emerged as New York cult attraction 1973 with re-vamped act and personnel as above. They followed in footsteps of Atlantic stablemate Bette Midler (♦), who first tapped nostalgia market on New York scene and established commercial potential of kitsch. Not that nostalgia was "new": Sha Na Na (♦) had long been packing in crowds as America's premier rock 'n' roll parodists, but Midler and the Transfer delved further back for their sources – through the '30s, '40s, '50s; with an occasional foray into the '60s en route.

Theatrically camp, the transfer's act is epitomized by Tim Hauser's Clark Gable moustache and Fred Astaire top hat and tails, and partner Alan Paul's Cab Calloway-style slicked-back hair and white tuxedo. Alongside them, the two girls – both fine singers in a multitude of styles – favour vamp wardrobe.

Both Hauser and Siegel have their roots in New York R&B. Ms Siegel was part of the famed Red Bird label's The Young Generation, who recorded under auspices of Leiber and Stoller (♦), while Hauser's singing career dates back to 1958 and the R&B group The Criterions. He subsequently worked as producer, DJ, and in folk-group that included late Jim Croce (♦).

Laurel Masse has been less forthcoming about her antecedents, but Alan Paul has perhaps the most diverse and interesting background of them all. New Jersey-born, a B.A. in Music and Drama and recipient of the Epstein Scholarship Award for Musical Achievement, he was an actor from age of six. Has appeared in several Broadway shows ("Oliver", "The King And I", "Camelot"), and movies ("The

*Left: Manfred Mann, plus 2
(the brass section), plus an
unidentified dancer.*

Pawnbroker", "The Pursuit Of Happiness"). In medium of TV, has featured in scores of well-known commercials.

The Good Earth.
Courtesy Bronze Records.

On their night, the Transfer's adroitly - reproduced nostalgia pastiches can make them one of the most wittily entertaining acts on the periphery of rock – that, in spite of the irritating sycophancy such acts seem to provoke in their audiences.

Yet their ability to outlast the nostalgia boom must be in question. Primarily a live act, they have on occasion broken in singles field, notably **Tuxedo Junction** – a U.S. and U.K. hit 1975–76.

Recordings:
Manhattan Transfer & Gene Pistilli (Capitol)
Manhattan Transfer (Atlantic)

Bob Marley (And The Wailers)

Marley was born 1945, the half-caste son of an English army captain and a Jamaican woman. He cut his first single, **One Cup Of Coffee,** in 1962 after Jimmy Cliff had introduced him to local promoter Leslie Kong.

Two years later, The Wailers were formed as a vocal outfit, with a line-up of Marley, Peter Tosh, Bunny Livingston, Junior Braithwaite and Beverley Kelso; as the group started to record, so they were augmented by session-men. Marley, however, always led the group, and provided the majority of material.

Wailers' first release for producer Clement Dodd was an up-tempo ska number, written by Marley, **Simmer Down.** It was a Jamaican hit, and over the next few years they had a succession of hits on the Coxsone label. In 1966 their single **Rude Boy** was first of a series that mythologised the activities of the infamous outlaws of Kingston's shanty town.

In 1966 the first changes began to take place. Braithwaite and Kelso left and were not replaced; The Wailers left their company, Coxsone, and began to produce themselves, as well as forming their own label Wailing Souls, though it folded after half-a-dozen releases.

Right: Bob Marley, reggae's
most commercial property,
who broke through in the U.S.
in 1976 with the bestselling
Rastaman Vibration.

Of more significance was Marley's association with Johnny Nash (✦) who went to Jamaica scouting for recording talent. Marley and Nash recorded some songs together, and they both went to Sweden, where Marley helped Nash compose score for a film in which he (Nash) was appearing. In 1971, Marley provided Nash with a U.K. hit single, **Stir It Up,** from the album **I Can See Clearly Now,** which contained another of Marley's compositions, **Guava Jelly.**

Back home, though, this was a barren period for The Wailers, partly due to the fact that both Livingston and Marley incurred jail sentences. From 1969, however, they began to start putting it together again, and recorded two albums with producer Lee Perry – **Soul Rebel** and **Soul Revolution,** and scoring hit singles with **Duppy Conqueror** and **Small Axe.**

In 1970 The Wailers formed another label, Tuff Gong, which had extensive local success with their own releases like **Trench Town Rock.**

Their releases were now beginning to preach the revolutionary doctrine of Rastafarianism; the manifestations of their faith are the regular use of the Rastafarian colours of red, orange and green, and their plaited hairstyle, known as dreadlocks. **African Herbsman** and **Rasta Revolution** were recorded at this time, though not issued outside Jamaica until 1973.

By this time Carlton Barrett (drms) and his brother Aston (bs) had joined the group, providing a fuller, more instrumental sound, before Chris Blackwell of Island Records advanced the band enough money to record the sophisticated **Catch A Fire** in 1973.

Island were ready to back The Wailers with a lot of money, but they did so gradually since Caucasian audiences could hardly be expected to adjust overnight to the subtle rhythms of reggae.

The stature of The Wailers did grow, however, as the band undertook low-key tours of Britain and America, and in late 1973 issued **Burnin'.** Though it was slightly disappointing, it nevertheless widened Marley's audience, because it included **I Shot The Sheriff,** a track recorded by Eric Clapton (✦) on **461 Ocean Boulevard,** and subsequently a major hit single.

In early 1975 came **Natty Dread,** credited to Bob Marley And The Wailers, and without Peter Tosh, who had opted to pursue a solo career, and Livingston. Al Anderson was on lead guitar, and Touter on keyboards. The album featured several of Marley's most memorable songs – **Lively Up Yourself, Them Belly Full, Natty Dread** and **No Woman No Cry.**

All attention was by now focused on Marley, and successful tours of America and Britain made him into a new cult figure, as did the unanimously favourable press he

received. A hit single, a live version of **No Woman No Cry,** recorded at the Lyceum in London, finally signalled the arrival of

Burnin'.
Courtesy Island Records.

Marley as a potent force on the music scene.

Marley is thus the first Jamaican artist to make a real breakthrough in the U.K. (and to an increasing extent, the U.S.), while retaining his support back home, where every Marley single is still an automatic No. 1.

The Bob Marley and Wailers **Live!** album consolidated their success in 1975, while **Rastaman Vibration** was released May 1976.

The Wailers have gone through other line-up changes, and are presently eight-strong, with Marley himself (rytm gtr), Aston Barrett (bs), Carlton Barrett (drms), Tyrone Downie (kybds), Seeco Patterson (pcsn) and China

Smith who has taken over from Al Anderson (ld gtr). Vocal backing is provided by Judy Mowatt, Marcia Griffiths and Rita Marley, the I-Threes. The latter is Marley's common-law wife.

Recordings:
Rasta Revolution (—/Trojan)
African Herbsman (—/Trojan)
Catch A Fire (Island)
Burnin' (Island)
Natty Dread (Island)
Live! (Island)
Rastaman Vibration (Island)

Steve Marriott

Born Bow, East London, Jan 30, 1947, he played in a variety of bands including Steve Marriott & The Moments (one of whom was actress Adrienne Posta) before he formed Small Faces (♦) 1965 with Ronnie Lane. Left that highly successful U.K. charts band to create Humble Pie (♦). After that outfit's ignominious dissolution 1975, he worked fitfully with own Steve Marriott All Stars band, recording solo album **Marriott,** mostly in New York, for 1976 release. In 1975–76 was also subject of Small Faces reunion rumours. (♦Faces.)

Recordings:
Marriott (A&M)

The Marshall Tucker Band

Tommy Caldwell bass, vocals
Toy Caldwell guitar, steel guitar, vocals
George McCorkel rhythm guitar
Doug Gray vocals, percussion
Paul Riddle drums, percussion
Jerry Eubanks sax, flute, vocals

One of wave of '70s U.S. bands which were handed their passport out of hitherto restrictive Southern bar/club circuit by international success of Allman Brothers (♦), all above were childhood friends from Spartanburg, South Carolina.

They were all working in various local bands when drafted into service in 1966. In first weeks after discharge four years later, Toy Caldwell resumed writing and penned **Can't You See?** composition which was to become Marshall Tucker Band's first U.S. hit single.

But first there was The Toy Factory, with Toy, Doug Gray and Jerry Eubanks, which metamorphosed after two years into Marshall Tucker in pursuit of "more creative format". Toy's brother Tommy joined new band, later recommending guitarist McCorkel and drummer Riddle.

On suggestion of Wet Willie (♦), approached Allmans mentor Phil Walden who signed them to his Capricorn label, for whom they cut eponymous first album for release in 1973. The group toured U.S. same year as support to Allmans, headlining in own right by time of second **Where We All Belong** (1975) is a double set, one album recorded in studio, the other live.

Recordings:
The Marshall Tucker Band (Capricorn)
A New Life (Capricorn)
Where We All Belong (Capricorn)
Searchin' For A Rainbow (Capricorn)

George Martin

Born Jan 3, 1926, Martin joined EMI in 1950, and as a staff producer for the Parlophone label signed The Beatles in 1962, before which he had produced Shirley Bassey and the Temperance Seven, and comedy albums by The Goons and Peter Ustinov.

He produced all the Beatles recordings from 1962–69, and was responsible not only for the group's recorded sound in early days, but also for giving expression to Lennon/McCartney's more complex ideas later on; he pieced together the arrangements for the **Sgt Pepper** album, and also tracks like **Tomorrow Never Knows** and **Strawberry Fields Forever.**

As a staff producer, he didn't really make much money from his success with The Beatles, until he set-up his own independent operation in 1965, when he formed AIR studios with producers Ron Richards, Peter Sullivan and Jim Burgess.

Martin produced other bands after The Beatles – Stackridge, for example – but had no real chart success until he started working with the band America (♦) and Jeff Beck (♦).

John Martyn

Born Glasgow in 1948, Martyn started playing guitar in 1967, and within a short time established a reputation on folk-club circuit, so that within three months he was cutting his first album for Island Records. Released later that year, **London Conversation** turned out to be his most unequivocally folk-based album; for his next, **The Tumbler,** he employed the services of noted flutist/saxophonist, the late Harold McNair.

The Road To Ruin.
Courtesy Island Records.

Stormbringer! was co-credited to him and his wife, Beverley, and was recorded in New York with noted American session-men, and helped bring Martyn to wider attention; Beverley again appeared with her husband on **The Road To Ruin** before family duties necessitated leaving her husband to continue solo again.

Bless The Weather extended jazz influences that had been creeping into Martyn's work, and it set a style which Martyn has developed closely since. **Solid Air** shows the pattern emerging, built around repetitive hypnotic melodies and extraordinary use of acoustic guitar through echoplex, which finds total expression on **Inside Out.**

With his partner, bassist Danny Thompson – formerly of Pentangle (♦) – Martyn continues to gather a following, particularly in the U.S., though it is doubtful if he will ever achieve general popularity, particularly as he utterly rejects all commercial devices in his work. His last album was indicative of his whole approach to the business, in that it was a live album, available only on mail-order from his home in Sussex. The fact that the initial pressing of 10,000 quickly sold out is evidence of his staunch support.

Recordings:
London Conversation (—/Island)
The Tumbler (—/Island)
Bless The Weather (—/Island)
Solid Air (Island)
Inside Out (Island)
Sunday's Child (Island)
With Beverley Martyn:
Stormbringer! (Warner Bros/Island)
The Road To Ruin (Warner Bros/Island)

Dave Mason

Born Worcester, England, May 10, 1946, Mason is something of an old hand in the rock business, having worked in different line-ups with many famous musicians.

A self-taught guitarist, he played in Birmingham area with a local group The Jaguars, and then joined The Hellians, which also included Jim Capaldi and Luther Grosvenor, before he and Capaldi broke away to form Deep Feeling, one of those semi-legendary formative bands.

Mason's first real introduction to the professional side of the rock business was as a roadie with the Spencer Davis Group; he also played with both Capaldi and Chris Wood on **I'm A Man.**

In 1967 he became a founder-member of Traffic (♦), and wrote band's second single, **Hole In My Shoe,** which reached No. 2 in British charts. At this point however it was evident that his aims were not compatible with those of the others, who were concerned with improvisation and the creation of musical moods – Mason's primary concern was in writing songs. The first Traffic album, **Mr Fantasy,** illustrates this dichotomy.

Mason first quit Traffic in December 1967; he went on to produce Family's classic debut album, **Music In A Doll's House.** He released two compositions, **Just For You** and **Little Woman** on a solo single, and towards the end of 1968 acted as a session musician on Hendrix's **Electric Ladyland.** (His other session credits include work on the Rolling Stones' **Beggar's Banquet,** and George Harrison's **All Things Must Pass.**)

Before this, however, in March 1968 he had re-joined Traffic, and his most celebrated composition, **Feelin' Alright,** appeared on their second album, **Traffic.** The song has since become something of a rock standard, having been recorded by everyone from Joe Cocker and Three Dog Night to Gladys Knight and the Pips.

Mason left Traffic again in October 1968 (a decision which soon caused the band to fold altogether). At that point he formed a short-lived group with Chris Wood, Jim Capaldi and Wynder K. Frogg, before moving to Los Angeles, where he had contacts in Gram Parsons, Mama Cass, and Delaney and Bonnie (♦), whom he had first met in 1967.

He was one of the Friends on Delaney & Bonnie's successful tours of U.S. and the U.K. in 1969, playing guitar alongside Clapton; his work is featured on the **On Tour** album. After this Mason was irregularly involved with Derek & The Dominos, and played at their debut gig in London in June 1970.

Prior to this Mason, armed with a contract from Blue Thumb, had finally put together his long-awaited solo album. **Alone Together,** which drew on the multifarious talents of the Delaney & Bonnie entourage, was received ecstatically by many critics; it was a bestselling album in the U.S., and a criminally overlooked one in the U.K.

Alone Together.
Courtesy Blue Thumb Records.

Ever industrious, Mason began working with Cass Elliott (♦ The Mamas And The Papas), and they made their debut together in Los Angeles in September 1970 before touring the States with a three-piece band. It was an intriguing, though quite unlikely, partnership, and sadly produced nothing of real consequence, though one album, **Dave Mason And Mama Cass** was issued before they went their separate ways in 1971.

He began working with Traffic for a third time, and appeared on the live album, **Welcome To The Canteen,** which showed the band to be quite revitalised.

After this Mason got together his own band in America, and recorded a double-album. However owing to problems with Blue Thumb, the album was issued in two parts – **Headkeeper** (1972) was a part-live, part-studio set, and **Dave Mason Is Alive** (1973) contained the rest of the live sessions. The latter was never issued in Britain.

Mason then moved to Columbia and, freed of contractual hassles, has since issued albums regularly. He clearly regarded **It's Like You Never Left,** released in U.S. late 1973, as his first solo album proper since **Alone Together;** his subsequent releases, **Dave Mason** and **Split Coconut,** have marked a progressive improvement in his work. For the latter album, he again formed a new backing band, which also accompanied him on a European tour that was nothing short of devastatingly successful. The line-up was: Jim Krueger (gtr), Rick Jaeger (drms), Gerald Johnson (bs), Jay Winding (kybds), and Mason himself (gtr, vcls).

Alone Together aside, Mason has never quite put everything together in the right way at the right time; but he remains a very talented and respected guitarist and songwriter, with a staunch following.

Scrapbook, released in 1972, is a double compilation set comprising selections from his work with Traffic as well as his solo albums **Alone Together** and **Headkeeper.**

Recordings:
Alone Together (Island)
Dave Mason And Cass Elliott (ABC-Dunhill/Probe)
Headkeeper (Blue Thumb/ Island)
Dave Mason Is Alive (Blue Thumb/—)
It's Like You Never Left (Columbia/CBS)
Dave Mason (Columbia/CBS)
Split Coconut (Columbia/CBS)

Matching Mole
◆ Robert Wyatt

Ian Matthews

Born Ian MacDonald in Lincolnshire, England, Matthews first worked professionally with Pyramid, an English surfing band (sic), after which he moved on to Fairport Convention (◆), where he shared vocal duties, played unobtrusive guitar and wrote the occasional song.

He stayed with band for two-and-a-half years, opting to leave to pursue a solo career before their third album, **Unhalfbricking,** was released. He then recorded **Matthews' Southern Comfort** for MCA, and as a result formed a band of same name with line-up of Gordon Huntley (pdl stl), Mark Griffiths (gtr), Carl Barnwell (gtr), Ray Duffy (drms), Andy Leigh (bs), and Matthews himself on vocals. At the time Huntley, who had wide professional experience, was generally considered the best steel-guitar player in England.

They recorded two albums, **Second Spring** and **Later That Same Year** in 1970, and in between found themselves with a hit single on their hands. Their version of **Woodstock** was a soft country interpretation of Joni Mitchell's song, and reached No. 1 in the U.K. and Top 20 in U.S.

Matthews' Southern Comfort made some good music, which was usually a blend of folk, country and their own compositions; but at the height of their success with **Woodstock,** Matthews, who thought the band's sense of purpose would be distorted by the hit single, suddenly left, leaving the others no alternative but to re-name themselves Southern Comfort, in which guise they made one more worthwhile album, **Frog City,** before splitting up themselves.

Thus Matthews resumed his solo career, with two albums, **If You**

Saw Thro' My Eyes and **Tigers Will Survive,** in 1971, that featured his own introspective songs.

Early in 1972 he found himself in a band once more, when he formed Plainsong with Andy Roberts, Dave Richards and Bobby Ronga. All four were guitarists, and as such the group was formed on a tidal wave of misplaced optimism which soon evaporated. The band separated in a matter of months, after making the concept album **In Search Of Amelia Earhart.** A second album, somewhat paradoxically titled **Plainsong III** was recorded, but never released. (Roberts went on to make two solo albums for Elektra – **Urban Cowboy** and **Andy Roberts And The Great Stampede,** both of which were issued in 1973.)

By now contracted to Elektra, Matthews resumed his solo career, this time in Los Angeles with the assistance of some very useful session-men. But neither **Valley Hi** (1973), which was produced by Mike Nesmith, nor **Some Days You Eat The Bear . . . And Some Days The Bear Eats You** (1974), despite the usual tasteful selection of material, met with much success.

Some Days You Eat The Bear . . . Elektra Asylum.

Matthews' contract was bought-up by Clive Davis at Arista, but since Davis rejected material as fast as Matthews came up with it, that arrangement proved entirely non-productive. Norbert Putnam then expressed a desire to produce Matthews, and a deal was put together with Columbia and **Go For Broke** released in 1976.

Matthews has a fine voice, and is a shrewd judge of material, but nevertheless after being the man-most-likely-to for so long, he is now beginning to look like the man-who-never-did.

Journeys From Gospel Oak is an album of material that Matthews recorded after **Tigers Will Survive;** it was released in Britain 1975 without his approval; similarly, **The Best Of Matthews Southern Comfort** was put together without his consent, and in a letter to "Melody Maker" he protested at the choice of material.

Recordings:
Matthews' Southern Comfort (Uni)
If You Saw Thro' My Eyes (Vertigo)
Tigers Will Survive (Vertigo)
Journeys From Gospel Oak (—/Mooncrest)
Valley Hi (Elektra)
Some Days You Eat The Bear . . . And Some Days The Bear Eats You (Elektra)
Go For Broke (Columbia/CBS)
With Matthews' Southern Comfort:

Second Spring (Uni)
Later That Same Year (Uni)
With Plainsong:
In Search Of Amelia Earhart (Elektra)
Compilation:
The Best Of Matthews Southern Comfort (—/MCA)

John Mayall

Born Manchester, England, Nov 29, 1933, Mayall is the Big Daddy of the British blues scene, in that his successive bands have virtually acted as a finishing school for many of Britain's leading instrumentalists.

Mayall became interested in blues at age of 13, and formed his first group, the Powerhouse Four, in college after his demob., but it wasn't until 1963 when, encouraged by Alexis Korner (◆), he left Manchester for London and began to establish himself. Even at this time, he had already acquired a reputation as a frugal eccentric, having lived in a treehouse for a time.

In London, he formed the first Bluesbreakers line-up, with John McVie (bs) and Bernie Watson (gtr), though by the time Mayall made his first album for Decca, Roger Dean had come in on guitar, and Hughie Flint on drums, alongside McVie. The album, **John Mayall Plays John Mayall,** was recorded live at Klook's Kleek, London.

In 1965 Dean was replaced by Eric Clapton (◆), who had just left The Yardbirds, and this team made **Bluesbreakers – John Mayall With Eric Clapton** (1966) – significantly it was the only time Mayall allowed anyone to be co-credited with him. **Bluesbreakers** was the first classic blues album, with Clapton enhancing the reputations of both Mayall and himself with some superbly imaginative guitar-playing (despite which, he received no more than the standard session fee).

Jack Bruce (◆) then came in as bassist, and when he and Clapton split to form Cream (◆), McVie rejoined and the group was completed by Aynsley Dunbar (drms) and Peter Green (gtr). This line-up produced **A Hard Road,** possibly Mayall's best album to date, with Green proving himself a perfectly adequate replacement for Clapton. The album bore liner notes, personally written by Mayall, on which he pledged himself never to augment the Bluesbreakers with a horn section.

Meanwhile, this Bluesbreakers also cut an EP with Paul Butterfield (◆), titled, obviously enough, **John Mayall's Bluesbreakers With Paul Butterfield,** while Mayall himself had made a solo album (supported solely by some occasional percussion by Keef Hartley), **The Blues Alone,** which had been recorded in one day in Hampstead, and was produced by Mike Vernon.

Green exited, shortly to form Fleetwood Mac with McVie, but he remains the most important right-hand man Mayall ever had. Though never given his due share of the limelight, Green had contributed much to Mayall's early sound, and shared vocal and composition duties with him. A Decca compilation, **Thru' The Years,** admirably docu-

ments this early period, and contains some interesting, and otherwise unissued, material (◆ Peter Green, Fleetwood Mac).

Mayall then expanded the Bluesbreakers to a sextet and, despite his pledge, brought in two horns players – Chris Mercer and Rip Kant; Mick Taylor (gtr) and Hartley (drms), who had previously been with The Artwoods, were also added to the line-up at this time. This band made **Crusade** (1967), an album on which the 18-year old and fairly raw Taylor turned in an impressive performance; the "Crusade" Mayall was leading was for the original American bluesmen who were not getting the recognition they deserved; Mayall was ever the zealous champion of the exploited bluesmen.

In early 1968 there followed a two-volume live album, **Diary Of A Band – Volumes I & II,** for which Heckstall-Smith had replaced Kant, and Keith Tillman had taken over from McVie on bass. The albums weren't very good, but they did emphasise that in 1968 bands like the Bluesbreakers were on the road virtually every day of the year.

Another set of Bluesbreakers came together for **Bare Wires** in June 1968. Personnel at this time: Henry Lowther (tpt, vln), Tony Reeves (bs), Jon Hiseman (drms), plus Taylor, Heckstall-Smith and Mercer. The album marked a change of direction for Mayall, who had hitherto been concerned essentially with material derived from Chicago-styled blues. **Bare Wires,** which contained only his own compositions, was his concession to contemporary progressive music – it was the thinking man's blues, though every time Mayall has tried for lyrical profundity, he has usually over-reached himself.

Bluesbreakers With Eric Clapton. Courtesy Decca.

The bare bones of the **Bare Wires** line-up left to become the nucleus of Colosseum (◆), and at this point Mayall ditched the term "Bluesbreakers", and he and Taylor returned to a quartet format, adding Steve Thompson (bs) and Colin Allen (drms). The only recorded work of this band was **Blues From Laurel Canyon,** which was Mayall's impressions of a three-week holiday in the States, and was a surprisingly satisfactory venture; this band, however, broke up – Taylor, Mayall's longest-serving guitarist, left, and was almost immediately offered the chair vacated by Brian Jones in the Rolling Stones (◆), while Allen also bowed out (though he was later reunited with Thompson as the rhythm section of Stone The Crows (◆)).

In mid-1969 Mayall defied the

whole blues-rock tradition and formed a band without a drummer or an electric guitarist, and announced his intention of exploring "seldom-used areas within the framework of low volume music". The new line-up consisted of Jon Mark (acoustic gtr), Johnny Almond (tnr, sxs, flute) and Thompson (bs). They made debut in U.S. and recorded **The Turning Point** at Fillmore East Jul 12, 1969. (Mayall was always scrupulously informative in his sleeve-credits.)

Bare Wires. Courtesy Decca Records.

The album was aptly titled. Although remaining within a blues framework, much of what the line-up attempted was nearer to jazz, and Almond's contribution was particularly impressive; altogether, it was an imaginative and successful move. **Empty Rooms** was recorded with the same line-up, though with the addition of Larry Taylor (bs). Thompson in fact had been ill, and he was sometimes replaced on tour by Alex Dmochowski. While this line-up was on the road, Mayall recruited as support act Duster Bennett, a "one-man blues band" who would usually join the band for closing number.

In December 1970, Mayall issued **U.S.A. Union**, on which he used American musicians for the first time. The new band was: Don "Sugarcane" Harris (vln), Harvey Mandel (gtr), Larry Taylor (bs). However, they had seemingly had little time to rehearse (something which Mayall normally recognised as an advantage), and the album was undone by the social conscience songs that Mayall had been writing since he'd discovered ecology around the time of **The Turning Point,** and which had been becoming increasingly more hackneyed.

The next year, Mayall got together all the various alumni of his bands, to make a guest-star double album, **Back To The Roots**; the album was clearly not the success it should have been, though the fact that Mayall had gathered together so many illustrious musicians showed the respect he was still accorded.

Since then, Mayall has worked increasingly in America – where he now lives – and increasingly in a jazz-blues style; for **Jazz-Blues Fusion** he assembled a band of: Blue Mitchell (tpt), Stax guitarist Freddy Robinson, Clifford Solomon (sxs), Larry Taylor (bs) and Ron Selico (drms). With some changes, this basic grouping made **Moving On** and **Ten Years Are Gone** (1973), the latter of which was produced by Don Nix; by then, Keef Hartley (♦) had been recalled to the first team,

Above: Eric Clapton. It was during his stint with Mayall that his early reputation as a guitar hero was consolidated.

Top: Mayall's Bluesbreakers take a break from recording. (Left to right) Clapton, Mayall, Flint and McVie.

and Victor Gaskin was on bass.

At the beginning of 1975, Mayall again came up with something completely different (for him), a female vocalist, Dee McKinnie. He'd also switched labels to ABC, and hence the album was called **New Year, New Band, New Company**; it was evident that Mayall's muse had long since departed – his songwriting had never been a particularly strong point, and now it was stretched very thin. Later that year in another complete departure, he went to New Orleans to record an album produced by Allen Toussaint. **Notice To Appear** was finally a John Mayall solo album proper.

Though his fierce determination to be forever moving on to something new has often led him up many musical cul-de-sacs, Mayall remains an innovative and influential figure of the last decade; however, he seems destined to be remembered more for the people he groomed for stardom,

than for his own contributions to the development of rock music.

Albums info: Polydor re-packaged **Empty Rooms** and **The Turning Point** as a double-album in 1974. **Looking Back** is a compilation of all the early Mayall singles.

Recordings:
John Mayall Plays John Mayall (London/Decca)
Bluesbreakers (With Eric Clapton) (London/Decca)
The Blues Alone (London/Ace Of Clubs)
A Hard Road (London/Decca)
Crusade (London/Decca)
Diary Of A Band, Vol. I (London/Decca)
Diary Of A Band, Vol. II (London/Decca)
Bare Wires (London/Decca)
Blues From Laurel Canyon (London/Decca)
The Turning Point (Polydor)
Empty Rooms (Polydor)
USA Union (Polydor)
Memories (Polydor)

Back To The Roots (Polydor)
Jazz-Blues Fusion (Polydor)
Moving On (Polydor)
Ten Years Are Gone (Polydor)
The Latest Edition (Polydor)
New Year, New Band, New Company (Blue Thumb/ABC)
Notice To Appear (Blue Thumb/ABC)
Compilations:
Looking Back (London/Decca)
The World Of John Mayall (—/Decca)
The World Of John Mayall, Vol. II (—/Decca)
Down The Line (London/—)
Beyond The Turning Point (—/Polydor)
Thru The Years (London/Decca)

Curtis Mayfield

Born Chicago June 1942, Mayfield was the creative force behind The Impressions (♦).

When he left to go solo in 1970, he had already set up his own record label, Curtom (now a flourishing independent company) and was beginning to broaden his horizons in fields of songwriting and production; but he could hardly have expected his solo career to take off in quite the way it did. His first solo album, **Curtis,** was one of the most successful of 1970, providing **Move On Up,** which in August, 1971 became his only British chart entry to date.

His next two albums, the double **Curtis – Live** and **Roots** helped consolidate his reputation; his vocals were soft but compelling, his songs often superb, his understanding of production techniques faultless; he was the perfect choice to provide the score for "Superfly", and in doing so he not only provided himself with the bestselling record of his career, but also ensured that a rather mediocre film would be remembered long after its natural lifespan was exhausted.

Superfly. Courtesy Pye Records.

Superfly was superbly conceived – it worked both as a soundtrack for the film, and as an album in its own right, as the very best of orchestral soul music. It went platinum in 1972, being one of the year's top albums, and provided two gold singles – **Freddie's Dead,** and **Superfly** itself. The momentum Mayfield built up was such that his next offering, **Back To The World,** went gold virtually as soon as it was released. **Curtis In Chicago** (a recorded television show, which featured guest appearances by old friends Jerry Butler and Gene Chandler), **Sweet Exorcist** and **Got To Find A Way** followed in rapid succession; and together with two more soundtracks which he wrote and produced – **Claudine**, for Gladys Knight and the Pips, and **Let's Do It Again**, for The Staple Singers, showed that he was in danger of over-extending himself.

Then in 1975 he released **There's No Place Like America Today**, which confirmed him as one of the great songwriters. Few people are able to analyse contemporary ills of society in quite the perceptive way that Mayfield achieves. What makes him special is the humanity and compassion of his writing. The day they made Curtis Mayfield, they threw away the mould.

Recordings:
Curtis (Curtom/Buddah)
Curtis – Live (Curtom/Buddah)
Roots (Curtom/Buddah)
Superfly (Soundtrack) (Curtom/Buddah)
Back To The World (Curtom/Buddah)
Sweet Exorcist (Curtom/Buddah)
Got To Find A Way (Curtom/Buddah)
There's No Place Like America Today (Curtom/Buddah)
Compilation:
Move On Up – The Best Of Curtis Mayfield (—/Buddah)

MC5

Wayne Kramer guitar
Fred "Sonic" Smith guitar
Rob Tyner vocals, harmonica
Michael Davis bass
Dennis Thompson drums

First came to prominence as figureheads of John Sinclair's revolutionary White Panther Party in Detroit, going to Chicago to play at 1968 Democratic Convention riots. Described retrospectively as the first '70s band of the '60s, the MC5 represented about equal parts dope and revolutionary ideology, macho flash and uncompromisingly violent high energy rock 'n' roll.

Above: Wayne Kramer of MC5.

First album was recorded live in 1968 and embroiled Elektra in controversy over lyric line "Kick out the jams motherfuckers!" This caused at least one U.S. record store to refuse to stock the album, the group responding by taking out a vigorously declamatory ad in a local underground paper. Elektra weren't too amused, especially when group went further and plastered "Fuck You" stickers over the record store's win-

Right: Paul McCartney, still rock's boss bass man. In autumn 1976 he announced plans to issue a Wings live album.

dows (these stickers bearing the Elektra logo) and band and label parted company shortly after.

(MC5 did cut a single for Elektra in which they modified offending line to "Kick out the jams brothers and sisters." Some copies of album contain this version, others the original.)

The '5 had also split from manager Sinclair (he served two-and-a-half years of 9 to 10 year marijuana sentence in a case which became a cause célèbre) and moved to Atlantic. For this label cut **Back In The USA** in 1970. Produced by rock critic Jon Landau, later to work in same capacity for Bruce Springsteen (♦), this is regarded by some as one of the greatest power-drive rock albums of all time. However, the '5 were out of step with public taste and sales failed to recoup Atlantic's advance.

The 1971 set **High Time** fared no better, and Atlantic subsequently dropped them from roster. The '5 went to England early 1972 to look for new opportunities but slowly fell apart, bassist Davis and drummer Thompson being the first to split.

Thompson (in Los Angeles) and "Sonic" Smith (in Detroit area) were, in 1976, working with new but still struggling outfits; while Rob Tyner had carved relatively successful career as writer/photographer. Bassist Davis, however, was in mid-'70s languishing in a Federal minimum-security jail, and, in February 1976, former lead guitarist Wayne Kramer pleaded guilty to a cocaine-dealing charge carrying a five-year prison sentence.

The '70s punk-rock revival was a scene the MC5 originally pioneered.

Recordings:
Kick Out The Jams (Elektra)
Back In The USA (Atlantic)
High Time (Atlantic)

Paul McCartney

The "Let It Be" film had shown McCartney doing his utmost to keep The Beatles (♦) intact; when it all proved to no avail, he became the first of the four actually to leave group, and two main points of dissension arose with other three – first of all, he angered them by deciding to issue **McCartney** only two weeks before the scheduled release of **Let It Be**. Secondly, he wanted to bring in Lee Eastman – his father-in-law – as financial adviser to the group. The others wanted Allen

Klein (➜), and this dispute was one of the starting-points of bitter and protracted litigation, with McCartney seeking to dissolve the group through the courts.

McCartney, issued April 1970, was an entirely home-made affair, featuring Paul's wife, Linda, whom he had married on Mar 12, 1969. McCartney played all instruments himself, and the album had a stark, unfinished quality to it, which was quite appealing, and contained **Maybe I'm Amazed,** which was covered by The Faces on **Long Player.**

Next time around, Linda was co-credited, and various New York session-men helped out. "Rolling Stone", however, called **Ram** the nadir of rock music; whether or not they were right at the time, McCartney soon showed he could do worse than this, and the album contained some good material, particularly **Back Seat Of My Car,** and **Uncle Albert/Admiral Halsey,** which became a U.S. No. 1. If the album evinced a decline into cosy domesticity, Paul has never pretended to like it any other way, and that side of his music was at its most candid on the single issued in February 1971, **Another Day.**

Later that year, McCartney, to his credit, formed a fully-fledged band. Unlike the ad hoc all-star aggregations favoured by the other Beatles, Wings was always intended as a permanent and viable recording and touring outfit. The initial line-up was: McCartney (bs, vcls), Linda McCartney (kybds), Denny Laine (gtr), Denny Seiwell (drms). Seiwell, previously had session experience in New York, and Laine had formerly been a member of the Moody Blues (➜). Nevertheless, the band's first album release, **Wild Life** (1971) was really tepid and showed McCartney's credibility sinking fast, a situation which **Red Rose Speedway** (1973) did nothing to rescue, though it did give McCartney another No. 1 U.S. single with **My Love,** and also reasserted his position as rock's boss bass-man. It also featured a new member of Wings, guitarist Henry McCullough (previously with Grease Band).

In between times, McCartney had made some strange singles. There was **Give Ireland Back To The Irish,** a single rush-released in wake of British soldiers shooting dead 13 Irish civilians in a demonstration in Londonderry on Jan 31, 1972, in an incident that became known as "Bloody Sunday"; in retrospect, the song, which was banned by the BBC, seems a token gesture by McCartney to demonstrate that Lennon wasn't the only ex-Beatle with a political conscience. The song was followed by the utterly innocuous **Mary Had A Little Lamb,** which did neither better nor worse than **Give Ireland Back To The Irish** in commercial terms. At the end of the year, Wings issued **Hi Hi Hi/ C Moon,** easily their best-ever single. **C Moon** especially showed McCartney had fully absorbed and understood reggae rhythms. The year 1973 was busy. He was arrested on a drugs charge, and in June had his own television special broadcast in Britain and America. Wings undertook their first full-scale tour of Britain, and McCartney wrote and recorded

Above: Band On The Run. Courtesy EMI. The McCartneys, Laine and assorted famous friends – a rogues gallery?

theme-tune for latest James Bond movie, "Live And Let Die", which provided him with a No. 2 single in America.

The band then went to Nigeria to record **Band On The Run,** but since Seiwell and McCullough had left after the tour, the McCartneys were accompanied only by the faithful Laine. The resulting album, however, was McCartney's best post-Beatle effort, and also became Wings' first platinum album (each of the others had gone gold). It provided two bestselling singles, **Jet** and the title track, and McCartney also finally replied to Lennon's vitriolic attack on him (**How Do You Sleep?**) on **Imagine** with a cutting song of his own, **Let Me Roll It,** complete with a primal scream.

Even the cover was interesting. It showed Wings in prison garb, as were various other show-biz celebrities/friends of the McCartneys' – Liverpool-born boxer John Conteh, film stars James Coburn and Christopher Lee, television interviewer Michael Parkinson, singer Kenny Lynch and Liberal M.P. and professional gourmet, Clement Freud.

The album restored McCartney's confidence, and Wings soon became a recognisable band again. When they went to Nashville to record in 1974 (where they made **Junior's Farm,** another fine single), Jimmy McCulloch, formerly of Thunderclap Newman and Stone The Crows, was recruited. The vacant drummer's stool was filled for a time by Geoff

Below: Red Rose Speedway. Courtesy EMI. Wings' second album; too bad there was only room for McCartney in the cover shot.

Britton, a British karate expert, but when he left the band found Joe English in New Orleans; the line-up of the band has thus been constant since early 1975.

Wings released **Venus And Mars** in the early summer of that year. Though the album went platinum, it was a largely uninteresting re-take of **Band On The Run.** The next album, **Wings At The Speed Of Sound** (1976), was the first real team effort, with McCartney delegating songwriting and vocal responsibilities to the other members, and the album suffered accordingly. Democracy was ever imperfect. However, on commercial terms alone, McCartney has been far and away the most successful of the four Beatles since the split – as indeed, everyone had predicted he would be.

Meanwhile, the band undertook their first world tour, which began in Britain in autumn 1975 and proceeded through Europe and Australia to go coast-to-coast in America in the summer of 1976.

Recordings:
Paul McCartney:
McCartney (Apple)
Paul And Linda McCartney:
Ram (Apple)
Wings:
Wild Life (Apple)
Red Rose Speedway (Apple)
Band On The Run (Apple)
Venus And Mars (Capitol/EMI)
Wings At The Speed Of Sound (Capitol/EMI)

Charlie McCoy

Doyen of Nashville studio musicians, McCoy is generally reckoned to be the premier harmonica session-man in the world; he says he has been playing the instrument since 1948.

A legendary figure in music circles, McCoy acts as session organiser in Nashville, being link-man between the resident musicians and the visiting artists. He played on Bob Dylan's **Highway 61 Revisited** and **Blonde On Blonde,** and was also a member of Area Code 615 (➜). He has made several solo albums, most of which feature unexceptional renderings (by Nashville standards) of unexceptional songs, distinguished by McCoy's superbly dexterous harmonica pyrotechnics. Because they are all of similar quality, only one is listed.

Recording:
The Nashville Hit Man (Monument)

The McCoys
➜ Rick Derringer

Country Joe McDonald

Perhaps the most endearing (and one of most enduring?) out-take of the politico-druggie awakening which spread out of San Francisco in the mid-'60s, McDonald epitomised that whole shambolically charming era arguably even more so than contemporaries Jefferson Airplane (➜) and Grateful Dead (➜).

He was born in El Monte, California, on New Year's Day 1942, and named after Joseph Stalin by his Leftist parents, Jewish on his mother's side. In his youth he listened mainly to country music, and wrote his first song **I Seen A Rocket** to support a friend's campaign for student president. Honourably discharged from the U.S. Navy after four years' service, he started writing politically-motivated songs which he performed in folk clubs around Berkeley, California.

His first recording was on an obscure album **The Goodbye Blues,** credited to Country Joe and Blair Hardman, released in 1964, after which he was part of The Berkeley String Quartet and the Instant Action Jug Band. Alongside McDonald in the approximately 13-strong latter act was guitarist Barry Melton, the pair forming the first incarnation of Country Joe & The Fish circa 1965 to record the legendary **Rag Baby** EPs for Takoma label, which have been described as "magazines in record form".

The Fish went through various personnel changes before their first album, **Electric Music For The Mind And Body,** was released in April 1967. This featured a line-up of McDonald (gtr, hrmnca, vcls), Melton (gtr), David Cohen (kybds, vcls), Chicken Hirsh (drms) and Bruce Barthol (bs). The latter was also an alumnus of the Instant Action Jug Band.

From the start they were a politically-oriented group, wildly eclectic and somewhat inconsistent, but they blended poetry, anarchism, politics and various strains of rock, blues, folk and country music with considerable skill.

The second album, **I-Feel-Like-I'm-Fixin'-To-Die** (1967), cemented their burgeoning reputation as the politically-conscious act of the day. The title track, an anti-war litany, was preceded by what was to develop into the famous Fish Cheer ("Gimme an F, Gimme a U, Gimme a C, Gimme a K", etc.), and had made its first appearance on one of Joe's **Rag Baby** EPs in 1965.

It was subsequently to become the group's best known and requested number, as well as the anthem of the whole West Coast politico-rock trip. McDonald performed it at the Woodstock Festival (1969), and had to be forcibly restrained from singing it in court as a witness for the defence in the trial of the Chicago Seven, the cause célèbre arising out of the 1968 Democratic Convention riots.

The early Fish albums were masterpieces, though the fourth, **Here We Are Again** (1969) showed signs of tension. In 1970 McDonald split from the Fish, which by then included ex Big Brother And The Holding Company (♦) members David Getz and Peter Albin, and commenced a series of solo albums and concerts.

He also became interested in medium of film soundtracks – scoring a Dutch movie of Henry Miller's novel "Quiet Days In Clichy", "Gas-s-s-s", "Que Hacer", a political film made in Chile, and "Zachariah". He and members of The Fish also appeared in the last-named.

Always politically conscious, in 1971 McDonald became associated with the Jane Fonda/Donald Sutherland anti-war revue FTA (Free The Army), but, ever the dissident, Joe pulled out after a tour of army bases lambasting Fonda's patronising attitudes towards the soldiers' lot.

In cohorts with various fluctuating line-ups, he subsequently became a regular fixture at festivals throughout the U.S. and Europe, never being allowed to leave the stage until he had led the audience into the legendary Fish Cheer.

He had worked in England extensively – his 1971-released **Hold On – It's Comin'** was cut in London with U.K. musicians including Spencer Davis – and in 1973 he made Europe his base of operations.

The Paris Sessions (1973) was recorded at the Chateau d'Herouville in France, and was the best of his solo releases to date, and in 1974–75 he reunited with Fish associate Barry Melton for an extensive U.K. club tour. The two played together and performed separate sets.

I Feel Like I'm Fixin' To Die. Courtesy Pye Records.

Now living in England, he continued to play concerts in 1975, but towards the end of the year returned to Berkeley, California, to sign a new record deal with Fantasy Records and record the 1976-released **Paradise With An Ocean View.**

That album not only saw him back in his homeland but also returning, in no uncertain terms, to the U.S. charts. Altogether, a quite remarkable character who has provided some of the most memorable moments in rock – not to mention 17 albums.

Recordings:
Country Joe & The Fish:
Electric Music For The Mind And Body (Vanguard)
I-Feel-Like-I'm-Fixin'-To-Die (Vanguard)
Together (Vanguard)
Here We Are Again (Vanguard)
C. J. Fish (Vanguard)
Compilations:
Greatest Hits (Vanguard)
The Life And Times Of Country Joe & The Fish From Haight Ashbury To Woodstock (Vanguard)
The Best Of Country Joe & The Fish (Vanguard)
Country Joe McDonald:
Country Joe And Blair Hardman (unknown)
Thinking Of Woody Guthrie (Vanguard)
Tonight I'm Singing Just For You (Vanguard)
Quiet Days In Clichy (Soundtrack) (Sonet)
Hold On – It's Comin' (Vanguard)

War War War (Vanguard)
Incredible! Live! Country Joe! (Vanguard)
The Paris Sessions (Vanguard)
Country Joe (Vanguard)
Paradise With An Ocean View (Fantasy)

Kate And Anna McGarrigle

Sisters from Canada, they grew-up in the French quarter of Quebec in a strong musical environment, and absorbed varying influences, from Stephen Foster and French Canadian folksongs to Gershwin and Edith Piaf.

In Montreal Kate and Anna were part of a group called the Mountain City Four, and in 1967 while Anna was at the L'Ecole des Beaux-Arts and Kate at McGill University, they were commissioned to write music for National Film Board of Canada's "Helicopter Canada".

In the '70s their compositions began to attract attention. Anna's **Heart Like A Wheel** was recorded in 1972 by McKendree Spring and later used on the soundtrack of "Play It As It Lays". It was subsequently recorded by Linda Ronstadt (♦).

Kate meanwhile moved to New York, where she met Maria Muldaur (♦), who recorded Kate's composition **The Work Song** on her debut solo album. Maria subsequently put a McGarrigle song on each of her next two albums – **Cool River** on **Waitress In A Donut Shop,** and **Lying Song** on **Sweet Harmony.**

Lenny Waronker, in charge of A&R at Warner Bros, was impressed with their songwriting, and Kate and Anna were accordingly flown to California to record an album with Joe Boyd (♦) producing.
Kate And Anna McGarrigle was released early 1976 to universal critical acclaim; it is an album of genuinely warming, romantic songs, and demonstrates the diversity of influences that have helped mould the sisters' musical direction.

Kate is married to (though separated from) Loudon Wainwright, and lives in New York; Anna lives on a farm in Alexandria, Ontario.

Recording:
Kate And Anna McGarrigle (Warner Bros)

Roger McGuinn

Born James Joseph McGuinn in Chicago, Jul 13, 1942 – he changed name to Roger in 1968 as result of adoption of Subud faith. The son of professional writers, he travelled country with them as a child. In his 'teens he began working as a folksinger and guitarist. Took familiar route to Greenwich Village in late '50s, and ended up backing '60s pop star Bobby Darin on U.S. tours.

A founder member of Byrds 1964; with his quaint Dickensian shades, McGuinn was the one constant factor in that seminal group's nine-year history. (♦ The Byrds.)

On demise of group, 1973,

McGuinn worked solo, producing three Byrd-soundalike albums for Columbia/CBS and touring firstly solo, then with own pick-up band. In late 1975 through 1976 turned-up as member of Bob Dylan's all-star Rolling Thunder Revue, after which he cut the excellent **Cardiff Rose** with fellow Dylan trouper Mick Ronson (♦) producing.

However, McGuinn still owns right to Byrds name and has been quoted as saying: "The Byrds may fly again one day . . . who knows?"

Recordings:
Roger McGuinn (Columbia/CBS)
Peace On You (Columbia/CBS)
Roger McGuinn And Band (Columbia/CBS)
Cardiff Rose (Columbia/CBS)

McGuinness Flint

After break-up of Manfred Mann (♦), Tom McGuinness formed McGuinness Flint with Hughie Flint, who had been one of the early drummers with John Mayall (♦); the band was completed by a couple of musicians/songwriters from Scotland, Benny Gallagher and Graham Lyle, and vocalist Dennis Coulson. Unlike the other alumni of Manfred Mann, McGuinness pledged himself and the band to unsophisticated, carefree music, a policy which resulted in two immensely enjoyable and very successful hit records, **When I'm Dead And Gone** and **Malt And Barley Blues** (1971), before Gallagher and Lyle (♦), who had written both songs, quit the band. Dixie Dean (bs, hrmnca) was recruited, and the band – now democratically named Coulson, Dean, McGuinness, Flint – made one album in the esteemed traditions of Manfred Mann. (In fact, it was co-produced by the four of them plus Mann himself.) **Lo And Behold** was an entire album of Dylan material, much of it obscure, some of which had not previously been unearthed; the songs were given treatments that were both imaginative and sympathetic, and the album remains the most successful album of Dylan material by artists other than Dylan.

Coulson made a solo album for Elektra in 1973, **Dennis Coulson.** He produced it himself, together with Gallagher and Lyle, who also wrote five of the compositions.
Discography is selective.

Recordings:
McGuinness Flint (Capitol)
Happy Birthday Ruthie Baby (Capitol)
C'est La Vie (—/Bronze)
Coulson, Dean, McGuinness, Flint:
Lo And Behold (—/DJM)

John McLaughlin

Born Yorkshire, England, 1942, McLaughlin studied violin and piano from the age of seven, and took up guitar in early 'teens under the influence of American blues recordings. By the age of 14 this interest had taken him into jazz, but it was as a member of

R&B bands (albeit jazz-tinged) that McLaughlin first gained attention as a virtuoso guitarist. He was a member of the Graham Bond Organization (◆ Graham Bond) in the early '60s with Jack Bruce and Ginger Baker, and also had a spell with Brian Auger Trinity (◆ Brian Auger).

In 1969 he dipped out of this circle to return to jazz roots and cut the extraordinary **Extrapolation,** with group including John Surman. The album made no impact commercially, but its dazzling virtuosity gave McLaughlin semi-legendary status and helped bring him to the attention of American jazz drummer Tony Williams.

In 1970, Williams invited McLaughlin to the U.S. to join his band Lifetime, subsequent to which Miles Davis (◆) came to hear of this rising young guitar star. During the next 18 months, McLaughlin was to play on two Lifetime albums, **Emergency** and **Turn It Over,** the second reuniting him with Jack Bruce (◆), and on the two seminal Miles Davis jazz rock sets **Bitches' Brew** and **In A Silent Way.** Around the same period, he found time to go to France to cut his own second solo album **Devotion** with Buddy Miles (◆).

McLaughlin had almost immediately found himself at odds with the pace of New York life. He first practised yoga as a means of relaxation, gave up meat, cigarettes and drugs, and subsequently became a convert to the philosophy of Bengal mystic Sri Chinmoy, an event which profoundly altered the course of his music.

Above: John McLaughlin, photographed in the U.K., 1974.

In 1971 he cut **My Goal's Beyond,** a meditational album of solo acoustic pieces and group improvisations on Indian scales. Accompanying him were Jerry Goodman, former violinist with U.S. jazz-rock band Flock, and drummer Billy Cobham (◆), another Miles Davis side-man.

These two, with additions of Jan Hammer (kybds) and Rick Laird (bs) comprised John McLaughlin's Mahavishnu Orchestra which made **The Inner Mounting Flame** and **Birds Of Fire** in 1972 and 1973 respectively. Both were innovatory releases in the jazz-rock genre, technically dazzling and breathtaking in emotional impact, and broke his name among rock audiences.

From that point, however, McLaughlin's spiritual awareness began to dissipate his hitherto unimpeachable taste. In 1973 he made a vapid, spiritually-obsessive jamming album with fellow Sri Chinmoy convert Carlos Santana (◆), **Love Devotion Surrender,** and then a Mahavishnu Orchestra album recorded live in Central Park, New York, August 1973, **Between Nothingness And Eternity.** This last was the final work of the Mahavishnu Orchestra I.

In January 1974 he disbanded his first orchestra and formed the Mahavishnu Mark II (though he preferred to call it the "real Mahavishnu Orchestra"). This greatly-expanded line-up featured the electric violin of Jean-Luc Ponty (◆), Michael Walden (drms), Ralphe Armstrong (bs), Gayle Moran (kybds, vcls), Steve Frankovitch and Bob Knapp (brass and reeds), and a four-strong string section of Stephen Kinder, Carol Shive, Marsha Westbrook and Phil Herschi.

Not content with stopping there, McLaughlin brought in the London Symphony Orchestra, under conductor Michael Tilson-Thomas, the production/engineering team of George Martin (◆) and Geoffrey Emory, both of Beatles/**Sgt Pepper** fame, and the arranging of Michael Gibbs, for the new group's massively-ambitious album debut, **Apocalpse** (1974).

Neither that or their second album, **Visions Of The Emerald Beyond** (1975), did anything to reverse widespread critical feeling that a substantial talent had disappeared over spiritual cliff.

In early 1976, from recordings at Chateau d'Heuronville, **Inner Worlds** appeared credited to a much-slimmed Mahavishnu Orchestra, subsequent to which McLaughlin was reputed to have severed links with Sri Chimnoy, re-discovered some of earlier vices and undergone re-think of direction. This took form of Shakti (1976), an acoustic album on which McLaughlin teamed with Indian group of same name.

In same year Polydor released **In Retrospect,** a two-album compilation of early recordings.

Recordings:
John McLaughlin:
Extrapolation (Polydor/ Marmalade)
Devotion (Barclay – import)
My Goal's Beyond (Douglas – import)
Love Devotion Surrender (Columbia/CBS)
In Retrospect (Polydor)
Shakti (Columbia/CBS)
Mahavishnu Orchestra:
The Inner Mounting Flame (Columbia/CBS)
Birds of Fire (Columbia/CBS)
Between Nothingness & Eternity (Columbia/CBS)
Apocalypse (Columbia/CBS)
Visions Of The Emerald Beyond (Columbia/CBS)
Inner Worlds (Columbia/CBS)

Don McLean

Born Oct 2, 1945 in New Rochelle, New York, where he grew up, McLean soon developed an interest in all forms of native American music, and when he left school in 1963 started playing in clubs as a folksinger – he has never held down a regular job.

From 1968 he made the Cafe Lena his home base, as it was through his connections with Lena Spender, who ran the club, that he became the Hudson River Troubadour, playing to 50 communities along the river. Pete Seeger got to hear of these activities and invited McLean to sail with him on the sloop "Clearwater", which sailed down the river from South Bristol, Maine to New York City, carrying the message of ecological salvation to the river community about to be infected by industrial pollution. McLean put together a book about this voyage, called "Songs And Sketches Of The First Clearwater Crew".

American Pie. Courtesy United Artists Records.

By the time the book was published, McLean was working regularly, building a reputation for himself, and writing songs. He recorded a tape of his songs and spent over two years trying to negotiate record contract; eventually **Tapestry** was released by a small company. It made a slight, though discernible impact, so that when the company folded his contract was bought-up by United Artists.

The album **American Pie** was issued in America towards end of 1971, and the title-song catapulted him to international fame. An elaborate allegory, it told the social and political history of a generation in terms of the rise and fall of its music, rock 'n' roll; it lasted over eight minutes, and has proved one of most outstanding singles of '70s so far.

Unfortunately for McLean the overwhelming success of that composition had tended to overshadow the rest of his career. Although his follow-up, also from the album, was a complete departure in that it was about the painter Van Gogh, and the song – **Vincent** – had some success of its own (reaching No. 12 in U.S., No. 1 in U.K., where it went one better than **American Pie**) nevertheless it is for **Pie** which he is best known in America.

The album, **Don McLean,** released late 1972 was all but ignored; it was a sombre and somewhat pained album as McLean, through songs like **The Pride Parade** and **Dreidel,** tried to resolve the traumatic effects of his sudden elevation to stardom – certainly it showed him to be a genuine creative talent.

In 1973 his career was given two fortuitous boosts. First of all, Perry Como had an international hit with **And I Love You So,** a song from McLean's debut album, and secondly Roberta Flack had a U.S. No. 1 with **Killing Me Softly With His Song,** which had originally been written by Lori Leiberman by Charles Gimbel and Norman Fox after seeing McLean in performance.

Certainly, McLean's years of apprenticeship had enabled him to develop into a skilled and versatile performer. (In 1971, Bob Elfstrum made "Other Voices", a film of one of his concerts, which was nominated for an Academy Award.) **Playin' Favourites,** an album of diverse material, none of it self-composed, showed both his depth of understanding of American music traditions and his own dexterity as an instrumentalist, both on guitar and banjo.

McLean in fact became far more popular in Britain than America; his annual tours of the U.K. are inevitable sell-outs, and singles like **Everday** and **Wonderful Baby** have enjoyed some success. In 1975 he gave a free concert in Hyde Park, London, at the conclusion of a particularly successful British tour.

In 1974 he released **Homeless Brother,** which was beautifully produced by Joel Dorn; it was an album of original songs such as **The Legend Of Andrew McCrew** which showed his flair for narrative. His recording career since has been interrupted by litigation with his record company.

Recordings:
Tapestry (United Artists)
American Pie (United Artists)
Don McLean (United Artists)
Playin' Favourites (United Artists)
Homeless Brother (United Artists)

Ralph McTell

Born Farnborough, Kent, McTell enlisted in army in 1965, and after that learned to play guitar and busked in Europe. On his return, he lived in Cornwall and began to write songs. He enrolled in teachers' training college, and during his time there 8 **Frames A Second** was released.

He toured British folk circuit for considerable time, gradually building-up a loyal following until **Spiral Staircase** was released 1969; this album included his most famous composition **Streets Of London** and brought him wider recognition; it was evident from his third release, **My Side Of Your Window,** that his writing was rapidly maturing.

Ralph McTell Revisited was a compilation of early recordings, re-mixed for release in America. **You, Well-Meaning Brought Me Here** received very enthusiastic reviews, before he moved to Reprise and issued **Not Till Tomorrow** (1972) and **Easy** (1973). He seemed likely to remain a performer very popular with minority following, until **Streets Of London** was issued as a single on Warner Bros label with all the trappings of instant commerciality (strings, and a girlie backing chorus); the song was a surprise No. 1 in Britain at beginning of 1975; McTell responded with his first-ever concert (rather than club) tour, for which he also broke with his customary habits by employing a supporting band, which included Steeleye Span's Maddy Prior, as backing vocalist.

At the conclusion of this tour, however, he suddenly announced his retirement to go away and write some new material in America. He has always seemed the dedicated folkie, to whom instant commercial success is anathema.

Recordings:
8 Frames A Second
(—/Transatlantic)
Spiral Staircase (—/Transatlantic)
My Side Of Your Window
(—/Transatlantic)
**You, Well-Meaning Brought Me
Here** (ABC)
Not Till Tomorrow (—/Reprise)
Easy (—/Reprise)
Streets (—/Warner Bros)
Compilation:
Ralph McTell Revisited
(—/Transatlantic)

Medicine Head

John Fiddler guitar, vocals
Peter Hope Evans harmonica,
Jew's harp

As duo playing small clubs around
Midlands area of England, broke
through when they sent a tape to
DJ John Peel, then running his
own Dandelion label. First album
in 1970, and single **His Guiding
Hand,** evidenced sparse understated style, and quaint mixture
of exotic love-songs and skeletal
R&B in Fiddler's writing. Their
Pictures In The Sky made U.K.
singles lists in summer 1971, after
which the eccentrically-reserved
Hope Evans split.

Fiddler re-formed Medicine
Head as a trio with ex Yardbird
Keith Relf on bass — Relf was at
time their producer — and John
Davies on drums. This trio made
1972 album **Dark Side Of The
Moon** (no relation).

When Hope Evans reappeared
later in 1972, he and Fiddler
worked as duo once again, although augmented by session
musicians on 1973 set **One And
One Is One,** produced by ex
Family keyboardsman Tony Ashton. Title track, and follow-up
Rising Sun, both made British
singles charts, after which group
expanded to quintet with addition of Rob Townsend (drms), also
ex Family, Roger Saunders (gtr)
and Ian Sainty (bs).

This line-up recorded **Thru' A
Five** for Polydor in 1974, but subsequently became involved with
now defunct WWA organisation.
Only Fiddler, Hope Evans and
Townsend emerged from this
barren, bitter period. The group
attempted to keep going by adding Charlie McCracken (bs), ex
Spencer Davis and Taste, but
finally submitted to ongoing managerial and economic pressures in
May 1975. Without the backing of
a record company, and unable to
issue their last album due to legal
disputes, they found it impossible
to continue. In 1976 resurfaced as
duo signed to Chas Chandler's
Barn label.

Recordings:
New Bottles, Old Medicine
(—/Dandelion)
Heavy On The Drum
(—/Dandelion)
Dark Side Of The Moon
(—/Dandelion)
One And One Is One (Polydor)
Thru' A Five (Polydor)

Melanie

Born Melanie Safka New York,
Feb 3, 1947, daughter of a one-
time jazz singer. Though Melanie
sang in East Coast bars, she
initially courted ambitions to be

an actress and attended drama
school.

She became a singer almost by
accident; she went to audition for
a small part in a play, but was
shown into the wrong office by
mistake, a music publisher's
office. As she was carrying a
guitar with her, she was asked to
sing, and out of that chance
meeting came a recording contract with Buddah Records, and
also her acquaintance with Peter
Schekeryk, who became first her
producer, and subsequently her
husband.

With her evident sincerity,
humanity and total lack of conceit,
she began to attract a following,
and with her album, **Candles In
The Rain** — which went gold —
she was accepted as the darling
of the contemporary peace 'n'
love movement, the champion of
the spiritually undernourished.

Her records, nonetheless, sounded no more than twee to many
listeners, but singles like **What
Have They Done To My Song,
Ma?** and the Jagger/Richard
song, **Ruby Tuesday** brought
her to a wider audience, and at
the beginning of 1972 **Brand
New Key** gave her a No. 1 U.S.
single, a No. 4 single in U.K.
Brand New Key was taken from
Gather Me, which became her
second gold album.

*Candles In The Rain.
Courtesy Pye Records.*

She and her husband formed
their own record label, Neighborhood Records in 1972, though
only Mike Heron's Reputation (➡
Incredible String Band) came
close to making the label a viable
proposition — and of course, her
own records continued to sell.
However, Neighborhood ceased
operations in 1975, though she
still retains the label as an outlet
for her product in U.K. In States,
she is now signed to Atlantic,
and has made an album in Los
Angeles, with Ahmet Ertegun
co-producing.

She still retains a large, but
minority cult following, though it
would seem that her historical
moment has passed.

Album notes: **Garden In The
City** is an album of unfinished
tapes, and other flotsam, that
Buddah released after Melanie
had moved to her own label and
without her approval.

Recordings:
Born To Be (Buddah)
Affectionately Melanie
(Buddah)
Candles In The Rain (Buddah)

Leftover Wine (Buddah)
All The Right Noises
(Soundtrack) (Buddah)
The Good Book (Buddah)
Gather Me (Neighborhood/
Buddah)
Stoneground Words
(Neighborhood)
Melanie At Carnegie Hall
(Neighborhood)
Madrugada (Neighborhood)
As I See It Now (Neighborhood)
Sunset And Other Beginnings
(Neighborhood)
Compilations:
From The Beginning (ABC)
The Four Sides Of Melanie
(Buddah)
The Very Best Of Melanie
(Buddah)
Garden In The City (Buddah)
Please Love Me (Buddah)

George Melly

Born Liverpool 1926, Melly is an
author, critic, journalist and bon-
vivant; during '50s he was the
vocalist in Mick Mulligan's Mag-
nolia Jazz Band, and when the band
broke-up in the '60s, he transferred his attention to literary
career. He wrote two books —
"Owning Up", his bawdy and
evocative memoirs of life on the
road with a band, and "Revolt
Into Style", his survey of the pop
aesthetics of '60s. At the same time
he was writing about pop, films
and television for The "Observer", and developing into something of a minor television personality himself. (He had his own
"chat" show on Anglia TV for
about six months.)

In 1973, under patronage of
Warner Bros executive Derek
Taylor (➡), he returned to his
first love and made **Nuts** and **Son
Of Nuts,** accompanied by John
Chilton's Feetwarmers. He also
returned to frequent live performance, and dusted off his
sleazy routines, which seemed as
fresh as ever.

Recordings:
Nuts (—/Warner Bros)
Son Of Nuts (—/Warner Bros)
It's George (—/Warner Bros)

Compilation:
'Fifties World Of George Melly
(—/Decca)

The Meters

Art Neville keyboards, vocals
Leo Nocentelli guitar, vocals
Joseph "Zig" Modeliste drums
George Porter bass, vocals
Cyril Neville percussion, vocals

The Meters started in New Orleans
as back-up group for Fats Domino
(➡), and spent some time gigging
around Bourbon Street area; they
were known as The Hawkettes,
and then the Neville Sound, at
which time both of Art's brothers
Cyril and Aaron were involved.
(Aaron Neville had a solo success
with **Tell It Like It Is** in 1967.)

After some sessions with Allen
Toussaint (➡) and Marshall
Sehorn, they changed their name to The
Meters; the line-up then was Art
Neville, Nocentelli, Modeliste and
Porter. They had an instrumental
hit, **Sophisticated Cissy** (No. 34
in U.S. charts), and became the
regular session-crew at Seasaint
Studios.

*Above: Art Neville, one of the
founders of The Meters.*

After three releases on Josie
label, mainly of funky instrumentals, they moved to Reprise,
and began to lean towards rock-
oriented material with **Cabbage
Alley** (released in May 1972),
with its heavy use of wah-wah
effects, and **Rejuvenation** (July
1974).

*Right: Cabbage Alley. Courtesy
Warner Brothers Records.
Released in May 1972 this
album embodied a move
towards more rock oriented
material.*

The Meters Cabbage Alley

In 1973 they came to Britain as part of Dr John package tour, and in 1975 played some U.S. dates as support to Rolling Stones, a gig they also acquired in 1976 on Stones' European tour.

Though a four-piece from the beginning, they added Cyril Neville to the line-up in 1975, prior to the recording of **Fire On The Bayou**. As the house-band at Seasaint Studios, they have worked on scores of albums, including Dr John's **In The Right Place**, Labelle's **Nightbirds**, Paul McCartney's **Venus And Mars**, and also albums for Jess Roden and Robert Palmer.

Album notes: **Cissy Strut** is a compilation of material from the three Josie albums, and **The Best Of The Meters**, originally issued in France, is comprised of tracks drawn from their Reprise material.

Recordings:
The Meters (Josie/—)
Look-Ka-Py-Py (Josie/—)
Chicken Strut (Josie/—)
Cabbage Alley (Reprise)
Rejuvenation (Reprise)
Fire On The Bayou (Reprise)
Compilations:
Cissy Strut (—/Island)
The Best Of The Meters
(—/Reprise)

Lee Michaels

Born Los Angeles Nov 24, 1945, first came to attention in band The Sentinels with John Barbata (later with Jefferson Starship). Went with Barbata into Joel Scott Hill's eponymous group but left after few months in 1965 to go to San Francisco and form own Lee Michaels band under influence of Jefferson Airplane (♦).

A multi-instrumentalist (he was also tutored on sax and trombone), Michaels featured on piano and organ in his own five-strong group which played Bay area clubs and festivals before signing to A&M for debut album **Carnival Of Life** (1968).

By the second album, **Recital** (1969), the band had been axed, and Michaels sang and played virtually all instruments himself, as well as writing, arranging and producing the project. With keyboards to the fore, his style had vaguely funk-jazz undertones but offered little that was new to the genre.

Public interest began to manifest itself, however, and his third effort, **Lee Michaels**, later in 1969, took him on to U.S. albums charts. This was essentially a studio jam (the whole thing cut in 6 hrs 45 mins) between Michaels and drummer Bartholomew Smith Frost, known as Frosty.

The pair toured U.S. as a top-billed attraction, until Frosty left to form own undistinguished group Sweathog.

Michaels, nevertheless, continued to dominate the best-seller lists. **5th**, in 1971, was a million-seller, also yielding the U.S. hit single **Do You Know What I Mean?** while in 1972 he repeated the pattern with single **Can I Get A Witness?** and **Space And First Takes**, the latter featuring drummer Keith Knudsen.

Michaels' contract with A&M was subsequently bought out for a considerable sum by Columbia

Records, and Michaels and Knudsen cut **Nice Day For Something** for that company in 1973. However, Knudsen then went off and joined the Doobie Brothers (♦), and Michaels sulked for a spell in Hawaii, flying aeroplanes, before returning to studio with old buddy Frosty to cut his **Tailface** set. A little more than average talent who happened to hit good at the right time, not much has been heard of him since.

In the U.K. Michaels was virtually unknown apart from appearance on Steve Miller Band's (♦) 1970 **Five** album.

Recordings:
Carnival Of Life (A&M)
Recital (A&M)
Lee Michaels (A&M)
Live (A&M)
Barrel (A&M)
5th (A&M)
Space And First Takes (A&M)
Nice Day For Something
(Columbia/CBS)
Tailface (Columbia/—)

Bette Midler

Born New Jersey 1945, grew up in Hawaii where her Jewish parents moved when she was a child. She had been named after her mother's favourite movie star, Bette Davis, and had early ambitions to be an actress. Worked for time in a pineapple cannery, then got 350-dollar job as movie extra in "Hawaii" musical (1965).

The money helped finance a trip to Los Angeles followed by New York. There she kept off the breadline by series of jobs – typist/filing clerk, salesgirl behind gloves counter at Stern's apartment store, etc. – while she practised singing and dancing and hustled for acting work.

First real breakthrough in this area was as member of chorus of the Broadway production of "Fiddler On The Roof". When she left that show three years later at the end of 1969, she had made her way out of chorus to take central role of Tzeitel.

It was at this point she determined to concentrate on career as singer, coming to prominence in the unlikely setting of a Turkish baths catering for homosexual clientele. This was the Continental Baths in New York which decided, in 1970, to put on cabaret shows to entertain their towel-clad gay customers. Playing piano and drawing on a wildly eclectic repertoire of show tunes, torch songs, rock and blues, all delivered in a brassy, archly camp style, The Divine Miss M (as she was known) established her Saturday night performances as the cult attraction of New York.

Word of this uniquely bizarre talent spread fast, with U.S. TV chat-show appearances helping break her overground through 1972. Sell-out concerts at venues such as New York Philharmonic Hall followed, eliciting rave reviews and the description of her as "the first cabaret star of the Beatle Generation."

Right: The Divine Miss M. Courtesy Atlantic Records. The darling of New York's gay set made her recording debut with the aid of four producers.

In 1973 her debut album, **The Divine Miss M**, not only sold a million but earned her a Grammy Award as Newcomer Of The Year. In same year she toured U.S. extensively with her musical director/conductor/pianist Barry Manilow (♦), who has since achieved fame in his own right.

Released second, eponymous album in January 1974 and a third, **Songs For The New Depression**, at the end of 1975. However, by this time, the early delirious press response had largely abated – those who had initially hailed her as an innovatory presence in rock backing off to adopt a more critical stance. Nevertheless, even as a freak out-take of the nostalgia boom, she retains a strong and loyal following, as evidenced by season of sell-out concerts in New York 1975.

Recordings:
The Divine Miss M (Atlantic)
Bette Midler (Atlantic)
Songs For The New Depression
(Atlantic)

Above: The industrious Buddy Miles.

Buddy Miles

Born Omaha, Nebraska, Sep 5, 1946 Miles has led a very full professional life as a rock drummer. He was playing professionally at the age of 15, backing the Ink Spots, and he was also on the

session that produced The Jaynettes' classic record, **Sally Go Round The Roses**. He later played in Wilson Pickett's back-up band and, at a New York gig, was approached by Mike Bloomfield to join him in the Electric Flag (♦). Bloomfield and Miles emerged as the two most successful instrumentalists in the Flag, with Miles' soul background and Bloomfield's rock orientation proving constructive points of reference.

Miles formed his own Buddy Miles Express from ruins of the Flag, and cut a powerful debut album, **Expressway To Your Skull**, which, though very much a rock album, still included a powerful base of soul music, as have most of his albums. The Express came to an end, however, when Miles worked temporarily with Jimi Hendrix (♦) in the Band Of Gypsies.

After Hendrix's death, Miles formed the Buddy Miles Band, for which he brought in Billy Cox, also from the Band Of Gypsies, and they had a U.S. hit single with title track of **Them Changes** in 1970.

By combining James Brown-style funk with brash brassy rock of Blood, Sweat & Tears, Miles continued to produce dynamic sets, but the unit never broke through to a mass audience.

In 1972 Miles was involved in another super-collaboration, when a series of gigs with Carlos Santana (♦) led to the unsatisfactory co-operative venture, **Carlos Santana And Buddy Miles Live**, which was recorded in a Hawaiian volcano crater. Miles' output continued to be prodigious, and **All The Faces Of Buddy Miles**, made in 1974, was produced by Johnny Bristol.

At this point, Miles went back to the reformed Electric Flag, though the second aggregation lasted an even shorter time than the first, and in 1975 he was back solo again, issuing **More Miles Per Gallon** on the Casablanca label.

Recordings:
Buddy Miles Express:

BETTE MIDLER · THE DIVINE MISS M ·

Expressway To Your Skull
(Mercury)
Electric Church (Mercury)
Buddy Miles Band:
Them Changes (Mercury)
We Got To Live Together
(Mercury)
A Message To The People
(Mercury)
Buddy Miles And Carlos
Santana:
Carlos Santana & Buddy Miles
Live (Columbia/CBS)
Buddy Miles:
Chapter VII (Columbia/CBS)
Booger Bear (Columbia/CBS)
All The Faces Of Buddy Miles
(Columbia/CBS)
More Miles Per Gallon
(Casablanca)
Compilation:
Buddy Miles Live (Mercury)

Frankie Miller

Born Glasgow, Scotland, discovered singing in London pubs and clubs end of 1971 by ex Procol Harum guitarist Robin Trower (♦) and ex Jethro Tull (♦) drummer Clive Bunker. Trower and Bunker had both quit their respective bands and were looking for a singer to complete minor-league "supergroup" Jude, having already picked-up bassist Jim Dewar from Stone The Crows (♦).

However, the whole project never got much further than press interviews in which Trower and Bunker praised unknown Miller's vocal talents, and Jude broke up early 1972 almost as quickly as it had assembled. Trower formed own band, taking Dewar with him, Bunker slipped into obscurity, while Miller ended up under solo contract to Chrysalis Records.

He was backed by now-defunct Brinsley Schwarz (♦) on debut album **Once In A Blue Moon** (1973), subsequently working as a kind of itinerant vocalist with Brinsleys and other pub-rock acts Bees Make Honey and Ducks Deluxe.

The Rock.
Courtesy Chrysalis Records.

Cut second album **Highlife** (1974) with producer Allen Toussaint (♦) in New Orleans – Miller having sent Toussaint, one of his long-time idols, a copy of his debut album. Resulting collection was critically well received but made little impact, Miller stepping up quest for permanent band.

Eventually assembled Frankie Miller Band out of former Grease Band and Wings stalwart Henry McCullough (gtr), Mick Weaver (kybds), Chrissie Stewart (bs) and Stu Perry (drms), taking them to San Francisco to record 1975 **The Rock** with producer Elliot Mazer. On return to U.K. dissolved band and re-grouped with Ray Min-

hinnitt (gtr), Charlie Harrison (bs), James Hall (kybds), Graham Deacon (drms).

Miller has yet to make any real impact on either side of Atlantic, despite excellent press, but is a fastly-maturing vocal talent whose style is firmly rooted in R&B and blues, displaying influences of other idols Sam Cooke and Ray Charles.

Recordings:
Once In A Blue Moon
(Chrysalis)
Highlife (Chrysalis)
The Frankie Miller Band:
The Rock (Chrysalis)

Steve Miller

Born Dallas, Texas, on Oct 5, 1943, Miller led his first group, the Marksmen, at age of 12. In 1961, while attending the University of Wisconsin, Steve and another ex Marksman, Boz Scaggs, started a white soul group called the Ardells, which also included Ben Sidran.

After college, Miller headed for Chicago, and after several near misses, including the potentially successful Goldberg/Miller Blues Band, the former half of which was Barry Goldberg (♦ Electric Flag), decided to check out the fast-growing San Francisco scene. He acquired a fine bass player in Lonnie Turner (who rejoined him in the mid-'70s) and sent for Tim Davis, leader of the Ardells' rival group in Wisconsin, who brought with him James "Curley" Cooke.

As the Steve Miller Band, the quartet of Miller (gtr, vcls), Turner (bs, vcls), Davis (drms, vcls), and Cooke (gtr, vcls) contributed three tracks to the sound track of the film "Revolution" in 1968, this being their recording debut. (The other tracks on the album are shared between Mother Earth and Quicksilver Messenger Service (♦).)

This combination lasted from late 1966 until autumn of 1967, although organist Jim Peterman joined during that time, and is included on Chuck Berry's **Live At The Fillmore** album, for which the Miller Band provide backing.

When Curley Cooke decided to leave in September 1967, Miller sent for his old friend Boz Scaggs (♦), who had become a noted folksinger in Scandinavia in the meantime, and the line-up of Miller, Scaggs, Peterman, Turner and Davis recorded two albums which are still regarded as milestones, **Children Of The Future** and **Sailor**. The former was regarded as perhaps the best example of progressive rock to emanate from 1968, while **Sailor** was one of the earliest albums to use stage-setting sound-effects to enhance the music. Many still consider it Miller's finest hour.

In August 1968, Scaggs left to pursue a solo career, and at the same time Peterman decided to become a producer, leaving Miller, Turner and Davis as the nucleus of the band.

With the addition at various times of Ben Sidran from the Marksmen, and British session-star Nicky Hopkins (♦), both playing keyboards, 1969 produced **Brave New World** and **Your Saving Grace**, before Turner left at the end of that year to be replaced by Bobby Winkelman, while

Hopkins threw in his lot permanently with Quicksilver Messenger Service, and Sidran left to become a producer, in which capacity he assisted Miller on the **Recall The Beginning** album three years later.

After attempting to record an album in San Francisco, Miller took Davis and Winkelman to Nashville, where they completed **Number Five**, released in July 1970, with the help of the celebrated Nashville sessioneers. After that, Davis left to launch a solo career, and Winkelman returned to the sessions from which he had come, their replacements being Ross Vallory (bs) and Jack King (drms).

This combination recorded **Rock Love**, with occasional assistance from David Denny (gtr), and lasted until the end of 1971, when **Recall The Beginning . . . A Journey From Eden** was recorded, with a nucleus of Miller, Jack King (drms), Dicky Thompson (kbds), and Gerald Johnson (bs).

At around the time it was released, Miller became seriously ill with hepatitis, and after a lay-off of six months re-convened the band, with John King replacing his namesake Jack on drums, and Lonnie Turner standing in for Gerald Johnson, who was also ill, plus Miller and Dicky Thompson.

Sailor.
Courtesy Capitol Records.

This combination, approximately the seventh Steve Miller Band, recorded **The Joker**, which became Miller's biggest album, with the title track reaching No. 1 in U.S. singles charts.

In May 1974, Miller decided to take a year off after almost non-stop gigging for nearly eight years, and little was heard from him during 1975, with the exception of a British visit with a pick-up band for a festival appearance.

During the early part of 1976, Miller came back with what many consider to be his strongest album since **Sailor**; back in harness with a regular band of Lonnie Turner (bs), Gary Mallaber (drms), Norton Buffalo (hrmnca, vcls), ex Commander Cody, and David Denny (gtr), Miller seemed set to re-start at the point at which he left off for his year's sabbatical.

Recordings:
Revolution (Soundtrack)
(United Artists)
Children Of The Future
(Capitol)
Sailor (Capitol)
Brave New World (Capitol)
Your Saving Grace (Capitol)
Number Five (Capitol)
Rock Love (Capitol)
Recall The Beginning . . . A
Journey From Eden (Capitol)

The Joker (Capitol)
Fly Like An Eagle (Capitol/
Mercury)
Compilation:
Anthology (Capitol)

The Miracles
➧ Tamla Motown

Joni Mitchell

Born Roberta Joan Anderson Nov 7, 1943 in McLeod, Alberta, Canada, Joni Mitchell attended school in Saskatoon and Saskatchewan before enrolling at Alberta College of Art in Calgary, intending to take up a career as a commercial artist.

She became interested in folk music, and took up ukelele before learning guitar from a Pete Seeger instruction record, and then sang traditional folk-ballads in a local coffee-bar called The Depression.

After going to Mariposa Folk Festival in Ontario 1964, Joni didn't return home; she started writing songs and working in Toronto coffee-bars. In June 1965 she married Chuck Mitchell, and the couple moved to Detroit, though the marriage was dissolved shortly afterwards. (A chapter of her life she later traced in **I Had A King** on **Songs To A Seagull**.)

Her success in Detroit led to engagements in New York; there too it was obvious that she was a special talent, but she achieved fame initially through the back door as other artists were impressed with her songs and recorded them – Judy Collins recorded **Both Sides Now** and **Michael From Mountains** for **Wildflowers** in 1967, Tom Rush recorded **The Circle Game,** and in the U.K., Fairport Convention did **Eastern Rain.**

In autumn 1967 she met Elliott Roberts, who became her manager, and signed for Reprise, recording **Songs To A Seagull** with David Crosby as producer; from here on, the following she accrued was entirely through her own efforts.

She is one of the few people who has shown an ability to progress with each successive release; every album shows a higher level of artistic and technical accomplishment than the one before. Both **Songs To A Seagull** and **Clouds** were essentially folk-based albums, with little supporting instrumentation. Stephen Stills played bass on the former album, and since Crosby, Stills, Nash and Young were handled by the same management, she soon became part of the same social circles, and moved out to California; she became notorious for various romantic attachments, including an affair with Graham Nash – she shared two cats in the yard with him, and wrote **Willy** about him.

Ladies Of The Canyon included **Big Yellow Taxi** (a major hit single in the U.K. and a lesser one in the U.S.) and also **Woodstock,** her contribution to the immortalisation of the hippie dream. The song had earlier been recorded by CSN&Y on **Deja Vu,** and shortly afterwards it became a hit in both Britain and America for Matthews Southern Comfort.

Blue, released in 1971, was an incomparable album, based mainly around a suite of songs to a former lover. From that moment on, she has been in a class of her own in the '70s, and only Dylan among contemporary songwriters is as important as she.

As her lyrics moved closer to poetry, so her musicianship equally became more refined; she was never again to record an album as stark musically as Blue.

With For The Roses, she moved to Asylum Records (for Roberts was in partnership with David Geffen, who owned the label) and acquired the services of many of the Los Angeles session-musicians, including Wilton Felder, Russ Kunkel, James Burton and Tom Scott; also both Nash and Stills were inevitably in attend-

The Hissing of Summer Lawns. Elektra Asylum Records.

ance. By time of Court And Spark (1974), Joni was working with Tom Scott's L.A. Express (and having an affair with the drummer, John Guerin) and her music was showing jazz influences; one of the songs on the album was Annie Ross' Twisted, the first outside composition she had ever recorded.

Later that year she issued Miles

Right: John Mitchell, as she was in the early '70s, when she was one of the Ladies living in Laurel Canyon. Also above.

Of Aisles, a live double-album of a tour with the L.A. Express; she has also toured with CSN&Y, but in recent years has performed live as infrequently as possible, and a 1976 European tour was cancelled because she was suffering from exhaustion. On the whole, she shuns attention of public, and hardly ever gives interviews to the press.

Towards end of 1975 came **The Hissing Of Summer Lawns,** a substantial leap forward, even for her. It contained songs that were her most complex and fascinating to date, both lyrically and musically. She played guitar, piano and synthesiser, and one track featured the warrior drums of Burundi.

Joni's album sleeves have been not the least interesting aspect of her work. All except **Blue** and **Miles Of Aisles** have featured her own original paintings – she obviously could have become a quite respectable artist – and she was photographed naked for the sleeve of **For The Roses** – not that it was sensational; like everything Joni does, it was very tasteful.

Recordings:
Songs To A Seagull (Reprise)
Clouds (Reprise)
Ladies Of The Canyon (Reprise)
Blue (Reprise)
For The Roses (Asylum)
Court And Spark (Asylum)
Miles Of Aisles (Asylum)
The Hissing Of Summer Lawns (Asylum)

Willie Mitchell

One of most distinctive producers in contemporary music, Mitchell is now president of Hi Records and a mainstay of Memphis soul scene. With Al Green's records, he devised a seminal and instantly recognisable sound, based on a laid-back regular rhythm and an overall lushness of production.

He was born in Memphis, learned trumpet at age of eight, and after advanced musical training, became proficient on a variety of instruments.

He put together a band which first became prominent in 1964 with an album called **20-75,** that proved to be the first of many; all were distinguished by highly disciplined playing, all were highly danceable.

With death of Hi Records president Joe Cuoghi, Mitchell assumed increasing administrative duties, but his band continued to tour, usually backing other Hi artists. The band's strongest line-up was/is James Mitchell – Willie's brother – (sx), Leroy Hodges (bs), Charles Hodges (kybds), Mabon Hodges (gtr), Howard Grimes (drms). Al Jackson was a long-time member of the band, and he also recorded with Hi artists, up to his death in 1975.

Other acts on Hi include Bill Black's Combo – which Mitchell continues to record in their original fashion, though Black himself is now dead – and sax man Ace Cannon. But Mitchell himself is most famous for his work with Al Green (➧), and the people who are virtually his understudies, Syl Johnson and Ann Peebles, who herself has made one modern classic of soul

music, **I Can't Stand The Rain.**

Moby Grape

Skip Spence guitar, vocals
Peter Lewis guitar, vocals
Jerry Miller guitar, vocals
Bob Mosley bass, vocals
Don Stevenson drums

Canadian-born Alexander "Skip" Spence was the original drummer with Jefferson Airplane (➧) but switched to guitar for formation of Moby Grape 1967. Above was original line-up. The group made its debut in Marin County and went on to attract cult following via gigs at Fillmore West and Winterland in San Francisco.

Signed to Columbia Records in 1967, that company made the foolhardy decision to launch them in a quite unprecedented blaze of national publicity. Their eponymous debut set was not only released as an album, but its 10 tracks were issued simultaneously as "A" and "B" sides of five different singles, all of which, needless to say, flopped.

This hype publicity not only caused the Grape to near self-destruct on the spot, but obscured the impact of what was in fact a classic rock album, regarded by some as a minor masterpiece. In the event, the Grape hung together, and paid their dues in front of audiences for a year before they could live down their disastrous start.

In 1968 they released **Wow,** another semi-classic set, which was issued with a "bonus" album **Grape Jam.** This, featuring Mike Bloomfield and Al Kooper on keyboards, was a precursor of later "supersession" albums involving permutations of Kooper, Bloomfield and Steve Stills. (U.K. audiences, though, had to make do with **Wow** alone.)

However, the album made little commercial impact, and, after a spell in the doldrums, the group broke up towards the end of 1968.

Without Skip Spence, they attempted first of a whole series of reunions in 1969–70, cutting a third fine album **Moby Grape '69** as four-piece, and embarking on a run of gigs which were alternatively disastrous and exhilarating. They soon broke-up again, with Mosley working first as a caretaker and then joining the U.S. Marines, the latter event again bringing down a storm of bad press on group's name.

Now without Spence and Mosley, group re-formed for second time, with bassist Bob Moore, to cut **Truly Fine Citizen** later in 1970 with producer Bob Johnston (➧).

Once more they split in album's wake; until coming together again in original five-piece form for the appalling **20 Granite Creek** (1972), a disillusioning postscript to one of the finest of the San Francisco bands.

Last-known chapter of the Moby Grape story was in 1974, when Lewis, Miller and Mosley announced their intention to tour with new version of band. However, due to original manager Matthew Katz's ownership of group name, they were forced to work under billing Maby Grope, and the whole escapade was yet another futile, short-lived exercise.

Outside of Grape, both Mosley

and Spence have recorded solo albums: **Bob Mosley** (Warner Bros) in 1972 and Spence's **Oar** (Columbia) in 1969. This last, which Spence cut in Nashville December 1968, wasn't released outside U.S. and is something of a collectors' piece. Spence, incidentally, was also instrumental in formation of The Doobie Brothers (➧), who have acknowledged heavy influence of Moby Grape.

Recordings:
Moby Grape (Columbia/CBS)
Wow/Grape Jam (Columbia/CBS)
Moby Grape '69 (Columbia/CBS)
Truly Fine Citizen (Columbia/CBS)
20 Granite Creek (Reprise)
Compilation:
Great Grape (Columbia/CBS)

The Monkees

Mickey Dolenz drums, vocals
Peter Tork bass, vocals
Mike Nesmith guitar, vocals
Davy Jones vocals

What America had always wanted was a home-grown phenomenon to be as successful as The Beatles; so in 1966 NBC-TV created The Monkees, a rock group which additionally had its own TV series; the style and themes of the show would follow those explored by The Beatles in **A Hard Day's Night** and **Help!** After auditioning The Lovin' Spoonful, it was decided that an already existing group would cause too many problems, so the company placed a few ads to see who arrived.

Eventually Dolenz, Jones, Tork and Nesmith were chosen; Tork was the last to be hired, and was recommended by Steve Stills (➧), who would have got the part himself if he'd had better teeth.

Dolenz had some experience as a child actor, having been the star of the children's TV show, "Circus Boy"; Jones, a native of Manchester in England, had taken the part of the Artful Dodger in the stage musical "Oliver". Only Nesmith had any real credentials as a musician.

Although they were initially hired as actors, the group's music from the show sold fantastically well – not surprisingly as the show's musical director was Don Kirshner (➧) and all the music was provided by his team of thoroughbred songwriters. **Last Train To Clarksville, Daydream Believer, A Little Bit Me, A Little Bit You** and **I'm A Believer** were all extremely successful.

After just over two years and 10 gold records, it was all over. The group came to resent the manner in which they were being manipulated (at a press conference in 1967 Nesmith told the world that they were not allowed to play on their own records); Tork left after the disastrous movie "Head" which tried so hard to be hip it alienated the last vestiges of their original pubescent audience. The other three stayed together as a trio until 1969, when Nesmith's growing interest in country music led him to form the highly praised First and Second National Bands.
(➧ Michael Nesmith.)
In 1975 Jones and Dolenz bravely tried to reform the band, with

Tommy Boyce and Bobby Hart, who had written many of the band's largest hits. They received a contract from Capitol Records, and made a U.S. tour, the success of which was not reflected in terms of record sales.

In retrospect, the Monkees' music was genuinely enjoyable, lightweight pop; since the marketing techniques used on them were considered very successful, they now bear the dubious honour of being rock music's first real weenybop phenomenon, and of paving the way for the Partridge Family and The Osmonds.

Recordings:
The Monkees (Colgems/RCA)
More Of The Monkees (Colgems/RCA)
Headquarters (Colgems/RCA)
Pisces, Aquarius, Capricorn & Jones Ltd (Colgems/RCA)
The Birds The Bees And The Monkees (Colgems/RCA)
Instant Replay (Colgems/RCA)
Head (Colgems/RCA)
The Monkees Present (Colgems/RCA)
Jones, Dolenz, Boyce & Hart (Capitol/—)

Montrose

Ronnie Montrose guitar
Bob James vocals
Jim Alciver keyboards
Alan Fitzgerald bass
Denny Carmassi drums

Originally from Colorado, Ronnie Montrose cut his musical teeth in San Francisco Bay Area firstly as a session-man – he plays on Beaver And Krause's **Gandharva** album. Coming to attention of Van Morrison, joined his touring band for a year and played on albums **Tupelo Honey** and **St Dominic's Preview** (in company of original Montrose bassist Bill Church). Played with Boz Scaggs 1972 before joining Edgar Winter (➧) for a year.

Warner Bros. Presents Montrose. Courtesy Warner Bros. Records.

On leaving Winter in early 1974, declined offer from British band Mott The Hoople in favour of forming own group, whose music is prototype heavy metal; Ronnie's guitar style owing debt to Jeff Beck.

Original vocalist Sam Hager was replaced by Bob James after second album **Paper Money** (late 1974), while by 1975 third set group had been boosted to five-piece by addition of keyboardsman Alciver.

Recordings:
Montrose (Warner Bros)
Paper Money (Warner Bros)
Warner Bros Present Montrose (Warner Bros)

Moody Blues

Justin Hayward guitar, vocals
Mike Pinder keyboards, vocals
Ray Thomas flute, vocals
John Lodge bass, vocals
Graeme Edge drums

The Moody Blues were formed in Birmingham, England 1964 as an R&B group by Pinder, Thomas, Edge plus Denny Laine (gtr, vcls) and Clint Warwick (bs, vcls). Their second singles release in January 1965 — a cover of the Bessie Banks' song **Go Now** — reached No. 1 in Britain, and No. 10 in America, becoming a million-seller, and a massive hit worldwide.

However, this proved an isolated early success, and after several minor hit singles, Laine and Warwick both left (Laine is now a member of Wings, ➡ Paul McCartney) to be replaced by Hayward and Lodge; their popularity declined, until they purchased a Mellotron and undertook a total change of direction.

Days Of Future Passed was an elaborate thematic work recorded with the London Symphony Orchestra, and was, on its own terms, a thoroughly successful enterprise; however, the album was partially responsible for creating a wave of concept records, and also for inspiring uninspired rock musicians to over-reach themselves by working with a full orchestra; nevertheless, **Days Of Future Passed** sold encourag-

ingly, and also spawned a hit single, **Nights In White Satin.** The song was actually more successful when it was re-released in 1972, moving higher-up British charts, and reaching No. 2 in America, where it also re-activated the sales of the album.

After this, **In Search Of The Lost Chord** and **On The Threshold Of A Dream** increased the Moodies' following to semi-Messianic proportions, and all their following albums, characterised by orchestral sumptuousness (and naive philosophising) had little difficulty in going gold.

At the end of '60s, they all settled in Cobham, Surrey, England, and formed their own Threshold Records (which since has released all their own group and solo product, but has been a non-starter in promoting outside talent); they have had hit singles with **Question** and **Isn't Life Strange?**

Self-managed, their following in U.S. still borders on the evangelical. They have an unyielding professionalism, often taking months to prepare albums, which are inevitably immaculately produced. However, they also seemed obsessed with their own importance, their lyrics became ever more burdened with cliched cosmic messages, and they showed a disinclination to change a winning formula (others might maintain that the band have already attracted more than their fair share of critical brickbats).

In 1974 they issued a compilation double-album, **This Is The**

Moody Blues, which had all the appearances of a posthumous set; in fact, the Moody Blues have never announced a cessation of activities, but since the release of **Seventh Sojourn** and accompanying world tour of 1973, they have not recorded or performed to-

In Search Of The Lost Chord. Courtesy Decca Records.

gether, and seem to have no plans to do so again. Their case-history is analogous to Simon & Garfunkel's: once they became an all-conquering team, there seemed little more to achieve as a unit, so they just concentrated on solo product.

During 1974 Graeme Edge worked in partnership with Adrian Ben Gurvitz, and they produced an album together, **Kick Off Your Muddy Boots,** before Gurvitz graduated to the Baker-Gurvitz Army (➡); Lodge and Hayward, working under the name of Blue Jays, achieved most independently, with a successful album, pro-

duced by members of 10cc, a major hit single, **Blue Guitar,** and a sell-out European tour. Ray Thomas issued his solo album, **From Mighty Oaks,** in 1975, and in 1976 Pinder filed his entry in the solo stakes, **The Promise.**

Album notes: The Magnificent Moodies was released in the U.S. as The Moody Blues No. 1.

The Magnificent Moodies
 (London/Decca)
Days Of Future Passed (Deram)
In Search Of The Lost Chord
 (Deram)
On The Threshold Of A Dream
 (Deram)
To Our Children's Children's Children (Threshold)
A Question Of Balance
 (Threshold)
Every Good Boy Deserves Favour (Threshold)
Seventh Sojourn (Threshold)
Compilation:
This Is The Moody Blues
 (Threshold)
Graeme Edge and Adrian Ben Gurvitz:
Kick Off Your Muddy Boots
 (Threshold)
Justin Hayward and John Lodge:
Blue Jays (Threshold)
Ray Thomas:
From Mighty Oaks (Threshold)
Mike Pinder:
The Promise (Threshold)

Below: The Moody Blues; (left to right) Ray Thomas, Justin Hayward, John Lodge, Mike Pinder and (front) Graeme Edge.

Right: Van Morrison; in the summer of 1976 he returned to live in the U.K. and immediately set to work recording an album for autumn release.

Dr Robert Moog

American electronics engineer (b. 1934) who in mid '60s pioneered significant development of audio synthesiser, the technological "toy" of a whole plethora of '70s flash-rock bands. Moog's own synthesisers are manufactured in New York State and are the most widely used in world.

The synthesiser is a complex electronic device composed of modular-linked oscillators and other waveform constructors, by which pure soundwaves can be created and shaped. Can be used in conjunction with keyboards; also as "treatment" for other instruments. Stage versions have been used by Emerson Lake And Palmer, King Crimson, Wings, Pink Floyd, Stevie Wonder, Yes, etc.

Van Morrison

Morrison, born George Ivan on Aug 31, 1945 in Belfast, Northern Ireland, grew-up surrounded by music. His mother had been a blues and jazz singer, and his father was a rapacious collector of blues and jazz recordings, particularly of people like Leadbelly, whose work was to be a strong early influence on Morrison.

By age 13, he was able to play guitar, harmonica and saxophone, and he left school in 1960 to become a professional musician, and immediately began touring throughout Britain and Europe with an R&B outfit, The Monarchs. In 1963 he formed Them with two Monarchs and two other friends, the original line-up of the band being: Billy Harrison (gtr), Alan Henderson (bs), Ronnie Millings (drms), Eric Wicksen (pno) and Morrison himself on vocals, harmonica and saxophone.

Them became the house-band at the newly-opened R&B club at Maritime Hotel, Belfast, and quickly became a local attraction, so much so that they recorded two singles – **Don't Start Crying Now**, which was a big hit in Ireland, and the Big Joe Williams number, **Baby Please Don't Go**, which, in January 1965, reached No. 8 in the British charts.

With this success, the band moved to London in 1965, and, with Bert Berns as producer, recorded his composition, **Here Comes The Night**, which reached No. 2 in British charts and No. 24 in U.S. in April 1965. An album was also recorded, though Morrison made no attempt to conceal his displeasure when Decca hired session-men (one of whom was Jimmy Page) to help out on the recording. This manipulation of the band's sound and even character (the image of Them as hard, surly, delinquent Belfast boys didn't exist outside the band's publicity kit) by the industry moguls not only crippled the group's chances of long-term success, but also left Morrison extremely suspicious of those

who call the tune in the music business.

It is no surprise that Morrison has since been quoted as saying that the only real Them was the one that played at the Maritime Hotel, but the band did lay down one absolutely classic single, **Gloria**, written by Morrison. It is a song that has become a juke-box and live gig favourite, and has been in the repertoire of many rock bands ever since (though it was never a hit).

The official line-up of Them underwent several changes – with Jackie McAuley playing keyboards, and, towards the end, Peter Bardens coming in, but the album **Them Again** was practically recorded with Morrison and session musicians. After a tour of U.S. that didn't work out (though for three weeks they played at the Whisky-A-Go-Go on a bill that also featured The Doors and Captain Beefheart), Morrison decided to disband Them on returning to England. The band, however, did reform without him, recruiting Ken McDowell as new lead vocalist, and making two more albums – **Now And Them** and **Time Out, Time In For Them** in 1968.

Morrison, however, had his own albums to do. After the collapse of Them, he returned to Belfast in a state of depression which was only relieved by the arrival of a plane ticket to New York.

Bert Berns had written **Hang On Sloopy** for The McCoys and **Twist And Shout** for the Isley Brothers, as well as **Here Comes The Night**, and had formed his own label, Bang Records. Being well aware of Morrison's potential, he invited him to New York to cut four trial singles.

One of the tracks that Morrison cut was **Brown Eyed Girl**, which

became a U.S. Top 5 hit when it was released in May 1967. Bang then put out an album, **Blowin' Your Mind**, about which Morrison knew nothing. It was merely a collection of the songs Morrison had cut, as he thought, as singles material. Berns pacified Morrison's anger by allowing him to make an album himself, the result of which was **The Best Of Van Morrison**, though yet again he did not really have the opportunity to exercise the artistic control he had been promised; he now suggests that the album is more accurately titled "The Worst Of Van Morrison".

Berns died suddenly of a heart attack on Dec 1, 1967, and Morrison was once again a free agent. For the next six months he played

Tupelo Honey.
Courtesy Warners.

small East Coast clubs for a pittance as a member of a trio, until Joe Smith, President of Warner Bros, bought-up his contract, and sent Morrison into the studio to record an album, the material for which Morrison had written some six months earlier.

Astral Weeks was recorded in New York in summer 1968 over a period of 48 hours, and to this day

remains one of the top 10 essential rock albums. Most critics have pointed out that it's virtually impossible to categorise, being acoustic and partly folk-based, while also revealing many of Morrison's blues influences. It is also tinged with jazz elements, with woodwind instruments featured regularly. At its simplest, it is a cycle of impressionistic songs linked by Morrison's Irish romanticism, with the music and lyrics fused together to create an album of compelling beauty.

Morrison says he was starving when the album came out; the lack of potential chart singles didn't help sales, which were merely moderate, despite the critical laurels. Warner Bros however were sensible enough to realise that it is an album that will still be selling consistently 20 years on.

In autumn 1969, Morrison began writing material for **Moondance**, which was released in February 1970. Though Morrison himself was not entirely satisfied with the album (something which reflects his hypercritical approach towards his own music), it is actually better than **Astral Weeks.** Certainly, Morrison avoided the necessity for invidious comparisons by making it brass-based where **Astral Weeks** had been string-based, and his songs also evinced a new maturity in his lyric writing; the songs functioned both independently and as a unit, and one track, **Into The Mystic**, is as finely constructed as any in the history of rock music.

These two albums helped Morrison establish an audience. **Van Morrison – His Band And His Street Choir** was released November 1970, and is disappointing, even though **Domino** provided him with another U.S. hit single. Apparently, he was very dissatisfied with the mix, and says that somewhere along the line he lost control of the album. It seems that business hassles were once again beginning to loom on the horizon. **Tupelo Honey** (1971) nevertheless showed Morrison again approaching his best form. He had moved to Marin County and the album, largely a suite of love songs to his wife Janet Planet, was excellent; four shots, three goals.

Moondance.
Courtesy Warner Bros. Records.

With release of **St. Dominic's Preview** (1972) and **Hard Nose The Highway** (1973), Morrison's audience had grown to the extent that his albums were fringe chart material. At this time, he was touring, having put together the Caledonia Soul Orchestra, an 11-piece band that included a string section, and which was composed of many of the musicians he had been playing with from **Moondance** onwards.

Though Morrison usually preferred playing small intimate clubs, he undertook a large-scale tour of U.S. and Europe, out of which, in February 1974, came the live double-album, **It's Too Late To Stop Now**, which contained a wealth of diverse material (Morrison had laced his own compositions with R&B standards) and which is one of the most successful live albums ever released. It is also one of the most absolutely live; Morrison refused to overdub a single note.

St. Dominic's Preview.
Courtesy Warner Bros. Records.

While Morrison has continued to work to the outer limits of his creativity, he has still encountered personal and professional problems. In 1973 he was divorced, and in 1974 he suddenly disbanded the Caledonia Soul Orchestra, and undertook a series of European gigs with a small five-piece band, playing saxophone and harmonica himself.

In 1973 he returned to Ireland for first time since he left in 1966, and wrote a batch of new songs which surfaced in 1974 as **Veedon**

Fleece; it was his most personally satisfying album since **Astral Weeks**, and certainly recalled the consistency of mood of that album.

Few people in rock music have put together a body of work as wide-ranging and uniformly impressive as Van Morrison. He remains an introspective, private person, who rarely gives interviews to the press, who prefers to work on his own, and who becomes irritated at the imperfections of others. There is no doubt that he is totally dedicated to his work, as few other performers are, and also that he sets exceedingly rigorous standards for himself. Since **Veedon Fleece** he is thought to have recorded four albums (including one with The Crusaders (♦)), but has deemed none of them fit for public release.

Ritchie Yorke, the one journalist in whom Morrison has frequently confided, has written "Van Morrison – Into The Music", a sort of biographical eulogy.

Recordings:
Them:
Them (Parrot/Decca)
Them Again (Parrot/Decca)
Compilation:
Them Featuring Van Morrison (Parrot/Deram)
Van Morrison:
Blowin' Your Mind (Bang/—)
The Best Of Van Morrison (Bang/President)
Astral Weeks (Warner Bros)
Moondance (Warner Bros)
Van Morrison: His Band And The Street Choir (Warner Bros)
Tupelo Honey (Warner Bros)
St. Dominic's Preview (Warner Bros)
Hard Nose The Highway (Warner Bros)
It's Too Late To Stop Now (Warner Bros)
Veedon Fleece (Warner Bros)

Compilation:
T.B. Sheets (Bang/London)

George "Shadow" Morton

New York producer: with Phil Spector (♦) and Jerry Leiber and Mike Stoller (♦Leiber and Stoller), a partner in influential Red Bird label founded in 1964. Despite antecedents of others, Morton was in fact the dominant figure – he drew on songwriting talents of Brill Building graduates, particularly Ellie Greenwich and Jeff Barry, but as Red Bird's chief producer he manipulated their raw material to develop a label identity and characteristic style.

This utilised pure teen lyrics against mixture of New York pop and lighter R&B, the label being one of the first to attempt to integrate musical tastes of black and white teenagers, employing artists of both races to create a sound which straddled boundaries.

Morton's finest moment was with the classic New York girl group The Shangri-Las (Betty and Mary Weiss, and Marge and Mary-Anne Ganser). Launching group in 1964, Morton supplied them with archly gimmicked songs, knitted together with brilliant

sound effects and distinctly shrill voice of lead singer Betty Weiss. Collaging musical references and lyrics based closely on the ethos of the romantic cartoon (the rock equivalent of the pop artist Roy Lichtenstein?), they had half a dozen hits mostly written either by Morton and Greenwich/Barry, including **Remember (Walking In The Sand), I Can Never Go Home Anymore, Give Him A Great Big Kiss, Past Present And Future** and the semilegendary **Leader Of The Pack.**

Morton's label had a number of other successes with Dixie Cups (**Chapel Of Love**), Jelly Beans (**I Wanna Love Him So Bad**), Trade Winds (**New York's A Lonely Town**) and Ad Libs (**The Boy From New York City**).

In its three years, Red Bird issued relatively few releases but had a significant influence on the subsequent development of pop. Morton remains active as producer in the '70s (New York Dolls, Isis, etc.), but his recent work pales into insignificance against his classics of the '60s.

Mickie Most

Born Michael Hayes in Aldershot, Most moved with his family to Harrow in North London, and at the time of the birth-pangs of British rock 'n' roll used to hang around Soho's 2 I's coffee bar, where he befriended Terry Dene and got to know Wee Willie Harris. While Dene moved on to transitory stardom, Most unsuccessfully formed the Most Brothers with Alex Murray (who later produced **Go Now** for the Moody Blues); in 1959 he married a South African girl and emigrated there, forming his own rock group and covering U.S. hits for the home market. As such, he had 11 consecutive No. 1s, and mastered the art of production.

He returned to the U.K. in 1962 and ran into the burgeoning R&B scene; he looked around for someone to produce while making a meagre living as a singer; he found The Animals in a Newcastle club, and had them record **Baby, Let Me Take You Home,** and then **House Of The Rising Sun,** which became a huge worldwide hit; Most quickly built on this foundation – **I'm Into Something Good** made Herman's Hermits a front-line group, and **Tobacco Road** did almost as much for the Nashville Teens.

Most seemed to have the Midas touch, and his services were in demand; he worked with Brenda Lee on **Is It True?**, and restored Lulu to the charts with **The Boat That I Row**. In 1966 he also produced for Donovan (♦) the hugely successful album **Sunshine Superman,** which included the single of the same name, a U.S. No. 1.

After recording Jeff Beck's **Hi-Ho Silver Lining** in 1967, he formed his own RAK label in 1969 which has since been singularly successful in creating chart product, usually aimed at an adolescent market; with writers Nicky Chinn and Mike Chapman, he made Suzi Quatro (♦) and Mud into indefatigable hit-machines, though the former has now faded and the latter have broken with RAK. Most merely turned his attentions to a group called Smokie instead.

Mott (The Hoople)

Overend Pete Watts bass
Dale "Buffin" Griffin drums
Morgan Fisher keyboards
Nigel Benjamin vocals
Ray Major guitar

Formerly Mott The Hoople, the above have worked under the truncated name "Mott" since bitter, late 1974 split from vocalist/writer/leader Ian Hunter (♦).

The original group's roots go back to Herefordshire, England, where Overend Watts and Dale Griffin went to school together and ended up in a group called Silence along with local musicians Verden Allen (kybds) and Mick Ralphs (gtr), the last-named being their original leader. In London they added vocalist Ian Hunter at suggestion of producer Guy Stevens and became Mott The Hoople, taking name from an obscure novel by Willard Manus.

With Stevens as producer/manager/Svengali, the group cut their eponymous debut album in August 1969, this being noteworthy for its brain-teasing Escher-illustrated cover and heavily Dylan or, more specific, **Blonde On Blonde**-influenced approach.

Their material varied between two styles of writing from Ralphs and Hunter. **Mad Shadows** (1970), a darkly satanic collection of songs still under Dylan influence, represented more forceful style of Hunter, while **Wildlife** (1971), in essence a somewhat chaotic album, reflected softer style of Ralphs.

Brain Capers, dedicated to James Dean, closed the first phase of the band in later 1971, and ended their association with Guy Stevens and Island. They had proved themselves as a live attraction – it was their concert at London's Albert Hall which caused a minor riot and led to a complete ban on rock at that venue – but they couldn't sell albums in sufficient quantities to maintain momentum.

The group did in fact split – on Mar 26, 1972 – but were encouraged to re-form by David Bowie (♦), who had seen them at a gig a few months earlier in Guildford. Bowie introduced them to his then-manager Tony DeFries and, more importantly, wrote and produced their first-ever hit **All The Young Dudes.** Bowie also produced their fifth album of the same name, providing Mott not only with desperately needed success but also a new image and stronger belief in their abilities. He tightened and focused their aggression, and then stepped aside.

At this point, encouraged by Bowie, Hunter assumed leadership of the band. He has claimed that the decision was also part-forced on him by manager DeFries' unwillingness to deal with all five personnel. Either way, this move was to cost Mott the services of Verden Allen and subsequently Mick Ralphs, their original leader, who went on to join Bad Company (♦).

Ralphs, however, was still around when the band made the excellent **Mott** (1973), which yielded two post-Bowie hit singles **All The**

Way From Memphis and **Hona-loochie Boogie**. (Ralphs had written **Can't Get Enough** for this session but neither he nor Hunter had the range to sing it. This was another reason for Ralphs' leaving. His song is now, of course, among Bad Company's "greatest hits".)

For their first headlining tour of the States in August 1973, the departing Ralphs was replaced by former Spooky Tooth guitarist Luther Grosvenor, who for some obscure reason decided to hide behind the pseudonym Ariel Bender for his spell with Mott, and Verden Allen by keyboardsman Morgan Fisher, ex of the British teenybop group Love Affair.

Thus reconstituted they cut the almost as satisfying **The Hoople** in 1974 and the in-concert set **Mott The Hoople Live** for release towards the end of that year. However, the Ariel Bender association didn't work out, and the story is that Hunter intended,

gether outside of Mott, began to flood the U.S. and U.K. rock press. Hunter was reported to have signed a lucrative solo deal with Columbia/CBS, but he has vehemently denied that the lure of a more financially-rewarding solo career was the reason for his splitting. One "pressure" not denied was Hunter's dissatisfaction with Dale Griffin's production of Mott's live album. Certainly the group had split into two warring factions, Hunter and Ronson vs the rest.

Either way, amidst a flurry of rumours, bitter recriminations on both sides, and charge and counter-charge, Hunter and Ronson went their own way while the rest of the band, having been tipped by the press to cave in under pressures, re-grouped after six months with the additions of singer Nigel Benjamin and guitarist Ray Major.

Major, a South Londoner, had in fact been approached to join the

Greatest Hits (Columbia/CBS)

Mountain

Leslie West guitar, vocals
Felix Pappalardi bass
Corky Laing drums
Steve Knight keyboards

Born in Bronx district of New York 1939 of Italian ancestry (his father a doctor), Felix Pappalardi worked Greenwich Village folkie circuit before turning in mid-'60s to production for likes of Joan Baez, Lovin' Spoonful, Youngbloods and Tim Hardin. In late '60s he came to international recognition as producer for Cream (♦), and was consequently for a spell the golden boy of American studios.

Working for Atlantic Records in 1968, he was asked by that company to knock into shape a New York group called The Vagrants which contained "this fat kid from Queens" on lead guitar. This "fat kid" – West's own description – was Leslie West (né Weinstein and b. Queens, New York, Oct 22, 1945).

Pappalardi wasn't over-impressed by The Vagrants, but he was by what he considered West's dynamite guitar work. Thus when the group broke up after two flop singles for Atco, Pappalardi took the guitarist into the studio for his **Leslie West-Mountain** solo album in 1969.

The album went so well that Pappalardi (Cream had by now disbanded) and West determined to team-up together in new group taking name from debut album. Steve Knight, whom Pappalardi had played with in the '60s outfit Devil's Anvil, was recruited as keyboardsman, and Boston drummer Norman Smart completed line-up.

Employing hard rock style that some critics regarded as "more Cream than Cream" – West played the Clapton part, Pappalardi was Bruce – Mountain took to the road, playing only their fourth gig before an audience of thousands at the August 1969 Woodstock Festival. Shortly after, however, drummer Smart was deemed unsuitable, and a young Canadian, Corky Laing (b. Montreal Jan 28, 1948), came in in his place. Line-up given above was group's best-known.

Their first album, **Mountain Climbing** (with Smart) was released in early 1970 and was certified gold in autumn of that year. Similarly, **Nantucket Sleighride** (1971 – with Laing) was a best-seller, and sell-out tours and singles **Mississippi Queen** and **For Yasgur's Farm** (i.e. Max Yasgur of Woodstock fame) kept them among forefront of U.S. heavyweight rock attractions – despite their derivative, and often heavy-handed style. Significantly perhaps, they never got off the starting grid in U.K.

Two more albums were forthcoming, **Flowers Of Evil** in late 1971 and a live set in 1972, before West and Laing split from Knight and Pappalardi; the latter wanted to ease-off live work and return to his studio, and teamed-up with former Cream bassist Jack Bruce (♦). Thus was formed the short-lived, opportunist West Bruce & Laing (♦) – which was little more than Mountain part two, or Cream part three!

When in summer 1973, Bruce got itchy feet (or perhaps pangs of conscience), West and Laing worked briefly in States as Leslie West's Wild West Show before re-forming Mountain January 1974 with Pappalardi back in the fold. Somewhere around this period Pappalardi and West appeared on a live album credited to Mountain and recorded in Japan. This, a double-set entitled **Twin Peaks**, was noteworthy for containing only three tracks over four sides of vinyl. In fact one cut, the live **Nantucket Sleighride**, not only occupies one whole LP but manages to encroach on its partner LP too. This album was never issued in U.K.

The re-formed group's first new studio collaboration was **Avalanche**, which featured rhythm guitar by David Perry, short-lived fourth component of the new band, and Pappalardi filling in keyboard colouring previously supplied by Steve Knight.

In early 1975 West released a tedious solo album **The Great Fatsby**, presaging second dissolution of Mountain, and now works with own Leslie West Band, still in cohorts with Laing, which released eponymous album towards end of same year.

Pappalardi is reputed to be medically deaf from playing on stage with Mountain.
(♦ also West Bruce & Laing.)

Recordings:
Mountain Climbing (Windfall/Bell)
Nantucket Sleighride (Windfall/Island)
Flowers Of Evil (Windfall/Island)
Mountain Live: The Road Goes Ever On (Windfall/Island)
Twin Peaks (Columbia/—)
Avalanche (Columbia/CBS)

Compilation:
Best Of Mountain (Windfall/Island)
Leslie West:
Leslie West – Mountain (Windfall/Bell)
The Great Fatsby (Phantom/RCA)
The Leslie West Band (Phantom/RCA)

The Move

Carl Wayne vocals
Roy Wood guitar, vocals
Trevor Burton guitar, vocals
Ace Kefford bass
Bev Bevan drums

The Move were formed 1965 as an amalgamation of artists from top Birmingham bands; since the five were each already individually accomplished, success was relatively instantaneous; they were also helped in no small way by the fact that they signed to Tony Secunda's management.

Secunda brought them to London 1966, where they opened at Marquee Club, and their dramatic stage presentation quickly won them critical plaudits and public support. By the end of the year they had a record contract with Deram Records, and **Night Of Fear**, a Roy Wood composition, reached No. 2 in the U.K. charts at the beginning of 1967. Wood, never less than a clever songwriter, found himself writing all the band's material, and though

The Hoople. Courtesy CBS Records. Released in 1974, this album was the first to feature Luther Grosvenor and Morgan Fisher.

once again, to split the band at Christmas that year after release of the live album and the single **Saturday Gigs**, with its nostalgic and valedictory feel. However, Bender wasn't prepared to wait that long, and instead, amid extensive publicity, former Bowie axe sideman Mick Ronson (♦) came into the band.

This was the second time Ronson had been involved in the saving of Mott The Hoople – the first during his associations with Bowie in the **All The Young Dudes** period – but, in the event, his arrival was to presage the second dissolution of the group.

Only a month or so after recruiting Ronson, Ian Hunter was admitted to a New Jersey hospital suffering exhaustion. Back in England, Dale Griffin, Morgan Fisher and Overend Watts were as stunned as Mott's British fans when their projected U.K. winter tour was cancelled a matter of days before the opening night.

Rumours of a break-up, with Hunter and Ronson working to-

band once before when Ralphs quit, but had to decline for contractual reasons. Prior to joining Mott 1975 he had worked with Hackensack, Andy Fraser Band and Frankie Miller. The unknown Benjamin was recommended to group by their erstwhile leader Ralphs, who saw him singing at London Marquee Club.
(♦ Ian Hunter, Mick Ronson.)

Recordings:
Mott The Hoople (Atlantic/Island)
Mad Shadows (Atlantic/Island)
Wild Life (Atlantic/Island)
Brain Capers (Atlantic/Island)
All The Young Dudes (Columbia/CBS)
Mott (Columbia/CBS)
The Hoople (Columbia/CBS)
Live (Columbia/CBS)
Mott:
Drive On (Columbia/CBS)
Shouting And Pointing (Columbia/CBS)
Compilations:
Rock And Roll Queen (Atlantic/Island)

his ability to mould his own niche has always been in question, he nevertheless quickly captured the essence of psychedelia and the swinging London underground of 1967, with **I Can Hear The Grass Grow** and **Flowers In The Rain.**

The latter became the first single to be played on Britain's first full-time pop music station, BBC Radio 1; also the publicity accompanying the record – a caricature of the then prime minister, now Sir Harold Wilson – became the subject of a legal dispute. Offended, he resorted to legal action, and won substantial damages, including all the royalties from **Flowers In The Rain,** which he donated to charity. Even so, as Al Clark points out in his sleeve-notes to **The Roy Wood Story** – "In terms of publicity, the affair probably just about covered its costs."

With this kind of publicity, and with their notorious stage image – Wayne once smashed a television set to smithereens – and Wood's facility for writing Top 20 material, The Move were rarely out of the limelight, even though they continued to spurn the metropolis and live in the Midlands.

Wood also began handling lead vocals, from **Fire Brigade** onwards, and he came to dominate the band. Soon after **Blackberry Way** had given the band a British No. 1, Burton left the band in early 1969, and Rick Price, also from Birmingham, came in. Kefford had left earlier in mid-1968, though he wasn't replaced.

The band made only two albums in the first four years of their existence – **The Move** (1967) and **Shazam** (1969), though both showed Wood's predilection for concise, melodic songs; in fact they began to be considered purely as a pop band in Britain, whereas in America they had a more serious, underground following.

It was this reputation that The Move sought unsuccessfully to overthrow, and Wood began to think in terms of an outfit which could combine classical and rock music – the Electric Light Orchestra, though he had conceived and named the band long before the idea came to fruition. Jeff Lynne joined the band because ELO (♦) was upcoming, and took the place of Wayne, who left in early 1970, and by 1971 when they made **Message From The Country** the line-up was reduced to Wood, Bevan and Lynne, though Price soon resurfaced in Wizzard.

The band had been wracked all through by contractual problems, and differences of opinions over the direction the group should take, and their albums had not sold well in Britain. They were all pleased to call it a day. They all went on to ELO, at last re-creating a studio sound on stage, but Wood was already fostering an idea for a parallel group with Wizzard, and he eventually left ELO in Lynne's capable hands, to hit the rock 'n' roll revival bandwagon. The Move's last single, **California Man,** was very much in this vein, and was the de facto debut single from Wizzard, who surfaced just a few months later in 1972 with **Ball Park Incident.** (♦ Roy Wood, ELO.)

The Best Of The Move is a double compilation issued 1975 in U.S. **California Man** is a British

compilation, though only of band's later material.

Recordings:
The Move (A&M/Regal Zonophone)
Shazam (A&M/Fly)
Looking On (Capitol/Fly)
Message From The Country (Capitol/Harvest)
Compilations:
The Best Of The Move (A&M/—)
California Man (—/Harvest)

Geoff Muldaur

Geoff Muldaur was a member of Jim Kweskin Jug Band (♦) for óver six years, during which time he married Maria d'Amato (♦ Maria Muldaur) and made two albums with her after they left the Jug Band.

Pottery Pie (1971) and **Sweet Potatoes** (1972) were full of eclectic material, which juxtaposed songs by artists such as Chuck Berry and Hoagy Carmichael. They were almost wilfully anti-commercial; produced by Nobody, proclaimed the sleeve of **Sweet Potatoes** defiantly, as though they were determined that their homespun music should not be tarted up for public consumption.

The albums also featured particular talents of guitarist Amos Garrett, with whom both Muldaurs have frequently worked since. In 1973, at a time when Geoff and Amos were both resident in Woodstock, they were members of Paul Butterfield's Better Days (♦ Paul Butterfield), and worked on both the albums made by that particular outfit.

In 1975, in wake of his estranged wife's abundant success, Geoff Muldaur made his own solo album, which was, like Maria's, produced by Joe Boyd (♦); it was titled **Geoff Muldaur Is Having A Wonderful Time,** which was quite possibly true since the album communicated little more than self-indulgence.

Recordings:
With Maria Muldaur:
Pottery Pie (Reprise/—)
Sweet Potatoes (Reprise/—)
Solo:
Geoff Muldaur Is Having A Wonderful Time (Reprise)

Maria Muldaur

Born Maria Grazia Rosa Domenica d'Amato on Sep 12, 1943 in Greenwich Village, New York, she grew up loving blues and big band music, even though it was against the better judgment of her mother, a teacher with a fondness for classical music. At high school, Maria formed The Cameos with three other girls, and they specialised in Everly Brothers harmonies; subsequently she formed The Cashmeres, who were offered a recording deal, though, Maria still being a minor, her mother stepped in and nixed it.

Maria nevertheless became involved in thriving activity on Greenwich Village folk scene, and found herself a member of the Even Dozen Jug Band, along with John Sebastian, Steve Katz, Stefan Grossman and Joshua Rifkin, who recorded one album for Elektra.

Also playing the same circuit was Jim Kweskin Jug Band (♦); Maria was much impressed with the vocalist, Geoff Muldaur. She joined the outfit shortly afterwards, contributing kazoo, tambourine and vocals, and later married Geoff.

When Mel Lyman came to hold the Jug Band in his thrall, Geoff and Maria cut two albums of their own for Reprise – **Pottery Pie** and **Sweet Potatoes.** When they split-up in 1972, Maria became involved in projects like the soundtrack of "Steelyard Blues", with Nick Gravenites, Mike Bloomfield and Paul Butterfield, before making her first solo album, **Maria Muldaur,** in Los Angeles in 1973, with Joe Boyd (♦) and Lenny Waronker producing, and some of Los Angeles' finest session-men assisting.

The album contained mostly contemporary material, from such diverse sources as Kate McGarrigle, Dr John, Dolly Parton and Dan Hicks. A song by Maria's guitarist, David Nichtern, was taken off as a single. **Midnight At The Oasis,** which was highlighted by a guitar solo of sustained dexterity and subtlety by Amos Garrett, became a hit single in both the U.S. and the U.K., and the album itself gradually climbed the U.S. charts, becoming one of surprise sellers of 1973, and ultimately being certified platinum.

Maria Muldaur.
Courtesy Warner Bros. Records.

In early 1973, Maria undertook some small club dates, and then during the summer went on a lengthy coast-to-coast tour with Stephen Stills, which obviously stimulated the sales of her album. By the autumn, she was a headlining star, and her prestige was such that she was able to persuade legendary jazz masters like Benny Carter to accompany her. Many of these old-time jazzers appear on her second album, **Waitress In A Donut Shop,** for which Warner Bros had allocated a huge budget, and which lacks something in spontaneous warmth, but was otherwise a follow-up of an excellent standard.

In 1975 she toured America and Europe, with a small band of her own which included Garrett and Dave Wilcox on guitars and Mike Finnegan on keyboards, and her third solo album **Sweet Harmony** (the title track was a Smokey Robinson composition) was released at the beginning of 1976; again, it was little short of immaculate.

Recordings:
Maria Muldaur (Reprise)
Waitress In A Donut Shop (Reprise)
Sweet Harmony (Reprise)

Michael Murphey

Born Dallas, Texas, Murphey originally envisaged a career in the Southern Baptist Church and to this end studied Greek at North Texas State University, before moving to Los Angeles to continue his education at UCLA, this time in creative writing. He worked for a time with Dillard & Clark Expedition, and was also a staff songwriter at Screen Gems for five years.

After performing at a gig in his home town of Dallas, he was recommended to producer Bob Johnston (♦), who got him a contract with A&M, and produced his first album in Nashville. **Geronimo's Cadillac** (1972) established him with a local cult following. The title track became one of the most widely recorded songs of recent years – in America it was covered by Hoyt Axton and Cher, in U.K. by Claire Hamill. Murphey's second album, **Cosmic Cowboy Souvenir,** bolstered his growing reputation, and he became one of the leading figures on progressive country scene in Austin, Texas, where he was then based.

In 1973 Murphey signed to Epic, while retaining Johnston as his producer, and made **Michael Murphey** (1974), and **Blue Sky – Night Thunder** (1975), which was recorded at James Guercio's Caribou studios, and contained **Wildfire,** a song which gave him a major U.S. hit single.

Recordings:
Geronimo's Cadillac (A&M)
Cosmic Cowboy Souvenir (A&M)
Michael Murphey (Epic)
Blue Sky – Night Thunder (Epic)

Elliott Murphy

Born Long Island, Murphy spent his youth playing in various bands, before becoming an itinerant folksinger in Europe. He returned to America, put a band together, and released a debut album called **Aquashow** in 1973. It received adulatory praise from several critics, something which persuaded company to back him with a considerable promotional push on the off-chance that he actually was, as some of the less sober critics were claiming, the new Dylan.

This immediately blighted Murphy's career. **Aquashow** borrowed extensively from Dylan, circa **Blonde On Blonde,** but he didn't quite pull it off. After a promising start, he was left with nothing, at which point he moved to RCA, concentrated on building up his audience more slowly, and again began to stimulate critical interest.

Recordings:
Aquashow (Polydor)
Lost Generation (RCA/—)
Nightlights (RCA)

Graham Nash

Born Blackpool, England 1942. Spent his youth in Manchester

where he met Allan Clarke at primary school and later formed The Two Teens with him during grammar-school years. The pair played in a number of groups together before they formed The Hollies (♦) in 1963, who for a lengthy period in the mid-'60s were Britain's most consistent hit singles group after The Beatles.

Nash was the acknowledged leader of the group, writing, singing and playing rhythm guitar, up to his split from them in December 1968. One reason was musical differences within the band: Nash had been nurturing ambitions to take the Hollies out of the pop bag in which public saw them, and was discouraged by failure of his ambitious **King Midas In Reverse** (1967) single to gain attention he thought it deserved (it was only No. 18 in U.K. lists); the crunch came when Nash expressed his outright opposition to a projected **Hollies Sing Dylan** album which he considered would be a disastrously retrogressive move on group's part. (The album was released without him in 1969.)

Another reason was that Nash had been hanging out on Hollies U.S. tour with David Crosby (♦) and Steve Stills (♦), musicians with altogether more credibility and talent, and it was in the company of the two Americans that Nash reappeared when he split from The Hollies in 1968. (♦Crosby Stills Nash & Young.)

Wild Tales.
Courtesy Atlantic Records.

However, Nash was the lightweight among heavy company in that collosally successful aggregation – compare the naive sentiments of his **Teach Your Children** and **Our House** to the work of Neil Young (♦) – and when CSN&Y disintegrated after **Deja Vu** (1970), Nash's solo albums revealed him as an essentially minor talent preoccupied with hippie-dippie philosophising.

The anti-war **Military Madness** and anti-political **Chicago** demonstrated this point on his first solo album **Songs For Beginners** (1971) although he retained a flair for melody. Many of the songs on that album are concerned with his brief affair with Joni Mitchell (♦). Ms Mitchell wrote the song **Willy** (Nash's nickname) about him on her **Ladies In The Canyon.**

Nash's high vocal harmonies had blended well with Dave Crosby's in CSN&Y and, concurrent with their solo work, the pair toured and recorded together. Between **Crosby And Nash** (1972) and the duo's **Wind On The Water** (1975) Nash recorded another distressingly anaemic solo album **Wild Tales** (1974), while both took part in the same year's CSN&Y re-

union tour.

This work aside, Nash is also part of the West Coast session-circle – vocalising on scores of albums – and has produced David Blue (♦) and Terry Reid (♦), latter on his **Seed Of Memory** album. **Whistling Down The Wire** issued summer 1976.

Recordings:
Songs For Beginners (Atlantic)
Wild Tales (Atlantic)
With Dave Crosby:
Crosby And Nash (Atlantic)
Wind On The Water (ABC/Polydor)
Whistling Down The Wire (ABC/Polydor)

Johnny Nash

Born Aug 19, 1940 in Houston, Texas, Nash has pursued careers in both acting and singing with some success. In his childhood he was leader of the choir at Progressive New Hope Baptist Church, and then worked in American television during his adolescence, ultimately declining a place at the University of California in Los Angeles to work in New York on a television programme, "Arthur Godfrey Talent Scouts", from 1956–63.

Nash also gave free rein to his singing ambitions, and in 1965 had a U.S. R&B chart hit, **Let's Move And Groove Together,** which showed that his vocal style owed not a little to Sam Cooke. He then took starring roles in films "Take A Giant Step" and "Key Witness".

In 1968 he suddenly made an impact in British charts, with three consecutive Top 10 records, **Hold Me Tight, Cupid** (the Sam Cooke song) and **You Got Soul,** which had all been recorded in Jamaica 1967; Nash was thus one of the first people to introduce Jamaican ethnic rhythms to a wide audience.

Despite this success, however, he went back to his acting career for four years, and made several films in Sweden.

In 1971 he made London his base, and signed with CBS Records. He recorded his debut album for them partly in his home town of Houston, and partly with Bob Marley (♦) in Kingston, Jamaica. The single that preceded the album, Marley's **Stir It Up,** was a Top 10 British hit in summer 1971.

The album was released 1972, and the title track, **I Can See Clearly Now,** was obviously something special. Nash had fused reggae back-beat with a finely arranged horn section and his own, almost ethereal vocals; with its mood of triumphant optimism, the song was a worldwide hit and undoubtedly one of classic songs of '70s. Though it only reached No. 5 in Britain, there was no such nonsense in America, where it went straight to No. 1.

A third single from the album, **There Are More Questions Than Answers,** also reached the Top 10 in Britain, while in America **Guava Jelly** was also a chart single.

Right: A shot of Ricky Nelson, teen idol, from the early '60s; pictured with him is guitar hero James Burton.

I Can See Clearly Now had been produced and arranged by Nash himself; it was an immaculate album.

He is certainly his own man; **My Merry-Go-Round** was no ordinary follow-up but an adventurous album that eschewed the simple approach of **I Can See Clearly Now** for sophisticated, allegorical lyrics that didn't always come off.

I Can See Clearly Now.
Courtesy CBS Records.

His subsequent releases have demonstrated both the fastidious manner in which he approaches his own work, and also his capacity for operating in the reggae or soul fields with equal facility. He had a further U.K. No. 1 in 1975 with **Tears On My Pillow** – ironically, a song that was lack-lustre by his own high standards.

Both **I Can See Clearly Now** and **Greatest Hits** – for which CBS did secure the rights to all of Nash's hits in the last 10 years – are highly recommended. Nash is certainly one of the great voices.

Recordings:
I Can See Clearly Now (Columbia/CBS)
My Merry-Go-Round (Columbia/CBS)
Celebrate Life (Columbia/CBS)
Tears On My Pillow (Columbia/CBS)
Compilation:
Greatest Hits (Columbia/CBS)

Nazareth

Dan McCafferty vocals
Manny Charlton guitar
Pete Agnew bass
Darryl Sweet drums

Roots lie in Dunfermline, Scotland, based semi-pro band The Shadettes in which McCafferty, Agnew and Sweet played for several years. Changed name to Nazareth when Charlton joined in 1969, but didn't turn professional until after release of eponymous first album in 1971.

Accrued reputation as no-frills hard-rock attraction in Scotland, but realised they would have to re-base themselves in London to achieve national recognition. Their third album, **Razamanaz** (1973), introduced ex Deep Purple bassist Roger Glover as producer, and yielded breakthrough British singles hit **Broken Down Angel** and follow-up **Bad Bad Boy.** In same year had third U.K. hit with somewhat bizarre rock treatment of Joni Mitchell song **This Flight Tonight.**

Follow-up album, **Loud 'n' Proud** (1974), again Glover-produced, established Nazareth in Europe (it went to No. 1 in Sweden, Switzerland, Finland, and No. 2 in Germany); also provided them with first taste of success in American charts.

The 1975 **Hair Of The Dog** set consolidated international success – concurrent with U.K. hit **My White Bicycle,** a British psychedelic oldie originally by Tomorrow (a group which included Steve Howe of Yes). Late 1975 **Rampant** album was certified Canadian gold prior to release. Both last-named albums produced by guitarist Charlton.

By that time group had established formidable bridgehead in U.S. and Canadian markets – backed up by 1975 singles success with Boudleaux Bryant oldie **Love Hurts,** which Jim Capaldi (♦) had earlier taken into U.K. lists.

In same year vocalist Dan McCafferty recorded own eponymous solo album.

Not exactly the most musically-talented of bands, Nazareth's achievements home and abroad are really quite remarkable for what many critics scornfully regard as an essentially lower division outfit. Nevertheless, as a gigging unit they have paid their dues many times over, and throw everything into an aggressive stage act which to their legions of fans compensates for any inherent musical shortcomings.

Loud 'n' Proud. Courtesy Mountain Managements.

Recordings:
Nazareth (Warner Bros/Mooncrest-Mountain)
Exercises (Warner Bros/Mooncrest-Mountain)
Razamanaz (A&M/Mooncrest-Mountain)
Loud 'n' Proud (A&M/Mooncrest-Mountain)
Hair Of The Dog (A&M/Mooncrest-Mountain)
Rampant (A&M/Mooncrest-Mountain)
Close Enough For Rock 'n' Roll (A&M/Mountain)
Compilation:
Nazareth's Greatest Hits (A&M/Mountain)

Dan McCafferty:
Dan McCafferty (A&M/Mountain)

The Nazz
→ Todd Rundgren

Fred Neil

Born in St Petersburg, Florida, in 1937, Neil was another of the many folksingers who emerged through the Greenwich Village scene in the late '50s and early '60s, and he cut two albums for Elektra, the first one of which, **Bleecker And MacDougal**, featured both John Sebastian and Felix Pappalardi as session-men, and the second of which was made with Vince Martin.

However, while his contemporaries went on to fame and fortune, Neil became reclusive and communicated with the outside world only by reputation. He settled to live in Coconut Grove, in South Florida, and built his own recording studio there, presumably from the royalties that his most famous compositions had accrued – these being **Candy Man** (recorded by Roy Orbison), **Dolphins** (Tim Buckley, It's A Beautiful Day) and **Everybody's Talkin'**, which was recorded by

Nilsson, and subsequently became the theme song of the highly successful movie, "Midnight Cowboy".

In 1970 Neil signed a contract with Capitol, and recorded **Other Side Of This Life.**

Bleecker And MacDougal was re-issued, retitled **A Little Bit Of Rain** in 1970, the same year that **Tear Down The Walls** was also re-issued.

Recordings:
Bleecker And MacDougal (Elektra)
Other Side Of This Life (Capitol)
With Vince Martin:
Tear Down The Walls (Elektra)

Rick Nelson

Eric Hilliard Nelson was born in Teaneck, New Jersey, May 8, 1940, into a show-business family. His parents had a radio show, "The Adventures Of Ozzie And Harriet", which transferred to TV in the '50s, at which point Ricky, as he was then known, and his brother, David, began to be featured.

After a girlfriend had told him in 1956 that she preferred Elvis Presley, Ricky decided to make a record himself, and came up with a string of hits, after being contracted to first Verve, and then Imperial, for whom he had the majority of his hits and all of the nine gold records he'd amassed by 1961, and which included **Poor Little Fool** and **It's Late.**

In 1963, having dropped the final "Y" from his christian name to signify maturity, he signed a 20-year contract with U.S. Decca (MCA), and produced the occasional hit, but otherwise went steadily downhill, particularly when his excellent band, which had included James Burton on guitar and Joe Osborn on bass, left him. A redeeming feature of these indifferent years can be found on the recommended albums **Country Fever** and **Bright Lights And Country Music** on which less manipulation was used than was normally the case.

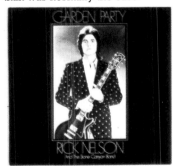

Garden Party.
Courtesy MCA Records.

In the '70s, Nelson enjoyed a new lease of life when he formed the Stone Canyon Band, a country rock-oriented five-piece. Among its members have been Randy Meisner, now with The Eagles (→); Steve Love, later with Roger McGuinn; Dennis Larden, once of Every Mother's Son; and Richie Hayward, who joined briefly during a period of uncertainty for Little Feat (→); but the outstanding musician in the band has always been Tom Brumley, pedal-steel guitarist, who played with

Buck Owens' Buckaroos for five years before joining Nelson, and who also manufactures the very popular ZB steel guitars.

Title track of **Garden Party**, an autobiographical account of his reception at a gig at New York's Madison Square Garden, was a major hit in America, producing another gold record for Nelson after an 11-year gap, but subsequently his commercial viability has deteriorated again, to the extent that MCA have released him from his contract and allowed him to look for another company.

Discography is selective. **Country Fever** and **Bright Lights And Country Music** were re-issued in 1973 on MCA, in the U.S. only, as a double-album, **Country.**

Recordings:
Country Fever (Decca/Brunswick)
Bright Lights And Country Music (Decca/Brunswick)
In Concert (MCA)
Rick Sings Nelson (MCA)
Rudy The Fifth (MCA)
Garden Party (MCA)
Windfall (MCA)
Compilations:
The Very Best Of Rick Nelson (—/Sunset)
The Legendary Masters: Rick Nelson (United Artists)

Willie Nelson

Though many of the performers who made Austin, Texas into the capital of breakaway contemporary country were college-educated folk and blues singers, Willie Nelson, leader and eminence grise of the movement was real hardhat country.

Born in 1933 near Waco, Texas, Nelson's parents parted early in his life leaving the boy's grandparents to raise him. Both these grandparents had mail-order music degrees and Willie was soon learning the basic guitar chords. Apart from some teenage gigs on the road, Willie worked as salesman and labourer before joining the air force.

He later hustled himself a small radio-station job in Texas and after further road work in bars and honky-tonks he made the trip to Nashville where he joined the then popular Ray Price and his Cherokee Cowboys. Nelson was writing prolifically, but he sold two of his best compositions for small outright fees to Price. One of these, **Nightlife**, became firmly associated with Price's name before Willie incorporated it again into his own act recently.

Although Nelson had written many songs he was by no means getting all his dues in Nashville and he was also becoming frustrated at its predictable musical style. Eventually he hired Neil Rashen (now his manager) to get him out of his RCA contract. He accepted Atlantic Records' offer of 25,000 dollars for his signature and started work in New York under Jerry Wexler.

The two resulting albums, **Shotgun Willie** (1973) and **Phases And Stages** (1974) are possibly the best Willie has done although **Red-Headed Stranger** and **The Sound In Your Mind** have found more favour commercially in the U.S. (The latter pair were recorded for Columbia, since Willie

left Atlantic after internal problems had caused the closedown of the label's Nashville office and the winding-down of their country policy.)

Now settled in Austin, Nelson is spearheading the outlaw movement, which appeals to both redneck and hip music fans. He has pared his music down to a personal, blues-influenced style and is generally considered to be writing some of the most intense country music around.

He has further spread the word by organising a series of 4th of July picnics in Texas, massive outdoor festivals which featured Leon Russell and Kris Kristofferson besides other, older country stars.

He is featured on **The Outlaws** album, with Waylon Jennings (→), Jessi Colter and Tompall Glaser. The discography is selective.

Recordings:
Shotgun Willie (Atlantic)
Phases And Stages (Atlantic)
Red-Headed Stranger (CBS)
The Sound In Your Mind (CBS)

Michael Nesmith

Born Houston, Texas, Dec 30, 1942, Nesmith claims he had no special interest in music until he was 20. In 1960 he had enlisted in the air force, and was discharged in 1962, when he first learned to play the guitar.

Though he first attracted attention as a songwriter – with songs like **Different Drum**, covered by Linda Ronstadt (→) – in 1965 he was selected to be one of The Monkees (→).

Nesmith was undoubtedly the most musical member of group, and it was his reaction against the band's manipulation that eventually allowed them to play on their own records (from **Headquarters** onwards).

By time he left, he had already produced an instrumental album of his songs, **The Wichita Train Whistle Sings**, in 1968, and he was able to put together his own group, The First National Band, which was swiftly snapped up by RCA.

The First National Band comprised Red Rhodes (pdl stl), John Ware (drms), previously of West Coast Pop Art Experimental Band, and John London (bs). This line-up backed Nesmith on his 1970 album, **Magnetic South** (from which came a hit single, **Joanne**, a song that was so successful it attracted cover versions by such as Andy Williams) and **Loose Salute.**

During the recording of **Nevada Fighter** in 1971, First National Band fell apart, and the album was completed with the aid of ubiquitous session-men James Burton and Glen D. Hardin. Nesmith now formed the Second National Band, which included Rhodes again, plus Michael Cohen (kybds), Johnny Meeks, formerly of Gene Vincent and the Blue-Caps, (bs) and Jack Ranelli. This line-up made only **Tantamount To Treason, Vol. I**; Nesmith's next album, in 1972, **And The Hits Just Keep On Comin'** featured just Rhodes and himself.

Meanwhile Nesmith founded his own label, Countryside, in conjunction with Elektra. Country-side was dedicated to bringing to public notice the talent to be found among the country performers in Los Angeles (hardly the traditional source of country music). However, the president of Elektra, Jac Holzman, resigned and was succeeded by David Geffen (♦), who was less amenable to Nesmith's ideas, and closed the Countryside subsidiary at a time when the label had made three recordings, and issued only two – although the specially-assembled Countryside Band (again including Rhodes) had backed Nesmith on his own album in 1973, **Pretty Much Your Standard Ranch Stash.**

With this experience of running his own record company, Nesmith persuaded RCA to allow his contract to lapse, and formed the Pacific Arts Corporation, of which the first release was the ambitious **The Prison** – a book with a soundtrack.

Pacific Arts is based in Carmel, Northern California, and allows Nesmith to be actively engaged in the worlds of films and books. Since his limited success with **Magnetic South,** his work has generally become more respected critically and more ignored publicly, making him something of a cult figure, especially in Britain where he has a small devoted following.

Nesmith has also produced albums for both Ian Matthews (♦) and Bert Jansch (♦).

Recordings:
The Wichita Train Whistle Sings (Dot)
Magnetic South (RCA)
Loose Salute (RCA/—)
Nevada Fighter (RCA)
Tantamount To Treason, Vol. I (RCA)
And The Hits Just Keep On Comin' (RCA/—)
Pretty Much Your Standard Ranch Stash (RCA)
The Prison (Pacific Arts)

New Riders Of The Purple Sage

David Nelson vocals, guitar
John Dawson vocals, guitar
Buddy Cage pedal steel
Spencer Dryden drums
Steve Love bass

Originally formed in 1970, partly as a showcase for Nelson and Dawson, and partly as one of the spin-off projects of the Grateful Dead (♦). Rest of the band was composed of Jerry Garcia (pdl stl), Mickey Hart (drms) and Phil Lesh (bs); inevitably, they were a permanent support group to The Dead.

This situation prevailed even after the band signed a recording contract with Columbia, although only Garcia remained both a member of The Dead and a New Rider. Dave Torbert, who had previously played with Dawson in such bands as the New Delhi River Band and the Mescaline Rompers, was brought in on bass, and Dryden, formerly of the Jefferson Airplane (♦), replaced Hart. This line-up produced **New Riders Of The Purple Sage,** a moderately-exciting debut album;

all the material had been composed by Dawson, and plainly showed the country-rock predilections of the outfit, as well as Dawson's sympathy with ecological causes.

Garcia then found himself over-committed, and Cage, previously with Ian and Sylvia's Great Speckled Bird, replaced him on pedal steel. This formation recorded four albums – three in the studio and one, **Home, Home On The Road,** live – from November 1971 until February 1974, after which Torbert departed to form Kingfish (♦ Grateful Dead). He was replaced by the vastly experienced Skip Battin, who had previously been a member of The Byrds (♦), and this line-up made **Brujo** and **Oh, What A Mighty Time;** Battin has now left again, to join Flying Burrito Brothers (♦).

The remaining members have signed with MCA, a move which could revive their flagging fortunes; the band seem to have deteriorated after an encouraging start.

Recordings:
New Riders Of The Purple Sage (Columbia/CBS)
Powerglide (Columbia/CBS)
Gypsy Cowboy (Columbia/CBS)
The Adventures Of Panama Red (Columbia/CBS)
Home, Home On The Road (Columbia/CBS)
Brujo (Columbia/CBS)
Oh, What A Mighty Time (Columbia/CBS)

Olivia Newton-John

Olivia Newton-John was born in Cambridge, England, on Sep 26, 1948 into an academic family, her grandfather having been a Nobel Prize-winning physicist. At the age of five, she moved with her family to Australia, and during her early 'teens, formed a group with three other girls, the Sol Four. When that ended, she sang solo in a coffee lounge, and impressed the customers so much that she was urged to enter a TV Talent competition, which she won.

The prize was a trip to England, though she didn't take it up until the following year, and shortly after arriving, formed a duo called Pat and Olivia with Australian Pat Carroll (later to marry Olivia's current record producer, John Farrar).

Come On Over.
Courtesy EMI Records.

After Pat was unable to renew her work permit, Olivia took the plunge as a solo artist, but not before she was part of an abortive manufactured group called Too-morrow, the brainchild of Don

Above: Randy Newman, one of the recluses of the rock world.

Kirshner (♦), who was seeking a replacement for The Monkees.

While still in Australia, Olivia had met Bruce Welch of The Shadows (♦), to whom she became engaged in 1971; he also acted as her record producer. In 1971 her debut album, **Olivia Newton-John** was released, and its sales were assisted by the fact that at the time she was making frequent appearances on television variety shows, and often worked with Cliff Richard, for example.

She also had isolated hit singles – **If Not For You** and **Banks Of The Ohio** (1971), **What Is Life?** (1972) and **Take Me Home Country Roads** (1973); however, that year she broke through in America, with a gold album and single, **Let Me Be There.** (This coincided with the termination of her engagement to Welch; John Farrar, also of The Shadows, took over production duties.)

After her 1974 entry for the Eurovision Song Contest failed to win, Olivia began to spend more of her time in America, where she almost inadvertently became rapidly established as a topselling country artist. In recent years, she has become the most successful female act in the U.S, bar none – something which represents a surprising about-turn in her fortunes. She now gains gold and platinum discs apparently at will, and has won dozens of top awards; she is the only English artist ever to have been voted best country-and-western artist in an American poll.

Recordings:
Olivia Newton-John (Uni/Pye)
Olivia (—/Pye)
Let Me Be There (MCA/—)
If You Love Me, Let Me Know (MCA/Pye)
Long Live Love (MCA/EMI)
Have You Never Been Mellow? (MCA/EMI)
First Impressions (MCA/EMI)

Clearly Love (MCA/EMI)
Come On Over (MCA/EMI)

New York Dolls

Arthur Kane bass
Sylvain Sylvain rhythm guitar
Johnny Thunder guitar
David Johannson vocals
Jerry Nolan drums

Formed late-1973 in New York, the Dolls were briefly that city's front-runners in the glam-rock stakes. First attracting attention on New York scuzz-club circuit, they took their wardrobe from the Rolling Stones circa 1973 and their music from the same source circa 1964 – vocalist Johannson was a ringer for Mick Jagger, guitarist Thunder a Keith Richard-lookalike par excellence.

Their first album, in 1973, was produced by Todd Rundgren (♦), and was intended to capture R&B raunch of early Stones; it succeeded in its own somewhat amateurish fashion but left a lot of raw edges to be ironed-out. Unhappily, the second, produced by the legendary George "Shadow" Morton (♦) in 1974, manifestly failed to deliver the goods. It was a prophetically-titled set.

The Dolls slipped rapidly from fashion as a whole breed of more innovative New York acts rose to local prominence (notably Patti Smith, Television), and the group was officially declared defunct in May 1975. "Falling interest" was cited as the reason.

Johannson and Sylvain announced their intention to continue in partnership; indeed, they resumed gigging in 1976 as New York Dolls, and talking of third album. Thunder has since worked with The Heartbreakers.

Recordings:
New York Dolls (Mercury)
Too Much Too Soon (Mercury)

Above: New York Dolls, revived in summer 1976 by Johannson (second from right) and Sylvain (centre).

Randy Newman

Born Los Angeles Nov 28, 1943 into a musical family – his uncles, Alfred and Lionel Newman had composed many movie scores; Randy's father got him classical music lessons from the age of seven, and eventually he graduated from University of California in Los Angeles in music composition.

He worked as arranger and songwriter, though with apparently little enthusiasm to undertake a career of his own. However, he began to become quite widely-known as his compositions were recorded by artists like Judy Collins (♦), who included **I Think It's Going To Rain Today** on her 1966 **In My Life** album, and later had a U.S. hit with the song. In Britain, Alan Price (♦) helped to familiarise the public with name of Randy Newman by recording several of his compositions, including **Simon Smith And His Amazing Dancing Bear.**

12 Songs was Newman's first recording, though he had intended it only as a demonstration tape, and it was eventually released in 1969 after **Randy Newman** (1968), a pioneering album featuring him with a large orchestra and his own highly original arrangements. In the event, it was too original, and sold very badly; it has long been unavailable, but it probably remains Newman's best record. After its release, he received a phone call from Paul McCartney, complimenting him on the album. **Live** (1971) was, like **12 Songs,** not originally intended for release, so that **Sail Away** (1972), could almost be said to be his debut album.

For **Good Old Boys** (1974) Newman plays Devil's Advocate on behalf of the maligned redneck south, and uses material from Huey Long's biography; but that doesn't compromise Newman's humanity, it is a work of real concern and helps to illustrate his enduring love for the little folk caught up in the mesh of large organisations.

Newman has never been a commercial success himself, nor is he ever likely to be, but he is one of the foremost living songwriters; his terse, finely ironic lyrics are complemented by a sophisticated musicality which balances perfectly between the poignant and the burlesque. However, it is all ideal material for other artists, and scores of people have tackled Newman's songs in recent years; Three Dog Night had a large transatlantic hit with **Mama Told Me Not To Come,** Bonnie Raitt and Joe Cocker recorded **Guilty,** Ringo Starr put **Have You Seen My Baby?** on the **Ringo** album, and Ray Charles covered **Sail Away.** In 1970 Nilsson recorded a whole album of his songs, **Nilsson Sings Newman.**

No doubt it is the regular royalties that Newman receives in this way that allows him to pursue his own career so sporadically and so self-effacingly.

Recordings:
Randy Newman (Reprise)
12 Songs (Reprise)
Live (Reprise)
Sail Away (Reprise)
Good Old Boys (Reprise)

The Nice

Keith Emerson keyboards
Brian "Blinky" Davison drums
Lee Jackson bass, vocals
David O'List guitar, vocals

The precursor of Emerson Lake And Palmer (♦), The Nice began in 1967 as a backing group for black British soul singer P. P. Arnold. who had a U.K. singles hit that year with **The First Cut Is The Deepest.** Emerson and Jackson, however, had been together previously in British R&B act Gary Farr & The T-Bones.

Five Bridges.
Courtesy Charisma Records.

The Nice played warm-up sets before P. P. Arnold's act and received such enthusiastic receptions that, by October 1967, they went on road as a group in their own right. Their forte was to delve into all manner of musical bags – from Bob Dylan's **She Belongs To Me** to Leonard Bernstein's **America** from "West Side Story" – and treat (or mistreat) their pickings via the increasingly flamboyant keyboards virtuosity of Keith Emerson.

Their first album, released in U.K. on early manager Andrew Oldham's Immediate label, contained Emerson's evergreen show-stopper **Rondo,** and, when O'List left the band shortly after, the keyboardsman became the unchallenged focal point of the trio. It was with The Nice that Emerson initiated the outrageous stage theatrics – stabbing, stomping and mauling his organ – that he was subsequently to develop in ELP.

The second and third LPs also evidenced Emerson's fondness for dislocating the classics, this trend coming to fruition in the ambitious **Five Bridges Suite** (1970) and the final album, **Elegy** (1971).

A considerable concert attraction throughout Europe (they were on the point of breaking in the U.S. when they split up), The Nice also displayed a penchant for attracting controversial but career-boosting publicity. They were heavily criticised in the national press for promoting their **America** single via a poster which had the faces of John and Bobby Kennedy and Martin Luther King superimposed over a group of children; and in June 1968 they were banned from London's Albert Hall (this long before the venue's absolute ban on rock music) after setting fire to the Stars and Stripes during their performance of the same number. None of this endeared them to composer Bernstein, who prevented group from releasing **America** in the U.S.

However, by 1970, with Jackson and Davison tiring of their secondary roles and Emerson flexing his muscles for greater things, the group split in a flurry of ill-feeling (♦ Emerson Lake And Palmer, Lee Jackson).

Recordings:
The Thoughts Of Emerlist Davjack (Mercury/Immediate)
Ars Longa Vita Brevis (Mercury/Immediate)
Nice (Mercury/Immediate)
Five Bridges Suite (Mercury/Charisma)
Elegy (Mercury/Charisma)

Nico

Born Berlin, circa 1940, she was a model and actress in Europe before arriving in London 1965 to pursue career as a singer. During this period she cut a flop single, **The Last Mile**, produced, arranged and co-written for her by Jimmy Page, later of Led Zeppelin, for Andrew Oldham's Immediate label; also appeared on ITV's "Ready Steady Go".

The following year found her in New York as part of Andy Warhol's Factory. She appeared in Warhol's famous "Chelsea Girls" movie, and was then teamed by Warhol with the legendary Velvet Underground (♦). They first worked as Nico and the Velvet Underground, and their first album similarly gave Nico star billing, even though Lou Reed (♦) and John Cale (♦) were the main protagonists of the group's unique musical vision.

Leaving the Underground after one album, Nico cut her first solo set, **Chelsea Girl** (1968), featuring songs by Cale, Reed and Jackson Browne (♦), the latter then 16 and reputedly one of Nico's lovers. Another, Bob Dylan, is said to have written **I'll Keep It With Mine** for her.

At leisurely pace she cut two more albums, **The Marble Index** and **Desertshore** with Cale producing/accompanying in 1969 and 1971 respectively, providing evidence that she possessed a unique vision of her own; both were bleak, sparsely instrumented (mostly just harmonium) collections of songs which evoked images of Gothic doom and High Romantic seriousness.

However, after release of the second, Nico mysteriously fled New York and took up self-exile in France. The apochryphal story is that she had got into a fight with a Black Panther luminary; and that she left to avoid the consequences. Either way, she produced nothing for three years until Island Records signed her up and brought her to England to record **The End** (1974), reuniting her with producer John Cale.

Prior to album release, Nico also appeared with Cale, Brian Eno (♦) and Kevin Ayers (♦) at ACNE concert at London Rainbow **June 1, 1974**, recorded on album of same name.

She was never the easiest of artists to work with, and Brian Eno had to intercede to stop Island dropping her during recording of **The End**, and she did in fact leave that label in late-1975. Future plans uncertain.

Recordings:
The Velvet Underground And Nico (Verve)
Chelsea Girl (Verve)

The Marble Index (Elektra)
Desertshore (Reprise)
The End (Island)
With Eno, Cale, Ayers:
June 1 1974 (Island)

Harry Nilsson

Born Brooklyn, New York, Jun 15, 1941, Nilsson is regarded by some people as a musical genius and by others as a tiresome dilettante.

He moved out to California as an adolescent, and took a job in the computing department of a bank, but gradually became involved with music through songwriting – his biggest early achievement was writing **Cuddly Toy** for The Monkees – and demo-singing. In 1968 he was contracted to RCA. His first albums for them, **Pandemonium Shadow Show** and **Aerial Ballet** established his quaint, idiosyncratic style, and were highly thought of by The Beatles (with whom he has since been associated in various ventures).

Harry (1969) contained his own compositions, while **Nilsson Sings Newman** (1970) contained Randy Newman's. Neither helped broaden his appeal much. However, his animated fantasy "The Point" won awards at some film festivals, and his soundtrack was well received. Up to this juncture, however, he was most famous for **Everybody's Talkin'**, which had been used as the theme-tune to "Midnight Cowboy", and which had been composed by Fred Neil (♦).

He recorded **Nilsson Schmilsson** in England with Richard Perry (♦) producing, and it went platinum in the States; it did less well in Britain, though it did produce a No. 1 single, **Without You**, which was a Badfinger (♦) song.

Nilsson repeated the formula for **Son Of Schmilsson**, and the result this time was a gold album. This was the high-water mark of his career. His songwriting has since deteriorated, and he has involved himself in some bizarre schemes. Meanwhile, his growing friendship with Ringo Starr led to his appearance on the Richard Perry-produced album **Ringo**; Nilsson supplied the backing vocals on **You're Sixteen**.

Pussy Cats.
Courtesy RCA Records.

A Little Touch Of Schmilsson In The Night found him performing straightforward renditions of old standards, with varying degrees of success. The album was produced by Derek Taylor (♦). He and Ringo made a film together, "Son Of Dracula", and the soundtrack to same was released on the Rapple label. Nilsson's next venture was the album, **Pussy Cats**, on which he and

Dream. Courtesy United Artists.

John Lennon set out to bring new life to old rock numbers; once again, the result was only partially successful. His releases since have indicated that his musical stature is being undermined by his ineffectual satirical approach. He remains the songwriter whose two own most famous recordings are songs by other people, the singer who never gave a public performance.

Recordings:
Early Years (Capitol/One Up)
Pandemonium Shadow Show (RCA)
Aerial Ballet (RCA)
Harry (RCA)
Skidoo (Soundtrack) (RCA)
Nilsson Sings Newman (RCA)
The Point (Soundtrack) (RCA)
Aerial Pandemonium Ballet (RCA)
Nilsson Schmilsson (RCA)
Son Of Schmilsson (RCA)
A Little Touch Of Schmilsson In The Night (RCA)
Son Of Dracula (Soundtrack) (Rapple)
Pussy Cats (RCA)
Duit On Mon Dei (RCA)
Sandman (RCA)

Nitty Gritty Dirt Band

John McEuen banjo, mandolin, guitar, accordion
Jeff Hanna vocals, guitar, percussion
Jim Ibbotson vocals, bass
Jimmie Fadden drums, vocals, harp

Came together in Long Beach, California in 1966 and, after surviving many vicissitudes, they have become something of an institution in American music circles. (Certainly, they play a wider range of American music than any other extant group.)

Bruce Kunkel and Hanna (b. Detroit, Michigan, Jul 11, 1947) started as a folk-song duo in Long Beach, and were joined by some of their student colleagues – Fadden (b. Long Beach, Mar 9, 1948), McEuen (b. Long Beach,

Dec 19, 1945) and Leslie Thompson and Ralph Taylor Barr, the resulting aggregation being known as the Illegitimate Jug Band; Jackson Browne (♦) was a member for a time.

After Kunkel and Hanna left school, the band was reorganised as Nitty Gritty Dirt Band, and John's elder brother, Bill McEuen, a well-known producer, took over the management of their affairs.

Their range of instrumentation attracted attention, and a debut single, **Buy For Me The Rain**, provided them with an early hit in 1967, even though the overt commerciality of the single (it had been arranged by David Gates (♦)) made it unrepresentative of their repertoire; for the next few years, the band consistently toured the U.S., and also released three albums, which mostly contained jug-band or vaudeville material. They were also featured in two films – the very successful "Paint Your Wagon" and the very unsuccessful "For Singles Only".

The line-up became more settled towards 1970. After his own band, Kaleidoscope, had broken up, Chris Darrow had been a member at the time **Rare Junk** and **Alive** were recorded, but he left and went on to back Linda Ronstadt. Kunkel also left, and Ibbotson (b. Philadelphia, Jan 21, 1947) came in to replace Barr.

Meantime, times were hard, and band members often took sabbaticals to pursue individual assignments – McEuen, for example, backed Andy Williams for a time.

The band's fortunes turned towards the '70s, however. Mike Nesmith's **Some Of Shelley's Blues** was a hit for them in 1969, and this was followed by their version of Jerry Jeff Walker's **Mr Bojangles**, which was a million-seller in 1970. This renewed interest in the band was reflected in the simultaneous success of their album, **Uncle Charlie And His Dog Teddy**, which included both **Mr Bojangles** and **House At Pooh Corner** (written by Kenny Loggins) which duly became their next hit in 1971.

They left Los Angeles to make their base in the Colorado mountains, and **All The Good Times** (1972) reflected their rural environment.

The band then outlined their plans for recording a triple-album set in Nashville of American country and bluegrass music, to be performed in conjunction with the original performers – Mother Maybelle Carter, Earl Scruggs, Doc Watson, Roy Acuff and Merle Travis, etc.

By every known law of the recording industry such an event should not have taken place, and even if it did, it should have been a disaster of Titanic proportions. Under the shrewd production guidance of Bill McEuen, however, the result was one of the most fulsome tributes to the beauties of American music, and many of its most outstanding personalities, ever devised. The three-record set was beautifully played, dexterously arranged, and lavishly packaged. It even sold well. Since the NGDB had performed in a modest and self-effacing manner, their stature was inevitably enhanced as a result.

Before the next album, **Stars And Stripes Forever**, (a double live), Thompson left, and the band have since operated as a four-piece. **Dream**, released in 1975, continued to demonstrate both their instrumental versatility, as well as their eclecticism, and their ability to utilise the paraphernalia of the recording studio to its best advantage.

Dream featured the Everly Brothers' **All I Have To Do Is Dream**, Hank Williams' **Hey! Good Lookin'**, short classical pieces, cajun music, hurdy-gurdy music and a Scottish pipe band – all put together beautifully.

Meanwhile, the members of the band continued their extra-mural activities. McEuen played on Bill Wyman's **Monkey Grip**, Hanna was featured on Richard Betts' **Highway Call**, and Fadden has played harmonica for both Linda Ronstadt and Jackson Browne.

In early 1976 Jeff Hanna left the band. They continued as a three-piece and abbreviated name to The Dirt Band.

The band's manager, William McEuen, has formed the Aspen Recording Society label which, at the time of writing, is looking for a distributor in America and Britain. The Aspen Recording Society is dedicated to preserving the ethnicity of American musical forms.

The members of group have stockpiled a considerable amount of recorded material. The Dirt Band as such have two albums ready for release – **Dirt, Silver And Gold** and **Jambalaya, Vol. I**, of which the latter is a triple set. There are also four solo albums in the can – John McEuen's **The Mountain Whippoorwill**, Ibbotson's **The Road Can Rule You**, Fadden's **Sleeping On The Beach** and Hanna's **Bayou Jubilee**.

British releases have differed slightly from the original American ones. **Pure Dirt** was a compilation from **The Nitty Gritty Dirt Band** and **Ricochet**, and likewise **Dead And Alive** was a compilation of material from **Rare Junk** and **Alive**.

Recordings:
The Nitty Gritty Dirt Band (Liberty/—)
Ricochet (Liberty/—)
Rare Junk (Liberty/—)
Alive (Liberty/—)
Uncle Charlie And His Dog Teddy (Liberty)
All The Good Times (United Artists)
Will The Circle Be Unbroken? (United Artists)
Stars And Stripes Forever (United Artists)
Dream (United Artists)
Compilations:
Pure Dirt (—/Liberty)
Dead And Alive (—/Liberty)

Jack Nitzsche

Nitzsche had extensive musical training before arriving in Hollywood and working with Sonny Bono as a music copyist at Specialty Records. He moved to Original Sound Records, and subsequently to an association with Lee Hazelwood, and then he met Phil Spector (➧) who was conveniently looking for an arranger at the time. Nitzsche worked with Spector right through from The Crystals' **He's A Rebel** to Ike and Tina Turner's **River Deep, Mountain High;** Nitzsche also worked other sessions, and it is claimed that in 1963 he was involved in the production of 26 chart records, of which 13 were for Spector.

At this time he also recorded three albums himself for Reprise, including **The Lonely Surfer,** and produced the Walker Brothers' first single, **Love Her.** Following Spector's temporary retirement in 1966, Nitzsche continued his friendship with the Rolling Stones, occasionally contributing keyboards and arrangements to their records. He also joined Crazy Horse (➧) for a time, and was featured on their excellent debut album as producer and pianist. He wrote the string arrangements on Neil Young's **Harvest,** and also appeared on Young's **Time Fades Away** (➧ Neil Young).

In 1972 he recorded an album in U.K. with the London Symphony Orchestra – called **St Giles Cripplegate**, which was the name of the church where the recording took place.

He is possibly the most talented and versatile arranger in rock music. He has recently been working in films, and came up with creditable and imaginative scores for both "Performance" and "One Flew Over The Cuckoo's Nest".

Don Nix

Born Memphis, Tennessee, Sep 27, 1941, Nix grew up loving R&B music, and at high school played in a group with Duck Dunn and Steve Cropper (➧). After learning to play alto and tenor sax while in the army, Nix became a member of The Mar-keys.

When he left the group, he moved to Los Angeles, and began to work with Leon Russell, before returning to Memphis as an independent producer, and working again with Stax Records, for people like Delaney & Bonnie.

In 1971 he received a contract from Russell's Shelter Records, and cut one album in Muscle Shoals', **In God We Trust,** and then made another solo album, for Elektra, **Living By The Days,** which again showed his love of blues, though the album was possibly too influenced by Leon Russell.

Nix was a member of the Alabama State Troopers, a trio of performers who made a low-budget, low-charge tour of the middle and southern states of America. The others were Lonnie Mack (➧) and Jeannie Green, but unfortunately Mack dropped out right at the beginning, and his place was taken by one of Nix's favourite blues singers, Furry Lewis. A double-album of the tour resulted – **The Alabama State Troopers.**

Nix has since made another solo album for Stax – **Hobos, Heroes And Street Corner Clowns** – and his other assignments include producing John Mayall, as well as the British group, Skin Alley. He is married to Claudia Linnear.

Recordings:
In God We Trust (Shelter/—)
Living By The Days (Elektra)
Hobos, Heroes And Street Corner Clowns (Stax)
With Jeannie Green and Furry Lewis:
The Alabama State Troopers (Elektra/—)

Ted Nugent

Born Detroit, Michigan, 1949 and a guitar-showman extraordinaire. Nugent came to attention as member of the Amboy Dukes in

Below: The doggedly determined Ted Nugent, who made it clear he just wasn't going to go away.

1965, an archetypal garage-band aggregation which, by all the laws that governed similar punk-rock one-shots, should have disappeared into oblivion after their sole stab at stardom – a slice of psychedelic nonsense entitled **Journey To The Center Of Your Mind** which hit the U.S. singles charts in 1968.

However, the Laws That Govern These Things hadn't reckoned on Ted Nugent. The man was nothing if not persistent. The Dukes had already been through several personnel changes (Rusty Day, later of Cactus, being the best known alumni) by the time of **Journey,** and Nugent slogged on through the '60s and into the '70s with a variety of line-ups. The only constant was that they all offered their leader's no-frills, heavy-metal chunderings as the main attraction.

Their gigging rate was a minor phenomenon – a reputed 150 a year mostly in the mid-West and South – with Nugent employing all manner of on-stage gimmicks to arrest flagging interest. Management hassles and personnel changes were commonplace. Nugent threw out anyone he suspected of taking drugs.

Ever the optimist, the guitarist laboured on – maintaining a minor reputation for pertinacity alone. In 1973–74 he attempted to capture further attention by a series of hammily-publicised guitar "duels" pitting the self-proclaimed greatest axeman in the world against the likes of Mike Pinera, Wayne Kramer (MC5), and Frank Marino (Mahogany Rush).

These were extraordinary affairs. Nugent would climax his feedback "battles" by bounding caveman-like from behind an amp, clad in loin-cloth and head-dress and sporting a bow and arrow; while another of his gimmicks was to demonstrate his ability to shatter a glass ball by the pitch of his guitar – it didn't always work, so a roadie with a hammer was always discreetly on hand to assist when necessary.

It may not have sold any albums but it did keep his name in the mid-West press, even as an object of ridicule, and helped freshen up his fading notoriety. Also much-publicised was the man's favoured pastime of wild-game hunting; he, his wife and young daughter eating the results of these expeditions on their Michigan farm.

Ted Nugent, it was clear, was simply not going to go away – and in 1975 his dogged persistence paid off in handsome style. Epic Records stepped in with a new recording contract, the management company which handles Aerosmith similarly preferred the dotted line, and the result was the 1975 **Ted Nugent** set which, backed by characteristically flamboyant concerts, edged its way up the U.S. charts.

He has no less than 11 Amboy Dukes albums behind him: four cut for Mainstream, one being the punk-rock collectors' piece **Journey To The Center Of Your Mind;** two for Polydor including the aptly-titled **Survival Of The Fittest;** and a further brace for Discreet as Ted Nugent & The Amboy Dukes, **Call Of The Wild** and **Tooth Fang And Claw.** The earlier material is collected on the 1975-released Mainstream

double set, **Journeys & Migrations.**

Recordings:
Ted Nugent (Epic)

Laura Nyro

Born The Bronx, New York 1947, of Italian/Jewish parentage. Her father was a jazz trumpeter, and she is said to have written her first songs when she was eight. Reputed to have undergone a harrowing LSD trip as teenager, an event which profoundly altered course of her life.

It was as a songwriter that she first came to prominence, her first two albums yielding such enormous U.S. hits as **Stoned Soul Picnic, Wedding Bell Blues** and **Sweet Blindness** for Fifth Dimension (♦), **And When I Die** for Blood Sweat & Tears (♦), **Stoney End** for Barbra Streisand and **Eli's Coming** for Three Dog Night (♦).

For a time she was the hottest songwriting property in the U.S. music industry, but within this statement lay the seeds of her dilemma. As British rock critic Ian MacDonald has noted in retrospect: "She had the uncomfortable knack of writing Instant Artiste Fodder whilst being too far out to get recognition as a performer in her own right."

Certainly, as regards the last part, she underwent an almost nightmarish experience when she played the Monterey Festival in 1967. Nyro, in gypsy Vegas garbs and backed by a black chick trio, thoroughly alienated the hippie audience by attempting to put on a soul revue and was all but booed off the stage.

It was only her second concert appearance, and after it she slunk back to New York to lick her wounds, having at this time recorded just the one album, **More Than A New Discovery,** for Verve in 1967 (this was later re-issued 1973 by Columbia/CBS as **The First Songs**).

Then into the picture came one David Geffen (♦), West Coast whizz-kid-to-be, under whose

Above: Laura Nyro, out of retirement and back in form.

management and guidance she recorded **Eli And The Thirteenth Confession** in 1968 with producer/arranger Charlie Callello (who also arranged 90 per cent of the hits for the Four Seasons (♦)). The hits for other acts were still there, but this displayed a maturity of vision astounding in a girl just turned 21.

With now only a cult audience to sustain her, she went on to cut two more devastating albums further revealing a singer and pianist of exceptional power and vision. Her music might loosely be described as a fusion of gospel and white soul, which at its best is of a broad novelistic design detailed by intense and elliptically poetic lyrics.

This trilogy was completed in 1970 by **Christmas And The Beads Of Sweat,** and she cut one more album, **Gonna Take A Miracle,** the following year in collaboration with LaBelle – a joyous, magnificent celebration of soul and R&B – and then retired to married life in Connecticut.

Always shy of interviews, little was heard of her until late 1975 when she returned to record her first album of original material for five years, **Smile,** which revealed that her remarkable talent remained intact.

The same critic quoted earlier

has credited her as being in the late '60s what Patti Smith (♦) has attempted to be in the '70s – the lady Rimbaud of rock.

Recordings:
More Than A New Discovery (Verve)
Eli And The Thirteenth Confession (Columbia/CBS)
New York Tendaberry (Columbia/CBS)
Christmas And The Beads Of Sweat (Columbia/CBS)
Gonna Take A Miracle (Columbia/CBS)
Smile (Columbia/CBS)

(A Band Called) O

Pix vocals, guitar
Ian Lynn keyboards
Mark Anders bass
Derek Ballard drums
Craig Anders guitar

Originally from the Channel Islands (off English coast), now based in Leicester, England. Formerly known as The Parlour Band, became "O" around 1972. Recorded first album 1974, second in following year. Lynn replaced Pete Filleul in May 1975.

Recordings:
A Band Called "O" (Epic)
Oasis (Epic)

Oblivion Express
♦ Brian Auger

Phil Ochs

Born Dec 19, 1940 in El Paso, Phil Ochs was sent to military academy, following the family tradition, before leaving to study journalism at Ohio State University.

He moved to Greenwich Village in early '60s and, like Dylan, was one of the leading lights on the burgeoning folk-scene. Dylan said: "I just can't keep up with Phil. And he's gettin' better and better."

Ochs in fact brought a semi-literary journalist's approach to his songs; he was certainly a more abrasive figure even than

Left: Gonna Take A Miracle. Courtesy CBS.

Gonna take a miracle
Laura nyro and Labelle

Dylan, and it was the overt political content and up-front nature of his writing that prevented him from making it. He was subject to a broadcasting ban which prohibited him from appearing on American television or radio at a time when public exposure was vital for his career. He signed with Elektra Records, and released **All The News That's Fit To Sing**; it made the charts, as did his next two albums, but the broadcasting ban prevented him widening his audience.

This was something he could only accomplish secondhand, when Joan Baez made his composition, **There But For Fortune** into a world-wide hit in 1965; in 1966 Ochs wrote the anthem of the anti-Vietnam war movement, **I Ain't Marching Anymore**; but this staunch politicising led to a rift between him and Dylan in 1966. Dylan said: "That stuff you're writing is bullshit, because politics is bullshit."

He was inevitably swept into the mid-'60s drug culture, and the new underground; he was always fighting for causes. He moved to Los Angeles and recorded **Rehearsals For Retirement** with the best Los Angeles session-musicians, and then in 1970 **Phil Ochs Greatest Hits** – which was a joke, as it contained all new material. His records were becoming less successful and, apart from a single released at the height of the Watergate scandal, **Here's To The State Of Richard Nixon, Greatest Hits** was the last Ochs record released – a live double-album of a Carnegie Hall concert was recorded, but never issued.

For much of the '70s he lived outside America; in London he occasionally wrote for the magazine "Time Out". In 1973, while in Africa, he was the victim of a savage assault which damaged his vocal chords – something which must have contributed to his growing depression, which culminated in his suicide in New York on Apr 8, 1976. His last public appearance had been with Dylan at benefit concert for victims of the military junta in Chile in 1974.

Recordings:
All The News That's Fit To Sing (Elektra)
I Ain't Marching Anymore (Elektra)
Phil Ochs In Concert (Elektra)
Pleasures Of The Harbour (A&M)
Tape From California (A&M)
Rehearsals For Retirement (A&M)
Gunfight At Carnegie Hall (A&M)
Phil Ochs Greatest Hits (A&M)

The Ohio Players

Johnny Williams (Diamond) drums
Leroy Bonner (Sugar) lead guitar, vocals
Clarence Satchell (Satch) saxophone, flute
Marshall Jones (Rock) bass
Ralph Middlebrooks (Pee Wee) trumpets, trombone, alto and tenor sax
Billy Beck keyboards, Moog, vocals
Marvin Pierce (Merv) trumpet, flugelhorn

The members of the band all hail originally from the vicinity of Dayton, Ohio, and the group first came together as the Ohio Untouchables, when Satch, Pee Wee and Rock (the group have now adopted their nick-names for almost permanent use) backed The Falcons (whose lead-singer at the time was Wilson Pickett) on **I Found A Love**. The song, recorded in Detroit, became a major hit in 1962, and on the strength of that the Untouchables had a record of their own released.

They had no success, however, and drifted back to Ohio, to emerge later in the '60s as the Ohio Players on the Compass label in New York; though they had a couple of minor R&B hits in 1968, they could again claim no solid success, and were allowed to move to Capitol, where they cut an album **Observations In Time** late in 1968, again with little joy.

After various personnel changes, the line-up was by now virtually established, and the band made an album for Westbound, having raised the necessary money – 400 dollars – themselves.

From this point they just got bigger and bigger. Their lengthy, instrumental funk pieces were originally no more than adequate, but the band gradually increased their popularity through their on-stage sartorial style (they enter like swirling dervishes, with scarlet capes over red and white jumpsuits), and through their album sleeves, which have invariably featured naked women in a variety of erotic postures. Claims that the Players' album sleeves were more interesting than their music have, however, been discredited. When they moved to Mercury in 1973, their music began to attain a greater precision; even though many of their pieces remain over-blown, there is often a compensating melodic attraction.

Skin Tight provided them with a Top 5 U.S. single, **Jive Turkey**, and on the strength of that the album went gold, as did both **Fire** (1974) and **Honey** (1975). They are currently one of the top selling U.S. acts.

Album notes: Their three releases for Westbound from 1970–72 – **Pain, Pleasure** and **Ecstasy** were issued in Britain in 1974 in a compilation form, **Pain + Pleasure = Ecstasy**. Meanwhile, Westbound issued a comparable album in the U.S., **Greatest Hits**, as well as a collection of outtakes, **Climax**. In view of their current status their earlier albums were reissued in 1975. The Compass recordings were issued on the Trip label in America and on the DJM label in Britain as **First Impressions**. **Observations In Time** was reissued in the U.S. as **The Ohio Players**.

Recordings:
First Impressions (Trip/DJM)
Observations In Time (Capitol/—)
Pain (Westbound/—)
Pleasure (Westbound/—)
Ecstasy (Westbound/—)
Skin Tight (Mercury)
Fire (Mercury)
Honey (Mercury)
Contradiction (Mercury)
Compilations:
Climax (Westbound/—)
Greatest Hits (Westbound/—)
Pain + Pleasure = Ecstasy (—/Westbound)

The O'Jays

Eddie Levert vocals
Walter Williams vocals
William Powell vocals

Originally a five-piece vocal group from Canton, Ohio (Bobby Massey, Bill Isles were the other members), The O'Jays were known as The Mascots in early '60s when they started singing together at high school. They came under guidance of local DJ Eddie O'Jay, who taught them their professional craft, and they changed their name out of deference to him.

In mid-'60s they signed with Imperial Records, though after a promising start achieved little and Isles left the group. After a period working in R&B clubs, and a brief interlude at Bell Records, The O'Jays signed with independent Gamble-Huff Productions in 1968.

Signed to Neptune Records, the band had several hits written for them by Gamble and Huff, including **Looky Looky**, but it wasn't until the latter started their own Philadelphia International Records, with The O'Jays as their major act, that the group began to assert themselves to a significant degree.

By this time, Massey had left, reducing the outfit to a trio; the first album on Philadelphia, **The**

Phil Ochs hugs Bob Dylan after the New York benefit concert in 1974 for the victims of the Chilean military junta.

173

O'Jays In Philadelphia, won some attention, but the album that really launched The O'Jays as a major U.S. vocal group, was **Backstabbers,** released October 1972, by which time Gamble and Huff were beginning to develop their smoothly orchestrated soul; the album spawned three large hits – the title track, **992 Arguments** and **Love Train.**

In 1973 came **Ship Ahoy,** a more major work, with an extended title track which fully allowed Gamble and Huff to explore production techniques which at the time were innovatory in the field of soul music – although Norman Whitfield at Tamla-Motown had been moving in a similar direction in his work with The Temptations.

Ship Ahoy also showed Gamble and Huff's increasingly ambitious lyrics, and their concern with ecological and humanitarian matters, themes which have been regurgitated on subsequent O'Jays albums, **Survival** and **Reunion** (1975), which, like their immediate predecessors, have gone gold within weeks of release.

Live In London was recorded on their successful European tour of 1974.

Recordings:
Backstabbers (Philadelphia International)
Ship Ahoy (Philadelphia International)
Survival (Philadelphia International)
Live In London (Philadelphia International)
Reunion (Philadelphia International)
Compilations:
Greatest Hits (United Artists/—)
The O'Jays (Bell/—)

Mike Oldfield

Born Reading, England, May 15, 1953, he began his career at the age of 14 as half-folk duo Sallyangie alongside elder sister Sally. They cut one album, **Sallyangie,** for Transatlantic in 1968 before Oldfield formed his own short-lived outfit Barefeet and subsequently joined Kevin Ayers And The Whole World. First as bassist, later as lead guitarist, he was with that band until its dissolution in 1971 (♦ Kevin Ayers).

Meanwhile, Oldfield had been nurturing an ambitious 50-minute composition, a demo tape of which he hawked around numerous British record companies without success. When he did find a taker, it was from a company which didn't yet exist. This was Virgin Records, the brainchild of one Richard Branson, founder of "Student" magazine as a teenager and at that time owner of a remarkably successful chain of discount record shops. Oldfield's arrival coincided with Branson's plans to launch his own label. The young composer was given time in a studio, where he overdubbed virtually every instrument himself, and his epic work – **Tubular Bells** – was Virgin Records' first release in May 1973.

It met with lavish critical acclaim – and the public was quick to latch on. **Tubular Bells** has since become one of the most remarkable success stories in rock – by early 1976 total world-wide sales stood at five million, and are still rising.

Breakthrough in the U.S. was helped immeasurably by a section of Oldfield's composition being used in the score of "The Exorcist" movie. This segment was released as a single in America with, again, enormous success – though Oldfield and Branson were so appalled by the editing of the U.S. 45 that, for the British market, they specially re-recorded another single (**Theme From Tubular Bells**) ostensibly to combat import sales.

In August 1974, the "wizard of a 1,000 overdubs" emerged from the studio with a follow-up, **Hergest Ridge.** Again a continuous thematical epic, this was a shade too close to being the Son Of Tubular Bells, and though it went straight into the British album lists at No. 1 (while his debut set still, incredibly, held down the No. 2 spot), its overall sales were comparatively disappointing.

For a time it appeared that Oldfield might have peaked on his phenomenal debut, but **Ommadawn,** released in October 1975, went a long way to dispel those fears – at least in commercial terms.

A thorough-going introvert, Oldfield has shied away from live work since his days with Ayers. He did, however, play guitar when David Bedford's **Stars End** composition was performed by the Royal Philharmonic Orchestra in 1975; and again, similarly with the RPO, for the live presentation of **The Orchestral Tubular Bells** conducted by Bedford. Oldfield also plays on Bedford's **The Rime Of The Ancient Mariner** (1975) album (♦ David Bedford).

Due to inflated gratuitous claims made on his behalf – "genius", "most important popular composer of the decade" and a host more in the same vein – it is not easy to make an objective assessment of Oldfield's contribution to rock. Albeit by no fault of his own, he has become the darling of the colour supplement set; beloved of arts-programme producers; the preserve of those "quality" newspaper music critics whose judgments on other acts are held in contempt by the mainstream rock press. The acceptable face of rock? Certainly. The future of rock? Posterity can sort that one out.

Recordings:
Tubular Bells (Virgin)
Hergest Ridge (Virgin)
Ommadawn (Virgin)

Andrew Oldham

In the early '60s, Oldham was the epitome of the teenage hustler determined to break into the burgeoning, lucrative British pop scene by whichever route would open for him. When he made an unsuccessful start as a singer, using the unlikely names Sandy Beach and Chancery Lane, he switched to PR – working as such for British fashion queen Mary Quant and, under Brian Epstein (♦), for The Beatles.

Oldham, however, was not a man to play second fiddle – he wanted a Beatles of his own. He went into partnership with one Eric Easton and, working on a tip from a journalist, saw the Rolling Stones (♦) performing at the Station Hotel, Richmond, in 1963. He signed them to a management contract, had the nous to recognise the potential in their embryonic rebel stance, and set about manipulating Stones' "outlaw" image using his acquired flair for publicity.

Oldham liked his share of it too; cultivating a mysterioso reputation modelled on that of the other whizz-kid of the '60s, America's Phil Spector (♦), even down to the omnipresent sunglasses. Encouraged use of name Andrew Loog Oldham because of more impressive ring.

He had "lost" Eric Easton early on, ousted original Stone Ian Stewart from the group because he didn't look the part – then, in 1967, Oldham himself was suddenly out in the cold; his relationship with Stones severed during sessions for the **Their Satanic Majesties Request** album. Did he jump or was he pushed? The question has never been answered.

The preceding year, however, Oldham had ambitiously launched his own record label Immediate (in collaboration with Tony Calder). Their roster of acts was impressive – The Nice (♦), Amen Corner, P. P. Arnold, Humble Pie (♦), Small Faces (♦), Chris

Tubular Bells. Courtesy Virgin.

Farlowe (♦), and briefly Fleetwood Mac (♦) — yet the company went bankrupt within three years.

Oldham went into semi-retirement, heading for America to try his hand at production. Little was heard of him, however, until his name turned up as producer on Donovan's 1973 **Essence To Essence** album. Also produced final Humble Pie set, **Street Rats**. In 1976, involved himself in a relaunch of the old Immediate logo, one of his first signings being Marianne Faithfull, whom he had originally coached to fame (♦ Marianne Faithfull).

Yoko Ono

Born in Japan Feb 18, 1933 into a wealthy family who sent her to the U.S. to study philosophy, Yoko Ono became well-known in early '60s New York avant-garde arts scene through her films and her impromptu happenings.

She was married with one child, Kyoko, when she met John Lennon (♦) at one of her art exhibitions in New York. When they'd both got divorced, they got married in Gibraltar on Mar 20, 1969, and Lennon later changed his middle name from "Winston" to "Ono".

She accompanied Lennon almost everywhere, including Beatles' recording sessions (she appears in the "Let It Be" film) and became a source of aggravation between Lennon and rest of group in final days.

John and Yoko projected themselves as the perfect far-out couple, were always photographed together, changed their styles of hair and dress together, and were publicised doing such things as sitting in bags, spending a week in bed together in Amsterdam in the cause of world peace, and sending a red rose to the Upper Clyde shipworkers.

Yoko also sang with the Plastic Ono Band whenever it existed, her contribution being mainly rising and falling squeaks and squeals. In 1970 she published "Grapefruit", a book of epigrammatic poems, and in 1972 her films "Apotheosis" and "Fly" were chosen for the avant-garde section of the Cannes Film Festival.

She made a series of experimental records with John while The Beatles were still extant, and since the group's demise she has helped out on John's **Sometime In New York City,** and made a series of albums of her own, though thankfully the cycle seems to have come to an end. Lennon claimed her song **Don't Worry Kyoto (Mummy's Only Looking For A Hand In The Snow)** was the best rock 'n' roll record ever.

In 1974 she and John lived apart for a year, but in 1975 they were reconciled and Yoko gave birth to a son.

Recordings:
Yoko Ono/Plastic Ono Band (Apple)
Fly (Apple)
Approximately Infinite Universe (Apple)
Feeling The Space (Apple)

The Classic Roy Orbison. Courtesy Decca Records. Recorded in 1966, this album, which contains none of his hits, is still on catalogue in Britain.

Roy Orbison

Born in Wink, Texas, Apr 23, 1936, Orbison, later known as The Big O, began his career as a rockabilly singer. He was first recorded by Norman Petty — Buddy Holly's manager — but Orbison did nothing of lasting importance for him. In 1956 he moved on to Sam Phillips and Sun Records in Memphis, after having sent them a copy of **Ooby Dooby,** which was his first taste of success. (The song was disinterred over a decade later by Creedence Clearwater Revival.)

However, he was basically miscast as a straight rock singer, and after the Everly Brothers had recorded his composition, **Claudette,** which he had written for his wife, he moved to Nashville to concentrate on his songwriting. There he was contracted to RCA, but, even though he was produced by Chet Atkins, it wasn't until he moved to Monument Records, and joined forces with producer Fred Foster, that things began to happen.

His first single for the label, **Paper Boy,** which had in fact been recorded at RCA's studios, sold encouragingly; his second, **Uptown,** did brisk business, and his third, **Only The Lonely,** a beautiful, commercial pop ballad, reached No. 1 almost everywhere it was issued.

During the next four years, Orbison had a staggering run of success. Though undoubtedly inspired by country singer Don Gibson (in 1967 Orbison recorded an album of his songs, **Roy Orbison Sings Don Gibson**), his material was utterly distinctive. Most of his songs were carefully constructed melodramatic ballads, often dolorous like **It's Over, Only The Lonely** or **Crying,** sometimes optimistic like **Oh! Pretty Woman,** or **Runnin' Scared.** The songs utilised sweeping strings, crashing choruses and powerful crescendos. At a time when pop music was irredeemably lightweight, Orbison stood head and shoulders above his contemporaries; his vocals were peerless, his range extraordinary. His songs compelled attention.

He had sufficient nous to diversify his material; **Mean Woman Blues** (the other side of **Blue Bayou**) was one of the loudest, rawest stabs at '60s rock 'n' roll, and **Candy Man** and **Dream Baby** demonstrated he could handle something a little funkier when necessary.

For some reason he became more popular in the U.K. than in the U.S. On his second British visit in 1963 (his first had been in 1962) he was initially top of a bill that also included The Beatles and Gerry and the Pacemakers.

He had a quiff of jet-black Brylcreemed hair, often dressed in black leather and rode motorcycles – an image of toughness which belied his natural shyness. He stood motionless on stage, letting the high notes bounce off the roof of his mouth. Though apparently the antithesis of star material, he had charisma to spare. In Britain his fan club following, outside Presley's, is reckoned to be the most loyal there is.

He had 16 Top 20 hits in Britain, but in the mid-'60s he was bedevilled by misfortune and personal tragedy. His wife, Claudette, was killed in a motorcycle accident on Jun 6, 1966, and that, coupled with the fact that he left Monument, took the steam out of his career.

His new contract with MGM promised much, but despite the surge of new product, the new songs were not as successful as the earlier ones. He made one film, "The Fastest Guitar Alive", but it was obvious his talents were not suited to movies.

In September 1968 his domestic life was shattered again when two of his three children died in a fire at his home near Nashville, and he abandoned writing new material. He has continued to perform regularly, especially in Britain, where his evergreen popularity was illustrated by the fact that a new compilation of his hits topped the album charts in 1976. Discography is selective.

Recordings:
The All-Time Greatest Hits Of Roy Orbison (Monument)
Original Sound Of Roy Orbison (Sun)
The Monumental Roy Orbison, Vol. I (—/Monument)
The Monumental Roy Orbison, Vol. II (—/Monument)
The Big O (—/Charly)

THE CLASSIC ROY ORBISON

Focus On Roy Orbison
(—/London)

Orleans

John Hall guitar, vocals
Larry Hoppen guitar,
  keyboards, vocals
Lance Hoppen bass, vocals
Wells Kelly drums, vocals

Formed February 1972 around noted American session-man and writer John Hall who, with Larry Hoppen and Wells Kelly, was formerly of group Boffalongo who did original of much-covered **Dancing In The Moonlight**. As session-guitarist Hall had worked with Taj Mahal, Al Kooper, Loudon Wainwright, etc.; as producer worked on Bonnie Raitt's **Takin' My Time** album; as writer with wife Johanna (lyricist) penned Janis Joplin's **Half Moon** and Tymes' hit **Ms Grace**.

Above: A young Roy Orbison.

The Halls wrote 10 songs for Orleans' eponymous debut album released 1973, also contributing heavily to second set **Let There Be Music** (1975) which yielded American Top 10 single **Dance With Me**. Originally a trio, later joined by Larry Hoppen's brother Lance.

Both albums have acquired for Orleans growing cult following as one of most intelligent, "musicianly" of new American bands; drawing on variety of sources – country, rock, soul, calypso – and embellishing the Halls' cleverly-constructed songs with rich vocal harmonies and inventive instrumental textures. A band to watch.

Recordings:
Orleans (ABC)
Let There Be Music (Asylum)

Osibisa

Teddy Osei flute, saxophone,
  percussion
Sol Amarfio drums
Mac Tontoh trumpet, flugelhorn,
  xylophone
Del Richardson lead guitar
Kiki Gyan keyboards, Moog
Kofi Ayivor percussion, vocals
Mike Odumusu bass

Osibisa was originally founded by Osei, who played in a band called The Comets in his native Ghana, before coming to London on a scholarship from the Ghanaian government to study at London College of Music; while there, Osei renewed a friendship with Amarfio, with whom he had played in several bands in Ghana, and together with Osei's brother, Tontoh, and Richardson, they formed Osibisa.

Purveying exciting and refreshing percussive African rhythms, overlaid with rock and diverse other influences, the group immediately made an impact when its debut album, **Osibisa**, was released 1971; the album entered the U.K. charts, and sold well in America.

In ensuing years, however, despite a regular album output, Osibisa never quite fulfilled their early promise, partly because of frequent personnel changes; Richardson, for example, left the band for a time to make a solo

*Welcome Home.
Courtesy Bronze Records.*

album, **Pieces Of A Jigsaw**, before returning in autumn 1975.

The band, however, concentrated on improving their stock through regular gigging; since there is an infectious ebullience about their live performance, their concerts are invariably successful, and in this way the band have been able to build up an audience wherever they have played; for example, they are highly touted in Africa – obviously – and also Australia and the Far East.

At the start of 1976, however, they were in clover. Signed to a new record company, their album, **Welcome Home,** sold well, and provided them with their first U.K. hit single, **Sunshine Day,** which finally seemed to be the forerunner of some prolonged and deserved success.

Recordings:
Osibisa (MCA)
Woyoya (MCA)
Heads (MCA)
Superfly TNT (Soundtrack)
(Buddah/—)

*Left: John Hall of Orleans:
their album Waking And
Dreaming, was issued in 1976.*

*Below: The Car Over The Lake
Album. Courtesy A&M Records.*

Happy Children (Warner Bros)
Osibirock (Warner Bros)
Welcome Home (Island/Bronze)
Compilation:
Best Of Osibisa (—/MCA)

Gilbert O'Sullivan

Real name Raymond O'Sullivan, born Dec 1, 1946 in Waterford, Ireland. On death of his father, a butcher, family moved to England when O'Sullivan was 12. He'd played piano from early age and performed with variety of semi-pro bands while at art school in Swindon – one of these was Rick's Blues, led by Richard Davies now of Supertramp (➡).

On leaving college, moved to London to break into music industry as songwriter, working for time as mail boy for large department store. Subsequently underwent unsuccessful periods with CBS (Columbia in U.S.) and Major Minor labels before discovery by Gordon Mills, manager of Tom Jones, Engelbert Humperdinck.

Mills signed him for management, changed name, and installed him in Surrey bungalow (near Mills' own home) to work on songwriting and new image for full year before release of **Nothing Rhymed** single in late 1970. This new "image" involved O'Sullivan being attired in ludicrous get-up of schoolboy shirt and short trousers, hob-nailed boots and pudding-basin haircut. Comparisons to Charlie Chaplin were encouraged in national press enticed by Mills' success record with Jones and Humperdinck.

On strength of this heavy media coverage, O'Sullivan survived initial guffaws of laughter to take his debut single into U.K. Top 10. This was the first of a long run of hits all displaying O'Sullivan's grasp of melody and song construction (an eclectic mix of influences, from Cole Porter through Beatles to Rogers & Hart), though his foolish appearance restricted

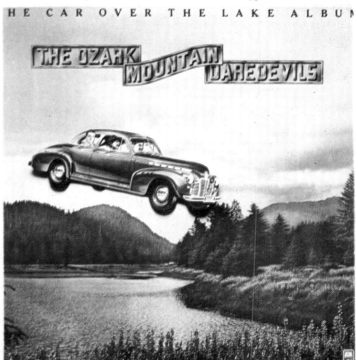

recognition to pop audience.

Among biggest successes was **Alone Again (Naturally),** in 1972, which made No. 3 in U.K. and broke O'Sullivan in U.S. – topping charts there and achieving gold status. **Claire,** a British No. 1, was also huge American hit same year, as was his debut album **Himself** (released one year after U.K. issue).

March 1973 British No. 1 **Get Down** marked shift of direction towards rock, and by this time the Chaplinesque trappings had been moth-balled away in favour of less contrived, audience-restricting apparel. Appearances in concerts and in charts have been less frequent since 1974, and he seems to be straining hard to recapture his earlier success.

Recordings:
Himself (MAM)
Back To Front (MAM)
I'm A Writer Not A Fighter (MAM)
A Stranger In My Own Back Yard (MAM)

The Outlaws

Billy Jones lead guitar, vocals
Hughie Thomason, Jnr. lead guitar, vocals
Henry Paul rhythm guitar, vocals
Monty Yoho drums
Frank O'Keefe bass

A Florida-based band, The Outlaws had the distinction of being Clive Davis' first signing to his Arista label; they attracted attention with their reasonably successful debut album, which was produced by Paul A. Rothchild. In 1975 they toured extensively in the States.

Recordings:
The Outlaws (Arista)
Lady In Waiting (Arista)

Ozark Mountain Daredevils

John Dillon guitar, piano, dulcimer, mandolin, harp, vocals
Steve Cash harp, vocals
Randle Chowning guitar, harp, mandolin, vocals
Michael "Supe" Granda bass, vocals
Larry Lee drums
Buddy Brayfield piano

Among the best of the new-wave country-rock bands, they were founded in Springfield, Missouri, accruing local reputation through gigs at Bijou Theatre where drummer Lee once worked as a bartender. None of above personnel had previous experience in top-line acts. Indeed, Steve Cash had never been in a band before, let alone played harp, when the Ozarks roped him in – he had, however, had poetry published in "Rolling Stone".

They cut a critically-acclaimed debut album in 1973, from which came the Cash-Dillon written American smash single **If You Want To Get To Heaven** (1974). Consolidated reputation as one of

finest '70s bands – in any field – with an equally-excellent second set in 1974.

Their repertoire draws on a potent fusion of melodic country and gritty rock 'n' roll, and invites certain comparisons with The Eagles (➧). Like the last-named, the Ozarks travelled to London to cut their first album with British producer Glyn Johns at Olympic Studios (along with co-producer David Anderle); while the same production team also worked on the second album, recorded for the most part at Randle Chowning's ranch home in Missouri.

In 1975 third album recorded in Nashville with Anderle producing.

Recordings:
Ozark Mountain Daredevils (A&M)
It'll Shine When It Shines (A&M)
The Car Over The Lake Album (A&M)

Pablo Cruise

Cory Lerios keyboards, vocals
David Jenkins guitar, vocals
Steve Price drums, vocals
Bud Cockrell bass, vocals

Emerged Bay Area of San Francisco July 1973 with Cockrell from It's A Beautiful Day and Stoneground alumni Lerios, Jenkins and Price. All four contribute material and vocals – often in multi-part ensemble fashion – to all-original repertoire which has links with lusher-textured elements of West Coast rock. Acclaimed first album released 1975; second in spring 1976.

Recordings:
Pablo Cruise (A&M)
Lifeline (A&M)

Robert Palmer

Born in Batley, Yorkshire, England, but raised in Malta until the age of nine. Developed interest in American R&B during 'teens, playing semi-pro in first band during art school and later while working during day as a graphic designer. At 19, Palmer was recruited to the Alan Bown Set as lead vocalist, but after a short while joined new jazz-rock aggregation Dada, which eventually metamorphosed into Vinegar Joe (➧). Palmer played rhythm guitar and shared vocals with Pete Gage and Elkie Brooks (➧) in this band until dissolution late 1973.

Palmer had been dissatisfied in Vinegar Joe for some months, and in early 1974 he put down in demo form some new song ideas and arrangements he had been formulating over a lengthy period. He took them to Island Records boss Chris Blackwell, and within three weeks he was on a 'plane to record his first solo album in New Orleans and New York under American producer Steve Smith. The Meters (➧) and Lowell George of Little Feat (➧) guested on the New Orleans cuts – George plays on Palmer's version of the Little Feat classic **Sailin' Shoes** – while the New York sessions made use of such studio luminaries as drummer Bernard Purdie

and guitarist Cornell Dupree.

Smith and Palmer returned to the States to cut the singer's second set, **Pressure Drop** (1975), half in Baltimore with Little Feat (this collection includes another Lowell George cut, **Trouble**), the rest in Los Angeles with an equally formidable line-up including noted Tamla Motown bassist James Jamerson.

Pressure Drop.
Courtesy Island Records.

Palmer's fusion of white-eyed soul and R&B hasn't found favour in all critical quarters, but favourable radio station reaction in U.S. has enabled him to establish minor foothold in market there that could be springboard to greater success.

Pressure Drop not released in U.K. until spring 1976.

Recordings:
Sneakin' Sally Through The Alley (Island)
Pressure Drop (Island)

Tony Palmer

Born in 1941, Palmer is a rock critic and TV producer. According to legend, he had never heard any rock music until 1967 when he asked a friend to introduce him to the genre via a selection of 10 seminal albums. One was **Sgt Pepper's Lonely Hearts Club Band,** and Palmer has been a True Believer ever since, frequently asserting that The Beatles were the greatest songwriters since Schubert, and bringing heavyweight/pretentious criticism to rock music through his column in the "Observer" – an extension of which was his book, "Born Under A Bad Sign".

As a television producer concerned with rock programmes, he has distinguished himself in a field of one. After the BBC's magazine programme, "How It Is", he went on to produce "All My Loving", which showed rock musicians as concerned human beings, and attempted to dispel the old cliches of them being teenage morons. His most successful venture was probably his film of Cream's farewell concert at the Albert Hall. He also directed a fondly-remembered film about Jack Bruce, "Rope Ladder To The Moon".

Van Dyke Parks

West Coast producer, songwriter and pianist session-man, Parks was born in Mississippi circa 1941 but moved to Hollywood with his

family at age 13. There he worked as a child actor, studied classical piano and composition, and signed to MGM ostensibly, so the story goes, to compose soundtracks for Walt Disney movies.

Instead he cut a couple of solo singles, gained a certain notoriety as the writer of folk-rock favourite **High Coin** (recorded by Bobby Vee, Charlatans, Harper's, West Coast Pop Art Experimental Band, etc.), and emerged as producer for likes of mid-'60s U.S. groups The Mojo Men (their baroque version of Steve Stills' **Sit Down I Think I Love You** was a 1966 Top 10) and the aforementioned Harper's Bizarre (**Anything Goes,** etc.).

He was prolific in many fields, a frail, aesthetic figure who accrued a reputation in West Coast musicians circles as being some kind of mysterious genius. Around 1966 he fell in with Brian Wilson of Beach Boys, and was taken on by Wilson to replace his current lyricist Tony Asher. This was the start of Wilson's freak-out drugs phase which alienated him (and Parks) from the rest of the band. The pair collaborated on the aborted **Smile** album, one of the most enigmatic projects in pop history. Further details can be found under Beach Boys entry, but it was Parks who wrote lyrics for such Wilson masterworks as **Heroes & Villains** and the hugely ambitious **Surf's Up** – planned for **Smile** but not released until some years later as lead track on the Beach Boys album of same name.

In 1968 Parks released his first solo album, **Song Cycle,** comprising material he had been working on for four years. Full of rococo imagery, by turns inspirational and outrightly pretentious, it was hailed in certain quarters as initiating a whole new genre – "Art Rock".

From that point on, Parks' name began to turn-up on an ever-increasing number of projects: as producer on Arlo Guthrie's **Running Down The Road** album, and Ry Cooder's and Randy Newman's eponymous debut albums; as session-pianist on such albums as Little Feat's **Feats Don't Fail Me Now,** Tim Buckley's eponymous album, and Judy Collins' **Who Knows Where The Time Goes?** An earlier notable session appearance was on Byrds' **Eight Miles High.**

Parks has shown no great desire to push his solo career. Four years elapsed before his next album, **Discover America,** in 1972, and another three years before his third, the late 1975 **The Clang Of The Yankee Reaper.** Both showed affinity for Caribbean music, nurtured by his production work for the Esso Trinidad Steel Band and calypso artist Mighty Sparrow.

Like his more illustrious contemporary Phil Spector (➧), Parks remains one of rock's most enigmatic characters.

Recordings:
Song Cycle (Warner Bros)
Discover America (Warner Bros)
The Clang Of The Yankee Reaper (Warner Bros)

Gram Parsons

Born in Winterhaven, Florida,

November 5, 1946, Parsons was brought up initially in Georgia, but upon the death of his father moved with relatives to New Orleans. He ran away from his adoptive home during the early '60s, aged about 14, and by the time he was 16 was singing protest songs in Greenwich Village.

Going to Harvard at the age of 18, he formed the International Submarine Band, which he led on guitar and vocals, with John Nuese (gtr), Ian Dunlop (bs) and Mickey Gauvin (drms). The group made two obscure singles, and then moved to Los Angeles, where a new line-up of Parsons, Nuese, Jon Corneal (drms) and Bob Buchanan (gtr) made **Safe At Home,** an album which is assumed to represent the beginning of country-rock and copies of which now change hands for a king's ransom.

Grievous Angel.
Courtesy Warner Bros. Records.

By the time the album was released, Parsons had already joined The Byrds (♦), though he spent only three months with the band before quitting on the eve of a South African tour, owing to his disapproval of apartheid. Even so, his participation in The Byrds produced far-reaching results; though his contribution was almost totally mixed out of **Sweetheart Of The Rodeo,** his vision of country-rock remained clear, and through this he has become one of the most seminal influences on the development of rock 'n' roll.

At the end of 1968 he formed the Flying Burrito Brothers (♦) with Chris Hillman, Chris Ethridge and Sneaky Pete Kleinow, and played a major role in the recording of both **The Gilded Palace Of Sin** and **Burrito Deluxe.** However, in April 1970, just prior to the release of the second album, Parsons left the group and came to Europe where he hung out with Keith Richard (♦ Rolling Stones). Various recording possibilities were suggested, but none taken up, before he began to make **G.P.** at the end of 1972, by which time he had met Emmylou Harris (♦), who was invited to be his co-vocalist.

Throughout the previous seven years, Parsons had been intrigued by the possibility of fusing country and rock 'n' roll music, presenting both forms to an audience previously biased against one or the other. **G.P.** and its successor, **Grievous Angel,** were reportedly the first of his records with which he was satisfied. Certainly, **Grievous Angel** is a truly magnificent album.

On Sep 19, 1973, Parsons died while rehearsing in the desert outside Los Angeles, and a week later, in a somewhat bizarre incident, his body was hijacked and burnt at the Joshua Tree National Monument, an act of loyalty by his long-time friend and road manager Phil Kaufman; it seems that, in the event of his death, Parsons had expressed a wish for his body to be cremated in this manner. (Hence no autopsy could be performed, and no conclusive cause of death established.)

After Parsons' death, Emmylou Harris assumed his mantle, and has already either recorded or put in her repertoire 90 per cent of the Parsons legacy.

Though his own recorded output was limited, the importance of Parsons can hardly be underestimated. Without his pioneering work, a large number of the '70s' most popular groups (The Eagles, for example) might never have achieved their present status. In 1974 The Eagles recorded **My Man,** written by Bernie Leadon, which is a moving tribute to Parsons.

Recordings:
International Submarine Band:
Safe At Home, (LHI/—)
Gram Parsons:
G.P. (Reprise)
Grievous Angel (Reprise)
Gram Parsons with the Flying Burrito Brothers:
Sleepless Nights (A&M)

Dolly Parton

Once a popular but straightforward country singer with the Porter Wagoner Show, Dolly Parton re-directed her career in '70s by going solo and eschewing the more stylised trademarks of Nashville country music.

She was born on a farm in Locust Ridge, in Sevier County, Tennessee, 1946, fourth child in family of 12. She made her first recordings at age 11, and appeared on Grand Ole Opry a year later. She left high school at 18, and headed straight for Nashville, where she barely earned a livelihood for four years, before she joined Porter Wagoner in 1967, the same year she signed with RCA. Thus began one of most successful partnerships in country music, the fruits of which can be sampled on **The Best Of Porter Wagoner & Dolly Parton,** a selection of some of the most thrilling mainstream country ever recorded.

Jolene.
Courtesy RCA Records.

Dolly's solo career began in 1974, with release of **Jolene,** a hit single and album in U.S. country charts. While retaining RCA's Bob Ferguson as producer, she settled for a lighter touch, and under-played the overt country influences. Her compositions became more lyrically ambitious, and transcended the limiting themes of standard country music.

She began to gain acceptance with rock audience indirectly as her material was covered by girl singers operating within rock milieu – Linda Ronstadt included **I Will Always Love You** on **Prisoner In Disguise,** Emmylou Harris recorded Parton's most famous – and also autobiographical – composition, **Coat Of Many Colours** on her debut solo album, and Maria Muldaur put **My Tennessee Mountain Home** on her debut solo album.

Dolly's own compositions continued to be automatic successes in U.S. charts, as she had hits with **Love Is Like A Butterfly** (1975) and **The Seeker** (1976); in Britain, **Jolene** finally became a hit in 1976.

Discography is selective.

Recordings:
Jolene (RCA)
Love Is Like A Butterfly (RCA)
The Bargain Store (RCA)
Compilations:
The Best Of Dolly Parton (RCA)
The Best Of Dolly Parton, Vol. II (—/RCA)

Les Paul

American guitarist – b. Lester Polfus in 1917 – who did much to pioneer electric side of guitar, including developing multi-tracking technique. With his partner and wife Mary Ford, Paul virtually invented many advanced recording devices, and this devotion to improved sound quality led to his famed Les Paul series of guitar designs which he produced for the Gibson Corporation.

These instruments represented a double jump on the evolutionary ladder, being both solid-bodied and fitted with multiple pick-ups; the necks were of superlative quality. They were only moderately popular until the Blues Boom of '60s, when they were discovered to be ideal for blues-playing, having a biting tone, tremendous power and good sustain quality. Gibson ceased to manufacture these guitars in early '60s, owing to disagreements with Paul.

Since then, however, a reconciliation has been effected and for the last four years an entirely new range of Les Paul designs – based on his earlier models – has been manufactured. Aficionados, however, openly prefer the "vintage" models; an original '50s Les Paul Gibson is now almost beyond price.

Pavlov's Dog

David Surkamp vocals, guitar
Doug Rayburn Mellotron, bass
Steve Scorfina guitar
David Hamilton keyboards
Richard Stockton bass
Tom Nickeson guitar, vocals

Originated out of St Louis, Missouri, 1973, original line-up consisting Surkamp, Hamilton, Rayburn, and ex REO Speedwagon guitarist Scorfina, plus one-time Chuck Berry drummer Mike Safron and violinist Siegfried Carver. Signed for reputedly grand sum to ABC Records, for whom they cut **Pampered Menial** debut.

However, before release, ABC mysteriously dropped band from their roster, and the group went to Columbia. When finally released (by both companies!) the album proved a daringly innovative debut set, totally reliant on original material, and revolving around the astonishing vocal gymnastics of David Surkamp – "like a choirboy on speed" as one (of the few) enthusiasts put it. A minor cult following resulted.

By time of second album, **At The Sound Of The Bell** (1976), star-turn fiddler Carver had gone, Nickeson had been added, and Safron's role taken over for sessions by British drummer Bill Bruford (♦ Yes, King Crimson). At that point, without permanent drummer, stability of above line-up looked in question – as did whether group's unique vision would be too far out for mass consumption.

Production/management handled by Murray Krugman and Sandy Pearlman (Blue Oyster Cult, Dictators).

Recordings:
Pampered Menial (Columbia/CBS)
At The Sound Of The Bell (Columbia/CBS)

Tom Paxton

Born Chicago, Illinois, Oct 31, 1937, Paxton studied at University of Oklahoma and did a stint of military service, before moving to New York in early '60s where he became one of the foremost young folksingers, along with Bob Dylan, Phil Ochs, et al. He signed with Elektra Records, and made seven records for them over a period of seven years. His first two albums, **Ramblin' Boy** and **Ain't That News** were particularly good, and showed his ability to combine biting satire (**Lyndon Johnson Told The Nation**) with songs of a tender, romantic nature (**My Lady's A Wild Flying Dove, The Last Thing On My Mind**), and also children's songs in the tradition of Woody Guthrie's (**We're All Going To The Zoo**).

Though his songs have been widely covered by other artists, he has never enjoyed wide commercial success himself, though he was very well received at 1969 Isle of Wight festival, where the brilliant satire **Talking Pot Luck Blues** held the audience enthralled.

He now performs with a small ensemble, though he has never attempted to commercialise his act. He has a loyal following, and his annual concert tours of Britain, where he now resides, are always popular.

Paxton's work evidences warmth, humanity and considerable wit; inevitably he will continue to be best-known through other recordings of his songs – as, for example, when John Denver covered **Whose Garden Was This?** or Judy Collins recorded **The Hostage,** his song about the Attica State prison massacre. Not a prolific composer, but on the other hand he does set himself exacting standards.

Recordings:
Ramblin' Boy (Elektra)
Ain't That News (Elektra)
Outward Bound (Elektra)

Above: Dolly Parton, who unfailingly won friends and influenced people in 1976.

Morning Again (Elektra)
The Things I Notice Now
(Elektra)
Tom Paxton No. 6 (Elektra)
The Compleat Tom Paxton
(Elektra)
How Come The Sun (Reprise)
Peace Will Come (Reprise)
New Songs For Old Friends
(Reprise)
Something In My Life (Private
Stock/MAM)

Pearls Before Swine

The single unifying feature of the almost totally undocumented career of Pearls Before Swine is Tom Rapp, whose only previous claim to fame was to have finished above Bob Dylan in a local talent contest.

The group, which, apart from Rapp, apparently consisted of surfers and unknown musicians, signed initially with the avant-garde ESP label, producing **One Nation Underground** and **Balaklava** in 1967 and 1968 respectively. Both were decorated with sleeve designs borrowed from Hieronymous Bosch.

After signing with the much more prestigious Reprise, **These Things Too** (1969) was leavened with a few notable studio musicians in addition to the unknowns, while **The Use Of Ashes** (1970) and part of **City Of Gold** (1971) were recorded in Nashville. The remainder of the last-named, and the whole of **Beautiful Lies You Could Live In** (1971) were made in New York.

Tom Rapp (1972), which passes for the composer-leader's first solo album (although the rest of the original group had long since departed), is partially a re-record

of some of the songs on earlier albums.

After this, Rapp signed with Blue Thumb, producing the final two listed collections. Since then nothing has been heard of him, though rumours abound that he lives in Holland. His songs have an undeniable quality, a semi-mystical other-worldliness set against swimmy arrangements, which has been claimed by critics as due to drug use – but when mixed with the classic songs of his peers like Leonard Cohen, Judy Collins and Jacques Brel, his albums have attracted a certain cultist following despite difficulties in obtaining them, particularly in the U.K.

Recordings:
One Nation Underground
(ESP/Fontana)
Balaklava (ESP/Fontana)
These Things Too (Reprise/—)
The Use Of Ashes (Reprise)
City Of Gold (Reprise/—)
Beautiful Lies You Could Live In (Reprise)
Tom Rapp (Reprise/—)
Stardancer (Blue Thumb/—)
Sunforest (Blue Thumb/—)

The Pentangle

Bert Jansch guitar, vocals
John Renbourn guitar, sitar,
vocals
Jacqui McShee vocals
Danny Thompson bass
Terry Cox drums, percussion,
glockenspiel

Formed late 1967 as an amalgamation of some of the foremost talents on the British folk-scene, particularly Renbourn (◆) and Jansch (◆), each of whom already had substantial solo reputations. They were joined by Jacqui McShee, who had previously sung with her sister in folk clubs and with Renbourn on **Another Monday.** Thompson and Cox were both experienced session-

men, familiar with jazz and blues, and had been part of Alexis Korner's Blues Inc. for a spell. The group, which was formed after trial sessions at the Horse-shoe Club in London's Tottenham Court Road, was thus designed as an experimental outfit, blending folk, blues and jazz.

Though this aim was never fully realised, as the band inevitably seemed to remain folk-based, they were nevertheless one of the most popular of contemporary bands at their height from 1968–71. They toured regularly in Britain and U.S., and were extremely accomplished in live performance; a concert programme was likely to include Thelonius Monk, gospel songs, and straightforward traditional folk music. Their albums, usually produced by Shel Talmy (◆) all sold well.

Basket Of Light.
Courtesy Transatlantic Records.

Towards the end they were criticised for being effete, and could not seem to take their musical ratatouille to any logical conclusion. In 1972 they were signed to Reprise in Britain, and their album **Solomon's Seal** turned out to be a valedictory one; the instrumental precision was still there, but the motivation wasn't.

The double-album **Sweet Child** (one live, one studio album)

remains their quintessential work, and **Basket Of Light** their bestselling album.

When they split up in March 1973, all resumed former occupations; Renbourn now lives on a farm in Wales; in 1974 he and McShee cautiously took steps to put together another group; after an unencouraging debut at the Cambridge Folk Festival, however, nothing came of it.

Recordings:
The Pentangle (Reprise/
Transatlantic)
Sweet Child (Reprise/
Transatlantic)
Basket Of Light (Reprise/
Transatlantic)
Cruel Sister (Reprise/
Transatlantic)
Reflections (Reprise/
Transatlantic)
Solomon's Seal (Reprise)
Compilations:
Pentangle History Book
(—/Transatlantic)
Pentangling (—/Transatlantic)

Carl Perkins

Born Apr 9, 1932 in Lake City, Tennessee, in conditions of some poverty (his father was a farmer), Perkins began his career in music by performing at country dances with his brothers Jay and Clayton; after several local radio spots, he signed to Sun Records, where Elvis Presley, who, like Perkins had been absorbed by both white country and black blues music, had already broken new ground with his version of Arthur Crudup's **That's All Right.**

Backed by his brothers, Perkins cut **Blue Suede Shoes,** which achieved the unprecedented (before or since) feat of topping the pop, R&B and country charts simultaneously. For Perkins it meant a gold record and instant stardom, but while he was on his way to a television show in March 1956 he was in a serious car accident, which killed his brother Jay and his manager.

Perkins was hospitalised for nearly a year; meanwhile Presley had cut a version of his **Blue Suede Shoes,** and was securing an unassailable position for himself. Though Perkins had other hits, including **Matchbox** (which was recorded by The Beatles, in his presence, in Britain 1964), Perkins quickly realised that the rockabilly scene had already passed its high point, and though he continued to record in that idiom, he introduced more and more country material into his repertoire.

Perkins joined the Johnny Cash television show in the later '60s, and has worked with him ever since. He has continued recording, but it was the impact he made in 1955–56 that is of lasting importance.

Discography is selective.

Recordings:
Dance Album (Sun/London)
Original Golden Hits (Sun)
Blue Suede Shoes (Sun)
King Of Rock (Columbia/CBS)
Boppin' The Blues (Columbia/
CBS)
The Man Behind Johnny Cash
(Columbia/CBS)
My Kind Of Country (Mercury)

Richard Perry

Born in Brooklyn, Perry spent his formative years working with a local sock-hop rock-band, but it wasn't until he moved to Los Angeles in later '60s that he began to rise to prominence.

He received the production credit for Captain Beefheart's critically-acclaimed **Safe As Milk**, and then helped Tiny Tim to international stardom with **God Bless Tiny Tim** and **For All My Little Friends.** This led to a succession of albums with Fats Domino, Ella Fitzgerald and Theodore Bikel, and, as an independent producer, with Fanny, Barbra Streisand and Andy Williams.

It was his work in MOR market that helped establish Perry's reputation; in particular his work on Streisand's **Stoney End.** Soon he became the premier West Coast producer, whose services were forever in demand. He worked with Carly Simon very successfully (especially with **No Secrets**, which included the massive hit single **You're So Vain**), and also Nilsson **(Nilsson Schmilsson** and **Son Of Schmilsson)** before going on to produce Ringo Starr's **Ringo**, easily his best solo album. The success of the Perry/Starr combination can probably be attributed to the fact that Perry favours an extravagant style of production, and hence it suited him to work with someone whose vocals were hardly of prima donna calibre.

He made another album with Ringo – **Goodnight Vienna** – that lacked the panache of the earlier one, and also worked with Art Garfunkel on **Breakaway.**

However, just as he had become the backroom-boy who was a glittering star in his own right, nemesis appeared in the shape of the **Martha Reeves** album. Perry asked for – and got – a fee that might have bankrupted an oil sheikh, and produced the album in a sumptuous, but cluttered, fashion. It went down like the "Titanic", the most expensive flop in the history of the record business.

Peter, Paul & Mary

Peter Yarrow guitar, vocals
Paul Stookey guitar, vocals
Mary Travers vocals

Yarrow, Stookey and Travers were brought together in New York's Greenwich Village in 1961 by Albert Grossman (♦), as an acoustic folk group in bestselling wake of Kingston Trio.

Yarrow (b. New York, May 31, 1938) graduated in psychology from Cornell University where he had lectured on folk ballads; he worked for a time as a solo artist, and was well-received at the 1960 Newport Folk Festival. Stookey (b. Birmingham, Michigan, Nov 30, 1937) had led a high school rock 'n' roll group on local television, and then become a stand-up comic in Greenwich Village clubs. Travers (b. Louisville, Kentucky, Nov 7, 1937) had appeared in several folk groups; after working on a flop Broadway show, "The Next President", with

Mort Sahl, she was encouraged back into singing by Stookey, and after seven months of intensive rehearsals, Peter, Paul & Mary set off on a blitzkrieg nationwide club tour which built them an enormous following, and they had a string of U.S. hits throughout the '60s.

In 1963 they covered **Blowin' In The Wind,** which reached No. 2 in U.S. charts and No. 13 in the U.K. In doing so, they helped to bring the name of Bob Dylan to a mass audience – in the same way that it was they who helped open the door for the widespread acceptance of both the folk and protest movements. Despite their conservative dress and orthodox singing style – characterised by simple acoustic guitar accompaniment and strident harmonies – they were familiar figures on campuses and protest platforms.

Their first hit was Pete Seeger's **If I Had A Hammer**, and others included Woody Guthrie's **This Land Is Your Land, Go Tell It On The Mountain** and **Puff (The Magic Dragon).** In 1968 they introduced another new writer – John Denver; his composition **Leaving On A Jet Plane** reached No. 1 in the U.S. and No. 2 in the U.K., where Lady Mary Wilson, the then Prime Minister's wife, quoted it as her favourite song.

By 1971 their historical moment had long passed, and they disbanded. They each made solo albums, and Mary was given a radio chat show; her most famous interviewee has been Bob Dylan.

Recordings:
Peter, Paul & Mary
(Warner Bros)
Moving (Warner Bros)
In The Wind (Warner Bros)
Peter, Paul & Mary In Concert
(Warner Bros)
A Song Will Rise (Warner Bros)
See What Tomorrow Brings
(Warner Bros)
Peter, Paul & Mary Album
(Warner Bros)
Album 1700 (Warner Bros)
Late Again (Warner Bros)
Peter, Paul & Mommy
(Warner Bros)
Paul Stookey:
Paul And (Warner Bros)
Mary Travers:
Mary (Warner Bros)
Morning Glory (Warner Bros)
All My Choices (Warner Bros)
Peter Yarrow:
Peter (Warner Bros)
That's Enough For Me
(Warner Bros)

P.F.M.

Franz Di Ciccio drums, vocals
Flavio Premoli keyboards, vocals
Franco Mussida guitar, vocals
Mauro Pagani flutes, violin, vocals
Patric Djivas bass
Bernardo Lanzetti guitar, vocals

Premiata Forneria Marconi – later abridged to the less unwieldy P.F.M. – were formed out of pop-group Quelli in Italy 1971 by Premoli, Mussida, Di Ciccio and Pagani. Fusing jazz, rock and classics in the manner so beloved by British "flash-rock" aggregations, the new band rapidly achieved status as Italy's foremost rock attraction.

Above: Paul, Mary and Peter photographed in the '60s. at the height of their success, when they helped pave the way for the emergence of performers like Bob Dylan.

In 1973, seeking international recognition, they commissioned former King Crimson lights man/writer Pete Sinfield (♦) to put English lyrics to their group compositions. Sinfield introduced them to Greg Lake of Emerson Lake And Palmer, and P.F.M. consequently signed to ELP's new Manticore label.

First result of this collaboration, **Photos Of Ghosts** (1973), which Sinfield also produced, made U.S. albums charts before band had worked there. The second set, **The World Became The World** (1974), introduced new bassist Djivas. Again Sinfield wrote lyrics, though production credit this time went to Claudio Fabi.

Third album, **P.F.M. Cook**, was recorded live at end of first North American tour during concerts in Toronto and New York Central Park – on release in 1975 this, too, made American lists.

However, the band were becoming increasingly dissatisfied with abilities of present personnel to handle lead vocals – a sixth member, Bernardo Lanzetti, being augmented primarily for this purpose. He made debut on 1976 set, **Chocolate Kings**, recorded in Milan. This also marked group's first attempts to write their own English-language lyrics.

Recordings:
Photos Of Ghosts (Manticore)
The World Became The World
Manticore)
P.F.M. Cook (Manticore)
Chocolate Kings (Manticore)

Philadelphia International

In late '50s and early '60s, Philadelphia was second only to New York as a root source of pop music – mainly due to Dick Clark's "American Bandstand" TV programme which originated there and provided exposure for

local artists. Freddy Cannon and others first came to attention in this way (and even Simon & Garfunkel, in the days when they were Tom & Jerry, were featured on programme), before the Cameo/Parkway labels were founded there at end of the '50s. The Cameo/Parkway roster included Chubby Checker, Bobby Rydell and The Orlons.

However, the city did not possess a proper four-track studio until late '60s when Kenny Gamble and Leon Huff, and their Sigma Sound Studio began to emerge as the dominant Philadelphia force, and soon as a major influence throughout the entire rock and soul music scene.

By the time Gamble & Huff established their own Philadelphia International Records in 1973, they had already developed a velvet-smooth orchestral soul style and, in combination with producer/arranger Thom Bell, it seemed likely for a time that Philly Records would present strong opposition to Tamla-Motown (♦), which was then in some turmoil, having just moved out to the West Coast.

However, although all the early releases on Philadelphia International were successful, few groups have lasted the course. The O'Jays (♦) have been the most consistent, while the Three Degrees had hits throughout 1974 and 1975, but hardly revealed themselves as the new Supremes. Harold Melvin and Blue Notes, The Intruders and Billy Paul were other company acts who achieved some measure of chart success; but ultimately Philly became known not for its own acts, but for its trend-setting sound, and for the session musicians, known collectively as MFSB, under which name they had hits of their own. Also for the quality of production work at Sigma Sound. Many soul and rock artists have opted to work there in recent years, including David Bowie, who recorded **Young Americans** there.

The offices of the Philadelphia International company are now located in the former Cameo-Parkway building.

"The Sound Of Philadelphia" by Tony Cumming, is a thorough exposition of the local music scene.

Sam Phillips

Phillips was born in Florence, Alabama in 1923. While working in Memphis as a DJ on Radio WRAC, he became aware of the dire lack of facilities for local black performers; most companies had to make do with makeshift arrangements (often tape-recorders in garages or hotel rooms) when scouring the South for likely talent.

Though white himself, Phillips set up his Sun studio in 1950 with the sole intention of recording black artists; he made records with Howlin' Wolf and B. B. King and others, selling the masters to companies like Chess in Chicago and RPM in Los Angeles.

By 1953 he was established enough to launch his own Sun label, and was initially successful with Rufus Thomas and Junior Parker. In 1954 a young white boy walked in and paid to record a couple of numbers for his mother. Phillips was impressed, signed the youngster, and the Elvis Presley (◆) legend was born.

When producing, Phillips used a recording technique that Charlie Gillett (◆) has described as "documentary", which allowed the singer to project himself more easily. Phillips found the most suitable vehicle for this style in Presley, whose Sun recordings display an unforced excitement that he was rarely able to recapture.

Like Phillips, Presley loved blues artists, especially Big Bill Broonzy and Big Boy Crudup, and it was Presley's recordings of **Mystery Train** (written and first recorded by Junior Parker) and Crudup's **That's All Right, Mama** that fused the blues and country traditions, in a style which became known as rockabilly; it was this sound that was effectively the

Below: The Pink Floyd, photographed on stage during their 1974 world tour.

beginning of rock 'n' roll as we know it today.

After Presley, Phillips switched his attention from blues back to white artists, from straight blues to rockabilly. He recorded Carl Perkins, Jerry Lee Lewis, Charlie Rich, Johnny Cash and Roy Orbison, before losing them all to major companies.

Phillips' most commercially successful recordings were Perkins' **Blue Suede Shoes,** a million seller, Cash's **I Walk The Line** and Lewis' **Whole Lotta Shakin' Goin' On.**

While original copies of these legendary rock recordings now change hands at saleroom prices, the Sun label itself ceased operations in 1968.

Shawn Phillips

Born Fort Worth, Texas, Phillips was a self-confessed recalcitrant child; he was thrown out of schools and into courts; he joined the navy in 1959, was severely disciplined almost straightaway, and left in 1961.

After learning to play guitar, he made his way to Los Angeles where he befriended Tim Hardin (◆). The pair then trekked east to Greenwich Village.

Phillips initially made his living as a dishwasher at The Night Owl, before picking up gigs in several New York clubs. During a concert tour, he met Ravi Shankar and determined to go to India to learn to play the sitar. He only got as far as London; there he made two acoustic albums, and starred in a film called, "Run With The Wind".

Phillips supported Donovan on a U.S. tour, and then threw over his folky stance and infused his music with the spirit of rock 'n' roll.

He returned to England to try filming again, but, without a work permit, was refused entry, and, after some bureaucratic hassles, was declared "persona non grata". So in 1967 he sought refuge in Positano, Italy, where he taught himself yoga and breath control, which enabled him to give free

rein to the amazing range of his voice.

After that, he found himself a manager and resumed his music career with some conviction. He has made seven albums for A&M since 1970.

Recordings:
Contribution (A&M)
Second Contribution (A&M)
Collaboration (A&M)
Faces (A&M)
Bright White (A&M)
Furthermore (A&M)
Do You Wonder? (A&M)

Pink Fairies

Paul Rudolph guitar
Larry Wallis guitar
Duncan Sanderson bass
Russell Hunter drums

Originally the name of an informal London drinking club-cum-terrorist organisation comprising Mick Farren, Steve Took and Twink, the Pink Fairies arose out of the ashes of The (Social) Deviants – a band which comprised Farren (vcls), Sanderson, Hunter and Rudolph. That group fell into disarray when Farren quit during U.S. tour.

On return to England and adoption of Fairies name, the band

augmented Twink as second drummer and followed in Deviants' footsteps as rough-and-ready Notting Hill Gate community band, playing numerous benefit gigs often in double feature with Hawkwind (◆).

They recorded flawed first album in 1971, after which Twink quit. The band continued as three-piece, completed a better second album **What A Bunch Of Sweeties** (1972) and for a time looked on verge of possible breakthrough. However, Rudolph then opted out and the band went through a series of experimental stages (including one with Mick Wayne, ex of Junior's Eyes) until they settled down with Larry Wallis, from UFO, on guitar.

This line-up made third album **Kings Of Oblivion** but stumbled deeper into omnipresent financial problems. Twink's return failed to stop the rot and the group disbanded end of 1973.

A one-off reunion gig featuring line-up as listed above took place in spring 1975; following year Fairies re-formed as trio, Rudolph having joined Hawkwind.

Recordings:
Never Never Land (—/Polydor)
What A Bunch Of Sweeties (—/Polydor)
Kings Of Oblivion (—/Polydor)

Pink Floyd

Rick Wright keyboards
Roger Waters bass
Nick Mason drums
Dave Gilmour guitar

Original Pink Floyd line-up had Syd Barrett on lead guitar instead of Dave Gilmour, otherwise personnel has remained constant. Roger Keith (Syd) Barrett was born January 1946 in university town Cambridge, England. Together with Waters and Gilmour he attended Cambridge High School for Boys. Moving to London, he attended Camberwell School of Art where, in addition to painting, he learned to play guitar. He played in various groups, Geoff Mott and the Mottos, The Hollering Blues, and, as a folk-duo, with Dave Gilmour who taught him Stones licks during their lunch-breaks.

George Roger Waters left Cambridge to study architecture at the Regent Street Polytechnic in London. Doing the same architectural course were Nicholas Berkeley Mason and Richard William Wright, both Londoners who arrived at the poly via Frensham Heights and Haberdashers'. Waters, Mason and Wright formed a group and called themselves Sigma 6. They were managed by Ken Chapman, an ex poly student but he had no luck in selling them to a record company. They tried for fame as The T-Set, also as The Abdabs, even as The Screaming Abdabs.

It was as The Abdabs that they were given their first interview, in the poly newspaper. At that time Clive Metcalf played bass and Roger Waters was on lead. The group had two singers: Keith Noble and Juliette Gale.

The Abdabs broke-up and Juliette Gale married Rick Wright. Mason, Wright and Waters tried again, this time bringing in jazz guitarist Bob Close. Waters also brought in Syd Barrett whom he knew from Cambridge. Barrett named the group after a record he owned by the Georgia bluesmen Pink Anderson and Floyd Council. He called them The Pink Floyd Sound. Musical differences between Bob Close and Barrett caused the former to leave.

The line up established, they played at a few dances and the like, but their first regular venue was a regular Sunday afternoon gig at The Marquee, called "The Spontaneous Underground" which began in February 1966. Here they built up their first small following and became more or less the "official" band of the London underground. It was here that Peter Jenner, their first manager saw them, and where they developed their electronic feedback techniques in-between playing Chuck Berry numbers.

In October 1966 they got a regular weekly gig at the London Free School's Sound/Light Workshop in All Saint's Church Hall, Notting Hill. Here, an American couple, Joel and Toni Brown from Tim Leary's Millbrook Institute, first projected slides over them and began to develop the idea of a lightshow to accompany the music.

On October 15 the "International Times", Europe's first underground newspaper, was launched at a huge party in the London Roundhouse. The Floyd played to an audience of 2,000 people with moving liquid slides projected over themselves and the audience. On December 3 they did another Roundhouse show, this time a benefit for Zimbabwe after Ian Smith had seized power in Rhodesia and on the 12th they did a benefit for Oxfam at the Royal Albert Hall.

Atom Heart Mother. Courtesy EMI Harvest.

Ummagumma. Courtesy EMI Harvest.

On Oct 31, 1966 the Floyd plus Pete Jenner and Andrew King set up Blackhill Enterprises as a six-way partnership to manage the group. In November they got in Joe Gannon to handle their lights as the Brown's returned to Millbrook. Dec 23, 1966 saw first of the UFO Club evenings, held every Friday night in an Irish Ballroom on Tottenham Court Road. The Floyd got the music and lights contract and became the house band. UFO became the "in" club of the burgeoning London underground scene and together with The Soft Machine (♦), The Crazy World of Arthur Brown, and Tomorrow, they were the archetypes of the new wave of "psychedelic rock" groups.

In January 1967, Joe Boyd (♦), musical director of UFO, produced their first single, a Syd Barrett composition **Arnold Layne.** It concerned a pervert-transvestite who stole ladies underwear from washing-lines, and was banned by the pirate station Radio London for being "too smutty". It scraped to No. 25 in the U.K. charts.

Barrett was very much leader of the group at this point. His lead guitar sound was distinctive; and he wrote almost all their material. They signed to EMI for a 5,000 pound advance, quite a big deal for its time, but one of the conditions was that they drop Boyd and use a staff producer, Norman Smith. This they did.

On Apr 28, 1967 they played at the famous Fourteen Hour Technicolour Dream Free Speech Festival for "International Times", held at Alexander Palace, North London. This was Britain's equivalent to the "be-in"'s held in U.S. and Floyd had the top spot: they appeared at dawn.

On May 12, they presented "Games For May" at London's Queen Elizabeth Hall. In the days when a "name" group only played for 30 minutes, it was an ambitious undertaking to do a full-length solo show. They used a rudimentary quadraphonic sound system with EMI installing two speaker stacks in rear of the hall. There were light projections, millions of bubbles and free daffodils given away. Barrett wrote new material including **Games For May.** With a change of title, **See Emily Play**, the song was issued as a single. By July it was at No. 5 in U.K. charts. They appeared on "Top Of The Pops" and were well on their way to becoming a "name" group.

Their first album, **The Piper At The Gates Of Dawn** (title taken by Barrett from one of the chapters of "Wind In The Willows") was released on Aug 5, 1967 and of the 11 songs on the album, 10 were by Barrett. He also did the drawing on the back sleeve.

In October, they did their first tour of U.S. playing at Fillmore East and West. While rest of the band had always been more into booze than drugs, Barrett was deeply involved in the psychedelic side of the Underground, taking large amounts of LSD and drawing the inspiration for much of his playing and writing from it.

He may have overdone it with the acid, or maybe it just assisted some more deep-seated problems in coming to the fore, but he had been behaving erratically prior to the tour and his condition worsened by the day. He became even more unpredictable, and on some gigs would only stand and stare at the audience while strumming the same chord all evening. There are many stories about his breakdown but they all added up to the same thing: Syd was becoming an acid casualty.

November 18 and another single, **Apples And Oranges** was released, the product of much recording at De Lane Lea, Sound Techniques and EMI Abbey Road. It flopped.

Meanwhile, things were getting totally out of hand with Barrett – and eventually it was decided to get in his old school chum Dave Gilmour to play guitar. He joined the Floyd on Feb 18, 1968 and for about seven weeks he and Barrett played together, but it was only a matter of time before Syd left. On April 6 he did (♦ Syd Barrett).

David Gilmour was born in Cambridge and went to same school as Barrett and Waters. Before joining Floyd he went to Paris and formed his own group, with whom he toured Europe. Fluent in French, among

his many jobs over there was working as a male model. Gilmour is the one member of Floyd who keeps in touch with music "scene"; the only one ever seen in clubs.

During this time the Blackhill partnership had been dissolved, though Syd Barrett stayed on with them. The Floyd were now playing to bigger venues and appearing regularly at Middle Earth Club, a more commercial successor to UFO. They played there seven times beginning Dec 16, 1967.

Shortly before Barrett left, they released **It Would Be So Nice,** which flopped. They didn't seem able to make singles any more.

Blackhill organised the first of their famed free concerts in London's Hyde Park and on June 29 the Floyd, together with Roy Harper and Jethro Tull, played to an enthusiastic audience. This, together with the critical acclaim which greeted their second album, **Saucerful Of Secrets,** released on the same day, gave them the confidence they needed to withstand loss of group's principal player and composer. Roger Waters emerged as new central figure, composing numbers such as **Let There Be Light** and **Set The Controls For The Heart Of The Sun.** The title track, in particular, pointed the way towards electronic embellishments.

They did American and European tours from July to September of 1968, perfecting their act until it became a full-scale concert production with special effects and light-show. At London Festival Hall on April 14, the Floyd presented "More Furious Madness From The Massed Gadgets of Auximenes" where they premiered their fabled Azimuth Co-ordinator. They toured with an act called "The Journey" featuring 360 degree sound and their Azimuth, a sort of joy-stick device for projecting sound around a hall. In July came release of soundtrack they had written for "More", a movie directed by Barbet Schroeder. Waters took lion's share of composing credits and his work shows an impressive development.

Other movie offers followed, and they also composed soundtrack to Peter Whitehead's "Tonite Let's All Make Love In London" and a remarkable score for Paul Jones' film "The Committee".

Then came **Ummagumma,** a double-album on EMI's new Underground label Harvest. It was released in October and featured two live sides, recorded at Mothers Club, Birmingham, and Manchester College of Commerce June 1969. The live versions of old favourites didn't add much to the originals but the other album was of interest: each member of the band had half a side to experiment with as they wished, Wright, Gilmour and Mason all writing single varying self-indulgent pieces, divided into numbered parts, and only Waters providing several individual tracks.

December 1969 saw them in Rome, writing and recording their score for Michaelangelo Antonioni's "Zabriskie Point". In the end not much was used though **Come In Number 51, Your Time Is Up** was a very effective backing to the scene of the desert mansion exploding, even though it was just **Eugene** with a new title. In March 1970, MGM released a soundtrack album of film including Floyd's three contributions. "It was hell, sheer hell", said Roger Waters of working with Antonioni.

In May 1970 David Gilmour joined Syd Barrett on stage at a show in Olympia. But the Floyd did nothing new until Bath Festival, where on 3 a.m. billing, they premiered their new **Atom Heart Mother** album complete with male and female chorus, a horn section and fireworks. The album was released in October and attracted vast public attention, reaching No. 1 in U.K. charts and projecting Floyd to superstardom. Looking back, however, it is certainly not one of their best albums.

A week before **Atom Heart Mother** was released, Syd Barrett's second solo album came out. It had been produced by Dave Gilmour and Rick Wright. That summer Floyd did a European tour and on July 18, another free concert in Hyde Park, this time attracting 100,000 people. Subsequently, toured U.S., having 40,000 dollars-worth of gear stolen in the process.

Atom Heart Mother had been jointly written by Floyd and electronics experimenter Ron Geesin and, in December, the soundtrack from "The Body", a film produced by Tony Garnett and directed by Roy Battersby, was released. Ron Geesin and Roger Waters jointly performed and produced score; Geesin writing majority of music.

On May 15 they did a two-and-a-half-hour star-billing set at a Crystal Palace Garden Party complete with fireworks and a 50-foot inflatable octopus which rose from the lake while they played **Return To The Sun Of Nothing** (later called **Echoes**). In teeming rain, they encored with **Astronome Domine.** Unfortunately the volume of the speakers killed the fish in the lake. They toured the far East, Japan, Australia and in October and November did another U.S. tour.

Meddle was released on November 13 to a lukewarm reception from critics. Like many other bands in both Britain and the U.S., the Floyd underwent a very bland period in early '70s.

The year 1972 saw very little of the group. They released one album **Obscured By Clouds,** another movie soundtrack – from "La Vallee", again a Barbet Schroeder film. This was recorded at Chateau d'Heronville in France where the equipment was, by their standards, primitive. Oddly enough, this was the album which broke them in the States, getting the F.M. airplay that had always eluded them.

Also in 1972 came the film of the Floyd at Pompeii, made by Adrian Maben for European TV, and first shown at the Edinburgh Festival in September. But most of the year was taken up with recording **Dark Side Of The Moon,** which altogether took nine months of meticulous work. It was premiered with a special presentation at the London Planetarium, March 1973.

This was their magnum opus – indeed, the album which to many latter-day aficionados "is" the Floyd. The group dealt with stress, lunacy and death in contemporary society; the whole conveyed via one of the classiest production jobs (by the Floyd themselves) on record. Cynics have suggested that the album's success was in large part due to the brilliance of its production – a stereo wet dream for hi-fi snobs everywhere – but it would be unfair to take credit away from the band for what was a considerable achievement.

Dark Side Of The Moon was a gigantic seller. It provided the Floyd with their first U.S. No. 1 and took-up permanent residency on the British charts for more than two years.

Roger Waters: "Not a bad album, though I do say so myself".

They toured the U.S. employing a girl backing-group, The Blackberries, who were more used to soul shows. On their return they played London's Earls Court before 18,000 people, hauling out a whole artillery of spectacular visuals: crashing aircraft, dry ice, lights, an inflatable man with blazing green eyes and a gong which burst into flames. They then retired for half a year, only emerging in December to play a benefit for Robert Wyatt (♦), the ex Soft Machine drummer who had broken his back. They raised 10,000 pounds.

In summer 1974, Dave Gilmour produced **Blue Pine Trees** by Unicorn on Transatlantic Records and he even did a few gigs with Sutherland Brothers & Quiver (♦) as a stand-in when their guitarist was ill. At the September Blackhill Free Concert in Hyde Park, he played guitar for Roy Harper (♦). Also in 1974, Nick Mason produced **Round One** for the now defunct Principal Edwards (his second for the group). He also worked on Robert Wyatt's **Rock Bottom** set, producing a very clean sound which he later repeated on **Shamal** for Gong (♦).

It was around this time that stories started filtering through the rock press (the Floyd have never readily made themselves available for interviews) that the band were experiencing real problems producing material to match calibre of omnipresent **Dark Side Of The Moon.**

In November, they toured the U.K., experiencing an unprecedented demand for tickets but turning in somewhat desultory performances. A bootleg recorded at their concert at Trentham Gardens, Stoke, on November 19 was mistaken by many people as their next official album;

Below: A saturnine Pink Floyd, in their early days. (Left to right) Wright, Barrett, Waters and Mason.

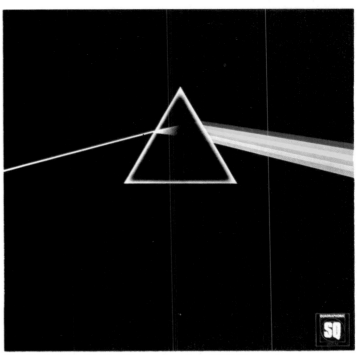

The Dark Side Of The Moon. Courtesy EMI Harvest.

and there were reports of its selling 150,000 copies in a matter of weeks.

In 1975 they completed another U.S. tour, spending June and July there and returning, without proper preparation, to Britain for the Knebworth Festival. They suffered from jetlag and were tired; the equipment developed technical problems and the group went to pieces, playing a disastrous set which resulted in them announcing that they would not play in the U.K. again.

They had spent the beginning of the year in the studios and finally, after six months labour, and two-and-a-half years after **Dark Side Of The Moon,** they produced their follow-up. This was **Wish You Were Here,** released in September 1975 to marked critical disappointment that was virtually inevitable considering the standard of its predecessor.

The track **Shine On You Crazy Diamond** (dedicated to Barrett) – possibly even the title itself – suggests that after all these years the Floyd still mourn the loss of Syd Barrett. It could just be that they need some of Syd's crazed energy to stop them lapsing into artistic slumber. And if that isn't enough, the shadow of **Dark Side Of The Moon** looks like hovering over them for some time to come.

First two albums below subsequently re-issued as double-set **A Nice Pair** on Harvest.

Recordings:
The Piper At The Gates Of Dawn (Capitol/Columbia)
A Saucerful Of Secrets (Capitol/Columbia)
More (Capitol/Columbia)
Ummagumma (Harvest)
Atom Heart Mother (Harvest)

Meddle (Harvest)
Obscured By Clouds (Harvest)
Dark Side Of The Moon (Harvest)
Wish You Were Here (Columbia/Harvest)
Compilations:
Relics (Harvest)

Plastic Ono Band

➡ John Lennon

Poco

Paul Cotton guitar, vocals
Rusty Young pedal steel, guitar, banjo
Timothy B. Schmit bass, vocals
George Grantham drums, vocals

Poco were founded in August 1968 by Richie Furay, an original member of Buffalo Springfield (➡) and Jim Messina, who had joined the band in its death throes. After completing the final Springfield album without the assistance of the other members of the group, Furay and Messina invited Young, who had played on one track, to join the new outfit; Young in turn recommended Grantham and Meisner (both, like himself, from Colorado) to complete the line-up.

Though the band had originally considered calling themselves Pogo, they decided on Poco; after auditioning for Apple Records (John Lennon seems to have been a bit slow on the uptake) the band signed for Epic Records, and released **Pickin' Up The Pieces**.

Meisner then left, to join initially Rick Nelson's Stone Canyon Band, and then The Eagles (➡). Messina therefore moved from guitar to bass until February 1970 when Schmit (previously with the New Breed, an early version of Redwing, in Sacramento) was brought in, and **Poco** and the very fine live album **Deliverin'** were released.

Poco Seven.
Courtesy Epic, CBS Records.

Further line-up changes ensued, however. Messina quit in November 1970, on the pretext that he was tired of touring, but almost immediately threw in his lot with Kenny Loggins to form Loggins And Messina (➡); his replacement was Cotton (previously with the Illinois Speed Press); as well as contributing lead guitar, he was a strong enough singer to supplement Furay's lead vocals. This line-up then managed three albums – **From The Inside** (1971), **A Good Feelin' To Know** (the title track of which provided the band with a bestselling single, and their most distinctive composition) and **Crazy Eyes** (1973).

In September 1973 Furay, frustrated by the band's lack of widespread success, left to form the Souther-Hillman-Furay Band (➡). After some indecision, the

four remaining members decided to continue rather than throw in the towel. They made two relatively poor albums, **Seven** and **Cantamos**, before signing a new contract with ABC Records in 1975, when their tenacity was rewarded as their first ABC release, **Head Over Heels,** proved to be their most successful to date. They are now playing with renewed vigour.

The Very Best Of Poco is a double compilation album that contains their best work on Epic.

Recordings:
Pickin' Up The Pieces (Epic/—)
Poco (Epic/CBS)
Deliverin' (Epic)
From The Inside (Epic)
A Good Feelin' To Know (Epic)
Crazy Eyes (Epic)
Seven (Epic)
Cantamos (Epic)
Head Over Heels (ABC)
Live (Epic)
Rose Of Cimarron (ABC)
Compilation:
The Very Best Of Poco (Epic)

The Pointer Sisters

Bonnie Pointer vocals
Ruth Pointer vocals
Anita Pointer vocals
June Pointer vocals

Born in the ghetto of Oakland, California, four of the six children of Elton and Sarah Pointer, both Ministers of the Church. Strictly-raised, they started singing in church, and, in fact, were denied access to any form of non-secular music until they started high school – at which point the sisters discovered the attractions of R&B, blues and jazz. That they quickly usurped parental control and made up for lost time is evidenced by the fact that Bonnie later worked, for a time, as a topless dancer.

After school they followed a variety of paths. Ruth sang; Anita went to secretarial college; Bonnie studied African and modern dance as well as piano. Then Bonnie and June (the youngest, and then still at high school) got their first

singing engagement which, though disastrous, led to club and party gigs and eventually to both joining Dorothy Morrison's Northern California State Youth Choir. When the Choir disbanded, first Anita and later Ruth linked with the others to form The Pointer Sisters.

At the prompting of their first manager, the girls collected all their possessions together and headed for Houston, Texas, expecting to strike gold. Instead, they ended up broke when promised engagements and recording sessions failed to materialise – and it was left to producer David Rubinson, a friend of a friend, to "rescue" them via wired air tickets to California. There, Rubinson found them session-work, first for Cold Blood and Elvin Bishop (who took them on tour with him) and subsequently for a whole host of acts, notable among which were Boz Scaggs, Grace Slick, Dave Mason and Esther Phillips – they also posed for the cover of one of Taj Mahal's albums.

In 1973 they decided to step out as a group in their own right; firstly via a series of ecstatically-received appearances at the Troubadour Club in Los Angeles. This was the year that Bette Midler (➡) was the toast of New York, and though they might not have consciously set out to mine the same territories of kitsch and nostalgia, The Pointer Sisters were by and large cast from a similar mould: utilising a highly eclectic repertoire (from Lambert, Hendricks & Ross to **Wang Dang Doodle**), garnishing their act with show-biz burlesque, decking themselves out in a wardrobe drawn from '40s styles. Nevertheless their sets at the Troubadour pretty soon made them the talk of the West Coast; TV bookings proliferated; and record success was quick to follow.

Under David Rubinson, they cut their eponymous debut album in 1973, providing their first U.S. singles hit with Allen Toussaint's **Yes We Can Can** in August that year. In 1974 they further evidenced their eclecticism by scoring an American country smash with **Fairy Tale**, written by Anita

Above: Iggy Pop, one of rock's more demented figures, noted for his outrageous stage performances.

and Bonnie. The single won a Grammy Award as Best Country Song of that year.

Recordings:
The Pointer Sisters (Blue Thumb)
That's A Plenty (Blue Thumb)
Live At The Opera House (ABC/Blue Thumb)
Steppin' (ABC/Blue Thumb)

Jean-Luc Ponty

Born in village in Normandy region of France, trained in classical music from early age by violin-professor father and piano-teacher mother. As whizz-kid violinist, Ponty played extensively on European jazz scene for five years, featuring with Jef Gilson Band, leading his own group, and recording with countless top-name artists – including **Violin Summit** with Stephane Grappelli and Stuff Smith for BASF in 1966.

Inclined towards amplification and drifting from "static" European jazz scene, Ponty went to the U.S. in 1969 where he hung out with Mothers Of Invention circle and "guested" on electric violin on Frank Zappa's 1970 **Hot Rats** album. Ponty's 1970 solo album **King Kong** was recorded under Zappa's direction, the violinist subsequently touring U.S. with Mothers pianist George Duke.

Later that year he returned to Europe, assembling the Jean Luc Ponty Experience for extensive touring through 1971–72. On his return to the U.S. in January 1973, Ponty was again approached by Zappa, joining the Mothers Of Invention (➡ Frank Zappa) through to October that year.

At this point he joined the restructured Mahavishnu Orchestra (➡ John McLaughlin), touring and recording with them throughout 1974. Quit that outfit spring 1975 to sign as solo artist with Atlantic Records and release **Upon The Wings Of Music**.

Has "guested" on several other albums, including Elton John's

1972 **Honky Chateau** set. Discography is selective.

Recordings:
Violin Summit (BASF)
Experience . . . (Ponty and George Duke) (Pacific Jazz)
The Electronic Connection (Pacific Jazz)
King Kong (Pacific Jazz)
Upon The Wings Of Music (Atlantic)
Compilation:
Portrait (United Artists)

Iggy Pop

"Iggy Pop is the Robert Johnson of Heavy Metal", stated one enthusiast of the most demented, bizarre figure ever to scrawl his name on a record contract, or disport his scrawny frame across a rock stage.

James Jewel Osterburg, as he was born to schoolteacher parents in Ann Arbor, Michigan, in 1947, adopted the name Iggy when he changed his affiliations and left The Iguanas, a Detroit punk combo, and joined local rivals The Prime Movers. After splitting to Chicago to play the blues with Paul Butterfield drummer Sam Lay, Iggy returned to Detroit with a uniquely demented vision. This was The Stooges – Iggy as vocalist, contortionist and all-purpose catalyst, the Asheton brothers Ron and Scott on guitar and drums respectively, and Dave Alexander on bass.

As a performer, Iggy pulled out a whole ragbag of outrageous on-stage gambits – he threw up on stage, was beaten up, indulged in fellatio with members of the audience – and generally plumbed the depths of depravity to earn The Stooges an unprecedented notoriety.

Elektra Records scooped them up along with The MC5 (➡) in 1969. John Cale (➡), on the loose from Velvet Underground, produced their first album that same year. Track after track of three-chord, banal, slobbering rock 'n' roll, it was quintessential punk-rock – hailed as such by aficionados of the genre, ridiculed by other sections of the rock press.

Various Stooges came, and went, though the nucleus of Iggy and the Ashetons remained intact, and in 1970 came **Fun House,** which enthusiasts describe as their second twilight-zone masterpiece.

After that, things deteriorated, and the band eventually split due to drug problems and general craziness (their punk credentials were second to none). Iggy cut lawns, played golf, lived with his parents and stalked the streets until David Bowie (➡) and his manager of the time, Tony DeFries, shipped him and latter-day ex Stooges/Chosen Few guitarist James Williamson to England.

The Asheton brothers were similarly wired air fares, and this four (with Bowie attempting to keep whatever control he could) recorded the 1973-released **Raw Power,** a heavy metal pièce de résistance.

Yet The Ig was untameable. Subsequently, the band split from DeFries and took another self-inflicted nose-dive into the compost. James Williamson was heard of working as a truck driver, later as forming a new band with

Ron Asheton; while Iggy Pop has simply got crazier and crazier hanging out around Los Angeles. In 1974 there were reports that he was working on an album project with Ray Manzarek, ex of Doors (➡), but nothing has materialised.

Whether he'll ever get anything together again is anybody's guess, although it has been rumoured that he and Bowie are once again in cahoots, preparing a new album.

Recordings:
The Stooges (Elektra)
Fun House (Elektra)
Raw Power (Columbia/CBS)

Elvis Presley

Whatever Little Richard might still be claiming to the contrary, Presley is the legitimate King of Rock 'n' Roll. It's pointless to total the number of records he's sold – by common agreement he seems to have sold more than anyone except Bing Crosby or The Beatles. After his first major hit, **Heartbreak Hotel,** he became the most potent symbol of rock music and teenage rebellion in America and Europe.

Golden Records, Volume Two. Courtesy RCA Records.

Born Elvis Aaron Presley Jan 8, 1935 in East Tupelo, Mississippi, near Memphis; his twin brother Jesse died at birth. He was raised by Vernon and Gladys Presley in a religious family atmosphere, and first sang hymns with his parents at local concerts. He won the 1943 Alabama-Mississippi State Fair talent contest singing **Old Shep** (a song he later recorded); in 1946 his parents bought him his first guitar, and he sang in high-school shows.

The Presley family moved to Memphis in 1948 and after leaving school Elvis took a job as a cinema usher; by 1953 he was working as a van driver for Crown Electric Co., when he took time off work to make a private recording of **My Happiness** to give to his mother as a birthday present. The studio in which he made the recording was owned by Sam Phillips (➡), who also ran Sun Records; Presley's name was noted by the staff there.

When Presley returned the following year, he was remembered, and Phillips set him to work with studio musicians Scotty Moore and Bill Black playing country songs to work out a sound, though without success until Phillips suggested they try some blues material by Arthur "Big Boy" Crudup, who also recorded for Sun. Elvis already knew and liked Crudup's material, and he cut **That's Alright, Mama,** with a

fast country backing and powerful vocals that, coming from a white singer, were quite a revelation.

The record was played by local DJ Dewey Phillips (who had to point out that the singer was white) and it received favourable audience response. Other local stations played the song, and Elvis appeared in local country shows singing his style of R&B through the efforts of local C&W booking agent Bob Neal, who became Presley's first manager in January 1955.

Presley then came to the attention of "Colonel" Tom Parker, an established country-music manager, who got him some work including his first-ever TV appearance on the Louisiana Hayride, Mar 3, 1955. That year, Presley had some minor hits on country charts, and in November Parker became his manager.

He signed Presley with RCA, who paid Sam Phillips 35,000 dollars for the contract and rights to all released and unreleased Sun material – a fantastic sum for the tapes of an almost-unknown singer.

Once in a position to be promoted nationally through RCA, Presley quickly became a sensation with young fans searching for something with more guts and sex appeal than the good-time rock of Bill Haley (➡). He created a new style of music, simply because he took black records, and enhanced the spirit of the original, with his light, but urgent vocal phrasing. His first recording with RCA, **Heartbreak Hotel** was released January 1956; it reached No. 1 in the U.S. and No. 2 in the U.K., and within a year Presley had won six gold discs. He aroused controversy – which was well-fanned by Parker – over his increasingly suggestive hip movements on stage that earned him the title Elvis the Pelvis, and en-

deared him even more to teenagers the world over. No one had heard music like **Blue Suede Shoes, Hound Dog, All Shook Up** and **Don't Be Cruel** before, simply because no one had created it before.

He made his first film, the Western "Love Me Tender" in 1956, followed by "Loving You" in 1957; in 1958 he made two more movies that each produced classic rock singles – "Jailhouse Rock" and "King Creole".

With Elvis the hottest property in America, he was conscripted into the U.S. Army on Mar 24, 1958 for national service. and Private 53310761 was posted to Frieburg, West Germany. It is a tribute both to the quality of Elvis' music, and the skilful marketing techniques of Colonel Parker (who had ensured that Elvis had a stack of first-class material in the can before he was conscripted) that on his discharge as sergeant two years later, having made no public appearances and having completed only one record session, he was still as much in demand as when he had joined up. (This can be contrasted with the Everly Brothers, who were almost forgotten by the time they'd completed their national service.)

Nevertheless, it was a mellowed Presley that emerged from army life; gone were the sideburns and hip-shaking, gone also were the classic rock songs. He concentrated on either medium-paced material like **His Latest Flame, She's Not You** and **Good Luck Charm,** slow ballads like **Are You Lonesome Tonight?,** or Latin melodrama like **It's Now Or Never.**

This change in style only seemed to increase his stature, as each

Below: Presley in the '70s, by which time he had returned to live performance.

successive single reached No. 1 on each side of Atlantic; but while the old fans demanded more rock numbers, all Elvis provided was an interminable series of appalling Hollywood movies, each one successively worse than the one

Blue Hawaii.
Courtesy RCA Records.

before. A further problem was that "Girls! Girls! Girls!", "Fun In Acapulco", "Viva Las Vegas!" etc., were not only turgid films, but that they came complete with equally turgid soundtracks. In retrospect, Presley's best movies were the ones he made shortly after leaving the army – "Flaming Star", "Follow That Dream", and "Wild In The Country", each of which had tried to illustrate Presley's acting ability.

In 1968 Parker tried a change of plan, and brought him out to the world again on NBC-TV's Elvis special with a live spectacular. Once again, Presley was doing what he did best, and his return to live appearances, and regular gigs in Las Vegas (with one of the most instrumentally proficient and highly-paid backing bands in the world – led by James Burton and Glen D. Hardin) revived the Presley fervour, though it is apparent that his audience is largely a mature one, since he has failed to maintain his appeal with younger generations–though as he has made only two memorable records in the last decade (**Suspicious Minds** and **Burning Love**) that is perhaps not surprising.

Above: Presley with Judy Tyler in Jailhouse Rock, 1958.

Nevertheless the Presley charisma should not be underestimated. In 1973 the soundtrack album of a television special, **Elvis: Aloha From Hawaii Via Satellite** topped the U.S. albums charts, and there were even two documentary films – "Elvis: That's The Way It Is" (1970) and the excellent "Elvis On Tour" (1972), which was made by Pierre Adidge and Robert Abel (who made the "Mad Dogs And Englishmen" movie), and probably told us as much about Elvis as we're ever going to find out.

On May 1, 1967, Presley married Priscilla Beaulieu, the daughter of a U.S. Army colonel, and a child, Lisa Marie, was born to them on Feb. 1, 1968; the marriage ended in lengthy and expensive, divorce proceedings in October 1973.

The separation undoubtedly had a traumatic effect on Presley, and reports of his declining health and increasing weight problems, whether true or not, certainly originated from this time. Meanwhile, he continues to work feverishly, playing Las Vegas for three months of each year, and recording regularly; his output over the years has been prodigious. Discography hopefully lists all his major album releases.

Though he remains one of the world's top performers, he is most revered for his early '50s work, and a compilation of his famous Sun recordings was not issued in Britain until 1975. When **The Elvis Presley Sun Collection** (which had been researched and compiled by Roy Carr) was eventually released, it entered the U.K. album charts, testimony to the lingering appeal of the most legendary work of a most legendary performer.

Recordings:
Elvis Presley (RCA)
Elvis (RCA)
Loving You (Soundtrack) (RCA)
Elvis' Christmas Album (RCA)
King Creole (Soundtrack) (RCA)
For LP Fans Only (RCA)
A Date With Elvis (RCA)

Below: The Pretty Things, with May (extreme right), who suddenly quit the band in 1976.

Elvis Is Back (RCA)
G.I. Blues (Soundtrack) (RCA)
His Hand In Mine (RCA)
Something For Everybody (RCA)
Blue Hawaii (Soundtrack) (RCA)
Pot Luck (RCA)
Girls! Girls! Girls! (Soundtrack) (RCA)
It Happened At The World's Fair (Soundtrack) (RCA)
Fun In Acapulco (Soundtrack) (RCA)
Kissin' Cousins (Soundtrack) (RCA)
Roustabout (Soundtrack) (RCA)
Girl Happy (Soundtrack) (RCA)
Elvis For Everyone (RCA)
Harum Scarum (Soundtrack) (RCA)
Frankie And Johnny (Soundtrack) (RCA)
Paradise: Hawaiian Style (Soundtrack) (RCA)
Spinout (Soundtrack) (RCA)
How Great Thou Art (RCA)
Double Trouble (Soundtrack) (RCA)
Clambake (Soundtrack) (RCA)
Speedway (Soundtrack) (RCA)
Elvis Sings Flaming Star And Others (RCA)
Elvis (TV Special) (RCA)
From Elvis In Memphis (RCA)
From Memphis To Vegas/ Vegas To Memphis (RCA)
On Stage: February 1970 (RCA)
Back In Memphis (RCA)
Elvis: That's The Way It Is (Soundtrack) (RCA)
The Wonderful World Of Christmas (RCA)
Elvis Country (RCA)
Love Letters From Elvis (RCA)
Elvis – Now (RCA)
He Touched Me (RCA)
Elvis As Recorded Live At Madison Square Garden (RCA)

Aloha From Hawaii Via Satellite (RCA)
Elvis (RCA)
Raised On Rock (RCA)
Good Times (RCA)
Elvis As Recorded Live On Stage In Memphis (RCA)
Having Fun With Elvis On Stage (RCA)
Promised Land (RCA)
Today (RCA)
From Elvis Presley Boulevard, Memphis, Tennessee (RCA)
Compilations:
Elvis' Golden Records (RCA)
50,000,000 Elvis Fans Can't Be Wrong: Elvis' Gold Records, Vol. II (RCA)
Elvis' Golden Records, Vol. III (RCA)
Elvis' Gold Records, Vol. IV (RCA)
Worldwide 50 Gold Award Hits, Vol. I (RCA)
Elvis: The Other Sides – Worldwide Gold Award Hits, Vol. II (RCA)
Elvis: A Legendary Performer, Vol. I (RCA)
Elvis: A Legendary Performer, Vol. II (RCA)
The Elvis Presley Sun Collection (RCA)

Billy Preston

Born Houston, Texas, Sep 9, 1946, Preston soon moved to Los Angeles with his family, and by the age of 10 had conducted the church choir, appeared with a local symphony orchestra, and played with the Mahalia Jackson show. He also took the part of the young W. C. Handy in his film biography, "St Louis Blues".

After touring with Little Richard

in 1962, he met Sam Cooke, and made **Sixteen-Year-Old Soul** in 1964 for Cooke's Sar Records. He then won a regular spot on the TV rock show "Shindig" and recorded both R&B and gospel instrumentals under the patronage of Ray Charles. From the album **The Most Exciting Organ Ever** came the British hit single, **Billy's Bag.**

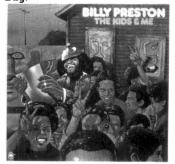

The Kids & Me.
Courtesy A&M Records.

Preston's work came to the attention of George Harrison, who invited him along to Apple. Preston almost immediately found himself part of the Apple inner sanctum, and was asked to play on **Get Back,** and in doing so became the first non-Beatle to be explicitly credited on one of their records ("The Beatles with Billy Preston"); he also played on the **Let It Be** album.

The Beatles bought out Preston's recording contract, and he cut **That's The Way God Planned It** and **Encouraging Words** with George Harrison co-producing; the title track of the former was a large British hit in 1969, and Preston spent increasing amounts of time in Britain.

After Harrison had given him another hefty shove up the ladder by giving Preston a solo spot at the Bangla Desh Concert, Preston signed a management contract with Bob Ellis (now Diana Ross' husband) and left Apple to join A&M, producing **I Wrote A Simple Song** with Harrison and David T. Walker on guitars and arrangements by Quincy Jones.

I Wrote A Simple Song provided Preston with a No. 1 U.S. single, **Outa Space,** and **Will It Go Round In Circles?** and **Space Race,** from his next two albums, gave him further large hits, though his record output has latterly become characterised by an automatic, stale funkiness.

Nevertheless, Preston takes a strong interest in the potential of electronic keyboards, and now has his own band entitled The God Squad, with three keyboard men sharing 16 instruments; he continues to be a keyboard sessioneer by appointment to rock royalty. He played on Harrison's comeback tour of the U.S. in 1974, and has also frequently toured with the Rolling Stones, including their 1975 Tour Of The Americas and 1976 slog through Europe. Discography does not include Preston's pre-Apple work.

Recordings:
That's The Way God Planned It (Apple)
Encouraging Words (Apple)
I Wrote A Simple Song (A&M)
Music Is My Life (A&M)
Everybody Likes Some Kind Of Music (A&M)
The Kids And Me (A&M)

It's My Pleasure (A&M)

The Pretty Things

Phil May vocals
John Povey keyboards, vocals
Peter Tolson guitar, vocals
Jack Green bass, vocals
Gordon Edwards keyboards, guitar, vocals
Skip Alan drums

Phil May is only surviving member of original group which he formed in 1963 with Dick Taylor (gtr), founder-bassist of embryonic Rolling Stones (➧). The Pretties originated from the Erith and Dartford areas of Kent and, apart from May and Taylor, comprised Brian Pendleton (rhy gtr), John Stax (bs) and, after a period with temporary drummers Viv Prince (drms).

Like most of London bands of time, their music was dirty, driving brand of R&B showing fondness for Bo Diddley (➧) rhythm – their name having come from a Diddley composition, **Pretty Thing.** Their image was the Stones taken one step further – dirtier, more objectionable – and they even managed to rival that group for a short period in 1964 when **Rosalyn/Big Boss Man** and **Don't Bring Me Down** showed

Silk Torpedo.
Courtesy Swan Song Records.

well on charts. The last-named was banned in the U.S. apparently because of lyrics.

However, this similarity to better-promoted Stones and inconsistent standards of their albums led to a slow but steady fall from popularity after one more U.K. hit single, **Honey I Need,** in March 1965. To the last, though, the original band kept up their "looning" image – on a 1965 Australian tour Viv Prince was involved in a fracas on a 'plane, and the local press reacted in suitably enraged fashion.

Prince was, in fact, replaced by Skip Alan later that year, following which there was a period of low morale and a two-year gap before the next album, the transitional **Emotions** (1967). Drummer Alan left during the sessions – reputedly fired – and Stax and Pendleton quit soon after. John Povey and Walley Allen, from Bern Elliott And The Fenmen, came in, along with drummer Twink (John Alder).

They made **S. F. Sorrow,** based on a short story written by Phil May and acknowledged as the first-ever rock opera. Pete Townshend (➧ The Who) is said to have listened to the album non-stop for four days after it came out, and then begun work on his own

group's **Tommy.** Townshend has always acknowledged the link, but unhappily the album was largely ignored on U.K. release in 1968 and when it eventually came out in America some 15 months later it received heavy panning for allegedly plagiarising **Tommy!**

Founder Dick Taylor, meanwhile, left group near completion of the album and Skip Alan, after working as a DJ in a French bar, returned to Pretties fold. Their next album, the hard rock **Parachute,** also sunk without trace on release in U.K. 1969, and though it was named Album Of The Year by "Rolling Stone" magazine in 1971 it fared little better in States.

By early '70s the group's career was well and truly in the doldrums. **Freeway Madness,** released early 1973, found them signed to Warner Bros, still getting good reviews but without making headway, although an American tour did attract some attention. By now they had acquired two more newcomers, Tolson and Edwards.

The group had a number of times hovered on verge of splitting, but seemed to have turned corner in 1974 when Led Zeppelin, long-time admirers of group, signed them to their newly-inaugurated Swan Song label. Jack Green, ex of T. Rex, joined prior to recording of first Swan Song album **Silk Torpedo.**

The group is also now managed by Zeppelin handler Peter Grant, and if they can't reap some success out of that heavy backing they might as well pack up and go home.

Recordings:
Pretty Things (Blue Thumb/Fontana)
Get The Picture (Blue Thumb/Fontana)
Emotions (—/Fontana)
S. F. Sorrow (Rare Earth/Harvest)
Parachute (Rare Earth/Harvest)
Freeway Madness (Warner Bros)
Silk Torpedo (Swan Song)
Savage Eye (Swan Song)

Dory Previn

Dory Previn started her music career writing film scores for Arthur Freed of MGM in Hollywood; it was through this connection that she met and married Andre Previn (former jazz pianist and now conductor of the London Symphony Orchestra), while two of her songs were nominated for an Academy Award.

A break-up of her marriage caused great emotional strain and led to a nervous breakdown and a rapid change in her music. She started to document some of her hang-ups, almost as a kind of therapy, and her second album, **Mythical Kings And Iguanas** (1971) remains one of the best records of its type.

All her albums have since expressed a naked sensitivity laced with traces of wry humour, with Previn recognised as one of the world's more unusual and expressive songwriters.

Nevertheless, she found it difficult to recapture the emotionally-charged intensity of her first albums; after some loss of direc-

tion, she moved to Warner Bros in 1974 where her lyrics became less harrowing and her music less plaintive; all her albums have been produced by Nik Venet.

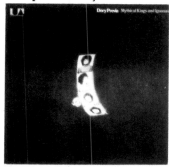

Mythical Kings and Iguanas.
United Artists Records.

At various times she has continued to work on film music, and has contributed to the scores of "Valley Of The Dolls" and "Last Tango In Paris". She has also written a highly-acclaimed book, "On My Way To Where?"

She rarely gives concerts, though **Live At Carnegie Hall** is a double-album set of a concert she gave there on Apr 18, 1973.

Recordings:
On My Way To Where? (United Artists)
Mythical Kings And Iguanas (United Artists)
Reflections In A Mud Puddle (United Artists)
Mary C. Brown And The Hollywood Sign (United Artists)
Live At Carnegie Hall (United Artists)
Dory Previn (Warner Bros)
We're Children Of Coincidence And Harpo Marx (Warner Bros)

Alan Price

Born Fairfield, Durham, England, Apr 19, 1942, Price was a founder member of The Animals (➧). On leaving in 1965, he formed the Alan Price Set, which was largely responsible for educating the British public in the special delights of Randy Newman (➧). The band made two worth-while albums – **The Price To Play** and **The Price On His Head,** and had a series of hit singles, including **I Put A Spell On You, Hi-Lili, Hi-Lo** (both 1966), and Newman's **Simon Smith And The Amazing Dancing Bear** (1967).

Following the group's break-up, Price became involved in a number of television specials, including one with Georgie Fame which led to the formation of a permanent partnership, which produced **Fame And Price, Price And Fame Together** (1971), and then split as their combined talents were less than the sum of their individual ones.

In any case, Price had other projects to get out of his system. He was invited to appear as himself and also write the score for Lindsay Anderson's film "O! Lucky Man" in 1973, which was a particularly successful venture for him.

Having been thus granted his stamp of artistic credibility, he embarked on a project of special significance, **Between Today And Yesterday,** a semi-autobiographical history of a boy from the working-class north-east who makes good in London. A single, **Jarrow Song** (1975), about the hunger marches in 1926 became a Top 5 British hit, and the album, benefiting from the consumer fall-out, was itself a hit. A television documentary about his life was produced to coincide with its release.

Between Today And Yesterday. Courtesy Warner Bros. Records.

Price left Warners for Polydor, and failed to emulate this success. It was felt that he had possibly over-reached himself; certainly **Metropolitan Man** did not carry much conviction. Nevertheless, he is an abiding talent, who will, no doubt, remain productive for some time to come.

Recordings:
The Price To Play (—/Decca)
The Price On His Head
  (—/Decca)
Fame And Price, Price And
  Fame Together (Columbia/
  CBS)
O! Lucky Man (Soundtrack)
  (Warner Bros)
Between Today And Yesterday
  (Warner Bros)
Metropolitan Man (—/Polydor)
Performing Price (—/Polydor)

John Prine

John Prine shares with Steve Goodman (♦) the distinction of having been discovered by the unlikely duo of Paul Anka and Kris Kristofferson (♦). The former helped out on the initial business deals of both Prine and Goodman, while the latter was quick to recognise a pair of kindred spirits.

John Prine.
Courtesy Atlantic Records.

Prine was born Oct 10, 1946 in Maywood, Illinois. He began to play guitar at the age of 14, but didn't take up music as a profession until 1969, having first been in the army and worked for the post office. Since he was discovered by Kristofferson in Chicago, his songs have been widely recorded by artists such as Al Kooper and Bonnie Raitt: in particular, **Sam Stone**, from his

debut album.

Though the fact that Dylan jammed on-stage with him in 1972 temporarily enhanced his standing, he has generally been regarded as a minority cult figure, who writes interesting songs with witty and clever lyrics, rather than someone who might potentially break through to a wide audience.

Recordings:
John Prine (Atlantic)
Diamonds In The Rough
  (Atlantic)
Sweet Revenge (Atlantic)
Common Sense (Atlantic)

Procol Harum

Gary Brooker piano, vocals
B. J. Wilson drums
Mick Grabham guitar
Chris Copping organ
Alan Cartwright bass
Keith Reid lyrics

Brooker, Copping and Wilson, along with guitarist Robin Trower, were originally members of The Paramounts, a Southend, England, -based outfit which cut a series of flop singles for Parlophone between 1963–65, one of which was their version of Coasters' R&B classic **Poison Ivy.**

Above: A Salty Dog. Courtesy Procol Harum.

However, Procol Harum was conceived when Gary Brooker struck out on his own and sought out lyricist Keith Reid to add words to the new, more adventurous material he was writing. Advertising in the British music press, they recruited first line-up which, aside of Brooker, comprised Bobby Harrison (drms), Ray Rowyer (gtr), Matthew Fisher (org) and David Knights (bs).

Thus constituted, Procol Harum released the mesmeric Brooker-Reid composed **Whiter Shade Of Pale** as their debut in May 1967. The single was astonishingly successful, racing in a matter of weeks to the No. 1 slot in the U.K. singles charts and breaking all kinds of records for copies sold per day. It made No. 5 in U.S.

But even as the music industry

appraised itself of this dizz-busting new phenomenon, dissent within the group was leading to crisis. Ray Rowyer and Bobby Harrison, the latter reputedly aggrieved because he had been passed over in favour of a session drummer during recording of the single, quit line-up, and for a time there were stories that Procol had split. The fact was they were totally unprepared for success so immense, so soon.

However, the band re-grouped bringing in ex Paramounts Trower and Wilson as replacements, and recorded first album later in 1967 although touring infrequently. They also released a follow-up single, **Homburg,** which although by and large a re-tread of **Whiter Shade Of Pale,** climbed into U.K. Top 10.

Two excellent albums, **Shine On Brightly** (1968) and **A Salty Dog** (1969) followed, but unhappily the group had come to be regarded as a one-hit (sic) wonder. Against this background, these albums – which many still consider as their most substantial achievements – received scant attention in U.K.

America, on the other hand, took to them with fewer preconceptions, and their 1969 Stateside tour attracted considerable acclaim. Despite this, the group

was again entering a period of disenchantment and disarray.

In mid-1969, after producing **A Salty Dog** Matthew Fisher quit the band (he subsequently worked as solo artist and producer). David Knights followed soon after.

Chris Copping, another ex Paramount, took both their places and, as a quartet, the group made the patchy **Home** (1970) and indifferent **Broken Barricades** (1971). After this last, Robin Trower, whose frustration was becoming increasingly evident with each recording, left to form Jude and later his own band (♦ Robin Trower).

Again the group resorted to ads in the music press, auditions providing newcomers Dave Ball, ex Big Bertha, on guitar, and Alan

Cartwright, formerly with Brian "Blinky" Davison's Every Which Way, on bass.

In Concert With The Edmonton. Symphony Orchestra.

In November 1971, accepting an offer set up by a Canadian rock writer/admirer, the band went to Canada to perform with the Edmonton Symphony Orchestra. The gig was beset with hassles and almost never happened, but the resulting live album was a tour de force that took Procol Harum completely by surprise. In fact it received such critical acclaim and audience attention in the North American market that the band postponed sessions on a planned new studio album and went out on a massively successful U.S. tour.

By the time they got round to completing the sessions – for **Grand Hotel** (1973) – Dave Ball had left the group and Mick Grabham, formerly with Cochise, had come in on lead guitar. The new line-up proved a stable one; and the album their most satisfying studio set for some time.

However, though by no means unpopular, the group hasn't yet been able to equal its U.S. status on home territory – despite a re-release **Whiter Shade Of Pale** making the U.K. Top 10 in 1972, and the new cut **Pandora's Box** similarly giving them home singles success in autumn 1975. This last came from **Procol's Ninth,** produced by Leiber & Stoller (♦).

In 1976 they are still noted for the qualities which brought them to prominence – Keith Reid's scholarly lyrics and Gary Brooker's superb piano work – yet remain one of the most unclassifiable of groups.

Recordings:
Procol Harum (Deram/Regal
  Zonophone)
Shine On Brightly (A&M/
  Regal Zonophone)
A Salty Dog (A&M/Regal
  Zonophone)

Above: Keith Reid, Procol's scholarly lyricist.

Home (A&M/Regal Zonophone)
Broken Barricades (A&M/
Chrysalis)
**Procol Harum In Concert With
The Edmonton Symphony
Orchestra** (A&M/Chrysalis)
Grand Hotel (Chrysalis)
Exotic Birds And Fruit
(Chrysalis)
Procol's Ninth (Chrysalis)
Compilations:
Best Of Procol Harum (A&M/—)
A Salty Dog (—/Music For
Pleasure)

Pure Prairie League

George Powell guitar, vocals
John Call pedal steel
Billy Hinds drums
Michael Connor keyboards
Larry Goshorn guitar
Michael Reilly bass

The group was originally formed
by Craig Fuller (gtr, vcls) from
Ohio, and Powell, from Kentucky,
with Call, Jim Lanham (bs) and
Jim Caughlan (drms) in 1971, and
they took their name from an
Errol Flynn movie. This line-up
produced an outstanding debut
album in 1972, though Lanham,
Caughlan and Call left soon afterwards, leaving the follow-up
album, **Bustin' Out**, to be made
by the nucleus of Fuller, Powell
and Hinds, with the aid of various
session-musicians, who included
Michael Connor and Mick Ronson.

These first two albums, produced
by Bob Ringe, are classics of the
country rock genre, and now
recognised as such, though PPL's
lack of contemporary success led
to their disbanding.

In 1974, RCA released a Fuller
composition, **Amie** – from **Bustin'
Out** – as a single, whereupon it
became a sizeable U.S. hit. The
group decided to reform, with
above line-up, and while they
have not yet reached the heights
of their initial work, they now have
a solid base on which to build,
and both **Two Lane Highway**
(1975) and **If The Shoe Fits** (1976)
have increased their popularity.

A feature of Pure Prairie League
album sleeves is their continuing
use of an elderly cowboy, drawn
cartoon-style by noted illustrator
Norman Rockwell.

Meanwhile, Fuller has formed a
promising band with Steve Katz,
Doug Yule and Eric Kaz.

Recordings:
Pure Prairie League (RCA)
Bustin' Out (RCA)
Two Lane Highway (RCA)
If The Shoe Fits (RCA)

Suzi Quatro

Born Detroit Jun 3, 1950, the
youngest among four girls and a
boy (Michael) born to semi-pro
jazz bandleader Art Quatro. All
the children gained early musical
experience in Art Quatro Trio,
Suzi playing drums, piano and
guitar. On leaving school at 14, she
adopted the stage name Suzi Soul
and formed The Pleasure Seekers
as all-girl rock group with sisters
Patti, Nancy and Arlene.

The Pleasure Seekers played the
seamier side of the U.S. gig circuit
and eventually changed name to
Cradle (with a tour of American
bases in Vietnam en route), and

it was at this point that British pop
entrepreneur/producer Mickie
Most (➧) came into picture. Most
was in Detroit recording Jeff
Beck (➧) when he saw Cradle at
local dance-hall and expressed
interest in managing their aggressive lead singer.

As Cradle were on verge of
breaking up, Quatro took up the
offer, travelling to England to
sign for Most's RAK Records. For
first year, Most encouraged her
songwriting – but debut single
Rolling Stone (1972) didn't work
out. Subsequently Most engaged
services of Nicky Chinn and Mike
Chapman, the most successful
English pop songwriters of their
day, and the new partnership
swiftly paid dividends in the shape
of a string of tailor-made U.K. hits:
**Can The Can, 48 Crash, Daytona
Demon** (in 1973), **Devil Gate
Drive, The Wild One** (1974). All
incredibly crass, but hits nonetheless.

At same time Most encouraged
her natural aggression, and promoted her relentlessly as the
"first raunchy female rock star",
a "rebel tomboy" in black leather
jumpsuits.

More recently Most's efforts have
been directed towards breaking
her internationally – she toured
U.S. twice in 1974 and had singles
hit there with **All Shook Up** – at
the expense of continued British
success, though the formula was
wearing decidedly thin by then
anyway.

Since first major U.K. appearance
as support on Slade tour in 1972,
she has worked on road with own
band – Quatro (bs, vcls), Len
Tuckey (gtr), Dave Neal (drms)
and Mike Deacon, ex Vinegar
Joe (➧), (kybds). Deacon replaced
original member Alastair Mckenzie.

Sister Patti has played with
Fanny (➧), while brother Michael
Quatro is signed as multi-instru-
mentalist with United Artists.

Recordings:
Suzi Quatro (Bell/RAK)
Quatro (Bell/RAK)
Mama Won't (Arista/RAK)

*Above: Freddy Mercury,
whose posturings helped
Queen become the major new
British band of the '70s, even
though their music was
blatantly derivative of many
'60s acts.*

Queen

Freddy Mercury vocals
Brian May guitar
John Deacon bass
Roger Taylor drums

Queen are as good an example as
any with which to approach the
theory of the vacuum effect in
rock: this states that when a topflight, proven rock attraction
withdraws into a period of inactivity the void thus created will
be filled by substitute, usually
lesser-talented, acts. In 1973–74
Led Zeppelin (➧) and David
Bowie (➧) were largely unavailable to British audiences – and
along came two acts (interestingly
enough from the same company)
to gratefully take advantage of
the vacuum. Cockney Rebel (➧)
plagiarised David Bowie, while
Queen ostensibly went one stroke
better: they hedged their bets by
sounding like an ersatz Zeppelin
but kept one foot in the glam-rock
area via the androgynous posturings of vocalist Freddy Mercury.

Of course, the band then and
now deny any such cold-blooded
manouvering – but their beginnings bore all the hallmarks of
careful planning (not to mention
lavish promotion).

They had come together in 1972
when May and Taylor, from the
disbanded, unknown, Smile outfit,
recruited former college friend
Mercury in a new project. They
auditioned for six months before
taking on John Deacon as bassist,
and spent some 18 months rehearsing and writing enough
material for three albums.

Their first eponymous album
was, as noted, released on the
back of a massive EMI promotional campaign in 1973 and immediately laid bare their debt to
Led Zeppelin. So did the second,

recorded while the first was still
the subject of vilification in the
rock press, and released in
spring 1974.

Yet Queen weren't the first band
to plunder the Zeppelin repertoire, and if critics couldn't
admire the content they could at
least acknowledge the style. After
all, heavy metal had never been
"fully" exploited as a commercial
force in the U.K.: what Queen did
was to take the hard-rock riffs,
overlay them with vocal harmonies and manifestly commercial
melodies and filter the whole via
superb production (by the band
and former engineer Roy Thomas
Baker). Contrived it may have
been, but it was undeniably well
crafted.

A good example of this was the
single from **Queen II, Seven
Seas Of Rhye**, a considerable
U.K. hit in early 1974. After this
first taste of success, the critics
didn't matter anyway, and Queen
went from strength to strength on
the back of a string of sell-out
concerts.

Killer Queen was a No. 2 hit
single in the British charts November 1974, and the third album
Sheer Heart Attack not only
notched up gold status in America
but swung a few of early critics
their way.

In 1975 the group produced the
hugely ambitious **A Night At The
Opera**, reputedly one of the most
expensive albums ever made – it
was still being re-mixed and refined right up to the eleventh
hour of release. Simultaneously
there appeared **Bohemian Rhapsody**, a single constructed along
epic lines, audaciously including
a snatch of opera as one of its
four sections. Both new pieces of
product hogged the British charts
for a lengthy spell. In fact **Rhapsody** broke a U.K. chart record by
holding down the top spot for
seven weeks, the longest stay in
that position for some eight years.

*A Night At The Opera.
Courtesy EMI Records.*

Queen's forte is their ability to
straddle barriers. With Mercury
camping up the front-man spot
(his kitsch rendition of the show
tune **Big Spender** is one of highlights of stage act), they are exotic
enough to attract a crossover
audience of bopper fans, yet
their records are equally well-
geared to hold the attentions of
the current generation of hard-
rock enthusiasts. Provided they
don't over-reach themselves, they
look set for a lengthy stay.

Recordings:
Queen (Elektra/EMI)
Queen II (Elektra/EMI)
Sheer Heart Attack (Elektra/
EMI)
A Night At The Opera
(Elektra/EMI)

189

Above: Bonnie Raitt, modest and likeable, continued to shun commercial success.

Quicksilver Messenger Service

Gary Duncan guitar, vocals
John Cipollina guitar
David Freiberg bass, vocals
Greg Elmore drums
Dino Valenti guitar, vocals

Quicksilver were formed in 1965 in San Francisco by Duncan, Cipollina, Freiberg and Elmore, briefly assisted by Jim Murray (vcls, hrmca), who left in early 1966 to study sitar music. Originally the band was also to have included Valenti, but he was inconveniently imprisoned on a drugs charge.

Prior to forming Quicksilver, each of the members had played either in bands or as folksingers, and they soon developed a strong local following, eventually signing with Capitol in 1968 – one of the last important San Francisco bands to get a record contract.

The group provided two songs for the soundtrack of the film "Revolution" (which also featured music by Mother Earth and the Steve Miller Band), before putting out **Quicksilver Messenger Service** in May 1968 and **Happy Trails** in March 1969. These remain the two best albums they have made, and two of the best examples of the San Francisco sound at its purest.

However, in January 1969 Valenti, released from jail, had taken Duncan to New York to form a group there, and English session-pianist Nicky Hopkins (♦) came in to repair the breach; the band's third album, **Shady Grove,** was however, first step on the downward path.

Valenti and Duncan failed to get anything together in New York and in February 1970 joined

Quicksilver, making the band a six-piece. This line-up produced **Just For Love** in September 1970, though Hopkins left just prior to its release. He was replaced briefly by percussionist Jose Reyes, who contributed to **What About Me?**, much of which had been recorded at the same time as the previous album.

Both Reyes and Cipollina split in October 1970, the latter to form Copperhead with Jim Murray, of the original Quicksilver (and in 1974 he was temporarily associated with Welsh band Man (♦)).

*Happy Trails.
Courtesy Capitol Records.*

The four surviving members – Duncan, Elmore, Valenti and Frieberg – carried on until September 1971 when Freiberg was jailed for marijuana possession. (Upon his release, he became a session-man, and eventually joined the Jefferson Starship (♦).) The others brought in Mark Ryan (bs) and Chuck Steaks (org) and produced two further albums, **Quicksilver** (November 1971) and **Comin' Thru** (April 1972).

From this point, the band seemed to disintegrate through apathy. Little of note occurred until the end of 1975, when the five mem-

bers who had contributed most to the group (i.e. the line-up as above) re-formed to make **Solid Silver,** an inappropriate title for a rather lacklustre album.

The only one of them who is now performing seems to be Freiberg, who is back with the Jefferson entourage. The activities of the others are currently somewhat under-publicised.

Recordings:
**Quicksilver Messenger
  Service** (Capitol)
Happy Trails (Capitol)
Shady Grove (Capitol)
Just For Love (Capitol)
What About Me? (Capitol)
Quicksilver (Capitol)
Comin' Thru (Capitol)
Solid Silver (Capitol)
Compilation:
Anthology (Capitol)

Quiet Sun
♦ Roxy Music

Quiver
♦ Sutherland Brothers & Quiver

Bonnie Raitt

Born in Los Angeles in 1950 into a musical family – her father was the Broadway singer, John Raitt – Bonnie mastered guitar, and became interested in classic blues singers, Robert Johnson, Mississippi John Hurt and Muddy Waters, in her adolescence, before moving east to the Cambridge folk scene in 1967.

She worked regularly on East Coast, and had initial success in Boston and Philadelphia area clubs, and acquired Dick Waterman as her manager. Waterman was also guiding the erratic careers of several blues singers, and soon Bonnie was sharing the stage with her idols – John Hurt, Fred McDowell, Son House and Sippie Wallace.

In 1971 she signed with Warner Bros, and made her debut album, **Bonnie Raitt,** which included compositions by Johnson and Wallace, and also utilised the services of Chicago bluesmen Junior Wells and A.C. Reed. She included more contemporary material on her second album, **Give It Up** (1972), including Eric Kaz's **Love Has No Pride,** a song of which hers remains the definitive version, despite the many covers since.

Takin' My Time (1974) was recorded on the West Coast, with John Hall of Orleans producing, and Lowell George, Bill Payne (♦ Little Feat) and Van Dyke Parks (♦) in attendance. The album covered a still wider range of material, and again assisted her slowly flowering reputation, through **Streetlights,** released later that year and produced by Jerry Ragavoy was thoroughly disappointing. Her fifth album, **Home Plate,** was recorded in Los Angeles with Paul Rothchild producing, and put her back on right track.

*Takin My Time.
Courtesy Warner Bros. Records.*

She performs regularly, with her own back-up band, and often gives charity concerts; coming from a middle-class background, she feels no urgency to enrich herself, saying: "I just want to make a living and throw something back into the community rather than buy a new pair of racing gloves for my Ferrari." Nevertheless, almost despite herself, her following is gradually building. In 1976 she made a short, but well-received, tour of Britain.

Recordings:
Bonnie Raitt (Warner Bros)
Give It Up (Warner Bros)
Takin' My Time (Warner Bros)
Streetlights (Warner Bros)
Home Plate (Warner Bros)

The Rascals

Felix Cavaliere vocals,
  keyboards
Eddie Brigati vocals
Dino Danelli drums
Gene Cornish guitar

The Young Rascals (they dropped the "Young" in 1967 when they all moved out of their teens) came together in New York in 1965, with Cavaliere, Brigati and Cornish all quitting Joey Dee's Starlighters simultaneously. All three had also had previous experience as session-men, and were attracted to soul and R&B music. Danelli had originally liked jazz, and had had a stint with Lionel Hampton's band, though a spell in Bourbon Street in New Orleans converted him to a love for R&B.

The four started playing gigs together on Long Island from February 1965, with material written by Cavaliere and Brigati. They acquired a manager in Sid Bernstein and a fast-spreading reputation as a hot live act; their music was soul-based, danceable, and totally immediate. They were signed by Ahmet Ertegun for Atlantic, despite opposition from Phil Spector and other well-known producers.

The band's first single, **I Ain't Gonna Eat Out My Heart Anymore,** aroused interest and encouraging sales; the second single, **Good Lovin'** was a U.S. No. 1, and was immediately followed by another massive hit, **You Better Run.** The band's earthy early material was produced by Tom Dowd, but when they moved towards fringes of jazz with **Groovin',** then Dowd left them in the capable hands of Arif Mardin. **Groovin'** was a marvellously atmospheric, superbly produced single that again gave them a

U.S. No. 1 and a gold record, and also cracked European market for them.

Since Cavaliere had taken over on vocals from Brigati for **Groovin'**, the lead vocals were henceforward shared; but, the heady success of **Groovin'** notwithstanding, the band had moved into areas they were less well equipped to handle, and never quite recovered their early poise. Records remained well produced, and slightly jazzy, but grew more lyrically pretentious. Despite further hits, and another No. 1, **People Got To Be Free** in 1968, their standing was irremediably on slide, and in 1971 they changed personnel and switched to Columbia.

Cavaliere and Danelli remained, and three new figures were brought in – Buddy Feiten, Robert Popwell and Ann Sutton. Feiten had previously been with Paul Butterfield (♦) and had also played on Bob Dylan's **New Morning** sessions.

This line-up issued **Peaceful World** in 1971; it aroused moderate interest, but little positive enthusiasm, and after **Island Of Real** in 1972, the Rascals finally disbanded.

Cavaliere moved to Warner Bros as a solo artist, and made two albums, **Felix Cavaliere** and **Destiny**, both of which displayed some energetic, high-class soul music, but somehow there was little public response; he remains on the sidelines, however, still a potential force.

Recordings:
The Young Rascals (Atlantic)
Collections (Atlantic)
Groovin' (Atlantic)
Once Upon A Dream (Atlantic)
Freedom Suite (Atlantic)
See (Atlantic)
Peaceful World (Columbia/CBS)
Island Of Real (Columbia/CBS)
Compilation:
Time Peace: Greatest Hits
(Atlantic)
Felix Cavaliere:
Felix Cavaliere (Bearsville/—)
Destiny (Bearsville)

Otis Redding

Born Dawson, Georgia, Sep 9, 1941, Redding grew up in nearby Macon. He first sang in church choir, and at school, an early inspiration being local hero Little Richard (Ray Charles also hailed from the same area).

He initially came to fame through his high-school friend Phil Walden, who helped Otis find gigs, and it was through Walden that Redding met a local R&B group, Johnny Jenkins and the Pinetoppers. In 1962 he was working with them as roadie, general assistant and occasional singer. When Jenkins went into Stax Studios in Memphis and the session finished early, Otis persuaded Jim Stewart, boss of Stax, to let him cut some songs.

One was a Redding composition, **These Arms Of Mine.** Stewart was sufficiently impressed to sign him up, even inaugurating the Volt label to deal with his releases. **These Arms Of Mine,** was issued as a single, and dented the U.S. Hot 100.

Pain In My Heart, another ballad, provided Redding with a second hit, and over the next four years most of his output met with

regular success. Songs like **I Can't Turn You Loose** emphasised his ability to handle up-tempo material, and he made other classic songs – **I've Been Loving You Too Long, Fa Fa Fa Fa (Sad Song)** and **Shake** (a tribute to another of his prime influences, Sam Cooke). Redding was less adept technically at handling slower material, but in Europe at least, **Otis Blue** (an album largely of ballads and containing his version of The Temptations' **My Girl,** which became a major hit single in U.K.) was regarded as a classic of its time.

Sittin' On The Dock Of The Bay.
Courtesy Atlantic Records.

Redding toured regularly in years 1964–67; he usually recorded with Booker T & The MGs – Steve Cropper (♦) was the Stax staff-man assigned to work with Redding – and worked on the road either with them or his protégè, the Bar-Kays.

He headlined the Stax-Volt European tour of 1965, and indeed had a greater following in Europe, at least until 1967 Monterey Pop Festival made U.S. rock audience realise what they'd been missing. He was a dynamic live performer, something captured for posterity in the film "Monterey Pop".

On Dec 10, 1967 Redding was killed, along with four of the Bar-Kays, when their plane crashed into an icy lake near Madison, Wisconsin. The Memphis soul community turned out in force for his funeral – Joe Tex, Joe Simon, Johnny Taylor, Solomon Burke, Percy Sledge, Don Covay and Sam Moore (of Sam and Dave) were all pall-bearers; everyone appreciated that Redding had been the most important soul artist of the decade, if only because he was the first to have broken through to a white audience (an achievement which his cover versions of white rock songs, like **Satisfaction** and **Day Tripper** had facilitated). Redding had also been instrumental in discovering raw talent, and had fostered the careers of Arthur Conley and William Bell.

His biggest hit was a posthumous one and his own composition (written with Cropper) **Sittin' On The Dock Of The Bay,** which reached No. 1 in U.S. and No. 3 in the U.K., and showed him moving towards more pop-oriented material, and possibly indicating that his appeal would have broadened still further had he lived.

Of the albums that he recorded during his lifetime, **Otis Blue** is easily the best. There have been many posthumous releases and compilations, of which the most complete is the double-album **The Best Of Otis Redding,** though even that contains a gross oversight by omitting the superb

Mr Pitiful.

In November 1973 Redding's son, Dexter Redding, who was 12 at the time, issued one single **God Bless** on Phil Walden's Capricorn label.

Discography is selective.

Recordings:
Otis Blue (Volt/Atlantic)
Dictionary Of Soul (Volt/ Atlantic)
Live In Europe (Volt/Atlantic)
Sittin' On The Dock Of The Bay (Volt/Stax)
Love Man (Atco/Atlantic)
Tell The Truth (Atco/Atlantic)
With Carla Thomas:
King & Queen (Volt/Stax)
With Jimi Hendrix:
Live At Monterey (Reprise)
Compilations:
The Immortal Otis Redding
(Alco/Atlantic)
The History Of Otis Redding
(Atco/Atlantic)
The Best Of Otis Redding
(Atco/Atlantic)

Helen Reddy

Born Melbourne, Australia, Oct 25, 1942, into a show-business family, Helen entered the entertainment profession when she was four years old, and ultimately had her own Australian TV show.

She felt there was limited scope for her in her own country, so she travelled to New York, with little immediate success; she was on point of returning when she met and married agent Jeff Wald in 1967. They struggled to make ends meet for four years, while Wald tried to get Helen's singing career under way; they moved to the West Coast and in meantime Helen took an external degree at University of California, Los Angeles. Eventually, Wald got his wife a recording contract with Capitol, and **I Don't Know How To Love Him** (from "Jesus Christ, Superstar") was issued as a single, as well as an album of same title.

The single was only moderately successful; however, when another song from the album, the self-composed **I Am Woman,** was issued as a single, it went straight to No. 1 in the U.S., as people saw Ms Reddy – not entirely accurately – as a passionate spokeswoman for the feminist cause.

No Way To Treat A Lady.
Courtesy Capitol Records.

It was nevertheless a badge she was willing to wear, and she began to talk about women's rights more eloquently than she discussed her music, though the hit songs continued unabated in the wake of **I Am Woman.** She has so far amassed five gold albums and four gold singles.

In Britain, she didn't break through until 1975, with **Angie Baby.**

Recordings:
I Don't Know How To Love Him (Capitol)
Helen Reddy (Capitol)
I Am Woman (Capitol)
Long Hard Climb (Capitol)
Love Song (Capitol)
Free And Easy (Capitol)
No Way To Treat A Lady (Capitol)

Lou Reed

New York born, leader of that city's seminal Velvet Underground (♦) until their disintegration amid apathy end of 1970. The Velvets had never achieved the attention their work warranted, and Reed was to claim that all the mistakes of his solo career were born out of this frustration, of a lust for some kind of success and for recognition of his former group's importance.

Transformer.
Courtesy RCA Records.

Either way, the Velvets split left Reed drifting in and out of music circles for a year – he worked for a spell with his father's accountancy firm in Freeport, Long Island – before RCA proffered a solo contract at the suggestion of New York writer and producer Richard Robinson. Interested in what was coming out of Britain, and with Reed having every reason to be disenchanted with New York, the pair travelled to London December 1971 to work on Reed's eponymous solo debut using an oddly mixed line-up which included Steve Howe, Rick Wakeman and Clem Cattini.

The result was less than satisfactory, but Reed persisted with British studios and players – though he did axe Robinson virtually at the point his producer was packing for return to London studios. This probably had less to do with Robinson as the fact that David Bowie (♦), nascent androgynous hero of British rock, had shown interest in producing Reed himself; Bowie's work and attitudes owing a large debt to Reed and Velvets.

The result of this coupling was **Transformer,** which appeared late 1972 and spilled forth a whole closet-full of twilight zone characters on a public whose appetite for this "daring" new turn in rock had been whetted by the likes of Reed disciples Bowie and Roxy Music (♦). It mattered not to them that the figures and scenarios of Reed's former (Velvets) work had been reduced to cartoon proportions, or that Reed was parodying Reed (as he would on each successive album) – this was what his new audience wanted to hear, and it had undeniable commerciality.

It even yielded a smash hit in **Walk On The Wild Side,** though how the single got played on BBC Radio 1 remains a mystery – presumably nobody there knew what "giving head" meant. Nonetheless, there was Reed in 1973 with the success he craved – a hit album and single in America and Britain.

But the rot had set in. Earlier, he had put on some exemplary performances for the enthusiasts – notably his U.K. tour with The Tots, a group of teenage New Yorkers – but after **Transformer** he hooked himself firmly into his role as Elder Statesman Of Ersatz Decadence and deteriorated at a rapid pace. This was a sobering sight for aficionados: Reed in eye-liner and phantom drag, aping Bowie the disciple of Reed.

In 1976 Reed was to tell a journalist: "I mimic me probably better than anybody, so if everybody else is making money ripping me off, I figured maybe I better get in on it. Why not? I created Lou Reed. I have nothing faintly in common with that guy, but I can play him well. Really well."

Reed stayed in Britain for his next album, the misunderstood **Berlin** (1973), bringing in American producer Bob Ezrin (Alice Cooper, etc.) and self-consciously returning to plumb the twilight zone with what he hoped would evince more credibility. It was intended as a magnum opus, but was much maligned by critics, and, being virtually inpenetrable to those who had discovered Reed via **Transformer,** died a commercial death.

Nevertheless, he managed to pick himself up sufficiently to assemble an excellent backing band out of guitarists Dick Wagner and Steve Hunter, from **Berlin** sessions, plus Prakash John (bs) and Whitey Glan (drms). All would later be spirited away by Alice Cooper (♦).

Reed could be alternately brilliant or horrifically parodic by the night, but the band was consistently fine on a repertoire which drew from Reed's Velvets period. One of their best performances – at New York's Academy Of Music – was captured on the 1974-released **Rock 'n' Roll Animal** set, which temporarily reconstituted a degree of Reed's fast-fading reputation. In general, however, it did more for his band.

But his next studio album, **Sally Can't Dance,** also released 1974, plummeted again into parody, and further devalued his dignity and status. Reed's own retrospective view was that it "sucked". Even so, the album went Top 10 in the U.S. charts.

In 1975 RCA issued another album from the Academy Of Music gig, **Lou Reed Live,** and towards the end of the year came the horrendous episode concerning **Metal Machine Music.** This was a double album, each side precisely 16.1 mins long, and purportedly an exercise in electronic experimentation. To the undiscerning ear (i.e. everybody except Reed and presumably the person at RCA who sanctioned its

Above: Lou Reed, with Velvet Underground colleague Nico paying close attention.

release) the four sides contained nothing except tape hum interrupted by the occasional high frequency burp. Reed went down in a torrent of abuse desperately trying to explain himself. To no avail.

Albums were returned in droves until RCA, duly embarrassed by their gullibility and culpability in the affair, were forced to take it off the market. Reed later claimed that he made the album to break his contract with his manager.

In 1976, taking stock of his decline and telling the press "no more bullshit, dyed-hair, faggot-junkie trip", Reed released **Coney Island Baby,** announcing that he was "as proud of this as anything I did with the Velvets". Unhappily, the majority of critics didn't share his opinion.

Reed produced his finest work between 1967–70 (♦ Velvet Underground). In 1976 both his attitudes and his work seem manifestly redundant.

Recordings:
Lou Reed (RCA)
Transformer (RCA)
Berlin (RCA)
Rock 'n' Roll Animal (RCA)
Sally Can't Dance (RCA)
Lou Reed Live (RCA)
Metal Machine Music (RCA)
Coney Island Baby (RCA)

Refugee
♦ Lee Jackson

Reggae

The origins of reggae go all the way back to Africa, but the immediate source can be traced back to the influence of post-war black R&B on the Jamaican music scene; the proximity of the Caribbean to the deep South of the U.S. meant the availability of black R&B radio stations, while the

migrant West Indian workers brought home U.S. discs.

The boogie-derived striding off-beat of New Orleans R&B artists like Fats Domino (♦) and Amos Milburn, together with the brass jump-bands, was taken over and imitated; gradually the prominent off-beat was accentuated further, while brass-blowing became increasingly bizarre. Influential in the transition were musicians of West Kingston, and travelling DJs – sound system-men – like Duke Reid and Coxsone Dodd, many of whom began to cut their own records.

The new beat, a neat inside-out of the original, was called "ska" and performed by artists like Byron Lee, Owen Grey and Prince Buster; it swept the Caribbean.

In Britain, the music remained underground, little known outside the West Indian communities, though Mods began to pick up on it. After the isolated success of Millie's **My Boy Lollipop,** in 1964, the market was taken more seriously; Chris Blackwell started Island Records, and Lee Gopthal helped him to form Trojan.

By 1966 the music had become more electric, more relaxed, while the simple off/on "ska" beat became increasingly complex. The emphasis switched from horns to bass and rhythm guitars, while the lyrics of some songs began calling attention to social conditions.

There were simultaneous influences; the religio/revolutionary creed of Rastafarianism began to win a fashionable cult following, while the rude boys – the outlaws – of Jamaica's shanty towns began to move into the studios, celebrating their own chosen life-style, which resulted in a spate of rude boy records, which ultimately led to a rougher and heavier style, which paved the way for Rock Steady.

In Britain, Prince Buster's **Al Capone** was among the early reggae hits, but it was not until two years later that reggae burst into the charts, sired by a gleeful "skinhead" audience, as well as black Britons. Desmond Dekker's **Israelites** reached No. 1 in the

U.K. (and No. 9 in the U.S.) in 1969. It was followed by **It Mek,** and a flurry of hits from Jimmy Cliff (♦), The Pioneers, Bob & Marcia, and others.

This commercial wave did not last but reggae, though still derided by many, was now established. It was further fired by the commercial success of Johnny Nash, working with Bob Marley, and of Paul Simon, who recorded **Mother And Child Reunion** in Kingston with local musicians.

Another important landmark was the film, "The Harder They Come", which portrayed the vicious and criminal nature of the Jamaican music scene, and garnered a cult reputation wherever it was shown (mainly in London).

In recent years, the music has become increasingly sophisticated, with the rise of the large West Indian studios, and also the investment of British record companies (particularly Island) in Jamaican acts. Bob Marley (♦) has already broken through with some chart success, and U.K. hit single with **No Woman, No Cry,** and The Heptones, Toots & The Maytals (♦) and Burning Spear, whose music is arguably the most potent and uncompromising roots music around, are knocking on the door.

Terry Reid

Born Huntingdonshire, England, Nov 13, 1949, arrived in London 1964 to join Peter Jay And The Jaywalkers as guitarist for brief period before forming own trio with Keith Webb (drms) and Pete Solley (kybds). Came under guiding hand of Mickie Most (♦) who produced single **Better By Far** and album, **Bang Bang You're Terry Reid** (1968).

Accrued reputation on London club circuit, but gained far more attention in the U.S., becoming almost a cult figure there after a 1968 tour with Cream. Lavishly praised for his singing ability, Reid's U.S. reputation was further enhanced by appearance at same year's Miami Festival. First and second eponymous album (1969) both good examples of style of time – rough, scratchy guitar work and powerful vocals.

Subsequently Reid settled in States, re-thinking his direction for considerable time before release of third album, **River,** for Atlantic in 1973. Something of a squandered talent, Reid has yet to reveal early promise. He signed to ABC Records September 1974 and finally in spring 1976 released **Seed Of Memory** for that label.

Recordings:
Bang Bang You're Terry Reid (Epic/—)
Terry Reid (Epic/EMI)
River (Atlantic)
Seed Of Memory (ABC)

Renaissance

Michael Dunford guitar, vocals
Jon Camp bass, vocals
John Tout keyboards
Terence Sullivan percussion
Annie Haslam vocals

Initial incarnation of Renaissance was evolved by ex Yardbirds (♦) singer/harp player Keith Relf and drummer Jim McCarty in Surrey, England, 1969. Other members included Relf's sister Jane and ex Nashville Teens keyboards man, John Hawken. Relf and McCarty further indulged their former R&B group's penchant for experimentation – this time attempting to fuse classical, folk, jazz, blues and rock – on eponymous debut album for Island that same year.

However, Relf and McCarty had every reason to be dissatisfied with this largely ineffectual effort, and both had left by the time Renaissance returned to a recording studio, by now signed to Sovereign label, for 1972 set **Prologue.**

This caused far more interest in U.S. than U.K. and the re-formed band – above line-up contains none of original members – made America their base and home for next two years. The group's music still aims towards classical-rock fusions, using lyrics by poetess Betty Thatcher, and the clear and controlled voice of Annie Haslam to further "colour" their sophisticated melodies. This often finds them lost in a kind of artsy no man's land – though they enjoy a cultish following in the U.S. and growing chart success with each release. Have yet to achieve any comparative breakthrough in U.K.

Turn Of The Cards released in U.S. 1974 but not issued in the U.K. until following year. Live album recorded New York in summer, 1975.

Recordings:
Renaissance (Warner Bros/Island)
Prologue (Capitol/Sovereign)
Ashes Are Burning (Capitol/Sovereign)
Turn Of The Cards (Sire/BTM)
Scheherazade & Other Stories (Sire/BTM)
Renaissance Live At Carnegie Hall (Sire/BTM)

John Renbourn

Renbourn played in an eccentric folk-rock band in the Richmond, Surrey, England, area before going solo and drifting on to the folk-club circuit. With Davy Graham and Bert Jansch (♦), he became a principal exponent of the new decorative style of acoustic guitar playing, developing in many ways into a better all-round instrumentalist than Jansch, although not so influential. However, the emergence of all three opened the door for the likes of Ralph McTell and John Martyn.

After striking-up an occasional partnership with Bert Jansch, they both joined Pentangle (♦), though Renbourn continued to make solo albums, of which **Sir John Alot** demonstrates his interest in medieval music.

Also a fine sitar player, he has been inactive since the demise of Pentangle, shunning the instant commercialism of the music business for his farm in Wales.

Recordings:
John Renbourn (Warner Bros/Transatlantic)
Another Monday (Warner Bros/Transatlantic)
Sir John Alot Of Merre Englandes Musik Thynge And Ye Grene Knyghte (—/Transatlantic)
The Lady And The Unicorn (—/Transatlantic)
Faro Annie (—/Transatlantic)
With Bert Jansch:
Bert And John (Warner Bros/Transatlantic)

Return To Forever

Chick Corea, keyboards, synthesisers
Stanley Clarke bass
Lenny White drums
Al DiMeola guitar

Return To Forever was founded by Chick Corea in 1973. Corea grew up in Chelsea, Massachusetts, and was taught music by his father, Armando Corea, an established professional musician in his own right. After being raised on a diet of jazz, Chick was sent to study classical music under concert pianist Salvatore Sullo from age of 11.

In 1960 he moved to New York, and over the next decade built-up a formidable reputation as a session-man, playing with such noted figures as Stan Getz, Herbie Mann and Mongo Santamaria, and also inaugurating his own solo career from 1965.

In 1969 he joined forces with Miles Davis (♦), and participated on many of the latter's most outstanding albums, including **In A Silent Way, Bitches' Brew** and **Live At The Fillmore.** Corea's work with Return To Forever has lent credence to the opinion that the creative centres of '70s jazz are to be found with the artists who reached their first maturity within Miles Davis' charmed circle.

Return To Forever (1972) was actually a Corea solo album, on which he was supported by Stanley Clarke, Joe Farrell and Airto Moreira. The album contained two compositions by Flora Purim.

Clarke had previously worked in New York with Gato Barbieri, Stan Getz and Pharoah Sanders; White, who joined the group at the start in 1972, has also worked with Miles Davis on **Bitches'** **Brew,** before moving on to work with Santana on **Caravanserai.** DiMeola is the most recent recruit to Return To Forever – he joined in 1974 – and had previously played with Larry Coryell, before enrolling at the Berklee College of Music; shortly after leaving Corea invited him to join Return To Forever.

Apart from Corea, all members of band have released solo albums; Clarke recorded **Journey To Love** (Atlantic 1975), White released **Venusion Summer** (also 1975), and DiMeola released his debut solo album in 1976.

Recordings:
Light As A Feather (Polydor)
Hymn Of The Seventh Galaxy (Polydor)
Where Have I Known You Before? (Polydor)
No Mystery (Polydor)
The Romantic Warrior (Columbia/CBS)

Rhinoceros

John Finley vocals
Michael Fonfara keyboards
Danny Weis guitar
Alan Gerber piano, vocals
Doug Hastings guitar
Jerry Penrod bass
Billy Mundi drums

Rhinoceros, an early aggregation of supersessioneers, was formed in 1968 with above line-up. Their debut album, **Rhinoceros,** contained **Apricot Brandy,** for several years used as a theme-tune on British radio.

The two best-known members of the band were Mundi, who had been a member of the Mothers Of Invention in 1966–67, and Doug Hastings, who had temporarily replaced Neil Young in Buffalo Springfield.

Penrod left before the recording of **Satin Chickens** in 1969 and was replaced by Canadian bass-player Peter Hodgson. Before **Better Times Are Coming,** their ironically-titled epitaph, Mundi, Gerber and Hastings had left and were replaced by Larry Leishman on guitar and Duke Edwards on drums and vocals. Much of the material had been provided by Guy Draper, who also produced the album.

Fonfara and Weis worked with Lou Reed in 1975 on his **Coney Island Baby** album.

Recordings:
Rhinoceros (Elektra)
Satin Chickens (Elektra)
Better Times Are Coming (Elektra)

Charlie Rich

A writer/singer from Arkansas whose career has influentially spanned both rock 'n' roll and modern country.

Rich was a later protégé of Sun Records' Sam Phillips (♦), who added Rich to his already famous rock 'n' roll stable and recorded him on the subsidiary Phillips International label.

The story, verified by Rich himself, is that Rich, then a budding jazz pianist, took some sides into Phillips with a view to a recording contract. The Sun boss gave him some demos of the then rising Jerry Lee Lewis and told him: "Listen to those and when you've learned to play piano as badly as that guy come back and see me."

Charlie was quick to learn because in 1958 he scored a hit with **Lonely Weekends,** a song that has become a rockabilly standard. Rich revived the rock 'n' roll sound in 1965 with the hit **Mohair Sam** on the Smash label and the '60s also saw him score with the slower-paced **Big Boss Man.**

Rich was widely reputed to have no real burning desire for stardom but stardom came nevertheless in the field of country music in 1973. The teaming of Rich with ace "Nashville Sound" producer Billy Sherrill on Columbia Records bore fruit in the **Behind Closed Doors** album and also in the two hit singles included on that album, **Behind Closed Doors** and **The Most Beautiful Girl.**

Sherrill had done well in America previously with Tammy Wynette and Tanya Tucker but with Charlie Rich he invented a new sound, "countrypolitan", a sound that appealed to those who, five years earlier, might have bought Frank Sinatra or Tony Bennett. Rich's stage shows are a mixture of all his influences and his early jazz and blues roots are demonstrated on **The Silver Fox.** Discography is selective.

Recordings:
Lonely Weekends (—/Charly)
Tomorrow Night (RCA)
Behind Closed Doors (Columbia/CBS)
The Silver Fox (Columbia/CBS)

Cliff Richard

Born Harry Webb in Lucknow, India, Oct 14, 1940, Richard worked as a clerk on leaving school, and in his spare time played in a group called The Drifters in his home town of Cheshunt, Hertfordshire.

The group – Terry Smart (drms), Ian Samwell (gtr, vcls) – built a strong local following and soon appeared at the 2 I's coffee-bar in Soho, the mecca for aspiring rockers in Britain in the late '50s, where Richard found Jet Harris (bs) and Hank Marvin (gtr). Smart was replaced by Tony Meehan.

Agent George Canjou discovered the group playing a gig at Shepherds Bush Odeon (in West London) in 1958 and arranged a solo recording contract for Richard, with The Drifters as his backing group. His first disc, **Move It** (a Samwell composition) became a major hit, and remains arguably his best record. He embarked on the first of many tours of the U.K. and as he quickly became well-known, the others changed their name from The Drifters to The Shadows (♦) to avoid confusion with the American vocal group.

Richard made his film debut in 1959 in "Serious Charge", singing his first million-seller, Lionel Bart's **Living Doll.** Though soon established as the best surrogate Elvis Presley Britain could produce, with the advent of The Beatles and also his own ceaselessly publicised Christian beliefs, he abandoned the black leather, white tie and sideburns of his early career to dress "respectably" and aim at a family audience. It was this emasculation of his music that probably accounted for his failure to make any impression on the U.S. market, even when his contemporaries were scoring regularly.

Nevertheless, the sequence of hits at home was unbroken, and **Travellin' Light** ('59), **Please Don't Tease** ('60), **The Young Ones** ('62), **The Next Time** ('63), **Summer Holiday** ('63), **The Minute You're Gone** ('65) and **Congratulations** ('68) all reached No. 1. Like Presley, he also made a series of dreadful movies – "The Young Ones" ('61), "Summer Holiday" ('63), "Wonderful Life" ('64), "Two A Penny" ('68), etc.

While his music continued to be shamelessly derivative, his own TV variety shows kept him in the public eye, and his apparently eternal youth acted as a telling advertisement for Clean Upright Living, his personal honesty-built him a measure of respect from his fellow professionals.

In 1976 he recorded **I'm Nearly Famous,** an album produced by Bruce Welch (♦ The Shadows), a conscious attempt to return to the uninhibited rock he had forsaken some 16 years earlier. Elton John signed him to Rocket Records for U.S. release, and "I'm Nearly Famous" badges were sported by real rock stars like Jimmy Page and Eric Clapton. With support from such luminaries, Richard's name became fashionable on the rock circuit and his single **Devil Woman** climbed into the U.S. Top 20 to give him his first success there after 49 hits in Britain.

Discography is selective.

Recordings:
Cliff's Hit Album (—/Columbia)
The Music And Life Of Cliff Richard (box set of 6 cassettes) (—/EMI)
I'm Nearly Famous (Rocket/ EMI)

Little Richard

Born Richard Penniman on Christmas Day, 1932 in Macon, Georgia, he was raised as a Seventh Day Adventist and spent his early years singing in church choirs. By age of 14 he was travelling with Dr Hudson's Medicine Show. At 16 he won a talent contest, and started making his first records for RCA in 1951; even this early, innovative, anarchic gospel-styled wailing, which was to influence James Brown, Otis Redding, et al., was apparent.

He was to record for a wide variety of labels, and while on Peacock was backed by Johnny Otis Band. In 1955 he made a private recording of **Tutti Frutti** with his group The Upsetters. The song was picked up by Specialty Records in Los Angeles, and the result was a million-seller for Richard, and a five-year contract, during which time he recorded six more gold records, including **Long Tall Sally, Rip It Up, Good Golly Miss Molly** and **Keep A-Knockin'.**

Then, while touring Australia in 1957, he decided to quit pop-music for religion, though he returned to music business full-time in 1963.

On completion of his theological studies, he signed first with Vee-Jay, who re-cut all his old Specialty

classics, and then with Okeh, who gave him the opportunity to prove his ability as a soul singer; his work for Modern was also impressive, especially with the great, rolling blues **Baby What You Want Me To Do?**

In 1970 Richard's career received new boost, partly through the widespread revival of rock 'n' roll and partly through a new contract with Reprise. **The Rill Thing** and **King Of Rock And Roll** are fine examples of modern R&B-cum-rock. He also recorded tracks with Delaney & Bonnie and Canned Heat, which, since they featured his keyboard work heavily, were widely acclaimed.

The movie "Let The Good Times Roll" showed Richard at his most irascible; he is a controversial character, much given to self-deification; with his bizarre apparel and heavy make-up, he is camp in the extreme. He believes he is the greatest, but in the '70s has more often than not seemed a tired performer, and one straining to recapture the past. He still has a loyal army of fans, especially in Britain, though most remember him for his golden years in '50s.

The discography is restricted to compilations of the original recordings of Penniman's most important '50s work on Specialty. Virtually all of the songs he has re-recorded at some time in an inferior form.

Recordings:
The Original Little Richard (Specialty)
Rock Hard, Rock Heavy (Specialty)
All-Time Hits (Specialty)

Above: Little Richard, flamboyant and irrepressible.

Joshua Rifkin

Born New York 1944, Rifkin had a background in classical music, although he began playing jazz and ragtime music on the piano from age of 10. He later obtained degrees in composition from Juilliard School Of Music, and in musicology from Princeton University.

Piano Rags By Scott Joplin, Vol. 3. Courtesy Nonesuch.

In 1960s he played piano and kazoo in Even Dozen Jug Band alongside such personalities as Maria Muldaur, John Sebastian and Steve Katz. In 1966 he put together **The Baroque Beatles Book** (what the early Lennon/ McCartney songs might have sounded like had they been written by J. S. Bach) for Jac Holzman's Nonesuch label, and as a result was invited to provide the arrangements for three of Judy Collins' most orchestrated albums – **In My Life, Wildflowers** and **Whales And Nightingales.**

Rifkin became a prime mover in the popularisation of ragtime

music in the '70s after recording a series of Scott Joplin's piano rags, again for Nonesuch. Joplin's dictum had always been, "It is never right to play ragtime fast", and Rifkin was never less than a most respectful interpreter.

When two of the rags, **Maple Leaf Rag** and **The Entertainer** were used in the highly successful film, "The Sting", the ragtime revival got under way, spearheaded by Rifkin, and overnight he became an unlikely household name, as **Piano Rags, Vols I & II** both became bestselling albums; Rifkin also gave concert tours, both throughout the States and Europe. Ever true to the spirit of the original, he played the rags slow.

He is now assistant professor of music at Brandeis University.

Recordings:
The Baroque Beatles Book (Nonesuch)
Piano Rags By Scott Joplin, Vol. I (Nonesuch)
Piano Rags By Scott Joplin, Vol. II (Nonesuch)
Piano Rags By Scott Joplin, Vol. III (Nonesuch)

The Righteous Brothers

Bill Medley vocals
Bobby Hatfield vocals

Bill Medley (b. Los Angeles, Sept 19, 1940) and Bobby Hatfield (b. Beaver Dam, Wisconson Aug 10, 1940) were the epitome of the phrase (sometimes used pejoratively) "blue-eyed soul" – so convincing were they in the soul genre that most people who heard their records for the first time automatically assumed they were a black act.

Medley's deep, rich timbre, though at times he seemed to be mimicking vocal technique (and material) of Ray Charles, made a perfect foil for the higher-pitched, gospel-flavoured range of Hatfield.

The Brothers (who were not related at all) scored their first sizable U.S. hit with untypical **Little Latin Lupe Lu,** which was showcased on debut album **Right Now** in 1963. The following year they appeared as show-openers on Beatles' American tour.

They really came to prominence, however, in early 1965 when under the supervision of king-pin pop production genius Phil Spector (➧) they released the classic **You've Lost That Lovin' Feelin'** (written by Spector, Cynthia Weill, Barry Mann). It featured a devastating, orgasmic vocal performance, behind which Spector marshalled all the considerable forces of his famed "wall of sound" technique, and went to No. 1 on both sides of Atlantic.

Widely regarded as one of the greatest singles ever, in Britain its success had extra significance. At that time most American hits which fell into soul/R&B bracket were "covered" by home-based acts, with chauvinistic radio DJs usually squeezing out the original to all but the collector.

Cilla Black made a monstrously squeaky "cover" of the Brothers' song and, true to form, hers was the version which got radio-plays and made charts. However, interest in Spector was growing in the U.K., and enough enthusiasts went out and bought the original to break it into lower reaches of charts (one of these enthusiasts, incidentally, was then-Stones manager Andrew Oldham who bought ad space in music press to laud the magnificence of Spector's production). Once in charts, DJs had to give both versions a spin. Quality won out in a neck-and-neck battle, and the Righteous Bros overtook the unfortunate Cilla who had to make do with No. 2. "Cover" artists never had it so easy after that.

The Brothers stayed with Spector's Philles label for two more lesser hits – including **Unchained Melody** – and four albums (listed below), though they produced much of material themselves, before moving to Verve.

Here their style mellowed somewhat, and they specialised in heavily-arranged, string-laden soul ballads. **You're My Soul And My Inspiration** – another Mann/Weill song – came close to standards of **Lovin' Feelin'**, while the Medley composition **Stand By,** from LP **Go Ahead And Cry** (1966) is a little-known but remarkable performance.

Working mainly with Bill Baker and ex Motowner Micky Stevenson, they produced a run of class albums until in 1968 they split up. Medley recorded solo and Hatfield tried, without much success, to keep Righteous Bros going with new partner Billy Walker. **Re-birth** (1969) was the result of

Right: The Righteous Brothers, masters of white soul. Bill Medley (left) and Bobby Hatfield (right).

this collaboration.

Medley's fine solo work included two excellent singles **Brown-Eyed Woman** and **Peace Brother Peace,** but somehow neither of the original Brothers' voices sounded as good without the other. Medley and Hatfield finally joined forces again in 1974 and had a freak U.S. hit, **Rock 'n' Roll Heaven,** a sickly death-disc lamenting dead rock stars such as Hendrix, Joplin, etc. Neither of reunion albums – **Give It To The People** (1974) was first – have been received with enthusiasm.

List below omits pre-Philles releases, the best of which is contained in the Moonglow **Best Of The Righteous Brothers** compilation (1966).

Recordings:
You've Lost That Lovin' Feelin' (Philles/London)
Just Once In My Life (Philles/London)
Back To Back (Philles/London)
Soul And Inspiration (Philles/London)
Go Ahead And Cry (Verve)
Sayin' Something (Verve)
Souled Out (Verve)
Righteous Brothers Standards (Verve)
One For The Road (Verve)
Re-Birth (Hatfield and Walker) (Verve)
Give It To The People (Capitol)
The Sons Of Mrs Righteous (Capitol)
Bill Medley:
100% (Verve)
Someone Is Standing Outside (Verve)
Gone (Verve)
Nobody Knows (MGM/—)
A Song For You (A&M)

Terry Riley

Avant-garde composer/performer, born Colfax, California 1935. Riley spent formative years touring night-clubs of America and Europe, playing ragtime piano, before joining experimental La-Monte Young group in 1962. He began to compose "systems music" and to perform live using electronic keyboards, soprano sax, and multiple tape-recorders – a sample of which is contained in **Poppy Nogood And The Phantom Band** from **A Rainbow In Curved Air** (1971).

In C (1970) was his first major

work, and remains the most successful Riley album, although **Curved Air** is more widely popular. Also in 1971, Riley collaborated with John Cale (➧) on **Church Of Anthrax** set.

The Riley cult died away somewhat after early '70s, but his lengthy excursions into dreamlike tape-delay effects around overlapping motto-themes have left their mark on rock – chiefly via Soft Machine (➧) – as well as drawing public attention to the contemporary classical avant-garde.

Recordings:
Keyboard Studies (BYG)
In C (Columbia/CBS)
A Rainbow In Curved Air (Columbia/CBS)
Church Of Anthrax (with John Cale) (Columbia/CBS)
Persian Surgery Dervishes (Shandar imp.)

Minnie Riperton

Minnie Riperton, who started taking opera lessons at the age of 11, signed to Chess Records in 1963, both as a solo artist and as a leading light of Rotary Connection, and it was as a result of her

Adventures In Paradise. Courtesy Epic, CBS Records.

work with that band that she originally came to notice.

In the '70s she went solo, and began to become well known on the West Coast, making her last album for the Chess company, **Come To My Garden** in 1973.

She then moved to Epic, where her debut album, **Perfect Angel** was produced by Stevie Wonder (➧), who also provided two compositions and played keyboards,

percussion and harmonica. The rest of the material had been written by Minnie and her husband Richard Rudolph; one of the tracks, **Loving You,** was issued as a single. It was a particularly haunting track, made more so by the incongruous bird whistling in the background. The song went to No. 1 in both Britain and America, a surprise hit of 1975; the album inevitably went gold, though her follow-up, **Adventures In Paradise,** was less successful.

The discography is selective.

Recordings:
Come To My Garden (Janus/—)
Perfect Angel (Epic)
Adventures In Paradise (Epic)

Johnnie Rivers

Johnny Rivers (b. New York City, Nov 7, 1942) grew up in Baton Rouge, Louisiana, and began performing at the age of 14. He was a proficient guitarist and singer by the time he moved to Los Angeles in early '60s.

Around 1962, he hit upon the idea of making live disco music, and his regular sessions at the Whisky A Go Go on Sunset Strip became enormously popular, producing several live albums.

During the latter part of the '60s, Rivers continued to perform, but also diversified, setting up his own record company, Soul City. An early signing in 1966 was the Fifth Dimension (➧), who were virtually ever present in the charts for the next two to three years, thanks to the songs of Jim Webb (another Rivers discovery), the production of Rivers and Bones Howe, and the backing musicians Hal Blaine (drms), Joe Osborn (bs) and Larry Knechtel (kybds).

Rivers can also be given credit for formulating the concept of a regular group of studio musicians, and perhaps more important, crediting them on the sleeves of records they made for him.

Right through the '70s, Rivers has continued to make highly professional records, using the best session-men, and frequently championing unknown songwriters who have subsequently been recognised as leaders in their field, notably Jackson Browne, Van Morrison and James Taylor.

A more recent coup was in persuading Brian Wilson to emerge from his self-imposed retirement to sing on the Rivers version of **Help Me Rhonda,** and there is no doubt that such items will consistently happen where Rivers is involved. Up to 1976, he has sold over 25 million of his own records, and won 16 gold discs, as well as winning two Grammy Awards, writing songs and running his own record label. Despite all this, he remains an under-rated talent – possibly because many of his own hits have been cover versions of already familiar songs.

Discography is selective. **New Lovers And Old Friends** was retitled **Help Me Rhonda** for U.K. release.

Recordings:
Slim Slo Slider (United Artists)
Home Grown (United Artists/—)
L.A. Reggae (United Artists)
Blue Suede Shoes (United Artists)
Last Boogie In Paris (Atlantic)
Road (Atlantic)
New Lovers And Old Friends (Epic)
Compilations:
Superpak (United Artists/—)
The Very Best of Johnny Rivers (United Artists/—)

Smokey Robinson
◆ Tamla Motown

Jess Roden

A veteran of minor league British rock scene, Roden has often appeared on fringes of success without making further headway. A vocalist, his first group was local Worcestershire outfit The Shakedown Sound. Left them to join The Alan Bown Set, a jazz-rock club attraction, after which he formed own Bronco outfit which cut two albums for Island in early '70s before dissolution.

Roden next turned up in the company of former Doors member Robby Kreiger and John Densmore in The Butts Band (◆) but this association lasted only for one album and a handful of gigs.

The singer recorded a solo album in London and New Orleans for Island label in 1974, and formed Jess Roden Band touring band from personnel of ailing Southampton-based outfit Iguana: Bruce Roberts (gtr), Pete Hunt (drms), John Cartwright (bs), Chris Gower (trom), Ronnie Taylor (sx). Steve Webb (gtr, vcls) was added to line-up for first Jess Roden Band-credited set, the excellent **You Can Keep Your Hat On** (1976).

Recordings:
Jess Roden (Island)
You Can Keep Your Hat On (Island)

Right: Keith Richard, whose unhappy series of drug busts continued during the Stones' 1976 tour of Britain.

The Rolling Stones

Mick Jagger vocals
Keith Richard guitar, vocals
Ron Wood guitar
Bill Wyman bass
Charlie Watts drums

Both born Dartford, Kent, Jagger (Jul 26, 1943) and Richard (Dec 18, 1943) first met at age of six at local Maypole County Primary School. Yet it wasn't until 1960 that their paths crossed again, and discovered that they had both been independently pursuing similar interests in blues and R&B. Also that they had a mutual friend in guitarist Dick Taylor, who had been at Dartford Grammar School with Jagger and was at that time at Sidcup Art School with Richard.

Jagger – who was student at London School of Economics – had discovered R&B via auspices of Taylor, this pair along with Bob Beckwith and Allen Etherington working under unlikely name Little Boy Blue & The Blue Boys. As result of Jagger and Richard's reunion, the latter added his Chuck Berry-influenced guitar to Blue Boys line-up. Even then Richard boasted punk credentials, having been expelled from Dartford Technical College for truancy.

Meanwhile, at around the same time, another young rebel of his period, Brian Jones (b. Lewis Brian Hopkin-Jones Feb 28, 1942) was trying to find work in musically-barren environment of home-town Cheltenham. He had already skipped school to play jazz as aspiring clarinetist and alto-saxist, and further enhanced his local notoriety by fathering two illegitimate children by the time he was 16.

Frustrated by lack of outlets for his musical ambitions in west country, Jones at one point split for sojourn in Scandinavia during which he improved ability on guitar. On return to Cheltenham he briefly joined local band The Ramrods and finally despaired of parochial life and drifted to London with his girlfriend and baby.

There he played occasionally with Alexis Korner's Blues Incorporated, having first met Korner on a Blues Inc. gig in Cheltenham, and nurtured ambition to front own authentic R&B band. To this end he advertised for like-minded musicians in "Jazz News", pianist Ian Stewart, singer Andy Wren and guitarist Geoff Bradford being recruited as a result.

Meanwhile, though still only of minority appeal, British R&B was on ascendancy – the pivotal venue for this exciting "new" music being the Ealing Blues Club where the highly-flexible Blues Inc. held a residency (◆ British R&B, Alexis Korner). It was here that Richard, Jagger, Taylor and Jones first met and exchanged experiences.

Jones by now had formed partnership with singer Paul Jones, later of Manfred Mann (◆), and then working under name P. P. Pond. (Jones, too, often used "ethnic" pseudonym – Elmo Lewis.) The Blue Boys went along to listen, and, a few weeks later, Jagger and Richard had summoned sufficient nerve to jam onstage at the Ealing club accompanied by mouth harpist Cyril Davies (◆) and Korner's drummer Charlie Watts.

Already some semblance of a new outfit was beginning to take shape. Jagger started rehearsing with Brian Jones, Geoff Bradford and Ian Stewart, and soon Richard and Dick Taylor were dropping by too. Of this aggregation, Bradford – a fine guitarist but too much the blues purist – was first to go; after falling out with first Richard and later Jones.

Meanwhile, Jagger made further appearances with Blues Inc., and by early 1962 was permanent singer for that band, which by then had graduated from Ealing to London Marquee Club. When he wasn't required by Korner, he worked out with Jones, Richard & Co.

Jagger, Jones and Richard were in fact so close at this time that they shared same (squalid) bedsit apartment in London borough of Hammersmith. They even got as far as cutting demo tape, which brought them first rejection – from EMI. These were lean times: Ian Stewart was the only one working, for chemicals giant ICI, and it was usually his money which kept band in food. Dick Taylor was the next to leave; he went to Royal College of Art, and later re-surfaced in Pretty Things (◆). By this time group had started using name Rolling Stones – from a Muddy Waters song.

In June 1962 came their first real break. Blues Inc. were booked for radio broadcast, but as budget only allowed for six players, singer Jagger was left out. Instead he took advantage of Korner's absence from Marquee to give embryonic Stones their London debut. First billed as "Brian Jones and Mick Jagger & The Rollin' Stones" they began to attract own audience.

But before they could progress any further, certain personnel changes needed to take place. Drummer Tony Chapman was deemed unacceptable and Stones worked for several months to persuade Charlie Watts (b. Jun 2, 1941) had by then been thrown in his gig with Blues Inc. due to pressures of drumming evenings and working by day as advertisement agency designer, and had instead joined group Blues By Six which made less demands on his time. Watts, a cautious man, wanted time to think before he threw in his lot with this new outfit.

In the meantime, auditions provided new bassist in Bill Wyman (né Perks, b. Oct 24, 1936) who had played in a previous band The Cliftons with Chapman. Then in January 1963 Watts took plunge and replaced Chapman. With these two important cogs in place, producing personnel of Jagger, Richard, Jones, Watts, Wyman and Ian Stewart, band went out on club circuit with repertoire of Berry/Diddley material and some of wildest R&B yet heard.

They recorded yet more demos, at IBC Studios, with a friend, Glyn Johns, and secured turning-point residency at legendary Crawdaddy Club at Station Hotel, Richmond. It was there, during their eight-month residency, that Stones attracted burgeoning cult following and, via a music press journalist, came to attention in April 1963 of first managers Andrew Oldham (◆) and Eric Easton, though latter was soon to drop out of picture. (George Harrison was one of many celebrities attracted to Crawdaddy by Stones' growing stature.)

Oldham, a former PR man and whizz-kid hustler, immediately sensed band's potential, obtaining a contract with Decca Records via executive

196

Dick Rowe, the man unfortunate enough to have once turned down The Beatles. Meanwhile, Oldham worked on group image – or rather simply amplified what they had already. He was shrewd enough to realise that the group's innate rebelliousness would provide perfect counterpoint to clean-cut fast-ascending Beatles; also shrewd enough to realise (as Stewart himself now recognises) that, however good he was as a musician, Ian Stewart physically just wasn't on a par with the rest.

It was not so much that Stewart was fired, more that he gradually drifted away from body of group though continuing to play on records, and often on stage too. This role he still fulfils with the Stones; along with sundry other duties including tour organisation.

From this point the group took off at a rapid pace. Jun 7, 1963 saw release of first single, Chuck Berry's **Come On** flipped with **I Want To Be Loved,** and first TV appearance – on ITV's "Thank Your Lucky Stars". During the transmission, according to author Roy Carr in his book "The Stones: An Illustrated Record", a TV producer advised Oldham that if Stones were to get anywhere it would have to be without the "vile-looking singer with the tyre-tread lips".

Come On wasn't massive hit (it sneaked into lower reaches of U.K. Top 30) but it helped band secure August gig at 1st National Jazz & Blues Festival at Richmond, and in September a support role on Everly Brothers/Bo Diddley/Little Richard package tour. In December 1973 their second single, Lennon/McCartney's **I Wanna Be Your Man,** made Top 20.

To coincide with first bill-topping U.K. tour (with Ronettes), an eponymous EP was issued January 1964 and a single, Buddy Holly's **Not Fade Away,** in February. This took them to No. 3 in U.K. charts in swaggering style, while also making first tentative inroads into U.S. market.

By now Stones had captured imagination of British youth and not-so-enthusiastic attention of national press, who branded them as dirty, unwashed enemies of decency and society. Naturally this, and stories told by outraged reporters of Stones urinating in public, only helped consolidate a growing legend.

This was further enhanced by their first U.K. album (early U.S. and U.K. releases differed greatly – see separate discographies). Released April 1964, this found group exploring a selection of standard R&B material and amounted to possibly the finest-ever rock album debut. June 1964 saw them embarking on first American tour, and **It's All Over Now** (the old Bobby Womack/Valentinos classic) providing first British chart-topper.

Riots broke out in Chicago when Stones attempted to give press conference outside Chess Records, where they recorded superb **Five By Five** EP. Subsequently **Little Red Rooster,** which was banned in States because of lyrics, became their last ethnically-daring single and racked up yet another U.K. No. 1. This cut was reputed to be Brian Jones' most cherished musical memory.

In January 1965 came second U.K. album, recorded mainly in States with emphasis on Chicago R&B, and, of even more significance, their first self-penned "A"-side **The Last Time.** (Jagger-Richard had previously been contributing material to albums and "B"-sides, often under group pseudonym Nanker, Phelge). This was U.K. No. 1 and made U.S. Top 10, although they only really took off in U.S. with the classic single, **Satisfaction.** From this point on all Stones' "A"-sides would be Jagger-Richard compositions. **Get Off Of My Cloud** similarly topped charts on both sides of Atlantic; this same year also producing another (U.K. only) EP **Got Live If You Want It,** culled from British concerts.

By this time the somewhat mysterious figure of New York accountant Allen Klein (♦) had appeared on scene as Stones "business manager", and Oldham's presence and influence was to wane as a result. Oldham

had done his job well, however, and no other act aside of Bob Dylan came near to rivalling Stones as outlaw heroes of rock 'n' roll. Wherever the group played riots ensued, while the national press continued to condemn them as a threat to the established order of the day.

Aftermath (1966) – with slight track variations between U.K. and U.S. versions – was the group's first all-original album, though initial impetus was minimised by almost simultaneous release of Beatles' **Revolver** and Dylan's **Blonde On Blonde.** In November came second live effort, again titled **Got Live If You Want It;** this time an album (U.S. only) but a somewhat unsatisfactory one from concert at London's Royal Albert Hall. The hit singles continued to pour forth.

In January 1967 yet more controversy surrounded the group when **Let's Spend The Night Together** was censored on Ed Sullivan U.S. TV show. No disaster in itself, but it was the start of a bad year for the group which saw them pursued by the establishment to the point of hounding via a series of drug busts which made international press at regular intervals.

First there was Jagger and Richard arrested during police raid on Richard's home; then the first of Brian Jones' busts. The establishment had hit back with a vengeance, but without doubt had gone over the top, and this time even the press found it hard to condone the subsequent jail sentences (eventually suspended on appeal) for such trivial charges. The whole affair became one huge disproportionate melodrama played out in full glare of public eye. Such a cause célèbre of its day that bishops and politicians argued the toss in public debate and finally that august organ "The Times" weighed in with its now famous "Butterfly On A Wheel" editorial to decry this abuse of the legal system.

The indifferent **Between The Buttons** emerged during these times of stress, as did the single **We Love You,** a toke of Stones' psychedelia employing Lennon/McCartney vocal harmonies and culminating with the sound of a slammed cell door.

The cell doors never did slam except for one night, but events had a lasting effect on Brian Jones whose estrangement from rest of group was increasing source of concern. Jones was getting into all sorts of weird scenes, and was hardly playing at all on records by 1967. If anyone was star-conscious in the Stones then it was Jones. As Ian Stewart has reminisced: "Brian loved it in that he was a Rolling Stone . . . but he forgot every so often that he was supposed to be playing guitar. Brian just got himself incredibly messed up very quickly . . . Brian was a very weak and easily-led character."

Though his sentence for possession of drugs was squashed, Jones began to suffer ill-health and in December 1967 was admitted to hospital. Earlier that year Jagger and his girlfriend Marianne Faithfull (♦) had visited Maharishi with Beatles and, besotted with quasi-mystic trappings, the group's November 1967 released **Their Satanic Majesties** album found them lost in space and hiding under terrestial shadow of **Sgt Pepper.**

In May 1968 Brian Jones was arrested yet again, committed for trial on 2,000 pound bail.

After traumas of previous year and the bewildering **Satanic Majesties** period, things looked somewhat bleak. But **Jumpin' Jack Flash** single restored faith in Stones as definitive rock 'n' roll band, and the much-delayed **Beggar's Banquet** collection in November that year proved to be the group's finest hour to date; it included such classics as **Sympathy For The Devil, Street Fighting Man** and **Stray Cat Blues,** but was also to be Jones' last album. Legend has it, however, that Jones made scant contribution to the set anyway. Dave Mason (♦) certainly guested on some tracks, while Eric Clapton (♦) is also rumoured to have taken part.

Get Yer Ya-Ya's Out. Courtesy Decca Records.

Sticky Fingers. Courtesy Rolling Stones Records.

'GET YER YA-YA'S OUT!'
The Rolling Stones in concert

Above: The Stones — a shot from the photo session that produced the cover of their 1976 album, Black and Blue.

Jones participated in Stones' never-to-be-seen TV special "Rock And Roll Circus" in December, and on Jun 9, 1969, a fortnight after another bust for Mick and Marianne – he quit the Stones.

The story at the time was, quote, that Jones no longer saw eye to eye with records the band was making, unquote, but it certainly went deeper than that. There seems good evidence to presume he was fired, because the Stones wanted to work again and Jones – who had made himself thoroughly unpleasant and unco-operative by this time – had no desire to go on the road.

It was to be another traumatic year: on Jun 13, 1969 Mick Taylor (b. Hertfordshire Jan 17, 1948) left John Mayall Band to join Stones. Brian Jones talked about forming new band with Alexis Korner, returning to ethnic roots, but on July 3 was found dead in swimming pool of his Hartfield home. He was 25. Coroners verdict: death by "misadventure".

Two days later Taylor made debut with Stones in Hyde Park, London, free festival at which Jagger read the assembly of 250,000 an excerpt from Shelley poem as memorial to Jones. On July 6 Jagger and Marianne flew to Australia for former to start work on first movie, the eponymous role in "Ned Kelly". (There Marianne would make first of suicide attempts, and Jagger would sunder their relationship.)

July 10: Brian Jones was buried. July 11: release of one of group's most swaggeringly-debauched singles **Honky Tonk Women.**

To tie in with first American tour for three years, another seminal Stones set, **Let It Bleed.** Then came the colossal mistake of Altamont (♦), ostensibly a free festival provided by the Stones as a "gift" to the kids of California. In the darkness as Jagger went through **Midnight Rambler, Under My Thumb** and **Sympathy For The Devil,** a young black was stabbed to death at foot of stage during a fracas involving Hell's Angels. Truly, it seemed, Hell had no fury than the devil invoked – and **Sympathy For The Devil** would not be performed on stage again by Stones for another six years. The full horrendous events of Altamont are captured on Maysles' brothers "Gimme Shelter" film of festival, distributed 1972.

The next album after a lengthy spell of inactivity was another live set, **Get Yer Ya-Ya's Out,** recorded at Madison Square Gardens, New York, November 1969, primarily as an effort to stem flood of Stones' bootlegs. At around same time Jagger made second, this time highly-praised, acting appearance in Nicholas Roeg's "Performance".

By now Stones had taken up residency in France for tax purposes, and finally broken always-antagonistic relationship with Decca (London in

Below: It's Only Rock 'n' Roll. Courtesy Rolling Stones Records.

U.S.), who responded by issuing whole series of poorly collated compilation sets. Another classic single, **Brown Sugar,** marked group's debut April 1971 on own Rolling Stones Records, concurrent with release of **Sticky Fingers**; a grand celebration of jet-set debauchery and chic demonic postures. Jim Price (tpt), Bobby Keyes (sx) and

Above: The Rolling Stones No. 2. Courtesy Decca Records.

pianist Nicky Hopkins (♦) now permanently augmented band for subsequent tours. In same year Jagger married to Nicaraguan model Bianca Perez Morena de Macias.

The double-set **Exile On Main Street**, arguably the most casually-dismissed but one of finest Stones albums, came in all fashionable flavours of rock and heralded another mammoth U.S. tour – these by now marshalled with considerable expertise by Cambridge University graduate Peter Rudge, who from that point on became nearest thing group had to a manager.

Albums deteriorated somewhat from that point, however, though both **Goat's Head Soup** (1973) and **It's Only Rock 'n' Roll** (1974) contained at least a couple of classics apiece; 1973 also saw immensely-successful American and European tours, the former recorded in infinite detail in Robert Greenfield's book "S.T.P.: A Journey Through America".

In December 1974, however, Mick Taylor quit group after making considerable contribution, and through following year rock press was rife with rumours of possible replacements (Ron Wood, Wayne Perkins, Harvey Mandel, etc.). Wood, then with Faces but close personal friend of Richard, was hottest tip but initially declined the offer. However, when summer 1975 Tour Of The Americas came round and still no permanent replacement was forthcoming, Wood agreed to "guest" with Stones while retaining links with Faces (♦). Since that last-named band fell into disarray (for which Rod Stewart blamed Wood's gigging with Stones), it now seems certain Wood will remain a permanent fixture, although by spring 1976 he had not yet been "officially" named as member of Stones.

Even though much-delayed early 1976 album **Black And Blue** met critical disapproval, the 1975 U.S. tour with Ron Wood and Billy Preston guesting revealed that Stones retained all of old live magic. Neither had their charisma diffused with time.

Though his pouts and poses these days have tendency to lapse into self-parody, Jagger retains full measure of agility and stage guile. By adopting up-front sexuality of black artists and developing it to unprecedented levels, he had long since set pattern for a whole generation of white rock singers. Yet the true essence of the Stones probably resides more comfortably with Keith Richard, whose impassive stage presence belies a keen musical brain unsurpassed in the rock genre. While legend may want us to believe that Richard permanently exists in drug-damaged limbo, his contribution to this most quintessential of rock bands is both immense and enduring.

Apart from aforementioned "S.T.P.", a number of books are available on Stones, among them Anthony Scaduto's bile-filled biography of Mick Jagger (who remains one of most inscrutable major characters in rock). By far the most minutely detailed account of group's career is Roy Carr's "The Stones: An Illustrated Record", from which most of early material in this article has been gleaned.

It wasn't until **Their Satanic Majesties** (November 1967) that U.S. and U.K. albums coincided. Before then, though some titles were same, there were often track differences. Hence different lists for early material; also for widely-different compilation sets, best assembled of which is 1975 **Rolled Gold**. There are also numerous Stones' bootlegs on market: best of these being **Liver Than You'll Ever Be** from Oakland Coliseum.

Recordings:
U.K. Releases:
The Rolling Stones (Decca)
The Rolling Stones No. 2 (Decca)
Out Of Our Heads (Decca)
Aftermath (Decca)
Between The Buttons (Decca)
Compilations:
Big Hits (High Tide And Green Grass) (Decca)
Through The Past Darkly

(Big Hits Vol. II) (Decca)
Stone Age (Decca)
Gimme Shelter (Decca)
Milestones (Decca)
Metamorphosis (Decca)
Made In The Shade (Rolling Stones Recs.)
Rolled Gold (Decca)
U.S. Releases:
The Rolling Stones – England's Newest Hit Makers (London)
12 x 5 (London)
The Rolling Stones, Now! (London)
Out Of Our Heads (London)
December's Children (London)
Aftermath (London)
Got Live If You Want It (London)
Between The Buttons (London)
Compilations:
Big Hits (High Tide And Green Grass) (London)
Flowers (London)
Through The Past Darkly (London)
Hot Rocks: 1964-1971 (London)
More Hot Rocks (Big Hits & Fazed Cookies) (London)
Metamorphosis (London)
Made In The Shade (Rolling Stones Recs)
Rolled Gold (London)
U.S. and U.K. releases post-1967:
Their Satanic Majesties Request (London/Decca)
Beggar's Banquet (London/Decca)
Let It Bleed (London/Decca)
Get Yer Ya-Ya's Out (London/Decca)
Sticky Fingers (Rolling Stones Recs)
Exile On Main Street (Rolling Stones Recs)
Goat's Head Soup (Rolling Stones Recs)
It's Only Rock 'n' Roll (Rolling Stones Recs)
Black And Blue (Rolling Stones Recs)
Mick Jagger (plus various):
Performance (Soundtrack) (Warner Bros)
Jagger, Wyman, Watts, Nicky Hopkins, Ry Cooder:
Jamming With Edward (Rolling Stones Recs)
Bill Wyman:
Monkey Grip (Rolling Stones Recs)
Stone Alone (Rolling Stones Recs)

Ronettes
♦ Phil Spector

Mick Ronson

From Hull, northern England, Ronson came to attention as guitarist in David Bowie's Spiders From Mars; an association resulting from Ronson's work with Michael Chapman (♦) and Bowie producer Gus Dudgeon. When Bowie announced his "retirement" from performing summer 1973, Ronson was already nurturing ambitions towards solo career – encouraged by sizeable personal following among Bowie aficionados, and by his (and Bowie's) manager Tony DeFries.

Unfortunately it went to their heads, and when Ronson solo was launched early 1974 the manufactured blaze of publicity set heights he could not hope to attain. His debut album, **Slaughter On Tenth Avenue**, and spring tour found him drowning in Bowie's slipstream, a good guitarist but patently inadequate as a singer and writer. The tour was an embarrassment long before it finished, so much so that everybody (including Ronson) appeared to believe the best solution was pretend it never happened.

Suitably chastened, Ronson dropped out of sight for a while, reappearing amidst much ballyhoo as a member of Mott The Hoople. However, this was a short-lived traumatic union that resulted in Ronson and Mott singer Ian Hunter leaving band to work together.

Ronson released second solo album, **Play Don't Worry**, January 1975, and subsequently toured with Hunter-Ronson Band, though that partnership was sundered – seemingly irrevocably – towards end of summer.

The guitarist next sprang surprise by turning up late 1975 as member of Bob Dylan's Rolling Thunder entourage, since when he has hung-out with other Dylan associates, producing Roger McGuinn's excellent **Cardiff Rose**. No longer contracted to RCA, future recording plans uncertain. (♦ David Bowie, Mott The Hoople, Ian Hunter, Roger McGuinn).

Recordings:
Slaughter On Tenth Avenue (RCA)
Play Don't Worry (RCA)

Linda Ronstadt

Born Jul 15, 1946 in Tucson, Arizona, Ronstadt had a musical upbringing, since her father was a guitar player. Determined to make a living as a singer, she left Tucson in 1964 and headed to Los Angeles, where she teamed up with an old friend, Bob Kimmel, and a Los Angeles musician Ken Edwards to form the Stone Poneys.

They received a contract from Capitol Records 1966, and made two albums in 1967, **Stone Poneys** and **Evergreen**, both full of fairly bland material and undistinguished three part harmonies; Capitol decided to project Linda more, and she was featured more prominently on **Stoney End**, an album which provided the hit single, Mike Nesmith's **Different Drum**.

Don't Cry Now. Courtesy Elektra Asylum Records.

In the wake of this, admittedly moderate, success, she broke with the other two to go solo (though Edwards re-joined her, and is now a member of her backing band); she made two more albums, **Hand Sown, Home Grown** and **Silk Purse**, the latter of which was produced by Elliot Mazer, and made with Nashville musicians. Linda has since been quoted as saying she hates the album. Certainly, though it featured mainly country material, it was hard to tell if she really knew in which direction she was headed.

In 1971, however, she hired Glenn Frey, Don Henley and Randy Meisner for her backing band. Though within six months, they'd split to form The Eagles (♦) with Bernie Leadon, nevertheless, The Eagles connection was to prove useful, and all four of them play on **Linda Ronstadt**, which was her most positive album to date.

After that she became part of David Geffen's stable of West Coast country-rock artists, and her debut Asylum album, **Don't Cry Now**, was produced by Peter Asher (♦). Linda had been progressively inching forward, but her career finally accelerated with the release of this album, which moved up U.S. album charts late 1973.

By 1974 her career had upturned dramatically, and **Heart Like A Wheel** (an album she owed to Capitol) provided three gold singles, including the No. 1 records **You're No Good** and **When Will I Be Loved?**; by the end of the year, she was the top-selling female artist in America, and her 1975 release, **Prisoner In Disguise**, confirmed her elevated status. She is also regularly in demand as a backing vocalist, and has appeared on literally scores of records.

Nevertheless, though she has toned down the overt sexuality which characterised her stage performances at beginning of '70s, it's still difficult to think of her as more than just a pretty face. While she hardly qualifies as an interpretative singer, her albums sell because of Asher's immaculate production work, the calibre of the supporting musicians and the excellent material – and because of astute marketing by Asylum.

Recordings:
Stone Poneys (Capitol/—)
Evergreen (Capitol/—)
Stoney End (Capitol/—)
Hand Sown, Home Grown (Capitol)
Silk Purse (Capitol)
Linda Ronstadt (Capitol)
Don't Cry Now (Asylum)
Heart Like A Wheel (Capitol)
Prisoner In Disguise (Asylum)
Compilation:
Different Drum (—/Capitol)

Tim Rose

Born September 1940, Rose was educated in Washington and won music awards at high school. A one-time student priest and navigator for Strategic High Command, he was one of the crop of quasi-folksingers who emerged in latter half of '60s in wake of Bob Dylan.

Before signing with Columbia Records he had been a member of the formative but financially unsuccessful Big Three with Cass Elliott; he possessed a gritty voice, ideally suited to bluesy themes, and was best known for his famous composition, **Morning Dew**, which attracted a host of cover versions.

Morning Dew was a track from **Tim Rose**, his debut album which featured black session-drummer Bernard "Pretty" Purdie, Cream producer Felix Pappalardi on bass, and guitarists Jay Berliner and Hugh McCracken in a small combo. The album also yielded an arrangement of the traditional song **Hey Joe** which was later picked up by Jimi Hendrix.

After making **Through Rose Coloured Glasses** in 1969, he left Columbia and signed with Playboy Records in 1971, for whom he made another album called **Tim Rose**, which wasn't issued in Britain until 1974.

His output in the '70s has been virtually negligible, although he has now signed for Atlantic and released one album for them, **The Musician**. He has also settled in Britain, and for a time teamed up with fellow U.S. expatriate Tim Hardin (♦), in a duo playing dates in selected London clubs, though after a few shambolic performances they dissolved the partnership.

Recordings:
Tim Rose (Columbia/CBS)
Through Rose Coloured Glasses (Columbia/CBS)
Tim Rose (Playboy/Dawn)
The Musician (—/Atlantic)

Diana Ross
♦ Tamla Motown

Roxy Music

Bryan Ferry vocals, keyboards
Andy Mackay sax, oboe
Eddie Jobson keyboards
Paul Thompson drums
Phil Manzanera guitars

Roxy Music was formed by former miner's son and fine-arts graduate Bryan Ferry and bass guitarist Graham Simpson in November 1970, Andy Mackay and Brian Eno joining in early 1971 and original drummer, Dexter Lloyd, in summer of that year. David O'List was lead guitarist for five months at their inception before being replaced by Phil Manzanera. Lloyd left prior to first album, his place being taken by Paul Thompson, who soon won a reputation for being among the genre's premier drummers.

None of the band had previously figured in name outfits. Ferry had sung with local, County Durham, groups, Banshees and Gas Board; Mackay had studied avant-garde music in England and electronic pioneers Morton Feldman and John Cage in Italy; Thompson had played with Smokestack while Manzanera had been part of the experimental Quiet Sun.

Perhaps Ferry's chief claim to fame at the time was to have failed an audition for King Crimson (♦), though Robert Fripp thought he had "potential" in other areas.

Even so, Roxy Music seemed destined for success after hugely favourable critical response to their early live performances (they supported David Bowie at a Christmas London Rainbow concert) and excellent coverage on British TV and radio. Their debut album, **Roxy Music** (1972), produced by erstwhile King Crimson lyricist Peter Sinfield hit top of U.K. national charts. With their amalgam of high art-school camp, an image that veered from mannered rock 'n' roll doowop to Noel Coward and Cole Porter-type crooning and a dress flair that matched their literate, musical eccentricity, they soon secured a firm following which has increased rapidly in England but less so in America.

A classic single, **Virginia Plain**, met with similar success; at that time Ferry's plan was never to release singles already available on albums, though after **Pyjamarama** this idea was forgotten.

Roxy Music.
Courtesy E.G. Records Ltd.

The second album, **For Your Pleasure** (1973), produced by Chris Thomas, who'd previously worked with Procol Harum, displayed more of their idiosyncracies, noticeably the avant-garde sounds of Terry Riley and John Cage that so influenced Eno's synthesiser contributions, and Mackay's sax and oboe in a cleaner setting. It also marked the departure of bassist Rik Kenton, replaced by John Porter, who had himself replaced Simpson after he suffered a nervous breakdown.

After a concert in Ferry's native Newcastle, the personality clashes that persisted between himself and Brian Eno as to the group's future direction came to a head with Eno leaving the band to pursue a solo career and fulfil his particular ambitions elsewhere (♦ Eno).

On **Stranded** (1973), 18-year old Eddie Jobson, formerly of Curved Air, joined band as violinist/keyboards player, immediately striking a melodic rapport with Mackay's reeds work though not filling the visual gap undoubtedly left by Eno.

Ex Big Three and Quatermass bassist, John Gustafson, succeeded Porter and has played on every album to date, but Roxy's policy of using different tour bass men persisted and little effort was ever made to find a regular performer.

Stranded revealed a new democracy within the group, Manzanera and Mackay now assisting with some lyrics, though Ferry's prominently urbane, English style still dominated their writing approach.

Nineteen-seventy-three also saw the development of Ferry's solo career outside the band with **These Foolish Things**, and constant press rumours of a group split that never materialised. Ferry's debut consisted of interpretations of personally admired numbers, including a hit single, Dylan's **A Hard Rain's Gonna Fall**. His second solo work, **Another Time Another Place** (1974), met with mixed response though Ferry had no trouble filling large venues like the prestigious Royal Albert Hall accompanied by a hand-picked band (including all of Roxy save Mackay), strings and a brass section.

Roxy's fourth album, **Country Life** (1974), showed band marking time neither progressing particularly nor falling behind their previous exacting standards.

Manzanera was quoted afterwards as not being entirely satisfied with the disc and, during a period of disguised friction between himself and Ferry, both he and Mackay worked on solo efforts. Mackay's **In Search Of Eddie Riff** (1974) was a quirky album and generally considered to be of dubious merit, the influences, ranging from King Curtis to Wagner, prevented it satisfying as an entity. Mackay later wrote music for ITV series "Rock Follies", an album of his score being released 1976 on Island. In contrast Manzanera's **Diamond Head** (1975) was an excellent combination of original material from Latin-American styles (Manzanera – real name Philip Targett-Adams – had been at school in Peru and Venezuela before coming to London) to hard rock with subtle use of electronics, a display of his varied guitar talents and a more relaxed atmosphere to that created by Roxy themselves.

Manzanera reformed Quiet Sun for the one-off **Mainstream** album with founder members Dave Jarrett, Bill McCormick and Charles Hayward, the resulting record being a stark, black-and-white representation of Manzanera's initial influences, including echoes of Terry Riley, Velvet Underground, Soft Machine.

It was not until **Siren** (1975) that Roxy eventually found the acclaim they'd been hoping for in States, and that after several strenuous tours that often threatened to break the band's morale. A hit single, **Love Is The Drug**, on both sides of the Atlantic, won them the right to play the full-size American venues they expected at home as a recent addition to the rock hierarchy.

Even so, many felt **Siren** to be their least satisfying record to date; the previous changes of style, experimentations in pastiche and an eclecticism made original were now replaced by something less imaginative if more widely commercial.

Siren.
Courtesy E.G. Records Ltd.

Rumours of impending splits, and inter-group warfare, continued, and in summer 1976 Ferry announced period of "trial separation", each member working on individual projects for unspecified time. This appeared to signal end.

For early albums, Roxy Music warranted acclaim as one of rock's most literate, provocative and entertaining bands. Regrettably, in later years initial spontaneous excitement seemed to have been usurped by ice-cold professionalism – this deterioration exacerbated by personality clashes.

Recordings:
Roxy Music (Reprise/Island)
For Your Pleasure (Warner Bros/Island)
Stranded (Atco/Island)
Country Life (Atco/Island)
Siren (Atco/Island)
Viva Roxy Music (Atco/Island)
Bryan Ferry:
These Foolish Things (Atlantic/Island)
Another Time, Another Place (Atlantic/Island)
Phil Manzanera:
Diamond Head (Atco/Island)
Quiet Sun: Mainstream (Antilles/Island)
Andy Mackay:
In Search Of Eddie Riff (—/Island)

Rufus

Chaka Khan vocals
Tony Maiden guitar
Bobby Watson bass
Kevin Murphy keyboards
Andre Fischer drums

Rufus were founded in Chicago 1972, original members of band being Murphy (who had previously played in the American Breed), Chaka Khan and Fischer. When the three of them moved to Los Angeles they acquired Maiden and Watson, both of whom had been featured on Billy Preston's **The Kids And Me.**

After a debut album that made little impact, they were recording their follow-up at Los Angeles Record Plant, when Stevie Wonder, impressed with Chaka's voice, checked out the session. He ended up giving the band some material, including **Tell Me Something Good,** which went gold when issued as a single in 1974.

The band followed it with one of Chaka's own compositions, **You've Got The Love,** and almost overnight the group were big business, with the album **Rags To Rufus,** which had been recorded when Chaka was eight months pregnant, going gold. Wonder then offered the band the support spot on his tour, and they later toured with Rolling Stones and Elton John. Nineteen-seventy-four was a very successful year – their next album, **Rufusised,** which was recorded in haste, with the record company needing fresh product urgently, was shipped gold.

Rufus play an assortment of styles, ranging from jazzy funk instrumentals to straight disco raves to mellow ballads. Possibly because the band is multi-racial – Murphy is no mere token honky – they are developing a hybrid soul-rock form which has an across-the-board appeal.

Chaka Khan – of the much-photographed bare midriff – is a forceful lead singer, and the band

acknowledged her role in their success by amending group name to Rufus Featuring Chaka Khan, which was also the title of the band's fourth album, released in 1975.

In early 1975, they made a brief tour of Britain, though they have yet to emulate their American success in Europe.

Recordings:
Rufus (ABC)
Rags To Rufus (ABC)
Rufusised (ABC)
Rufus Featuring Chaka Khan (ABC)

Todd Rundgren (And Utopia)

Todd Rundgren guitar, vocals
John Siegler bass, vocals
Roger Powell Moog, trumpet vocals
Ralph Shuckett keyboards, vocals
Moogy Klingman keyboards, vocals
John Wilcox drums

Enigmatic whizz-kid, virtuoso guitarist and studio master Todd Rundgren was born in Philadelphia suburb of Upper Darby. He began his band life in a local rock 'n' roll outfit, Woody's Truckstop, before forming English Mod-influenced flash-rock outfit The Nazz in 1968. The Nazz were unusual in Philadelphia for providing a viable alternative to the San Francisco sound dominating American music at time, as they attempted to personify everything "swinging London", from their clothes to their Beatle-influenced material. With Rundgren on guitar were Robert "Stewkey" Antoni (kybds, vcls), Carson van Osten (bs) and Thom Mooney (drms).

Nazz were characterised by recording and playing sophistication that heralded the end of the '60s era and a newer, more professional sound. Probably too advanced for their period they succeeded with two minor U.S. hit singles, though only **Hello It's Me** (Boston's most requested, four times re-released AM song) made it to the bottom rungs of national charts.

Three Nazz albums were issued, all of which are extremely rare collectors' items. The first **Nazz** (1968) was a moderate-seller but **Nazz Nazz** (1969) and **Nazz III** (1969) sank without trace; none were released in Britain, where, as in America, Rundgren has always been a highly regarded cult underground figure.

With end of Nazz, Rundgren concentrated on playing the studio as much as his instruments, performing and producing single-handed the album bearing his then-nickname **Runt** which included a minor hit **We Gotta Get You A Woman.** Interest in his precocious ability, allied to the continued faith in Rundgren's undoubtedly varied talents placed in him by head of Bearsville, Albert Grossman (♦), led to Rundgren becoming one of States' most sought-after producers, engineers, session-men and songwriters.

Among the huge number of acts that Rundgren has worked with in studio are The Band, Jesse Winchester, Butterfield Blues Band,

New York Dolls, Fanny, Grand Funk, Halfnelson (later Sparks), Janis Joplin, Badfinger, Hello People and James Cotton.

Meanwhile his own solo career blossomed with **Ballad Of Todd Rundgren** (1971) assisted by the sons of New York society figure, Soupy Sales, Hunt (bs) and Tony Sales (drms). Always attempting to push the barriers of rock to new heights Rundgren made an initial attempt to launch his Utopia Road Show with a lighting system and effects that could match visually his futuristic music.

The plan failed for lack of finances but was later revived, in modified format, when his radical departures into the stranger echelons of intensely complex heavy-metal space rock met with an appreciative and larger audience.

A double, **Something/Anything** (1972), contained Rundgren's most diverse styles to date; he had seemingly mastered every angle from soul to Beach Boys to raw daring of a Hendrix. Many of songs represent his finest hour in eyes of fanatical following that began to worship Rundgren as a rock 'n' roll saviour. Certainly, there is no doubting the appeal of numbers like **I Saw The Light, It Wouldn't Have Made Any Difference** or **Couldn't I Just Tell You?**

A Wizard, A True Star (1973) continued in this vein, juxtaposing Rundgren's unique vision with carefully chosen soul and Tamla ballads. As examples of a solo artist at the peak of his creativity, both these albums remain fresh, essential to any record collection.

Todd.
Courtesy Warner Bros. Records.

Rundgren's inexhaustible capacity for hard work and an output unequalled for proliferation led to another double in 1974, called simply **Todd,** which revealed once more that the multi-coloured hair and customised Putney synthesiser kid was capable of astounding, confounding, amusing and confusing both fans and critics alike.

Many found the album's louder moments, and sheer volume of material, too much of a departure from the previous melodic flair and short, constructed songs, but Rundgren, as ever, was keeping several steps ahead of interested listeners and concentrating almost solely on engineering technique plus a genius for electric guitar eclecticism that fused Brian Wilson with John McLaughlin and occasionally out-did allcomers at their own game.

Utopia, the name of his new band and performing concept, featured most of the above musicians with Kevin Ellman on per-

cussion and M. Frog Labat on synthesisers. The result, half-live, half-studio, released in 1974, angered many who felt Rundgren had over-reached himself.

A cosmically supposed enlightenment, lyrical obscurity and musical bombast made this his least accessible work to date but live audiences were suddenly flocking to witness America's most zany rock 'n' roll personality developing his own acidic visions rather late in the day. Rundgren himself became something of a recluse, forgoing interviews and repudiating allegations that he'd become a junkie.

Initiation (1975), despite the pretentious flirtations with half-baked versions of Zen Buddhism and Alice A. Bailey's "A Treatise On Cosmic Fire" that influenced his lyrics and Eastern mystic scores, contained a perceptible undercurrent of his former melodic invention while one could ascertain traces of self-parody and wry humorous debunking of what Rundgren appeared to be holding up as on the other hand valid. At a shade over one hour **Initiation** is also amongst the longest albums ever made, evidence of his engineering abilities, if not his sense of self-control.

Another Live (1975) is a far more listenable reflection of his dynamic stage abilities, including a nod to his roots in a version of The Move's **Do Ya?**, and the song that has come to represent Rundgren's personal philosophy, both for himself and the role of the audience in **Just One Victory.**

The 1976 album, **Faithful,** is an aptly-named combination of original material and covers of 1966 songs – a year Rundgren holds as the definitive period of rock innovation – that he claims as leading influences on his own inimitable style. Included are note-for-note re-makes of **Good Vibrations,** Hendrix's **If Six Were Nine** and **Strawberry Fields Forever.** The result is an affectionate if rather pointless exercise but Rundgren's enthusiasm, and an innate talent that borders on actual genius, prove he will always be a valid, interesting if not entirely satisfying character in the forefront of radically unusual rock.

Recordings:
Nazz (Screen Gems Columbia/—)
Nazz Nazz (Screen Gems Columbia/—)
Nazz III (Screen Gems Columbia/—)
Runt (Bearsville)
Runt, The Ballad Of Todd Rundgren (Bearsville)
Something/Anything (Bearsville)
A Wizard A True Star (Bearsville)
Todd (Bearsville)
Utopia (Bearsville)
Initiation (Bearsville)
Another Live (Bearsville)
Faithful (Bearsville)

Tom Rush

Tom Rush (b. Portsmouth, New Hampshire, Feb 8, 1941) was a product of the great American folk revival, the same as Dylan, Joan Baez, Phil Ochs, Tom Paxton, Fred Neil, etc.

He studied at Harvard, became one of the coterie of dedicated folk artists working in Boston area, and signed to Elektra Records while still a student, and long before that label had moved from folk into rock.

Unlike most of his contemporaries, he cast his musical horizons far and wide from beginning, and was unafraid to use electric instrumentation or mix acoustic numbers with Bo Diddley and Buddy Holly, and self-composed love ballads with traditional folk and blues material – as he did on **Take A Little Walk With Me;** though his earliest offerings are to be found on two albums on Prestige, recorded 1963 and 1964.

He was, in fact, one of few authentic-sounding white interpreters of blues material, as the frighteningly intense **Galveston Flood** on **Take A Little Walk With Me** showed. His bottle-neck and twelve-string guitar work attained a very high standard.

With **The Circle Game,** Rush became one of the first Elektra artists to move out of the folk scene altogether (another was Judy Collins ♦), using lavish string arrangements to underline poetic strength of thoughtful and reflective lyrics. Bringing together material by Joni Mitchell, Jackson Browne and James Taylor (all hardly known at the time), **The Circle Game** was one of the earliest concept albums. It also contained the original version of his most well-known composition, **No Regrets.**

After four albums for Elektra, Rush moved to Columbia in 1970, and again his debut for that label showed that he spanned the whole vista of American music. Though he was by now becoming more and more esoteric listening, **Merrimack County** was a strong album; it chronicled his love for the simple, rural life, though in unabashed, unsentimental and uncliched terms – the simplicity of the music evoking the simplicity of the daily round.

TOM RUSH WRONG END OF THE RAINBOW

Wrong End Of The Rainbow. Courtesy CBS Records.

Ladies Love Outlaws was comparatively disappointing, though it did contain a fresh arrangement of **No Regrets,** which was used by the Walker Brothers as the basis of their comeback hit single in Britain 1976.

Rush remains one of the most idiosyncratic of contemporary performers. He is also one of the most reclusive, and hardly one of the most prolific – only four albums in six years since he signed with Columbia.

Rush has so far been with three different companies, and has called his debut album with each one **Tom Rush;** he is now without a recording deal, having been dropped by Columbia in summer 1975; so to fit in with established

practice, his next album will also have to be titled **Tom Rush.**

Recordings:
Tom Rush (Prestige/Xtra)
Blues/Songs/Ballads (Prestige/Xtra)
Tom Rush (Elektra)
Take A Little Walk With Me (Elektra)
The Circle Game (Elektra)
Tom Rush (Columbia/CBS)
Wrong End Of The Rainbow (Columbia/CBS)
Merrimack County (Columbia/CBS)
Ladies Love Outlaws (Columbia/CBS)
Compilation:
Classic Rush (Elektra)

Ken Russell

Born in 1927, Russell established himself as a television director of great original vision and flair before entering the film industry and charting his own increasingly idiosyncratic style, from "Women In Love" through to "The Devils".

When he came to direct Pete Townshend's rock opera, "Tommy", in 1974, his flamboyance and taste for excess proved invaluable; "Tommy" was filmed as an opera, with no dialogue, and the music – which was heard in quintrophonic, itself a technical breakthrough – was handsomely matched to the photography. Though the net result was a form of audio-visual assault and battery, "Tommy" nevertheless has some claim to being the first rock movie (even including "Woodstock") since it was the first time that the cinema had grappled with all the audaciousness and extravagance of rock music on its own terms.

After this, Russell declared that rock music in general and Pete Townshend in particular were going to save the world, and then went on to make "Lizstomania", once again with Roger Daltrey, who'd played Tommy in "Tommy", in the leading role (♦"Tommy").

Leon Russell

One of the first of the super-sessionmen, Russell played with a whole host of artists from Jerry Lee Lewis through to The Crystals, Herb Alpert, The Byrds, Delaney & Bonnie and Rolling Stones.

A multi-instrumentalist, he was born in Lawton, Oklahoma, Apr 2, 1941 and grew up in Tulsa. He studied classical piano from age of three for 10 years, but then grew tired of the disciplines of formal music.

At 14 he learned to play trumpet and put together his own band; he lied about his age so that he could work in a Tulsa night-club, where he played with Ronnie Hawkins (♦) and the Hawks (now The Band). Later, Jerry Lee Lewis took Russell's band on the road with him.

In 1958 he moved to Los Angeles, and began to hustle gigs as a sideman on recording sessions – something his instrumental versatility enabled him to do with relative ease. He met James Burton (then with Rick Nelson ♦), who taught him guitar, and worked in studio with Dorsey Burnette, Glen Campbell and others. He worked on nearly all the Phil

Above: The Mad Dogs ensemble, with Cocker and Russell.

Spector (♦) hit productions – from The Crystals' **He's A Rebel** to the Righteous Brothers' **You've Lost That Lovin' Feelin',** as well as on isolated hits like The Byrds' **Mr Tambourine Man,** Herb Alpert's **A Taste Of Honey** and Bob Lind's **Elusive Butterfly.**

He spent some time as an executive with a small record company, Viva, and tried in vain to interest people in Delaney & Bonnie (♦), with whom he was very friendly. From 1967 he quit the business for two years in order to build his own sophisticated home studio, though he occasionally appeared with Delaney & Bonnie on the TV show "Shindig", and sometimes played sessions.

In 1968 he and Marc Benno were signed by Mercury for the Smash label, and made the **Asylum Choir** album, which sold disappointingly.

Meanwhile, he became one of the Friends of Delaney & Bonnie when they got their show on the road, while Joe Cocker cut Russell's composition **Delta Lady** – written for Rita Coolidge – at his (Russell's) studio; Booker T. (Rita's brother-in-law) also cut part of his solo album there.

Russell teamed with English producer Denny Cordell to form Shelter Records – which shortly signed the wonderfully down-home J. J. Cale – and then went to London together where, with engineer Glyn Johns, they laid down the tracks for Russell's debut solo album, **Leon Russell.**

At the beginning of 1970, Russell put together the Mad Dogs and Englishmen all-star entourage to back Joe Cocker (♦) on his mammoth American tour; though as the film of the tour illustrates, the whole enterprise served to elevate Russell into the star attraction at the expense of Cocker.

If Russell was by now considered a man of some stature in the rock business, this reputation was fortified when he was invited to work with and produce Bob Dylan, although the resulting tracks (of which two, **Watching The River Flow** and **When I Paint My Masterpiece** appear on **More Bob Dylan Greatest Hits)** were recorded when Dylan seemed to be creatively at a low ebb, and Russell did not re-acquaint him with his muse.

Russell, in any case, was developing his own solo career. Throughout 1972–73, he was enormously popular in the U.S. He developed a strong on-stage personality with his long, wispy hair and beard, and familiar stovepipe hat; he was one of the artists featured at the Concert For Bangla Desh. His own albums usually employed super-star line-ups, and were of variable quality, though after **Carney,** a gold album and a triple live affair, which had been recorded at the Ontario Race Track, and which immediately went gold, Russell's standing as a solo artist declined.

A second Asylum Choir album was recorded in 1969 with Benno, but Mercury were reluctant to release it, so Russell bought the tapes and released it on his Shelter label in 1971.

Leon Russell severed his associations with Shelter Records in 1976, and initiated a new label, Paradise Records, with his **Wedding Album.** The album celebrated his marriage to Mary McCreery, who had released one solo album on Shelter in 1973, **Butterflies In Heaven,** and had composed **Singin' The Blues,** a track on Eric Clapton's **There's One In Every Crowd.**

Recordings:
Leon Russell (Shelter)
Leon Russell And The Shelter People (Shelter)
Carney (Shelter)
Live (Shelter)
Hank Wilson's Back (Shelter)
Stop All That Jazz (Shelter)
Will O' The Wisp (Shelter)
Wedding Album (Paradise)
With Marc Benno:
Asylum Choir (Smash/Mercury)
Asylum Choir II (Shelter)

Sadistic Mika Band

Kazuhiko Katoh guitar, vocals
Mika Katoh vocals
Rei Ohara bass, vocals
Yukihiro Takahashi drums
Mayayoshi Takanaka guitar
Hiroshi Imai keyboards, sax

Led by Kazuhiko and his stunning wife Mika, Japan's top rock export. Kazuhiko Katoh was founder, a former university graduate who enjoyed considerable home-based success with his group

Folk Crusaders from 1966–70.

Katoh soloed as acoustic performer for two years until formation of Mika Band 1972. Wife Mika, Ohara, and Takahashi were former graphic-design students. Takanaka, half-Japanese half-Chinese, was previously in group Flied Egg (sic), while Imai didn't join band until 1975 and second album.

First eponymous album was released in Japan 1973 and to Western ears was arrestingly frenetic concoction of Western rock and incomprehensible, gabbled Japanese lyrics. Its somewhat "tinny" production only added to music's idiosyncratic charm.

Unfortunately this was a quality (sic) lost when, for second album **Black Ship** (1975), band employed services of British producer Chris Thomas, who had worked extensively for Roxy Music. This was far more Westernised set, though lyrics still made no concession to foreign ears, and despite aforementioned misgivings earned the group widespread critical favour. However, subsequent British tour supporting Roxy Music proved somewhat bewildering experience for U.K. fans. Thus far, outside Japan, Mika Band remain unproven commodity.

Hot! Menu!
Courtesy EMI Harvest.

In addition to pivotal roles in band, Kazuhiko and Mika Katoh have worked as DJs with own separate shows on Japanese radio. Kazuhiko is also prolific hit-writer for other home-based acts.

Recordings:
Sadistic Mika Band (Harvest)
Black Ship (Harvest)
Hot! Menu! (Harvest)

Doug Sahm

Sahm, born Nov 6, 1941, is a native Texan who brought a realistic touch of blues and country to San Francisco during mid-'60s.

He had originally formed a country-blues band called The Knights in 1955, but when he moved to 'Frisco formed Sir Douglas Quintet, who had a simple but classically memorable hit single in 1965, **She's About A Mover**. After an album called **Honkey Blues**, issued in 1968 and credited, somewhat strangely to the Sir Douglas Quintet + 2, they had another success in 1969 with **Mendocino**; the quartet had pioneered a unique sound in which Sahm's thick-toned voice was backed by simple chopping guitar chords and garage band organ from Augie Meyer.

After commercially unsuccessful albums in the following years, Sahm signed to Atlantic, for whom he made **Doug Sahm And Band** in 1973. Since the sidemen included Bob Dylan, Dr John and David Bromberg, and the album was produced by Jerry Wexler, Arif Mardin and Sahm himself it attracted attention, but after a second Atlantic album **Texas Tornado** – which again featured the omnipresent Dr John – he moved to Warner Bros and recorded **Groover's Paradise** (1974) with a new backing band that included the rhythm section from Creedence Clearwater Revival (◆), Stu Cook and Doug Clifford (who in 1976 moved on to act in the same capacity for Don Harrison).

Sahm's personal dilemma was probably summed up by the song **Lawd I'm Just A Country Boy In This Great Big Freaky City**, and when the "cosmic cowboy" scene began in Austin he went back there to settle. His albums have always been good-time and varied, and on any one of them it's possible to find convincing blues, rock, country, or even Mexican music; he actually branded the **Groover's Paradise** album as The Tex-Mex Trip.

Sahm has also made it his business to encourage local talent, and Chicano country star Freddie Fender dedicated a track from his first album to him.

Mendocino was reissued in the U.K. in 1975 on Charlie Gillett's Oval label.

Recordings:
Sir Douglas Quintet + 2:
Honkey Blues (Smash/—)
Sir Douglas Quintet:
Mendocino (Smash/Mercury)
Together After Five (Smash/Mercury)
1 + 1 + 1 = 4 (Philips/—)
The Return Of Doug Saldana (Philips/—)
Compilation:
The Best Of The Sir Douglas Quintet (Tribe/—)
Doug Sahm And Band:
Doug Sahm And Band (Atlantic)
Sir Douglas Band:
Texas Tornado (Atlantic)
Doug Sahm:
Groover's Paradise (Warner Bros)

Sailor

Georg Kajanus guitar, vocals
Henry Marsh nickelodeon, piano, vocals
Phil Pickett nickelodeon, bass, vocals
Grant Serpel drums

Somewhat self-consciously attired in white sailor-suits, emerged on U.K. rock scene 1974 sounding like some sort of European cousin twice removed of Roxy Music. Previously unknown, most of material and idiosyncratic style derive from mannered singer and 12-string guitarist Kajanus, who claims Russo-Nordic origins. Highly eclectic, another major contribution to bizarre musical textures is group's custom-built "nickelodeon", a double-sided keyboards box of tricks played by Marsh and Pickett simultaneously.

First single **Traffic Jam** (1974) flopped on release in U.K., but gradually picked up sufficient interest in European market to make No. 1 in Holland and do almost equally as well in Belgium. United Kingdom recognition, after mostly unfavourable early press, helped by support roles on Cockney Rebel and Kiki Dee tours 1975, subsequent to which they achieved British singles breakthrough with the Roxy-esque **Glass Of Champagne**. Followed-up 1976 with **Girls Girls Girls** in Top 10.

American producers Rupert Holmes (◆) and Jeffrey Lesser flown into London for recording of second album, **Trouble** (1976).

Recordings:
Sailor (Epic)
Trouble (Epic)

Buffy Sainte-Marie

Born in Maine, Feb 20, 1941 of Cree Indian descent, Buffy Sainte-Marie first came to prominence in mid-'60s; she obtained a contract from Vanguard Records after producer Maynard Soloman had seen her performing in a Boston club. Her first album contained **Universal Soldier**, a song that became a classic protest song, though it only came to public notice through cover versions by Donovan and Glen Campbell.

Her early recordings blended traditional songs with original compositions by her and her friends – she has a very distinctive style of singing which nevertheless allows her to give convincing renditions of songs from many different cultures.

She initially worked solo in concert, but as her career progressed, recorded with rock bands, orchestras, electronics and country artists, thus creating a vast and challenging range of material, admittedly, not all of it successful. Her first major departure from the folk-styled settings of her early albums was with **I'm Gonna Be A Country Girl Again** (1968), an all-country album recorded in Nashville, the title track of which has resolutely refused to become a hit single in Britain or America despite the fact that it's been released several times and is a song of considerable merit.

Illuminations (1970) was even more adventurous in that it featured the work of electronics expert Michael Czakhowski, and also contributions from a rock-band led by guitarist Bob Bozina.

For **She Used To Wanna Be A Ballerina** (1971) she acquired the services of Neil Young, Crazy Horse and Ry Cooder, and the album provided her with her biggest hit single to date – **Soldier Blue**, the title song from the successful movie about the massacre of Indians in the last century.

Besides **Universal Soldier**, her greatest success as a composer came when Elvis Presley recorded **Until It's Time For You To Go** which reached No. 5 in the U.K. and No. 40 in U.S. 1972.

Her compositions are emotional, sensual, and much subtler than they at first appear; like most of the other folksingers of her generation, she holds fierce Left-wing views, particularly concerning the plight of the American Indian. Over 12 years she has built up an impressive song-cycle

of Indian consciousness material, much of which was collected together on the Vanguard compilation album, **Native North-American Child: An Odyssey**; on her 1976 **Sweet America** album, she actually infused Indian musical elements into her songs for the first time, though her record company insisted they be placed on Side 2 of the album because of their lack of commercial appeal.

I'm Gonna Be A Country Girl Again. Courtesy Pye Records.

With her old man, Sheldon Peters Wolfchild (who is also a member of the backing band she now uses) she has set up a project called Creative Native to help provide for the education and cultural enlightenment of American Indian children.

In 1973 she left Vanguard after almost a decade and signed with MCA, though after two largely unsuccessful albums for them, moved again to ABC. **Sweet America** is generally considered her strongest album in some time.

Recordings:
It's My Way (Vanguard)
Many A Mile (Vanguard)
Little Wheel Spin And Spin (Vanguard)
Fire And Fleet And Candlelight (Vanguard)
I'm Gonna Be A Country Girl Again (Vanguard)
Illuminations (Vanguard)
She Used To Wanna Be A Ballerina (Vanguard)
Moonshot (Vanguard)
Quiet Places (Vanguard)
Buffy (MCA)
Changing Woman (MCA)
Sweet America (ABC)
Compilations:
The Best Of Buffy Sainte-Marie (Vanguard)
The Best Of Buffy Sainte-Marie, Vol. II (Vanguard)
Native North-American Child: An Odyssey (Vanguard)

Santana

Carlos Santana guitar, vocals
David Brown bass
Ndugu Leon Chancler drums
Tom Coster keyboards
Francisco Aquabella percussion
Armando Peraza percussion
Greg Walker vocals

Born Autlan, Mexico, Jul 20, 1947, son of a Mariachi musician, Carlos Santana spent formative years working night-clubs of dubious repute in red-light area of Tijuana. His move to San Francisco coincided with Haight-Ashbury musical explosion.

Virtually in at beginning, he first attracted attention when he guested on **The Live Adventures Of**

Mike Bloomfield And Al Kooper album, meanwhile organising electric blues bands with which he gigged at local clubs, bars and dance-halls.

Attempting different approach to distinguish his music from similar SF bands, he added Mike Carrabello (congas) and Jose "Chepito" Areas – Central America's poll-winning percussionist – to produce commercial brand of Latin rock. With aforementioned personnel, plus David Brown (bs), Gregg Rolie (kybds, vcls) and Mike Shrieve (drms), recorded eponymous first album 1969 and garnered immediate public and critical acclaim. Their appearance in "Woodstock" movie, performing Soul Sacrifice, was one of most exciting segments of that documentary and established band on international basis, pushing debut album to platinum sales status.

On second album, Abraxas (1970), they elaborated original format with Oye Como Va, written by acknowledged King Of Latin Swing Tito Puente. Also added more authenticity by augmenting with a number of respected Latin artists. The result was another monster seller and a string of ecstatically-received sell-out U.S. concerts.

Santana 3 in 1972 introduced new members to band, Coke Escovedo and Carlos Santana's young guitar protégé Neil Schon, and appeared to bring band's format to logical conclusion.

Carlos Santana's "solo" outing, Carlos Santana & Buddy Miles Live (1971), was little more than casual jam which did nothing to enhance the guitarist's reputation – if anything it pin-pointed his limitations when working outside of own band.

Nevertheless, Santana subsequently disbanded his group and, guided by his friend Mahavishnu John McLaughlin (♦), embraced teachings of guru Sri Chinmoy, through which he assumed new name Devadip.

The 1972 set Caravanserai found Santana working with looser aggregation of musicians, the product being a heady fusion of Latin, jazz and rock devices. Schon and Rolie were on album but omitted from 1973 version of Santana band which comprised, apart from guitarist/leader, Doug Rauch (bs), Richard Kermode and Tom Coster (kybds), James Mingo Lewis and Armando Peraza (congas), plus originals Areas and Shrieve.

Years 1973–74 again found Santana working outside of group, first with aforementioned McLaughlin on jointly-credited Love, Devotion, Surrender and subsequently with another Chinmoy convert "Turiya" Alice Coltrane on Illuminations.

Again Santana band was re-shuffled extensively, producing new line-up of founder-member Brown (bs), plus Chancler, Coster, Walker, Peraza, from current personnel: 1975 found group touring U.S. co-billed with Eric Clapton and at relatively low ebb, Borboletta having failed to achieve sales of its predecessors.

However, 1976 Amigos set represented something of a return to past form and more earthy roots, and renaissance of interest followed. Columbia Records were reportedly so pleased with

new set they re-signed him to five-year, seven-album contract with the company's biggest-ever artist guarantee.

Now managed by American rock entrepreneur Bill Graham (♦), who promoted their early gigs and "talked" them on to Woodstock billing while they were still unknown.

Caravanserai.
Courtesy CBS Records.

Santana married wife Urmila in 1973, with whom he runs San Francisco health-food restaurant dedicated to the mission of Sri Chinmoy. Santana hasn't yet followed McLaughlin's example and dropped the guru in favour of old vices, but, under direction of Graham, he has latterly been self-consciously rediscovering less flighty areas of musical exploration.

At his best, distinctive characteristics of Santana's guitar improvisations have been their purity and sweetness of tone, plus his ability to sustain notes on feedback for any length of time.

Lotus (1975) is a lavishly-packaged three-album set recorded live in Japan; released in West after demand for Japanese import copies.

Recordings:
Santana (Columbia/CBS)
Abraxas (Columbia/CBS)
Santana 3 (Columbia/CBS)
Caravanserai (Columbia/CBS)
Welcome (Columbia/CBS)
Borboletta (Columbia/CBS)
Lotus (Columbia/CBS)
Amigos (Columbia/CBS)
Compilations:
Greatest Hits (Columbia/CBS)
Carlos Santana and Buddy Miles:
Carlos Santana and Buddy Miles Live (Columbia/CBS)
Carlos Santana and John McLaughlin:
Love, Devotion, Surrender (Columbia/CBS)
Carlos Santana and Alice Coltrane:
Illuminations (Columbia/CBS)

Sassafras

Dai Shell guitar
Terry Bennett vocals
Ralph Evans guitar, vocals
Ricky John bass, vocals
Robert Jones drums, vocals

Formed by Shell and Evans in native South Wales area 1972, though they subsequently split and re-formed in January 1973 for release of debut album. Above is original and current line-up, although both Ricky John and Robert Jones (ex Love Sculpture) have both left then re-joined group – replacing, respectively, interim members Steve Finn and

Chris Sharley. A hard gigging band, have yet to rise above club and college level popularity.

Recordings:
Expecting Company (Polydor)
Wheelin' 'n' Dealin' (Chrysalis)
Riding High (Chrysalis)

Savoy Brown

Kim Simmonds guitar
Paul Raymond keyboards, guitar, vocals
Ian Ellis bass, vocals
Tommy Farnell drums

Classic example of British band which achieved massive American following while remaining un-lauded at home, Savoy Brown has endured an endless succession of personnel changes during its traumatic life-span, with guitarist Simmonds the only constant factor.

They were formed 1966 as Savoy Brown Blues Band with earliest line-ups drawn from Simmonds (brother of band's manager Harry), Martin Stone (gtr), Ray Chappell (bs), Bob Hall (kybds), Bryce Portius (vcls) and Leo Mannings (drms). The group joined nascent British blues circuit alongside contemporaries Chicken Shack (♦), Fleetwood Mac (♦), and first album, in 1967, was strictly blues in form.

By second set, Getting To The Point (1968), Portius had been replaced by Chris Youlden, who shared most of writing credits with Simmonds, and personnel altered frequently.

Train To Nowhere, from 1969 Blue Matter album, was group's tour de force, filled out with brass. However, the British blues boom was winding down by this time and, with A Step Further (1969) and Raw Sienna (1970), the group edged sideways towards boogie-based rock though retaining blues undertones. At same time, Savoy Brown began to concentrate activities primarily on American market where constant touring soon brought them to headlining status.

Blue Matter.
Courtesy Decca Records.

However, virtually every tour brought yet another new line-up change. Chris Youlden left before 1970 Looking In set, which featured reduced personnel of Simmonds, Lonesome Dave (vcls, pno), Roger Earl (drms) and Tone Stevens (bs). But last three were shortly to break away to form Foghat (♦).

In 1971 Simmonds set about assembling new band with Dave Walker (vcls), and Paul Raymond (kybds), Andy Silvester (bs) and Dave Bidwell (drms) from various editions of then-defunct Chicken Shack (♦). Silvester was replaced

by Andy Pyle 1973.

Band continued to enjoy considerable reputation in America but Simmonds in particular began to lose interest and declared Savoy Brown defunct around Christmas 1973. Simmonds then began hanging out with fellow British bluesmen Stan Webb, former Chicken Shack guitarist/leader, and Miller Anderson, ex Keef Hartley Band, whose own Hemlock aggregation was having difficulty getting off ground.

In spring 1974, the three decided to pool their resources, using Eric Dillon (drms) and James Leverton (bs) from Hemlock. They retained name Savoy Brown (subtitled Boogie Brothers) due to its pulling power in U.S., where new outfit subsequently toured. It was a short-lived, confused affair, however, which found Miller Anderson leaving to re-join Keef Hartley (♦) and Stan Webb forming new band Broken Glass with Eric Dillon.

Simmonds once again re-grouped Savoy Brown, bringing back Paul Raymond and adding other members as above.

Recordings:
Shake Down (—/Decca)
Getting To The Point (Parrott/Decca)
Blue Matter (Parrott/Decca)
A Step Further (Parrott/Decca)
Raw Sienna (Parrot/Decca)
Looking In (Parrott/Decca)
Street Corner Talking (Parrott/Decca)
Hellbound Train (Parrott/Decca)
Lion's Share (Parrot/Decca)
Jack The Toad (Parrot/Decca)
Boogie Brothers (London/Decca)
Wire Fire (London/—)
Skin 'n' Bone (London/—)

Leo Sayer

Born Shoreham, Sussex, England, May 21, 1948, Sayer enjoyed a remarkably speedy rise to prominence. He had done little except busk on London streets and briefly lead outfit Patches when, in 1972, he met up with agent/musician Dave Courtney and singer/actor Adam Faith (♦), the latter becoming his manager.

Sayer (lyrics) and Courtney (music) entered into prolific song-writing partnership, with Faith producing Sayer's first album, Silverbird, at Who vocalist Roger Daltrey's Sussex studio. Daltrey himself took an interest in what was going on, so much so that he used all Sayer/Courtney songs for his 1973 solo album, from which the team's Giving It All Away was smash hit for him early 1973.

Later that year, Sayer's Silverbird, featuring cover shot of the artist in pierrot costume (in which guise he would subsequently play early concerts), was edging up British charts assisted by his own smash hit, The Show Must Go On.

As manager and discoverer of this nascent kid hero, Faith looked to be on to a winner. Sayer followed in 1974 with gold album Just A Boy and two more hits, One Man Band and Long Tall Glasses, the second of which provided American chart breakthrough.

By 1975, however, and the Another Year set, Courtney had

sundered the partnership to pursue own solo career, his place being taken by former Supertramp bassist/writer Frank Farrell who had been member of Sayer's back-up band. This produced a further smash hit, **Moonlighting**.

With distinctive, unrefined voice, Sayer has displayed penchant for arresting and mostly successful singles. However, certain question marks remain. The early clown's attire and make-up was a gimmick which became a handicap; and the release of Sayer's flop version of Beatles standard **Let It Be** Christmas 1975 proved a gross error of taste and judgment.

Nevertheless, if Farrell can acquit himself as adequately as Courtney, Sayer could yet have a lot more to offer.

Recordings:
Silverbird (Warners/Chrysalis)
Just A Boy (Warner/Chrysalis)
Another Year (Warners/Chrysalis)

Boz Scaggs

William Royce (Boz) Scaggs was born Ohio, Jun 1944, and raised in Oklahoma and Texas. At the age of 15 he met Steve Miller (♦) at school in Dallas, and was asked to join Miller's band, The Marksmen, as vocalist and tambourine-player while Miller taught him rhythm-guitar.

My Time.
Courtesy CBS Records.

Scaggs followed Miller to the University of Madison in Wisconsin, and joined the latter's Ardells group – which also worked under the name of the Fabulous Night Train – playing a mixture of R&B and rock 'n' roll.

Returning to Texas, Scaggs formed an R&B band, The Wigs. In 1964 they all quit university to go to Britain, Scaggs being accompanied by George Rains (drms), John "Toad" Andrews (gtr), and Bob Arthur (bs). They found on arrival that there was already a plethora of R&B bands there, so while the others returned to the States, eventually to form Mother Earth, Scaggs roved Europe as a folksinger, and stayed for a while in Stockholm, where he cut **Boz**, an album that was issued by Polydor only in Europe.

He returned to the U.S. to join Steve Miller in San Francisco in 1967, but after two highly acclaimed albums, **Children Of The Future** and **Sailor,** Scaggs split, citing, inevitably, musical differences as the reason.

Jann Wenner, editor of "Rolling

Right: Leo Sayer, in his pierrot outfit. His success survived a change of costume.

Stone" and a neighbour of Scaggs', arranged a new record deal for him, and produced **Boz Scaggs** at Muscle Shoals; with the assistance of the local session-musicians, augmented by Duane Allman; it remains his best album to date.

Scaggs subsequently signed with CBS, and has since produced a series of stylish but patchy albums of what might be termed white soul. **My Time** (1972), with the exciting opening track **Dinah Flo,** is probably the best of the bunch.

Although Scaggs has been placed in the hands of influential producers like Glyn Johns and Johnny Bristol, he seems set to remain a minor cult figure, with a faithful following which has hardly deviated since the release of **Boz Scaggs.**

Recordings:
Boz Scaggs (Atlantic)
Moments (Columbia/CBS)
Boz Scaggs And Band (Columbia/CBS)
My Time (Columbia/CBS)
Slow Dancer (Columbia/CBS)
Silk Degrees (Columbia/CBS)

Gil Scott-Heron (and Brian Jackson)

Son of Jamaican pro soccer player and librarian, Scott-Heron was born in Chicago and raised by his grandmother in Jackson, Tennessee. Wrote detective stories as teenager, and further explored literary leanings – particularly modern black poets – when brought to New York by his mother to continue studies. Attended Pennsylvania's Lincoln University where he first met collaborator-to-be Brian Jackson.

At 19 Scott-Heron's first novel, "The Vulture", was published; this being followed by volume of rap verse "Small Talk At 125th And Lenox" and second novel "The Nigger Factory".

Although his books were moderately successful, he turned to music to achieve wider communication. Along with Brian Jackson, recorded three albums

for Bob Thiele's Flying Dutchman label: the aforementioned poems set **Small Talk At 125th And Lennox; Pieces Of A Man,** his first work of songs which included rap poem **The Revolution Will Not Be Televised** (brought to wider attention via Labelle's **Pressure Cookin'** album), and **Free Will.**

Fourth set, **Winter In America,** was recorded for Strata/East label, which had somewhat better distribution service, although album was still only available in few East Coast cities. Nevertheless, from this came disco hit **The Bottle.**

Major break came in 1974 with signing to Clive Davis' Arista label; in fact they were first act on roster. Arista debut **The First Minute Of A New Day** brought this talented new team to public notice, along with back-up aggregation, the Midnight Band. Second album, **From South Africa To South Carolina** (1975) yielded smash international hit **Johannasburg.**

Scott-Heron and Jackson's music is pungent mix of jazz-based city funk laced with highly literate black consciousness lyrics.

Recordings:
Small Talk At 125th And Lenox (Flying Dutchman/—)
Pieces Of A Man (Flying Dutchman/Philips)
Free Will (Flying Dutchman/—)
Gil Scott-Heron and Brian Jackson:
Winter In America (Strata-East/—)
The First Minute Of A New Day (Arista)
From South Africa To South Carolina (Arista)
The Adventures Of Baron Von Tripp (Soundtrack) (Arista)
Compilation:
The Revolution Will Not Be Televised (Flying Dutchman/RCA)

Seals & Crofts

Jim Seals and Dash Crofts, both born in Texas, met in junior high school. They first achieved success as members of The Champs, who had a huge instrumental hit in 1958 with **Tequila,** though

only Seals had been in band at time. Seals (gtr) and Crofts (drms) remained in group until mid-'60s, when they constituted a new band called The Dawnbreakers; this in turn broke up when all the members were converted to the Baha'i faith, and Seals & Crofts retreated to consider their musical direction in the light of their new religion.

I'll Play For You.
Courtesy Warner Bros. Records.

They emerged in 1970, with Crofts by now playing mandolin, as a soft-rock harmony duo, who quickly established a large following. After two albums on TA Records, **Seals And Crofts** and **Down Home,** they moved to Warner Bros, since when all of their albums have gone gold, and one platinum.

It is difficult to account for their overwhelming success, but it is certainly true to say that they happened at the right historical moment. Though they now use a backing band for live appearances, their music is generally lightweight, and their lyrics have dealt in a rather naive manner with Matters Of Concern – e.g. their album **Unborn Child** was a thematic work protesting the evils of abortion.

Despite the fact that they are undoubtedly the super-wimps of the '70s, they have come up with one classic composition, **Summer Breeze,** which was turned to good advantage by the Isley Brothers (♦).

Their first two albums, **Seals & Crofts** and **Down Home** have been acquired by Warner Bros and reissued as **Seals & Crofts I & II.**

Recordings:
Seals & Crofts I & II (Warner Bros)
Year Of Sunday (Warner Bros)
Summer Breeze (Warner Bros)
Diamond Girl (Warner Bros)
Unborn Child (Warner Bros)
I'll Play For You (Warner Bros)
Compilation:
Greatest Hits (Warner Bros)

Sea Train

Richard Greene violin
Andy Kulberg bass, flute
Don Kretmar sax, bass
John Gregory guitar, vocals
Roy Blumenfeld drums

Formed Marin County, California, with above line-up (plus lyricist Jim Roberts) by Kulberg and Blumenfeld after they quit New York outfit Blues Project (♦) and gigged their way west. Critically-acclaimed debut album (1969) placed heavy emphasis on violin virtuosity of Greene, native of Beverly Hills who had played in Nashville with bluegrass veteran

Bill Monroe and briefly with Jim Kweskin's Jug Band.

Sea Train went through several personnel changes, however, and by time of second album, recorded in London with former Beatles producer George Martin (♦), only Greene, Kulberg and writer Roberts survived. Newcomers were Peter Rowan (gtr, vocals), another ex-associate of Monroe, Larry Atamanuik (drms), Lloyd Baskin (vcls, kybds). This line-up stayed intact for third album, again Martin-produced.

Considerable changes took place before 1973 Warner Bros set **Watch**. Kulberg and Baskin were only survivors, new arrivals being Julio Coronado (drms), William Elliott (kybds) and Peter Walsh (gtr, bs, vcls). The last-named, from Pacific Gas & Electric, proved dominant new force, his strident guitar-playing being most noticeable characteristic of new album, subsequent to which the group folded.

Recordings:
Sea Train (A&M)
Sea Train (Capitol)
Marblehead Messenger (Capitol)
Watch (Warner Bros)

John Sebastian

Sebastian was born New York into a showbiz family – his mother was an administrator for Carnegie Hall, his father a famous harmonica virtuoso. He lived with his family in Rome for five years, although he was schooled in New York.

In his adolescence he joined the many ambitious folkies hanging around Greenwich Village (others included his friends David Crosby and Roger McGuinn). Sebastian himself played guitar, harmonica, autoharp, and also sang. One night, he found himself backing Fred Neil and Felix Pappalardi on mouth-harp, and he was offered session-work by producer Paul Rothchild. He worked with both the Even Dozen Jug Band – under the pseudonym of John Benson – and Tim Hardin, and accrued wide experience in studio and live-work before forming The Lovin' Spoonful (♦) 1965.

Since he was very much the main creative force of the band, he seemed to be in a position to pursue a satisfactory solo career when the Spoonful disbanded in 1968; however, Sebastian has never fulfilled this potential.

He moved to Los Angeles, though his first major solo appearance was an unscheduled one at Woodstock in 1969. Although obviously high most of the weekend, Sebastian's ingenuous hippie routine won him a place in the affections of the festival crowd and later the moviegoers who caught the film.

With this platform of solo success, he released his debut solo album, **John B. Sebastian**, which included a couple of worthy compositions in **She's A Lady** and **How Have You Been?**

Nevertheless, the latter song indicated the problem; his period of de facto retirement had blunted the edges of his wit, and his latter songs have shown him taking himself too seriously. Also both

his recorded material and his live repertoire have included a goodly dosage of golden Spoonful, which seems to indicate he writes fresh material only with difficulty. He has been backed on his solo albums by a variety of star musicians, and usually performs live with a band of hand-picked Los Angeles musicians; all to little avail, as his career has gone steadily downhill.

Tarzana Kid.
Courtesy Warner Bros. Records.

In 1976, however, he appeared to be making a valiant attempt at a comeback, with a single, **Welcome Back**, which reached No. 1 in the U.S.

Recordings:
John B. Sebastian (Reprise)
Cheapo Cheapo Productions Present The Real Live John Sebastian (Reprise)
The Four Of Us (Reprise)
The Tarzana Kid (Reprise)
Welcome Back (Reprise)

The Section
♦ James Taylor

Neil Sedaka

Born New York, Mar 13, 1939 Sedaka was initially trained as a concert pianist, being educated at

Below: Sedaka, with Carole King; both were colleagues working for Don Kirshner.

Juilliard School of Music. In 1956 he was selected by Arthur Rubinstein as the best New York classical pianist.

However by then Sedaka was already more interested in writing pop songs, which he did in partnership with a friend from Brooklyn, Howard Greenfield (the former wrote music, the latter the lyrics). The first person to accept their songs was Jerry Wexler at Atlantic, who placed their material with Laverne Baker. They also wrote for The Tokens and Dinah Washington. It was when Connie Francis recorded **Stupid Cupid** in 1958 that the team really became established.

Sedaka was already signed to Aldon Publishing, the organisation of Don Kirshner (♦) and Al Nevins which operated out of the hothouse conditions of the New York Brill Building; Sedaka and Greenfield were one of the teams of prolific writers there.

In 1959 Sedaka managed to convince Steve Sholes at RCA Victor, that he had a future as a singer as well as a songwriter. His first release, **The Diary** was moderately successful. The second, **I Go Ape**, was a Top 5 record in Britain. But it was his fourth single, **Oh! Carol**, written for his sweetheart of the time Carole King (♦), that really established him as a front-line performer. Hits rolled off the drawing-board – **Happy Birthday Sweet Sixteen, Calendar Girl** and **Breaking Up Is Hard To Do** were engagingly cute, unprepossessing pop material, and few people could do that sort of thing better.

By 1963 he and Greenfield had written over 500 songs which had sold over 20 million records; but that was the year the lights went out for Sedaka and his contemporaries, as Beatlemania washed away the music-industry establishment.

Sedaka abandoned his personal performing career, but continued to be active, if not flourishing, as a songwriter, creating hits for Fifth Dimension and Tom Jones. By 1971, still working in harness with Greenfield, he was persuaded by Don Kirschner to enter

the ring again. He chose to promote his comeback album, **Emergence**, through a concert at the London Albert Hall. (Sedaka, who'd been discouraged by Aldon from performing in U.S. at the height of his fame, had always been a more popular live artist in the U.K.) The concert was a success, and the album began to attract attention.

More importantly, Sedaka began to work with a group called Hot Legs at Strawberry Studios near Manchester. They made an album together, **Solitaire**, which, though it didn't sell particularly well, was thought of sufficient quality to warrant another – **The Tra-La Days Are Over** (1973). At this point, Hot Legs became better known as 10cc (♦), and Sedaka began to happen again. The album sold well in England, and also produced a hit single, **That's Where The Music Takes Me**; the next, **Laughter In The Rain**, this time recorded in Los Angeles, showed that Sedaka's stock was once again rising.

Nevertheless, he now had no record company in the States. Elton John (♦) literally fainted when he heard this, and immediately signed Sedaka to his Rocket Records. The album, **Sedaka's Back**, was thus a combination of material from **Solitaire, The Tra La Days Are Over** and **Laughter In The Rain**.

The single, **Laughter In The Rain**, gave him his first U.S. No. 1 for over 10 years in 1975.

Since then Sedaka's level of success, both as recording artist and concert performer, has been consistently high; his songs have been regularly covered by other artists. The Captain And Tennille's version of **Love Will Keep Us Together** became the biggest-selling U.S. single in 1975, and **Solitaire** did well for The Carpenters. Sedaka's second album issued in America on Rocket, **The Hungry Years** (a graphic but quite inappropriate title), became a No. 1 album.

In 1973 Sedaka and Greenfield dissolved their lengthy professional partnership, and Sedaka now works with lyricist Phil Cody. One of their first compositions together, **Bad Blood**, gave Sedaka the second U.S. No. 1 of his new career. His present success can probably be attributed to the fact that he was determined to re-establish himself through his fresh material, which combined his ear for melody with a more mature lyrical approach.

A point of interest is that since their adolescence, and the Oh! Carol/Oh! Neil affair, the careers of Carole King and Neil Sedaka have charted similar courses; both have shown a talent for survival that one would hardly have thought possible at end of '50s, and both are now established as singer/songwriters of some significance.

A Sedaka discography is difficult, since his American releases, **Sedaka's Back** and **The Hungry Years,** have been compilations of material from albums previously issued in Britain. **Steppin' Out** is actually the first of his '70s albums that has been issued in an identical form in Britain and America.

Recordings:
Emergence (—/RCA)
Solitaire (—/RCA)

The Tra La Days Are Over
(—/MGM)
Laughter In The Rain
(—/Polydor)
Sedaka's Back (Rocket/—)
**Live At The Royal Festival
Hall** (—/Polydor)
The Hungry Years (Rocket/—)
Overnight Success (—/Polydor)
Steppin' Out (Rocket/Polydor)
Compilations:
24 Rock 'n' Roll Hits (—/RCA)
Greatest Hits (RCA/—)
**Laughter And Tears: The Best
Of Neil Sedaka Today**
(Polydor/—)

Pete Seeger

Born May 3, 1919 in New York
City, Seeger is the big daddy of
folk/protest singers. His mother
was a violin-teacher, and his
father a noted musicologist.
Seeger learned to play ukelele
and banjo, and developed an
interest in folk music of America
when he was about 16.

He spent some time with Alan
Lomax the famous collector of
folk-songs, in the archives of
Library of Congress in Washington, D.C., before, typically, taking
his banjo and hoboing around the
mid-West and Southern States,
soaking up the music of rural
America.

He was educated at Harvard,
and in the war served in the
armed forces, though mostly he
was entertaining other troops.

He started The Weavers folk
group in 1949, after working for a
while with a vocal group that included Woody Guthrie (➡). His
spell with The Weavers was
hugely successful, and they helped to popularise songs like
**Goodnight Irene, On Top Of
Old Smokey,** and Seeger's own
Kisses Sweeter Than Wine.

He has long been involved with
left-wing U.S. politics, and was
the person who originally gave
the protest movement **We Shall
Overcome.** He also helped to
popularise scores of old American folk ballads, and personally
composed many anthems of the
times – **If I Had A Hammer,
Where Have All The Flowers
Gone?** and **Little Boxes.**

Though he tended to be overshadowed by the new breed of
angry young folk-singer at the
beginning of '60s, there is no
gainsaying his massive contribution. He is married with three
children, and his sister Peggy
lives in the U.K. with Ewan MacColl
(whose own folk-songs, **Dirty
Old Town** and **First Time Ever
I Saw Your Face,** have been
accorded some prominence by
Rod Stewart and Roberta Flack
respectively).

Seeger has made over 50
albums; in 1973 CBS in Britain
issued **The Best Of Pete Seeger.**

Bob Seger

Born in Detroit, Seger is quite
possibly one of the great lost
figures of rock 'n' roll; despite
regular gigging and albums output, he has never approached
anything more than minor cult
status; yet, he is very popular
on his home territory in Detroit,
and writes fierce, driving rock
music in a style not unlike John
Fogerty's.

Seger has always seemed des-

tined to miss out on the big time,
right from the moment in 1966
when one of his first singles,
Heavy Music, entered the U.S.
charts the week his record company, Cameo Parkway, wound up.
After making four albums for
Capitol, he temporarily retired
from the business in 1969 to go
back to college, but in 1971 was
back on the road, working with a
duo who themselves made a few
recordings, Teegarden and Van
Winkle. The fruit of this partnership was Seger's first album for
Reprise, **Smokin' O.P.'s** (1972).

In 1973 Seger made **Back In '72,**
an album that received high praise
from the critics, which had been
recorded partly in Muscle Shoals
– with J. J. Cale numbered
amongst backing musicians – as
was **Seven,** an album that included one dynamite song, **Get
Out Of Denver,** that was issued
as a single, though without
success.

After three albums for Reprise,
Seger reverted to Capitol, and
started working with his own back-
up group, The Silver Bullet
Band; they have since toured the
U.S. as support to Bachman-
Turner Overdrive, and recorded
two albums – **Beautiful Loser**
(1975) and **Live Bullet** (1976).

In mid-'60s, Seger, in the guise
of the Beach Bums, made a parody
single, **The Ballad Of The Yellow
Beret,** which was issued on Are
You Kidding Me Records.

Two of Seger's early albums,
Ramblin' Gamblin' Man and
Mongrel were re-issued by Capitol in U.S. 1975; as yet, his first
four albums not issued in U.K.

Recordings:
Ramblin' Gamblin' Man
(Capitol/—)
Noah (Capitol/—)
The Bob Seger System (Capitol/
—)
Mongrel (Capitol/—)
Smokin' O.P.'s (Reprise)
Back In '72 (Reprise)
Seven (Reprise)
Beautiful Loser (Capitol)
Live Bullet (Capitol)

Sensational Alex Harvey Band

Alex Harvey vocals, guitar
Zal Cleminson guitar, vocals
Chris Glen bass
Hugh McKenna keyboards
Ted McKenna drums

At 41, Britain's oldest living
punk, with a face that looks like
it's survived a hundred bar-room
brawls, Alex Harvey is one of the

Above: Alex Harvey in 1976.

The Impossible Dream. Courtesy Phonogram Ltd.

genuine characters in U.K. rock.
A hard-nosed Scot, he was born
in Glasgow's notorious slum district The Gorbals, Feb 5, 1935.
Leaving school at 15, he took
numerous odd jobs (he claims
"musician" as his 36th occupation!) before playing guitar in
various skiffle-groups in 1954. In
1956 he won local talent contest
and was acclaimed as "The
Tommy Steele Of Scotland".

Three years later he formed the
legendary Alex Harvey Big Soul
Band, an outfit which played in
its own right and backed artists
like Eddie Cochran and Gene
Vincent on U.K. tours. In the early
'60s they spent a lot of time
playing in Germany, where first
album **Alex Harvey's Big Soul
Band** (1964) was recorded, and
became popular in British clubs
for combination of rock and blues
laced with inimitable Harvey
humour.

In 1967, however, the group tired
of constant gigging for little reward, and split up. Harvey worked as a solo artist in night clubs,
subsequently joining band
assembled for London theatre
production of "Hair" musical for
some three years by which time
he yearned to return to rock.

Harvey travelled north where he
saw Cleminson, Glen, and
McKennas working as Scottish
hard-rock band Tear Gas, who
had at that time cut two poorly-
received albums.

Returning south, appeared again
on club circuit as Alex Harvey
and Tear Gas which gradually
metamorphosed into Sensational
Alex Harvey Band in 1972. Gigging consistently, group survived
early hostility and began to
attract cult following via gradually
evolving use of rock theatricals,
involving various vaundevillian
props and guitarist Cleminson
adopting clown's mask make-up.
The younger Cleminson makes
perfect foil for veteran punk
raconteur Harvey, who is currently reaping success he's worked hard to achieve over some 22
gruelling years.

The sight of a fanatical audience

of Harvey lookalikes, most of
them young enough to be his
children (two of them, aged 15
and eight, in fact are), is one of
the most engaging in rock.

Despite 1975 British singles success with live re-work of old
Tom Jones' tub-thumper **Delilah**
and more-than-healthy sales for
albums, Harvey has yet to satis-
factorily transfer excitement of
stage act to record. However, in-
concert reputation is strong
enough to sustain the band for
some time, and probably bring
American breakthrough in near
future.

By introducing his younger
brother Leslie to Maggie Bell (➡),
Harvey was also instrumental in
formation of Stone The Crows (➡).

Recordings:
Alex Harvey's Big Soul Band
(Polydor)
Roman Wall Blues (—/Fontana)
**Sensational Alex Harvey Band:
Framed** (Atlantic/Vertigo)
Next (Atlantic/Vertigo)
The Impossible Dream
(Atlantic/Vertigo)
**Sensational Alex Harvey Band
Live** (Atlantic/Vertigo)
Tomorrow Belongs To Me
(Atlantic/Vertigo)
The Penthouse Tapes
(Atlantic/Vertigo)

Sha Na Na

Scott Powell vocals
Johnny Contardo vocals
Frederick Dennis Greene
vocals
Don York vocals
Chris Donald guitar
Bruce Clarke bass
Screamin' Scott Symon piano
John Bauman (Bowzer) piano
Lennie Baker saxophone
Jocko Marcellino drums
Ritch Joffe vocals
Elliot Cahn guitar, vocals
Henry Gross guitar, vocals

Sha Na Na were formed 1969 at
Columbia University, in the vanguard of the rock 'n' roll movement, being totally nostalgia-

Above: The Shadows, in the days when the going was good.

oriented, completely specialising in '50s rock 'n' roll, and impersonations of artists like Gene Vincent and Eddie Cochran. Their powerful visual act took in slick choreography, dazzling gold lame costumes (soon to become commonplace in glam-rock period) and teddy boy suits, and lots of grease. The only genuine '50s rocker was Baker, who had been with Danny and Juniors. Above was original line-up.

Straightaway, the band stole the limelight at Woodstock Festival (♦) in 1969, but they were hardly able to build on this, mainly because although they were a visual and dynamic stage act, their records, being largely retreads of '50s material, were not especially interesting. **Rock 'n' Roll Is Here To Stay** was issued in 1969, with David Bromberg (♦) as one of the session musicians, and **Sha Na Na** in 1970.

Their third album, **The Night Is Still Young** (1972), did contain an original song, **Bounce In Your Buggy,** that almost became a hit single in Britain, but on the whole the lack of strong original material was their Achilles heel.

For such a large group, they were subject to surprisingly few personnel changes, though Vinnie Taylor replaced Donald in 1970.

In 1973 they made a double-album, **The Golden Age Of Rock 'n' Roll** (released in Britain as a single-album), after which there were certain changes. Singer Elliot Cahn left in June 1973, because he'd had enough of life on the road, and the constant inevitable in-fighting; (something he later wrote about in an article for "New Musical Express"). Another vocalist Ritch Joffe also left, and Bruce "Zoroaster" Clarke was replaced by Chico Ryan. Neither Cahn nor Joffe were replaced.

As a 10-man unit, Sha Na Na made **From The Streets Of New York** in 1974, an album that was recorded live in Central Park, New York, and featured Sha Na Na stage act, complete with jiving competition; needless, to say, it didn't work particularly well on record.

Their sixth album, **Hot Sox** (also 1974), was produced by Jack Douglas, with Bob Ezrin as executive producer (i.e. the team now handling Aerosmith (♦)), but still availed the band little, as did the regular changes of persona – Elliot Cahn had been Gino; Scott Powell became Captain Outrageous, and then Tony Santini; when Elliott Randell joined the band in 1974 he became Enrico Ronzoni.

Meanwhile, the group had been working hard for five years, and some of the strains began to tell. Vinnie Taylor died of a heroin overdose in April 1974, Screamin' Scott Symon had a nervous breakdown, and Bowzer has undergone major surgery to repair collapsed lungs. Despite, all this, Sha Na Na are still in business; possibly if rock 'n' roll is here to stay, so are they.

Gross left to go solo in 1970, and had two albums released on A&M – **Henry Gross** and **Plug Me Into Something,** both of which received encouraging reviews. In May 1976 he had a major U.S. hit single with **Shannon.**

Recordings:
Rock 'n' Roll Is Here To Stay (Kama Sutra)
Sha Na Na (Kama Sutra)
The Night Is Still Young (Kama Sutra)
The Golden Age Of Rock 'n' Roll (Kama Sutra/K-Tel)
From The Streets Of New York (Kama Sutra)
Hot Sox (Kama Sutra)
Sha Na Now (Kama Sutra/—)

The Shadows

Hank B. Marvin guitar, vocals
Bruce Welch guitar, vocals
John Farrar bass, vocals
Brian Bennett drums

In 1958, Cliff Richard, then a teenybop idol, needed a backing group with whom he could go on the road. He had a drummer in Terry Smart, an old friend, and a bass-player in Ian Samwell, who had written his first hit, **Move It,** and they were augmented by Hank B. Marvin (b. Oct 28, 1941), and Bruce Welch (b. Nov 2, 1941).

The group were known as The Drifters, and supported Richard on his first tour, the bill-toppers being the Kalin Twins.

Also on the bill was an act called the Most Brothers, one of whom was Mickie Most (♦), and in their backing-group was a bass guitarist named Jet Harris. After the tour, Harris (b. Jul 6, 1939) was brought in to The Drifters to replace Samwell, who left to concentrate on songwriting and production, and Harris introduced a friend of his, Tony Meehan (b. Mar 2, 1943), to replace Smart, who was leaving the music business.

During 1959, The Drifters changed their name to The Shadows, due to the fact that the American group of the same name objected. The new name was the brainchild of Harris, who felt that as Cliff's backing group, they were in Richard's shadow. Also during that year, the group had their first records released without Cliff Richard, although they remained his backing group, and appeared on his records.

During a British tour 1960, The Shadows met Jerry Lordan (an artist on the same bill), who played them a tune he had written called **Apache.** In July 1960, this became the first No. 1 for The Shadows, and the first of over 20 hits during the next five years. The Shadows completely captured the imagination of would-be guitarists, with Marvin being the model for thousands of guitar styles all round the Western world, and a similar number of groups imitating the "Shadow Walk", a fairly simple but effective set of stage movements.

During this hit period, several personnel changes occurred within the group. Tony Meehan, who eventually moved into production, was the first to leave; he was replaced by Brian Bennett. In 1962, Jet Harris left, and almost immediately got back together with Meehan, the duo producing three Top 5 records in 1963, before Harris became ill, and dropped from the public eye almost completely. He was replaced by Brian "Licorice" Locking, who himself left at the end of 1963, to devote more time to the Jehovah's Witnesses.

John Rostill came in on bass just in time to make "Wonderful Life", the least successful film in a series starring Cliff and the Shadows, which had started with "The Young Ones" and "Summer Holiday", and in this form the group continued until end of 1968, when Welch decided that 10 years with The Shadows was enough, and the group effectively ceased to exist.

In 1970, Marvin and Welch enlisted the help of Australian John Farrar, whom they had met on a tour of Australasia in 1966, and under the name of Marvin, Welch and Farrar, they made two reasonably successful albums, but split up when Welch became ill after breaking up with his then fiancée, Olivia Newton-John (♦).

In 1973, John Rostill died in mysterious circumstances, and a planned Shadows reunion album, **Rockin' With Curly Leads,** was made by Marvin, Welch, Farrar and Bennett, who in the meantime had been working as a producer and session-drummer with great success. The Shadows were again asked to re-form in 1975, this time to perform as Britain's entry in the Eurovision Song Contest, and another album, **Spec's Appeal,** was released containing some of the suggested songs from the contest, and several instrumentals of the type that had made the group famous in the first place.

Bennett continues to be an in-demand studio musician, Welch is writing and producing for Cliff Richard, Farrar is doing the same for Olivia Newton-John, both with great success, and Marvin is also involved in similar undertakings, but so far he has not been able to emulate the achievements of his colleagues.

Though where they go from here is not certain, it is undeniable that The Shadows, and especially Marvin, changed the lives of many budding guitarists during the early '60s. Their influence cannot be understated.

Discography is selective.

Recordings:
The Shadows' Greatest Hits (—/Columbia)
More Hits (—/Columbia)

Shangri-Las
♦ George "Shadow" Morton

Sharks
♦ Chris Spedding

Shotgun Express
♦ Camel, Peter Green, Rod Stewart

Carly Simon

Born New York Jun 25, 1945 into upper middle-class culturally inclined family with book-publishing affiliations. She attended exclusive Sarah Lawrence College, at which point she first sang with elder sister Lucy as Simon Sisters. They played folk-clubs around New York area, including Bitter End, but split when Lucy married.

Carly Simon travelled to France not singing for year before she met Bob Dylan manager Albert Grossman (♦) who, she claims, wanted to groom her as "female Dylan". To this end, Grossman set up New York record sessions late 1966 with Bob Johnston producing, and likes of The Band, Al Kooper, Mike Bloomfield as support. Dylan even wrote lyrics for one of songs.

However, Simon fell out with Grossman over handling of her career and tracks were never released. Instead, she re-surfaced late 1969–70 signed by Jac Holtzman to Elektra. Her close friend, Jacob Brackman, film critic for "Esquire" magazine, co-wrote

Playing Possum. Courtesy Elektra Asylum Records.

material with her for first and second albums.

From first eponymous set, released early 1971, **That's The Way I've Always Heard It Should Be** not only made American singles lists but delineated her by the smoother, glossier, more sophisticated style from other female singer/song-writer contemporaries.

Major success on both sides of Atlantic came with 1972 album **No Secrets,** and goldseller single **You're So Vain** featuring Mick Jagger among back-up vocals. Subject of song increased interest, with actor Warren Beatty most popular public choice, though Ms Simon refused to be drawn. Politically conscious,· she had added support to George McGovern's presidential campaign, signing up for celebrity appearances on request of Beatty.

Marrying singer / songwriter James Taylor (♦) in 1973 (they have one child, Sarah), recordings and concert appearances – she did few guest spots with Taylor – subsequently became sporadic. **Hotcakes,** released 1974, was American Top 10 seller, though met mixed critical reaction, and there was 18-month gap before next set, **Playing Possum** (late 1975).

No Secrets, Hotcakes, Possum produced by Richard Perry (♦),

who she claimed had liberated her from self-conscious artiness of early work. However, she used Ted Templeman for production on **Another Passenger** (1976), with all-star backing cast; yet critical favour still eluded her.

Recordings:
Carly Simon (Elektra)
Anticipation (Elektra)
No Secrets (Elektra)
Hotcakes (Elektra)
Playing Possum (Elektra)
Another Passenger (Elektra)
Compilation:
The Best Of Carly Simon (Elektra)

Above: Carly Simon. Her recording success proved as durable as her marriage.

Paul Simon

Born Oct 13, 1941 in Newark, New Jersey into a Jewish/Hungarian family, Simon was raised in a middle-class residential district of New York, and knew Art Garfunkel (♦) from childhood. They went to school together in New York.

They first enjoyed short-lived success in 1957 as a derivative bee-bop high-school duo called Tom (Graph) & Jerry (Landis); they went into a local recording studio, laid down a couple of tracks, of which one, **Hey! Schoolgirl,** became a Top 40 hit in the U.S. It was an auspicious beginning, but when little else happened they both just went back to school.

At Queens College in New York, Paul met Carole Klein (King), and they made some demos together; Paul was also occasionally involved with semi-professional groups, such as The Passions and The Mystics, and he sang lead for the latter on one occasion.

Simon went to Law School, but dropped out in early 1964 and went to England, where he performed at folk-clubs, and impressed most of

those who saw him; one of them, Judith Piepe, started touting his compositions in England on his behalf (and for her efforts was later rewarded when she appeared on the front-cover of **The Paul Simon Song Book**).

On returning to America, Simon hawked around his own tapes, and finally succeeded in interesting Columbia. He and Garfunkel – who had by now reverted to using their real names (Simon's recurrent themes have included honesty and deception, though he also used the song-writing alias Paul Kane) – played acoustic guitars, and clambered aboard the folk-song bandwagon, borrowing protest from Dylan and harmonies from the Everly Brothers. They made a debut album in 1964, **Wednesday Morning 3 A.M.,** on which they worked with Tom Wilson as producer. (Wilson had been involved with all the Dylan albums from **Freewheelin'** at that point.) The album consisted partly of Simon's own songs, and partly of standard folk material. Its initial impact was minimal.

By May 1965 Judith Piepe had persuaded CBS in London to record an album of Simon's songs; he flew back post-haste and recorded **The Paul Simon Song Book** in London. The album showed Simon's quietly reflective compositions to their best advantage, as he accompanied himself solely on guitar. All the songs were his own, and the album clearly showed that he was a major talent. On the strength of it, Simon was able to work in England and Europe throughout the summer.

Meanwhile, in America, Tom Wilson had decided to try to activate interest in the **Wednesday Morning 3 A.M.** album by issuing one of the tracks, **The Sound Of Silence,** as a single and, in the absence of both Simon and Garfunkel, he augmented the song with electric guitar, bass and drums to give it a contemporary folk-rock sound. **Sound Of Silence** made No. 1 in the U.S. charts, and thus the success formula had been accidentally established. Simon, who had been producing an album for Jackson C. Frank in London, returned again to New York, and he and Garfunkel lined up a string of college dates.

In 1966 they issued a new album, **Sounds Of Silence,** which included **Homeward Bound,** a song that Simon had written while stranded in Widnes, Lancashire. Aside from Davy Graham's **Anji,** all the songs were Simon's own, though it featured much material previously recorded on **The Paul Simon Song Book,** though now given a specious and unsatisfying rock instrumentation, something which detracted from the quality of the songs. It was nevertheless a more commercial proposition, and **Homeward Bound** – one of the fresh compositions – duly became a hit single in America (No. 5) and Britain (No. 9).

Garfunkel's role in all this was minimal – he simply provided the close harmonies that helped give the duo a distinctive sound. The compositions were always Simon's own; his lyrics were usually emotionally stark, and sometimes self-consciously poetic, often using the theme of the individual in society; but too regularly his emotions strayed into whimsy and sugariness, a facet underscored by the formidable use of strings on the next album, **Parsley, Sage, Rosemary And Thyme** (produced, as was **Sounds Of Silence,** by Bob Johnston (♦), Wilson having left the company), and particularly on one track **The Dangling Conversation.**

That track was nevertheless a hit, as was **I Am A Rock,** and Simon and Garfunkel established themselves as the campus cuties in America, though on a tour of England in early 1967 they played to half-full houses.

Their following began to consolidate with **Bookends,** a reasonably ambitious album, with songs that dealt with people in positions of despair and anxiety. Even then, the second side of the album was given over to "B"-sides of previously-issued singles (Simon was never a prolific writer), with one exception, **Mrs Robinson,** a song Simon had written for the soundtrack of "The Graduate". It was that soundtrack that enabled Simon & Garfunkel to reach unscaled heights of popularity in both Britain and America; indeed, their own success paralleled the runaway commercial success of the movie.

Total world domination needed one more heave, and this was achieved with **Bridge Over Troubled Water.** The title track, with piano by Larry Knechtel, reached No. 1 on both sides of the Atlantic, and assisted the album in its inexorable march to becoming the third highest-selling album of all time, with sales of over eight million.

The key to Simon & Garfunkel's success was probably that they offered safe, synthetic protest; they questioned society's values without challenging them; what drug references there were in their songs were oblique. Essentially, they were all-American boys; with their lavish, wide-screen production jobs, theirs was the ultimate coffee-table music.

It was a situation Simon probably didn't enjoy and there was also the problem of topping **Bridge Over Troubled Water;** when Art Garfunkel accepted a role in "Catch-22", he and Simon decided to call it a day and concentrate on solo activities.

Though Simon has made only three albums of new material in the six years they have been apart, it does now seem as though during the whole Simon & Garfunkel era he was merely serving his apprenticeship, so much more forceful and stimulating has his music become since the split.

Probably he felt inhibited within the partnership from writing too directly about his own experiences. Certainly, he seemed to react against the saccharine over-production of much of the material, and having kept the customers satisfied for so long, it was now time for a change.

Simon's material since has become more disarmingly honest and personal. The first solo album, **Paul Simon,** which employed a spare, lean production in contrast to the excesses of the S&G catalogue, gave him a Top 10 hit single in both Britain and America, **Mother And Child Reunion.** And his continuing popularity was emphasised by his second solo album, **There Goes Rhymin' Simon,** which again spawned a hit single – **Kodachrome** in the U.S. and **Take Me To The Mardi Gras** in the U.K., where it was felt that radio stations might bypass

Above: Simon and Garfunkel; success is a serious matter.

The Paul Simon Song Book.

There Goes Rhymin' Simon.

Parsley Sage Rosemary
& Thyme.

Paul Simon, circa 1967.

Kodachrome because of advertising difficulties.

One remarkable quality of his solo work was its tastefulness; he began working with many of New York's top session-musicians, and in 1973 he undertook an American and European tour with a gospel group, the Jessy Dixon singers, and also a South American outfit, Urubamba; out of this tour came a live album, though it contained no new Simon compositions, and one or two that he had recorded at least twice before.

With the release of **Still Crazy After All These Years** in the autumn of 1975 – an album which concerned in part the break-up of his marriage

– he again toured, this time with the Jessy Dixon singers, and a group of session-musicians that included David Sanborn (sx), Richard Tee (kybds), Hugh McCracken (gtr) and Steve Gadd (bs), as well as the famed jazz harmonica-player, Toots Thielmans. It must have cost a bundle to get that show on the road.

Paul Simon now says that many people don't arrive at the full flood of their creative powers until they are in their '30s. He seems to have only recently engaged his, and he and Joni Mitchell are the two contemporary singer/songwriters whose work has met with equal and abundant commercial and critical success.

"Paul Simon – Now And Then" by Spencer Leigh (Raven Books) examines Simon's career and work up to 1973.

All the Simon & Garfunkel albums have gone at least gold, and they haven't yet invented categories for what **Bridge Over Troubled Water** and **Simon and Garfunkel's Greatest Hits** (released in June 1972) have sold.

Wednesday Morning 3 A.M. was issued in the U.S. in November 1965, and in Britain in October 1968. Paul Simon is the first to admit that it's a fairly dreadful album, and yet it is a measure of the phenomenal success of Simon & Garfunkel that even that, their lowest-selling album, has sold more than any Rolling Stones album except **Sticky Fingers.**

Recordings:
Wednesday Morning 3 A.M.
(Columbia/CBS)
The Sounds Of Silence
(Columbia/CBS)
Parsley, Sage, Rosemary &
Thyme (Columbia/CBS)
Bookends (Columbia/CBS)
The Graduate (Soundtrack)
(Columbia/CBS)
Bridge Over Troubled Water
(Columbia/CBS)

Compilation:
Greatest Hits (Columbia/CBS)
Paul Simon solo:
The Paul Simon Song Book
(Columbia/CBS)
Paul Simon (Columbia/CBS)
There Goes Rhymin' Simon
(Columbia/CBS)
Live Rhymin' (Columbia/CBS)
Still Crazy After All These
Years (Columbia/CBS)

Simon & Garfunkel
➧ Paul Simon

Nina Simone

Born Eunice Waymon in Tryon, North Carolina, Feb 21, 1933, she was one of eight children, had an upbringing in gospel music, and sang in the church choir with two of her sisters. Since she obviously had musical talent – she taught herself piano and organ before she was seven – she was given a formal music training, and her teacher was so impressed with her, she organised a fund to pay for Nina's education at the high school in Asheville, North Carolina, and then at the Juilliard School Of Music.

Her family moved to Philadelphia, and Nina began to work in night-clubs on East Coast. An engagement in Atlantic City led to a recording contract which yielded a massive hit version of **I Loves You Porgy** in 1959. In the '60s her work veered away from jazz towards R&B, and she recorded **Please Don't Let Me Be Misunderstood** and Screamin' Jay Hawkins' **I Put A Spell On You**, both of which were later picked up by The Animals (➡).

As her style became even more contemporary, so her records became more commercial, and she had two large hits in Britain, with **Ain't Got No – I Got Life** (from "Hair") in 1968 and the Bee Gees' **To Love Somebody** in 1969. However, she became increasingly involved with black-power movements, something which necessarily alienated much of her white audience, and moved her from the plush supper clubs to black political rallies and soul venues. Since 1974 she has not worked at all within the music business.

Discography is selective.

Recordings:
Nina Simone Sings The Blues (RCA)
Silk & Soul (RCA)
'Nuff Said (RCA)
To Love Somebody (RCA)
Black Gold (RCA)
Here Comes The Sun (RCA)
Emergency Ward (RCA)
Gifted And Black (Canyon/Polydor)
It Is Finished (RCA/—)

Pete Sinfield
➡ King Crimson, P.F.M.

Peter Skellern

Born Bury, Lancashire, England in 1947, first sang in local church choir and learned to play piano

Below: Rhymin' Simon triumphs again.

and trombone. By age 16, he was organist and choirmaster of St Paul's Church, Bury, later studying at London Guildhall School Of Music from which he graduated with distinction 1968.

Joined rock group The March Hare later known as Harlan County, which released album on Nashville label 1971 before split due to personnel problems. Skellern worked briefly for music publishers Chappells, and then began new career as singer/songwriter/pianist 1972.

His first single, the lavishly orchestrated **You're A Lady**, made No. 3 in U.K. charts and has since been widely covered, though he had to wait some time for second hit **Hold On To Love** (1975).

An admirer of Randy Newman, with whom he shares penchant for dour but wittily observant love songs, Skellern has proved very much his own man. His publically-neglected **Not Without A Friend** album (produced by Derek Taylor) was highly-eclectic concoction paying little regard to commerciality or prevailing trends; all Skellern originals bar Hoagy Carmichael's **Rockin' Chair**.

Now signed to Island label, he has gradually earned admiration of fellow musicians as unclassifiable but highly-creative new talent. George Harrison's quote that Skellern was one of few interesting new artists happening in Britain was widely used in 1975 Island music press ads.

Recordings:
Peter Skellern With Harlan County (—/Nashville)
Peter Skellern (—/Decca)
Not Without A Friend (—/Decca)
Holding My Own (—/Decca)
Hold On To Love (—/Decca)
Hard Times (Island)

Slade

Noddy Holder vocals, guitar
Dave Hill guitar
Jimmy Lea bass, piano
Don Powell drums

Holder (b. Walsall, Staffordshire,

Jun 15, 1950), Lea (b. Wolverhampton, Staffs, Jun 14, 1952), Hill (b. Fleet Castle, Devon, Apr 4, 1952) and Powell (b. Bilston, Staffs, Sep 10, 1950) first came together in Midlands as The 'N Betweens, playing routine club material – Beatles, Motown, etc. They changed their name to Ambrose Slade, at which point Chas Chandler (➡) caught their act at Rasputin's Club in Bond Street, London, February 1969, and became their manager and producer.

Chandler abbreviated their name to Slade, and also heightened their skinhead image – cropped hair, Dr Marten's, Ben Shermans, though it was no more than a specious attempt to grab hold of a transitory adolescent market. The gambit failed, mainly because Slade played hard rock, and skinheads were into reggae.

However, Slade's natural exuberance, and the power of Holder's vocals, began to win them a young audience anyway, and a reworking of a Little Richard song, **Get Down And Get With It**, gave them their first hit in May 1971. The song featured the boot-stomping routine that was to become their early trademark.

With the Holder/Lea composition, **Coz I Luv You**, the band established a formula that saw them become the top teenage band in Britain, with each single being direct and aggressive; they were promoted as a working-class group – something the characteristic mis-spelling of each song-title was intended to enhance.

For a two-year period from 1972–74 the group could do no wrong, and songs like **Tak Me Bak 'Ome, Mama Weer All Crazee Now, Gudbuy T'Jane** – easily their best – and **Cum On Feel The Noize** were all massively successful. Their songs were even enjoyed by the rock's critical establishment – mainly because no other band could supply the same gut energy and dynamic enthusiasm.

However, they ran into problems when they tried to broaden their appeal, and also move into more ambitious fields. A film, "Flame",

was set up; its aim had probably been to build up the band to a level of public acceptability similar to that which The Beatles achieved after "A Hard Day's Night". Despite the fact that the band members made creditable acting debuts, and despite the moderately encouraging reviews, "Flame" failed to catch the imagination of the public, and Slade were left to pick up their career where they had left it.

Their moment seemed to have passed. In 1973 they were hot, and in 1976 they were lukewarm; also, their regular attempts to crack the American market in a big way all floundered unsuccessfully. Nevertheless, Slade were the one pop-rock band to emerge in the '70s who gave the impression that they were both intelligent and talented enough to survive; though many of their army of fans had no doubt tired of seeing the same stage act recycled year after year, they are a band who will undoubtedly come again.

Recordings:
Beginnings (—/Fontana)
Play It Loud (—/Polydor)
Slade Alive! (Polydor)
Slayed? (Polydor)
Old, New, Borrowed And Blue (Polydor)
Flame (Soundtrack) (Polydor)
Nobody's Fools (Polydor)
Compilation:
Sladest (Reprise/Polydor)

Slapp Happy

Anthony Moore piano, vocals
Peter Blegvad guitar, clarinet, vocals
Dagmar piano, vocals

A motley assembly of characters, Slapp Happy coalesced into group form 1972 with British-born Moore, New Yorker Blegvad and German Dagmar having been previously involved together on a variety of projects. Dagmar had composed and performed extensively in Hamburg, while Moore had made soundtracks for underground movies in Germany and Switzerland. He and Blegvad had first met and formed a group early 1968.

The three came together in winter 1971 as part of circle of friends and musicians surrounding German avant-garde outfit Faust, at that group's Wumme studios. As Slapp Happy, with backing from members of Faust, they recorded first album, **Sort Of**, at Wumme 1972. Blegvad later toured for spell as member of Faust.

Second album, **Slapp Happy**, was recorded 1974 for England's Virgin label, and revealed a quirkily refreshing and unclassifiable new talent, the three writer/performers having drawn on European musical and literary heritage to inspire their own idiosyncratic creations.

Subsequently became closely allied with Virgin label stablemates Henry Cow (➡) and eventually the two groups merged into one, though retaining separate names. Together they recorded **Desperate Straights** (1974) and **In Praise Of Learning** (1975), but during recording of the latter Blegvad and Moore became estranged from rest and quit taking

name Slapp Happy with them. Dagmar opted to remain with Henry Cow. However, Slapp Happy subsequently folded, Blegvad returning to New York and Moore working as solo artist for Virgin. His **Out** album was released July 1976.

Recordings:
Sort Of (Polydor)
Slapp Happy (Virgin)
Slapp Happy & Henry Cow:
Desperate Straights (Virgin)
In Praise Of Learning (Virgin)

Sly And The Family Stone

Sly Stone vocals, keyboards, guitar
Freddie Stone guitar
Cynthia Robinson trumpet
Larry Graham, Jnr bass
Greg Errico drums
Rosie Stone vocals, piano
Jerry Martini saxophone

Sly Stone (b. Sylvester Stewart, Mar 15, 1944, in Dallas, Texas) formed several bands with his brother Freddie after the family moved to California in '50s; he performed as lead singer with The Viscanes, who had a local hit song called **Yellow Moon.**

After leaving school, Sly took on a variety of jobs in the industry, and became a successful record producer, working with Bobby Freeman, The Mojo Men and The Beau Brummels. He also made a name for himself as a DJ.

There's A Riot Going On.
Courtesy CBS Records.

In 1966 he formed his own group, The Stoners; though he disbanded it within a year, it was in this way that he discovered Cynthia Robinson, a girl trumpet-player who has been with Sly ever since.

He put together a new band, The Family Stone, line-up as above. Apart from Freddie and Rosie, Graham was another relative of Sly's (his cousin). The band was thus founded as an inter-racial (Martini and Errico were white), inter-sexual outfit. They played everything, from James Brown soul riffs through acid-rock guitar and electronics, adding a jazzy horn-section and wild vocal harmonies; they won a local following as a live act, as they moved away from the black dance-halls to the predominantly white psychedelic ballrooms.

The band's first album, **A Whole New Thing,** wasn't quite all its title suggested, but it did contain one gem of an exuberant single, **Dance To The Music,** which reached No. 7 in U.K. and No. 8 in U.S. in 1968.

It was an encouraging start, and both **Dance To The Music** and

Above: Original Small Faces (l to r), Steve Marriott, Kenny Jones, Jimmy Winston, Ronnie Lane.

its sequel **M'Lady** were highly influential, recharging a flagging soul scene with fluent jazz phrasing, complex arrangements, a sense of humour and an individual identity.

Dance To The Music also served as the title of the band's third album; although basically a dance record, Sly's innate lightness of touch and the band's sheer energy overcame any possible monotony. In 1969 they improved still further, with **Everyday People,** which went gold as a single, as did the album it was taken from, **Stand!,** the title track of which was the Black Power anthem. This album also included the ebullient **I Want To Take You Higher,** the song which featured as the high point of their dynamic act at Woodstock Festival (♦) that year; it was a performance which sealed their status as one of the most fashionable groups on the rock circuit.

However, this was followed only by anti-climax, as the band blew out several gigs, and there were rumours of drug problems. Only one single was put out – **Thank You (Falettinme Be Mice Elf Agin),** which was a postscript to the first phase of the Family Stone's collective existence. With no other new product forthcoming, Epic issued **Greatest Hits,** which immediately went gold.

In 1971 Sly put out **There's A Riot Going On,** an album that was a complete departure from the band's previous material and established him as a writer, and set further new directions for soul music; it was certainly low-key, emphasising Sly's disillusionment in his newly-cast role of superstar. English rock critic Andrew Weiner called it "an elegantly constructed portrait of personal and social disintegration".

Meanwhile, The Family Stone, which was by now gigging rather infrequently, endured line-up changes. Graham, whose bass-lines had been so prominent in the band's early work, departed to form his own group (Graham Central Station) and was replaced by Rusty Allen; Andy Newmark came in for Errico on drums, and saxophonist Pat Ricco was added. It was this line-up that made **Fresh**

(1973), an unconvincing album, as Sly backed off the despair of **There's A Riot Going On,** but was unable to replace it with anything very positive.

His albums subsequently have been of little interest, but Sly has always been an unpredictable and frequently baffling character, advancing in oblique, sideways steps. In 1974 he got married on the stage before a gig at Madison Square Garden, to Kathy Silva who had borne him a child some months previously. Father and mother and baby are pictured on the front cover of **Small Talk** (1974).

There were more line-up changes for **Small Talk;** Bill Lordan had replaced Newmark, and the band had been augmented by Sid Page (♦ Dan Hicks and his Hot Licks) on violin.

Album notes: Sly's first two albums, **A Whole New Thing** and **Life,** were reissued by Epic as a double-album **High Energy** in 1975.

Recordings:
A Whole New Thing (Epic/—)
Life (Epic/—)
Dance To The Music (Epic)
Stand! (Epic)
There's A Riot Going On (Epic)
Fresh (Epic)
Small Talk (Epic)
High On You (Epic)
Compilation:
Greatest Hits (Epic)

Small Faces

Steve Marriott vocals, guitar
Ronnie Lane bass
Ian MacLagan organ
Kenny Jones drums

If The Who (♦) were the mid-'60s heroes of West London's Mods, then the Small Faces sprang from their East London equivalent. In 1965 they broke into British charts with single **Whatcha Gonna Do About It?** and the whole country picked up on this physically small and sharply-dressed group, led by a former child actor Steve Marriott who was later to admit that he could barely play guitar in early days.

Original group contained Jimmy Winston on keyboards, but he was replaced by MacLagan immediately after first success and above was best-known line-up of band which continued to dominate U.K. singles charts over

next three years. **Sha La La La Lee** was a second smash, followed by **Hey Girl, All Or Nothing** (their first No. 1), and **My Mind's Eye** in 1966; **Here Comes The Nice, Itchycoo Park, Tin Soldier** (1967); and **Lazy Sunday** and **The Universal** in 1968.

For **Here Comes The Nice,** group switched to Immediate label, scoring biggest U.S. hit with **Itchycoo Park.** By and large, however, their greatest success was on home turf.

As time went by, group and Marriott in particular grew frustrated by label of Top 10 singles band. They tried hard with albums, but the results were never satisfying – not until the **Ogden's Nut Gone Flake** collection which charted at No. 1 in 1968. With its revolutionary circular cover, this has since been accorded quasiclassic status.

In 1969 Marriott left to form Humble Pie, and the press prepared to write off the chances of the rest. However, Lane, Jones and MacLagan survived this nearfatal blow, eventually re-grouping as Faces with Ron Wood and Rod Stewart and going on to surpass Marriott's Pie in success and acclaim. (♦ Faces, Humble Pie, Steve Marriott, Ronnie Lane.)

Ogdens' Nut Gone Flake.
Courtesy NEMS Records.

Recordings:
Small Faces (—/Decca)
From The Beginning (—/Decca)
Ogden's Nut Gone Flake (Immediate)
Autumn Stone (Immediate)
Compilation:
Vintage Years (Sire/—)

Patti Smith

Rock fan extraordinaire, poet, singer, songwriter, and punk princess of New York, Patti Smith was born in Chicago in December 1946 but grew up in south Jersey. Arrived New York 1967 where, fuelled by influences of Rolling Stones, Dylan, Hendrix, Jim Morrison, William Burroughs and Arthur Rimbaud (there's a little of each in her work and attitudes), she began to evolve form of rock 'n' roll poetry.

She was introduced to rock business by Bob Neuwirth, and during 1971 worked on variety of projects – including co-authoring play, "Cowboy Mouth", with Sam Shepard, and appearing in BBC-TV special.

Her boyfriend Allen Lanier of Blue Öyster Cult (♦) encouraged her to write and sing (she co-composed **Career Of Evil** track on BOC's 1974 **Secret Treaties** album), as did guitarist/rock writer Lenny Kaye who accompanied her on poetry readings at St Mark's Church, New York.

Began to attract cult following enhanced when U.S. "Cream" magazine first put her work into print September 1971. Two volumes of writings and poems, "Seventh Heaven" and "Witt", followed.

By 1974 the poems were giving way to songs, performed to growing following in Manhattan clubs with back-up of Kaye and pianist Richard Sohl. In 1975 group grew to five-piece with additions of Ivan Kral (gtr, bs) and Jay Daugherty (drms), and became focus of New York's emergent new rock scene.

Horses.
Courtesy Arista Records.

First album, produced by John Cale (♦) for Clive Davis' Arista label and released towards end 1975, was real tour de force; juxtaposing rock and literary allusions against a raw-nerved, high-energy musical backdrop evocative of early Stones and Velvet Underground.

Recordings:
Horses (Arista)

Phoebe Snow

Phoebe Snow was born Manhattan, Jul 17, 1952, though when she was three, her parents moved to Teaneck, New Jersey, and she has lived there ever since. It wasn't until the late '60s that she began taking an interest in music – fusing the blues of John Hurt and Big Bill Broonzy, torch songs, and jazz licks to develop her own style.

Even so, she pursued her career with some shyness and reluctance, but when she started playing Greenwich Village folk-clubs, her unique voice, with its amazing range, soon brought her to public attention, and in 1973 she was signed to a contract with Shelter Records, by Dino Airali, who was so excited by her potential, he produced her debut album himself, and acquired the services of prominent musicians, including Dave Mason and David Bromberg. Her first album, **Phoebe Snow,** was a minor revelation, because of the strength of her material, the luscious, quasi-jazzy settings, and her own hypnotic vocals. The single from the album, **Poetry Man,** became a U.S. Top 5 single, and the album went gold with little difficulty. It was an amazing debut; her voice seemed to belong to a mature black singer, rather than a young white one.

Paul Simon was one of the people who were impressed with her, and she sang vocals with him on **Gone At Last,** a track from his **Still Crazy After All These Years** album. She also joined him on several U.S. dates, and moved to Columbia Records

to make her second album, **Second Childhood.** Again, she was provided with the best session-men available; mostly, they were the same crew Simon had used on **Still Crazy;** producer was likewise Phil Ramone. However, **Second Childhood** was slightly disappointing, probably because public expectations were already too extravagant, possibly because her compositions were somewhat weaker. The album, nevertheless, went into the U.S. Top 10. Phoebe Snow is unquestionably one of the brighter talents to emerge in recent years.

Recordings:
Phoebe Snow (Shelter)
Second Childhood (Columbia/CBS)

Soft Machine

Karl Jenkins reeds, keyboards
John Marshall drums
Roy Babbington bass
John Etheridge guitar
Alan Wakeman saxes

The above is approximately the 14th incarnation of this durable British unit, which like so many of its rock avant-garde contemporaries evolved out of activities of outfit Wilde Flowers, which in turn had its origins at Simon Langton School, Canterbury. In 1961 this numbered among its pupils Mike Ratledge, Hugh Hopper, Robert Wyatt (né Ellidge), and David Sinclair.

This group used to congregate at home of Wyatt's writer/broadcaster mother playing latest jazz releases, until in 1962 Wyatt split to enrol at Canterbury College Of Art where he stayed for only short period before drifting penniless across Europe. There he first met Daevid Allen, a 21-year old Australian beatnik with impressive avant-garde credentials. Hugh Hopper joined the pair in Paris, where he became immediately infatuated with Allen's "tape loop" experimentations with then-unknown Terry Riley (♦).

Meanwhile, back in Canterbury, Wilde Flowers had been formed. Personnel changed weekly but included Hopper, Wyatt, Kevin Ayers, and all four original members of Caravan.

They played a little jazz, a touch of rock, but when Daevid Allen came across from France the balance was tipped in favour of rock and free-form improvisation.

Bored with studies at Oxford University, Mike Ratledge returned to Canterbury, his arrival proving some kind of catalyst. Hugh Hopper went off with Pye Hastings and Richard Coughlan to form next version of Wilde Flowers later to become Caravan (♦); while Ratledge (kybds), Wyatt (drms), Ayers (bs, vcls), Allen (gtr) formed own band. They used variety of different names but finally settled on Soft Machine, from William Burroughs' novel. (Allen phoned Burroughs in Paris to get writer's permission.)

Arriving in London, one of earliest gigs was playing opposite early Pink Floyd at UFO Club. Met West Coast eccentric Kim Fowley (♦) who produced group's first single **Feelin' Reelin'**

Squeelin'/Love Makes Sweet Music, the sessions featuring rhythm guitar by Jimi Hendrix who was cutting own debut single **Hey Joe** at same studio.

The record made no impact on release mid-1967, and Softs travelled to France. In St Tropez they become involved in "total environment" happenings surrounding Alan Zion's production of Picasso play "Desire Attrappe Par La Queue", this multi-media experiment eventually being broken up by local gendarmerie. It was beginning of group's considerable reputation in France.

Unfortunately, on their return to Britain, Daevid Allen was denied re-entry. He made way back to Paris and later emerged as founder of Gong (♦).

Reduced to trio, 1968 found Softs working as support on Hendrix's first American tour, at end of which they recorded first album with producer Tom Wilson in New York. Both were somewhat stressful experiences, and Soft Machine subsequently disbanded.

Soft Machine Seven.
Courtesy CBS Records.

Ayers went to Majorca to write songs; Ratledge returned to London; while Wyatt hung around in New York before travelling to Los Angeles.

Finally, in 1969, Probe label decided to release first album, pressuring Wyatt to reassemble band. Ratledge agreed but Ayers couldn't be tracked down (♦ Kevin Ayers). Instead, Wyatt recruited aforementioned Hugh Hopper (bs) to record 1969 second set **Volume Two.**

They embarked on arduous string of U.K. gigs, towards end of which they boosted line-up to seven-piece by additions of jazzers Elton Dean (sx), Marc Charig (tpt), Nick Evans (trom) – all from Keith Tippett Group – and Lyn Dobson (sitar, flt, sx).

This is widely regarded by aficionados as best-ever Softs line-up. Unfortunately they never recorded together. By time of **Third** (1970) Evans, Charig and Dobson had left, largely because band could no longer afford them. Founder-member Wyatt was also now becoming estranged from Ratledge and rest. In early 1971 came **Fourth,** the band's first album to appeal to jazz-rock cross-over audience, after which Wyatt split to form Matching Mole (♦ Robert Wyatt).

For **Fifth** (1972) Phil Howard took drum stool, but was dismissed during recording after clash with Ratledge, and John Marshall (ex Nucleus, Jack Bruce Band) completed sessions.

By May 1972 Dean had been replaced by another former Nucleus sideman Karl Jenkins, and after

Sixth (1973) Hopper, too, went own way. He recorded **1984** solo album and then joined Isotope (♦). Another jazzer, Roy Babbington, took his place.

Seventh, not surprisingly, demonstrated growing jazz influence. However, it also evidenced a certain dearth of feeling and wit, the latter quality seemingly having left band along with Wyatt.

In Feb 1974 Alan Holdsworth (gtr) came in for year's stay before replaced by Etheridge. Ratledge quit, severing last link with original Softs, band then joined by Alan Wakeman, cousin of Rick Wakeman (♦).

With their revolutionary structures and harmonies, their unusual jazz voicings, and free-form improvisation, Soft Machine have profoundly influenced European rock scene. However, their most exciting periods are to be found on earlier work, particularly first four albums.

Recordings:
The Soft Machine (Probe)
Volume Two (Probe)
Third (Columbia/CBS)
Fourth (Columbia/CBS)
Fifth (Columbia/CBS)
Sixth (Columbia/CBS)
Seventh (Columbia/CBS)
Bundles (Harvest)
Softs (Harvest)

Sonny & Cher

Husband/wife team who first came to international attention in middle '60s. Sonny was born Salvatore Bono on Feb 16, 1935 in Detroit, son of Italian immigrants who later journeyed to Los Angeles.

In 1951 he wrote his first song, **Koko Joe,** while working as market box-boy (in 1964 it was a minor hit for the Righteous Brothers (♦)); he was then employed with his father on aircraft assembly line until the family broke up.

He married in 1954, and a daughter was born 1958; took a succession of jobs to support his family (e.g. waiter, masseur) but continued to write songs and, while working as a truck-driver in Hollywood, took time out to audition them.

On strength of this, he was given a job as apprentice producer with Specialty Records, and from then on worked in the record industry – later moving to Hi-Fi records – though with little initial success.

He was divorced at this time, and shortly after started working for Philles Records as assistant to Phil Spector (♦). He also met half-Indian girl, Cherilyn Sakisian (b. May 20, 1946 in El Centro, California). She had moved to Hollywood because she wanted to be an actress. She met Sonny in 1963; the next year they took a day trip to Tijuana and got married.

Sonny had been trying to persuade Spector to record Cher; Spector was reluctant, but Cher did get to sing back-up on recording of **Da Doo Ron Ron** when Darlene Love failed to turn up for session. Sonny had some personal success when one of his compositions, **Needles And Pins** (co-written with Jack Nitzsche) became No. 1 hit in U.K. for The Searchers.

They worked together as Caesar And Cleo before reverting to

their real names, and using Sonny's business connections to make a record – **Baby Don't Go** for Reprise. They shifted to Atlantic to make **Just You** and then **I Got You Babe** in 1965.

It was a magnificent single, perfectly moulded in the folk-rock sound of the time (i.e. that identified with The Byrds) and had lyrics about groovy true love. Almost overnight Sonny & Cher became one of the most commercially successful and well-publicised of contemporary acts. They dressed eccentrically, and were regularly asked to leave hotels and restaurants. They made marriage and love fashionable, and became prominent on hippie high-society circuit – they gave parties for visitors like Twiggy, and Rolling Stones slept on their floor when they were an unsuccessful act in the U.S.

With Cher's dark good looks and Sonny's talent as a composer and appearance of looniness, they enjoyed a succession of hit singles, both together and separately – Cher recorded **Bang Bang** and Dylan's **All I Really Got To Do**, and Sonny **Laugh At Me**. In 1966 they moved into movies, with "Good Times", which was directed by William Friedkin (whose later works include "The French Connection" and "The Exorcist").

There was a lull in their fortunes during the acid-rock period. Sonny was very puritanical about drugs; in 1968 he and Cher made an anti-dope film for schools. Also, as everyone else was by now dressing as wildly as they did, so they became less distinctive. They made a second film, "Chastity" (the name of their daughter), but it was a flop.

In 1970 they moved into the Las Vegas night-spots and television, with their own one-hour show,

Below: Togetherness for Sonny and Cher, the couple who made marriage hip, but finally proved that all they ever needed was more than each other in their lengthy and bitter divorce proceedings.

after which they became bigger than ever before, and even had another hit single, **All I Ever Need Is You.** They continued to be involved with social and political issues (both were on the board of the Drug Abuse Council and Cerebral Palsy Foundation), and have worked for Democratic Party presidential candidates (Robert Kennedy and Hubert Humphrey).

But it was becoming more evident that Cher was the real star; in 1974 they began protracted and bitter divorce proceedings. After which they had individual shows – Sonny's flopped, but Cher's ratings improved after a less healthy start (Cher).

Recordings:
Look At Us (Atco/Atlantic)
Wondrous World Of Sonny And Cher (Atco/Atlantic)
In Case You're In Love (Atco/Atlantic)
Good Times (Atco/Atlantic)
Sonny & Cher Live (MCA)
All I Ever Need Is You (MCA)
Mama Was A Rock 'n' Roll Singer, Papa Used To Write All Her Songs (MCA)
Compilations:
The Best Of Sonny And Cher (Atco/Atlantic)

Sons Of Champlin

Bill Champlin vocals, keyboards, guitar
Geoff Palmer keyboards, horns, vocals
Terry Haggerty guitar
Dave Schallock bass, vocals
Jim Preston drums
Phil Wood brass, keyboards
Mark Isham brass, synthesiser, keyboards
Michael Andreas woodwinds

Probably the longest-lived second division San Francisco band, the Sons Of Champlin formed in 1966 with Champlin, Palmer and Haggerty from the current line-up, together with Jim Myers and Bill Bowen (drms), Al Strong (bs) and

Tim Caine (sax). An album was recorded at this time but never released, and it wasn't until the group signed with Capitol in 1969 (minus Myers, who entered the services) that their first album, a double, hit the streets.

Only a few months later, a second was released under the name of The Sons, with the temporary addition of a trumpet player, but the group broke up in early 1970, with the members playing in various small-time bands around the Bay Area. At the end of 1970, they decided to re-form as The Sons, and a third album was released in April 1971, this time with a line-up of Champlin, Palmer, Haggerty, Strong and Bowen.

In the summer of 1971, Strong and Bowen left after personal differences at the same time as the band changed its name to Yogi Phlegm, and were replaced by David Schallock on bass (ex Big Brother and the Holding Company) and Bill Vitt on drums. The latter didn't stay for too long, and was replaced by Jim Preston at about the same time as the group changed its name back to (variously) The Sons or The Sons Of Champlin. An album was recorded for Columbia but was unsuccessful, and it wasn't until 1975 that the band made another album for yet another company, the newly-formed Ariola America.

Undoubtedly a product of the drug culture, the Sons Of Champlin seem to have no great desire to succeed in the terms of their peers like the Jefferson Airplane/Starship or Grateful Dead, but their first and fourth albums, together with a limited edition live album, are recommended if they can be found.

Recordings:
Loosen Up – Naturally (Capitol/—)
The Sons (Capitol/—)
Minus Seeds And Stems (Limited Edition)
Follow Your Heart (Capitol/—)
Welcome To The Dance (Columbia/CBS)
The Sons Of Champlin (Ariola America)

Circle Filled With Love (Ariola/America)

Joe South

One of the first session-men to become a star in his own right, South was born in Atlanta, Georgia, Feb 28, 1942. He learned to play guitar at age 11, and in 1957 was invited to join a band led by Pete Drake; by the early '60s he had cut a few tracks for a local record company, and his dexterity as a guitarist regularly brought him session-work in Nashville and Muscle Shoals, working with artists such as Bob Dylan and Aretha Franklin. In 1966 Columbia flew him to New York to play on Simon & Garfunkel's **Sounds Of Silence.** In the meantime, he picked up experience of practically every aspect of the recording business, on both the creative and the business sides, and also worked as a country DJ for a time.

His compositions began to be widely recorded, and he wrote **Untie Me** for The Tams, **Down In The Boondocks** for Billy Joe Royal, and **Hush**, which was successfully covered by Deep Purple.

By 1968 South had decided he could do well in his own right, and acquired a contract with Capitol, and recorded an album, **Introspect.** One of the tracks, **Games People Play,** began to be widely covered, and hence Capitol reissued the album in 1969, making that song, which was also issued as a single, the new title track. Both single and album went gold (the single reached No. 12 in the U.S. and No. 6 in the U.K.).

South made two further albums, **Don't It Make You Wanta Go Home?** (1969) and **So The Seeds Are Growing** (1971), which contained more celebrated compositions – particularly the title track of the former, **Walk A Mile In My Shoes,** and **Rose Garden,** which became a massive hit for Lynn Anderson on both sides of the Atlantic.

In 1971, however, South dropped out of the business for three years, as a result of the joint strain of the pressures he had suffered during three years as a top-notch country-rock performer, and of the death of his brother, Tommy South. Joe lived in the jungles of Maui, in Hawaii, in the intervening period, before re-emerging in 1975 with a new album, **Midnight Rainbows,** which had been recorded in Atlanta with the assistance of some members of the Atlanta Rhythm Section ().

Recordings:
Games People Play (Capitol)
Don't It Make You Wanta Go Home? (Capitol)
So The Seeds Are Growing (Capitol)
Midnight Rainbows (Island/—)
Compilation:
Greatest Hits (Capitol)

Souther Hillman Furay Band

John David Souther guitar, vocals
Chris Hillman bass, guitar,

mandolin, vocals
Richie Furay guitar, vocals
Paul Harris keyboards
Al Perkins steel guitar
Jim Gordon drums

Formed in September 1973 as a ready-made supergroup á la Crosby, Stills, Nash and Young the SHF Band boasted talents from just about every seminal West Coast group. Furay had been in The Buffalo Springfield and Poco, Hillman in the Byrds, The Flying Burrito Brothers and Stephen Stills' Manassas, Souther in Longbranch Pennywhistle with Glenn Frey of The Eagles, as well as making a solo album and being a noted songwriter for such as Linda Ronstadt and Bonnie Raitt, Harris having played on sessions for anyone who was anyone, likewise Gordon, and Perkins, also a Burrito and a member of Manassas.

Despite the obvious promise displayed, the chemistry was wrong, and after one album with the lineup as above, and a second with Ron Grinel replacing Gordon, the group evaporated into a number of solo projects.

Recordings:
The Souther Hillman Furay Band (Asylum)
Trouble In Paradise (Asylum)
John David Souther:
John David Souther (Asylum)

Spanky And Our Gang

Elaine "Spanky" McFarlane lead vocals
Nigel Pickering guitar, vocals
Bill Plummer bass, vocals
Marc McLure steel guitar, banjo, vocals
Jim Moon drums

The original Spanky and Our Gang was formed in 1966, comprising Spanky, Nigel Pickering, John Seiter (drms), Malcolm Hale (gtr, vcls), Geoffrey Myers (bs, vcls) and Lefty Baker (gtr, vcls), and in this aggregation, or with the substitution of Kenny Hodges for Geoffrey Myers, produced several excellent harmony-based hits until 1969, when Spanky retired to tend to her children.

Their best-known songs from that period include **Sunday Will Never Be The Same, Lazy Day** and **Like To Get To Know You,** typified by Spanky's crystal-clear voice penetrating the harmonies of the male voices surrounding her.

After the group's demise, Pickering went on a world cruise, while the whereabouts of the rest of the original group are uncertain. During 1975, Spanky and Pickering reunited, and with the help of Jim Moon (ex Byrds) and numerous session-musicians – Marc McLure, maker of several solo albums, and Bill Plummer, featured on the Rolling Stones' **Exile On Main Street** and leader of his own group, the Cosmic Brotherhood – made a fine album which instantly recreated the glories of the group's past.

Recordings:
Spanky And Our Gang (Mercury)
Like To Get To Know You (Mercury)
Without Rhyme Or Reason

B/W Anything You Choose (Mercury)
Live (Mercury/—)
Change (Epic/—)
Spanky's Greatest Hits (Mercury/—)

Sparks

Ron Mael keyboards
Russell Mael vocals
Dinky Diamond drums
Ian Hampton bass
Trevor White guitar

Originally Halfnelson, formed as trio Los Angeles 1968 by Mael brothers (Ron the eldest) with guitarist Earle Mankey. Received first recording contract 1970 when Maels sent demo tape to Todd Rundgren (♦), who arranged signing to Albert Grossman's Bearsville label and flew to Hollywood to produce first album, at which point band was augmented by Harley Feinstein (drms) and Jim Mankey (bs, gtr), younger brother of Earle.

Kimono My House.
Courtesy Island Records.

Thus constituted, they released first album January 1971 to little success after which they changed management and name – to Sparks. The album was released a second time, re-credited to Sparks, but again didn't sell, although a single, **Wonder Girl,** enjoyed minor U.S. chart success.

At this point group embarked on three-month European tour, returning to U.S. 1972 in time for release of second album, **A Tweeter In Woofer's Clothing.** But this failed to register too, and it was largely out of a sense of desperation that the Maels travelled to Britain to sign new contract with Island Records. When work permit problems denied them use of former associates, the brothers recruited new support (of which Dinky Diamond is only survivor) via ads in music press.

Their first album, **Kimono My House** (1974), produced by Spencer Davis alumnus Muff Winwood, was widely hailed in U.K. rock press as a significant breakthrough. Ron Mael's lyrics evidenced a keen wit which, when backdropped 'against outrageously ambitious arrangements, revealed a highly literate yet ostensibly innocent and fresh approach to jaded pop modes. The single, **This Town Ain't Big Enough For The Both Of Us,** raced into the U.K. Top 10.

Propaganda (1974) continued this innovative style, with slightly less success. Subsequently, however, the Maels displayed an inability to develop the format. Furthermore, they proved manifestly unable to handle live performances on anything other than

teenybopper level.

Subsequent singles failed to meet earlier success, and group began descent into contrived pastiche and embarrassing plays for bopper market. Maels have since returned to States to resume residency there.

First two albums originally unreleased in U.K., but were packaged together in Warner Bros double-set released 1975.

Recordings:
Sparks (Bearsville/—)
A Tweeter In Woofer's Clothing (Bearsville/—)
Kimono My House (Island)
Propaganda (Island)
Indiscreet (Island)

Phil Spector

The First Tycoon Of Teen, as Tom Wolfe described him in his book "The Kandy Kolored Tangerine Flake Streamline Baby", Phillip Harvey Spector is one of the single most enigmatic figures in rock history while also being among the most seminal of pioneers in the genre.

He was born in The Bronx district of New York, Dec 25, 1940, but was taken by his widowed mother to Los Angeles at age 12. He started to play guitar and piano while at high school, and first influences were emergent R&B typified by work of writer/producers Jerry Leiber & Mike Stoller (♦) with whom young Spector began hanging out during Los Angeles studio sessions.

Started own career in 1958 when he formed trio The Teddy Bears (Spector, Annette Bard, Marshall Lieb) and enjoyed massive international success with his song **To Know Him Is To Love Him.** Spector was nine when his father, Benjamin, died, and is said to have got inspiration for song title from inscription on tombstone.

Phil Spector's Christmas Album. Polydor Records.

When Teddy Bears failed to consolidate on initial success, Spector turned to production first on West Coast with Lester Sills (who was producing Duane Eddy) and later in New York as understudy to Leiber and Stoller at Atlantic Records. He co-wrote with Leiber Ben E. King's **Spanish Harlem** and played guitar break on Drifters' **On Broadway.** First self-produced New York hit was Ray Peterson's **Corinna Corinna,** a U.S. Top 10 Christmas 1960. Other hits followed, including Curtis Lee's **Pretty Little Angel Eyes** and Gene Pitney's **Every Breath I Take.**

It was around this time boy-genius Spector evidenced first signs of extrovert nature, cutting

a bizarre figure on Manhattan boulevards with his flowing hair, black cloak and wraparound dark glasses. However, New York apparently became too overpowering for him and he returned to West Coast to form own label Philles with Lester Sill, the name deriving from combination of partners' Christian names.

His first signing was The Crystals (Barbara Alston, Pat Wright, Deedee Kennibrew, Lala Brooks) who he found in New York, and intended to groom as his own version of that city's then topselling girlie group The Shirelles (**Will You Still Love Me Tomorrow?**). Their first single was a song Spector had co-written, **There's No Other (Like My Baby),** which went to No. 20 in national charts October 1961 and gave first hints of production techniques later to be employed.

In 1962 Spector assumed full control of Philles by buying out Sill's share, and recorded second Crystals' single in Hollywood, the stunningly innovative teen anthem **He's A Rebel,** using session support of the likes of Leon Russell (♦), jazzman Barney Kessell and Sonny Bono (♦ Sonny & Cher). Also present was Jack Nitzsche, who became regular Philles arranger, and studio engineer Larry Levine who worked on every Spector record for next eight years. Nitzsche would later turn up in Crazy Horse (♦).

He's A Rebel became U.S. million-seller, and in mid-1963 Spector strengthened his roster by signing another New York girl group The Ronettes (Veronica "Ronnie" Bennett, Estelle Bennett, Nedra Talley). Two sisters – one of whom, Ronnie, would later marry Spector – and a cousin, they were spotted by the producer working at New York's Peppermint Lounge, and were to prove an even more potent vocal force than Crystals.

With the Spector/Ellie Greenwich/Jeff Barry composition **Be My Baby** their first release, they also sold a million that same year, following with **Baby I Love You, The Best Part Of Breakin' Up, Do I Love You** and a string of what are now regarded as pop classics.

Meanwhile Crystals continued to ring up cash registers with **Da Doo Ron Ron** and **Then He Kissed Me,** and hits for new signings Bob B. Soxx And The Blue Jeans (**Zip-A-Dee-Doo-Dah**) and Darlene Love (**Today I Met The Boy I'm Gonna Marry**) established this eccentric young production genius – a dollar millionaire by age 21 – as the hottest property in American music business.

Spector's talent lay deeper than simply with his astounding production expertise; after his own enigmatic fashion, he was also a shrewd business operator taking on only those acts he could manipulate to success, releasing only those records he knew would sell. This resulted in a comparatively low product rate, but highly lucrative turnover per release.

One of his few failures was due to events beyond his control. This was the semi-legendary Spector Christmas album, originally titled **A Christmas Gift To You.** It comprised various aforementioned Philles acts working through a repertoire of Christmas standards, all treated with characteristically lavish Spector production, a labour of love on which he toiled for over a year. But on the day scheduled for release, Nov 22, 1963 John Kennedy was assassinated and few Americans felt inclined to pick up on Spector's jolly Christmas gift.

The album was never shipped or promoted, and when Spector's Philles operation ceased in 1966 it became a prized collectors' item. Subsequently, however, the album has thrice been repackaged and is now regularly re-promoted each Christmas.

Another sign of Spector's shrewdness was his use of instrumental flip-sides to Philles singles, the notion being to prevent DJs avoiding "A"-side for even infrequent air-plays. On these he gave his session-men free reign.

Thus emerged Spector The First Tycoon Of Teen, although his best was yet to come. In 1964 he signed The Righteous Brothers (♦) and produced what many have acclaimed as the ultimate pop record, **You've Lost That Lovin' Feelin'**. Here his genius for production truly blossomed to create a single of epic proportion, the zenith of his so-called "wall of sound" technique. It was a smash hit across the world Jan 1965.

In the following year Spector pulled off another comparable all-time classic with **River Deep Mountain High** for Ike And Tina Turner (♦), but this time the American public failed to accord him the attention this new masterpiece deserved – though it would be more accurate to say they weren't given the chance.

It is now recognised that Spector had simply become too successful for his own good, and that jealousy within U.S. music circles was conspiring to thwart his meteoric progress. Certainly **River Deep** was boycotted: white radio stations declared it too black; black stations declared it too white. In all except Britain where the record was a smash, Spector's magnum opus fell on stony ground – it was a blow to his pride which was to contribute to his virtual retirement from music business and closure of Philles shortly after.

From that point Spector became ever more the eccentric, leaving New York to take up residence in closely-guarded Hollywood home. Apart from cameo appearance as dope-pusher in "Easy Rider" movie, and work for new findings The Checkmates (on their 1969 **Proud Mary** hit he reputedly used some 300 musicians, losing money in process despite minor hit), he remained virtually inactive until turn of the '70s.

During mid-'60s Spector had visited Britain on couple of occasions – he co-wrote Rolling Stones' **Little By Little** with Mick Jagger – and it was in company of The Beatles, long-time aficionados of his work, that he finally re-surfaced.

He was first brought in by John Lennon to produce **Instant Karma**, and later to doctor final controversial Beatles set **Let It Be** – much to the chagrin of Paul McCartney (♦ Beatles). However, he stayed on to work with other solo Beatles – producing George Harrison's **All Things Must Pass**

and **Bangla Desh** albums, and successive albums for John Lennon and Plastic Ono Band. Close relationship with Lennon remains (♦ John Lennon).

Rarely giving interviews, his life shrouded in rumour and mystique, Spector survived two near-fatal car crashes in early 1975. Recent activities include returning Philles' catalogue to circulation in U.K. via Phil Spector International – virtually all early product can now be attained on compilation albums – and working on West Coast with Cher, Dion, Darlene Love, Nilsson and newest discovery Jerri Bo Keno. Still uses Gold Star Studios in Los Angeles where he produced most of classic singles.

Other less-known facets of Spector's intriguing career are that he was a close friend and supporter of satirist Lenny Bruce (he is said to have paid large sum to buy police photos of Bruce's corpse to prevent them getting into circulation); and that he financed Kung Fu superstar Bruce Lee's last movie "Enter The Dragon". The deaths of Bruce and Lee, and of other close friends Bobby Darin, Tom Donahue (♦) and Ralph Gleason, have contributed to his long-standing withdrawal into privacy.

To this day Spector's pioneering production techniques remain a monumental influence on contemporary rock, while the innocence of his teen-pop masterpieces of the '60s will never likely be surpassed.

There are two excellent books available on Spector's career; "Out Of His Head" by Richard Williams and "The Phil Spector Story" by Rob Finnis. The latter contains a minutely-detailed chronological list of all Spector's production and writing credits.

Chris Spedding

During 1975 Spedding wasn't the only guitarist approached by Rolling Stones as possible replacement for Mick Taylor. But he was most certainly the only one whose previous credits included appearances on BBC-TV's "Top Of The Pops" disguised under furry costume as one of kiddies' favourites The Wombles (♦ Mike Batt)! As for the Stones, Spedding claims to have turned them down.

Born Sheffield, England, 1943, Spedding's first instrument was violin, which he gave up in early 'teens to learn guitar. From Sheffield band The Vulcans he arrived in London 1960, playing for three years with unknown country group which mostly toured U.S. bases. During 1964–65 he entertained passengers on the P&O liner Himalaya, subsequent to which he played bass briefly for Alan Price (♦) and later guitar for Paul Jones.

In 1967 he formed The Battered Ornaments with Pete Brown (♦), and through Brown met Jack Bruce (♦). This brought him first of session gigs – on Bruce's 1969-released **Songs For A Tailor**, the year the Ornaments sundered. Spedding next turned up, again briefly, in Ian Carr's Nucleus jazz-group, but from this point mainly concentrated on session-work. Lulu, Gilbert O'Sullivan, John Cale, Dusty Springfield, David Essex, Donovan are just a

few of disparate acts he has worked with. For Donovan's **Cosmic Wheels** (1973) album, he also wrote string arrangements. In 1971 and 1972 took time out to record two solo albums.

His background was similar in a way to Jimmy Page (♦ Led Zeppelin). He was one of the hottest young session-players of his day when, in autumn 1972, he got together with ex Free (♦) bassist Andy Fraser and formed Sharks. This was a band which had everything going for it – when Fraser left after first album, **First Water** (Island 1973), outfit comprised, apart from Spedding, Buster Cherry Jones (bs), Snips (vcls), Nick Judd (kybds) and Marty Simon (drms) – and indeed they were one of Island Records' Great White Hopes of '70s.

They were a good band too, highly rated by critics, especially for Spedding's tasteful guitar work, but somehow they never realised their potential. After second album, **Jab It In Yore Eye** (Island 1974), Judd and Simon quit, and the group finally disintegrated in November that year in somewhat bitter circumstances. In 1975 Spedding was back in familiar role as session-man, though he also worked for time with Roy Harper (♦) band Trigger. However, one of characteristics of Spedding's latter-day career had been an almost success-at-any-cost approach; and this, towards the middle of year, saw him quit Island to reappear in somewhat strange company of pop producer Mickie Most (♦).

The pair connived to produce for him a somewhat tardy James Dean image, and a slice of punk bubblegum, **Motorbikin'**, which took Spedding into U.K. singles charts for debut hit. A subsequent album from this collaboration, the eponymous **Chris Spedding** (1976), found the guitarist/singer going through his paces on a remarkable set of rock pastiches, performed with cold-blooded brilliance.

Jazzman turned Womble turned supersideman turned pop star at age 32, truly the chameleon of rock.

Recordings:
Backward Progression (—/Harvest)
The Only Lick I Know (—/Harvest)
Chris Spedding (—/RAK)

The Spencer Davis Group

Spencer Davis vocals, guitar, harmonica
Stevie Winwood vocals, guitar, keyboards
Muff Winwood bass
Pete York drums

Above: The Spencer Davis Group, with Stevie Winwood (second left).

Original line-up as above, formed 1963 out of varied backgrounds: Muff Winwood had led eight-piece mainstream jazz band with brother Stevie sometimes on piano and vocals; Pete York was into likes of jazzers Kirk, Ellington, Basie; while Davis worked with trad jazz band and had his own solo blues spot playing 12-string guitar and singing Leadbelly and Big Bill Broonzy material.

Having sat in on occasions with each others' bands, Davis – a former lecturer at Birmingham University – initiated the new unit which started August 1963 with residency at Golden Eagle public house in Birmingham. They played R&B of different flavours, ranging from John Lee Hooker to Betty Everett, and were immediately distinctive due to the prodigious vocal prowess of Stevie Winwood.

Winwood (b. Birmingham, May 12, 1948) was only 16 on group's formation but his keyboard style and high-pitched and emotive vocals, evincing strong influence of emergent Motown sound, displayed a maturity far beyond his years. Davis, some years his senior, appeared a paternal figure by comparison.

It was when the group got together with West Indian writer Jackie Edwards that the hit format came. **Keep On Running** (1965), **Somebody Help Me** (1966) were both U.K. No. 1 singles; the group's own **Gimme Some Lovin'** making No. 2 spot later in 1966. Island label founder Chris Blackwell was early producer.

By 1967, however, Stevie Winwood was flexing his muscles for greater things, and after the group's last big hit in 1967 with **I'm A Man** (written by Stevie and producer Jimmy Miller) he left them to form Traffic (♦).

Band subsequently drifted apart – Muff Winwood now works for Island Records as executive – until Davis pulled together a new Spencer Davis Group retaining York and bringing in Eddie Hardin (kybds), Phil Sawyer (gtr), and Charlie McCracken (bs). But without Stevie the magic had gone, and the band never settled sufficiently to make much headway. Sawyer was replaced by Ray Fenwick, and Hardin & York split to form own eponymous duo.

After another attempt with rhythm section of Nigel Olsson and Dee Murray (later with Elton John), Davis eventually wrapped the group up in 1969 when he moved to California.

There he worked fitfully, forming an acoustic duo first with Alun Davies (who later worked with Cat Stevens band) and later with Peter Jameson. He also recorded with bluesman Fred McDowell. Personal problems forced him

Mark Andes (bs) and Jay Ferguson (vcls) were joined by John Locke (kybds) and Ed Cassidy (drms). The last-named, reputedly California's stepfather though they now deny it, was a colourful character. Born sometime around 1930, he had had a chequered career spanning modern jazz (as sideman for likes of Cannonball Adderley, Gerry Mulligan, Thelonius Monk) and was, for short time, part of Rising Sons with Taj Mahal (♦) and Ry Cooder (♦). He was certainly one of the few bald-headed drummers in rock.

Twelve Dreams of Dr. Sardonicus. Courtesy Epic, CBS.

Basing style on Ferguson's songs and jazz affiliations of new recruits, Spirit recorded a quartet of exceptional albums over next three years – first two in 1968, third in 1969 – before breaking up during recording of highly-acclaimed 1970 set **The Twelve Dreams Of Doctor Sardonicus.** This was subsequently pieced together by producer David Briggs.

Though they enjoyed loyal following and good reviews, they never achieved comparative success. Following the split, Andes and Ferguson formed Jo Jo Gunne (♦), while California convalesced after a riding accident – he didn't return to recording until sub-standard 1973-released Epic solo album listed below.

Locke and Cassidy continued Spirit in company of Texas-born twins Al and Christian Staehely. This line-up lasted only until sessions for disappointing **Feedback** (1971), at which point the two originals quit, leaving Staehelys

Mike ...... keyboards, vocals
Luther Grosvenor guitar
Greg Ridley bass
Mike Kellie drums

Original line-up as above, Spooky Tooth were a product of the late '60s progressive boom and became an integral part of the British underground rock scene without ever attaining heavyweight status. What success they enjoyed was usually on foreign soil, and they often appeared as more an academy for musicians than a band in their own right.

Keyboardsmen Wright and Harrison were the leaders, the group's basically hard rock music being characterised by their contrasting writing and singing styles. They had vastly different backgrounds: Harrison (b. Carlisle, England, 1945) had worked as an export clerk before joining The V.I.P.s (alongside Mike Kellie); while Wright was born in New Jersey, U.S. (also 1943), and had been a child actor in the U.S. before studying psychology. It was these studies which first brought him to Europe.

With original line-up, group cut first and second albums in 1968 and 1969, providing later versions of the band with some of most-requested material – viz. **Sunshine Help Me, Evil Woman, Better By You.** They were sometimes compared to Traffic, with whom they shared the same record producer, American Jimmy Miller.

(First album was not released in U.S. until early '70s under new title **Tobacco Road.**

By **Ceremony** (1969) Greg Ridley had left to join Humble Pie (♦). Initiated by Wright, this was a strange album on which they shared credit with Pierre Henry, a French pioneer of electronic music; Wright wrote music and lyrics and Henry added electronic overdubs. There was nothing in band's past to suggest this somewhat bizarre new turn. Nevertheless, the album took group into the U.S. charts and stayed there for some months.

Wright quit at this point, however, to form own short-lived

Wonderwheel, and other members fell by the wayside – Luther Grosvenor later re-surfaced with Mott The Hoople (♦) under unlikely pseudonym Ariel Bender. As a final gesture, Harrison brought in former Grease Band (♦) stalwarts Henry McCullough, Chris Stainton and Alan Spenner, and recorded the excellent **The Last Puff,** which again put Spooky Tooth name in U.S. charts but was largely ignored in homeland.

You Broke My Heart So I Busted Your Jaw. Courtesy Island.

At this point Harrison, too, decided on solo career, and Spooky Tooth was officially defunct. However, neither Wright or Harrison were overburdened with individual acclaim, and in 1973 they reconstituted their old band, retaining Kellie on drums and bringing in Mick Jones (gtr) and Chris Stewart (bs). This band cut two albums, both in 1973, again without a great deal of success. Vocalist Mike Patto joined them for the 1974 **The Mirror** set, but the group disintegrated for second time in November same year.

Wright and Harrison are again pursuing solo careers, the former this time with considerable success (♦ Gary Wright).

Recordings:
It's All About (—/Island) retitled **Tobacco Road** (A&M) for later U.S. release
Spooky Two (A&M/Island)
Ceremony (with Pierre Henry) (A&M/Island)
The Last Puff (A&M/Island)
You Broke My Heart So I Busted Your Jaw (A&M/Island)
Witness (Island)
The Mirror (Island/Good Ear)
Compilation:
The Best Of Spooky Tooth (—/Island)

Dusty Springfield

Born Mary O'Brien, Apr 16, 1939 in Hampstead, London, she was the best female rock singer Britain ever produced.

With Tom Springfield (her brother) and Tim Field, she formed The Springfields, an antiseptic British equivalent of Peter, Paul & Mary, in 1960. After Field had been replaced by Mike Hurst (who later went on to produce Cat Stevens ♦) and The Springfields had had a couple of respectable British hit records **(Island Of Dreams, Say I Won't Be There)** and an impressive American one **(Silver Threads And Golden Needles),** the group

suddenly disbanded in September 1963.

Dusty's solo career immediately took off with **I Only Want To Be With You** in December 1963 as she threw over the commercial folkiness of The Springfields and flirted with the new rhythmic sounds emanating from Detroit, via the Tamla-Motown studios. Though Motown was her first love, she was nothing if not versatile, and recorded a wide range of material by top songwriters – **I Just Don't Know What To Do With Myself** and **Wishin' And Hopin'** by Burt Bacharach and Hal David, **Some Of Your Lovin'** and **Goin' Back** by Carole King and Gerry Goffin, as well as the dramatic Italian ballad **You Don't Have To Say You Love Me,** which reached No. 1 in the U.K. and No. 4 in the U.S. 1966.

Her best album, and the one which fully demonstrated her capabilities as an interpreter of soul music, was **Dusty In Memphis,** produced by Jerry Wexler with the aid of the top local sessioneers. The album engendered the hit single, **Son Of A Preacherman,** a classic song of which Dusty's remains the supreme interpretation.

Dusty Springfield had 14 British hits between 1963–68, after which her level of success, which had become increasingly fitful, began to drop off as the problems of her personal life intruded on her professional one. She has not performed publicly in Britain since 1972, and has not released an album since 1973. Though the passing years only enhance, Garbo-like, the Springfield myth, she now lives reclusively in America, occasionally turning-up as a backing vocalist (e.g. on Anne Murray's **Together**). Elton John was understood to want to sign her to Rocket Records and launch a comeback for her (in the mid-'60s, Kiki Dee had been little more than an ersatz Dusty Springfield, but the projected deal fell through.

A Girl Called Dusty. Courtesy Phonogram Ltd.

Dusty's last album, **Cameo,** was recorded in 1973 on the West Coast with ABC staff producers Steve Barri and Lambert and Potter, and included a version of Van Morrison's **Tupelo Honey.** It was heavily under-publicised. Discography is selective.

Recordings:
A Girl Called Dusty (—/Philips)
Everything's Coming Up Dusty (—/Philips)
Where Am I Going ? (—/Philips)
Dusty In Memphis (Atlantic/Philips)
A Brand New Me (Atlantic/Philips)
Cameo (Dunhill/Phonogram)

Compilation:
Golden Hits (Philips)

Bruce Springsteen

Springsteen was born Sep 23, 1949, in Freehold, New Jersey, and in 1965 began commuting to Greenwich Village to play guitar at the Cafe Wha. He was young and ambitious and wanted desperately to be a rock star. He formed bands called Steel Mill, and Dr Zoom and the Sonic Boom. After a short spell at New Jersey Community College, he went to the West Coast, but failed an audition with a local record company and returned East, to begin gigging in clubs again.

In 1972 he met Mike Appel, who became his manager and producer. Appel took him to John Hammond (♦) at Columbia, and Springsteen was signed immediately, as a solo artist. Towards the end of the year, he cut **Greetings From Asbury Park NJ**, which was released in January 1973. It was a successful debut album – it served its purpose, it attracted rock media attention, his name was noised abroad; it was close to Dylan, but it was equally apparent that Springsteen had more vitality and imagination than run-of-the-mill Dylan plagiarists.

His second album, **The Wild, The Innocent And The E-Street Shuffle** marked the beginnings of his back-up group, the E-Street Band, and also saw the intensification of the rock press campaign, which swelled to an hysterical pitch.

He also developed his act into a lengthy show that dramatised his narrative pieces. Many of his songs were too long or too self-indulgent, he tried too hard to be special, to be everything that everyone was saying he was – yet despite all this, the talent was there; and then Jon Landau of "Rolling Stone" made his well-intentioned, but ultimately disastrous, quote, "I have seen the future of rock 'n' roll, and it's called Bruce Springsteen", that became a millstone round Springsteen's neck when Columbia used it as the basis of an intensive publicity campaign.

Born To Run.
Courtesy CBS Records.

He had difficulty recording his third album, since it obviously had to be good enough to ride the wave of media promotion, and – ironically – Landau himself was called in to help out on the production. **Born To Run** was issued in the autumn of 1975, and it did the trick, becoming a gold album in U.S. (where its success

stimulated the sales of the previous two albums) and breaking into the bottom reaches of U.K. charts.

Born To Run emphasised the Springsteen technique absolutely; what it lacked in lyrical subtlety and melodic strength, it compensated for in sheer bravado and panache. It was melodramatically produced, in a style that owed something to Phil Spector.

Springsteen has not yet had the opportunity to develop his own style naturally, but now has solid public support, so he can work with less pressure; throughout 1975 his U.S. shows were entirely successful, and he made a brief visit to Britain late in the year, and again received a rapturous reception.

By 1974, Springsteen had brought together the E-Street Band. The personnel are: Gary Tallent (bs), Max Weinberg (drms), Roy Bitten (kybds) and the charismatic Clarence Clemons, once one of James Brown's Famous Flames, on saxophones.

Recordings:
Greetings From Ashbury Park NJ (Columbia/CBS)
The Wild, The Innocent And E-Street Shuffle (Columbia/CBS)
Born To Run (Columbia/CBS)

Stackridge

Mutter Slater vocals, flute
Crun (James Walters) bass
Andy Davis vocals, guitar, Mellotron
Keith Gemmell sax, clarinet, flute
Peter Van Hooke drums

Totally unclassifiable, they were formed around Bristol area firstly as Stackridge Lemon with constantly changing personnel which sometimes included manager Michael Tobin. Slater, Crun and Davis are survivors of this initial aggregation which gathered minor reputation in west country before arriving in London for debut album. Released 1971, this featured such Stackridge inventions as Percy The Penguin, Dora The Female Explorer, and Marzo Plod.

With manic vocalist Mutter Slater to fore, group made a virtue of eccentricities virtually incomprehensible outside of staunch following, which they achieved via consisten U.K. gigging. Dances and props such as dustbin lids and rhubarb stalks were all part of repertoire; true aficionados turning up to concerts brandishing own lids and stalks.

Second album **Friendliness** contained group's theme song, **Lummy Days**, and saw return of Crun, who had left before debut set to resume career as bricklayer.

However, band's attempt to move towards more serious musical approach while retaining essence of humour, proved unpopular among most avid section of following and before release of third album, the George Martin-produced **The Man In The Bowler Hat/Pinafore Days** (1973), Mutter Slater quit in a bout of disillusionment.

Stackridge gigged on without him, bringing in Gemmell (formerly of Audience) and key-

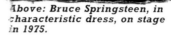
Above: Bruce Springsteen, in characteristic dress, on stage in 1975.

boardsman Rod Bowker, but suffered to certain degree through loss of irreplaceable Slater, who had been central character in stage act. Also around same time Bill Bent, drummer on first three albums, replaced by John White.

In 1974 group were first signing to Elton John's Rocket Records, recording **Extravaganza** for that label in 1975, at which point Mutter Slater rejoined line-up. New drummer Van Hooke is a former Van Morrison sideman.

Both played on 1976 album **Mr Mick**, along with former Greenslade keyboardsman Dave Lawson who subsequently "guested" on spring U.K. tour. Despite early problems Stackridge now seem to have achieved balance of lunacy and musicianship – though old favourites like **The Stanley** are still trotted out for the faithful. Recent Martin-produced albums evince somewhat self-conscious striving for Lennon/McCartneyesque feel.

Recordings:
Stackridge (MCA)
Friendliness (MCA)
The Man In The Bowler Hat/Pinafore Days (Sire/MCA)
Extravaganza (Sire/Rocket)
Mr Mick (Sire/Rocket)

The Staple Singers

Roebuck "Pop" Staples guitar, vocals
Mavis Staples vocals
Cleo Staples vocals
Yvonne Staples vocals

Born in Drew, Mississippi in 1915, Pop Staples moved north with his wife Oceola to Chicago in the '30s. In 1948, so the story goes, he was left a guitar as security for a loan. He formed a family gospel group, singing in local churches, and building a growing reputation, so that the family became one of America's top gospel groups

in the post-war years.

In '60s the group began to move into rock and R&B markets. As Pop got older and Mavis turned out to be first-class singer, so she took over lead vocals from him. When the group signed with Epic Records, they began recording more contemporary rock material – such as Stephen Stills' **For What It's Worth** – but it was when they moved to Stax in 1968 that they became particularly successful, with Mavis' urgent vocals, Pop's typically fat, rolling guitar lines (his guitar technique is among the most original extant, as is demonstrated on **Jammed Together**, an album he made with Albert King and Steve Cropper) and some very funky arrangements.

Be What You Are.
Courtesy Pye Records.

Soul Folk In Action became their first bestselling R&B album in 1968, and their stock improved with **We'll Get Over**, before the title track of **Heavy Makes You Happy** in 1971 gave them a major U.S. single. For the next few years they were one of America's top vocal groups.

The year 1972 was their most successful yet. **Bealtitude: Respect Yourself** became a gold album, and provided two gold singles – **Respect Yourself** and **I'll Take You There,** the latter of which was quoted by Mick Jagger as his favourite record of '70s.

The Staples' next album, **Be What You Are,** also sold heavily, and provided the title track to become another U.S. No. 1 single, while in the U.K. **If You're Ready**

(Come Go With Me) gave them a minor chart breakthrough in 1974. They also made a short European tour that year, though they have rarely played outside the States.

They explain their move from gospel to secular music by pointing out that their lyrics are inevitably exhortations to universal peace and brotherly love. Their music is so compelling and hypnotic, however, they don't really need a justification.

In 1975 they worked with Curtis Mayfield (♦) on the soundtrack of the film "Let's Do It Again". Mavis Staples also issued two solo albums in 1970, **Mavis Staples** and **Only For The Lonely**.

Discography is selective.

Recordings:
Soul Folk In Action (Stax)
We'll Get Over (Stax)
Heavy Makes You Happy (Stax)
Bealtitude: Respect Yourself (Stax)
Be What You Are (Stax)
City In The Sky (Stax)
Let's Do It Again (Curtom)

Ringo Starr

After break-up of The Beatles (♦), Ringo always seemed the one likely to be left out in the cold, since he had little flair for composition, and his singing had been acceptable rather than noteworthy.

His first solo project, though, came to fruition before the demise of The Beatles. **Sentimental Journey** was an album of show-biz standards Ringo apparently recorded to please his mother. Apart from the device of using a different producer for each track, it was of little interest. All it proved was that few people were less well-fitted to sing that material than Ringo, and everybody already knew that.

His second solo album, released September 1970, was a considerable improvement. **Beau-'coups Of Blues** had been recorded in Nashville, with some hand-picked local musicians, including Charlie McCoy, Jerry Reed, Charlie Daniels and The Jordanaires. The songs, mostly lachrymose ballads well-suited to Ringo's lugubrious vocals, had all been specially commissioned. The project could be accounted a success.

He made two excellent singles, **It Don't Come Easy** (1971) and **Back Off Boogaloo** (1972), which were both Top 5 records in Britain and America, and guested on albums for John Lennon and George Harrison, as well as playing at events like the Concert for Bangla Desh.

Ringo also conducted a parallel film career, having already had a cameo part in "Candy" (1968), and also a leading role, with Peter Sellers, in "The Magic Christian" (1970). He made a Western called "Blindman", and in 1973 starred in "That'll Be The Day" with some personal success. However he over-reached himself in directing "Born To Boogie", a documentary film about Marc Bolan.

In the winter of 1973 he released **Ringo**, a lavishly-packaged album that he regarded as his solo debut proper. He and his pro-

ducer, Richard Perry (♦), seemed to understand each other, and the result was an extraordinarily good album, with several hit singles being culled from it – **Photograph, You're Sixteen** and **Oh My My**, of which the latter two were both U.S. No. 1's. Ringo had triumphantly proved himself as a solo artist.

Goodnight Vienna.
Courtesy Apple, EMI Records.

The album was also interesting because it marked a reunion, of sorts, of The Beatles, in so far as all were featured, and each of the other three had provided a song for Ringo. John's **I'm The Greatest**, George's **Sunshine Life For Me**, and Paul's **Six O'Clock** were all very good. There is no doubt that Ringo relished the role of peace-maker.

Ringo tried to repeat the formula with **Goodnight Vienna**, but it was hardly up to the same standard, even though it did provide yet another U.S. No. 1 – **No No Song**, written by Hoyt Axton. **Blast From The Past** (1975) was a premature collection of hit singles.

Like all the Beatles, Ringo now enjoys more consistent commercial success in America than Britain, and it isn't surprising that that's where he is based. He still runs a furniture-designing business with his partner Robin Cruickshank, and appears frequently on television in America. In 1975 he set up his own record label, Ring' O Records, and signed a new deal himself with Polydor. He continues to do nothing in particular, and to do it very well.

Recordings:
Sentimental Journey (Apple)
Beaucoups Of Blues (Apple)
Ringo (Apple)
Goodnight Vienna (Apple)
Compilation:
Blast From Your Past (Apple)

Status Quo

Francis Rossi guitar, vocals
Alan Lancaster bass
Rick Parfitt guitar, vocals
John Coughlan drums

The worst band in the world, or the true progenitors of working-class punk heavy metal? Status Quo are Britain's very own Grand Funk (♦): almost universally condemned by rock cognoscenti, but supported by a veritable denim army of banner-waving, head-shaking British fans.

They began in 1962 when south Londoners Rossi, son of an ice-cream man, and Lancaster formed first group with Coughlan. They turned professional 1966 and were playing British holiday camps, or backing visiting U.S.

singers, as The Spectors when joined by Parfitt from Woking, Surrey.

As Status Quo (Rossi then known as Mike Rossi), broke through early 1968 with a piece of lightweight pop psychedelia **Pictures Of Matchstick Men**, which was Top 10 U.K. hit. Followed through with similarly successful **Ice In The Sun**, same year, but had all the hallmarks of a transient chart-oriented attraction. At this point line-up included keyboardsman Roy Lynes.

However, when the hits dried up the Quo took time out to re-think their direction, and set about accruing new image and reputation via progressive rock circuit. They had to live down their past and create a whole new audience from scratch to achieve their ends. Against the odds they did just that, and re-emerged in early '70s as an unashamed 12-bar boogie band, musically unadventurous but successful nonetheless.

They returned to charts with refurbished image via 1970 hit **Down The Dustpipe**, a somnambulistic piece of pop boogie, while continuing to build following on club circuit. Scored unprecedented success at 1972 Reading Festival, and in 1973 notched up first chart album **Piledriver** on new label, Vertigo. In same year enjoyed three more hit singles, **Paper Plane, Mean Girl, Caroline**, all performed in same listlessly laid-back fashion earning them tag "Poor man's Canned Heat".

However, group had the last laugh as sales of subsequent albums grew with each release, the 1975 set **On The Level** taking them to No. 1 spot at same time as single **Down Down** topped singles charts.

They remain unfashionable and musically unadventurous, but have achieved considerable cross-over pop/rock audience evidenced by sell-out tours in U.K. attended by fanatical following. Have so far made several tours of U.S. in search of elusive breakthrough there.

Recordings:
Picturesque Matchstikable Messages (—/Pye)
Status Quotation (—/Pye)
Ma Kelly's Greasy Spoon (—/Pye)
Dog Of Two Head (—/Pye)
Piledriver (A&M/Vertigo)
Hello (A&M/Vertigo)
Quo (A&M/Vertigo)
On The Level (Capitol/Vertigo)
Blue For You (Capitol/Vertigo)

Stealers Wheel

Gerry Rafferty vocals, guitar
Joe Egan vocals, keyboards

Stealers Wheel are a perfect example of a group who threw it all away – their history is one of turmoil and internal dissension, when it could so easily have been one of considerable success.

The story begins with Gerry Rafferty, who joined Billy Connolly (♦) and Tam Harvey in The Humblebums, who were re-billed as The New Humblebums, and cut one album of that title.

When they disbanded, Rafferty made one solo album, **Can I Have My Money Back?**, for the same

label, Transatlantic, before forming Stealers Wheel with Joe Egan. The other original members of the band were Rab Noakes and Roger Brown, so that originally the line-up comprised four singer/songwriters. However, before they made any recordings Noakes and Brown both left, as did Ian Campbell, a bass-player they had brought in.

Rafferty and Egan recruited Paul Pilnick (an original member of the semi-legendary Liverpool group, The Big Three) on guitar, Rod Coombes on drums and Tony Williams on bass; A&M meanwhile paid Transatlantic for Rafferty's contract, so the band started recording in December 1972, and released **Stealers Wheel** the following year. The album. which had been produced by Leiber and Stoller (♦) was thought to be remarkably good, and contained three songs that were later lifted as singles – **Stuck In The Middle With You, You Put Something Better Inside Me** and **Late Again**, all joint Rafferty/Egan compositions.

However, before the album had had an opportunity to make a commercial impact, Rafferty left the band, and Williams was ousted. The others brought in Delisle Harper to take the place of Williams, and Luther Grosvenor (later to surface as Ariel Bender in Mott The Hoople) was recruited to fill Rafferty's place.

At this point, in May of 1973, **Stuck In The Middle With You** began to happen. It was in fact a superlative folk-rock single, for all that the vocals were deliberately pitched somewhere between John Lennon and Bob Dylan. Ultimately, the single reached No. 6 in the U.K. and No. 2 in the U.S. Hence, the group's manager suggested to Rafferty that it was only logical that he should return – which he did, though as a result all the rest were dismissed with the exception of Egan.

Rafferty and Egan completed some gigs on the strength of their success, and then went into the studios to make **Ferguslie Park**, another Leiber-Stoller production. **Ferguslie Park** (1973) was again critically acclaimed, although this time it didn't produce a major hit – though **Star** went Top 50 in the U.S. Dispirited, Rafferty and Egan nevertheless started to put together another album, though they fell out with Leiber and Stoller, and started recording with Mentor Williams as producer. At this point, the sessions were held up due to managerial hassles and the album was finally issued in March 1975, 18 months after **Ferguslie Park,** by which time the public had lost interest, and in any case Rafferty and Egan were at that point reportedly again no longer on speaking terms.

Recordings:
Stealers Wheel (A&M)
Ferguslie Park (A&M)
Right Or Wrong (A&M)

Steeleye Span

Maddy Prior vocals
Tim Hart vocals, guitar, dulcimer
Peter Knight fiddle, mandolin, vocals
Bob Johnson lead guitar, vocals

Rick Kemp bass, vocals
Nigel Pegrum drums, flute

Steeleye Span were formed 1969 when Ashley Hutchings, then just out of Fairport Convention (➧) met up with two duos – Tim Hart and Maddy Prior, who had started singing in St Albans, England, and were very popular on the folk circuit, having recorded three albums; and Gay and Terry Woods, the latter of whom had been part of a formative electric folk band, Sweeney's Men. The five of them decided the time was then right for a solidly traditionally-oriented electric folk band.

Hark! The Village Wait was recorded in 1970 under the direction of Sandy Roberton's September Productions. During the sessions, it became apparent that the Woods were incompatible with the other three – they left and were replaced by Martin Carthy, a leading figure in the traditional folk revival, and fiddler Peter Knight.

With this line-up Steeleye went on the road, and recorded **Please To See The King** and **Ten Man Mop** in 1971. At the end of the year a general upheaval took place – Sandy Roberton left the picture, both as manager and producer. Jo Lustig took over the band's management, and Hutchings left to form the Albion Country Band, to be shortly followed by Carthy.

Knight's old folk-club partner Johnson was induced to forsake his secure career in accountancy to join the band, while Hutchings was replaced by Kemp, who'd worked with Mike Chapman (➧) for a couple of years and with King Crimson for about a week.

Commoners Crown.
Courtesy Chrysalis Records.

This line-up began to achieve considerable success in Britain during 1972, and issued their best album to date, **Below The Salt**, from which their accapella version of the Latin hymn, **Gaudete, Gaudete** was extracted to become a hit single in 1973. Meanwhile, **Below The Salt** was soon followed by **Individually And Collectively**, a compilation of material from **Please To See The King** and **Ten Men Mop** as well as solo recordings by Hart, Prior and Carthy.

In 1973 they issued **Parcel Of Rogues**, which showed their material was continuing to get stronger, and augmented to a six-piece by adding ex Gnidrolog drummer Pegrum. By this time the band were very popular in Britain, embarking on several sell-out nationwide tours, but their failure to crack the American market, despite regular attempts, continued to rankle.

Now We Are Six thus referred both to the number of albums and the number of personnel. It was produced by Jethro Tull's Ian Anderson, and was illuminated by Johnson's sombre murder ballads, particularly **Thomas The Rhymer**, which still stands as the quintessential Steeleye track. It also included a version of **To Know Him Is To Love Him**, which featured David Bowie on saxophone. (The band had previously demonstrated their interest in old rock material by recording an accapella version of Buddy Holly's **Rave On**.)

All Around My Hat.
Courtesy Chrysalis Records.

Their stage act at this time was a weird and wonderful affair, since it included both a film (illustrating the narrative of Hart's song **The Bold Poachers**) and a Mummer's Play – also conceived by Hart. Their audience was large and loyal, but in some ways it wasn't large enough. **Commoner's Crown** was very much the mixture as before, though it was enriched by two fine tracks in **Demon Lover** and **Long Lankin**, and also the guest appearance of Peter Sellers, who played ukelele on **New York Girls**.

Though this was a somewhat disappointing period for the band, they rallied well, engaged a new manager, Tony Secunda, who had previously handled The Move (➧), and a new producer, Mike Batt (➧), well known for his inventive and enthusiastic work as the man behind The Wombles, the rock band for the under-fives. **All Around My Hat** was the band's most commercially successful album to date; it gave them a major British hit single (the title track) and a first foothold in the U.S. charts.

During a lull in Steeleye's activities in 1976, Maddy Prior recorded **Silly Sisters** with June Tabor, a traditional singer, and the two embarked on a short British tour.

All of Steeleye's material is currently available in Britain, as all the non-Chrysalis product was reissued on Mooncrest in 1975–76.

Recordings:
Hark! The Village Wait (—/RCA)
Please To See The King (—/B&C)
Ten Man Mop Or Mr Reservoir Butler Rides Again (—/Pegasus)
Below The Salt (—/Chrysalis)
Parcel Of Rogues (Chrysalis)
Now We Are Six (—/Chrysalis)
Commoner's Crown (Chrysalis)
All Around My Hat (Chrysalis)
Compilations:
Individually And Collectively (—/Charisma)
Steeleye Span Almanack (—/Charisma)
Tim Hart & Maddy Prior:
Folk Songs Of Olde England, Vol. I (—/B&C)
Folk Songs Of Olde England, Vol. II (—/B&C)
Summer Solstice (—/B&C)
Maddy Prior & June Tabor:
Silly Sisters (—/Chrysalis)

Steely Dan

Donald Fagen keyboards, vocals
Walter Becker bass, vocals

Every other critic's choice as The Band Most Likely To when they first leapt to prominence with one of the most dazzling debut albums ever, Steely Dan is and always has been the progeny of songwriter/players Becker and Fagen and producer Gary Katz.

Becker and Fagen were New Yorkers, attending Bard College together in up-state New York, after which they wrote score for Zalman King movie "You Gotta Walk It Like You Talk It (Or You'll Lose That Beat)" – their music for film was released on Spark label album **The Original Soundtrack** – and made abortive attempt to form band in Long Island with guitarist Denny Dias.

Neither events showered them with honours and the next two years found them both gigging to pay the rent as back-up men for '60s act Jay And The Americans

It was during this period they met producer Katz, who eventually rescued them and took pair to West Coast ostensibly as staff writers for ABC/Dunhill Records. However, Katz saw wider possibilities and set about assembling a band to showcase Becker and Fagen's songs: the aforementioned Dias travelled west with his guitar, followed by Boston drummer Jim Hodder, New York singer Dave Palmer, and pedal steel guitarist Jeff Baxter. Also from Boston, Baxter was a fine musician who had interesting credentials, having played with the band Ultimate Spinach; as side-man for Buzzy Linhardt and as sessioner for Carly Simon.

They called this new six-piece Steely Dan – taking name from a steam-powered dildo in William Burroughs' novel "The Naked Lunch" – and in June 1972 recorded **Can't Buy A Thrill** in Los Angeles.

Below: The earliest extant publicity photograph of Steely Dan.

Comprising all Becker-Fagen material, replete with inscrutable collegiate lyrics to be found on all successive releases, it was an astonishingly accomplished debut set: a collage of pure pop, Latin rhythms and close harmonies – the whole performed with immaculate panache. Apart from some brilliant Baxter guitar work, particularly on **Change Of The Guard**, it contained two of 1972's finest rock singles, **Do It Again** and **Reelin' In The Years**, which American public (if not British) had the good sense to take warmly to their hearts.

Countdown To Ecstasy (1973), their second set, found them minus Palmer, and perhaps a shade too obtuse for comfort and commerciality, but the third album, **Pretzel Logic** (1974), was yet another tour de force. Every style they touched was rendered with immaculate taste and playing, from bossa nova of **Rikki Don't Lose That Number** (another U.S. hit) through to jazz echoes of **Parker's Ball** and Duke Ellington's **East St Louis Toodle-oo**.

Can't Buy A Thrill.
Courtesy Anchor Records.

The band looked set for great future, even if their rare live performances were somewhat diffident, but aficionados weren't to know of conflicts which existed within group. The problem derived primarily from Becker and Fagen's reluctance to tour. As writers and thus receivers of royalty cheques, there was little pressure on them to do so anyway. On other hand, rest of band had no comparable source of income; and apparently weren't too enamoured with the idea of hanging around Los Angeles waiting for Becker and Fagen to book next studio session.

Matters came to a head when Baxter and Hodder quit band in summer 1974. Baxter had resolved the dilemma by "guesting" on tour with friends The Doobie Brothers (whom he's since joined), and was in England July 1974 with them when a transatlantic phone call told him he was no longer a member of Steely Dan. Rumours of a total group break-up were rife for several months afterwards.

The Fagen-Becker attitude, when they again started giving interviews, was that Steely Dan was "more a concept than a rock band", revolving around them, their songs and various satellite musicians.

The "satellites" on the next studio set, **Katy Lied** (1975), apart from faithful Denny Dias, were Jeff Pocaro (drms) and Mike McDonald (kybds) – with guest "satellites" Rick Derringer and Eliot Randall. But this to enthusiasts, who had endured the split stories with increasing despair, was a disappointing anti-climactic return. Subsequently, McDonald followed Baxter into Doobie Brothers (➧).

This apparent decline was arrested by the 1976 set, **The Royal Scam**, showing Becker and Fagen back on decidedly more creative turf – even though, as players, they had chosen to become little more than "satellites" themselves, just two of 24 sessionmen. No question, however, that the stylish **Royal Scam** re-asserted Steely Dan's right to be ranked among best new acts of '70s.

Recordings:
Can't Buy A Thrill (ABC/Probe)
Countdown To Ecstasy (ABC/ Probe)
Pretzel Logic (ABC/Probe)
Katy Lied (ABC)
The Royal Scam (ABC)

Steppenwolf

John Kay vocals, guitar
George Biondo bass, vocals
Jerry Edmonton drums, vocals
Bobby Cochran guitar
Wayne Cook keyboards

Leaving aside Herman Hesse for moment, Steppenwolf was brainchild of singer Kay, who was born East Germany Apr 12, 1944, but fled with his mother to Canada in 1958. In Toronto he formed blues band Sparrow but met with little success; until group drifted via New York to California and there metamorphosed into Steppenwolf (taking name from Hesse novel at suggestion of first producer) in 1967.

Line-up, apart from Kay, comprised Goldy McJohn (org), Jerry Edmonton (drms), Michael Monarch (gtr) and, after brief spell with original bassist Rushton Moreve, John Russell Morgan (bs).

Retaining elements of blues from Sparrow but leaning more towards macho hard-rock with political undertones, band released eponymous debut album in January 1968 from which came monster U.S. hit single **Born To Be Wild**, the ultimate bikers' anthem, and the much-requested **The Pusher**, written by Hoyt Axton (➧).

Magic Carpet Ride from **Second** album kept group on charts, while use of two Steppenwolf numbers in "Easy Rider" movie greatly enhanced reputation. In fact, between 1969 and 1971 group were constantly on U.S. album charts with series of goldsellers, among them **Monster,** most overtly political of their works thus far. A series of benefit gigs followed, for likes of Vietnam Moratorium Day Committee.

However, group underwent several line-up changes during lifespan. Monarch and Morgan left end of 1969 to be replaced by Larry Byrom (gtr) and Nick St Nicholas (bs). The last, like Kay, was German-born, but survived only until mid-1970 when George Biondo took over bass chores. A further change replaced Byrom with Kent Henry.

Despite enormous success – eight gold albums – in February 1972 founder members Kay, Edmonton and McJohn called Hollywood press conference to announce Steppenwolf's dissolution due to creatively-stifling atmosphere of group situation. Kay launched solo career, see albums list, while Edmonton and McJohn (two of the Toronto originals) assembled own band Manbeast.

However, none of members' individual efforts were as successful as previous group and, after two year lay-off, Steppenwolf was revived in early 1974 with line-up of Kay, McJohn, Edmonton, Biondo and Bobby Cochran. First result of reunion was **Slow Flux** album (1974) since when Wayne Cook has replaced McJohn, who now leads own eponymous outfit.

Recordings:
Early Steppenwolf (Dunhill/Stateside)
Steppenwolf (Dunhill/Stateside)
Steppenwolf The Second (Dunhill/Stateside)
At Your Birthday Party (Dunhill/Stateside)
Monster (Dunhill/Stateside)
Live Steppenwolf (Dunhill/Probe)
Steppenwolf 7 (Dunhill/Probe)
For Ladies Only (Dunhill/Probe)
Slow Flux (Epic)
Hour Of The Wolf (Epic)
Skullduggery (Epic)
Compilations:
Steppenwolf Gold (Dunhill/Probe)
Rest In Peace (Dunhill/Probe)
16 Greatest Hits (Dunhill/Probe)
John Kay:
Forgotten Songs And Unsung Heroes (Dunhill/Probe)
My Sporting Life (Dunhill/Probe)

Cat Stevens

Born Steven Georgiou in London, July 1947, the son of Greek parents, Stevens took up folk-music while still at Hammersmith College in 1966. He met independent record producer Mike Hurst (formerly of The Springfields), who expressed an interest in his material. Hurst had been on point of emigrating to the U.S., but at the last minute decided to invest his savings in the session which produced Stevens' first disc, **I Love My Dog.**

This was released as first record on Decca's newly-formed quasi-progressive label, Deram, and the song became a minor hit; with his dark good looks, Stevens quickly became a teen idol, and his next disc, **Matthew And Son** reached No. 2 in Britain in spring 1967; it was one of the few pop discs of '60s to evince any form of class-consciousness, with a sharp lyric and a strong melody. He seemed set for a lengthy career, as his compositions were recorded with some success by other artists – P. P. Arnold recorded **The First Cut Is The Deepest,** and The Tremeloes **Here Comes My Baby** – and he toured on package shows with Engelbert Humperdinck and Jimi Hendrix.

Tea For The Tillerman.
Courtesy Island Records.

In early 1968, after **I'm Gonna Get Me A Gun,** Stevens' success at Deram began to peter out; this was partly because he was already becoming ambitious to write material of a more adventurous kind – he wanted to score his songs in a classical manner. However, later that year he contracted TB, and spent a year recuperating in a clinic.

Stevens took his time and didn't attempt to re-enter the spotlight until he had a group of compositions with which he was satisfied. The songs he'd written while he was recovering from his illness were finally issued as **Mona Bone Jakon** which was released on Island in 1970.

The album came out at the right historical moment, the beginning of the singer/songwriter phase, and it did well; a single taken from it, **Lady d'Arbanville**, about a former girlfriend, restored him to the British charts, but in a very different style. **Mona Bone Jakon** was recorded solely with the support of Alun Davies (gtr), John Ryan (bs) and Harvey Burns (drms), and just this nucleus of support was used for his next album – **Tea For The Tillerman**. Again, the spare production was by Paul Samwell-Smith, and Stevens' sensitive but essentially straightforward songs like **Father And Son** and **Wild World** seemed to strike responsive chords in the populace. **Tea For The Tillerman** sold very quickly in Britain, and it went gold in America in 1971 – as have all of Cat's albums.

Nevertheless, his best work is generally agreed to be found on **Tea For The Tillerman** and **Teaser And The Firecat** (1972), which contained **Moonshadow, Morning Has Broken** and **Peace Train**. After this, he became involved with Eastern mysticism, and his work grew ever more complex, when the appeal of his previous work had been in its simplicity. The first side of **Foreigner** (1973), for example, was wholly devoted to **The Foreigner Suite,** a rambling work which was concerned with his usual themes of love and freedom, and used piano, brass, strings and synthesiser.

Unknown to the masses, Stevens had at this time become a tax exile, living for most of the year in Brazil, though he continued to give freely to various charities, and international organisations, such as UNESCO.

He continued to chart his own musical course, though most critics felt that **Buddha And The Chocolate Box** was fairly vacuous, and **Numbers** again found Stevens' music being stifled by complex themes and orchestrations.

In line with his increasing sophistication on record, Cat's tours have become more unwieldy. For his European tour late 1975 he used his basic unit of Alun Davies (gtr), Jean Roussell (kybds) and Gerry Conway (drms), augmented by a second guitarist and a Brazilian percussionist, as well as a group of girl backing-singers. Furthermore, he performed under a huge arch, with a backdrop of an enormous mandala, that had been specially sewn for the tour.

Stevens, meanwhile, continues to live reclusively; he is a thorough professional who is painstaking in his attention to detail in his various projects, and hence there was a gap of over 18 months between releases of **Buddha And The Chocolate Box** (1974) and **Numbers** (1975), which was only partially filled by a **Greatest Hits** album (1975).

Recordings:
Matthew And Son (Deram)
New Masters (Deram)
Mona Bone Jakon (A&M/Island)
Tea For The Tillerman (A&M/Island)
Teaser And The Firecat (A&M/Island)
Catch Bull At Four (A&M/Island)
Foreigner (A&M/Island)
Buddha And The Chocolate Box (A&M/Island)
Numbers (A&M/Island)
Compilations:
Very Young & Early Songs (Deram/–)
View From The Top (—/Deram)
Greatest Hits (A&M/Island)

Al Stewart

Glasgow-born and a public school drop-out, one of early gigs was as lead guitarist behind singer turned DJ Tony Blackburn in Bournemouth, south England, band. From there he travelled to London, accruing following as singer/guitarist via folk-clubs Bunjies and Les Cousins.

Dylan influenced, his first album **Bedsitter Images** (November 1967) was soft-rock collection with orchestral backings. Early material evinced obsession with unrequited love, this brought to head on **Love Chronicles** (January 1969) which featured then session-man Jimmy Page on guitar. The title track was an anguished 18-minute autobiographical account of Stewart's lost love; it earned certain dubious notoriety for containing word "fucking" in lyric, this also being boldly reprinted on record sleeve.

It sold in no great quantity but

immediately established Stewart as troubadour of bed-sit land; and a regular U.K. college circuit favourite. The subsequent **Zero She Flies** (1970) again examined relationship breakdowns in somewhat self-pitying style, but contained interesting historically-oriented **Manuscript** composition, a direction Stewart was to pursue almost totally on highly ambitious 1974 set **Past, Present And Future**, replacing bed-sit dolefulness for fatalistic reflections on European history. **Orange**, which appeared 1972 between these two, appeared to mark time while Stewart rethought direction.

Up until **Past, Present And Future** none of previous albums had been released in States. But by now Stewart was working with electric band – using nucleus of defunct Home – and made first U.S. tour March 1974, attracting growing cult following which has since seen his popularity in America far exceed that in Britain. Now works consistently with amplified band (Gerry Conway, Pat Donaldson, Simon Nicol and Simon Roussell provided back-up for 1975 tours) and has used Sutherland Brothers & Quiver guitarist Tim Renwick on 1975 **Modern Times** and 1976 **The Year Of The Cat**. Stewart has been quoted as decrying all work previous to **Past, Present And Future**.

Recordings:
Bedsitter Images (—/CBS)
Love Chronicles (—/CBS)
Zero She Flies (—/CBS)
Orange (—/CBS)
Past, Present And Future (Chess-Janus/CBS)
Modern Times (Janus/CBS)
The Year Of The Cat (Janus/RCA)

John Stewart

Born San Diego, California, Sep 5, 1939 to a father who trained racehorses (which may account for the equine flavour of many of his songs), Stewart learnt how to play the chords of **Streets Of Laredo** from Frank Zappa, when they were both at college in Pomona during mid-'50s.

His first band was of the garage variety, John Stewart And The Furies. They recorded a single for a local label in late '50s in California. Also by this time, two of Stewart's compositions had been recorded by The Kingston Trio, as a result of which he was informed by Frank Werber, that group's manager, that Roulette Records in New York were looking to sign up an act with a similar format.

Stewart, playing guitar and banjo, collected a friend, John Montgomery (gtr), and his glee-club teacher, Gil Robbins (bs), and the all-singing trio went to New York to become the Cumberland Three, who had made three albums by mid-1961, by which time John Montgomery had left to be replaced by Mike Settle.

In July 1961, Dave Guard, one of original members of Kingston Trio, decided to leave, and Stewart auditioned as his replacement. He was taken on as a salaried member from 1961 until 1967, when the group ceased to function. During Stewart's time

with the group, they made nearly 20 albums, most interesting of which are **New Frontier** (1962) and **Number 16** (1963), both on Capitol.

Even before he left The Trio (he gave the group a year's notice in 1966), Stewart was looking for other ways to present his music, and plans for a group which would include John Phillips (before The Mamas and Papas) and Scott McKenzie (pre-**San Francisco**) failed due to McKenzie's reported breakdown. The next possibility was a duo of himself and John Denver, and a demo tape was produced by the two containing what amounted to their greatest hits at the time, **Daydream Believer** by Stewart, and **Leaving On A Jet Plane** by Denver, but both realised after a short time that the combination wouldn't work, and went their separate ways.

Stewart then had **Daydream Believer** recorded by The Monkees, which enabled him to survive for long enough to launch a solo career, which began with an album called **Signals Through The Glass**. On this he was joined by Buffy Ford, whom he eventually married in 1975. The album was not a commercial success, and his next attempt, in 1969, was to team himself with Nik Venet as producer, and the massed musicians of Nashville as backing, for an album, **California Bloodlines**, which remains his most celebrated to this day. (Simultaneously, across the street, Bob Dylan was laying down the tracks for **Nashville Skyline**.)

In 1970, Stewart was introduced to Peter Asher by Chris Darrow, at the time a member of his backing band, and David Geffen, at the time Stewart's agent, and Asher produced **Willard**, which includes back-up contributions from Carole King and James Taylor. This album was less successful than **Bloodlines**, and Stewart left Capitol for Warner Bros.

The first of his two albums for the new Company was **The Lonesome Picker Rides Again**, released 1971, and produced by Michael Stewart, his brother, and an ex-member of We Five. On this album, John finally recorded his own version of **Daydream Believer**, although it is likely that he had also tried to record it before during sessions in his Capitol days.

Sunstorm followed in 1972, ending Stewart's brief stay with Warner Bros. Despite the help of Hollywood's finest session-men, and with production again by his brother, the album failed to excite too many people, and John Stewart moved to RCA.

His debut for that label, **Cannons In The Rain**, is regarded as his most accessible. Recorded in Nashville, and produced by Fred Carter, this looked set to be the album to finally establish Stewart; it was not to be.

The next was a double album, **The Phoenix Concerts**, recorded live in March 1974 in Phoenix, Arizona, where Stewart commands a fanatical audience. While this album was his first to make the American charts, it failed to stay there long.

In 1975, Stewart, who had reunited with Nik Venet for the live album, returned with him to the studio to cut **Wingless Angels**,

certainly the low point of his career thus far. At the time of writing, Stewart is negotiating for a new contract, and at the same time, a Kingston Trio reunion album is planned for late 1976.

John Stewart remains a cult figure, with a small, but loyal following.

Recordings:
Signals Through The Glass
(with Buffy Ford) (Capitol/—)
California Bloodlines (Capitol)
Willard (Capitol)
The Lonesome Picker Rides Again (Warner Bros)
Sunstorm (Warner Bros/—)
Cannons In The Rain (RCA)
The Phoenix Concerts Live (RCA)
Wingless Angels (RCA)

Rod Stewart

Stewart was born in north London, Jan 10, 1945, though his brothers were born in Scotland and he later found it convenient to gloss over his Sassenach origins. He attended the same secondary school as Ray and Dave Davies (of The Kinks ♦), and his parents owned a newsagents shop along the Archway Road, in Holloway.

On leaving school, he took a few temporary jobs – fence-erecting, grave-digging, etc.; thoroughly obsessed with soccer from an early age, he signed as an apprentice with Brentford F.C., but became disillusioned with the wages and having to clean the boots of the first-team players.

Instead he adopted the contemporary beatnik course, and took to the road. He bummed around Europe for a while, in particular in Spain, with English folksinger Wizz Jones, who taught him how to play banjo; this was Stewart's formative period (he later cited his vocal influences as Sam Cooke, Eddie Cochran, Al Jolson and Ramblin' Jack Elliott). He had to be repatriated from Spain as he was destitute. Apparently, he still owes British Airways the cost of the fare.

He also learned to play guitar, and obtained a semi-pro gig on his return to Britain, singing and playing harmonica with the Birmingham outfit, Jimmy Powell and the Dimensions, though as Stewart tells it, Powell kept him pretty much in the vocal shadows.

In 1964 he made one record for Decca, **Good Morning Little Schoolgirl** (on which John Paul Jones was one of the session-musicians), though it amounted to little. The following year he joined the R&B-oriented Hoochie Coochie Men (formerly the Cyril Davies All Stars) to link with Long John Baldry (♦) in the vocal front line.

When Baldry disbanded Hoochie Coochie Men, Stewart was unemployed for two months; meanwhile Baldry was forming the London-based Steampacket R&B revue with Brian Auger (♦) and Julie Driscoll; on Baldry's invitation, Stewart joined the project. For years, no recordings existed of this formative outfit, but some material was recently traced and issued in Germany as **Early Days** on 2001 Records.

Stewart left after clashes of personality (he claims that Auger fired him) to join the like-minded Shotgun Express. This had a distinguished line-up: permutations of Stewart (vcls), Beryl Marsden (vcls), Peter Green (gtr), Mick Fleetwood (drms), Peter Bardens (kybds) and Dave Ambrose (bs). The band failed however – according to Stewart – because it strived too self-consciously to ape the earlier Steampacket, on which it was admittedly modelled.

Below: Rod Stewart, with Tetsu behind, on tour with The Faces.

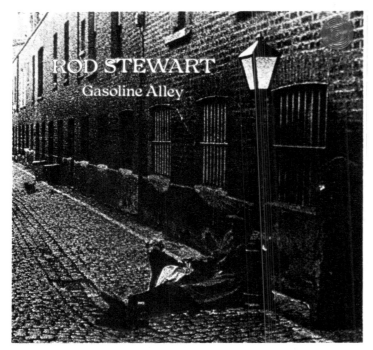

Gasoline Alley. Courtesy Phonogram Ltd.

Never A Dull Moment. Courtesy Phonogram Ltd.

During this time Stewart was also making occasional advances with his solo career (he cut a single of a Michael D'Abo composition and recorded once under the "patronage" of Mick Jagger); in 1968 he and Ron Wood joined the Jeff Beck Group. Beck's was a prestigious name in the U.S., and it was as his vocalist that Stewart began to receive wider recognition (➡ Jeff Beck).

Also at this time Stewart did sessions, for which he was paid a straightforward fee, with the studio-group Python Lee Jackson; the band never did any gigs, or achieved anything at the time, though after Stewart's leap to fame a single, **In A Broken Dream,** was issued in 1972, and reached No. 3 in the U.K. charts, becoming something of a '70s classic.

Stewart recorded two albums with Beck Group – **Truth** (1968) and **Beck-Ola** (1969), on both of which Stewart's sandpapery vocals are very effective; in Britain, the albums made little commercial impact, but they did help bring Stewart to public attention, and in 1969 he signed a contract as a solo artist with Mercury Records.

Meanwhile, he left Beck after the latter had wanted to alter the composition of the band and sacked Wood. Later that year, he and Wood both joined The Faces, who were at that time looking for a vocalist, Steve Marriott having just moved on to Humble Pie (➡).

Stewart's name still meant little in the U.K., even though the group were occasionally billed as Rod Stewart And The Faces. In the U.S. however, it was a different story, and he was more successful at establishing himself; his first two albums, **An Old Raincoat Won't Ever Let You Down** (1969) and **Gasoline Alley** (1970), though largely ignored in Britain, sold creditably in the U.S., and certainly received critical attention.

The first was retitled **The Rod Stewart Album** for U.S. release; it highlighted Stewart's abundant talent, showing him as a fine interpretative singer of folk-songs (**Man Of Constant Sorrow,** Ewan MacColl's **Dirty Old Town**) as well as having a sure touch with rockers, and being no mean composer himself. **Gasoline Alley** amply confirmed first impressions, and to this day is arguably his finest album. It revealed him as a topflight composer, with fine autobiographical songs (**Jo's Lament, Lady Day**); it deservedly established Stewart as an important solo singer in the U.S., a standing that was reinforced by two successful Stateside tours with The Faces in 1970. The British public, as ever, remained more diffident.

At this time, it was Stewart's firm intention to pursue parallel careers, both as a solo artist and as lead singer of The Faces; accordingly he released one solo album, and recorded one Faces album per year. At the same time, he announced that he would not tour except with The Faces: "If I chose a band, I'd choose the same guys I got in the band anyway."

It was the release of **Every Picture Tells A Story** in summer 1971 that finally accorded him superstar status. At least one side of the album (strangely, the second) was devastatingly brilliant, and **Maggie May,** a tale of a schoolboy's liaison with a hooker, is a quintessential rock song. It was lifted as the single from the album, and at one period in September 1971 Stewart occupied the No. 1 spots in both the albums and singles charts on both sides of the Atlantic.

Stewart and The Faces were pre-eminent for the next few years, playing sell-out gigs throughout the world to wildly enthusiastic audiences. The band generated a magical live atmosphere – Stewart is a first-class stage performer; he referred to his legion of British fans as The Tartan Hordes (Stewart adopted the Scottish tartan as a personal favour, and thus pre-empted the Bay City Rollers (➡)) and the band regularly kicked footballs into the audience; they were as fervently worshipped as a soccer team by their followers.

There were, however, constant rumours that Stewart would eventually strike out on his own, though this hardly seemed to affect the cohe-

siveness of the band; even when Ronnie Lane left in 1973, Tetsu was brought in as bassist, and the stability of the band seemed assured.

In 1972 Stewart's next solo album, **Never A Dull Moment,** was inevitably as commercially successful as the previous one, and immediately went gold, while **You Wear It Well** was a worthy successor to **Maggie May.**

Though two singles were issued in 1972 and 1973 – **What Made Milwaukee Famous** (U.K. only) and **Oh No Not My Baby** – Stewart's career was then handicapped by contractual problems, and the release of his next album was delayed while Mercury and Warner Bros wrangled in the courts over whose album it should be. In the interim, a compilation album, **Sing It Again, Rod** was issued; this featured all old material, with the exception of **Pinball Wizard,** which Stewart had sung in Lou Reizner's stage presentation of Tommy (➡) at the Rainbow Theatre in London.

Smiler was issued late in 1974, and it proved disappointing; the standard of Stewart's own compositions had fallen, with the exception of **Farewell,** another of his beautiful lyrical ballads; he also included two Sam Cooke songs – **Bring It On Home To Me** and **You Send Me,** which he handled with loving care, and the songs became an integral part of The Faces' stage show. The rest of the material fell flat somehow; it seemed a mistake for Stewart to have relied on material from his superstar colleagues, Elton John (**Let Me Be Your Car**) and Paul McCartney (**Mine For Me**).

It seemed that Stewart was inevitably becoming drawn into the showbiz celebrity circuits, and his recordings were losing something of

Above: Atlantic Crossing. Courtesy Warner Bros. Records.

their natural charm.

Smiler was his last album for Mercury. It sold somewhat disappointingly, and Stewart sensed public dissatisfaction; his response was to record the next one in Muscle Shoals, with Tom Dowd producing, and Steve Cropper among the backing musicians. It proved to be the nadir of his solo work so far; what shall it profit Rod Stewart if he gain the whole world of technical accomplishment and studio sophistication and lose his own soul? The answer was another gold album, but, on the whole, a declining critical interest in his work. Stewart's unaffected working-class charm had been entirely dissipated; he was by now existing in the stratosphere of Hollywood celebrities, and having a much-publicised affair with film actress Britt Ekland. (It was at her suggestion that **Atlantic Crossing** had been divided into a slow side and a fast side.) Stewart meanwhile met the British press in Dublin, Eire; for tax reasons, he wanted to avoid returning to England.

After a U.S. tour in summer 1975 (for which Wood had joined The Faces immediately following a similar slog with the Rolling Stones), The Faces again became becalmed, and in December 1975 Stewart finally announced his decision to go solo; it was almost as though The Faces had broken because no one any longer had the necessary will-power to pull them together.

Stewart had no real immediate solo plans; he did suggest that he would perform live with some of the Muscle Shoals musicians who had backed him on **Atlantic Crossing,** but these plans did not come to fruition, and he cited insufficient rehearsal time as the reason. He did however record another album in the States, and **A Night On The Town** was issued in 1976.

In 1976 Mercury reissued **An Old Raincoat Won't Ever Let You Down** and **Gasoline Alley** as a double-set entitled **The Vintage Years.**

Recordings:
The Rod Stewart Album/An Old Raincoat Won't Ever Let You Down (Mercury/Vertigo)
Gasoline Alley (Mercury/Vertigo)
Every Picture Tells A Story (Mercury)
Never A Dull Moment (Mercury)
Smiler (Mercury)

Atlantic Crossing (Warner Bros)
A Night On The Town (Warner Bros)
Compilation:
Sing It Again, Rod (Mercury)
The Best Of Rod Stewart (Mercury/—)
Recorded Highlights And Action Replays (—/Mercury)

Below: Stephen Stills. In 1976 he made an album with Neil Young and was sued for divorce by his wife, Veronique Sanson.

Robert Stigwood

Born 1934 in Australia, Stigwood first appeared on the British music scene working for Brian Epstein's NEMS Enterprises, and therefore being involved with the mid-period Beatles.

When he struck out on his own, it was as manager of Australian group The Bee Gees (◆), and then of Cream (◆) and it is his involvement with Eric Clapton (◆) that has ensured his continuing pre-eminence on the managerial and entrepreneurial side of the rock business.

Seeing openings elsewhere, and having the financial wherewithal to exploit them, he moved into tangential projects, and promoted both "Hair" and "Jesus Christ Superstar", two of the most commercially successful theatrical ventures of the last decade. Ever resourceful, he then financed Ken Russell's film of "Tommy" (making sure that Eric was given a small part in it), and also handled two Beatle spin-offs – he produced "John, Paul, George, Ringo . . . And Bert" in London's West End, and also the stage version of "Sergeant Pepper's Lonely Hearts Club Band" in New York.

He now owns his own record label, RSO Records, which includes on its roster Clapton, Jack Bruce (though he rarely makes solo albums) and Barbara Dickson, whose career he successfully launched after she had been in the cast of the original Liverpool production of "John, Paul, George, Ringo . . . And Bert".

Stephen Stills

Born Dallas, Texas, Jan 3, 1945, he moved around U.S. South as a child. Majored in political science at University of Florida. A singer and something of a multi-instrumentalist – guitar, keyboards, drums – he played local folk-clubs, before dropping out of university to go to New York. There he performed with various groups, including Au Go Go Singers with Richie Furay, but was eventually lured to Los Angeles by what he felt was more creative musical environment.

He made abortive attempt to form a band with Van Dyke Parks (◆), auditioned unsuccessfully for membership of Monkees (◆), and finally called the aforementioned Furay from New York to assist him assemble new band which became the legendary Buffalo Springfield. It was Stills who wrote Springfield's first U.S. hit in early 1967, the politically-conscious **For What It's Worth**, plus other group stand-outs **Bluebird** and **Rock And Roll Woman**. When group split May 1968 (◆ Buffalo Springfield), Stills worked on variety of projects: he turned down offer to replace Al Kooper (◆) in Blood Sweat & Tears (◆) but did cut **Supersession** jam album, August 1968, with Kooper and Mike Bloomfield (◆); also played guitar for his girlfriend Judy Collins on her **Who Knows Where The Time Goes?** album (Nov 1968); and bass on first Joni Mitchell album (July 1968).

He is also said during this period to have taken guitar lessons from Jimi Hendrix and cut a number of unreleased tracks with drummer Dallas Taylor.

Then in December 1968 was announced team-up of Crosby Stills & Nash, which would produce astonishing eponymous debut album evidencing Stills at peak of creativity. His epic-length **Suite: Judy Blue Eyes**, written for Judy Collins, was that outfit's first U.S. hit (◆ Crosby Stills Nash & Young).

Stills recorded first solo album during latter days of this colossally-successful aggregation's traumatic life-span. When CSN&Y ended world tour at London's Royal Albert Hall, February 1970, Stills stayed in England purchasing Ringo Starr's Surrey mansion for some £90,000. Employing variety of stellar musicians – Jimi Hendrix, Eric Clapton, John Sebastian, Crosby, Nash, Booker T., Cass Elliott, etc. – **Stephen Stills** was cut at Island Studios, London, and Wally Heider's and Record Plant in Los Angeles and was impressive solo debut. Hendrix had "OD"ed between recording and release in November 1970, and the set was dedicated to "James Marshall Hendrix".

Stills returned to CSN&Y for last few months of band's existence, then formed first own group line-ups using Calvin "Fuzzy" Samuels (bs), Dallas Taylor (drms), both ex CSN&Y side-men, plus Paul Harris (kybds), Stephen Fromholz (gtr) and Memphis Horns brass section for tour purposes. Nucleus of band came together at Stills' Surrey home and embarked on 52-date U.S. tour to promote second album, the somewhat less assured **Stephen Stills II** (July 1971).

Stephen Stills.
Courtesy Atlantic Records.

This band metamorphosed into Manassas October 1971 via Miami recording sessions on which Stills used services of singer/guitarist Chris Hillman (ex Byrds, Flying Burritos) and Al Perkins (pdl stl). Hillman was virtual second-in-command to Stills' often outstanding and widely-acclaimed outfit; other members being Samuels, Taylor and Harris, and newcomer Joe Lala (prcsn). Samuels later replaced by Kenny Passarelli.

The band toured extensively and recorded two albums, the double-set **Manassas** (May 1972) and **Down The Road** (January 1973). However, in September 1973, Hillman, Perkins and Harris split to form Souther-Hillman-Furay Band (◆). Stills, who had married French singer Veronique Sanson in spring 1973 and was by then living in Colorado, formed a second version of Stephen Stills

Band retaining Lala, Passarelli, and bringing in guitarist Donnie Dacus, keyboardsman Jerry Aiello and noted session-drummer Russ Kunkel (James Taylor, etc.).

This was only short-lived aggregation, however, because in May 1974 occurred the much-rumoured reunion of Crosby Stills Nash & Young. Lala and, briefly, Kunkel joined CSN&Y back-up squad for highly lucrative, widely-publicised one-off world tour ending in London February 1975.

By this time Stills had severed long-standing contract with Atlantic and signed to Columbia, who released **Stills** in June 1975. Something of a hotch-potch of material dating over previous five years, this failed to halt widespread opinion that Stills' talents were on decline – although the album was notable for record debut of aforementioned Donnie Dacus. Dacus, a young protégé of Stills, co-wrote a number of tracks, and was important fixture in third incarnation of Steve Stills Band formed March 1975. Other personnel were Lala and Aiello, plus Ronald Ziegler (drms) and George Perry (bs).

Second Columbia album **Illegal Stills** (May 1976) was more spirited attempt to recapture former glory; also spotlighting growing relationship with Dacus. Also in early 1976 Stills was reported to be working at Criteria Studios, Miami, with Neil Young (◆) – with a joint album the likely outcome.

Supersession (with Al Kooper, Mike Bloomfield) (Columbia/CBS)
Stephen Stills (Atlantic)
Stephen Stills II (Atlantic)
Manassas (Atlantic)
Down The Road (Atlantic)
Stills (Columbia/CBS)
Stephen Stills Live (Atlantic)
Illegal Stills (Columbia/CBS)

Alan Stivell

Stivell was born in Brittany in 1943, son of a harp-maker, Jord Cochevelou; he was given his own first harp when he was nine, and subsequently became expert on the instrument. He has since used those skills, as well as his knowledge, both practical and academic (he has a degree in Celtic and English studies) to spearhead a renaissance of the Breton and Celtic cultures Strangely enough, he was able to popularise traditional music through the unlikely channels of rock 'n' roll. He divided his concerts between straightforward traditional music, and electric music, for which he put together a rock band, which included the widely-respected guitarist Dan Ar Bras, and the superb fiddler, Rene Werneer.

After four early solo albums – the first two of which were released in France only, and are devoted exclusively to harp music – he made **Alan Stivell At The Olympia**, a convincing live-rock album, conveying as it does both a rhythmic looseness, and a fine sense of atmosphere.

From Celtic Roots (1973), probably his best album, includes **Ian Morrison Reel**, one of the most effective set-pieces of his stage act.

Throughout 1974–75 Stivell toured Europe to capacity crowds,

provoking scenes of wild enthusiasm wherever he played; he recorded a second live album in Dublin in November 1974. For his 1975 concert tour, he emphasised the political purpose of his concerts by using a back-projection of slides of demonstrations for Breton independence.

Stivell considers that his political and artistic aims are of equal importance; however his progress as champion of Breton populist movement was halted in 1976 when his band split from him, and Dan Ar Bras went on to join Fairport Convention (◆).

Recordings:
Reflections (—/Fontana)
Renaissance Of The Celtic Harp (—/Philips)
Alan Stivell A L'Olympia (—/Fontana)
From Celtic Roots (—Fontana)
Alan Stivell In Dublin (—/Fontana)
E Langonned (—/Fontana)

The Stone Poneys
◆ Linda Ronstadt

Stone The Crows

Maggie Bell vocals
Les Harvey guitar
Jim Dewar bass
John McGinnis keyboards
Collin Allen drums

Above was original line-up. The Crows began out of Glasgow, Scotland, when a young Maggie Bell got up on stage to sing with Alex Harvey (◆ Sensational Alex Harvey Band) and got £2 for her cheek. Harvey introduced her to his younger brother Leslie, then leading Kinning Park Ramblers.

Maggie joined group performing American soul hits, and when Ramblers folded she sang first with Mecca Band at Sauchiehall Street Locarno, Glasgow, and later for rival Denison Palais Band.

Eventually she rejoined Les Harvey in band called Power which toured clubs and U.S. bases in Germany and was discovered and renamed Stone The Crows (line-up as above) by Peter Grant (◆ Led Zeppelin).

Their first two albums, both released in 1970, were notable for tight, soul-based sound, Harvey's superb guitar work and Maggie's gut-bucket singing. However, public acclaim wasn't arriving as fast as was hoped, and McGinnis and Dewar quit in February 1971. The group were near to breaking up when Ronnie Leahy (kybds) and Steve Thompson (bs) came in as replacements. **Teenage Licks** (1971) produced strong upsurge in group's fortunes, Maggie Bell winning first of many awards as Britain's Top Girl Singer in 1972.

But, in same year, came tragic death of Les Harvey, killed on stage by a "live" microphone during gig at Swansea University. The group attempted to carry on – failing to draw Peter Green (◆) out of retirement and settling for Jimmy McCulloch (from Thunder-

clap Newman) as new guitarist –
but the writing was on the wall.

'Ontinuous Performance, already half-completed, was finished by the new line-up and released to critical acclaim. But still there was no commercial success to sustain them, and in June 1973 the band broke up.

Maggie Bell (♦) now solo; McCulloch with Wings (♦).

Recordings:
Stone The Crows (Atlantic/
Polydor)
Ode To John Law (Atlantic/
Polydor)
Teenage Licks (Atlantic/Polydor)
'Ontinuous Performance
(Atlantic/Polydor)

The Stooges
♦ Iggy Pop

Strawbs

Dave Cousins vocals, guitar,
banjo, dulcimer
Rod Coombes drums
Chas Cronk bass
Dave Lambert guitar, vocals

Cousins is only surviving founder member of this chameleon-like band which has been through a variety of musical and personnel changes.

They started out as bluegrass group The Strawberry Hill Boys, formed 1967 by Leicester University student Cousins and former schoolfriend Tony Hooper, the pair having previously played folk-clubs individually and together. Mandolin player Arthur Philips completed first line-up, group drawing influences from likes of Ewan McColl, Peggy Seeger, Flatt & Scruggs. Took name from Strawberry Hill district of London in which they initially rehearsed.

Playing folk clubs as Britain's first bluegrass band, a series of personnel changes followed Philips' departure. Eventually Ron Chesterman emerged as bass player, group began to be referred to more simply as Strawbs, and were joined by highly-gifted folk-singer/writer Sandy Denny (♦).

However, Denny had gone own way – to Fairport Convention (♦) – by time Strawbs secured record deal with A&M, being that American company's first U.K. signing, though an album of earlier recordings **Sandy Denny & Strawbs: All Our Own Work** appeared on a budget label five years later. This contained first recording of Denny's much-covered **Who Knows Where The Time Goes?** composition.

Strawbs first album proper was released by A&M 1969, produced by Gus Dudgeon, to unprecedented acclaim. Classical cellist Claire Deniz augmented band for second Tony Visconti-produced album, **Dragonfly** (1970). This set disappointed early support and, after period of re-appraisal, Cousins and Hooper totally re-grouped bringing in Richard Hudson (drms) and John Ford (bs) – ex of Velvet Opera – and Rick Wakeman (kybds). The latter, who had contributed to **Dragonfly,** was highly-

Above: The Stylistics, doyens of sophisto-soul, with lead singer Russell Thompkins Jnr. (left) who sings just as sweet as he looks.

talented virtuoso graduate of Royal Academy of Music.

Cousins became more interested in electric guitar, while Wakeman added classical overtones – it resulted in somewhat uncertain identity but clearly had to take Strawbs out of folk-club circuit. Indeed, their next album, **Just A Collection Of Antiques And Curios,** was recorded live at July 1970 London Queen Elizabeth Hall concert, this gig resulting in Wakeman being hailed in rock press as major new discovery of year.

Wakeman was already finding difficulty containing his talents on 1971 **From The Witchwood** set, and in that year after yet more individual critical attention he quit to join Yes (♦). Blue Weaver, ex of Amen Corner came in to replace him.

Other internal pressures were taking place, with Cousins and Hudson and Ford at loggerheads over composing contributions. Cousins suffered mental collapse – following gig at Luton 1971.

After 1972 set **Grave New World,** their biggest commercial success thus far, band started using lights, slides and back projections to heighten effect on stage. This move further from early roots led to departure of Tony Hooper after Strawbs last folk gig, at Chelmsford Folk Festival 1972. He was replaced by Dave Lambert. In same year Cousins took time out to record a solo album.

At end of 1972 group enjoyed first singles success in U.K. with

Lay Down, and in January 1973 an even bigger hit with **Part Of The Union,** written by Hudson-Ford.

However, this only exacerbated policy disagreements and, after traumatic American tour and **Bursting At The Seams** album, Hudson-Ford (♦) split to pursue independent career. During this tangled, emotionally - stressful period an embittered Blue Weaver fell by wayside, while Cousins retired to Devon home to piece together a new band. Lambert was retained, with newcomers being John Hawken (ex Nashville Teens, Renaissance, Vinegar Joe), unknown Chas Cronk, and former Stealers Wheel drummer Rod Coombes.

By now, band's appeal had significantly declined in the U.K. – and 1974 **Hero And Heroine** set received both public and critical thumbs down. In America, however, the band began to accrue a burgeoning following. A 1974 British tour flopped badly and throughout 1975 they made no attempt whatsoever to gig in U.K.; the view of home critics at least was that Strawbs had sunk into the deepest of ruts.

Breaking U.S. market these days seems the main concern of this unpredictable aggregation. **Ghosts** (1975) was notable for return of cellist Claire Deniz and enlistment of Charterhouse School Choir. By **Nomadness** (1976), keyboardsman Hawken had departed, reducing group to quartet.

Recordings:
**Sandy Denny & The Strawbs:
All Our Own Work**
(—/Hallmark)
Strawbs (—/A&M)
Dragonfly (—/A&M)

**Just A Collection of Antiques
And Curios** (A&M)
From The Witchwood (A&M)
Grave New World (A&M)
Bursting At The Seams (A&M)
Hero And Heroine (A&M)
Ghosts (A&M)
Nomadness (A&M)
Compilation:
Strawbs By Choice (A&M)
Dave Cousins:
Two Weeks Last Summer (A&M)

Streetwalkers
♦ Chapman
Whitney
Streetwalkers

The Stylistics

Russell Thompkins, Jnr lead
vocals
Herb Murrell vocals
Airrion Love vocals
James Dunn vocals
James Smith vocals

Composed of two earlier local Philadelphia groups, The Percussions and The Monarchs, they first came to attention in mid-70s as leading exponents of soft soul sound of Philadelphia, with Thompkins' ethereally light falsetto lead vocals. Though in some ways their music is little more than superior supper-club schmaltz, the point about The Stylistics is that not only are they better than everyone else at it, there's not even anyone in same league.

Most of their early material, recorded at Sigma Sound Studios, was provided by celebrated songwriting team of Thom Bell and Linda Creed, from **I'm Stone In Love With You** (1972) to **You Make Me Feel Brand New** (1974). Their compilation album, **The Best Of The Stylistics** was the biggest-selling album of 1975 in Britain (and also the biggest-selling album ever by black artists) and within 12 months of its release, they practically had enough hit single material for a Volume II. Thom Bell ceased controlling their productions in 1974, and they were placed under the experienced aegis of the Hugo & Luigi songwriting team, with the equally experienced Van McCoy arranging and conducting the music. The success rate of the group was unaffected, and they had a 1976 U.K. No. 1 with **I Can't Give You Anything (But My Love),** though by now Bell's lightness of touch was missing, their material seemed over-orchestrated, and there was a danger of the Stylistics becoming the Bombastics.

In 1976 they moved to H&L, Hugo & Luigi's own label.

Heavy was re-titled **From The Mountain** for U.K. release.

The Stylistics (Avco)
Round II (Avco)
Rock'n'Roll Baby (Avco)
Let's Put It All Together (Avco)
Heavy/From The Mountain (Avco)
Thank You Baby (Avco/—)
You Are Beautiful (Avco)
Fabulous (H&L)
Compilation:
The Best Of The Stylistics (Avco)

Sun Records
→ Sam Phillips

Supertramp

Rodger Hodgson vocals, guitar, keyboards
Dougie Thompson bass
John Anthony Helliwell sax, clarinet, vocals
Richard Davies vocals, keyboards
Bob C. Benberg drums

United Kingdom flash-rock aggregation, founder members Davies and Hodgson teaming up after former's band The Joint failed to make impact (another of Davies' earlier groups, Rick's Blues, had included Gilbert O'Sullivan).

Original Supertramp line-up, apart from Davies and Hodgson, featured Richard Palmer (gtr), Dave Winthrop (sxs) and Bob Miller (drms). They came together in late '60s under sponsorship of benevolent millionaire. First eponymous album released 1970, after which Miller suffered nervous breakdown and was replaced by Kevin Currie, selected from auditions involving some 200 drummers.

Frank Farrell came in on bass for second album, **Indelibly Stamped** (1971), allowing group's original bassist Hodgson to switch to lead guitar. However, interest in album was negligible and the band faded following a particularly disastrous Norwegian tour.

Currie, Palmer and Winthrop split, to be replaced by Benberg, formerly of Bees Make Honey, and Helliwell and Thompson from Alan Bown Set.

Eventual breakthrough came with **Crime Of The Century** in 1974, a semi-concept affair which was immaculately produced by Ken Scott. It also yielded 1975 hit-single **Dreamer. Crisis? What Crisis?,** another Scott production, followed closely format set by predecessor and attained similar degree of chart success.

Crisis? What Crisis? Courtesy A&M Records.

Recordings:
Supertramp (A&M)
Indelibly Stamped (A&M)
Crime Of The Century (A&M)
Crisis? What Crisis? (A&M)

Screaming Lord Sutch

David Sutch, the London-born self-styled "Lord", was one of the most colourful characters of British rock in '60s. For though he never had a hit (his **Jack The Ripper** and re-moulding of Coasters' **I'm A Hog For You** came closest in early '60s), he had a flair for self-publicity which kept him in British press headlines; whether for attempting to start own "pirate" radio station; for being chased at gunpoint by girlfriend's

Below: Lord Sutch, most active and publicity-conscious of U.K. '60s rock performers.

irate father; or for seeking election to parliament on "Votes For 18 Year Olds" platform.

An original long-hair well before Beatles and Stones, Sutch was unsurpassed on British club circuit for his outrageous showmanship; being brought on stage in coffin for **Jack The Ripper,** or wearing toilet seat as hat. Many of his gimmicks were straight pinch from black American singer Screamin' Jay Hawkins, but, unlike Hawkins, Sutch lacked real vocal force, a failing even presence of super-session friends Jimmy Page, Nicky Hopkins, Jeff Beck and Keith Moon couldn't hide on his two early '70s albums listed below.

Sutch's real claim to fame was as one-time employer of some of today's rock heroes. Page, Beck, Hopkins and Ritchie Blackmore were all at various times members of Sutch's Savages back-up band.

Recordings:
Lord Sutch & Heavy Friends (Cotillion/Atlantic)
Hands Of Jack The Ripper (Cotillion/Atlantic)

Sutherland Brothers & Quiver

Iain Sutherland rhythm guitar, vocals
Willie Wilson drums, vocals
Gavin Sutherland bass, vocals
Tim Renwick lead guitar, vocals

The Sutherland Brothers Band and Quiver amalgamated in 1972. Prior to that, the Sutherlands had made two folk-rock albums for Island. Quiver had also made two albums, and further gained a place in the annals of British rock as the band who played the very first set at Britain's first full-time rock music venue, the Rainbow in Finsbury Park, London. (They were supporting The Who.) However, the Sutherlands needed a good backing group, and Quiver needed some good material, so a union seemed a likely proposition.

Despite hard, regular gigging in

both the U.K. and the U.S., and a favourable critical reaction, public recognition was not immediately forthcoming.

There was, however, one isolated hit when **You Got Me Anyway** reached Top 20 in U.S. early 1973, and on the strength of this the band toured the States as support to Elton John.

In Britain the tide didn't turn in their favour until Rod Stewart, a long-time admirer of the Sutherlands' compositions, included **Sailing** on his **Atlantic Crossing** album. When issued as a single, it reached No. 1 in Britain September 1975. In the wake of this indirect breakthrough, the band moved to CBS and released **Reach For The Sky,** an album of no small merit. The single taken from it, **Arms Of Mary,** became a U.K. Top 10 hit in 1976. Although much of their material is lyrically feeble, they have a strong grasp of melody, and the hard work finally seems to be paying off.

Original line-up included keyboards-player Pete Woods, who left in 1975.

Album notes: the U.S. album **Lifeboat** is not the same as the U.K. album but a compilation of material from the two albums by the Sutherland Brothers Band, plus the singles they had recorded with Quiver – the compilation thus includes their version of **Sailing,** which wasn't available on an album in Britain until Island issued a compilation in 1976.

Recordings:
The Sutherland Brothers Band:
The Sutherland Brothers Band (—/Island)
Lifeboat (—/Island)
Quiver:
Quiver (Warner Bros)
Gone In The Morning (—/Warner Bros)
The Sutherland Brothers and Quiver:
Dream Kid (—/Island)
Beat Of The Street (—/Island)
Reach For The Sky (Columbia/CBS)
Compilations:
Lifeboat (Island/—)
Sailing (—/Island)

Billy Swan

Born in Cape Girardeau, Missouri, he first came to notice when **Lover Please,** a song he had written at age 16 for his band of the time, Mirt Mirley and the Rhythm Steppers, became a huge hit for Clyde McPhatter.

He lived off the royalties for a time, and moved to Nashville, taking odd jobs. He replaced Kris Kristofferson as janitor at Columbia's Nashville Studios.

It was while working for Columbia Music that Swan became involved with Tony Joe White, and produced the latter's first three – and most important – albums. Others of his sundry achievements include playing in Kristofferson's band at 1970 Isle of Wight Festival, backing Kinky Friedman as a member of Texas Jewboys, and roadying for various country stars. He also lived for a while in house of Elvis Presley's uncle (he now owns a pair of Presley's socks).

In August 1974 he released an isolated single, **I Can Help,** which subsequently became an international hit. The album of the same title showed Swan's restrained, but goodtime mixture of rock 'n' roll and country-funk to excellent effect, and yielded another hit, a stately reworking of Presley's **Don't Be Cruel**. **Rock 'n' Roll Moon**, released 1975, consolidated his reputation and provided another large hit, **Everything's The Same**.

I Can Help. Courtesy Monument, CBS Records.

Meanwhile, he began to undertake live appearances, and played in Paris with some of Nashville's finest session-musicians (including Charlie McCoy and Kenny Buttrey) in 1975; he also toured Britain in 1976 with Willie Nelson (♦).

Swan is one of the rock world's endearing figures. He is very popular with fellow professionals, and since his recent success both Kristofferson and Friedman have recorded **Lover Please** (as indeed he has himself), and Presley has recorded **I Can Help**.

Recordings:
I Can Help (Monument)
Rock 'n' Roll Moon (Monument)

Sweet

Brian Connolly vocals
Andy Scott guitar
Steve Priest bass
Mick Tucker drums

Formed 1968 by Tucker and Connolly who first met as members of pop outfit Wainwright's Gentlemen. As Sweet, recorded four flop singles before meeting British songwriting team Nicky Chinn and Mike Chapman in 1970. Chinn-Chapman, who also managed them, produced whole string of instantly catchy, immediately forgettable bubblegum singles, which kept Sweet permanently on U.K. charts for two years: **Funny Funny, Co-Co** (both 1971), **Poppa Joe, Little Willy, Wig Wam Bam** (1972) and **Blockbuster, Hell Raiser, Ballroom Blitz** (1973).

Strung Up.
Courtesy RCA Records.

Derided by rock press, Sweet

worked ballroom circuit with vulgar, bopper-baiting act. Achieved certain notoriety by being banned by Mecca circuit of dance halls for overt sexual nature of repertoire.

In 1974, attempting to rid themselves of restrictive bubblegum image, group split amid rancour from Chinn-Chapman stable, proving immediately that they could survive on own when group-penned **Fox On The Run** made U.K. Top 10 that year.

Subsequently Sweet have attempted further inroads into hard rock market, thus far with only limited success in U.K. but with considerably more impact in America where, even during **Little Willy** period, some rock critics had accorded them "trash aesthetic" status. U.S. version **Desolation Boulevard** contains cuts from U.K. namesake and **Sweet Fanny Adams**.

Recordings:
Funny How Sweet Co Co Can Be (—/RCA)
Sweet Fanny Adams (—/RCA)
Desolation Boulevard (—/RCA)
Give Us A Wink (Capitol/RCA)
Compilations:
Greatest/Biggest Hits (Bell/RCA)
Strung Up (—/RCA)
Desolation Boulevard (Capitol/—)

Shel Talmy

Born in Chicago 1938, Talmy is one of the most influential producers from one of rock's most creative periods. He came to Britain in the early '60s, and worked with The Who (♦) on their first four singles (**I Can't Explain, Anyhow, Anyway, Anywhere, My Generation** and **Substitute**) and their debut album, **My Generation**. He also produced all early Kinks (♦) singles, up to and including **Waterloo Sunset,** and therefore was the person responsible for putting on record the fat, heavy, aggressive guitar riffs that characterised that early sound.

He had a stack of hits to his credit in the mid-'60s, as he was also involved with Manfred Mann, Amen Corner and The Easybeats. He additionally produced Pentangle's early albums.

In the '70s, he stepped back from the record industry to become involved with a book publishing firm, and also wrote a novel himself, "The Ichabod Deception". In 1976 he returned actively to recording, and produced an album for Ralph McTell.

Tamla Motown

The Tamla-Motown organisation, which is today the largest black-owned corporation in America, was the brain-child of Berry Gordy Jnr who, when not working on the production-line of a Detroit car factory, spent his time writing songs.

It was in 1958 that he first won renown, when his composition **Lonely Teardrops** became a million-seller for Jackie Wilson. The next year, he wrote another one – **You Got What It Takes** for Marv Johnson.

Convinced he could do even better with his own label, Gordy

borrowed 700 dollars from his sister Anna who, with her husband Harvey Fuqua, already had her own label.

Gordy had wanted to call his new label Tammy, but there was already one of that name, so he called it Tamla, later adding Motown, from "Motortown" (i.e. Detroit), and subsequently others as well – Soul and Gordy for example.

Tamla distributed Anna, Gordy's sister's label, and it was that label that produced the first million-seller, Barrett Strong's **Money**. Then, on Tamla itself, came The Miracles' **Shop Around,** the label's first gold record. Concentrating on developing the local talent within Detroit itself, Tamla Motown built up a strong roster of acts that included The Supremes, with Diana Ross, The Miracles, with Smokey Robinson, Marvin Gaye, Four Tops, Stevie Wonder, The Temptations, Martha and the Vandellas and Junior Walker.

The company's second gold disc was acquired with The Marvelettes **Please Mr Postman** – also the label's first U.S. No. 1; meanwhile, a potentially fine songwriting team was evolved when Eddie Holland started to concentrate on writing and producing with his brother Brian and their friend Lamont Dozier. The staff producers – Smokey Robinson, Harvey Fuqua, Johnny Bristol and Berry Gordy himself – all played a part in evolving the distinctive "Motown Sound", which made R&B palatable to white as well as black audiences – "The Sound Of Young America" as they called it. By 1964, Motown was the largest independent label in America, dominating the R&B market with 42 bestselling songs, and sales of over 12 million; these figures dramatically increased in each of the ensuing years.

The two most commercially-successful acts in the mid-'60s were The Supremes and Four Tops (♦). Material for both acts was generally composed by the now-prolific team of Holland-Dozier-Holland. Other acts were brought in – the Isley Brothers (♦) and Gladys Knight & the Pips (♦), each of whom could boast of pre-Motown success.

However, many acts also began to leave Motown – Mary Wells and Kim Weston, for example, both of whom were doomed to subsequent obscurity; Jimmy Ruffin, Four Tops and the Detroit Spinners all left too, though only the latter, who went to Philadelphia to work with Thom Bell, had more success after leaving Motown than while they were there.

As the company got bigger, so it looked to expand its horizons, and it launched the Rare Earth rock label, with the white group of the same name, and in 1971 uprooted itself to the West Coast, where the music seemed to become less funky and more smooth and sophisticated in line with the environment.

This had possibly been Motown's first wrong move, though in any case their pattern of automatic success had been broken. Both Gladys Knight and the Isley Brothers left and subsequently enjoyed greater commercial success; and the Jackson 5 (♦), who had for a time been Motown's hottest property, also moved.

Meanwhile, Marvin Gaye (♦) and Stevie Wonder (♦) continued to release million-selling albums unerringly, and Diana Ross, as a solo artist, became Motown's first all-round entertainer, when she seemed to veer into the cabaret market, and also starred in two major film productions launched by Motown – **Lady Sings The Blues,** the biography of Billie Holiday, and **Mahogany.** In 1975 Motown further emphasised its position as one of the top record companies by offering to Stevie Wonder a 12 million dollar contract that was massive even by the exaggerated standards of the record industry.

Tangerine Dream

Edgar Froese synthesisers, keyboards, guitar
Christoph Franke synthesisers
Peter Baumann synthesisers, keyboards, flute

Founded Germany 1967 by Froese and Franke originally as rock band, though music tended towards improvisation as realised on first album **Electronic Meditation** released (Germany only) 1970. At this point group abandoned "restrictions" of conventional instruments and recruited Baumann on keyboards. Early live appearances in this new experimental form provoked hostile receptions, but group persevered and began to accrue following.

Ricochet.
Courtesy Virgin Records.

Alpha Centauri cut 1971, **Zeit** 1971 and **Atem** in following year, subsequent to which T. Dream quarrelled with German record company and signed for England's Virgin Records. One of the few German experimental bands to survive early '70s interest in European avant-garde scene, the group brought with them already sizeable audience and first two albums for Virgin, **Phaedra** (1974) and **Rubycon** (1975), went into U.K. album lists. Brought to even wider attention via controversial concert at Rheims Cathedral in December 1974, where some 6,000 aficionados attempted to fill the 2,000-capacity building. Apart from concerts in more conventional venues, T. Dream have attempted to repeat cathedral gigs where possible – undoubtedly, Gothic overtones of their always-improvised electronics are ideally suited to these settings.

October 1975 saw them appear at York Minster, and Coventry and Liverpool Cathedrals as part of sell-out British tour, subsequent to which release of live album **Ricochet** drawn from 40 hours of tapes from British and French concerts.

Froese recorded first solo album 1974, second in 1975. Ohr albums, aside of first, now issued on Virgin. **Alpha** and **Atem** previously also on Polydor.

Recordings:
Electronic Meditation (Ohr import)
Alpha Centauri (Ohr import)
Zeit (Ohr import)
Atem (Ohr import)
Phaedra (Virgin)
Rubycon (Virgin)
Ricochet (Virgin)
Edgar Froese:
Aqua (Virgin)
Epsilon In Malaysian Pale (Virgin)

Taste
➧ Rory Gallagher

Bernie Taupin
➧ Elton John

Chip Taylor

Born James Wesley Voight in Yonkers, New York (brother of the actor Jon Voight), Taylor was best-known in the '60s as a songwriter, his most famous composition being **Wild Thing**, for The Troggs, a major hit on both sides of the Atlantic (No. 2 in the U.K., No. 1 in U.S.); other song credits include **Angel Of The Morning** (Merrilee Rush), **Any Way That You Want Me** (American Breed and The Troggs), **Storybook Children** (Billy Vera and Judy Clay), **I Can't Let Go** (The Hollies) and **Take Me For A Little While** (Vanilla Fudge).

Taylor then became involved with other projects – he produced an album for the Flying Machine (➧ James Taylor) and a single for Neil Diamond. He then became

part of a trio (Al) Gorgoni, (Trade) Martin and Taylor; they released two hybrid country albums on Buddah in 1971 and 1972, and Taylor remained to cut a solo album, **Gasoline,** which included his version of **Angel Of The Morning.**

He then moved to Warner Bros, and in 1973 made the critically-acclaimed and ironically-titled **Chip Taylor's Last Chance;** a second album, almost as good followed immediately, though **This Side Of The Big River** (1975) was a disappointment. Taylor's original charm had lain in the fact that he was that ethnic half-breed, a New York country singer, who contrived to make fine country albums outside Nashville.

Recordings:
Gorgoni, Martin & Taylor:
Gotta Get Back To Cisco (Buddah)
G, M & T (Buddah)
Chip Taylor:
Gasoline (Buddah)
Chip Taylor's Last Chance (Warner Bros)
Some Of Us (Warner Bros)
This Side Of The Big River (Warner Bros)

Derek Taylor

Born Liverpool 1932, Taylor was a show biz columnist for the "Daily Express" who became press officer for The Beatles in the early '60s at the suggestion of Brian Epstein. Taylor was invaluable, since he could always be relied upon for the quotable quote that didn't really tell you anything. In America in the mid-'60s, he was active in the early careers of The Byrds (➧) and The Beach Boys (➧); back in England, he presided over the chaos that was Apple, and wrote a book about his experiences – "As Time Goes By".

In the '70s he joined Warner Bros in U.K., and helped re-launch the career of George Melly (➧). Though he became Managing Director of Warner

Bros (UK) Ltd in 1975, he was eased aside when Nesuhi Ertegun arrived in London in 1976 to oversee the integration of the Warner Bros, Elektra and Atlantic labels in Britain.

James Taylor

Born Mar 12, 1948 in Boston, Massachusetts, Taylor was brought up in conditions of some prosperity. His father was Dean of the Medical School of the University of North Carolina, and his mother had been a lyric soprano at the New England Conservatory of Music. They owned two houses, of which one was a summer residence at Martha's Vineyard, which is where James met Danny Kortchmar in 1963.

He was educated at Milton Academy, a boarding school just outside Boston; in his final year he sank into depression and admitted himself to a local mental hospital. Nine months later he discharged himself and went to New York where Kortchmar (Kootch) was putting together a coffee-bar group, The Flying Machine, which Taylor joined; before the group broke up in spring 1967, they made some recordings which were issued in 1972 at the height of Taylor's fame as **James Taylor And The Original Flying Machine.**

Taylor then went to live in Notting Hill Gate in London, where he made a demo tape of some of his songs; after auditioning with several companies, Peter Asher (➧) showed some interest, and so Taylor signed to The Beatles' Apple Records.

James Taylor was released 1968, and it went largely unnoticed; some of it was marred by unsympathetic arrangements, but it contained much good material, including one of his best autobiographical songs, **Carolina In My Mind.**

However Taylor now had drug problems, and on his return to the States re-entered mental hospital, although Asher kept faith in him and, with Apple in complete disarray, negotiated a contract for Taylor with Warner Bros. When Taylor came out, he and Asher went to California in December 1969 to record **Sweet Baby James.**

The album was released to enthusiastic reviews, and gradually the public sat up and took notice, until it has now become one of the largest-selling albums of all time. Sales of the album were aided by a hit single – **Fire And Rain;** with consecutive verses about Taylor's heroin addiction, his period in a mental institution, and the suicide of a close friend, it was one of the most harrowing songs ever to hit the U.S. singles charts; certainly Taylor has not since matched the dramatic impact of the song.

Sweet Baby James, however, set Taylor some problems; laid-back and relaxed, it was essentially the right product at the right time, a necessary antidote to the Zeppelin heavy-metal syndrome, and, though it paved the way for a million singer/songwriters of questionable talent,

Left: James Taylor and Dennis Wilson in "Two Lane Blacktop".

placed Taylor himself in a false position of pre-eminence. Despite the qualities of many of his later albums – and especially the brilliance of parts of **Mud Slide Slim** – he was never quite able to match up to the public's expectations of him for another five years. ⸰

James Taylor.
Courtesy Apple, EMI.

Meanwhile, some of the singer/songwriters whose first break came in the wake of **Sweet Baby James** proved to be some of his own family. His elder brother, Alex, who had formed a rock band in 1964 called the Fabulous Corsairs, was a keen musician, and in 1971 he made an album, **Alex Taylor** with a group named Friends And Neighbours for Phil Walden's Capricorn Records, and a second one, **Dinnertime,** the following year.

Like James, Livingston and Kate Taylor had both had spells in the local sanitorium, McLean Hospital. Livingston made three albums for Capricorn in the early '70s – **Livingston Taylor, Liv,** and **Over The Rainbow;** Peter Asher produced an album for Kate in 1971, called **Sister Kate,** released on Cotillion/Atlantic Records.

Above: Mud Slide Slim straightens his feet.

To return to James: **Mud Slide Slim And The Blue Horizon** was released in May 1971. It was in a similar acoustic style to **Sweet Baby James,** and contained a clutch of good songs of his own, and one of Carole King's, **You've Got A Friend,** which was issued as the single and reached No. 4 in the U.K. and No. 1 in the U.S.

Taylor's concerts at this time, in America and Europe, were very successful; he was usually backed by a line-up of: Carole King (pno), Danny Kootch (ld gtr), Lee Sklar (bs), Russ Kunkel (drms) – these personnel, minus Carole King but with Craig Doerge on keyboards, formed themselves into an outfit called The Section, and as such backed Taylor on **One Man Dog,** and made two albums of their own for Warners Bros – **The Section** and **Forward**

Motion.

In early 1973, he married Carly Simon (➧), a major event on the social calendar of the new rock aristocracy, and their joint success at this time can be gauged by the fact that in 1973 Taylor and Simon were reckoned to be the highest-paid married couple in the world, with the exception of Richard Burton and Elizabeth Taylor.

That year, Taylor also starred in his first movie – sharing the honours with Beach Boy Dennis Wilson in "Two Lane Blacktop".

In the three years after **Mud Slide Slim** was released, he made only two albums – **One Man Dog** and **Walking Man,** neither of which was very exciting, though in 1974 he was restored to the U.S. singles charts via **Mockingbird,** a duet with Carly Simon from her **Hotcakes** album.

In 1975 he released **Gorilla,** produced by Lenny Waronker and Russ Titelman, and it was a bona fide re-emergence, since it gave him another U.S. Top 10 album, and also another hit single, again with Carly, **How Sweet It Is** (the old Marvin Gaye number); he now seems to have recovered the self-confidence that had deserted him.

Recordings:
James Taylor And The Original Flying Machine (Euphoria DJM)
James Taylor (Apple)
Sweet Baby James (Warner Bros)
Mud Slide Slim And The Blue Horizon (Warner Bros)
One Man Dog (Warner Bros)
Walking Man (Warner Bros)

Below: 10cc; (left to right) Gouldman, Stewart, Godley and Creme.

Gorilla (Warner Bros)
In The Pocket (Warner Bros)

Tempest
➧ Colosseum

10cc

Eric Stewart guitar, vocals
Lol Creme guitar, vocals
Graham Gouldman bass, vocals
Kevin Godley drums, vocals

Formed Manchester, England, 1972 as natural outcome of four friends and colleagues returning to home town. Creme and Godley had been at art school together (they designed sleeve of first 10cc album) and in various groups; while Stewart and Gouldman played together in The Mindbenders, who had 1966 British Top 5 hit with **Groovy Kind Of Love.**

Gouldman had in fact joined in later days of this last group, working previously as a prolific and highly successful songwriter. His credits turn up on a whole string of '60s British hits including **For Your Love** and **Heart Full Of Soul** for Yardbirds (➧), **Bus Stop** and **Look Through Any Window** for Hollies (➧), **No Milk Today** for Herman's Hermits and **Tallyman** for Jeff Beck (➧). He also recorded solo album in late '60s **The Graham Gouldman Thing.**

When Mindbenders split 1968, Gouldman went to America to work as songwriter for Kasenetz-Katz organisation, while Stewart was instrumental in setting up Strawberry Studios in Stockport, inviting Creme and Godley to work with him there.

First result of this experimental studio doodling was single **Neanderthal Man** which the trio released on Fontana label under name Hotlegs in 1970. This went to No. 2 in U.K. charts, and was followed by nationwide tour with Moody Blues during which Gouldman returned from U.S.

The four returned to Strawberry Studios filling in time between writing with production and session-work. It was while experimenting in studios that Godley/Creme composition **Donna** received the treatment which turned it into clever parody of U.S. hits of late '50s.

They took song to Jonathan King (➧) who suggested name 10cc, and within weeks of release on King's new UK label the single was at No. 2 in British charts late 1972.

In July 1973 came an even defter piece of pop parody, **Rubber Bullets,** which went to No. 1, followed by the equally-brilliant **The Dean And I.** Initial categorisation as transient pop band was dissipated by highly literate skills of aforementioned cuts, and with release of eponymous debut album (1973) the group achieved sudden and considerable critical acclaim. Out of nowhere Britain had acquired its first consistently entertaining singles group since the mid-'60s.

All four members of band write songs individually and together and draw on variety of influences ranging from Beatles through Beach Boys to Four Seasons. The wit of lyrics distinguished them from other parodists.

They released a second, acclaimed album on UK 1974 before signing for reputedly handsome sum to Mercury in 1975. From that year's **The Original Soundtrack** came one of 1975's most illustrious singles, Eric Stewart's chart-topping **I'm Not In Love.**

Soundtrack and 1976 offering **How Dare You** have both been subject to certain criticism as evidencing loss of warmth due to over-indulgence in recording techniques, plus self-conscious artiness, but there's no denying this most professional and gifted of bands their place among Britain's finest rock acts of '70s.

Recordings:
10cc (UK)
Sheet Music (UK)
The Original Soundtrack (Mercury)
How Dare You (Mercury)
Compilation:
100cc (UK)

Ten Years After

Alvin Lee guitar, vocals
Leo Lyons bass
Chick Churchill keyboards
Ric Lee drums

Alvin Lee and Leo Lyons first met in the former's home town, Nottingham, England. They played together in Hamburg, Germany, before being joined by Ric Lee (no relation) to form The Jaybirds. Chick Churchill brought group up to four-piece, and as such they built considerable grass-roots following around Nottingham area, before changing name to Ten Years After in 1967.

Nationally they emerged as one of the top bands of the second-wave British blues boom, although drawing on rock more

heavily than "authentic" contemporaries such as Fleetwood Mac, Chicken Shack. They gained a residency at the prestigious Marquee Club, London, and a spot on the Windsor Blues Festival which drew a standing ovation.

By then they had established a style which they adhered to closely in succeeding years – basically blues-based and fronted by the speedy, highly taut and accomplished guitar playing of Alvin Lee.

They released their first album in 1967, and shortly after put in the first of their many visits to the U.S. (up to demise of band TYA held distinction of undertaking 28 American tours, more than any other British group).

Watt.
Courtesy Chrysalis Records.

Undead (1968), a live album, and **Stonedhenge** (1969), the quintessential early TYA albums, made impact in Europe and America. Both in writing and playing Alvin Lee came more to the fore, being elevated to superstar status after the band's appearance in movie of Woodstock Festival (➧), held August 1969. TYA were accorded 11 minutes in the movie, their epic workout on **Goin' Home** proving one of the most popular segments of same.

It was a turning point for the band on two counts: as noted, it thoroughly established them in international rock hierarchy of their day; at same time, however, it signalled a marked deterioration in their musical credibility. From that point on, audiences all over would demand of Lee the same flash-fingered "Fastest Guitar In The West" pyrotechnics of "Woodstock" and eventually reduce TYA to little more than a high-speed freak-show.

After extensive touring, and a U.K. hit single with **Love Like A Man** from **Cricklewood Green** (1970), they took time off in 1971–72 to cure "Woodstock hangover" and to make **A Space In Time.** The group utilized electronic effects and evidenced an altogether more subdued ambience. The album garnered them a U.S. gold but the experiment was only partially successful.

In 1973 Alvin Lee was talking candidly to the rock press about his disillusion with the group, describing them as a "travelling jukebox". After **Rock And Roll Music To The World** in 1972, they had again gone off the road for six months late 1972 into 1973 to pursue solo projects. Lee himself retired to his 15th-century home in Berkshire, England, to build his own studio, and record an album with American gospel singer Mylon LeFevre, using heavyweight session support from likes of Ron Wood, Steve Win-

wood, Jim Capaldi and George Harrison (credited as Harry Georgeson). Chick Churchill, meanwhile, recorded an album of his own, **You And Me.** Both were released November 1973.

There had been one "token" TYA album that year, **Recorded Live,** culled from four concerts in Amsterdam, Rotterdam, Frankfurt and Paris.

In early 1974 the group announced U.K. concerts, but on March 22, a month before TYA were due to play the London Rainbow Theatre as a group, Alvin Lee arranged his own hurriedly - organised concert there, using a nine-piece support band assembled only 10 days earlier. Their set was recorded live for the double album, **Alvin Lee & Co In Flight.**

TYA went on to play the Rainbow, a sell-out gig, but it was apparent that the end was at hand. This concert proved to be their last British appearance. In spring 1974 came the ironically-titled **Positive Vibrations,** the last TYA studio set – and later in the year Alvin Lee announced plans for a worldwide solo tour employing the services of Ronnie Leahy (kybds), Steve Thompson (bs) – both ex Stone The Crows (➧) – and Ian Wallace (drms) and Mel Collins (sxs) – both ex King Crimson (➧). The latter two appear on **In Flight.**

Nevertheless, a TYA split was denied by the group's management. The situation appeared to be clarified in May 1975 when Alvin Lee declared the group defunct, and it was announced that Ric Lee had formed his own band. Yet only one month later the group completely bamboozled anyone who could still muster interest in their activities by turning out for yet another American tour, most likely due to unavoidable contractual obligations. This did little to halt TYA's rapidly-descending status, and the year ended with the news that Columbia in the U.S. had dropped the act from their roster due to falling sales.

Above: Alvin Lee, 1 year after the demise of Ten Years After.

Since that mid-1975 tour, Alvin Lee has released two more solo albums, **Pump Iron** and **Saguitar,** and formed a new touring Alvin Lee & Co with Tim Hinckley (kybds), Andy Pyle (bs) and Bryson Graham (drms); Ric Lee has formed his own production company; Chick Churchill has been appointed professional manager for Chrysalis Publishing; and Leo Lyons has worked as a producer (➧UFO).

Although TYA have never "officially" disbanded – the most their U.K. record company will concede is that their future looks

"decidedly uncertain" – they have to all intents and purposes ceased to exist. It was without doubt the messiest of deaths.

Recordings:
Ten Years After (Dream)
Undead (Deram)
Stonedhenge (Deram)
Ssshh (Deram)
Cricklewood Green (Deram)
Watt (Deram)
A Space In Time
(Columbia/Chrysalis)
Rock And Roll Music To The World (Columbia/Chrysalis)
Recorded Live
(Columbia/Chrysalis)
Positive Vibrations
(Columbia/Chrysalis)
Compilation:
Goin' Home
(Columbia/Chrysalis)
Alvin Lee:
Alvin Lee & Co/In Flight
(Columbia/Chrysalis)
Pump Iron (Columbia/Chrysalis)
Saguitar (Columbia/Chrysalis)
Alvin Lee & Mylon LeFevre:
On The Road To Freedom
(Columbia/Chrysalis)
Chick Churchill:
You And Me
(Columbia/Chrysalis)

Them
➧ Van Morrison

Thin Lizzy

Phil Lynott vocals, bass
Brian Robertson guitar
Scott Gorham guitar
Brian Downey drums

Formed Dublin, Ireland, 1970, arrived in London March 1971

with original line-up of Lynott, Downey and Eric Bell (gtr). Released first album 1971. Worked club/college circuit in U.K., and broke into British singles chart early 1973 with new arrangement of traditional **Whiskey In The Jar** although follow-up **Rudolph's Tango** failed to register.

Eric Bell quit group suffering ill-health and Gary Moore (ex Skid Row, now with Colosseum II) joined for short spell, before Lynott and Downey re-grouped June 1974 with two new guitarists Gorham, an American, and Robertson a Scot.

This four-piece cut **Night Life** for November 1974 release, and **Fighting** in September 1975. Fronted by Lynott, a black Irishman who writes most of group's material, Thin Lizzy are basically a hardrock band – though later material evidences more subtle (and eclectic) use of the genre.

This brought handsome rewards in summer 1976 when **Jailbreak** and single **The Boys Are Back In Town** won considerable critical and commercial acclaim in U.S. and U.K.

Recordings:
Thin Lizzy (London/Decca)
Shades Of A Blue Orphanage (London/Decca)
Vagabonds Of The Western World (London/Decca)
Night Life (Vertigo)
Fighting (Vertigo)
Jailbreak (Mercury/Vertigo)

Below: Thin Lizzy, with Phil Lynott (centre) exuding macho cool. After years in the business, the band became overnight the most exciting new act of 1976.

Richard and Linda Thompson

Thompson was born and educated in London and, with Ashley Hutchings and Simon Nicol, formed Fairport Convention (♦) immediately he left school, though he also worked for a time designing stained-glass windows.

Having been one of the main creative forces in the illustrious history of Fairport (his compositions for the band included **Meet On The Ledge, Genesis Hall** and **Sloth**), he left in January 1971, because he felt he'd been in the band too long and was no longer extending himself.

I Want To See The Bright Lights Tonight. Island.

His immediate post-Fairport activities were nevertheless rather desultory. Being adept at both acoustic and electric guitar, he did a large amount of session-work, and was featured on large proportion of the folk-rock projects in early '70s, later averring that the most pleasing sessions he'd worked on had been those for Mike & Lal Waterson's **Bright Phoebus** and Gary Farr's **Strange Fruit**.

He was a member of two ad hoc assemblies (mainly composed of Fairport alumni) that recorded albums for Island in 1972; as one of The Bunch, he recorded **Rock On** in April 1972, an album of rather lacklustre treatments of old rock 'n' roll songs, and **Morris On,** an album of traditional dance music recorded with Hutchings, Dave Mattacks, John Kirkpatrick and Barry Dransfield.

In June 1972 he issued his first solo album, **Henry The Human Fly,** which contained such compositions as **Shaky Nancy** and **Nobody's Wedding,** but it was an isolated offering, and he began to work the folk-club circuit in partnership with Nicol, who had also left Fairport by this time, and Linda Peters, a friend of Sandy Denny's and back-up session-singer whom Thompson later married.

After also playing for a time as support to Sandy Denny (♦), Thompson recorded another album in 1973 – it was not issued until a year later – and decided to return to electric music. He put together a band, Sour Grapes, with Linda as lead-singer and Nicol, plus a drummer and bassist. The band played several gigs in Britain spring 1974 as support act on a Traffic tour, but it was a disastrous line-up, and was sundered at the completion of the tour; Thompson never did learn the surname of the bass-player.

I Want To See The Bright Lights Tonight, the first album jointly credited to Richard and Linda Thompson, was finally released at the same time. It was an album that attracted ecstatic reviews, and sold encouragingly, and henceforth the Thompsons worked together, using a pick-up band for touring purposes instead of a regular line-up.

Though the album contained songs of some gravity, title track was one of the most joyous songs of the '70s; the standard of the work was maintained on **Hokey Pokey,** on which Thompson's characteristically humanistic compositions were placed in less sombre settings; Thompson had the gift of being able to explore complex themes in a simple framework. **Pour Down Like Silver** was released late 1975, and that juxtaposed songs like **Jet Plane In A Rocking Chair** with some of Thompson's most dexterous guitar work since he left Fairport.

He toured Britain twice in 1975, using the same back-up musicians – Dave Pegg (bs), Dave Mattacks (drms) and John Kirkpatrick (accordion).

They made a shambling stage crew; Thompson has always firmly eschewed the more glamorous accoutrements of the rock business, and his live act has an air of studied amateurishness about the presentation (though not about the quality of the music). He is unlikely ever to become a fully-fledged rock star, simply because he would always take steps to avoid commercial success, and partly because his introverted Moslem faith leaves little room for such considerations. However his devoted following throughout Britain is ample testimony to the fact that he is one of the most important of contemporary songwriters.

In 1976 Thompson issued **(guitar vocal)** (neat title), a double-album of flotsam and jetsam from his work over the previous eight years.

Recordings:
Henry The Human Fly (Island)
(guitar, vocal) (Island)
Richard And Linda Thompson:
I Want To See The Bright Lights Tonight (—/Island)
Hokey Pokey (Island)
Pour Down Like Silver (Island)

Three Dog Night

Danny Hutton vocals
Chuck Negron vocals
Cory Wells vocals
Mike Allsup guitar
Jim Greenspoon keyboards
Joe Schermie bass
Floyd Sneed drums

Among most commercially successful of rock acts in U.S., Three Dog Night have amassed a total of 14 gold albums (i.e. their entire output) and nine gold singles; their record company says they have sold over 40 million records. Most critics do not understand why.

The concept of group originated with Danny Hutton who was born in Buncrana, Eire, but raised

Above: A fish-eye's view of Thunderclap Newman (Keene, Newman and McCulloch), posing in Hyde Park in London.

in U.S. He thought a line-up with three lead singers would have amazing versatility, so he recruited Wells (who had previously toured with a band supporting Sonny & Cher) and then Negron.

They then added the rest of line-up – Schermie, who came from the Cory Wells Blues Band; Sneed, a black drummer from Canada who had worked with Jose Feliciano; Greenspoon (the son of silent screen star Mary O'Brian) grew up in Hollywood and Allsup, whose background was in country and gospel music, came from a band called The Family Scandal. The members of the band thus brought a diversity of musical influences with them, though the critics never forgot that they had been assembled for the primary purpose of producing hit singles.

The outfit worked in clubs on West Coast gaining experience – both Brian Wilson and Van Dyke Parks worked with them in the studio, but when they signed to ABC-Dunhill, their first album was produced by Gabriel Mekler, the Hungarian-born classical pianist who had previously produced albums for Steppenwolf.

The first album exemplified the Three Dog Night technique – they merely re-worked songs from other sources, though they selected the material with some care and were responsible for bringing to attention songwriters previously underexposed.

Their debut album provided them with three hit singles, **Nobody, Try A Little Tenderness** and Harry Nilsson's **One,** respectively, the latter becoming their first gold single. The album subsequently went gold, as did the next nine, as Three Dog Night became one of the most popular recording and live bands in the States, probably because they concentrated on singles-oriented "songs", when other bands were concentrating on more adventurous material.

Suitable For Framing, the band's second album, released in 1969, contained **Easy To Be Hard,** which became one of the first hit singles from the musical "Hair", the Laura Nyro composition **Eli's Coming,** and **Lady Samantha,** by the then almost unknown songwriting partnership of Elton John/Bernie Taupin. This album also contained compositions by members of band, though their forte was to remain cover versions.

Two other songwriters they helped to push were Randy Newman, whose **Mama Told Me Not To Come** gave the band their solitary hit single in Britain, and Hoyt Axton, whose **Joy To The World** went gold in 1971.

Though basically a post-psychedelic heavy-rock band, attracting a youthful audience, Three Dog Night's music possessed strong R&B undertones, which was clearly evidenced on **Freedom For The Stallion,** from their **Seven Separate Fools** album.

In 1973 Schermie left the band, to be replaced by Jack Ryland, and Skip Konte joined as a second keyboard player to bring the personnel up to eight. Nevertheless, the heady days when they were one of the top box-office attractions in America seem to be over.

Recordings:
Three Dog Night (Dunhill/Stateside)
Suitable For Framing (Dunhill/Stateside)
Captured Live At The Forum (Dunhill/Stateside)
It Ain't Easy (Dunhill/Stateside)
Harmony (Dunhill/Probe)
Naturally (Dunhill/Probe)
Seven Separate Fools (Dunhill/Probe)
Recorded Live In Concert – Around The World With Three Dog Night (Dunhill/Probe)
Cyan (Dunhill/Probe)
Hard Labour (Dunhill/Probe)
Dog Style (Dunhill/ABC)
Coming Down (ABC)
American Pastime (ABC)
Compilations:
Golden Biscuits (Dunhill/Probe)
Joy To The World – Their Greatest Hits (Dunhill/ABC)

Thunderclap Newman

Andy Newman keyboards
Jimmy McCulloch guitar
John "Speedy" Keen vocals, drums

A product of Pete Townshend's ever-fertile imagination, Thunderclap Newman was an instantly-successful group during 1969, though they were never able to follow up the enormous success gained with their first single, which reached No. 1 in British charts.

Newman, an ex Post Office engineer, was a traditional jazz pianist who idolised Bix Beiderbecke, while McCulloch was a 16-year old guitarist from Scotland whom Townshend had seen at Middle Earth Club in a group called One In A Million. Keen was a songwriter and ex roadie for such as John Mayall, and had contributed **Armenia, City In The Sky** to **The Who Sell Out** album. From these essentially diverse people, who were generally unable to communicate with each other, Townshend as producer and bass player (under the alias Bijou Drains) conjured a Keen song **Something In The Air** into one of the most successful and memorable singles of the period.

In order to both capitalise on the single's success, and to allow Speedy to front the group from the front, rather than from behind his drum kit, Jim Avery (bs) and Jimmy McCulloch's brother Jack (drms) were brought into the group for live work, but this move was disastrous, and the group folded during 1970, leaving behind one absurdly underrated album.

Keen has since made two fine solo albums, continuing the songwriting quality shown on **Hollywood Dream**, while Newman produced a bizarre solo effort on which he played a large number of both normal and weird instruments. McCulloch is currently holding the lead guitar chair with Wings (♦), having previously done stints with John Mayall, Stone The Crows and Blue.

Recordings:
Hollywood Dream (MCA/Track)
John "Speedy" Keen:
Previous Convictions (—/Track)
Y'Know Wot I Mean? (Island)
Andy Newman:
Rainbow (—/Track)

Tomita

Isao Tomita was born in Tokyo in 1932, and graduated from Tokyo University in the history of art. His main interests, however, already lay in the areas of music and electronics, and he began to compose choral pieces. He was commissioned to write the theme music for the 1964 Tokyo Olympics and later wrote pieces for the Japanese Philharmonic Orchestra.

He provided the music for the Toshiba Hall at the 1970 Expo exhibition, and in 1973 established Plasma Music, which is dedicated to the creation of a new form of synthesiser music.

In April 1974 his first piece of recorded music was issued in the the U.S. Called **Snowflakes Are Dancing**; it was his synthesiser interpretation of music by Debussy, and it gradually proved a huge and unlikely bestseller, both in the U.S. and in the U.K. The healthy sales of Tomita's albums since (in which he has given the technological treatment to, respectively, Mussourgsky and Stravinsky) have shown that his success with **Snowflakes Are Dancing** was no fluke.

Recordings:
Snowflakes Are Dancing (RCA Red Seal)
Picture At An Exhibition (RCA Red Seal)
Firebird (RCA Red Seal)

"Tommy"

It had always been Pete Townshend's major ambition to write a rock opera (♦ The Who). He had listened to **S. F. Sorrow** by The Pretty Things (♦), arguably the first rock opera and then created **Tommy**, the story of a boy who is struck deaf, dumb and blind at an early age after witnessing his mother's fornication, but who develops into a pinball champion through his heightened sense of smell, and who recovers his faculties after a nebulous mystical experience, and becomes a Messiah leading an adolescent crusade until he retreats from the excessive fanaticism which the crusade has unleashed.

Sounds silly, doesn't it?

When **Tommy** was released by Track Records in May 1969, it was received ecstatically by the swelling legion of Who devotees, and more hesitantly by the uncommitted who were naturally suspicious of a double concept-album. **Tommy** produced a hit-single, however, in **Pinball Wizard**, and gradually the album began to reach a large audience, both in Britain and America.

In April 1970 The Who presented **Tommy** in its entirety on-stage at the New York Metropolitan Opera House, but it was in December 1971 that the first logical extension of the work took place when Lou Reizner presented the stage version of **Tommy**, with an all-star cast, at the Rainbow in London. A slightly different studio version of this, recorded with the participation of Ringo Starr, Peter Sellers and the London Symphony Orchestra, was released by Ode Records in 1972.

The next logical extension was a film, which was duly set up in 1974 by Robert Stigwood (♦) and directed by Ken Russell (♦); it was released to generally favourable acclaim in 1975. The film starred Daltrey as Tommy, and also featured Keith Moon, Eric Clapton, Tina Turner, Arthur Brown, Ann-Margret and Oliver Reed. There was, of course, a double soundtrack album accompanying the movie. It featured The Who, augmented by scores of experienced sessioneers.

Tommy has thus become a celebrated artefact of rock music, and possibly of the 20th century. Certainly, the music is often very good; equally certainly, Townshend missed the boat (as he once admitted) with the libretto, which was rather more superficial than he would have liked. Never-less, it has been the longest-running show in rock-biz, and The Who are beginning to wonder if it will ever go away.

Toots & the Maytals

Fred "Toots" Hibbert vocals
Raleigh Gordon vocals
Jerry Matthias vocals

One of the most popular native bands in Jamaica, Toots & the Maytals are perhaps now right behind Bob Marley in line for international recognition.

After singing in Baptist choirs as a child, Toots moved down to Kingston from his birthplace of Maypen and linked up with Matthias and Gordon. For a time they worked with producer Clement "Sir Coxsone" Dodd as The Vikings, and following this they recorded for other leading Jamaican producers – Prince Buster, Byron Lee and Leslie Kong – and became one of the island's top acts. This success was interrupted in 1965 when Toots served a two-year prison sentence on a drugs charge; he returned, however, to renewed popularity. Toots & the Maytals have won the Jamaican National Song Festival three times.

In 1971 Leslie Kong died, and Toots & Maytals moved back to work with Byron Lee, who had by this time set up his Dynamic Sounds Studio. They recorded two albums there – **Funky Kingston** and **In The Dark**, both of which were released in Britain on the Dragon label, thus helping to swell the band's overseas support.

In 1975 they were signed by Island Records, and in 1976 released **Reggae Got Soul**, produced by Warrick Lynn and Joe Boyd, and toured Britain, using a back-up band of: Earl "Hux" Brown (gtr), Rad Bryan (gtr), Jackie Jackson (bs), Winston Wright (org) and Paul Douglas (drms); it was Jackson and Brown who helped give Paul Simon's **Mother And Child Reunion** the ring of authenticity.

In U.S., Island issued **Funky Kingston**, a compilation of material from both **In The Dark** and **Funky Kingston** itself.

Recordings:
Funky Kingston (—/Dragon)
In The Dark (—/Dragon)
Reggae Got Soul (—/Island)
Compilation:
Funky Kingston (Island/—)

Allen Toussaint

Born 1938, Toussaint has spent his entire working life in New Orleans, and has been an integral part of two separate golden eras of music there. In the late '50s he worked with Fats Domino (♦), often playing piano on Domino's records. When Minit Records was set up in 1960 he became the company's chief songwriter, producer, bandleader and pianist. As such, he manufactured hits such as Ernie K. Doe's **Mother-In-Law** and, later on, Aaron Neville's **Tell It Like It Is**. Toussaint also acted as an independent producer for other local companies, and was thus involved in creating a string of hits for both Clarence "Frogman" Henry and Lee Dorsey; he was especially associated with the latter, for whom he wrote **Holy Cow** and **Working In A Coal-Mine**, both big hits in mid-'60s, and then in 1970 helped Dorsey make a comeback album **Yes We Can**.

Toussaint had written all but one of the compositions, which included **Yes We Can Can, Sneakin' Sally Through The Alley** and **Occapella**, since recorded by the Pointer Sisters, Robert Palmer and Ringo Starr respectively.

Meanwhile, in 1965 Toussaint had gone into partnership with Marshall Sehorn, setting up a local company and building the Seasaint Studios, which have been frequented, especially in the recent '70s, by outside artists hoping to capture some of that elusive southern funk. Frankie Miller (♦) recorded **High Life** there in 1974, and again since Toussaint had written some original material, the album was plundered by the other artists; **Shoorah, Shoorah** became a hit in the U.K. and the U.S. for Betty Wright, and **Brickyard Blues** was a U.S. hit for Three Dog Night, there was also a version on Maria Muldaur's **Waitress In A Donut Shop**. Since, under Toussaint's astute control, and with his tasteful productions, his New Orleans studios have become a most fashionable place in which to record; literally scores of artists have worked there, including Paul McCartney, Labelle, and the latest person to test the holy waters is John Mayall, whose 1976 solo album, **Notice To Appear**, was produced by Toussaint.

The Meters (♦) have been used as regular session-men at Seasaint, and Toussaint has also regularly worked with Dr John (♦), another native of the area. In 1973 Toussaint accompanied Dr John on a series of European concerts.

Toussaint has made his own solo albums – **Life, Love And Faith** in 1972, and **Southern Nights** in 1975, but admits he is satisfied with neither. Certainly he seems unable to bring to his own recordings the magic that he infuses in others.

Recordings:
Life, Love And Faith (Reprise)
Southern Nights (Reprise)

Tower Of Power

Hubert Tubbs vocals
Lenny Pickett saxes, flute
Emilio Castillo sax, vocals
Steve Kupka sax, vocals
Greg Adams trumpet, flugelhorn, vocals
Mic Gillette trumpet, trombone, vocals
Bruce Conte guitar, vocals
Chester Thompson keyboards, vocals
Frank Prestia bass
David Garibaldi drums

Formed early '70s in Oakland, California, a weighty funk-rock ensemble which has enjoyed a number of bestselling U.S. singles such as **So Very Hard To Go, You're Still A Young Man** and **What Is Hip?**, while also regularly placing albums high on charts.

Moved to Warner Bros label 1972 when they released **Bump City** set. **Tower Of Power** appeared 1973; **Back To Oakland** in 1974; **Renewal** and **In The Slot** in 1975, the latter of which yielded **You're So Wonderful, So Marvellous** single.

A multi-talented band, Castillo and Kupka form mainstay of songwriting force; while Adams provides bulk of arranging. Hubert Tubbs, born Frankston, Texas, joined group as new vocalist March 1975.

Aside from group activities, Tower Of Power horn-section has been widely used on other artists' albums, notably Elton John's **Caribou**, while arranger Adams has also worked for likes of Elton John, Santana and Jose Feliciano.

Last listed album is live set containing **You're Still A Young Man** and **What Is Hip?**, and was recorded at Sacramento Memorial Auditorium and Cerritos College.

Recordings:
East Bay Grease
(San Francisco/—)
Bump City (Warner Bros)
Tower Of Power (Warner Bros)
Back To Oakland (Warner Bros)
Urban Renewal (Warner Bros)
In The Slot (Warner Bros)
Live And In Living Color
(Warner Bros)

Traffic

Stevie Winwood guitar, keyboards, vocals
Chris Wood saxophones, flute
Dave Mason guitar
Jim Capaldi drums

Traffic were formed with above line-up in 1967 shortly after Winwood had left The Spencer Davis Group (➧) to enable him to expand his musical horizons. He had already played with Eric Clapton in a short-lived studio band, Powerhouse, which contributed some tracks to the Elektra sampler, **What's Shakin.**

Winwood (b. in Birmingham May 12, 1948) had also jammed with Wood (b. Birmingham Jun 24, 1944) and Capaldi (b. Evesham, Worcestershire Aug 24, 1944) and Dave Mason (➧) in clubs around the Birmingham area prior to leaving Spencer Davis.

The four of them repaired to a cottage in Aston Tirrold in Berkshire for six months in order to – as the saying went – get it together in the country.

They achieved this with some aplomb, and introduced themselves with the idyllic summer single **Paper Sun**, which reached No. 5 in Britain. That and its sequel, **Hole In My Shoe**, encapsulated the summer of 1967 as accurately as any overt flower-power anthem. The debut album, **Mr Fantasy,** was a successful vehicle of the talents of the entire group, and served notice that Traffic would be more than merely a backing band for Winwood.

However, Mason's flair for light melody was straightaway at odds with the more jazz-oriented ambitions of the other members, and he departed December 1967, though he returned in a matter of months to help out on the second album, **Traffic,** to which he con-

tributed **Feelin' Alright.**

In 1968 Traffic were also featured, along with the Spencer Davis Group, on the United Artists soundtrack to the film, "Here We Go Round The Mulberry Bush".

Later that year, Mason quit again, leaving the entire band to call it a day and offer **Last Exit** as their farewell album. Island Records, their British company, administering the last rites, issued a **Best Of Traffic** in 1969.

Mr. Fantasy.
Courtesy Island Records.

Winwood meanwhile had again joined Clapton in Blind Faith (➧), and when that collapsed, temporarily enlisted in Ginger Baker's Air Force. Wood, meantime, did sessions with Dr John.

In 1970 Winwood planned a solo album, tentatively entitled **Mad Shadows**. He called in Wood and Capaldi to help out on the sessions, and as a result Traffic was reformed as a trio, and in April released the incomparable **John Barleycorn Must Die,** which showed the band's ability to merge jazz, rock and traditional folk-music and was also a magnificent tribute to Winwood's superb versatility, since he contributed the lion's share of the instrumentation.

Since Winwood was handling all guitars, keyboards and vocals, the pressure on him inevitably proved too great, and in November Rick Grech (➧) was added to the line-up; in 1971 they expanded the personnel again with a percussionist, Reebop; and for a short British tour in the summer of 1971, ex Domino Jim Gordon came in to bolster the rhythm section, and the errant Mason again returned to the fold. This line-up played only a few dates together, but the live recording **Welcome To The Canteen** was recommendation enough of their corporate abilities.

At the end of the year **The Low Spark Of The High-Heeled Boys,** was issued while the band were touring America; it went gold in U.S. in 1972, and was made by the line-up as before, with the inevitable exception of Mason who had left again; when the band returned from America, Grech and Gordon, too, had departed along the way.

The band was now again in a state of flux, despite the excellence of their last albums. It proved an academic problem, since Winwood fell ill with peritonitis, and Capaldi adjourned to Muscle Shoals to make a solo album, **Oh! How We Danced;** while there he established connections with Muscle Shoals sessioneers David Hood (bs) and Roger Hawkins (drms) who joined the band for **Shoot Out At The**

Fantasy Factory, which was recorded in Jamaica in 1972.

With Winwood recovered, the band set out on a 1973 world tour, for which they added Barry Beckett, also from Muscle Shoals, on keyboards. The vitality and strength of this line-up was fully demonstrated on the made-in-Germany live double-album, **On The Road.**

The Muscle Shoals recruits bowed out after this tour, and for an English tour in 1974 Rosco Gee, the bass-player from Gonzales, was added; since Reebop disappeared somewhere along the way, the band completed the tour in the form in which they had originally started. After a final album **When The Eagle Flies,** which was very good instrumentally, but marred by some over-ambitious Capaldi lyrics, the band again went into one of its periods of hibernation; this time, it proved to be for good, since no one apparently any longer had the will-power to hold it all together. In any case, Capaldi was embarking on a bouyant solo career (➧ Jim Capaldi).

Traffic, one of the many British bands more popular in the States, will be fondly remembered; few groups provided such consistently stimulating music, few groups contained musicians of such a high calibre.

Shoot Out At The Fantasy Factory. Courtesy Island.

Winwood, released in the U.S. in 1973 is a compilation of some of Stevie Winwood's finest moments, from all stages of his career.

Mr Fantasy
(United Artists/Island)
Traffic (United Artists/Island)
Last Exit (United Artists/Island)
John Barleycorn Must Die
(United Artists/Island)
Welcome To The Canteen
(United Artists/Island)
Low Spark Of The High-Heeled Boys (Capitol/Island)
Shoot Out At The Fantasy Factory (Capitol/Island)
On The Road (Capitol/Island)
When The Eagle Flies (Island)
Traffic compilation:
Best Of Traffic
(United Artists/Island)
Winwood compilation:
Winwood (United Artists/—)

Robin Trower

Born Mar 9, 1945, he was member of Southend, England, based R&B group The Paramounts which metamorphosed into Procol Harum via a somewhat devious route (➧ Procol Harum). Trower played guitar with that band up to 1971 **Broken Barricades**

album, long before which his frustrations within Procols had been apparent.

On departure, first attempted to form new band, Jude, with ex Jethro Tull drummer Clive Bunker, singer Frankie Miller (➧) and ex Stone The Crows (➧) bassist Jim Dewar. This proved abortive, and Trower pursued solo career in cahoots with Dewar mid-1972.

For Earth Below.
Courtesy Chrysalis Records.

Released first solo album **Twice Removed From Yesterday** in 1973, first incarnation of Robin Trower Band comprising himself on guitar, Dewar on bass and vocals, and Reg Isadore on drums. Trower's undoubtedly Jimi Hendrix-influenced guitar playing was and remains dominant factor, and it was as nascent guitar hero that second set, **Bridge Of Sighs** (1974), became considerable American hit.

Early efforts were, in fact, concentrated on U.S. market, backed by heavy tours, with belated British recognition arriving largely as result of Stateside status. Before **For Earth Below** (1975) Isadore was replaced by ex Sly Stone drummer Bill Lordan, and that and 1976 **Robin Trower Live** were again top U.S. sellers, marginally less so in U.K.

Recordings:
Twice Removed From Yesterday (Chrysalis)
Bridge Of Sighs (Chrysalis)
For Earth Below (Chrysalis)
Robin Trower Live (Chrysalis)

The Tubes

Fee Waybill vocals
Bill Spooner guitar
Vince Welnick keyboards
Rich Anderson bass
Michael Cotten synthesisers
Roger Steen guitar
Prairie Prince percussion

Brought together in San Francisco 1972 by founder Spooner, the group rapidly achieved notoriety and cult following around Bay Area as one of the most outrageously bizarre acts yet perpetrated in name of rock.

Mixing driving rock with satire and outright theatrical presentations, Tubes became known along West Coast for crazed happenings such as their Streakers Ball, which admitted all naked members of public free, and their leather-and-chains production number **Mondo Bondage**. Also appeared in skin flick "The Resurrection Of Eve", and indulged in various projects creating murals and theatre and environmental designs.

Innumerable props are used for live performances, including electronic special effects, a succession of costumes, glitter-rainstorm and fog machines, and, frequently, theatrical sets built around certain numbers – at larger venues, the whole spectacle is transmitted over closed-circuit video.

After building cult audience, group signed to A&M for release of 1975 eponymous debut album produced at Record Plant, Los Angeles by Al Kooper (♦). With one of best covers of year, this successfully translated Tubes high-energy onto vinyl, and included **Mondo Bondage** plus other group "standard", **White Punks On Dope.**

Recordings:
The Tubes (A&M)
Young and Rich (A&M)

Ike and Tina Turner

Ike Turner, born in Clarkesdale, Mississippi Nov 5, 1931 has had a career that spans virtually the gamut of post-war popular music. He grew up deep in the delta blues country, worked as a DJ, and founded his own band, the Kings of Rhythm, which played in vicinity of Mississippi in early '50s; the band cut one disc, **Rocket 88** (with Jackie Brenston as lead vocalist), that has often been claimed to be the first rock 'n' roll record (but then, so have many others . . .); meanwhile, Turner worked as a talent scout for Sam Phillips (♦) and was responsible for the discovery of Howlin' Wolf.

Turner continued to cut blues and R&B singles and, with the arrival of rock 'n' roll moved to St Louis, and developed his act into a revue-style show, featuring him on guitar and piano and spotlighting various vocalists. Annie Mae "Tina" Braddock (b. Brownsville, Tennessee, Nov 26, 1938) had performed in the church choir at home, but in the mid-'50s moved to St Louis with her sister in the hope of making a career as a singer. Eventually, Ike Turner agreed to let her sing, and she joined the show. They were married in St Louis in 1958.

In 1960 Ike had written a song called **A Fool In Love;** when the singer didn't show up for the session, Tina recorded the song, which was credited to Ike & Tina Turner and became their first million-selling single; for the next few years they had a string of U.S. hits on the Sue label, including **I Idolize You** and **It's Gonna Work Out Fine.** Meanwhile, the foundations of the Ike & Tina revue had been laid when Tina hired a trio of girl back-up singers, The Ikettes (the personnel of which has, at various times, included P. P. Arnold, Bonnie Bramlett, and Merry Clayton).

After their success on Sue began to flag, they moved to various other companies, and worked on the West Coast for Warner Bros, and Ray Charles' Tangerine label, cutting a single, **Anything You Wasn't Born With,** that was produced by Charles himself. However, the fortunes of the Turners veered sharply upwards when they worked on the soundtrack of a film called "The T'N'T Show". On the film set they met Phil Spector (♦), who expressed an interest in producing Tina.

Ike therefore took a back seat during the recording of **River Deep, Mountain High,** a song which has a curious history. It went straight to No. 3 in the charts in Britain, where it has since become one of the top-selling singles, and has also been freely acclaimed as one of the Top 10 singles of all time. Certainly, Tina's strong, surging vocals were ideally suited to a production job that was extravagant and grandiose even by Spector's exceptional standards.

However, the song reached only No. 88 in the U.S. charts, and this comparative failure was apparently one of the reasons why Spector temporarily quit the business in a state of disillusionment. The album **River Deep Mountain High** was not even produced entirely by Spector, so that it juxtaposed his full-scale pop productions with some of Ike's work that were lean and R&B styled; nevertheless, it all fused together, and the result is one of the few totally successful albums the Turners have made.

With Spector leaving the picture as rapidly as he had entered it, the Turners looked to relatively small labels, before Ike met up with an old associate Bob Krasnow, who was by now president of Blue Thumb. Krasnow produced Ike & Tina for his label, and the result was a string of successes that included **The Hunter** and Otis Redding's **I've Been Loving You Too Long.**

In 1969 the Ike & Tina Turner Revue toured the States as support act with the Rolling Stones, and since then they have steadily increased their standing with the U.S. rock audience. The Revue was by now a thoroughly professional show – The Ikettes were well-choreographed, the dramatic set - pieces well arranged. The stage act became ever more flamboyantly sexual, with The Ikettes dressed in the miniest of mini-skirts, performing suggestive routines, and Tina the focus of the show, simulating orgasms and trading innuendos with Ike on an extended version of **I've Been Loving You Too Long** that became the centre-piece of the show.

River Deep Mountain High. Courtesy A&M Records.

They looked increasingly to the rock market for both their material and their audience, and when they moved to Liberty/United Artists in 1971 earned a gold disc with their version of **Proud Mary,** and also recorded material like **Get Back** and **Honky Tonk Women.**

In 1973 they suddenly produced another classic single – **Nutbush City Limits,** one of Tina's own compositions – though again it achieved more in the U.K. (where it reached No. 2) than in the U.S.

So the Ike & Tina Turner Revue (with the support band now called the Family Vibes) rolls on; by now it has become thoroughly jaded, as the routines have changed little in the last five years. However, it still plays to capacity audiences everywhere, and Ike and Tina Turner presumably have the versatility to develop something new as soon as it is required.

In 1972 Ike made a solo album **Blues Roots,** which possibly indicated that that is the musical direction in which he would like to be heading.

In her role of the Acid Queen, Tina, giving an overtly sensual performance, was generally thought to be one of the successes of the Ken Russell film of "Tommy".

Since Ike & Tina Turner have recorded at least 30 albums (many of them of shoddy quality), for almost as many companies, the discography is selective. **River Deep, Mountain High,** which was released on Philles/ London in 1966 was reissued on A&M in 1971.

Recordings:
River Deep Mountain High (A&M)
The Hunter
(Blue Thumb/Liberty)
Her Man, His Woman (Capitol)
Workin' Together (Liberty)
'Nuff Said (United Artists)
Nutbush City Limits (United Artists)
Sweet Rhode Island Red (United Artists)
Compilations:
Souled From The Vaults (—/DJM)
16 Great Performances (ABC)
The Very Best Of Ike & Tina Turner (United Artists)
Ike Turner:
Blues Roots (United Artists)
Tina Turner:
Acid Queen (United Artists)

Turtles

♦ Flo & Eddie

UFO

Phil Mogg vocals
Michael Schenker guitar
Danny Peyronel keyboards
Pete Way bass
Andy Parker drums

British band formed 1970 by Mogg, Way, Parker and guitarist Mick Bolton. First hard rock album **UFO 1,** recorded 1971, went totally unrecognised in U.K. but by one of strange quirks of fate was picked up by audiences in Japan, France and Germany.

In Japan group's rendition of Eddie Cochran rocker **C'mon Everybody** raced up singles lists 1972, and UFO subsequently embarked on frenzied Japanese tour, recording live album **UFO Lands In Tokyo** for local market.

Bolton left 1973 and it wasn't until some 18 months later he was replaced by German-born Schenker. The 1974 debut album on Chrysalis label, **Phenomenon,** produced by Ten Years After bassist Leo Lyons, as was 1975 set **Force It** and 1976 **No Heavy Petting.** Lyons called in TYA keyboards colleague Chick Churchill to augment sessions, plus Robin Trower Band's Jim Dewar for vocal harmonies.

Peyronel, from Heavy Metal Kids (♦), added to line-up August 1975.

Group remain virtually unknown on home territory, though the three Chrysalis LPs have seen them making inroads into American market.

Recordings:
UFO (— Decca)
Flying (—/Decca)
Phenomenon (Chrysalis)
Force It (Chrysalis)
No Heavy Petting (Chrysalis)

United States Of America

Joseph Byrd keyboards
Dorothy Moscowitz vocals
Gordon Marron violin
Rand Forbes bass
Craig Woodson drums

Pioneering electronics band from New York led by experimental composer Joseph Byrd. Only recording, the eponymous 1968 set, was an uneven but nevertheless remarkable mixture of intellectual satire and cultivated decadence. After group split, Byrd went on to make **The American Metaphysical Circus** with a unit called The Field Hippies, but succeeded only in creating embarrassing self-parody.

Recordings:
The United States Of America (Columbia/CBS)
The American Metaphysical Circus (Columbia/CBS)

Uriah Heep

Mick Box guitar
Ken Hensley keyboards
John Wetton bass
Lee Kerslake drums

One of the many bands who shamelessly plagiarised the heavy-metal trail blazed by Led Zeppelin (♦), Uriah Heep were launched in 1970 to almost unanimous rock press hostility – one American critic being driven to write: "If this group makes it, I'll have to commit suicide".

Their roots lay in an outfit The Stalkers which London-born Box joined at age 17. They later recruited services of David Byron, born Epping, Essex, who at one stage in his career had sung sessions for anonymous cover-version hits and compilation albums alongside Elton John and Dana Gillespie (♦ Elton John). Byron and Box subsequently formed Spice, recruiting bassist Paul Newton from The Gods, which also included Ken Hensley and Mick Taylor, the latter of whom would later join Rolling Stones (♦).

As Spice turned into Uriah Heep, Hensley followed Newton's path into new group after short spell with Cliff Bennett's Toe Fat. Drummer Keith Baker was last to join.

Thus constituted they released critically-reviled debut album

Very 'eavy . . . Very 'umble in 1970. Neither that or the second set, **Salisbury** in 1971, made public impact and the group had to sustain itself with recognition in Germany until U.K. breakthrough later in 1971 with **Look At Yourself**. American success was quick to follow.

However, the rhythm section went through a number of changes during this period – in addition to Newton and Baker, bassist Mark Clarke and drummers Al Napier, Ian Clarke and Nigel Olsson (on loan from Elton John) all put in stints with band. Personnel didn't settle down until fourth album **Demons And Wizards** (1972) which featured Gary Thain (bs) and Lee Kerslake (drms).

Though they remain critically unfashionable to this day, Uriah Heep's popularity began to grow at rapid pace. **Demons And Wizards**, **Magician's Birthday** (1972) and the double-set **Uriah Heep Live** (1973) all went gold in U.S. and U.K., while American singles hits included **Easy Living** and **Blind Eye/Sweet Lorraine**.

By 1974, however, dissent was beginning to reveal itself among members of the band, with "musical director" Hensley letting it be known in British rock press that he was unhappy with group's musical progress. Box and Byron disagreed.

In same year bassist Thain suffered a near-fatal electric shock while performing with Heep on stage in Dallas, Texas. This brought him into open conflict with group's manager Gerry Bron, Thain claiming that insufficient consideration was shown for his injuries. Thain was also suffering personal problems preventing group working on next album and in Feb 1975 was "invited" to leave the band. Both Bron and Heep have refuted allegations that he was sacked. (On Mar 19, 1976, Thain was found dead in flat, after taking pills.)

High And Mighty.
Courtesy Bronze Records.

In March 1975 the group found a replacement in John Wetton, who had similar roots in Bournemouth area to Heep drummer Kerslake. An excellent bassist, Wetton's antecedents included roles with Family (♦) and King Crimson (♦), although prior to joining Heep he had been acting as "hired" bass-player for Roxy Music (♦). Wetton also appeared on Roxy guitarist Phil Manzanera's **Diamond Head** solo album.

Turning his back on an altogether more musically credible background, the cynics' view was that Wetton took up the Heep offer attracted purely by financial rewards. Thus reconstituted, group cut **Return To Fantasy**

for 1975 release and **High And Mighty** for 1976, after which (in July) Byron was fired from band. Heep's future, at time of writing, distinctly uncertain.

Ken Hensley solo albums listed below released 1973 and 1975.

Recordings:
Very 'eavy . . . Very 'umble (Mercury/Vertigo)
Salisbury (Mercury/Vertigo)
Look At Yourself (Mercury/Bronze)
Demons And Wizards (Mercury/Bronze)
Magician's Birthday (Mercury/Bronze)
Uriah Heep Live (Mercury/Bronze)
Sweet Freedom (Warner Bros/Bronze)
Wonderworld (Warner Bros/Bronze)
Return To Fantasy (Warner Bros/Bronze)
High And Mighty (Warner Bros/Bronze)
Ken Hensley:
Proud Words On A Dusty Shelf (Mercury/Bronze)
Eager To Please (Warner Bros/Bronze)

Frankie Valli
♦ Four Seasons

Van Der Graaf Generator

Peter Hammill piano, guitar, vocals
Hugh Banton keyboards, bass
David Jackson saxes
Guy Evans drums

Three times split and reformed, they were founded at Manchester University, England in 1967 from flexible line-up of Hammill, Banton, Evans, Keith Ellis and Chris Judge Smith. The latter gave them their name but split soon afterwards, and the whole band broke-up towards end of 1968.

Hammill continued to play fill-in gigs and recorded an intended solo set, **Aerosol Grey Machine**, which featured most of aforementioned musicians and was eventually released as Van Der Graaf's debut album.

Thus haphazardly reconstituted, the group released three more albums, **The Least We Can Do Is Wave To Each Other** (1969), **H To He Who Am The Only One** (1970) and **Pawn Hearts** (1971). Nic Potter (bs) had replaced Ellis but quit halfway through sessions for second of this trilogy. Jackson joined at same time as Potter, and personnel was as listed above when group split for second time in 1972.

Despite cult following for Hammill's doom-laden musical experimentations, Van Der Graaf had made little to no impact in the U.K. – yet were considered a top-line act among rock fans in Italy, also being popular to varying degrees in other European countries.

Just before **Pawn Hearts**, Hammill had released his first solo album **Fool's Mate** (1971) and after the split he continued working solo – to little commercial success. He recorded five albums

in total, of which the 1975 set **Nadir's Big Chance**, a rock satire, was the most notable.

However, he had kept in touch with former colleagues (including Chris Judge Smith, with whom he wrote songs) and in early 1975 the personnel listed above reformed VDGG and undertook a French tour. Their British concert return at Victoria Palace Theatre in July 1975 was ecstatically received by the VDGG faithful, although they have still to make mass breakthrough.

Their 1975 album **Godbluff** was recorded at Rockfield Studios, Wales, as was 1976 set **Still Life**.

Recordings:
Aerosol Grey Machine (Mercury)
The Least We Can Do Is Wave To Each Other (Mercury/Charisma)
H To He Who Am The Only One (Dunhill/Charisma)
Pawn Hearts (Mercury/Charisma)
Godbluff (Mercury/Charisma)
Still Life (—/Charisma)
Peter Hammill:
Fool's Mate (Charisma)
Chameleon In The Shadow Of Night (—/Charisma)
The Silent Corner (—/Charisma)
In Camera (—/Charisma)
Nadir's Big Chance (—/Charisma)

Vangelis

Full name Vangelis Papathanassiou (which makes it easy to see why RCA promote him via forename only). He was born in Southern Greece, but was in France at time of Greek political upheavals 1968. Unable to return, he formed band Aphrodites Child – with Demis Roussos – which had immediate European smash single with **Rain And Tears**.

A keyboard virtuoso, Vangelis was widely tipped in 1974 to replace Rick Wakeman in Yes (♦). Although he didn't join, he hung around in London and signed contract with RCA. Heavily-promoted debut album features Vangelis playing every instrument through grand piano to assorted percussive devices. Yes singer Jon Anderson wrote lyrics for **So Long Ago So Clear** composition, on which he also sings.

Recordings:
Heaven And Hell (RCA)

Vanilla Fudge

Mark Stein keyboards, vocals
Vince Martell guitar, vocals
Tim Bogert bass, vocals
Carmine Appice drums, vocals

Variously known as "first of the heavy bands" and "doyens of punk mysterioso", this New York band first came to public attention in 1967 with hit revival of old Supremes hit **You Keep Me Hangin' On**. Fudge had slowed song down to half its original tempo, inserted plenty of neo-classical organ melodramatics and pseudo-Indian guitar licks and swelled it up into an almost Spectoresque extravaganza.

1967 debut album included full seven-and-a-half minute version of single, plus Fudged-up arrangements of such songs as

Eleanor Rigby, Ticket To Ride, Bang Bang, and People Get Ready. Their almost fussy neo-gospel harmonies and cinerama arrangements irritated a lot of people, but it was certainly an exhilarating sound.

Vanilla Fudge.
Courtesy Atlantic Records.

The Beat Goes On (1968) was one of most gallant disasters in annals of rock, being nothing less than a musical record of last 25 years, including the entire history of music in less than 12 minutes.

Third album same year featured mainly original songs, plus a nine-minute version of Donovan's **Season Of The Witch**. Unhappily, when their extended treatment was lavished on their own songs, it simply sounded tedious.

By 1970, Fudge had issued final album and disbanded. Carmine Appice and Tim Bogert formed Cactus (♦) and eventually ended-up in Beck, Bogert, and Appice (♦). Mark Stein formed ill-fated band called Boomerang. Vince Martell disappeared from public view.

Recordings:
Vanilla Fudge (Atlantic)
The Beat Goes On (Atlantic)
Renaissance (Atlantic)
Near The Beginning (Atco)
Rock And Roll (Atco)

The Velvet Underground

Lou Reed guitar, vocals
John Cale bass, viola
Sterling Morrison guitar
Maureen Tucker drums

The seminal New York City band and one of the most important influences in rock, though never accorded during their existence the recognition their pioneering music warranted. They were formed in 1966 with line-up as above, of whom Lou Reed, an accountant's son from Long Island, and John Cale, a Welshman who had arrived in New York on a music scholarship to Eastman Conservatory, were the key figures.

Reed had attended Syracuse University, following which he drifted through journalism and acting courses before working for Pickwick Records in New York as a songwriter. He also wrote poetry which was published in "Fusion" magazine in the U.S., and occasionally delivered by Reed in poetry readings at St Mark's Church. In 1964 Reed first encountered Cale, who had by then discarded his classical studies to pursue his growing interest in the contem-

Above: The Velvet Underground.

porary New York avant-garde, having joined LaMonte Young's experimental group on electric viola.

However, nothing came of this initial meeting and Reed went on to assemble various groups, The Warlocks and The Primitives recruiting first Sterling Morrison and later the Beatle-cropped Maureen Tucker. Cale joined them in 1966 and they became The Velvet Underground taking their name from a pornographic paperback.

Their earliest engagement was a residency at the Cafe Bizarre in Greenwich Village, where they started performing in winter 1966, immediately arousing localised controversy. Reed has reminisced: "They said, 'One more song like that and you're fired'. So we played one more song like that and, sure enough, they fired us."

Fortunately they had by that time come to the attention of Andy Warhol, pioneer of the New York "pop art" school, who was looking for a suitable rock group to add to his multi-media freak-show unit The Factory. Warhol put them on his touring "total environment" show The Exploding Plastic Inevitable, after augmenting them with German-born singer Nico.

The show opened in New York and toured the U.S. and Canada, polarizing opinion wherever they played. John Cale has described one concert in Ohio where the audience listened in stunned silence, while the group's first album quotes various reviews on its inner sleeve: "Screeching rock 'n' roll – reminded viewers of nothing so much as Berlin in the decadent '30s" – "Los Angeles Magazine"; "A three-ring psychosis that assaults the senses . . . discordant music, throbbing cadences, pulsating tempo" – "Variety"; ". . . an assemblage that actually vibrates with menace, cynicism and perversion. To experience it is to be brutalized, helpless . . ." – "Chicago Daily News".

This first album, nominally produced by Warhol who also provided the famous "banana" cover, was recorded in 1967, and put down on vinyl some of the most startlingly innovative music heard in rock. From the off, the Velvets had set out to counter the peace-love vibes emanating from the U.S. west coast and at that time

holding sway over contemporary music. There were no beads and caftans in the menacing scenarios the Velvets chose to explore; this was an altogether more demonic sub-culture whose subject matter had hitherto been regarded as taboo in mass media, i.e. drugs (as in **Heroin, I'm Waiting For The Man)** and sado/masochism **(Venus In Furs).**

Warhol's name and Nico's death's-angel face may have predominated in initial period, but the music was very much Reed and Cale. To Reed's startling mixture of musical primitivism and lyrical worldliness, Cale added authentic touches of avant-garde elements from his studies with LaMonte Young, experimenting with the possibilities inherent in noise and monotony as embodied in **European Son.**

Quite obviously the album was years ahead of its time. Not surprisingly, in view of the up-front nature of its lyrics, it garnered no commercial airplay and all but sank without trace once reviewers had recovered from the initial shock.

Later in 1967 Nico left to pursue a solo career and Warhol began to lose interest. So did the press.

White Heat/White Light was released in U.S. December 1967 and featured few of the softer songs Reed had previously written for Nico. Instead, it struck out even more determinedly into urban realism and musical experimentation, containing the classic **Sister Ray,** and still stands as one of rock's most uncompromising records. Unhappily, it was at the time also one of the most ignored, the Velvets by then having alienated all but a handful of fans.

The band went on the road, playing to diminishing audiences, and a rift began to develop between Reed and Cale resulting in the latter leaving the band before the third set, **The Velvet Underground,** in March 1969. He was replaced by the comparatively pedestrian Doug Yule, and the Velvets became Lou Reed's band, this third album being the work of a quieter, less supercharged group. Much of it still remains an enigma, however, and it certainly cost the group even further devotees.

In fact, the Velvets' commercial status had been near to non-existent since the first album, and in mid-1969 they parted company with MGM/Verve, spending some few months without a contract before signing with Atlantic.

In 1970 they returned to New York to record for this label, with Billy Yule having replaced Maureen Tucker, and played a summer residency at Max's Kansas City. They hadn't played New York since April 1967 and this reappearance even managed to provoke a certain interest among local aficionados. However, it wasn't enough to maintain Reed's belief in the band as a continuing entity and in August that year, in a bout of disenchantment, he walked out on the group never to return.

The following month saw release of their Atlantic album (it wasn't issued in U.K. until April 1971), to a rare degree of critical acclaim. Although Reed has criticised it heavily for the production and the mix (he had no hand in the running order of the songs), it demonstrates that the group were capable of greatness even at the point of dissolution. Whatever its faults, **Loaded** is a dynamic rock 'n' roll album containing at least one more solid classic in the genre in **Sweet Jane.**

Sterling Morrison went off to teach in Austin, Texas; while Lou Reed followed Nico and Cale into a solo career. Doug and Billy Yule made an ill-advised attempt to keep the Velvets going with new members, touring and releasing the Velvets-in-name-only album **Squeeze** in 1972, but eventually they too chucked it in. (Doug Yule in fact turned up as member of Reed's backing band on a 1975 tour, presumably having been forgiven for his part in **Loaded** editing and ersatz Velvets.)

Two Velvets live albums have been posthumously released: the double set **1969,** which is a recording of the group in Texas and San Francisco that year; and **Live At Max's Kansas City.** The last-named was recorded during their aforementioned 1970 New York engagement, on a cassette machine belonging to the group's friend Brigit Polk.

The Velvets' considerable accomplishments were that they increased the scope of lyrical and instrumental expression in rock with an aggressive infusion of documentary realism, drawing their inspiration from the street life of New York. Unwelcomed at the time of San Francisco's flower-power movement, this new direction was unhappily to remain generally unacknowledged until some two years or more after the band folded (⯈ Lou Reed, Nico,

John Cale).

Recordings:
**The Velvet Underground &
 Nico** (Verve)
White Light/White Heat (Verve)
The Velvet Underground
 (MGM)
1969 (Mercury)
Loaded (Atlantic)
**The Velvet Underground Live
 At Max's Kansas City**
 (Atlantic)
Squeeze (Atlantic)
Compilations:
Archetypes (MGM/—)
 **Andy Warhol's Velvet
 Underground** (Kama Sutra)

Vinegar Joe

Elkie Brooks vocals
Robert Palmer vocals, guitar
Peter Cage guitar
Steve York bass
Mike Deacon keyboards
Peter Gavin drums

Emerged as remnant of Dada, an ambitious but unsuccessful British 12-piece jazz-rock outfit featuring dual vocal line-up of Brooks and Palmer. Superfluous brass and percussion dispensed with, a streamlined six-piece evolved late 1971 as Vinegar Joe. Emphasis was on hard, raunchy R&B style, but extrovert live feel of band proved almost impossible to capture on record. After three albums (first two in 1972) band broke-up late 1973. Robert Palmer (⯈) and Elkie Brooks (⯈) now solo.

Recordings:
Vinegar Joe (Atlantic/Island)
Rock 'n' Roll Gypsies
 (Atlantic/Island)
Six Star General (Atlantic/Island)

The Wailers
⯈ Bob Marley

Loudon Wainwright

Born in Chapel Hill, North Carolina in 1947, Wainwright is the son of an established American writer, though Loudon himself has always shunned the establishment. His first two albums, **Album I** and **Album II,** released in 1971 and 1972 respectively, were characterised by a macabre humour and an atmosphere of tastelessness – for – tastelessness' sake, which was evidenced by numbers like **Suicide Song.** Wainwright delivered this biting, satirical material in an emotive, whining voice.

However he has never recaptured the stark, penetrating acidity of some of those early compositions. When he moved to Columbia in 1973, he mellowed his approach for **Album III** with songs of a more slapstick nature. He also made full use of session-musicians. Simultaneously he increased the purely humorous side of his stage act through the use of glib, comic antics; which was fine – he even collected a U.S. Top 40 single with **Dead Skunk** – but though he was getting slicker, and increasing his audience, his material was becoming less demanding, and **Attempted Moustache** (1974), which was played for laughs all the way, was a complete disappointment.

In 1975 **Unrequited** was more successful. It was a synthesis of all the new elements he had introduced into his music since **Album II**, and once again the humour was used to make serious points, and not just for cheap laughs. It is nevertheless probable that he will remain a figure of minority appeal; a new contract with Arista in 1975 resulted in album **T-Shirt**.

Wainwright married Kate McGarrigle (➧ Kate and Anna McGarrigle) in 1973 but they are now separated.

Recordings:
Album I (Atlantic)
Album II (Atlantic)
Album III (Columbia/CBS)
Attempted Moustache
(Columbia/CBS)
Unrequited (Columbia/CBS)

Tom Waits

Born Dec 7, 1949 in Pomona, California, Waits first came to notice in '70s as a live performer in smoke-filled West Coast nightclubs whose act fused lengthy humorous raps with the free verse of the beat generation of the '50s; he was a cross between Lord Buckley and Jack Kerouac. Backed only by piano, drums, sax and upright bass, Waits has built his reputation through live-work, and supporting gigs with acts such as Frank Zappa, Charlie Rich and Jerry Jeff Walker. His most famous composition is **Ol' 55**, which The Eagles included on their **On The Border** album.

Nighthawks At The Diner.
Courtesy Elektra Asylum
Records.

He has so far released three albums, of which **Nighthawks At The Diner** (1975) was a double live-set which most accurately reflected the nature of his work. Currently a cult figure of rapidly growing status, he paid his first visit to Europe in 1976.

Recordings:
Closing Time (Elektra)
The Heart Of Saturday Night
(Elektra)
Nighthawks At The Diner
(Elektra)

Rick Wakeman

Born West London, May 18, 1949 into musical family. At 16 Wakeman decided he wanted to be a concert pianist and studied at The Royal College of Music. He came to attention of music in-

dustry playing pub gigs and began to miss lectures to fulfil fast-increasing engagements as session-man, finally being dismissed from college without his degree.

Wakeman worked extensively as in-demand session-player for likes of Cat Stevens, T. Rex, David Bowie (**Hunky Dory**) before joining The Strawbs (➧) early 1970 to immediate critical acclaim. From there, he took his considerable keyboard skills and classical influences into Yes (➧) in 1971, releasing his first acclaimed solo album while a member of that band in 1973.

The Myths And Legends of King Arthur. Courtesy A&M Records.

However, musical and personality clashes eventually forced him to leave that band towards the close of 1973, since when he has pursued solo career.

Second album **Journey To The Centre Of The Earth,** his musical interpretation of a story by Jules Verne, was recorded live at London Royal Festival Hall in January 1974 and went to No. 1 in U.K. lists and No. 3 in the U.S.

He subsequently performed the work at an open-air Crystal Palace Garden Party in London July same year, using an orchestra and choir and embellishing the production with inflatable prehistoric monsters bobbing on the lake in front of the stage. Shortly after, Wakeman suffered a minor heart attack, the culmination of this ambitious venture on top of some 12 U.S. and U.K. tours with Strawbs and Yes.

Undaunted, he pursued grand-concept / big - production theme, coming to peak with release early 1975 of his **Myths And Legends Of King Arthur** composition, on which he used a 45-piece orchestra and 48-piece choir. The live premiere of this work took place at London Empire Pool in May 1975 as a musical pageant on ice, again employing massive orchestral and choral support in addition to his own group, The English Rock Ensemble.

Wakeman lost a small fortune on this ill-advised enterprise, though he had the compensation of another recording topping the British charts, plus gold albums coming from America, Brazil, Japan and Australia.

He subsequently reorganised English Rock Ensemble into smaller unit – Ashley Holt (vcls), Roger Newell (bs), John Dunsterville (gtr) and Tony Fernandez (drms), plus brass section of Reg Brooks and Martyn Shields – for later 1975 tours of America and Brazil.

Same year saw release of the Ken Russell movie "Lisztomania", for which Wakeman wrote score.

In March 1976 came release of his next solo album, **No Earthly Connection.**

He has several other interests outside of performing, being a director of 11 companies. These include a firm which manufactures instruments, a recording studio, and a company which hires out his collection of (eight) Rolls Royce cars. He also owns a racehorse, and lives with wife Ros and two sons in mansion in Buckinghamshire countryside.

With full-blown classical influences that on occasions verge on sheer pretension despite displaying considerable technical expertise, Wakeman's work has managed to avoid over-much criticism due to the genuinely engaging and fallible nature of the man's character.

Recordings:
The Six Wives Of Henry VIII
(A&M)
Journey To The Centre Of The Earth (A&M)
The Myths And Legends Of King Arthur And The Knights Of The Round Table (A&M)
Lisztomania (Soundtrack) (A&M)
No Earthly Connection (A&M)

Wendy Waldman

Wendy Waldman was born in Los Angeles 1951; her father composed soundtrack music for films. She spent part of her childhood in Mexico, and then started performing in Los Angeles from age of 16 – firstly as a solo performer, then with a jug-band.

In 1973 she signed a contract with Warner Bros and released her debut album, **Love Has Got Me;** simultaneously, Maria Muldaur used two of her songs, **Mad Mad Me** and **Vaudeville Man** on **Maria Muldaur,** an album that subsequently went platinum, thus helping to launch

Ms Waldman's name as a songwriter.

Wendy Waldman quickly became part of the Muldaur/Harris/ Ronstadt emergent school of female singers, who all appeared on each other's records, and contributed back-up vocals to Linda Ronstadt's **Don't Cry Now** and **Heart Like A Wheel,** as well as writing **Gringo En Mexico** for Maria Muldaur's 1974 album **Waitress In A Donut Shop.** Judy Collins recorded her composition **Pirate Ships** on **Judith.**

Her second solo album, **Gypsy Symphony,** was released 1974. This exhibited a variety of compositions and styles, and was warmly reviewed by critics; **Wendy Waldman** was issued in 1975, but it was then apparent that a breakthrough would be no simple operation, since there was an overdose of direct female competition.

None of her albums have yet been issued in Britain.

Recordings:
Love Has Got Me
(Warner Bros/—)
Gypsy Symphony
(Warner Bros/—)
Wendy Waldman
(Warner Bros/—)

Jerry Jeff Walker

Walker was born in New York State Mar 16, 1942, and performed with his guitar on the road as soon as he was able to leave home. In 1966, he helped to form a band called Circus Maximus, with whom he stayed for a first album, but left when the group began to move into a jazzier field which could not

Below: Joe Walsh; the will-he-won't-he quit The Eagles saga kept the rock press busy in '76.

accommodate Walker's essentially folk-rock songs.

He thus returned to his solo career, making an album for Vanguard; using famed Nashville pickers like Wayne Moss, Kenny Buttrey and Norbert Putnam, and with assistance from David Bromberg on guitar, this was to be the blueprint for much of what has followed.

Leaving Vanguard, Walker signed up with Atco, for whom he made three albums. Undoubtedly the most significant item from this period is a song called **Mr Bojangles,** written by Walker, which has received literally dozens of cover versions. However, Walker was not fond of the life he was forced to lead, and returned to Austin, Texas, where he has lived ever since. When signing with MCA in 1972, Walker was able to exercise the artistic control he wanted over his records; his definition of artistic control was the opportunity to make albums as and when he felt like it.

His debut album for the label was made in Texas, but had to be mixed in New York, so he decided that he would do the next one, **Viva Terlingua,** with a mobile truck in a ghost town in Texas called Luckenbach, which has an official population of one. That album, released in 1973, was followed by another recorded in Texas, and then by **Ridin' High,** which had a basic backing provided by his own group, the Lost Gonzo Band, who in fact made their own album in 1975.

It's A Good Night For Singing was recorded entirely in Nashville; as well as his own songs, Walker uses material by the members of his band, in particular by Gary Nunn, and by Guy Clark, a very promising writer also from Austin. Along with Willie Nelson, Waylon Jennings and several others, Walker, Clark and Nunn are at the heart of the "red-neck rock" movement which is centred in Austin, Texas. Their main aim appears to be to enjoy life to the full, rather than to worry about whether their records are successful, and this has undoubtedly prevented them from reaching the wider audience that such as Walker undoubtedly deserve.

Recordings:
Driftin' Way Of Life (Vanguard)
Mr Bojangles (Atlantic)
Five Years Gone (Atlantic/—)
Bein' Free (Atlantic/—)
Jerry Jeff Walker (MCA)
Viva Terlingua (MCA/—)
Walker's Collectibles (MCA)
Ridin' High (MCA)
It's A Good Night For Singing (MCA/—)

Joe Walsh

Born New York, was attending Kent State University, Ohio, when, after playing with local band The Measles, he joined The James Gang as lead guitarist and singer. Once described by The Who's Pete Townshend as his favourite guitarist, Walsh made four best-selling albums with James Gang and was responsible for some of their biggest hits, such as **Funk 49** and **The Bomber,** before quitting group November 1971 (♦ James Gang).

The Smoker You Drink, The Player You Get. Courtesy ABC.

Retaining hard rock of previous band but placing increasing emphasis on harmonies and more subtle arrangements, he recorded first solo album with musicians who took group name from record title, **Barnstorm.** These were Kenny Passarelli (bs) and Joe Vitale (drms), who were joined by Rocke Grace (kybds) and Manassas' Joe Lala (prcsn) for second Walsh solo set, **The Smoker You Drink, The Player You Get** (1973).

This album went gold in U.S., as did his hit-single **Rocky Mountain Way.** Third album, **So What** (late 1974), featured Barnstorm aggregation on only a couple of tracks, while also using support of Eagles, J. D. Souther and Dan Fogelberg (Walsh produced and played on Fogelberg's successful **Souvenirs** album).

Subsequently Walsh organised new stage band comprising Ricky Fataar (drms), ex of Beach Boys, Bryan Garofalo (bs), David Mason (kybds) and Paul Harris (kybds), also ex of Manassas.

Live album released end of 1975 by which time Walsh had teamed-up with Eagles (♦) as replacement for Bernie Leadon, a move indicative of the singer/guitarist's swing from heavy rock towards soft-rock territory. He and Eagles share same manager in Irv Azoff. However, Walsh's stay with Eagles will possibly prove only temporary one; and solo recordings are likely to continue.

Recordings:
Barnstorm Featuring Joe Walsh (Dunhill/Probe-Anchor)
The Smoker You Drink, The Player You Get (Dunhill/Probe-Anchor)
So What? (Dunhill/Anchor)
You Can't Argue With A Sick Mind/Live (ABC)

War

Harold Brown drums, percussion, vocals
Papa Dee Allen percussion
B. B. Dickerson bass, percussion, vocals
Lonnie Jordan keyboards, ARP, vocals
Charles Miller clarinet, saxophones, vocals
Lee Oskar harmonica, vocals
Howard Scott guitar, percussion, vocals

Miller, Brown, Scott and Dickerson originally came together in mid-'60s as a high-school group in San Pedro, California, playing small clubs in the area. When Dickerson moved to Hawaii, Peter Rosen joined on bass, while Allen came in on congas.

After Scott had had a spell in the U.S. Army, the various personnel drifted back together in Los Angeles, at which time they were called Night Shift. Rosen introduced the band to producer Jerry Goldstein, who was suitably impressed, and in turn introduced the band to Eric Burdon (♦), who at that time had just disbanded the New Animals and was hanging-out with Danish-born white harmonica player Lee Oskar. Burdon began to work with the band, bringing in Oskar and stream-lining the personnel by dropping all the hornmen except Miller to increase the funk potential of the outfit. He also changed their name to War.

Rosen died of an overdose, and Dickerson was induced to return from Hawaii and rejoin the band; with the line-up thus complete, the aggregation began to achieve colossal immediate success; their first single, **Spill The Wine,** topped the U.S. charts, and both their two albums sold well. Eric Burdon And War toured Europe in 1970, when they jammed with Jimi Hendrix at Ronnie Scott's Jazz Club, and then again in 1971 when Burdon, exhausted, was unable to complete the itinerary. War finished the tour themselves, and won excellent reviews.

The split became permanent, and the members began to handle all the vocal duties themselves.

After a debut album that attracted some attention, the band began to emerge as a potent force in their own right as a soul/jazz/funk band; **All Day Music,** the title track from their second album, was a hit single in late 1971, and a second single, **Slippin' Into Darkness** made the charts the next year; the album went gold as have all the band's subsequent albums.

Both **The World Is A Ghetto** (1972) and **Deliver The Word** (1973) spawned two major hit singles, of which **The Cisco Kid** (from **The World Is A Ghetto**) is the most celebrated. By retaining their roots as a street-funk outfit, and blending their natural jazz rhythms with some infectious melodies and some dexterous instrumentation, the band have now emerged as one of the top-selling American acts. Both **Why Can't We Be Friends?** (1975) and the single taken from it, **Low Rider,** topped their respective U.S. charts. The latter was also a hit in Britain.

Recordings:
War (United Artists)
All Day Music (United Artists)
The World Is A Ghetto (United Artists)
Deliver The Word (United Artists)
War Live (United Artists)
Why Can't We Be Friends? (United Artists/Island)
With Eric Burdon:
Eric Burdon Declares War (MGM)
Black Man's Burdon (MGM)

Clifford T. Ward

Clifford T. Ward was born in Kidderminster, Worcestershire, Feb 10, 1946, and began to play piano and sing with local bands while still at school.

Early ventures, which included Cliff Ward and the Cruisers, and The Secrets, had little success, and a contract with Immediate Records was aborted when that company crashed in 1970.

Having by this time become a school-teacher, Ward continued his songwriting in his spare time, and this situation continued even after he was signed by the ill-fated Dandelion label, owned by John Peel and Clive Selwood, who saw in Clifford an artist with rather more appeal than the majority of their more ethnic acts on the label.

After making a critically successful first album for Dandelion, the company collapsed, and Ward moved to Charisma Records in 1973, soon afterwards achieving a Top 10 single hit with **Gaye,** a track from his first album for the label.

Since that time, Ward has made three other albums, but has so far failed to break into the singles chart again. He is a cult figure for an audience which otherwise does not admit to the existence of cults; he writes tasteful, melodic songs, but as he obstinately refuses to perform them live, it is unlikely his audience will increase in the near future.

Recordings:
Singer Songwriter (—/Dandelion)
Home Thoughts (Atlantic/Charisma)
Mantle Pieces (—/Charisma)
Escalator (—/Charisma)

No More Rock And Roll
(—/Phonogram)

Dionne Warwick

Born East Orange, New Jersey, Dec 12, 1941, she was trained at Hart College of Music in Hartford, Connecticut, before moving to New York with her sister Dee Dee to gain early experience as a back-up singer on record sessions.

In 1962 she came to the attention of songwriting team of Bacharach and David, who arranged a contract for her with Sceptre Records. The first song they wrote for her, **Don't Make Me Over,** reached No. 21 in U.S. charts and, thus established, the Bacharach/David/ Warwick team became one of the most successful hit-making partnerships of '60s, Dionne proving the perfect interpreter of Bacharach/David's superior ballads. Both **Anyone Who Had A Heart** (1963) and **Walk On By** (1964) were major hits, and both earned her gold discs; success was automatic, with songs like **You'll Never Get To Heaven** (1964), **Message To Michael** (1966) and **I Say A Little Prayer** (1967).

Nevertheless, as the Bacharach/ David material began to veer towards a more formulated, cabaret approach, and they began to compose for movie scores and stage musicals, so her songs gradually began to lose impact, though there was always the occasional song of genuine class – **Do You Know The Way To San Jose?** was a Top 10 record in Britain and America in 1968.

In 1971 Dionne left Sceptre for Warner Bros, since when her chart appearances have been less frequent, although she has experimented with different producers. **Just Being Myself** (1973) featured material by Lamont Dozier and Brian Holland; then

Below: An early shot of Dionne Warwick, who has yet to repeat her '60s success in the '70s.

in 1974 she was teamed with The Detroit Spinners, and a song produced by Thom Bell, **Then Came You,** took her back to the top of the U.S. singles charts; her 1974 album of the same title contained that track, though the rest of the album was produced by Jerry Ragavoy. In 1975 she finally recorded a whole album, **Track Of The Cat,** which was written, produced and arranged by Bell; the music was interesting, the sales disappointing. It is nevertheless clear that Ms Warwick has avoided the role of a bland MOR performer that began to seem her destiny at the close of the '60s.

Meanwhile, in 1975 she dropped the "E" she had added to her surname in 1971; plus ça change.

Discography is (very) selective.

Recordings:
Dionne (Warner Bros)
Just Being Myself (Warner Bros)
Then Came You (Warner Bros)
Track Of The Cat (Warner Bros)
Compilation:
The Very Best Of Dionne Warwick (United Artists/—)

Muddy Waters
→ Blues – American

Weather Report

Josef Zawzinul keyboards, synthesiser
Wayne Shorter saxes
Alejandro Neciosup Acuna percussion
Chester Thompson drums
Jaco Pastorius bass
Alphonso Johnson bass
Narada Michael Walden drums

Zawinul and Shorter are constants and leading figures in band which has undergone a number of personnel permutations since formation in 1970, the above being their constitution at time of writing (i.e. at time of 1976 release **Black**

Market) – this representing more a "pool" of musicians than a fixed group.

Both key members were previously with Miles Davis (→) during his experimental jazz-rock period in late '60s, Zawinul having written title track of the pivotal Davis album **In A Silent Way** (1969).

Mysterious Traveller.
Courtesy CBS Records.

A native of Vienna, Zawinul had arrived in U.S. on scholarship to Berkley School of Music in Boston. Apart from Davis, his antecedents include spells with Maynard Ferguson, Yusef Lateef and Cannonball Adderley. During nine years with Adderley, Zawinul wrote most of group's music, including 1967 Grammy Award-winner **Mercy Mercy Mercy.**

Black saxophonist Shorter, from Newark, New Jersey, first gained attention during five-year stint as composer/tenorist for Art Blakey Group, before being recruited by Miles Davis for some six years' stay. He and Zawinul have both recorded several solo albums.

Weather Report was originally formed as vehicle for talents of Zawinul and Shorter plus Czech bassist Miroslav Vitous, the latter leaving after the band's fourth album **Mysterious Traveller.**

Consistent jazz poll-winners, Weather Report are considered the most inventive exponents of the jazz-rock fusion, garnering accolades and a considerable following in both markets.

Of current "personnel", Johnson previously played with Chuck Mangione and Horace Silver; Thompson with Frank Zappa.

Recordings:
Weather Report (Columbia/ CBS)
I Sing The Body Electric (Columbia/CBS)
Sweetnighter (Columbia/CBS)
Mysterious Traveller (Columbia/CBS)
Tale Spinnin' (Epic)
Black Market (Columbia/CBS)

Jimmy Webb

Son of a Baptist minister, Webb was born Aug 15, 1946 in Elk City, Oklahoma. In 1962, he moved with his family to San Bernadino, California. After dropping out of music college, he took a job as a contract composer for Motown's Jobete Music, the company that published his first hit, **Honey Come Back,** in 1965.

It was through his work in the industry that Webb got to know Johnny Rivers (→), who recorded Webb's composition **By The Time I Get To Phoenix** on his 1967 **Changes** album; though the song had no immediate success,

Rivers did put Webb in touch with a group he had just signed to his own label, the Fifth Dimension (→). They recorded Webb's **Up, Up, And Away,** and the song was an immediate success. (In Britain, it was also a hit, but in a cover version by the Johnny Mann Singers.) A fruitful partnership was established between Webb and the Fifth Dimension.

Meanwhile, Glen Campbell had found **By The Time I Get To Phoenix,** recorded it himself, and the song became a major U.S. hit for him.

The Webb/Campbell association proved equally productive, with Campbell achieving worldwide hits with two more Webb compositions, **Wichita Lineman** and **Galveston.**

In 1968 Webb captured eight Grammy Awards; offers poured in for him to provide material for established artists, though he took up few of them. He wrote the whole of actor Richard Harris's debut album, **A Tramp Shining.** The album contained **MacArthur Park,** an elaborately-orchestrated song that was memorable for the uneven standard of the lyrics – which managed to combine sensitivity, romanticism, and utter bathos in just about equal proportions – and for the fact that, at seven-and-a-half minutes, it was one of the longest singles ever issued. It reached No. 1 in the U.S. charts at Concorde speed, and virtually repeated the performance in Britain.

Webb collaborated with Harris on his next album – **The Yard Went On Forever** – but by that time Webb, at 21, was not only a multi-millionaire, but the hottest songwriting property on the market.

He withdrew for a time to labour over a solo album, and try to achieve the same kind of response as a singer/songwriter. However, none of his solo albums have caught the imagination of the public; it seems as though it is only when his songs are interpreted by other artists that they take on an added dimension; possibly, it is simply that he has been trying too hard with his own material.

He has often taken on outside projects, including several production commitments, which have included an album for The Supremes in 1972, one for Cher (Stars) in 1975, and one for his sister Susan Webb, also in 1975. In addition, he wrote and produced a comeback album with the Fifth Dimension called **Earthbound,** something which the album appositely remained.

In 1973 he provided two songs for Art Garfunkel's solo album, one of which, **All I Know,** was a major U.S. hit single.

Land's End was released in 1974; he is thought to be working on a new solo album.

Recordings:
Jim Webb Sings Jim Webb (Warner Bros)
Jimmy L. Webb: Words And Music (Warner Bros)
And So: On (Warner Bros)
Letters (Reprise)
Land's End (Asylum)

Howard Werth

Former moving force behind

British band Audience, which, when it folded in July 1972, featured line-up of Werth (vcls, gtr), Trevor Williams (vcls), Patrick Neubergh (sx), Nick Judd (kybds) and Tony Connor (drms). Group recorded four critically well-received albums for Charisma label but never enjoyed mass acceptance and appeared to lose direction and heart after departure of founder member Keith Gemmell to Stackridge (♦).

Werth spent some two years making his first solo album, **King Brilliant** (1975), with producer Gus Dudgeon. While with Audience, he wrote music for "Bronco Bullfrog" movie, performed by group.

Recording:
King Brilliant (Rocket/Charisma)

Leslie West
♦ Mountain

West, Bruce & Laing

Leslie West guitar, vocals
Jack Bruce bass, vocals, keyboards
Corky Laing drums

Formed 1972 when bassist-producer Felix Pappalardi left American band Mountain to return to studio projects and Leslie West and Corky Laing joined forces with Scottish bassist Jack Bruce (♦).

Like Mountain, WB&L was a twice-removed cousin of Cream, Bruce's earlier band; exploiting same heavy format which original group had developed in 1967. They made two unsatisfactory studio albums before Bruce left summer 1973 and the others returned to the U.S. to eventually re-form Mountain (♦). Third, live, album released posthumously in 1974.

Recordings:
Why Dontcha (Windfall/CBS)
Whatever Turns You On (Columbia/RSO)
Live 'n' Kickin' (Windfall/RSO)

Wet Willie

Jimmy Hall vocals, sax, harmonica
Rick Hirsch guitar
Jack Hall bass
John Anthony keyboards
Lewis Ross drums
Donna Hall vocals
Ella Avery vocals

First five members above all from Mobile, Alabama, where they worked under name Fox. In 1971 they were one of the many Southern boogie-rock bands signed by Allman Brothers (♦) manager Phil Walden to his newly-inaugurated Capricorn Records, for whom they cut first eponymous album same year under production of Eddie Offord.

Offord, best known for his work with Emerson, Lake & Palmer, also produced second album **Wet Willie II**, at Muscle Shoals studios, but it was the third album, **Drippin' Wet**, a live recording of a New Year's Eve concert 1972 at the Warehouse in New Orleans, that broke band into U.S. lists. Early in 1973 backing vocalists Hall and Avery – The Williettes – augmented Wet Willie line-up. **Keep On Smilin', Dixie Rock**, produced by Tom Dowd (♦).

Recordings:
Wet Willie (Capricorn)
Wet Willie II (Capricorn)
Drippin' Wet (Capricorn)
Keep On Smilin' (Capricorn)
Dixie Rock (Capricorn)
The Wetter The Better (Capricorn)

Barry White

Born Galveston, Texas, in 1944, White first made a professional breakthrough as co-producer of some hit singles in later '60s – Bob & Earl's **Harlem Shuffle**, Jackie Lee's **The Duck**, and Felice Taylor's **I Feel Love Comin' On**.

He began to chart a more independent course in the '70s, however; with his three-girl vocal group Love Unlimited (one of whom is his wife) he created a No. 1 U.S. hit single – **Walkin' In The Rain (With The One I Love)**, and then scored an instrumental success, **Love's Theme**, with the velvet strings of his Love Unlimited Orchestra.

With both units supporting him, White then went on to establish himself as a solo star, oblivious of the fact that his husky vocals had an extremely limited range. His usual technique was to half-speak, half-sing the lyrics, which would characteristically extol the virtues of L-O-V-E **(Never, Never Gonna Give You Up, You're My First, My Last, My Everything)**. What made his records enormous hits – especially in Britain – was the sweeping strings and the brash orchestral overkill; subtlety or restraint is hardly his forte.

White is nevertheless an artist who has evolved his own distinctive sound, and his own style of production, even if it means he now has as much to do with soul music as the Royal Scots Dragoon Guards. He is both physically huge, and huge in terms of popularity; his concerts – with his orchestra and Love Unlimited in attendance – have become lavish set-pieces. He could be around for a long time.

Recordings:
I've Got So Much To Give (20th Century/Pye International)
Stone Gon' (20th Century/Pye International)
Can't Get Enough (20th Century)
Just Another Way To Say I Love You (20th Century)
Let The Music Play (20th Century)
Compilation:
Greatest Hits (20th Century)
Love Unlimited:
Love Unlimited (MCA)
Under The Influence Of Love Unlimited (20th Century/Pye International)
In Heat (20th Century)
Love Unlimited Orchestra:
Rhapsody In White (20th Century/Pye International)
White Gold (20th Century/Pye International)
Music Maestro Please (20th Century)

Tony Joe White

Born in Oak Grove, Louisiana, Tony Joe White formed his first band, Tony Joe and the Mojos, while still in his 'teens. A subsequent band, Tony and the Twilights, headed for Texas, and when they broke up, White remained there as a solo singer, developing his songwriting talents. In 1968 he went to Nashville and with production help from the then unknown Billy Swan, put out the first of three fine albums recorded variously in Nashville and Memphis, utilising the session-musicians of those areas. From this period, which lasted until 1970, came the best music that Tony Joe White has so far produced, including such notable songs as **Polk Salad Annie, Soul Francisco, Rainy Night In Georgia** and **Groupy Girl**, which all attracted numerous cover versions from Presley downwards.

White's trademark of a deep soulful voice – originally not believed to belong to a white artist, and a highly-stylised guitar technique, which he referred to as "whomper stomper" – combined with some interesting songs, made him a significant figure.

However, when he moved to Warner Bros, his novelty appeal began to wear off, so that the three albums he made for that label, the last being in 1973, were of far less interest to the record-buying public. Ironically, a compilation album of the Monument tracks was released on Warner Bros in 1975, and seems to have led to a re-birth of activity, and he is now recording for 20th Century.

Recordings:
Black And White (Monument)
Continued (Monument)
Tony Joe (Monument)
Tony Joe White (Warner Bros)
The Train I'm On (Warner Bros)
Home Made Ice Cream (Warner Bros)
Compilation:
Best Of Tony Joe White (Warner Bros)

The Who

Roger Daltrey vocals
Pete Townshend guitar
John Entwistle bass
Keith Moon drums

Daltrey (b. Mar 1, 1944), Townshend (b. May 19, 1945), and Entwistle (b. Sep 10, 1944) were the original members of the band, when they were known as The Detours; Moon (b. Aug 23, 1946) was acquired along the way.

The band's recording debut took place when they met publicist Peter Meaden, who transformed their image, gave them the name The High Numbers, put them in Mod clothes, and re-wrote Slim Harpo's **Got Live If You Want It** as **I'm The Face**. It was a clever stab at breaking into the London Mod market, which was heavily into R&B sounds. However, although Meaden's plan was well-timed and executed, the record itself wasn't a hit, and he disappeared from the scene.

However, as the band's following grew in the pubs where they gigged in London's Shepherds Bush area, so Kit Lambert and Chris Stamp took note of their popularity and took over their management. They decided the Mod image was just right, and merely altered the name of the band – to The Who – and encouraged an open aggression in their act to match the physical aggression of the Mods in their contemporary battles with Rockers.

So The Who came to be the musical representatives of the Mod subculture, claiming affiliations with contemporary pop-art movement (viz. the cover of **My Generation**) and incorporating auto-destructive elements in their stage act. Nevertheless, they didn't immediately win a record contract, and only got one with American Decca on the recommendation of Shel Talmy (♦), who produced Townshend's **I Can't Explain**. It was released in January 1965, and wasn't successful until the band – and their audience – were seen on "Ready Steady Go", a programme that enormously helped The Who in their early days. (And The Who conceded as much by titling one of their EPs **Ready Steady Who**.)

The chic existentialism of **Anyway, Anyhow, Anywhere** reached No. 10 in the U.K. charts, and helped to establish the crashing, heavyweight guitar riffs that were initially the band's trademark, but it was **My Generation** that became the archetypal Who song of the early days.

My Generation was one of the songs that helped turn pop-music into rock-music; it was fierce, it was brash, and it represented an individual statement by one of the most articulate of the new wave of English rock stars – though the lyric, paradoxically, was stuttered by Daltrey. **My Generation** reached No. 2 in Britain in 1965, and No. 75 in America, where The Who had not had much exposure at that time; the song nevertheless became a set-piece of their stage act, and to this day they have hardly ever failed to perform it.

The first album, again titled **My Generation**, was reputedly the result of two projected albums – one straight R&B, the other of auto-destruction. Nevertheless, the result was their most exciting and spontaneous work, and helped to convey the life-style of the Mod as well as anything Townshend ever did (even on his weighty **Quadrophenia**). Talmy bowed out after this album and the first four singles – the fourth of which, **Substitute**, reached No. 5 in Britain in 1966, and offered one of Townshend's most clever lyrics yet. The Who's output for the next few years was placed in the hands of Kit Lambert.

By 1966 the band were hugely popular in Britain, though their notorious destructive set-pieces on stage had placed them heavily in debt, and indeed they were not to start making money for another two to three years. **A Quick One** was issued in 1966, and it showed Townshend's penchant for bizarrely ironic lyrics (though Entwistle too weighed in

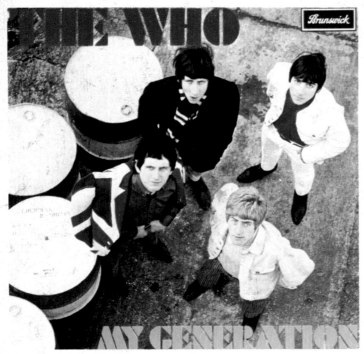

Above: My Generation. Courtesy Decca Records.

THE WHO SELL OUT

Replacing the stale smell of excess with the sweet smell of success, Peter Townshend, who, like nine out of ten stars, needs it. Face the music with Odorono, the all-day deodorant that turns perspiration into inspiration.

THE WHO SELL OUT

This way to a cowboy's breakfast. Daltrey rides again. "Thanks: to Heinz Baked Beans every day is a super day", Those who know how many beans make five get Heinz beans inside and outside at every opportunity. Get saucy.

Above: The Who Sell Out. Courtesy Polydor Records.

with **Boris The Spider**) and also his aspirations towards major art-form; the title track, deliberately referred to as a mini-opera, ran for 10 minutes, and was a clear indication of Townshend's intentions. Meanwhile, after **I'm A Boy,** the group issued **Happy Jack,** which at last brought them recognition in America, the song reaching No. 24. The band's image, their unrepentant destructiveness, was natural publicity fodder, and they were undoubtedly helped by the fact that they were the one band – with the exception of The Beatles – who were composed of four distinct and individual personalities.

They gigged long and hard in the States in 1967, and finally cracked the market with a performance of typical brio at the 1967 Monterey Festival.

Their 1967 album release, **The Who Sell Out,** saw them treading water. Again, it demonstrated Townshend's predilection for doing something more ambitious than the mere ordinary album form, and the songs on **The Who Sell Out** were linked by jingles from the various offshore pirate radio stations which had been outlawed by the British Parliament from August 1967. The album also concerned itself with advertising spoofs; it wasn't wholly successful on this tack either; it seems that Heinz were very annoyed by the front cover, though their anger was assuaged when it was pointed out to them how much free advertising they'd be getting.

Nevertheless, the album contained songs of genuine merit, like **Mary Anne With The Shaky Hand;** there was another mini-opera, **Rael (Parts I & II),** a Speedy Keen composition, **Armenia City In The Sky,** and a classic piece of seminal psychedelia, **I Can See For Miles,** which had already been a Top 10 single in both Britain and America.

With the band established as one of the top live attractions on both sides of Atlantic (a position that was absolutely sealed with their performance at Woodstock in 1969), Townshend finally took the time to realise his master-plan; **Tommy** was a 90-minute rock-opera that has become one of the landmarks of rock music. Although people had tried concept albums before (and Townshend admits he had been impressed by the Pretty Things' **S.F. Sorrow**), there had never been a project as ambitious as this carried off as successfully. Though hindsight and over-exposure has made everyone more aware of **Tommy's** faults, it remains musically superb; one criticism is that it weaned The Who away from classic three-minute songs, but that would probably have happened anyway, as it did with The Kinks; and anyway, Townshend made a desultory attempt to return to the singles market at the end of 1971 with **Let's See Action** and then **Join Together.**

For the moment, **Tommy** yielded **Pinball Wizard,** a Top 5 single in Britain in 1969. The double album was not an immediate success, either critically or commercially, but over a matter of months it generated interest, and the album was to sell consistently well for the next two or three years; the group meanwhile found themselves burdened with it, seemingly for ever. Though they performed it in its entirety only twice – once in London and once in New York – they featured a large dosage of it in their stage act, and some of it was included again on **Live At Leeds,** a 1970 album that was an accurate representation of their current stage act; the release of the album also served as a useful fill-in to conceal the fact that Townshend was having difficulty in writing material that could compare in impact with **Tommy.**

Tommy had been dedicated to Meher Baba, Townshend's guru, about whom he wrote an article for "Rolling Stone". From being the spokesman for the mid-'60s rebels without causes, Townshend began to concern himself with matters spiritual, and was often featured on television's religious programmes. The other members of the band remained constant personalities, with Moon often the focal point of

fracas and unruly incidents; he has remained irrepressible.

Soon **Tommy** (♦) began to develop an existence outside of The Who, with Lou Reizner's stage production in London, and the ensuing double-album, and then Ken Russell's film in 1975, and another double-album. **Tommy** just wouldn't go away.

In 1971 the band released **Who's Next,** their first album of (new) songs for four years; it was the bits that Townshend had salvaged from an abortive **Lifehouse** project. Nevertheless, the album, which went gold in the U.S., hardly wasted a track, and **Baba O'Reilly, The Song Is Over** and **Won't Get Fooled Again** were all lengthy pieces, which were nevertheless well-constructed and successful. A shortened version of **Won't Get Fooled Again** became a hit single.

As the '70s unfolded, however, members of the band began to indulge more frequently in solo activities. In 1972 Townshend issued a solo

Below: Keith Moon – rehearsing, apparently, the role of Scrooge.

Above: The Who, in characteristically dynamic pose. In autumn 1976 they issued a double retrospective album.

album, which was rather egotistically titled **Who Came First,** which he had put together himself in his home studio. Critics who averred that the release of the album presaged the end of The Who were wide of the mark; Townshend was soon putting his energy into another complex work which returned to the themes of the early Who songs. "One of the things which has impressed me most in life was the Mod movement in England, which was an incredible youthful thing", said Townshend in a 1968 "Rolling Stone" interview.

Quadrophenia returned to the inarticulate, directionless Mod, with each member of the band representing one of the four sides of his personality. It enjoyed some success, and spawned a first-class single **5.15,** but in many ways it was too ambitious, both thematically and musically, and the more heavily-orchestrated style didn't suit the band; but again, for all its faults, the album was a worth-while and valuable experiment.

Below: The Who By Numbers. Courtesy Polydor Records.

After a British and American tour to promote the album, the members of the band returned to their individual lives, while Entwistle spent time sorting through the material that had been deposited in the band's out-tray during the previous decade, and emerged with **Odds & Sods,** an album that reflected the changes the band had been through, and was of considerable interest. This penchant of the band for tidying-up loose ends had earlier been noted in 1972 when Townshend had personally supervised the compilation of a "greatest hits" album, **Meaty, Beaty, Big And Bouncy.** Because of contractual problems, some of the material had had to be re-recorded.

In 1975 The Who went on the road again, and released a new album, **The Who By Numbers,** that articulated Townshend's disillusionment with the trappings of success, and reaffirmed his position as the thinking-man's rock-musician, rock-music's thinking man.

Ten years on from their first days of heady success, The Who are one of the institutions of contemporary culture; they have survived, despite constant personality clashes within the band, because they have always so far managed to retain a sense of direction and a sense of purpose. Keith Moon issued a solo album, **The Two Sides Of The Moon,** in 1975. It wasn't very good. (➧ Roger Daltrey; John Entwistle).

Album notes: **My Generation** was called **The Who Sing My Generation** in the U.S. **A Quick One** was retitled **Happy Jack,** and that track added to the album for U.S. release. **Magic Bus,** a U.S.-only album, was a compilation of tracks previously issued in Britain. After its initial success, **Tommy** was retailed in the U.K. as two separate albums. **A Quick One** and **The Who Sell Out** were reissued in 1974 as a double-back in both Britain and America, and additionally in America the first two albums were issued as a double. **Odds & Sods,** though a compilation album; was composed of fresh material, and is listed as an original album.

Recordings:
My Generation
  (MCA/Brunswick)
A Quick One (MCA/Brunswick)
The Who Sell Out (MCA/Track)
Magic Bus (MCA/—)
Tommy (MCA/Track)
Live At Leeds (MCA/Track)
Who's Next (MCA/Track)
Quadrophenia (MCA/Track)
Odds & Sods (MCA/Track)
The Who By Numbers
  (MCA/Polydor)
Compilations:
Direct Hits (MCA/Track)
Meaty, Beaty, Big And Bouncy
  (MCA/Track)
Pete Townshend:

Who Came First (MCA/Track)
Keith Moon:
Two Sides Of The Moon (MCA)

Wilde Flowers

➧ Soft Machine,
Caravan

Hank Williams

Williams is a legendary figure who was one of the most important

Above: Johnny and Edgar Winter recorded an album together in 1976.

country-music stylists ever and whose rootsy Southern music also contributed to the evolution of rock 'n' roll.

Born in a log cabin in Alabama in 1923 he acquired a guitar early in life and took lessons from a black street-singer. A stormy career followed. Hank became a member of the Grand Ole Opry but was fired in 1952. Life on the road saw ecstatic receptions all over America but there were also stories of drinking, drugs, Hank shooting-up hotel rooms or sometimes not turning up on stage. In Southern country circles this was strong stuff.

The rumours regarding Hank's death in 1953 en route to a gig vary. A quack doctor was found to have prescribed Hank with an illegal dosage of a particular sedative, but the full details of his death have never been revealed.

His life was more than reflected in his music – lonesome, uncompromising and full of taut emotion. His slower songs, such as **Your Cheating Heart** and **So Lonesome I Could Cry** are some of the bluesiest pieces ever written by a white performer while his up-tempo numbers, **Honky Tonkin'** and **Move It On Over** are early echoes of rockabilly with their restless sound, hollow recording and strong backbeat.

Discography is selective.

Recordings:
Hank Williams Greatest Hits, Vol. 1 (MGM)
Hank Williams Greatest Hits, Vol. 2 (MGM)

Paul Williams

Born Omaha, Nebraska, 1940, his father was killed in an automobile crash when Williams was 13. He was moved to Long Beach, California, to be raised by an aunt and uncle until the age of 18.

His career interests first took him into movies where he worked as a set-painter and stunt man (skydiving, motorcycle-riding, etc.) before he made acting debut as a "punk kid" delivery boy in an ammonia commercial – a baby-faced, diminutive figure, Williams was a natural for "child" acting roles. The commercial led to a part in Tony Richardson's satirical "The Loved One" (1964) in which Williams, then aged 24, was cast as the 10-year old eccentric boy genius Gunther Fry. In 1965 he appeared in the Marlon Brando film "The Chase" – again playing a child punk.

It was while on the set for this last-named that Williams made his first attempt at songwriting, but it wasn't until two years later that he took up a parallel career as a pop-song writer in collaboration with professional composer Roger Nichols. (In the meantime Williams had written sketches for comedian Mort Sahl.) Together they wrote such million-selling hits as **We've Only Just Begun** (which began life as a TV jingle for a banking house!) and **Rainy Days And Mondays** for The Carpenters (♦), **Just An Old Fashioned Love Song** and **Out In The Country** for Three Dog Night (♦), plus a string of MOR compositions for the likes of Tom Jones, Andy Williams, Dionne Warwick, The Monkees, Johnny Mathis and Tiny Tim.

In 1970 Williams added a further facet to his burgeoning career by recording and performing as a singer/writer, making debut on Reprise with that year's **Someday Man**. He has since pursued a variety of careers simultaneously, appearing as guest artist on U.S. TV music and chat shows, writing and performing scores and title songs for several U.S. TV dramatic productions, and acting in movies such as "Battle For The Planet Of The Apes" and the musical "Phantom Of The Paradise". In the last-named, Williams played lead role, as well as scoring film and singing title song.

For fourth album, **Here Comes Inspiration** (1974), Williams inaugurated new writing partnership with producer/arranger/pianist Ken Ascher, this continuing via **A Little Bit Of Love** early in 1975. Both continue his predilection for MOR love songs, using rock-trained musicians to achieve extra edge to sound.

Recordings:
Someday Man (Reprise)
Just An Old Fashioned Love Song (A&M)
Life Goes On (A&M)
Here Comes Inspiration (A&M)
Phantom Of The Paradise (Soundtrack) (A&M)
A Little Bit Of Love (A&M)
Compilation:
The Best Of Paul Williams (A&M)
Ordinary Fool (A&M)
Bugsy Malone (Soundtrack) (Polydor)

Jesse Winchester

Winchester was born in Shreveport, Louisiana, in 1945, and spent most of his formative years in Memphis, where his parents moved as a result of the fact that his father was in the services.

He learned piano at age of six, and was a church organist at 14, while simultaneously learning guitar. His main idols of the time were Ray Charles and Jerry Lee Lewis; he joined various unsuccessful rock 'n' roll bands.

In 1967, shortly before his draft papers arrived, Winchester had gone to study in Munich; instead of returning to America he settled in Canada, which has remained his home ever since.

In 1970, he met Robbie Robertson of The Band, and was introduced to Robertson's manager, Albert Grossman (♦) who signed Winchester to the Ampex label, for whom he recorded his first album. Produced by Robertson, it contains several very fine songs which have attracted a number of cover versions, notably **Biloxi, Yankee Lady** and **The Brand New Tennessee Waltz**. The Ampex label became defunct shortly afterwards and Winchester reverted to Ampex's parent company, Bearsville.

In October 1972, he released his second album, partly produced by Bearsville golden-boy Todd Rundgren, and partly by Winchester himself. Despite help from noted guitarist Amos Garrett, this album was generally less successful, but the release of **Learn To Love It** in late 1974 reassured his following.

Winchester finally widened his previously narrow spectrum of live appearances in 1976 by playing selected dates in Europe; however, he is still unwilling to return to America, despite President Ford's amnesty for draft-dodgers.

Let The Rough Side Drag was released in 1976; his first two albums were then re-issued as a double set.

Recordings:
Jesse Winchester (Ampex/—)
3rd Down, 110 To Go (Bearsville)
Learn To Love It (Bearsville)
Let The Rough Side Drag (Bearsville)

Pete Wingfield

Educated at Sussex University, England, where he formed blues-band Jellybread in late '60s, recording two albums with them for Blue Horizon label. On break-up, hired himself out as pianist to a number of acts – including Colin Blunstone, Maggie Bell, and Van Morrison – while also working as session-man. He appeared on albums by aforementioned names (writing three songs for Blunstone's **Journey** set, and one for Maggie Bell's **Suicide Sal**) as well as contributing piano to recordings by Jess Roden, Freddie King, Mud, Al Stewart and Bloodstone.

He also contributed articles on soul and R&B to specialist British magazines, having previously published his own R&B fanzine "Soul Beat" prior to college days.

In June 1974 signed to Island Records for whom he recorded solo album **Breakfast Special** (1975). From this came the wittily-observed blue-eyed R&B single **18 With A Bullet**, with double-entendre lyrics built around expressions used in American music trade. It was a hit in U.K. and U.S. where, for one week, it quite rightly resided at 18 with a "bullet" in trade charts before climbing higher in lists.

Recording:
Breakfast Special (Island)

Wings
♦ Paul McCartney

Edgar Winter

Born Beaumont, Texas, Dec 28, 1946, he spent 'teens playing with his older brother Johnny Winter (♦) in group Black Plague which performed at go-go clubs on Southern U.S. gig circuit. Brothers – both albinos – went separate ways in later years, with Edgar taking a correspondence course to get his high school diploma, but opting out of college to join a jazzband instead.

Shortly after Johnny Winter's sudden rise to fame, Edgar joined his brother's band, where he attracted attention via his vibrant solo work on keyboards and alto sax.

However, while Johnny veered towards blues and rock-oriented approach, Edgar chose to experiment with neo-jazz roots on his album **Entrance** (1970) after being encouraged to pursue solo career by his brother's manager Steve Paul. A big production work on which Edgar Winter played virtually all the instruments himself, it was favourably received by critics but made little public impact.

Aiming for a wider audience, he formed Edgar Winter's White Trash with Jerry LaCroix (vcls, sax, harp), Jon Smith (vcls, sx), Mike McLellan (vcls, tpt), Bobby Ramirez (drms), George Sheck (bs) and Floyd Radford (gtr). A strongly R&B oriented band drawn mostly from musicians Edgar had played with prior to Johnny's success, they cut one relatively successful eponymous album 1971 which helped establish band as headlining attraction in U.S. Their double-live album **Roadwork** (released 1972) was Edgar's biggest-seller to date.

They toured for over a year – one of the gigs was closing night at New York's Fillmore East – but parted ways due to Winter's desire to forsake R&B for more experimental pastures.

This led him to form The Edgar Winter Group with Dan Hartman (vcls), Ronnie Montrose (gtr) and Chuck Ruff (drms). Assembled in approximately three days, they started work on an album which would provide the million-selling international hit **Frankenstein**, on which Winter experimented with an Arp synthesiser. This instrumental was the last track to be added to the album because Winter feared the rest of material – written by him and Hartman – lacked commerciality.

Frankenstein was originally released as the "B"-side to **Hangin' Around**, another track from the album, but radio requests were such that the record was flipped by public demand – after Winter had edited it down in length – and went to No. 1 on the U.S. singles lists. When the album, **They Only Come Out At Night**, followed a few weeks later, it too soared to No. 1, eventually achieving platinum status.

In October 1973, Rick Derringer (♦) came into the group as replacement for Jerry Weems; Weems himself having replaced Ronnie Montrose, who left to form own eponymous group (♦ Montrose). Derringer had previously worked with brother Johnny as well as producing the studio **White Trash** album, and **They Only Come Out At Night**. Billed as The Edgar Winter Group Featuring Rick Derringer, they became one of major attractions on U.S. gig circuit. **Shock Treatment** (1974) was another big U.S. seller.

Continuing his experiments of **Entrance**, Winter in 1975 cut another all-his-own-work solo album **Jasmine Nightdreams**, then later in the same year demonstrated his versatility by producing another group rock 'n' roll album **The Edgar Winter Group With Rick Derringer**. Derringer has since left band to form own outfit.

Apart from work on brother Johnny's albums **Johnny Winter** and **Second Winter**, Edgar appears on Rick Derringer's solo albums **All American Boy** and **Spring Fever** and on Bette Midler's **Songs For The New Depression**.

Recordings:
Entrance (Epic)
Edgar Winter's White Trash (Epic)
Roadwork (with White Trash) (Epic)
They Only Come Out At Night (Epic)
Shock Treatment (Epic)
Jasmine Nightdreams (Blue Sky)
The Edgar Winter Group With Rick Derringer (Blue Sky)

Johnny Winter

Born February 1944 in Leland, Mississippi, though he grew up in Beaumont, Texas. An albino, Winter was shunned by most of his schoolmates and turned for solace to the radio, where he listened to rock, country and blues. It was this that determined him to get into music.

After series of abortive groups with younger brother Edgar (♦ Edgar Winter), he worked as a back-up man for local bluesman and made various records for regional labels – these would all later be released after Winter's rise to fame, including **First Winter, About Blues** and **Early Times**.

Eventually he cut an album for local Sonobeat label which he intended to hawk around the bigger companies as a kind of glorified demo. Before he could carry out his plan, a writer on "Rolling Stone" magazine eulogised this incredible albino blues guitarist in an article on rock in Texas. Entrepreneur Steve Paul (owner of the Scene Club in New York and then manager of Tiny Tim) read the piece, traced Winter to Texas and signed him to management contract. Immediately the guitarist became the talk of New York for his appearances at the Scene, and by December 1968 he had graduated to an ecstatically-received concert at the prestigious Fillmore East.

Second Winter.
Courtesy CBS Records.

Steve Paul signed him to a reputedly massive Columbia Records contract in 1969, with his "first" album **Johnny Winter** following soon after. However, the Texas "demo" tape had in the meantime been leased to Imperial Records, and under title **The Progressive Blues Experiment** was issued simultaneously with the Columbia set, causing not only much embarrassment but also disappointing sales.

Neither did Winter's inexperience in large halls serve him in good stead when he made his first major tour, and some early gigs were near-disastrous. However, his follow-up Columbia album, recorded in Nashville late 1969 and featuring brother Edgar on keyboards and saxophones, proved an excellent set which went a good way to rescue his reputation from poor start.

By this time, with his aforementioned old material flooding the market, Winter had retired his old rhythm section of Red Turner (drms) and Tommy Shannon (bs), in favour of a union with three former members of The McCoys – Rick Derringer (gtr, vcls), Randy Hobbs (bs), and Randy Z (Zherringer) (drms) (♦ Rick Derringer). Randy Z was replaced by Bobby Caldwell after recording of the 1971 **Johnny Winter And** album.

This new group produced an excellent live album, **Johnny Winter And Live** (also 1971), but

Winter's heavy life-style and mounting drugs problems forced him into lengthy semi-retirement later that year from which he didn't re-emerge until 1973 with the again outstanding **Still Alive And Well**. This contained **Silver Train** written for him by Mick Jagger and Keith Richard.

Saints And Sinners appeared in 1974 and **John Dawson Winter III** later same year, but the critical concensus is that Winter hasn't produced a good album since **Still Alive And Well**. His reputation as an exceptionally fine guitarist rests on earlier work, which made him one of the most exciting blues-based rock musicians of the early '70s. In terms of sales, he has in latter years been eclipsed by success of brother Edgar.

First four pre-Imperial albums below are hard to date, and are listed in no particular order of recording. The British version of **The Johnny Winter Story** was double set compilation of tracks from U.S. album of same name plus selections from **About Blues**.

Recordings:
First Winter (Buddah)
About Blues (Janus/—)
Early Times (Janus/—)
The Johnny Winter Story (GRT/Marble Arch)
The Progressive Blues Experiment (Imperial/Liberty-Sunset)
Johnny Winter (Columbia/CBS)
Second Winter (Columbia/CBS)
Johnny Winter And (Columbia/CBS)
Johnny Winter And Live (Columbia/CBS)
Still Alive And Well (Columbia/CBS)
Saints And Sinners (Columbia/CBS)
John Dawson Winter III (Blue Sky)
Captured Live (Blue Sky)

Stevie Winwood
♦ Spencer Davis Group; Traffic; Blind Faith

Wishbone Ash

Andy Powell guitar
Laurie Wisefield guitar
Martin Turner bass, vocals
Steve Upton drums

Formed 1969 by Martin Turner and Steve Upton who had played together in various groups around south-east of England. They arrived in London, joined with Powell and Ted Turner (no relation) as Wishbone Ash and spent nine months on the road before release of their eponymous first album in 1970, this featuring fairly straight-forward rock fronted by the twin guitars of Powell and Ted Turner.

From here they accrued an impressive following on the U.K. club and college circuit, developing into an accomplished English-styled rock band, though lacking slightly in vocal ability and personality. They reached peak with the strong seller **Argus**, in 1972, which is possibly

the definitive Wishbone album.

Wishbone 4 (1973) saw them returning to more basic rock style, strangely perhaps after the more eclectic **Argus**. A certain loss of direction followed, with Ted Turner eventually leaving group in June 1974. He was replaced by Laurie Wisefield, ex of the defunct Home, and Wishbone travelled to Miami for recording of **There's The Rub**; released October 1974, some 18 months since their last studio album.

Argus.
Courtesy MCA Records.

Subsequently the group took up residence on the U.S. east coast as escape from punitive British tax laws. This has severely restricted U.K. appearances – one concert in 1975, at Reading Festival – though they have regularly toured the U.S. Now signed to Atlantic in U.S., **Locked In** (1976) produced by Tom Dowd (♦), featuring session-man Peter Wood (ex Sutherland Bros & Quiver, Al Stewart Band) on keyboards.

Recordings:
Wishbone Ash (MCA)
Pilgrimage (MCA)
Argus (MCA)
Wishbone 4 (MCA)
Live Dates (MCA)
There's The Rub (MCA)
Locked In (Atlantic/MCA)

Bill Withers

Born Jul 4, 1938 in Slab Fork, West Virginia, youngest of six children. Withers had a rural upbringing and evinced no particular inclination to follow a career in music; in any case, he had a speech impediment during his adolescence. He served in U.S. Navy for nine years, and only started singing and playing guitar when he left in 1964; while working in an aerospace factory in Los Angeles, he began composing songs in his spare time, and hawked round some of his demonstration tapes. He was manufacturing toilet seats for Boeing 747s when Clarence Avant, head of the small independent Sussex Records, showed an interest and introduced Withers to Booker T. Jones, who not only produced and arranged Withers' debut album in 1971, but also acquired the guest services of Stephen Stills.

When the album was released in spring 1971 Withers was still not a full-time performer, and photographs for the album sleeve had to be taken during his factory lunch-break.

The single from the album, **Ain't No Sunshine**, began to get air-play, moved into the charts during the summer, ultimately reached No. 3, and gained Withers a gold record; the song has subsequently become something of a modern soul standard; in Britain, where Withers' version had not been successful, Michael Jackson (➧ Jackson 5) had a Top 10 hit with the song in 1972.

Withers made his professional debut in a club in Los Angeles just a few weeks short of his 33rd birthday. Nevertheless, he quickly made up for lost time. **Grandma's Hands,** a second single from his debut album, provided him with another hit, and in 1972 his second album, **Still Bill,** was even more successful, going gold itself and spawning two gold singles – **Lean On Me** and **Use Me,** the former of which has attracted a plethora of cover versions.

His music had strong rhythmic qualities, and also possessed strong melodies – so that he often recorded with little supporting instrumentation. His songs were also evidently gospel-influenced, and this was a quality particularly reflected in **Live At Carnegie Hall,** a double-album recording of his own debut at a major venue. The album was thoroughly successful, probably because his lengthy introductions were interesting, pointing up the fact that Withers' songs were all born of his own varied experience. Throughout 1972 and 1973 Withers toured successfully in both America and Europe.

However, this live album has so far proved to be the climax of Withers' career, and he now seems to be suffering from a malaise common to rock performers. All his most effective songs, which he had written before his climb to fame, were spirited and evocative; as soon as he began to rely on freshly-written material, he obviously had to struggle to find interesting subject matter, and his popularity began to decline accordingly. Of his recent work, neither + **'Justments** (1974), on which Jose Feliciano guested, nor **Making Music,** his debut album for Columbia in 1975, has garnered heavy sales.

It is a sad, but inevitable conclusion that, for all the excellence of his early work, Withers seemed a spent force at the beginning of 1976.

Recordings:
Just As I Am (Sussex/A&M)
Still Bill (Sussex/A&M)
Live At Carnegie Hall
  (Sussex/A&M)
+ **'Justments** (Sussex)
Making Music (Columbia/CBS)
Compilation:
The Best Of Bill Withers
  (Sussex)

Wizzard
➧ Roy Wood

Howlin' Wolf
➧ Blues – American

Bobby Womack

Womack was born in Cleveland, the third of five brothers; their father was a minister, and the brothers formed themselves into a group, working out tight gospel harmonies, and playing mid-West gospel circuit.

Then known as The Womack Brothers, they toured with The Soul Stirrers, a group that included Sam Cooke (➧): Cooke asked Womack to be his guitarist, and also took the brothers to California to record for his Sar Label. It was hence Cooke who tilted Womack from gospel music towards R&B.

To coincide with their shift in musical focus, the Womack Brothers became The Valentinos, and as such recorded two classic compositions by Bobby – **Lookin' For A Love,** which was later revived by the J. Geils Band, and **It's All Over Now,** which became a big hit for the Rolling Stones.

After The Valentinos folded and Cooke died, Womack continued working as a songwriter and session-musician; in particular, he was closely involved with the career of Wilson Pickett. In 1968 he signed as a solo artist with Minit Records, and later its parent company United Artists. Since then Womack has become one of the major artists working with music that is a hybrid of rock and roll. He has worked with many leading rock names, including The Rolling Stones and The Faces, Jim Keltner and Sneaky Pete Kleinow. He has gigged several times with Rod Stewart, Ron Wood and Mick Jagger.

As yet, he is still an artist granted more recognition by his colleagues than the public; he still writes most of his own songs (and had also worked with Leon Ware, who composed material for Marvin Gaye's **I Want You**), and his albums are perfect examples of the slick soul-rock genre of the '70s.

Recordings:
The Womack Live (Minit/—)
My Prescription (Minit/—)
Communication (United Artists)
Understanding (United Artists)
Facts Of Life (United Artists)
Across 110th Street (Soundtrack)
  (United Artists)
Lookin' For A Love Again
  (United Artists)
**I Don't Know What The World
  Is Coming To** (United Artists)
Safety Zone (United Artists)
Compilations:
I Can Understand It
  (—/United Artists)
Greatest Hits (United Artists/—)

Stevie Wonder

Stevie Wonder is one of the most remarkable figures in contemporary rock music, something to which the fact that he recently signed a 12 million dollar contract with his record company is ample testimony. The contract is not only the highest ever negotiated; it is just about equal to the sum of the two previous highest.

He was born Stephen Judkins in Saginaw, Michigan, May 13, 1950, being blind from birth. His family moved to Detroit when he was three, and when he was 12 he was introduced to Tamla head Berry Gordy by Ronnie White, one of The Miracles. Gordy immediately signed up the youngster; not only did he sing with an urgent, if piping, sense of excitement, but he was an adept harmonica- and bongo-player too. Berry sensed that here was a potential hero for America's young blacks, and in May 1963, by the time of **Fingertips,** Wonder's third single, this promise had been realised. The record stayed at No. 1 in U.S. for several weeks; Little Stevie Wonder – as he was then called – was just 13.

His first album, **Recorded Live – The 12-Year-Old Genius,** was released at this time; the genius tag was mainly a result of comparisons between him and Ray Charles (➧), but future events were to demonstrate that it was not altogether inappropriate.

He began touring occasionally with Motown shows, and in 1965 played some dates in Britain as a member of the somewhat premature Motown package tour, though later that year **Uptight (Everything's Alright),** which again prominently featured his frenzied harmonica-playing, was another major hit in both U.S. and U.K.

With Dylan's **Blowin' In The Wind** (1966) and his own frenetic composition **I Was Made To Love Her** (1967) Wonder embarked on a succession of hit singles for the next five years, most of which reached Top 10s on both sides of Atlantic. During this period Stevie was concentrating intensively on his work and soon reached a point where he was practically self-sufficient in that he was producing and arranging his own records, as well as playing all the instruments and singing.

Hence with the release of his album, **Where I'm Coming From,** in 1971, he entered a new phase of his career; when he reached the age of 21 he received all his childhood earnings, and henceforward concentrated not on producing bread-and-butter hit singles, but took an altogether more ambitious path, by recording albums as whole units. He was thus running ahead of the Motown machine (then still thinking in terms of singles market) and little attention was paid to **Where I'm Coming From.**

However, everything changed with **Music Of My Mind,** an album that was absolutely all his own work, and won acclaim from the rock audience as well as the black audience, to whom he was already endeared. Throughout the summer 1972 he supported The Rolling Stones on a series of U.S. dates, so that by the time of **Talking Book** his following had reached massive proportions. Two singles from **Talking Book, Superstition** and **You Are The Sunshine Of My Life,** both became No. 1's in U.S. charts, and did almost as well in the U.K. The latter song had a lingering melody that attracted a host of cover versions.

By the time **Innervisions** was issued in August 1973, he was so popular the album went platinum within a month; however, four days after its release, Wonder was injured in a car accident in Winston-Salem, North Carolina, though not as seriously as was at first feared. He spent some time recovering in hospital, but by the end of September was jamming with Elton John at Madison Square Garden.

Fulfillingness' First Finale was issued in 1974, completing a quartet of truly remarkable pieces of work. Again, two tracks were selected for release as singles –

Below: Stevie Wonder in familiar pose – receiving an award.

246

Boogie On Reggae Woman, and **You Haven't Done Nothin',** the latter of which was an indictment of Richard Nixon.

Shortly before release, Wonder announced his intention of retiring two years hence, to work with and for handicapped and underprivileged children in Africa. However, this apparently has since been forgotten, or lost in the general confusion surrounding Wonder's career. A certain amount of mystery also existed around his projected releases; he played some dates at Rainbow in London in 1974, which were reputedly recorded for a live album, though never issued. There was also reported to be several albums' worth of material in the can, though none of it was deemed suitable for release. Probably only Wonder himself knows how much material has been recorded, since he tends to work in isolation, quite independently of the Motown organisation. A new album **Songs In The Key Of Life** was finally scheduled for release in summer 1976.

Wonder's two-year silence is particularly strange in view of the fact that he has inexhaustible energy, and a seemingly insatiable appetite for work. As well as his own projects, he has acted as writer/producer for other people, most of whom have had their status improved as a result. He has produced the following albums: B. B. King's **To Know You Is To Love You;** Minnie Riperton's **Perfect Angel;** Rufus' **Rags To Rufus;** the Main Ingredient's **Afrodisiac.** (Both **Perfect Angel** and **Rags To Rufus** subsequently went gold in the U.S.)

He has also worked with Syreeta Wright, whom he married in 1970. Though they are now separated, Wonder produced two albums for her, **Stevie Wonder Presents Syreeta** and **Syreeta.**

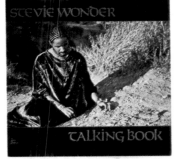

Talking Book. Courtesy Tamla Motown Records.

Despite Wonder's prolific workrate, he is extremely frail physically, and at one point was reportedly existing on a diet of two lemons a day. Though he remains a very private person, he is occasionally found gigging in strange places, and played with Bob Marley in Jamaica in 1975.

It was in the summer of 1975 that he signed his multi-million dollar contract; since Wonder is the single most respected performer in the whole of rock music, it is fitting that he should also be the most highly paid.

Discography is limited to his recent work.

Recordings:
Signed Sealed Delivered (Tamla)
Where I'm Coming From

Above: Wizzard Brew. Courtesy EMI Harvest.

(Tamla)
Music Of My Mind (Tamla)
Talking Book (Tamla)
Innervisions (Tamla)
Fulfillingness' First Finale (Tamla)
Songs In The Key Of Life (Tamla)
Compilations:
Greatest Hits, Vol. I (Tamla)
Greatest Hits, Vol. II (Tamla)

Roy Wood

Wood was born Birmingham, England, Nov 8, 1946, and attended Moseley College of Art, from which he was expelled; he then began to play in local groups, and first had one of his compositions recorded as a member of Mike Sheridan and the Nightriders. The song was called **Make Them Understand,** and it achieved only obscurity on its release in 1965. The following year, Wood joined Birmingham super-group, The Move (♦).

Despite their level of success, The Move were continually beset by problems, either managerial or contractual, or just occurring as a result of differences of opinion among band members; certainly it seems they all wanted the band to head in different directions. Eventually, Wood evolved an idea for his own futuristic band, the Electric Light Orchestra; he wanted to be able to recreate on stage the kinds of sound The Beatles were achieving on tracks like **Strawberry Fields Forever** and **I Am The Walrus.**

However, before he could inaugurate this scheme, it was necessary to fulfil the contractual obligations of The Move, and it wasn't until after release of their last album, **Message From The Country** in 1971 that he was able to go ahead with ELO (♦).

ELO, however, spawned its own difficulties; after just one album, Wood was prepared to leave the outfit to Jeff Lynne, while he engaged himself with another idea, creating a rock 'n' roll revival band, Wizzard.

For Wizzard, he recruited Rick

Price, who had been a short-term member of The Move; other original members of the band were: Bill Hunt (pno, hrpschd, Fr hrn), Hugh McDowell (elec cello), Nick Pentelow (sax), Mike Burney (sax), Keith Smart (drms) and Charlie Grima (drms). However, though the band's debut album **Wizzard Brew,** amply demonstrated Wood's ear for melody, his determination to prove that every member of the band was a multi-instrumentalist resulted in some very sloppy arrangements, and a rather self-indulgent album.

When Wizzard were pared down to essentials, they were, however, brilliant. They had two U.K. No. 1 singles in 1973 – **See My Baby Jive** and **Angel Fingers,** as well as another Top 5 hit, **I Wish It Could Be Christmas Everyday;** Wood, as the central personality in Wizzard, painted his hair various garish colours, wore elaborate make-up, and for a time tapped an adolescent audience who were presumably unfamiliar with his stint with The Move.

Wizzard might have conquered the world, but again Wood moved on to another idea, and he made an album with the nucleus of Wizzard, crediting it to **Eddy And The Falcons;** the album was an affectionate pastiche of various styles of '50s rock music; and it met with a disappointing public response.

Since then Wood has concentrated on fulfilling his ambitions of a lifetime – he has written songs for Elvis Presley, and has made two solo albums – **Boulders** (1973) and **Mustard** (1975) which have been his own work from start to finish.

He continues to have the knack of writing hit singles almost at will, even though his recent releases have been having an irregular. He is presently having an affair with Annie Haslam of Renaissance (♦), and sorting out his next rock 'n' roll masterwork. In the meantime, Harvest issued **The Roy Wood Story** in 1976, a beautifully compiled album that includes selections from every stage of his career.

Recordings:
Boulders (United Artists/Harvest)
Mustard (Jet)
Compilation:
The Roy Wood Story (—/Harvest)
Wizzard:
Wizzard Brew (United Artists/Harvest)
Eddy And The Falcons (United Artists/Warner Bros)
Compilation:
See My Baby Jive (—/Harvest)

Woodstock

The Woodstock Music And Arts Fair, to give it its full and proper name, was not the largest festival ever (Watkins Glen, in July 1973, also in up-state New York, holds that distinction) but it was certainly the most celebrated.

On Aug 21, 1969 some 450,000 kids trekked out to a farm belonging to dairyman Max Yasgur 50 miles from Woodstock in upstate New York for a three-day festival which would come to represent the peaking of the peace'n'love vibe which had emanated out of San Francisco earlier in the '60s.

A galaxy of rock talent appeared, but they had to share equal billing with the kids who proved that the population of a fair-sized town could gather in a field in the middle of nowhere virtually without incident. In fact there were three deaths (one O.D., one kid run over by a tractor, one burst appendix) but there were also two births, and no real fights except for a clash between Who guitarist Pete Townshend and Yippie leader Abbie Hoffman. On the first day, with thousands more present than the organisers had allowed for, the whole bash was declared a free festival, and the joyous celebrations of "peace and music" were not halted by a torrential downpour on Day 2.

The event was documented on Michael Wadleigh's "Woodstock" full-length feature movie which went on general release in 1970. A triumph of back-room editing, it proved both a significant development of split-screen techniques and a breakthrough for rock documentary – becoming a box office smash throughout the world.

Woodstock.
Courtesy Atlantic Records.

Several of the acts virtually made their names on the strength of "Woodstock" the movie – most notably Ten Years After (♦), Santana (♦), Sha Na Na (♦), and Richie Havens (♦), though it was also to prove the undoing of the first-named band. Then there was the case of John Sebastian (♦), who had gone to Woodstock simply to hang out, but, when the rain prevented amplified bands appearing, found himself projected onto the stage with his acoustic guitar and etched into celluloid history. Others who made the festival and the movie were Joan Baez, Arlo Guthrie, The Who, Country Joe, Sly And The Family Stone, Canned Heat, Joe Cocker, Jimi Hendrix, and Crosby, Stills, Nash & Young, whose music opened and closed the documentary.

Equally legion (but many of them forgotten) are the acts who made festival but not the film: Jefferson Airplane (the sound crew were apparently too tired to carry on recording when they came on in the early morning), The Grateful Dead, The Band, Blood, Sweat & Tears, Creedence Clearwater, Incredible String Band, Johnny Winter, Paul Butterfield, Janis Joplin, Melanie, Ravi Shankar, Mountain and Keef Hartley.

Some of these, however, did manage to get themselves on the two **Woodstock** albums (10 sides of music in total) released on Cotillion/Atlantic; while Joni Mitchell even managed to write a song about the festival without even being there. Her **Woodstock** was recorded by CSN&Y on **Deja Vu,** and was a hit single for Matthews' Southern Comfort (in both U.S. and U.K.). As for Max Yasgur, he was immortalised in the Mountain number **On Yasgur's Farm** and became a rock celebrity of sorts overnight. He died in Florida in February 1973, aged 53.

What was never widely known was that the festival nearly didn't happen at all. It was originally planned for a different site, nearer Woodstock itself, and almost capsized six weeks before the event until Warner Bros (distributors of the movie) infused sufficient funds to keep the organisation going.

From Woodstock came the terms Woodstock Generation and Nation, which have come to describe (pejoratively in later years) the hippie age. In retrospect, Woodstock can be seen as no great new dawn; rather, it was the last flag-waving of a sinking sub-culture, one which would in succeeding months be rocked by the horror of Altamont (➡), the warfare at the Isle Of Wight, the Chicago Conspiracy Trials, and the Manson nightmare.

Link Wray

Wray's status as a near legend is founded on just one weirdly primitive instrumental single, titled **Rumble** and written by Wray and DJ Milt Grant for the Cadence label. It is said to have been recorded in 1954 but didn't start selling until some two or three years later. A brooding, menacing sound, it shifted more than a million copies and stayed on the U.S. charts for 14 weeks.

Part Indian, Wray was born 1930 in Fort Bragg, North Carolina, his family later moving to Arizona where he learned to play guitar in the open-tuned bottleneck style. Wray's early experience was in a country band with brothers Doug and Vernon (sometimes known as Ray Vernon), playing bars and whorehouses.

Above: Link Wray, one of those musicians whose lack of commercial success belies his professional reputation.

Vernon recorded for Cameo in 1957 and Link played on session. Wray also worked on Milt Grant's TV show in Washington, backing Fats Domino and Ricky Nelson among others, and collaborated with Vernon to produce and back the Bunker Hill collectors' piece **Hide And Go Seek.**

The story of **Rumble** is that Wray's band were performing at a dance hall in Fredericksburg, Virginia, when a gang fight broke out. **Rumble** was intended as a musical simulation of that fight, featuring a murderously heavy guitar riff which pre-dated heavy metal rock by some 15 years. Wray had another massive American hit with **Rawhide** in 1959, but a string of rather mediocre follow-ups met with little success. Along with **Rumble,** they are collected on the compilation album **There's Good Rockin' Tonite.**

In 1965 Wray quit music to work on family farm commune in Maryland, playing occasionally in local bars and recording prolifically in his now-famous Three Track studio built in a shed on the farm. Legend has it that when Wray's backing musicians couldn't afford drums he had them stomp the floor and rattle cans instead.

The brilliant **Link Wray** (1971) was a result of these primitive recordings, the guitarist by this time enjoying a renaissance of interest due to various superstar-status musicians citing him as a major early influence, most prominent among them being Pete Townshend of The Who. Jeff Beck, The Kinks, Bob Dylan are others who have either expressed their admiration, or been directly influenced by Wray's pioneering guitar style.

He cut two somewhat disappointing albums for Polydor, on which he was swamped by San Francisco session heavies, while in 1973 England's Virgin Records released the more ethnic **Beans And Fatback,** which comprised further takes from his Three Track days.

In June 1975 Wray signed for Virgin and recorded the 1976 album **Stuck In Gear** at Ridge Farm studios in Dorking, England.

A remarkable man who's been married three times and fathered eight children, Wray appears somewhat embarrassed by his latter-day fame.

Recordings:
Ling Wray (Polydor)
Beans And Fatback (Virgin)
Be What You Want To (Polydor)
The Link Wray Rumble (Polydor)
Stuck In Gear (Virgin)
Compilation:
There's Good Rockin' Tonite (Union Pacific)

Gary Wright

Born Creskill, New Jersey, U.S. in 1943, he was firstly a child actor and played keyboards in various high school bands before studying psychology at universities in New York and, from 1965, in Berlin. There, Wright dropped his studies to form his own group New York Times which gigged throughout central Europe. On one occasion, in Norway, they appeared as support to Traffic – that group's manager Chris Blackwell being impressed by Wright's dexterity on keyboards. Blackwell, who was also founder of Britain's Island Records, suggested he go to Britain and find a more receptive audience.

The Dream Weaver.
Courtesy Warner Bros. Records.

In London, Wright got together with American producer Jimmy Miller and with the musicians who would subsequently comprise the newly-formed Spooky Tooth (➡). Wright was co-leader of that band, as well as supplying a large part of their material. He left them in 1970 to form Gary Wright's Wonderwheel. During

this time, Wright recorded two solo albums, **Extraction** and **Footprint,** but attracted little attention and eventually re-formed/re-joined Spooky Tooth in 1973.

However, this second incarnation of the group was even more short-lived than the first, and in February 1974 Wright travelled to Los Angeles to begin work on his third solo album, the keyboards-dominated **The Dream Weaver.** Released July 1975, this and the single of same title were among "sleeper" hits of year in the U.S. By early 1976 the album had gone gold, while the single had made the No. 1 spot in the American lists.

Wright has also worked sessions for George Harrison, as well as producing albums for Splinter and Tim Rose.

Recordings:
Extraction (A&M)
Footprint (A&M)
The Dream Weaver (Warner Bros)

Robert Wyatt

Born in Bristol, raised in Dulwich, London, the son of writer/broadcaster Honor Wyatt (née Ellidge). It was during schooldays in Canterbury that he met musicians who were to form nucleus of The Wilde Flowers, which split to produce two groups, Caravan (➡) and The Soft Machine (➡). Wyatt went with the latter as drummer/vocalist, appearing on four Softs albums.

Before he left in September 1971, Wyatt recorded a solo album, the punningly-titled **The End Of An Ear.** During this period he also made an (unreleased) single with Jimi Hendrix; was occasional drummer with Kevin Ayers (➡) & The Whole World; and contributed to **Banana Moon** album by Daevid Allen (➡ Gong). When he left the Softs, the group lost a great deal of their wit and a certain amount of their profundity too.

In December 1971 he formed his own band Matching Mole with personnel of Bill McCormick (bs), Phil Miller (gtr), David Sinclair (kybds), the latter later replaced by Dave Macrae. They cut two albums but disbanded towards end of 1972.

Wyatt had reconstituted Matching Mole and was about to start work with new line-up in summer 1973 when he fell out of the window of an apartment block leaving him paralysed from the waist down.

During his six months in hospital, he composed the material for **Rock Bottom,** his second solo album which, in mid-1974, elicited unanimously enthusiastic reviews. It was certainly one of the most literate and incisive (almost painfully personalised) albums of its year, and went on to win the top French music award, the Prix Charles Cross 1974. Production was by Pink Floyd drummer Nick Mason, the Floyd having earlier raised 10,000 pounds for Wyatt via a benefit concert.

Two months later Wyatt turned up in the U.K. singles lists with a quite inspired re-working of the old Monkees hit **I'm A Believer,** a feat which acquired him an appearance on BBC-TV's "Top Of The Pops" – despite the

BBC's "concern" that the sight of a man in a wheel-chair might disturb sensitive viewers. Naturally Wyatt's incapacity has severely limited his concert appearances, but he did make an enthusiastically-received return to stage at London's Drury Lane Theatre September 1974 and subsequently put in a couple of critically-lauded concert collaborations with fellow Virgin Records' act Henry Cow (♦).

Ruth Is Stranger Than Richard. Courtesy Virgin Records.

Third solo album **Ruth Is Stranger Than Richard** released mid-1975, was somewhat disappointing after **Rock Bottom** tour de force. Nevertheless, Wyatt remains one of the most articulate of contemporary British composer/musicians.

Recordings:
The End Of An Ear (Columbia/CBS)
Rock Bottom (Virgin)
Ruth Is Stranger Than Richard (Virgin)
Matching Mole:
Matching Mole (Columbia/CBS)
Little Red Record (Columbia/CBS)

Tammy Wynette

The Queen of middle-American country music, Tammy Wynette was born in Redbay, Alabama, worked in a beauty salon in Birmingham, had an early unsuccessful marriage and then went to Nashville to try and sell her songs and land a recording contract.

She had the luck to be teamed up with Columbia's Billy Sherrill, then a new producer himself, and to become part of what has since been termed "The Billy Sherrill Sound".

The Billy Sherrill Sound itself was part of "The Nashville Sound". During the 1960s country-music in America was gaining a new respectability, many of its original fans had moved to the cities, and Nashville was smoothing out the sound and adding strings alongside the steel guitars.

The singers were still allowed their "image" though and Tammy's was that of the platinum, middle-American housewife, waiting faithfully for her man to return from work, a little isolated and vulnerable and perhaps dreaming of a better life somewhere in the city.

Also, she sang with a crying, "country-soul" voice which, coupled with the mundane subject-matter of the songs, spawned some intrigued coverage by one or two noted rock journalists.

It helped too that Tammy was

married then to George Jones, an influential country-stylist whom many consider to be somewhere near Hank Williams in musical stature. Tammy made several duet albums with George and in the latter days their well-publicised marriage problems added spice to the music. Tammy's solo hit **D.I.V.O.R.C.E.,** a track some years old, was released in Britain by CBS with incredibly good timing or incredibly bad taste, depending upon how you look at it. Discography is selective.

Recordings:
The Best Of Tammy Wynette (Epic)
Tammy Wynette and George Jones:
Let's Build A World Together (Epic)

Stomu Yamash'ta

Yamash'ta was born in Kyoto, the old capital city of Japan in 1947. His father is leader of Kyoto Philharmonic Orchestra, and it was through his enthusiasm that Yamash'ta, from an early age, attended Kyoto Music Academy. By the time he was 13 he was already working as a percussionist in his father's orchestra, and had also been hired to write the scores of two Kurosawa films, "Yojimbo" and "Sanjuro".

He then went to America to study at Interlochan Summer Music School, and became subject to Western musical influences. At the age of 19, he began to undertake solo appearances as a percussionist. He also worked with Peter Maxwell Davies on the soundtrack of Ken Russell's "The Devils", and provided the theme music for Robert Altman's "Images".

While Kachaturian was lauding him as the world's greatest percussionist, he was already beginning to move into rock music, and started to perform in concert with a three-piece jazz-rock outfit called Suntreader; he also recorded with them his first album for Island Records in 1973.

He then toured Europe and America with a troupe he had founded, The Red Buddha Theatre, in two acclaimed productions – "The Man From The East" and "Raindog", basing his success on the way he juxtaposed Western and Eastern musical influences, with neither predominating over the other.

He has remained versatile, and open to accept fresh musical challenges; in 1976 he worked on supersession project **Go** with Stevie Winwood and Mike Shrieve.

Recordings:
Floating Music (—/Island)
The Man From The East (—/Island)
Freedom Is Frightening (—/Island)
One By One (—/Island)
Raindog (—/Island)

The Yardbirds

Keith Relf vocals, harmonica
Eric Clapton guitar
Chris Dreja rhythm guitar
Paul Samwell-Smith bass

Jim McCarty drums

Formed 1963 as the Metropolis Blues Quartet, original line-up featured Anthony "Top" Topham who was replaced after a matter of months in October that year by Eric Clapton (no commercial recordings available by first line-up). London-based, most of personnel being drawn from southeast England, the "Most Blues-wailing Yardbirds" – as they were soon dubbed – relied totally at first on Chicago originated Chess/Checker/Vee-Jay catalogues for inspiration and material.

The band amassed a fervent following on London and Home Counties club circuit, blossoming into a cult attraction when they took over Rolling Stones residency at the legendary Crawdaddy Club in Richmond. They began to appear regularly at the then-prestigious Marquee Club in London and toured Europe with American blues veteran Sonny Boy Williamson. An album of this partnership, **Sonny Boy Williamson & The Yardbirds,** was released in 1965 (long a collectors' item, it was re-issued 1975 with Clapton's name featured prominently in title).

The group's first album proper, **Five Live Yardbirds** (U.K. only), had been released in 1964, and in 1965 they scored their first U.S. and U.K. hit single with **For Your Love,** written by Graham Gouldman now of 10cc (♦).

(Though there is some repetition of tracks, U.S. and U.K. albums apart from Sonny Boy Williamson set at no time coincided – hence separate listings below. The group's first and second American albums were **For Your Love** (August 1965) and **Having A Rave Up** (January 1966). Both featured Eric Clapton, though on only four cuts on latter release.)

Clapton, however, declined to go along with this denial of the group's ethnic roots and quit to pursue the blues in the company of John Mayall (♦). Another nascent guitar hero, Jeff Beck (♦), took his place, and the Yardbirds consolidated on their new-found

commercial appeal with two more chart successes, **Heart Full Of Soul,** again written by Gouldman, and the double "A"-side **Evil Hearted You/Still I'm Sad.**

Nineteen sixty-six was a turbulent year, despite two more hits, **Shapes Of Things** and **Over Under Sideways Down.** Samwell-Smith was first to quit. Chris Dreja switched to bass and noted session-man Jimmy Page was recruited, in July that year, as rhythm guitarist. (Page had initially been approached as replacement for Clapton but at that time had declined.) Only one single resulted from this line-up, **Happenings Ten Years Time Ago.**

When Beck was taken ill, Page switched to lead guitar, the pair playing twin leads on the former's return to the group. However, this was for only a short period before Beck, too, left the band.

Pop producer Mickie Most (♦) took over recording duties for the disastrous 1967 set, **Little Games.** With the exception of the title track, this was a mish-mash of demos, first takes, and material the band is reputed not to have intended for public consumption. In the event, it was only ever released in the U.S.

By this time the group's fortunes were at a low ebb. In an attempt to revive American chart interest in the group, the singles **Ten Little Indians** and **Ha, Ha, Said The Clown** (both U.S. only) were issued to little avail. The Yardbirds disbanded after a gig at Luton Technical College in England in July 1968.

After the break-up Keith Relf, who had cut two solo singles during time with Yardbirds, teamed up with Jim McCarty to form ill-fated folk duo Together and subsequently Renaissance (♦). After an inauspicious post-Yardbirds career, Relf died through electric shock at his home on May 14, 1976. Dreja became photographer while Jimmy Page, left with rights to the group name and a string of contracted dates, set about forming The New Yardbirds . . . the band which became Led Zeppelin (♦).

Below: Yardbirds. Courtesy Columbia, EMI Records.

A posthumous Yardbirds album was briefly on the American market in 1971. Titled **Live Yardbirds,** it had been recorded a couple of months before **Little Games,** during a performance at the Anderson Theatre, New York, on Mar 30, 1968. It is said to have been recorded on condition that its release was dependent on group consent. This they never gave, and the album was withdrawn from sale within days of release. It has subsequently appeared in bootleg form, and is interesting in that it includes material later to appear in early Zeppelin repertoire.

In retrospect, The Yardbirds were the prototype of both the guitar-dominated and heavy metal psychedelic bands of later '60s and '70s. Their status as one of the truly legendary rock bands is beyond question. Virtually all Yardbirds releases are now recognised as collectors' items. Apart from albums below, group also appear as session-men on Philamore Lincoln album for Epic, **The North Wind Blew South,** although only Dreja is credited on sleeve.

Recordings:
U.S. Albums
Sonny Boy Williamson & The Yardbirds (Mercury)
For Your Love (Epic)
Having A Rave Up With The Yardbirds (Epic)
Over Under Sideways Down (Epic)
Little Games (Epic)
Live Yardbirds (Epic)
Compilation:
The Yardbirds' Greatest Hits (Epic)
U.K. Albums
Sonny Boy Williamson & The Yardbirds (Featuring Eric Clapton) (Fontana-Philips)
Five Live Yardbirds (Columbia)
The Yardbirds (Columbia)
Compilation:
Remember The Yardbirds (Starline)

Yes

Jon Anderson vocals
Steve Howe guitar
Chris Squire bass
Patrick Moraz keyboards
Alan White drums

With original line-up comprising Anderson and Squire, plus Peter Banks (gtr), Tony Kaye (org), Bill Bruford (drms), they were formed 1968 after a chance meeting between the first two named musicians in a London music business drinking club, La Chasse in Soho.

Anderson (b. Oct 25, 1944) was from Accrington, Lancashire. At point of meeting Squire, he had spent some 12 years on the road with various unsuccessful bands, having started with his brother Tony's group The Warriors – a track by this band featuring Anderson appears on 1975 British beat compilation album **Hard-up Heroes** (London/Decca).

In contrast, Squire was a Londoner (b. Mar 4, 1948) educated at Haberdasher's Aske public school in Elstree, Middlesex. He had taught himself music, and briefly played in a band The Syn before forming Yes with Jon Anderson.

An early influence on the new group were contemporaries The

Nice (♦), featuring Keith Emerson. Like The Nice, Yes drew on classical influences to flesh out elaborate arrangements, while Tony Kaye's Hammond-playing evidenced a certain debt to Emerson. Their musically self-conscious debut album, **Yes** (1969), included covers of Byrds and Beatles compositions among original works and was tentative step on road to experimentation.

The Yes Album.
Courtesy Yes.

Their second, the 1970-released **Time And A Word,** was if anything even less satisfactory, the group being augmented by an orchestra to flail around on over-arranged material drawn from within band and outside sources Richie Havens and Steve Stills.

In 1971 Banks quit to form own (unsuccessful) group Flash and Steve Howe (b. London Apr 8, 1947) came in as replacement. Howe had an interesting background, having played with various bands The Syndicate, The In Crowd, Bodast and Tomorrow, being best-known for the last-named who had a minor late '60s U.K. hit with the quasi-psychedelic **My White Bicycle.**

Howe was an altogether better player than Banks, providing Yes with much more colour and scope on their 1971 **The Yes Album,** produced by Eddie Offord. Moreover, the material had radically improved, and from then on all numbers would be written within the group.

Yes picked up their first really positive music press reviews and began to accrue a sizeable following. However, Tony Kaye then left to form his own (unsuccessful) band Badger.

In his place came Rick Wakeman, who had previously drawn critical attention to his overflowing abilities on keyboards via his work with The Strawbs (♦), a group which was unable to provide the necessary scope for the full range of this classically-trained musician's talents.

Wakeman brought his whole artillery of keyboard trickery to Yes – inviting further comparisons with Keith Emerson – and pushed the group further into the realms of what has become known as "flash-" or "techno-rock". Emerson's ELP (♦) are the other leading exponents of this technically dazzling but generally overblown and pretentious school of rock.

With Yes, this took the form of a dependence on the technical accomplishments of individual members to carry complex, quasi-orchestral arrangements of the sometimes slight compositions of Jon Anderson or various writing permutations within group. Lyrically inaccessible, at worse banal,

but on their night they could be often exciting and impressive.

That this music had its adherents in enormous numbers was evidenced by the success of both Yes and ELP (and individual members in instrumental categories) in music-paper polls, and massive sales. **Fragile** (1971), the Wakeman debut album which found them more confident if a trifle coldly accomplished, was followed by the group's first American tour, on the strength of which the album went into the U.S. Top 10 and provided a hit single there with **Roundabout.**

Then, in 1972, there came release of **Close To The Edge,** another massive seller. However, shortly after recording of same, Bill Bruford threw in his highly lucrative position to join Robert Fripp in King Crimson (♦). (Jon Anderson had earlier sang lead on parts of the King Crimson album **Lizard.**

Alan White (b. Pelton, County Durham Jun 14, 1949) came in as replacement in a strange choice in view of his antecedents in no-frills rock 'n' roll, most notably with the Plastic Ono Band (♦ John Lennon). He had also worked as session-man for likes of George Harrison, Joe Cocker, Alan Price and Air Force.

He made his debut on the ambitious **Yessongs,** a triple live set of material from previous three albums. This was another huge seller in both U.K. and U.S., the group by this time having risen to headline status on American tours.

However, in between release of these two, Rick Wakeman had evidenced his need to work outside of Yes with a solo album **The Six Wives Of Henry VIII** in early 1973. Rumours of a split subsequently began to circulate based not only on musical differences but also on the well-known personality estrangement of Wakeman from rest of band – their general health-food lifestyle being alien to Wakeman's publicised fondness for liquor.

However, Wakeman stayed around long enough for the next Yes set, the ponderous and pretentious **Tales From Topographic Oceans** which featured one continuous Anderson/Howe composition over its four sides. It was released to mixed reviews.

After this, the Wakeman clash came to a head and he quit band late 1973 to pursue a solo career (♦ Rick Wakeman). After much speculation and touting of names (♦ Vangelis), Patrick Moraz was recruited from Refugee (♦ Lee Jackson) in August 1974. Born Morges, Switzerland Jun 24, 1948, Moraz had been classically-trained on a variety of instruments at various academies in his homeland as well as at Columbia University, New York. Before joining Refugee early 1974 he had led his own groups, as well as composing prolifically for films.

Since this change, Yes' line-up has remained stable, as has their popularity. Latterly, however, there have been signs of a slight flagging of interest in "flash-rock" as a whole, a genre which tends to be lauded by older critics as the most exciting development of rock but denigrated by the rock press as an outright denial of same. Though they produced some interesting work mid-period, latter-day activities of the group have plunged headlong into pretension, lyrical obscurity and cold artistry.

Nowhere was the grand conceit of this particularly self-conscious stream of music better evidenced than in this group's decision in 1975 that each member – from vocalist to drummer – was capable of producing a solo album worthy of public interest.

Compilation **Yesterdays** (1975) includes **Dear Father** and 9.40 minute version of **America,** neither of which appear on previous albums.

Recordings:
Yes (Atlantic)
Time And A Word (Atlantic)
The Yes Album (Atlantic)

Below: Tales From Topographic Oceans. Courtesy Yes/Dean.

Jesse Colin Young
♦ Youngbloods

Neil Young

The most enigmatic and arguably the most powerfully inventive figure to emerge from the singer/songwriter proliferation at the turn of the '70s, Young was born in Toronto, Canada, Nov 12, 1945 the son of a noted sports journalist. He spent his formative years in Winnipeg, where he formed the pop-oriented Neil Young And The Squires but abandoned that to work Canadian and Border club circuit as a folk-singer. He first met Steve Stills (♦) during these travels – and in 1966 drove across the American continent in his 1953 Pontiac hearse with the notion of seeking out Stills in Los Angeles.

Together they formed Buffalo Springfield (♦), one of the seminal West Coast groups, where Young's distinctively high-pitched quavery vocals and penchant for melodic rock 'n' roll songs (**Broken Arrow, Mr Soul, Nowadays Clancy Can't Even Sing, I Am A Child, Out Of My Mind,** etc.) marked him out as an original talent.

Young has since revealed that he worked illegally during his Springfield period, possessing neither a musician's union card nor the necessary papers to work in the U.S.

With persistent friction existing between him and Stills, Springfield survived until May 1968 when Stills joined forces with Dave Crosby and Graham Nash in CS&N, and Young resumed gigging in smaller American clubs as a singer/guitarist, reportedly to largely indifferent audiences.

In January 1969, after a period of seclusion in Topanga Canyon, he released his first solo album, **Neil Young,** which was a considerable disappointment after the quality of his work for Buffalo Springfield. It suffered from fussy arrangements and relatively weak compositions, though another version subsequently re-mixed by Young showed some improvement.

It was while recording this album that Young encountered long-serving West Coast outfit The Rockets which contained Danny Whitten (gtr, vcls), Ralph Molina (drms) and Billy Talbot (bs). Renamed Crazy Horse (♦), they backed Young on his second solo set, the July 1969 **Everybody Knows This Is Nowhere,** which

Above: Young. He recorded Long May You Run with Stills 1976.

contains the track **Running Dry (Requiem For The Rockets)** and the stand-out group workouts **Cowgirl In The Sand** and **Down By The River.** This was an altogether more assured rock 'n' roll album, featuring some potent electric guitar interplay between Whitten and Young.

On a commercial level, however, Young's progress was at this time taking a back seat to the highly-publicised Crosby, Stills & Nash aggregation. There are probably several reasons why Young took up their offer to join the group (♦ Crosby, Stills, Nash & Young) – the one propounded by the cynics, in which there is probably a certain amount of truth, is that Young was attracted by the prospect of a cut of the highly lucrative action.

Whatever, Young was able to keep Crazy Horse ("My rock 'n' roll band" he once told a reporter) to one side – they had a separate career anyway – and in June 1969 teamed-up with CS&N. His presence was felt in no uncertain terms on the April 1970 CSN&Y **Deja Vu.** Young's contributions, **Helpless** and **Country Girl,** overshadowed those of any other participant, and brought him to international recognition.

His third solo album, **After The Goldrush** (September 1970), recorded with Crazy Horse plus whizz-kid guitarist Nils Lofgren (♦), was an absolute tour de force. Rich in powerful melodies and evocative imagery, it opened whole new vistas of Young's talent and nearly ran away with all the critical accolades of its year.

From this point on, Young's burgeoning charisma and commercial standing began to rapidly outgrow the swiftly disintegrating CSN&Y outfit.

For whatever reasons, however, Young failed to seize the opportunity to establish himself beyond doubt as the premier singer/writer of the day. Eighteen months were allowed to elapse before the eagerly-awaited release of **Harvest** (March 1972). Largely on the strength of his previous accomplishments it was an immediate international million-seller, but any kind of examination revealed it to be a bland retread of the ground covered in **Goldrush.** The melodies may have remained as strong but the incisiveness of the earlier lyrics had been replaced by self-pitying declamations of the superstar's lot (Young hasn't been alone in falling victim to that particular trait).

Young's stock began to deteriorate almost as rapidly as it had flourished. The December 1972 basically-retrospective double-set **Journey Through The Past,** compiled as a soundtrack for the film of the same name, appeared to reveal him as bereft of new ideas.

At the same time stories began to circulate about Young's erratic behaviour and a series of shambolic American gigs. Towards the end of 1973 came **Time Fades Away,** a live album recorded at seven different U.S. venues and featuring the back-up band for **Harvest,** The Stray Gators – Jack Nitzsche (kybds), Ben Keith (pdl stl gtr), Tim Drummond (bs) and Johnny Barbata (drms) – plus Crosby and Nash on vocals. It was everything rumour had suggested it would be – a sloppily recorded, indifferent set that greatly eroded Young's commercial standing.

It is hard to understand Young's

motives here without accepting the theory that he was acting out of some perverse desire to destroy his own credibility as a sign of contempt towards the music industry. Without doubt he was greatly affected by the overdose deaths of Danny Whitten and one Bruce Berry, a former roadie for CSN&Y and Crazy Horse.

Through to the end of 1973 Young toured with another version of Crazy Horse – Nils Lofgren, Ben Keith, Billy Talbot and Ralph Molina – on what is known as the "Tonight's The Night" tour. It was a monumentally bizarre event in which an embittered Young seemed to deem it his personal mission to convey the death vibe he felt resonating from Whitten and Berry. The actual song **Tonight's The Night** would be performed on stage twice sometimes three times a night in varying forms, recounting the stories of the Whitten/Berry deaths, each version a more chilling experience than the last.

Young was virtually destroying himself on stage, and there are stories told of how his manager Elliot Roberts persistently throughout the tour attempted to re-direct his charge towards more commercial pastures – or, at least, token recognition of the fact that audiences had a right to make demands of their own.

In July 1974 came the magnificent and powerfully evocative **On The Beach,** in which a character (assumed to be Elliot Roberts) tells Young he is "pissing in the wind". However, as fine an album as it was, it scarcely returned Young to his former commercial status. Neither did the June 1975 set **Tonight's The Night** which, as the title suggests, was the culmination of Young's period of being haunted by the ghosts of his deceased, O.D.'d friends. The album was dedicated to Berry and Whitten and the sleeve featured a picture of Crazy Horse with an empty space where Whitten should have been. Among the tracks was Whitten's drug-oriented **Downtown.** Talking of **Tonight's The Night,** Young has said: "I'm not a junkie and I won't even try it to check out what it's like." Certainly, as an epileptic and diabetic, any such notions on Young's part could have had fatal results.

It was a demanding, uncompromising album which documented the rock wastelands of the '70s in quite harrowing style, and at no point did it make any concessions to commercial appeal. In fact, it represented a further decline in Young's status – each of the previously-mentioned three albums showing a 50 per cent decline in sales on its predecessor.

Earlier, in May 1974 through to February 1975, Young had regrouped with CSN&Y for a lengthy American tour, and again his were the most potent contributions.

In 1976 came **Zuma,** heralded as signalling a return to public favour, and a series of concerts, again with a new-look Crazy Horse, Molina, Talbot and newcomer Frank Sampedro (rhym gtr), which revealed Young as apparently having finally exorcised the influences of Whitten and Bruce.

Latterly he has appeared a

much more relaxed, at ease with himself figure in personal and public life, and in spring 1976 was believed to be working at Criteria Studios, Miami, with Steve Stills; a joint album being the likely outcome.

Despite the enigmatic and unpredictable nature of much of his work, Young remains one of the single most important figures in rock. Also, despite his fall from former glory, he retains a Messianic following. All his albums are worthy of investigation, even though his latter-day work does not represent the most "comfortable" of rock listening.

Recordings:
Neil Young (Reprise)
Everybody Knows This Is Nowhere (Reprise)
After The Goldrush (Reprise)
Harvest (Reprise)
Journey Through The Past (Reprise)
Time Fades Away (Reprise)
On The Beach (Reprise)
Tonight's The Night (Reprise)
Zuma (Reprise)

The Youngbloods

Jesse Colin Young guitar, bass, vocals
Jerry Corbitt guitar, vocals
Joe Bauer drums
Banana (Lowell Levinger) guitar, keyboards

Perry Miller assumed the name Jesse Colin Young in 1963, when he was working the folk circuit of the East Coast of America, and made a solo album in 1964 which took four hours to record. A second album was made the next year, which also featured John Sebastian of the Lovin' Spoonful on harmonica and dobro-player Pete Childs, which was as unsuccessful as the first, so Young formed a duo with Jerry Corbitt, a Massachusetts folksinger.

The need for a rhythm section became apparent, and Joe Bauer and Banana were added at the end of 1965, the first few recordings of the group, which assumed the name of The Youngbloods, being released at a much later date on the **Two Trips** album.

Having satisfied the contractual requirements of Mercury, the group signed with RCA, and from their New York base, produced **The Youngbloods** and **Earth Music**, both produced by Felix Pappalardi, before moving to the West Coast, where they produced their best work with RCA, **Elephant Mountain**, released in 1969. Subsequently, almost every-

thing the group recorded for RCA has been repackaged and re-compiled.

During the recording of **Elephant Mountain**, Jerry Corbitt left the group, and the group continued as a trio, signing with Warner Bros, who granted them their own Raccoon label in America. Their first two albums under the new deal, **Rock Festival** and **Ride The Wind** were live recordings, the latter produced by Charlie Daniels (➤).

During the early part of 1971, Michael Kane was added on bass, and The Youngbloods made their final two albums before breaking up into a number of solo projects, a sad end to the career of a much-loved band.

In the meantime, Corbitt made two solo albums, the last of which appeared around 1971, and seems to have subsequently vanished.

Bauer and Banana each made an album, and also appear to have vanished, leaving Jesse Colin Young as the only currently active ex-member.

A band called Noggins, which included Banana, Joe Bauer and Michael Kane, made **Crab Tunes** on Raccoon in 1972.

The Youngbloods was reissued as **Get Together** in the U.S. in 1976.

Recordings:
Jesse Colin Young:
The Soul Of A City Boy (Capitol)
Youngblood (Mercury/—)
Jesse Colin Young & The Youngbloods:
Two Trips (Mercury)
The Youngbloods:
The Youngbloods (RCA/—)
Earth Music (RCA/—)
Elephant Mountain (RCA)
Rock Festival (Raccoon/ Warner Bros)
Ride The Wind (Raccoon/ Warner Bros)
Good And Dusty (Raccoon/—)
High On A Ridgetop (Raccoon/—)
Compilations:
The Best Of The Youngbloods (RCA)
Sunlight (RCA)
This Is The Youngbloods (RCA/—)
Jerry Corbitt:
Corbitt (Polydor)
Jerry Corbitt (Capitol)
Jesse Colin Young:
Together (Raccoon/—)
Song For Juli (Warner Bros)
Light Shine (Warner Bros)
Songbird (Warner Bros)
On The Road (Warner Bros)
Joe Bauer:
Moonset (Raccoon/—)
Banana And The Bunch:
Mid Mountain Ranch (Raccoon/—)

Frank Zappa

Francis Vincent Zappa Jnr was born of Sicilian-Greek parentage on Dec 21, 1940 in Baltimore, Maryland. In November 1950 FVZ Snr took his family to the West Coast, first to Monterey, then three years later to Pomona, San Diego and finally, in 1956, to Lancaster, California in the Mojave Desert where Frank went to Antelope Valley High School until he graduated in 1958. While at school he had an eight-piece combo called The Blackouts. He collected R&B records and listened to Edgar Varese. In 1959 another move took him to Chaffee Junior College and marriage to his first wife, Kay, which lasted five years.

He spent 10 months playing cocktail-lounge music and wrote the score for a "B" grade movie, "The World's Greatest Sinner" ("It was rancid" – Zappa). In 1963 his old English teacher got an advance for a cheap western movie "Run Home Slow", for which Frank had written the

score. With his share of the money he bought an electric guitar and a recording studio. The studio was a three-track, which Frank christened Studio Z and it was located in Cucamonga. Frank, Jim "Motorhead" Sherwood and two girls lived there. Among the people he recorded was Don Van Vliet, a friend of his from high school, whom Zappa named Captain Beefheart. They were going to start a band called The Soots but it never happened. A 10-volume set of albums of these recordings are promised from Zappa.

Money was very short and Zappa was lured into making a sex tape by the San Bernadino Vice Squad. He did 10 days in jail and three years on probation during which time he was not supposed to be with an unmarried woman under 21. He bailed the girl involved out of jail with royalties he was able to raise on **Memories Of El Monte** which he and Ray Collins wrote for The Penguins. Having been in jail got him out of the draft.

Zappa joined a group called The Soul Giants whom he soon renamed The Mothers (the "of Invention" part was added by MGM Records later because they were nervous). The original line-up was Roy Estrada (bs), Jimmy Carl Black (drms), Ray Collins (vcls) and Dave Coronada (sax), though he left when he discovered Zappa's plans for the group.

They had a hard time of it but were finally heard playing at the Whiskey A Go-Go on the Strip by Tom Wilson, the producer of Bob Dylan, the Velvet Underground, Cecil Taylor, et al. Wilson liked their song **Trouble Every Day**, about the Watts Riots and wanted to make it a single. Once in the studio he heard **Any Way The Wind Blows** and **Who Are The Brain Police?** and he decided to make an album, **Freak Out**.

In the end he spent 21,000 dollars on it, unheard of in those days. No one had done a double rock album before, particularly a new group. It was also the first "concept" album, if you like, the first rock opera. It represented the entire underground scene in Los Angeles at that time, most of them are either namechecked or actually on the record. Zappa captured the freaks, the energy, the weirdness and was able to translate it to disc. He advertised it in comic books and in underground papers – he knew his audience read.

The line-up on **Freak Out** was Ray Collins, Roy Estrada, Jimmy Carl Black and Elliott Ingber, who played alternate lead and rhythm guitar to Zappa. Among the 24 other people in the crowd scenes was Kim Fowley. It was recorded early 1966, and released in August that year.

Ingber left to join The Fraternity of Man and later became Winged Eel Fingerling with Captain Beefheart. Collins, Black and Estrada were joined by Don Preston (kybds), Bunk Gardner (saxes), Billy Mundi (drms) – Black changed to congas and trumpet – and Jim "Motorhead" Sherwood (saxes and roadie). They recorded **Absolutely Free** in late 1966; it was released in May 1967.

The group then moved to New York City and did a six-month stint at the Garrick Theater in Greenwich Village doing 14 shows a week beginning late November, 1966. The show was very theatrical with Zappa persuading marines from the audience to break up dolls on

Below: Zappa, his new partnership with Beefheart was a brief one.

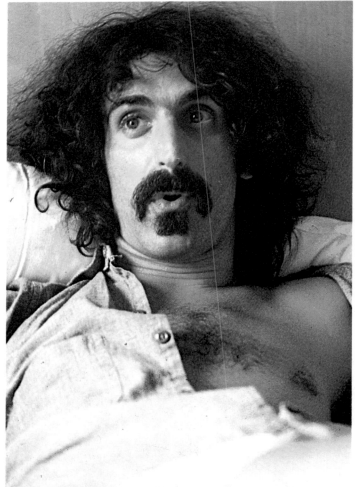

stage and a lot of crazy audience participation. In August 1967 Zappa added Ian Underwood to the band on piano and woodwinds.

They recorded **We're Only In It For The Money** between August and October 1967 during the middle of which they visited London and played the Royal Albert Hall. Zappa spoke to McCartney on the telephone about getting permission to parody **Sgt Pepper** on the cover of **We're Only In It For The Money,** but McCartney was suspicious and referred him to the Beatles management. Afterwards McCartney said: "He kept talking about 'product' so it sounded like a business matter"; Zappa felt annoyed and the matter held up the release of the album.

The first three MGM albums were reissued in a variety of compilations but only one has the space and sensibility needed to put that material together and that is the one Zappa himself did, **Mothermania.** The others are very badly done.

Back in New York City, Zappa hired Apostolic Studios on East 10th Street on a weekly basis and worked on his first solo album, **Lumpy Gravy** with the Abnuceals Emuukha Electric Symphony and Chorus, a 50-man session-band including many of the Mothers. It was a serious work in which he explored the possibilities of Varese and Stravinsky and his other modern classical influences within the genre of rock 'n' roll.

Billy Mundi left in December 1967 to join Rhinoceros (♦) and was replaced by Art Tripp III. During the five-month period October 1967 to February 1968 Zappa worked simultaneously at Apostolic Studios on two albums, with **Ruben And The Jets** falling more towards the middle of the time and being dated as November on the album. The other album was **Uncle Meat.** Though seemingly representing the two poles of Zappa's music, there are many cross-references between the two albums.

Ruben And The Jets was so authentic a re-creation of '50s rock that many people bought it believing it was 15 years old. **Uncle Meat** was written in the studio; as the musicians would play one section Zappa would sit in the control booth writing the next. It was the music for a movie which was never finished, a flickering underground super-imposition of Zappa family home movies, concerts, and other strange footage. For the album Ruth Komanoff on marimba and vibes and Nelcy Walker, soprano, were added but they did not stay on when the group moved back to Los Angeles.

In Los Angeles, Zappa took the Log Cabin, Tom Mix's old ranch under which Mix had buried his horse. It was a huge place and became the centre of a very active social scene. He married Gail Sloatman.

Burnt Weenie Sandwich was recorded in 1969 and is "sandwiched" between two '50s doo-wop numbers **WPLJ** and **Valarie;** a Zappa "return to the roots"? The album was the last that the group made since **Weasels Ripped My Flesh** was a composite of good live tracks and studio recordings over the period 1967–69. It was released in 1970 after Zappa had broken up the group.

In October 1969 Zappa issued a long press release: "The Mothers of Invention, infamous and rocking teen combo, is not doing concerts any more. It is possible that, at a later date, when audiences have properly assimilated the recorded work of the group, a re-formation might take place . . . ."

The huge expense of keeping such a large band together combined with public apathy in the U.S. (though not in Europe) towards his music, finally caused the termination of the group.

All through 1968–69 Zappa was very involved with record production. He produced quasi-sociological albums of such Los Angeles phenomena as The GTOs **Permanent Damage** and **An Evening With Wild Man Fischer,** a crazed young man who used to sing original songs for a dime on the Strip.

He played on Jeff Simmons' **Lucille Has Messed My Mind Up** album which Straight Records released. (Straight and Bizarre were two record companies that Zappa and Herb Cohen launched at this point.) His best-known production from this period is probably the double album **Trout Mask Replica** by Captain Beefheart.

When the group was disbanded Lowell George moved on to Little Feat, as did Roy Estrada. Jimmy Carl Black and Bunk Gardner formed their own group Geronimo Black. Art Tripp joined Beefheart's Magic Band and was renamed Ed Marimba. Only Ian Underwood stayed on with Zappa and played with him on his second solo album, **Hot Rats.**

The line-up included a guest appearance from Captain Beefheart, Sugar Cane Harris (vl), Jean-Luc Ponty (vln), John Guerin (drms), Paul Humphrey (drms), Ron Selico (drms), Max Bennett (bs), and Shuggy Otis (bs); not all at once, of course, but spread over August and September 1969.

It is regarded by many as his finest album, being very melodic and having some superb solos yet experimenting with a variety of new forms of modern rock 'n' roll.

Zappa did further work with Jean-Luc Ponty after **Hot Rats,** producing, composing and arranging **King Kong: Jean-Luc Ponty Plays The Music Of Frank Zappa.** Legal reasons prevented Zappa's name appearing as producer.

In May 1970 Zappa formed a new Mothers, mainly to play the score for his movie "200 Motels". The new line-up was originally going to have a new name but ultimately finished-up as The Mothers. The band still included Ian Underwood and added George Duke (kybds and trmbne), Aynsley Dunbar (drms), Howard Kaylan and Mark Volman, "The Phlorescent Leech and Eddie" who were previously "The Turtles", and Jim Pons, also from The Turtles (bs), who didn't fully join until the following year, 1971.

Zappa made a third solo album **Chunga's Revenge** the vocals being a preview of what was to come on **200 Motels.**

200 Motels itself came out on United Artists, who released the film. It was written and filmed in London where Zappa was living. The movie received a very mixed reception, most critics feeling that Zappa should stick to music. In May 1971 Zappa played at one of the final concerts at the Fillmore East, appearing on stage with John Lennon and Yoko Ono. He was finally in the realm of the superstars. His performance was included on John and Yoko's **Sometime In New York**

Below: Overnite Sensation Mothers. Zappa (centre) with Ian Underwood just behind his right shoulder.

City album.

In the spring of 1971 Don Preston returned, replacing George Duke. Jim Pons finally took over on bass from Jeff Simmons when Simmons left during the rehearsals for **200 Motels** because he couldn't relate to Zappa's musical ideas.

This group cut two live albums: **The Mothers: Fillmore East – June 1971** with Bob Harris added on keyboards and with a sleeve like a bootleg, possibly because Zappa was annoyed about the various European bootlegs of him in circulation. The other album was **Just Another Band From L.A.** which was recorded at the University of California in Los Angeles on Aug 7, 1971 and featured one of Zappa's mini-operas, **Billy The Mountain.**

The Mothers had a disastrous European tour in 1971. First their equipment was completely destroyed by fire at the Montreux Casino in Switzerland and then, in December, Zappa was seriously injured when he was pushed from the stage of the Rainbow Theatre, London, by the husband of one of his fans.

In 1972 came another solo album, **Waka Jawaka.** Don Preston and Aynsley Dunbar play on it, helped by ex Mothers Jeff Simmons and George Duke. In addition there is Erroneous (bs), Janet Ferguson (vcls), Sal Marquez (tmpt), Tony Duran (sl gtr), Ken Shroyer (trmbne), Joel Peskin (tnr sax), Bill Byers (trmbn), Mike Altschul (piclo and flts).

As usual, once Zappa got a team together he used them again, and this new line-up became the Mothers with the exception of Jeff Simmons and play on **Grand Wazoo.**

The **Grand Wazoo** album added yet more to the line-up: Earl Dumler, Tony Ortega, Ernie Watts, Joanne McNabb, Johnny Rotella and Fred Johnson were all added on horns. Malcolm McNabb (brass), Bob Zimmitti, Alan Estes and Lee Clement (prcsn) complete the band.

In 1973 Zappa produced Ruben and the Jets' **For Real,** a group of guys using the Mothers' pseudonym for real, including ex Mothers Jim "Motorhead" Sherwood and Tony Duran in the line-up.

Nineteen seventy-three also saw Zappa cut **Overnite Sensation.** Though Ian Underwood was not on **Grand Wazoo** or **Waka Jawaka** he was on the 1972 European tour, along with his wife Ruth Underwood on marimba, vibes and percussion; they, together with Bruce Fowler (trmbne), and Sal Marquez (trmpt), who were on the European and U.S. 1972 tours, formed the basis of the new Mothers. Zappa added ex Mothers George Duke on keyboards and synthesiser, Jean Luc Ponty (vln), Tom Fowler (bs) and Ralph Humphrey (drms).

Almost as if he were determined to gain commercial success Zappa now concentrated on very simple rock music with bizarre lyrics. No longer were his lyrics critical or threatening and no longer was his music weird or experimental; he was almost dealing in straight pop songs.

Apostrophe (') is another solo album in the same vein, only even more uncomplicated. Zappa fans were amazed and confused. For the album he used the following current, temporary or ex Mothers: Johnny Guerin, Ralph Humphrey, Aynsley Dunbar, Erroneous, Tom Fowler, George Duke, Jean Luc Ponty, Sugar Cane Harris, Ian Underwood, Sal Marquez, Bruce Fowler and Ray Collins. Jack Bruce played bass, Napoleon Brock played sax and Ruben Guevara and Robert Camarena from Ruben and the Jets did back-up vocals. It was a bland period.

An album of good unreleased material, mostly live, came next, **Roxy And Elsewhere,** mostly from a three-day residence Dec 10, 11 and 12, 1973 at the Roxy, Hollywood. The remaining tracks are from 1974. The line-up is the same on all tracks. Basic group: George Duke, Tom Fowler, Ruth Underwood, Napoleon Murphy Brock and Chester Thompson. Temporary group: Jeff Simmons, Don Preston, Bruce Fowler, Walt Fowler and Ralph Humphrey.

For **One Size Fits All** the basic group remains, the temporary group goes and is replaced by James Youman (bs), Johnny Guitar Watson and Bloodshot Rollin Red (hrmnca). The tracks come from a variety of sources including live TV and a 1974 concert in Helsinki, Finland. Zappa produced it between December 1974 and April 1975.

Bongo Fury reunited Zappa and Beefheart. Beefheart came out of his two-year retirement and accepted Zappa's offer of a tour. A live album, **Bongo Fury** was recorded at Armadillo World Headquarters, Austin, Texas, May 20 and 21, 1975. The album also has two studio tracks. Its line-up is George Duke, Napoleon Murphy Brock, Brian Fowler, Tom Fowler, Chester Thompson and Denny Walley on slide guitar and Terry Bozzio on drums.

Because Virgin Records claimed to have Beefheart signed to them, they brought an injunction forbidding Warner Bros to distribute the album in England.

After that, Zappa went on tour again, this time without Beefheart.

Recordings:
Freak Out (MGM/Verve)
Absolutely Free (MGM/Verve)
We're Only In It For The Money (MGM/Verve)
Lumpy Gravy (Solo) (MGM/Verve)
Cruising With Ruben And The Jets (MGM/Verve)
Uncle Meat (Bizarre/Reprise)
Hot Rats (Solo) (Bizarre/Reprise)
Burnt Weenie Sandwich (Bizarre/Reprise)
Weasels Ripped My Flesh (Bizarre/Reprise)
Chunga's Revenge (Solo) (Bizarre/Reprise)
Fillmore June 1971 (Bizarre/Reprise)

200 Motels (United Artists)
Just Another Band From L.A. (Bizarre/Reprise)
Waka/Jawaka (Solo) (Bizarre/Reprise)
The Grand Wazoo (Bizarre/Reprise)
Over-Nite Sensation (DiscReet)
Apostrophe (') (Solo) (DiscReet)
Roxy And Elsewhere (DiscReet)
One Size Fits All (DiscReet)
Bongy Fury (With Captain Beefheart) (DiscReet/—)
Compilations:
Mothermania (MGM/Verve)
Live Jam album with John & Yoko Lennon. Included in:

Some Time In New York City (Apple)
King Kong: Jean-Luc Ponty

Plays The Music Of Frank Zappa (World Pacific)

Zombies

Colin Blunstone vocals
Rod Argent keyboards
Paul Atkinson guitar
Chris White bass
Hugh Grundy drums

Formed 1962 around St Albans, England, area by five schoolkids who entered newspaper talent competition in 1964 and were subsequently signed to Decca Records. First single **She's Not There,** written by Rod Argent, made British Top 20 1964 and raced to top of American charts.

Above: The Zombies, clean-cut boys all.

However, further success was not forthcoming and group folded in 1967 within weeks of completing **Odyssey And Oracle** album. Ironically, a track from this set, **Time Of The Season,** became chart-topper and million-seller in America and Japan, more than a year after band had split. Colin Blunstone (➧) retired from music business until return in early '70s, while Rod Argent went on to form own eponymous band (➧ Argent).

Recordings:
Begin Here (Parrot/Decca)
Odyssey And Oracle (Columbia/CBS)
Compilation:
Time Of The Zombies (Epic)

Z. Z. Top

Billy Gibbons guitar, vocals
Dusty Hill bass, vocals
Frank Beard drums

The champions of Texas rock in their Nudie's Rodeo Tailors' suits, ten-gallon hats and cowboy boots, Z.Z. Top were formed towards the end of 1970, and first came to attention as the support group headlining acts were reluctant to follow.

Gibbons was the prime mover, a former graphic art student who played lead guitar in Houston-based psychedelic outfit Moving Sidewalks, whose regional hit **99th Floor** topped Texan charts for five weeks. The Sidewalks had once opened in New York for Jimi Hendrix, causing the guitarist to refer to Gibbons during an appearance on the Johnny Carson Show as one of America's most promising young players.

However, at same time as this

acknowledgment was being broadcast, Moving Sidewalks fell apart and Gibbons began to audition for new group in company of newly-acquired manager/producer Bill Ham. Beard was first to join, and, after a fruitless six-month search for a bass-player, he recommended Hill. Both had previously played in Dallas band American Blues.

Drawing their music from south-western blues and R&B – Robert Johnson, John Lee Hooker, B. B. King, etc., suffused with contemporary power rock – the new trio initially faced hostile audiences but began to accrue a reputation around Texan clubs and bars as an aggressively hard-working, high-energy band.

Their **First Album** was recorded late 1970 and attracted considerable local interest, as did the second set **Rio Grande Mud** which eventually went gold after release in early 1972.

Outside of home territory, they were often critically denigrated but nevertheless demonstrated their burgeoning grass-roots popularity as support band on tours in mid-West and western states. They often caused near-riots and invariably piled encore upon encore to the point where many headline acts refused to have them on the same bill. In 1972, they cemented home state popularity with headlining gig before 10,000 fans at Dallas Memorial Coliseum.

Tres Hombres. Courtesy Decca Records.

Third album, **Tres Hombres,** yielded hit single **LaGrange,** and widened group's appeal. Between this and release of **Fandango** 18 months later, Z.Z. Top took their power-drive rock from support to national headliner status, with **Tres Hombres** eventually being certified a platinum-seller.

Fandango, likewise, was a platinum success. This featured one studio side, the other cut live before an SRO concert at New Orleans' famed Warehouse. Among live tracks is group's concert standard **Thunderbird.**

Culmination of Z.Z. Top's remarkable rise to fame came in July 1974 when they played the Texas Memorial Stadium, Austin, to 80,000 fans, bill-topping over Bad Company, Joe' Cocker and Santana.

Recordings:
First Album (London)
Rio Grande Mud (London)
Tres Hombres (London)
Fandango (London)

INDEX

This index does not set out to be comprehensive, but concentrates on those personalities whose names recur throughout. It also provides an alphabetical guide to any acts and artists of stature not given their own entry in the book, and supplements the cross-reference system (denoted by ➡) used throughout. The main A-Z entries are not included so please check with the main listing first. References to main entries are indicated here by **bold** type.

255